Greek Oratory

KU-206-187

Greek Oratory

Tradition and Originality

STEPHEN USHER

OXFORD
UNIVERSITY PRESS

*This book has been printed digitally and produced in a standard specification
in order to ensure its continuing availability*

OXFORD
UNIVERSITY PRESS

Great Clarendon Street, Oxford OX2 6DP

Oxford University Press is a department of the University of Oxford.
It furthers the University's objective of excellence in research, scholarship,
and education by publishing worldwide in

Oxford New York

Auckland   Cape Town Dar es Salaam Hong Kong   Karachi
Kuala Lumpur Madrid Melbourne Mexico City   Nairobi
New Delhi Shanghai Taipei Toronto
With offices in
Argentina Austria Brazil Chile Czech Republic France Greece
Guatemala Hungary Italy Japan South Korea Poland Portugal
Singapore Switzerland Thailand Turkey Ukraine Vietnam

Oxford is a registered trade mark of Oxford University Press
in the UK and in certain other countries

Published in the United States
by Oxford University Press Inc., New York

© Stephen Usher, 1999

The moral rights of the author have been asserted

Database right Oxford University Press (maker)

Reprinted 2007

All rights reserved. No part of this publication may be reproduced,
stored in a retrieval system, or transmitted, in any form or by any means,
without the prior permission in writing of Oxford University Press,
or as expressly permitted by law, or under terms agreed with the appropriate
reprographics rights organization. Enquiries concerning reproduction
outside the scope of the above should be sent to the Rights Department,
Oxford University Press, at the address above

You must not circulate this book in any other binding or cover
And you must impose this same condition on any acquirer

ISBN 978-0-19-925002-8

Short Loan Collection

WITHDRAWN

UNIVERSITY
OF
GLASGOW
LIBRARY

To My Wife

PREFACE

The immense vitality and inventiveness of the Greek orators ensured their popularity in their own times, and also the transmission of some, at least, of their work, initially through the stalls of the fourth- and third-century booksellers, and later into the Hellenistic libraries. Interest in them survived the movement of the cultural centre of gravity to Rome, where Greek men of letters, under the enlightened patronage of a philhellenic Roman aristocracy, maintained the literary status of their language and even enhanced it. Of these men, one of the most interesting is Dionysius of Halicarnassus, whose literary circle studied the orators as the prime models for eclectic imitation ('Which characteristics of each should we imitate, and which should we avoid?' (*On the Ancient Orators*, 4)). His essays on the individual orators (Lysias, Isocrates, Isaeus, Dinarchus, and Demosthenes) also contain judgements of literary merit which are purely aesthetic and not directed towards practical utility.

The influence of Dionysius, and of other critics, of whom the greatest was the author of *On Sublimity*, was strong enough to prevail through the Renaissance and affect the attitudes of nineteenth- and twentieth-century scholars. Dionysian opinions provide the first point of reference for many of their discussions, with the consequence that these incorporate not only his strengths but also his weaknesses. These latter include technical vagueness in stylistic criticism, and generalization instead of detailed examination.

Such an examination is attempted in the present book. It includes most of Greek oratory, considering each speech from two main standpoints: as its author's response to the difficulties of the case, which depends on his ability to present the facts favourably, deploy the most persuasive arguments, and display his rhetorical skills; and, more importantly, the degree of adaptation and innovation which he brings to his oratory, bearing in mind the richness of the early tradition that he inherited, the content of which is assembled in the opening chapter. This emphasis on each orator's individual contribution to the genre and on its development differentiates my approach from those of illustrious predecessors such as Blass, Jebb, Dobson, and Kennedy. It also complements the utilitarian view of oratory which partly accounts for the recent welcome revival of interest in it, and aims to encourage students of law, society, and history to appreciate their oratorical sources as literature which is peculiarly sophisticated, and which rewards the technical analysis offered in these pages.

Most of the speeches examined are forensic. Most of the deliberative or symbouleutic oratory is by Demosthenes; and ceremonial or epideictic oratory (apart from that of Isocrates) is examined in a brief chapter because of its mainly stereotypic character. The summaries at the ends of chapters should be read only as general guides to their contents.

It is my pleasant duty to thank Christopher Carey for reading the entire script and making many shrewd and constructive observations as well as saving me from a number of errors. I am grateful to Douglas MacDowell for his detailed examination of the early chapters, and the many comments which have enabled me to make improvements and corrections. Michael Edwards kindly supplied me with materials for Appendix A, and corrected the proofs. I have also acted on a number of suggestions made by the anonymous reader who reported to the Press, whose copy-editors I also thank for their hard work. I am solely to blame for any inadequacies that have survived their scrutiny.

S.U.

Royal Holloway College

PREFACE TO THE PAPERBACK EDITION

I am glad of the opportunity to make a number of typographical corrections noted by reviewers, thanking them both for their vigilance and the mainly favourable reception they have given the book. Additions to the bibliography reflect the continuing interest that scholars and students are showing in Greek Oratory in all its aspects.

ADDITIONAL BIBLIOGRAPHY

DOVER, K. J., *The Evolution of Greek Prose Style* (Oxford, 1997).

EDWARDS, M. J., *Lysias: Five Speeches (1, 12, 19, 22, 30)* (Bristol CP/Duckworth, 1999).

FISHER, N., *Aeschines: Against Timarchus* (Oxford, 2001).

GAGARIN, M. (ed.), *The Oratory of Classical Greece* (University of Texas Press, Austin): A complete collection of translations in progress. Volumes so far published: *Antiphon and Andocides*, trans. D. MacDowell and M. Gagarin (1997); *Lysias*, trans. S. C. Todd (2000); *Aischines*, trans. C. Carey (2000).

MacDOWELL, D. M., *Demosthenes: On the False Embassy* (Oxford, 2000).

OBER, J., *Mass and Elite in Democratic Athens* (Princeton, 1989).

SINCLAIR, R. K., *Democracy and Participation in Athens* (Cambridge, 1988).

WHITEHEAD, D., *Hyperides: The Forensic Speeches* (Oxford, 2000).

WORTHINGTON, I., *Greek Orators II: Dinarchus and Hyperides* (Warminster, 1999).

YUNIS, H., *Taming Democracy: Models of Political Rhetoric in Classical Athens* (Ithaca N.Y., 1996).

CONTENTS

LIST OF ABBREVIATIONS

Blass *AB*	F. Blass, *Die Attische Beredsamkeit*, i–iii/2 (Leipzig, 1887–98, repr. 1962).
Burtt *MAO* ii	J. O. Burtt, *Minor Attic Orators*, ii (Loeb; London, 1954).
Carey *GO* vi	C. Carey, *Greek Orators*, vi: *Apollodorus* (Warminster, 1992).
Cawkwell *PM*	G. L. Cawkwell, *Philip of Macedon* (London, 1978).
Davies *APF*	J. K. Davies, *Athenian Propertied Families* (Oxford, 1971).
Denniston *GPS*	J. D. Denniston, *Greek Prose Style* (Oxford, 1952).
Dobson *GO*	J. F. Dobson, *The Greek Orators* (London, 1919).
Dover *GPM*	K. J. Dover, *Greek Popular Morality* (Oxford, 1974).
Dover *LCL*	K. J. Dover, *Lysias and the Corpus Lysiacum* (Los Angeles, 1968).
Edwards *GO* i	M. J. Edwards, *Greek Orators*, i: *Antiphon* (Warminster, 1985).
Edwards *GO* iv	M. J. Edwards, *Greek Orators*, iv: *Andocides* (Warminster, 1995).
Ellis *PMI*	J. R. Ellis, *Philip II and Macedonian Imperialism* (London, 1976).
Goodwin *MT*	W. W. Goodwin, *Syntax of the Moods and Tenses of the Greek Verb* (New York, 1875, repr. 1965).
Harrison *LA*	A. R. W. Harrison, *The Law of Athens*, i–ii (Oxford, 1968–71).
Jebb *AO*	R. C. Jebb, *The Attic Orators from Antiphon to Isaeus*, i–ii (London, 1893, repr. 1962).

Kennedy *APG*   G. Kennedy, *The Art of Persuasion in Greece* (Princeton and London, 1963).

MacDowell *AHL*   D. M. MacDowell, *Athenian Homicide Law* (Manchester, 1963).

MacDowell *DAM*   D. M. MacDowell, *Demosthenes: Against Meidias* (Oxford, 1990).

MacDowell *LCA*   D. M. MacDowell, *The Law in Classical Athens* (London, 1978).

Maidment *MAO* i   K. J. Maidment, *Minor Attic Orators*, i (Loeb; London, 1941).

Meiggs and Lewis *GHI* R. Meiggs and D. M. Lewis, *A Selection of Greek Historical Inscriptions* (Oxford, 1969).

Pearson *AD*   L. Pearson, *The Art of Demosthenes* (Meisenheim, 1976).

Radermacher *AS*   L. Radermacher, *Artium Scriptores* (Vienna, 1951).

Rhodes *CAP*   P. J. Rhodes, *A Commentary on the Aristotelian* Athenaion Politeia (Oxford, 1981).

Sealey *DT*   R. Sealey, *Demosthenes & His Time* (Oxford, 1993).

Sp.   L. Spengel, *Rhetores Graeci*, i (1853), ii (1854), iii (1856).

Todd *SAL*   S. C. Todd, *The Shape of Athenian Law* (Oxford, 1993).

Trevett *ASP*   J. Trevett, *Apollodorus the Son of Pasion* (Oxford, 1992).

Usher *GO* i   S. Usher, *Greek Orators*, i: *Lysias* (Warminster, 1985).

Usher *GO* iii   S. Usher, *Greek Orators*, iii: *Isocrates* (Warminster, 1990).

Usher *GO* v   S. Usher, *Greek Orators*, v: *Demosthenes De Corona* (Warminster, 1993).

Walz   C. Walz, *Rhetores Graeci*, 9 vols. (1832–6).

Wyse   W. Wyse, *The Speeches of Isaeus* (Cambridge, 1904).

I

THE EARLY RHETORICAL TRADITION

Oratory became a more or less distinct genre of Greek prose literature some time around the middle of the fifth century BC.[1] The
uncertainties surrounding its beginnings do not allow a more precise dating. On one important aspect of its early development, however, confident assertion is possible: unlike other genres, oratory
evolved under the stimulus of two agencies, that of the preceptor
and that of the practitioner. From the start there were teachers
instructing would-be orators in what to say, how and in what order
to say it. By the time of Antiphon, the first Greek orator whose
speeches have survived, the work and influence of the teachers had
crystallized into a body of topics and types of argument which only
the most talented (or foolhardy) might ignore. An attempt, such as
is envisaged in the present enquiry, to assess the literary achievement
of each of the Attic orators, must logically approach their texts with
the initial intention of trying to identify what they received from
the first teachers, before examining the merit of what may seem
idiosyncratic and original. The tradition begins with these early
teachers, and it is necessary to clarify the form in which their
instruction was transmitted. The sources use the terms *techne* and
technai to describe the vehicle(s) of that instruction, but the words

---

[1] The idea that Homer invented rhetoric, or the theory of oratory, originated in the
Sophistic view of his central status in education (Plato, *Ion* 540b; *Rep.* 606e), became established (see Radermacher *AS* A iii–iv), and its persistence in modern times is attested by many
attempts to conform the speeches in the *Iliad* and *Odyssey* to later rhetorical theory. The latest of these attempts, P. Toohey, 'Epic and Rhetoric' (in I. Worthington (ed.), *Persuasion:
Greek Rhetoric in Action* (London and New York, 1994), 153–62; for other bibliography see
his nn. 170–3), shares the ingenuity of its predecessors but also their failure to find true parallels with Attic oratory, except perhaps in the use of *paradeigmata* (historical examples).
Homeric oratory, while vigorous and fertile in emotional appeal, is in the main loosely and
informally constructed, though both epics contain evidence for the importance and variety
of types of oratory in Homeric society. See Usher *GO* i. 5–6.

'handbook' and 'handbooks' into which these terms are most usually translated can misrepresent their true nature.[2] On balance, our evidence indicates that they were not analytical treatises, foreshadowing the *Rhetoric* of Aristotle or the *Rhetorica ad Alexandrum*, but model speeches, whose continuous texts were read or listened to by students of oratory and/or prospective litigants. Their contents were varied by different imaginary, but possible, forensic situations, and perhaps graded according to difficulty, some dealing with straightforward cases, others with those involving conflict between existing laws, customs, and religion.[3]

The idea that a speech should have distinct sections was probably established early, and may indeed have been the most important element of early doctrine. Corax[4] may have conceived schemes of oratorical division (*partitio oratoria*). The part assigned to his pupil and fellow-Sicilian Tisias by the sources can, in spite of some difficulties of interpretation, be summarized without distorting its nature. He incorporated his master's teaching in model exercises, and circulated these among his pupils and clients. These were the

---

[2] Nevertheless I shall continue to use them in the interest of convenience.

[3] Since A. Gercke, *Hermes* 32 (1897), 348–59 presented the evidence and arguments for this view of *technai*, most scholars have accepted it. See G. A. Kennedy, *AJP* 80 (1959), 169–78; K. Barwick, *Philol.* 107 (1963), 42–63. Yet the existence in the 5th cent. of prescriptive manuals containing topoi in standard forms of words, which could be learnt and applied individually, cannot be ruled out entirely, in view of the frequency of similar formulae in extant speeches. (Gercke, art. cit. 358, is prepared to admit that a 'gradual transition' to the systematic manuals of Theodectes, Anaximenes, and Aristotle could have taken place.) The published (though unfortunately undatable) teachings of Theodorus of Byzantium, Euenus of Paros, and possibly of Licymnius may have taken this specialized form (Plato, *Phaedrus* 266c–267c). Far too little is known about the contribution of these 5th-cent. rhetoricians (and too much about Antiphon) to justify the central claim of T. Cole, *The Origins of Rhetoric in Greece* (Baltimore, 1991) that 'Greek literature before Plato is largely "arhetorical" in character' (p. x). See my review, *CR* 2nd ser. 42 (1992), 58–60.

[4] The traditional pioneer of instruction in oratory. References to his teaching on *partitio oratoria* (henceforth to be termed 'division') concern deliberative oratory, and are late (5th to 14th cent. AD: see Radermacher *AS* A v. 16 (Johannes Doxopater and an anonymous rhetorician (Walz vi. 11, *Proleg. Syll.* p. 24, 8), who concludes the section thus: καὶ τὰ μὲν πρῶτα ἐκάλεσε προοίμια, τὰ δὲ δεύτερα ἐκάλεσεν ἀγῶνας, τὰ δὲ τρίτα ἐκάλεσεν ἐπιλόγους). Troilus (*Proleg.*, Walz vi. 48) begins by describing Corax as a political figure, but ends with reference to ἔγκλημα, κατηγορία, and δικασταί. But the value of these late sources has been much disputed. P. Hamberger, *Die rednerische Disposition in der alten TEXNH PHTOPIKH* (Paderborn, 1914), 36, opines that the tradition which they preserve is sound, but S. Wilcox, *AJP* 64 (1943), 1–23 regards them as worthless. Plato's discussion of division in *Phaedrus* 266d ff. establishes that it was one of the main preoccupations of the early rhetoricians. It would therefore be unwise to suppose that Corax contributed nothing of significance to the theory of division. That his teaching also included probability-argument is suggested by Aristotle (*Rhet.* 2. 24. 11). But see next note.

first 'technai'.[5] Tisias' *technai* illustrated the division of speeches, perhaps adding the proof section to Corax's tripartite division, and subdividing it. Indeed, the most recurrent of Tisias' interests cited by the sources are concerned with proof, and specifically with the use of argument from probability (*eikos*).[6] Then, a much-told story concerning the two Sicilians may seem to broaden the scope of argument covered in their teaching. It tells how Tisias had agreed to pay his master's fee after he won his first case, but refused to do so. Corax took him to court, where he argued that if he succeeded in persuading the jury, he should of course be absolved from payment, and if he failed to persuade them, Corax's teaching would be proved useless and consequently no fee was due.[7] We may sympathize with the court for throwing out the case and pronouncing Tisias 'a bad egg from a bad *crow*' (*corax*), but before passing on it is worth observing its specific effect. It is a 'double-catch' (*dilemmaton*), ensnaring the opponent under either of the two hypotheses described.[8]

Any further details of the contents of the earliest handbooks must be largely conjectural. In reviewing those few which the sources have preserved, the first point to notice is that they are confined to

[5] The name of Tisias is nearly always present when τέχνη (or *ars*) is mentioned. (The only exceptions are Aristot. *Rhet.* 2. 24. 11 and *Rhet. ad Alex.* 1421ᵇ2–3.) Tisias' status as the author whose work could be examined by later generations tended to make Corax the more shadowy figure for some (Plato, *Phaedrus* 273c: ... τέχνην ἀνευρεῖν ὁ Τεισίας ἢ ἄλλος, ὅστις δή ποτ' ὢν τυγχάνει ...; Aristot. *Soph. El.* 33 183ᵇ29: Τεισίας μετὰ τοὺς πρώτους). Again, no source says that Corax composed speeches for particular clients, but Tisias is credited with at least one, for a Syracusan woman (Pausanias 6. 17. 8). On the other hand, Corax but not Tisias is said to have engaged in politics around the time of the fall of the tyrants in Sicily (465 BC). See further, D. A. G. Hinks, *CQ* 34 (1940), 61–9; Kennedy, *APG* 58–61.

[6] Plato, *Phaedrus* 273a–c is the first to quote the hypothetical case of a weak man accused of assaulting a strong man and arguing not the facts (or the truth) of the case but the probability: Πῶς δ' ἂν (past potential) ἐγὼ τοιόσδε τοιῷδε ἐπεχείρησα; ('How could a man of my physique have attacked a man of his?'). (M. Gagarin, 'Probability and Persuasion', in I. Worthington (ed.), *Persuasion: Greek Rhetoric in Action* (London and New York, 1994), 51–2)) felicitously describes this as 'reverse probability argument' after showing that Tisias or Corax did not 'invent' probability-argument.) The judgement of probability depended upon day-to-day experience and the common sense of a jury, and enjoyed the great strength that it could not be bribed like witnesses (Aristot. *Rhet.* 1. 15. 17).

[7] Sopatros in Walz v. 6; Troilus in Walz vi. 48; O. Navarre, *Essai sur la rhétorique grecque avant Aristote* (Paris, 1900), 12, who calls the story 'une fable'. Its authenticity is to some extent undermined by the fact that it was also told of Protagoras and his pupil Euathlus (Diog. Laert. 9. 8. 56; Radermacher *AS* A v. 15). But its casuistical flavour is characteristic of the type of argument used by the Sophists to 'make the worse case seem the better'.

[8] On dilemmaton, or rather ἐνθύμημα ἐκ διλημμάτου, see Apsinus, *Tech. Rhet.* 10 (Sp. i. 376, 378, who quotes [Dem.] 26 *Ag. Aristog. B* 14).

the proof section of a speech. Although the evidence presented above is sufficient to indicate that Corax and Tisias envisaged three or more parts for a speech, actual discussion of prooemium, narrative, and epilogue is almost wholly lacking.[9] It is necessary to abandon the Sicilian pioneers and look elsewhere. The Sophists Protagoras and Prodicus[10] seem to have preferred the medium of the lecture to that of the handbook, for the practical reason that the former afforded a continuous source of income, whereas the availability of the latter, in the absence of laws of copyright, could drastically reduce the size of their audiences. But this disadvantage does not seem to have deterred Gorgias: on his famous visit as chief spokesman of the Leontinian embassy to Athens in 427 BC, he not only delivered a rhetorical *tour de force* to the Ecclesia, which persuaded the Athenians to agree to an alliance against Syracuse, but is said to have brought some form of written teaching material, a *techne*.[11]

The two complete surviving speeches of Gorgias, the *Helen* and the *Palamedes*, together with a fragment of a *Funeral Oration*, provide our only evidence for the form and content of his rhetorical instruction.[12] Unfortunately, none of these pieces can serve the present purpose of identifying early rhetorical material because the dates of their composition are quite uncertain. Indeed, authorship

---

[9] The only reference to topics concerns prooemium and epilogue, with a fleeting allusion to narrative: Κόραξ . . . ἤρξατο λόγοις πρότερον θεραπευτικοῖς καὶ κολακευτικοῖς τὴν ὄχλησιν καὶ τὸ θορυβῶδες καταπραῦναι τοῦ δήμου, ἅτινα καὶ προοίμια ἐκάλεσε, μετὰ δὲ τὸ καταπραῦναι καὶ κατασιγῆσαι τὸν δῆμον ἤρξατο, περὶ ὧν ἔδει, συμβουλεύειν τῷ δήμῳ καὶ λεγειν ὡς ἐν διηγήσει καὶ μετὰ ταῦτα ἀνακεφαλαιοῦσθαι καὶ ἀναμιμνῄσκειν ἐν συντόμῳ περὶ τῶν φθασάντων καὶ εἰς σύνοπτον καὶ ὑπ' ὄψιν ἄγειν τὰ λεχθέντα τῷ δήμῳ. καὶ τὰ μὲν πρῶτα ἐκάλεσε προοίμια, τὰ δὲ δεύτερα ἐκάλεσεν ἀγῶνας, τὰ δὲ τρίτα ἐκάλεσεν ἐπιλόγους (anonymous rhetorician, loc. cit. (n. 4) (*AS* p. 17)). This late source may well be suspected of anachronism by taking his topics from 4th cent. or later rhetoric.

[10] See p. 5.

[11] Sopatros (Walz v. 7, 10 (see Radermacher's notes, *AS* pp. 16, 19)). Diodorus' statement that Gorgias τέχνας ῥητορικὰς πρῶτος ἐξεῦρε (12. 53. 1) may have been written from an Athenian standpoint, meaning that before Gorgias brought his rhetoric to Athens, stay-at-home Athenians had had no opportunity to study rhetorical texts. This still leaves the precise nature of these texts uncertain, and in Gorgias' case a contemporary source (Plato, *Hippias Major* 282b) mentions only his public oratorical displays (*epideixeis*) and his lucrative teaching (συνὼν τοῖς νέοις χρήματα πολλὰ ἠργάσατο καὶ ἔλαβεν). For the Leontinian embassy of 427, see Thuc. 3. 86. 3–4.

[12] It is perhaps worth suggesting, by the way, that his rather flamboyant style and character, as portrayed by Plato in *Gorgias*, make him the unlikely author of a dry, didactic manual like those written by later rhetoricians.

of the two complete works as we now have them must be questioned, since they are written in the Attic dialect. The possibility
that their present form is due to an Athenian editor or transcriber
must be considered seriously. Again, if this *Helen* and that of
Isocrates (see p. 314) are in some way related, a date of publication
around 393 is probable. Blass (*AB* i. 646) tentatively proposes 'after
390' for the *Palamedes*. As a quasi-forensic speech on a mythical
subject, it is of sufficient interest for its contents to be examined
elsewhere (Appendix B).

This brief survey of early rhetoric would be incomplete without
some discussion of the Sophists' contribution to it. But the extent
to which rhetoric came within their purview is difficult to assess.[13]
The most frequently cited interests of Protagoras are in grammar,
and these, together with his avowed general aim of making his
pupils 'better citizens' (Plato, *Prot.* 318e–319a) make him a seemingly high-minded figure, incompatible with the sophist who
could 'make the worse argument appear the better' (Aristot. *Rhet.* 2.
24. 11). But both the sophists and Plato were aware of the possible
ambivalence and contrivable confusion between being 'good' and
being 'good at (something)'; and Protagoras' teaching must have
contained techniques of disputation which included the ability to
turn arguments on their head; and these techniques were found as
useful by speechwriters as by students learning to think for themselves. Actual evidence as to whether litigants obtained direct help
from Protagoras or his teaching is tenuous.[14] The tradition surrounding Prodicus of Ceos makes him interested in the mechanics
of persuasion—how to attract and keep an audience's attention and
arouse its emotions (Aristot. *Rhet.* 3. 14. 9; Quint. 3. 1. 12)—as well
as sharing Protagoras' interest in correct expression (*orthoepeia*).
Definition of certain terms used in legal arguments may be trace-
able to him.[15] Hippias of Elis was a versatile, much-travelled
sophist. The tradition that he claimed ability to speak on any subject in a new way (Xen. *Mem.* 4. 4. 6) would suggest an interest in

[13] For detailed examination of the subject, see H. Gomperz, *Sophistik und Rhetorik*
(Leipzig and Berlin, 1912); M. Untersteiner, *The Sophists*, trans. K. Freeman (Oxford, 1954);
and in general, W. K. C. Guthrie, *The Sophists* (Cambridge, 1971); G. B. Kerferd, *The
Sophistic Movement* (Cambridge, 1981); J. de Romilly, *Les Grands Sophistes* (Paris, 1988).

[14] See, however, Plato, *Crat.* 391b: Socrates advising Hermogenes: ἐπειδὴ δὲ οὐκ
ἐγκρατὴς εἶ τῶν πατρῴων, λιπαρεῖν χρὴ τὸν ἀδελφὸν καὶ δεῖσθαι αὐτοῦ διδάξαι
σε τὴν ὀρθότητα περὶ τοιούτων, ἣν ἔμαθεν παρὰ Πρωταγόρου.

[15] See Radermacher's note, *AS* B viii. 11 (p. 69).

epideixis rather than the genres of practical oratory.[16] Technical innovations in prose style are attributed to Thrasymachus of Chalcedon,[17] though the fragment of his writing preserved by Dionysius of Halicarnassus (*Dem.* 3), rather than breaking new ground, applies the existing stylistic resources of balance and hypotaxis with clarity and restraint.[18] Finally, it seems probable that the public discourses of the Sophists contained, in varying proportions, both performance and instruction—declamation and commentary.

THE ANTIPHONTEAN *TETRALOGIES*

This collection of twelve short speeches in groups of four, two each for prosecution and defence,[19] dealing with three imaginary homicide cases, is the most authentic source of early rhetorical material. Although both date and author are disputable, the *Tetralogies* are most probably the earliest extant model speeches,[20] and therefore hold a prime position in this study of the resources available to the Attic Orators from the beginning. The circumstances created for each case rule out its resolution purely by means of direct evidence, which is either not available, as in the *First Tetralogy*, or open to interpretation, as in the *Second* and *Third Tetralogy*. All three thus require rhetorical treatment: facts, or alleged facts, play a secondary role to arguments and pleas, which assume their highest level of sophistication and intensity when dealing with the religious and moral conflicts that are peculiar to cases of homicide.[21]

---

[16] Plato, *Hipp. Min.* 363a: Hippias 'declaimed' (ἐπιδειξαμένου) on the characters of Homeric heroes.

[17] His is the first name linked with prose rhythm (Aristot. *Rhet.* 3. 8. 4; Cic. *Orat.* 52. 175); and he was associated with Gorgias as a pioneer of artistic prose (Cic. *Orat.* 12. 39).

[18] Denniston *GPS* 15 pronounced the passage 'good, if not very distinguished'. It contains little of the emotional appeal for which he was renowned (Plato, *Phaedrus* 267c–d); but it is genuine periodic writing, and includes an early example of hypothetical inversion (ἐβουλόμην μὲν . . . ἐπειδή). Its originality could be assessed if it could be dated.

[19] The confusing concept of three *Tetralogies* is compounded by their traditional position in the Antiphontean corpus, which is 2, 3, 4. In this book they will be designated *Tetralogy* (*Tetr.*) 1, 2, and 3, ignoring the traditional numbering.

[20] See Appendix A, in which the main arguments for a date in the late 430s are set out.

[21] Hence perhaps the choice of homicide cases for model exercises: they enabled the speechwriter to display the widest range of his skills.

Tetralogy 1. 1: Prosecution 1

A citizen has been murdered on his way home from a dinner-party. The only witness to accuse the defendant is a slave who died soon after identifying him, so that his evidence could not be tested under torture.[22] Thus, with the direct evidence as to fact being sufficient for accusation but too tenuous to secure conviction, the case is ideal for the exploration of probability-argument for both sides. This appears even in the prooemium (1–3), where the defendant is assumed, by a bold *petitio principii*[23] to be an experienced criminal who is not likely to leave material evidence, so that it will be necessary to rely on probabilities (εἰκότα). No other extant homicide speech incorporates probability in its prooemium. After this the aim is to eliminate improbabilities (4). These define different classes of suspects—criminals (κακοῦργοι) seeking gain, men in their cups, men quarrelling, men killing in error—by reference to the place and circumstances of the murder. These circumstances are allowed to emerge in the course of the argument rather than through a continuous narrative. With these improbabilities out of the way, he is free to allege premeditation and to proceed to motive (5–8): enmity (and desire for revenge for past wrongs), fear (of conviction in an impending lawsuit), hope (double hope—of escape, or if not of escape, at least of the satisfaction of requital). This catalogue of motive is the kernel of the case. Witnesses are merely mentioned almost as an afterthought (9), and the prosecutor's success or failure is made to depend on whether the motives furnished would have been likely to induce any man (not just this particular man, as nothing is done to try to individualize his character), to commit murder. There is a short epilogue (10–11), which interestingly introduces the idea of *expediency* alongside that of justice.[24]

---

[22] The evidence of slaves was admissible only under torture in classical Athens. Rhetoricians provided standard arguments both to affirm the validity of such evidence and to discredit it (Aristot. *Rhet.* 1. 15. 26; *Rhet. ad Alex.* 16). See, in general, Harrison *LA* ii. 147–50; S. Todd, 'The Purpose of Evidence in Athenian Courts' in P. Cartledge *et al.* (eds.), *Nomos: Essays in Athenian Law, Politics and Society* (Cambridge, 1990), 33–5; and in particular, G. Thür, *Beweisführung vor Schwurgerichtshöfen Athens: Die Proklesis zur Basanos*, Sitzungsberichte der Österreichischen Akademie der Wissenschaft, Phil.-Hist. Kl. vol. 317 (Vienna, 1977).

[23] Aristot. *Soph. Ref.* 167ᵃ37, 168ᵇ23.

[24] The question of strict adherence to the law in Athenian courts frequently arises later. The enjoyment of sovereign power by the people, together with the inchoate state of some Athenian legislation afforded scope for leniency when a man was able to provide an array of

Tetralogy 1. 2: Defence 1

The remarkable pathos of the prooemium was noticed by Blass.[25]
The need to use strong methods to obtain the jury's goodwill has
been created by the prosecutor's concluding argument, which has
doubled the danger for the defendant. After complaining that he is
the most unfortunate of men, he turns the imputation of being
experienced (*Tetr.* I. I. I) on its head, arguing from probability that
acting as he is accused of doing would show him to be a simpleton
(3) (cf. Lys. 7 *Sac. Ol.* 12). He also complains (4) that he is required
not only to prove his innocence but also to find the murderer (cf.
5 *Her.* 64–6). He cannot point to an individual, so he suggests possible classes of people—robbers, hooligans, his other enemies (5–6).
Turning to the slave's testimony (7–8), he seeks to substitute for the
prosecution's probability-argument one which purports to be more
probable: the principle that slaves' evidence is unreliable unless
obtained under torture, as was not the case here. Next (9) he
applies the argument of 'the greater danger' to the prosecutor's reference (*Tetr.* I. I. 6) to an impending lawsuit which the dead man
had been about to bring against him: to lose his property from that
was a less daunting prospect than losing his life on conviction of
murder (9). Naturally, but sophistically, he does not weigh the
relative chances of apprehension and conviction. 10 contains the
figure of concession: if the probability-arguments secure his conviction, where the facts have failed to do so, *even so* he deserves
acquittal on grounds of self-defence, because those arguments arise
from the perception that he was the original victim. He may be trying to provide for justified homicide as his fall-back position. But
the kind of contorted logic used here is typical of the *Tetralogies*:
nothing marks them more clearly as academic exercises. After it the
author returns to more mundane devices: the recital of the
speaker's services and benefactions to the state, and his profession
of patriotic behaviour (12). The speech ends curiously with a paraleipsis, to the effect that he will not attack his dead enemy's character.

his benefactions to the state or to his family and friends. Hence a plea for simple justice might
not suffice. The prosecutor has to say something like: 'He *is* guilty, but you must also realize that it would be disadvantageous to acquit him.'

   25 *AB* i. 148, 156. The pathetic theme is his unique misfortune in having an enemy who
is capable of injuring him even in death.

Tetralogy 1. 3: Prosecution 2

In his short prooemium (1), the speaker matches his opponent's emotional appeal with a striking personification of 'misfortune' (ἡ ἀτυχία ἀδικεῖται), and repeats his statement of his guilt, adding the defilement (μιαρίαν) peculiar to a murderer. In the rest of the speech he systematically attempts to refute each of the defendant's arguments.

In 2 he tries to reinstate the dying slave's evidence, but because the defendant's point that it was technically inadmissible is hard to rebut, he returns to it again in 4 with the statement that a slave in these circumstances is given his freedom. The prosecutor continues his practice of making unproved assumptions in 5, where he devises a conspiratorial role for the defendant. In 6 the same level of ingenuity is applied to the rebuttal of 9, where he shifts the idea of the 'greater danger' from the prospect of conviction to that of his being caught in the present crime. In 7, by giving universal application to the defendant's argument, he reduces it to absurdity.[26] In 8 he provides what no doubt became the standard argument against the recital of leitourgiai, that such services prove only that a man was rich; and he shrewdly adds that fear of loss of that wealth was a good motive for murder, implying that this probability was the stronger evidence. He uses notably colourful language in his final attack: τὰ ἴχνη τῆς ὑποψίας ('the footprints of suspicion') . . . προστρόπαιος ('avenger', frequently used of a god) . . . ἀγνεύετε τὴν πόλιν ('purge the city'); and he concludes with the topos of example to other potential wrongdoers. It is perhaps the most interesting and accomplished of the four speeches.

Tetralogy 1. 4: Defence 2

The emotional tone is set by the opening word Ἰδού ('Behold!'), an unparalleled imperative. The prooemium matches the prosecutor's first for length, and is directed mainly at establishing his motivation. The defendant's 'misfortune' (ἀτυχία) as victim of malicious prosecution dominates the section (1–4).[27]

---

[26] Aristot. *Soph. Ref.* 174ᵃ32.

[27] Note also the figure of correction: καινότατα . . . εἰ χρὴ καινότατα μᾶλλον ἢ κακουργότατα εἰπεῖν (2).

He then argues probability in regard to the behaviour of (alleged) witnesses of the murder (4–5), a very hazardous piece of rhetoric, as Maidment points out.[28] In 7 he returns to the topos of the reliability of the dying slave's evidence (2. 2. 7), extending his argument sophistically by comparison with the evidence of a free man who survives and may face perjury charges. After this unpromising material the author obviously feels that something sensational is needed, and he introduces it in the form of a piece of direct evidence—an alibi, with witnesses (8). But direct evidence is not the prime material of rhetorical exercises, and we revert (9) promptly to probabilities, this time with a gnome[29] to the effect that prosperous people like himself prefer a quiet life as the best way of avoiding a change in their circumstances.

The rest of the speech does little more than contradict, without further argument, the allegations of the prosecutor. It is the weakest speech of the four, and raises the interesting question of the author's intention: did he intend his pupils to view this *Tetralogy* as a model of a successful prosecution in a case which depended on argument rather than evidence?

Tetralogy 2. 1: Prosecution 1

This case is technically one of homicide admitted as accidental by both sides. Herein lies the prosecutor's main problem. The specific instance under trial, accidental killing in the course of athletic activity, was exempt from prosecution in the time of Demosthenes,[30] but the distinction between voluntary and involuntary

---

[28] *MAO* i. 78–9. He notes 'a portentous *petitio principii*, which of course entirely neglects the fact that passers-by had come forward with very different information'. The defendant is apparently trying to exploit the confusion inherent in the prosecutor's argument in 1. 3. 2 by concentrating on the 'passers-by' he has himself imagined as the reason for the murdered man's not having been robbed (1. 2. 5) and ignoring the men who found him and questioned the dying slave.

[29] Three gnomic sentences, in fact (τοῖς μὲν γὰρ ἀτυχοῦσι . . . καθίστανται). The quick reversion from direct evidence to rhetoric may perhaps undermine Gagarin's suggestion (in *Persuasion*, ed. Worthington, 52–3) that the purpose of introducing the alibi was to show that facts, when available, will overcome arguments from probability.

[30] Dem. 23 *Ag. Aristocr.* 53: ἐάν τις ἐν ἄθλοις ἄκων . . . μὴ φεύγειν κτείναντα. Cf. Plato, *Laws* 9 865a; [Aristot.] *Ath. Pol.* 57. 3 and Rhodes *CAP* 644–6. MacDowell (*AHL* 74) points out that the victim was not a competitor but a bystander. Nevertheless, the argument that he met his death through trespassing on forbidden ground seems cogent. (Plutarch's brief account of the case discussed by Pericles and Protagoras (*Per.* 36. 5) does not describe the victim as a spectator or a competitor, and cannot therefore be cited as a parallel.)

homicide was made much earlier.[31] All types of homicide, however, raised the issue of *miasma* (pollution), which was deemed to
affect the whole community and demanded that the killer be
debarred from public and sacred places. His first speech concentrates on this. It is too short to be subdivided. He simply states the
above position and describes, in one sentence, the circumstances of
the killing: his son has been killed by a javelin thrown by the defendant 'in the gymnasium'. He then makes a plea to other parents in
the jury to show fellow-feeling for his bereavement,[32] but makes
sure to end with a reference to the law of miasma.

Tetralogy 2. 2: Defence 1

The defence has a well-defined prooemium, where we encounter
the first oratorical use of the frequent topos of the quiet citizen, the
ἀπράγμων.[33] Its purpose as an instrument of captatio benevolentiae
becomes clear as the speaker talks of his συμφορά ('misfortune') and
ἀνάγκη ('necessity'), but he also sees a danger. He is going to have
to argue with unusual subtlety (ἀκριβέστερον) because the truth
(ἀλήθεια) (by which he means the definition of the legal (and religious) position) is difficult to attain, whereas a particular view of it
(δόξα) can be persuasively put by a clever advocate.

The defence proceeds to the question of definition (*status gener-
alis*), i.e. the nature of the action which has taken place. He summarizes the view he is going to argue in the words ἄλλου δ᾽ εἰς
αὐτὸν ἁμαρτόντος εἰς ἀκουσίους αἰτίας ἦλθεν ('he accidentally
came to be blamed for an error committed by another against himself', 3). He now examines the central fact which confirms this
view: the alleged victim, not the defendant, by running into the
path of the javelin, which was cast within the proper area, brought
about his own death. With agreement that the death was accidental established, the question hinges on who committed an error (6)
and so became the killer. The use of the word φονεύς ('slayer') at

---

[31] See R. J. Bonner and G. Smith, *The Administration of Justice from Homer to Aristotle*, i
(1938) 111–14, ii (1930) 203–20; Rhodes *CAP* 643 (Laws of Draco and Solon).

[32] This plea is sharpened by the idea of 'conscience' (ἐνθύμιον), implying a burden of
guilt upon those who failed to avenge a murder.

[33] Such a citizen expected popular approval. See Aristoph. *Clouds* 1007; *Wasps* 1040–1;
Birds 39–44; *Peace* 191 (contrasted with *sycophantes*); Dem. 18 *Cor.* 308. See W. Nestle,
Ἀπραγμοσύνη, *Philol.* 81 (1926), 129–40; D. Lateiner, 'The Man Who Does Not Meddle
in Politics', *CW* 76 (1982), 1–12.

this stage is dramatic, and will be in the jury's minds as the speaker next describes the obedient, correct, and lawful action of the thrower (7) and the contrasting error of the victim, who is punished with requital (δίκην) for it (8). He becomes the perpetrator (τὸν δράσαντα) and thereby frees the defendant from blame. The reversal of accusation[34] is completed by returning to the law. He makes no reference to miasma, presumably on the logical ground that he has proved his son's innocence of the crime which would incur it.

The plea which concludes the speech (10–12) insists intensely[35] upon that innocence, but also manages to include a reply to the demand for requital: he says that the boy's death 'is not unavenged' (11), showing recognition of the strength of primitive beliefs about homicide, but insisting that the 'error' was not his son's but the victim's.

Tetralogy 2. 3: Prosecution 2

The author has already sought to illustrate the inappropriateness of attack on personal character in a case of this kind. This accords with the carefully chosen words used by both sides at important points, e.g. the prosecutor has asked for pity rather than revenge (*Tetr.* 2. 1. 2), while the defendant describes the death as πάθος ('that which was suffered') and expresses sympathy and sorrow even while he is proving that it was self-inflicted (*Tetr.* 2. 2. 8). He makes the prosecutor begin his second speech in the same vein by saying that the defendant had spoken with uncharacteristic recklessness, thereby forcing him to follow his simple statement with a more elaborate one. This is a novel variant of the prooemium-topos of abundance.[36] Then, after pleading with the jury to observe their sacred duty as ἔργων τιμωροί, ὁσίων δὲ διαγνώμονες ('avengers of wrong deeds and arbiters of right'), he shows that for him the 'truth' lies in a literal interpretation of the fateful action, whereas acceptance of the defendant's argument would require belief that 'he who struck and killed neither wounded nor killed, whereas he

---

[34] Later a standard method of refutation, e.g. Lys. 21 *Def. Brib.* 16, 17. The principle is noted by Aristotle, *Rhet.* 2. 23. 7, but his examples do not correspond closely with the above: closer is that of λύσις ἐκ περιτροπῆς given in Apsinus, *Tech. Rhet.* 9 (Sp. i. 376).

[35] Note esp. the metaphor ζῶν ἔτι κατορυχθήσομαι ('I shall be buried though yet alive'), and the plea not to be left childless in old age.

[36] Lys. 10 *Ag. Theomn.* 1 (of witnesses); 12 *Ag. Eratos.* 1 (of evidence).

who neither touched the javelin nor had any intention of throwing it . . . pierced his own side with it' (5).[37]

In 6 he introduces a new piece of evidence (cf. 2. 2. 8), alleging that an instructor had ordered the victim to retrieve some javelins, and he was hit 'because of the thrower's indiscipline'. He then claims that the gravamen of the case is the question of who threw the javelin that killed his son (7). He then argues (8) that punishment is due for the taking of life whether it was willingly or unwillingly taken, and failure to exact it would be to impede divine will.[38] In 9 the roles of 'the innocent' and 'the guilty' are reversed (περιτροπή, n. 34). In 10 he falls back on a secondary argument, to the effect that if guilt falls on one it must fall on both, so that the survivor should not go unpunished. The speech has a clear-cut epilogue (11–12), in which law, religion, and blood-guilt figure largely, as might be expected. In particular, he protests against the injustice of being found guilty.[39]

Tetralogy 2. 4: Defence 2

In his final speech, the defendant has to reaffirm where the responsibility for the death lies, and he points out that it was not necessary for the victim actually to have thrown the javelin to be responsible. If he had stood still, he would not have been killed (4).[40]

The idea of 'general and particular', designed to focus responsibility on the dead boy, is used in the next argument, which is that any thrower could have suffered the same misfortune as the defendant, but the victim behaved uniquely (5). A consequence of this is that all throwers were potential killers (6). Praise of the law (8), a frequent topos in later oratory, appears for the first time here, but only in order to reinforce the main thesis, which is reversal of accusation,[41] establishing the defendant as free from blame (καθαρὸς

---

[37] This is the rebuttal of the 'argument by definition' on which the defence has drawn. Such arguments would naturally have found a place in the teachings of the Sophists, who were greatly interested in defining the meanings of words. Definition (finitio) is discussed at length by Quintilian, and his examples include one concerned with different kinds of homicide (7. 3. 7). Cf. Aristot. Rhet. 2. 23. 8.

[38] He also says that ἀτυχία should be expected to entail συμφορά.

[39] οὔτε . . . αὐθένται καταγνωσθέντες ὅσια ἀλλ' ἀνόσι' ἂν πάθοιμεν ὑφ' ὑμῶν.

[40] οὐ γὰρ ἀτρεμίζων ἀπέθανε.

[41] translatio criminis (Ad Herenn. 1. 14. 24), ἀντέγκλημα (Hermog. Stas. 2 Sp. ii. 139–40).

τῆς αἰτίας, 9). The ideas of 'atonement' in προστρόπαιον and of 'conscience' in ἐνθύμιον (9) are followed by a quiet ending.

Tetralogy 3. 1: Prosecution 1

The speaker is trying to rebut a plea of self-defence in an admitted homicide, in which the defendant alleges provocation. The case is complicated by the possibility that the victim might have survived with proper medical treatment.

The most striking feature of the prooemium is the religious and philosophical tone, with its reference to a single god creating the human race and placing high value on life. This may be an archaic element, out of place in the routine prooemia of later practical oratory, though it is not entirely absent from them.[42] The religious standpoint is highlighted by the reference to the accused as τὸν ἀσεβήσαντα ('the sinner') and to his deed as having created a miasma (5). The short description of the manner of the killing (6) is an interesting example of what might be termed an 'economical narrative'—telling the absolute minimum required to support the speaker's contention that an old man was brutally and wantonly killed by a younger man, with no reference to actions preceding or following the killing.

Tetralogy 3. 2: Defence 1

The well-defined prooemium contains the topoi of the prosecution's discreditable motive—enmity (ἔχθρα)—and their freedom from risk. The defendant's spirited reply, alleging that the victim was in fact the aggressor, boldly suggests that as such he deserved to receive more punishment than he gave (cf. Soph. *O.T.* 810–12).

By way of a procatalepsis (ἐρεῖ δέ, 3), the *status coniecturalis* of the case is explored. Was it murder? The man was attended by a doctor who should have restored him, but failed (4). He moves on quickly from this point, however, and directs his main argument towards the question of who was guilty, applying the prosecution's reference to the gods to his own position, and using some of their language (7). He ends (9) by attributing the ἀσέβημα to the prosecution.

---

[42] e.g. Dem. *Proem.* 27, 30; 18 *Cor.* 1.

Tetralogy 3. 3: Prosecution 2

The main interest of this speech lies in the drawing of probability from the use of character types. 'Young men are more likely to be aggressive than older men' (2).[43] It is very apposite here. The speaker proceeds to enlist the jury's sympathy by dwelling on the inequality of a contest between young and old. By a rather sophistic argument, he tries to link 'the hands' with 'the intentions' (4), deliberately confusing intention with outcome through a clever antithesis.[44] Seemingly realizing the precariousness of this argument he then turns to the possibility of mischance (ἀτυχία). A rare early use of hypostasis (εἰς τοῦτο τόλμης καὶ ἀναιδείας ἥκει, ὥστε . . . ('he has reached such a level of rash impudence that . . .', 6), a device of deinosis, seems to confirm that the speaker is being represented as insecure with his shaky arguments. Indeed, the speech ends on a note of protestation, another indication of insecurity.

Tetralogy 3. 4: Defence 2

The speaker is a synegoros (advocate, supporting speaker), the defendant having withdrawn into exile. Naturally, he must begin by denying that the withdrawal is due to consciousness of guilt. But his appearance as a newcomer to the trial enables him to introduce some fresh ideas. Perhaps the most interesting of these concerns the meaning of 'tekmeria', which here appears to be 'indications drawn from arguments', as distinct from physical evidence. The prosecution's tekmeria are said to fail the test of reasonableness (εἰκός), because universal application of the assumption that young men are more aggressive than older men would render the examination of other evidence superfluous. He urges as more realistic the particular proposition that some young men are self-controlled, and some older men are violent in their cups. Thus in successive speeches the standard antilogical enthymemes (rhetorical syllogisms) have been examined. The speaker now reintroduces (3) the direct evidence, the witnesses, to tilt the balance once more in his favour. He then

---

[43] Aristot. *Rhet.* 2. 12. 13.

[44] 'If in each case our hands carry out our intentions, he who struck but did not kill willed only the blow, but the man who struck the fatal blow willed the death, for it was as a result of an intentional act that the man was killed.'

rebuts the 'argument from intention' by saying that the defendant's intention extended only as far as the delivery of a blow in his own defence (4). His role as a new speaker enables him to give a new account of the killing which emphasizes the defendant's reactive part throughout, contradicting his statement that he gave more than he received. Aware of this weakness, he follows it with two topoi of reversal of accusation, switching the blame first to the victim (6–7), then to the doctor (8). The speech ends (11) with the topos of time (χρόνος—'allow time to pass, do not decide hastily'), uniquely suited to homicide cases, where an unfavourable verdict leads to irreversible punishment (cf. Ant. 5 *Her.* 14, 86).

RHETORIC IN THE DRAMATISTS

Fifth-century tragedy contains material which could have derived ultimately from rhetorical teaching, and since many plays were written before the earliest published speeches, examination of these is of particular interest. Disappointingly but perhaps predictably, the earliest tragedian, **Aeschylus**, does not add much to our knowledge of early rhetoric. However, the trial of Orestes in the *Eumenides* shows some of the mechanics of legal procedure in operation, with the prosecutor (ὁ διώκων[45]) speaking first (583–4), and Apollo as witness for the defence (576). He is an unusual witness in that he accepts responsibility for the alleged crime (579–80), thus taking some of the wind out of the prosecution's sails. But they press on with their case, directly questioning the defendant to establish the fact of the crime and to confirm under whose authority he committed it (585–603). This interrogatory procedure was probably illustrated in the *technai*.[46] The other feature of the trial that may relate to rhetorical theory is the distinction between justified and unjustified homicide, which, together with other distinctions gave rise to formal treatment under heads, later called *staseis*, Lat. *status*.[47] Apart from these features, the trial seems to

---

[45] Aeschylus follows the technical usage of the singular even though there is a plurality of prosecutors—the eponymous chorus.

[46] Lys. 12 *Ag. Eratos.* 25; 22 *Ag. Corndealers* 5; Andoc. 1 *Myst.* 101. See E. M. Carawan, 'Erotesis: Interrogation in the Courts', *GRBS* 24 (1983), 209–26.

[47] Evidence that the questions of fact, of justification, and of the precise category of an alleged offence were a part of early rhetorical theory has tended to be overlooked in the face of the tradition that Hermagoras of Temnos (2nd cent. BC) invented *stasis*-theory. This

have few points of contact with the theory or practice of fifth-century oratory. Dominated by deities, its atmosphere is prophetic and expository; and, curiously, when Athena casts her deciding vote, she explains her action by her own birth, not by her judgement of the merits of the arguments (734–43).

Whereas the *Oresteia*, produced in 458 BC, belongs to the new democratic age at Athens by only a few years, the plays of **Sophocles** are firmly embedded in it. The earliest of those that we have is *Ajax*, dated between 445 and 444.[48] It is the first extant play to contain identifiable rhetorical devices, though these are present only on a very modest scale. There are two successive instances of the later hackneyed hypothetical inversion (εἰ μὲν . . . ἂν . . . νῦν δέ, 442–53). Forceful use is made of rhetorical question in 1097 ff. and elsewhere. The plot of *Antigone*, produced probably in 442, should have provided opportunities for quasi-forensic argument about guilt, responsibility, and the nature of law, but in the event the play contains nothing relating to rhetorical usage. Moreover, the uncompromising standpoints taken by the main characters seem to rule out persuasion and debate. Of the other extant plays only *Oedipus Tyrannus* probably antedates the first Attic orations,[49] but it yields no rhetorical material.

Although not directly contributory to the present search, the occurrence of rhetorical devices in the later plays[50] is of interest, since it could stem from the poet's awareness of the growing art of speechwriting in his later years.[51] In *Electra* we find a good example of hypophora (535–41), antithesis with anaphora (959–61), the transitional topos 'to cut a long story short' (688), and enumeration (967–72). In *Philoctetes*, there is a related transitional formula ταῦτα μὲν τί δεῖ λέγειν; (11–12), hypophora (1350 ff.); and, perhaps influential on later oratory more than influenced by contemporary speeches, characterization (79, 88 ff., 108, 336–8, 902–13).

evidence includes, in addition to the above Aeschylean example, its presence in the *Tetralogies* (2. 2. 3, 3. 2. 3); also Lysias 12 *Ag. Eratos.* 35, 29 *Ag. Philocr.* 5 (q.v.). O. Navarre, *Essai sur la rhétorique grecque avant Aristote* (Paris, 1900) 261 is one of the few to acknowledge the probable antiquity of *stasis*-theory, and also notes traces of it in Aristotle *Rhetoric* (1. 13. 9 ff.).

[48] For this dating, see V. Ehrenberg, *Sophocles and Pericles*, Appendix C, who follows Jebb in identifying it as an early play. Jebb noted Aeschylean influence in the structure of this play and *Antigone*. More recently, scholars have argued for a later date.

[49] *c.*429 BC is suggested by Ehrenberg, *Sophocles and Pericles*, 114.

[50] *Electra* has been dated around 413, *Philoctetes* and *Oedipus Coloneus* later.

[51] Sophocles was actually involved in litigation at this time (Aristot. *Rhet.* 3. 15. 3).

Thus Sophocles appears to have drawn little upon the material of the nascent genre of practical oratory. The third great tragedian, **Euripides**, shows much clearer affinities with it,[52] and these are manifested in some of his earlier plays, which were composed before the first Attic speeches and the ambassadorial visit of Gorgias, thereby increasing the likelihood that the rhetorical material in them may derive from early *technai*. The agon in *Heraclidae* (*c*.430 BC) contains an early working of the deliberative themes of justice and expediency, and there is already a degree of sophistication as the two speakers, the herald and Iolaus, dispute about two kinds of justice. On a practical level, and contributing to a rhetorical flavour, the play contains a good example of paraleipsis (951–2),[53] and a passage of carefully balanced antithetical argument followed by rhetorical questions (153–65). *Hippolytus* (428 BC) has a passage which takes the recognizable form of a defence speech (983–1035), but the poet shows himself so conversant with two topoi that he adapts them to character. For captatio benevolentiae the self-righteous Hippolytus substitutes remonstration against his father's anger. Then he adapts the plea of the inexpert speaker by saying that he is happier addressing a few intelligent people than a large crowd (986–7). One is justified in assuming that the original forms of both topoi will have been familiar to the audience. Then follows regret of the necessity to plead, another forensic commonplace (990–1). Next, he proposes to divide up his defence, as rhetorical theory prescribes. First he gives a catalogue of his virtues—in general his *sophrosune* ('self-control') (995) and his sexual chastity in particular (1002–6) which provide an implied *eikos*-argument against the main charge—his best defence against the strong factual evidence of Phaedra's corpse and her letter denouncing him. Then he turns on his accuser and demands that he state possible motives (1008), suggesting some and dismissing them as

---

[52] Th. Miller, *Euripides Rhetoricus* (Göttingen, 1887) examines division and other rhetorical features of the plays, in furtherance of his thesis that Euripides' speeches followed the rules laid down in rhetorical handbooks. For a more balanced and cogent assessment of Euripidean rhetoric, see M. Lloyd, *The Agon in Euripides* (Oxford, 1992). Of the thirteen scenes which he recognizes as *agones*, the following qualify chronologically for inclusion in the present discussion: *Heraclidae* 120–283, *Hippolytus* 902–1089, *Medea* 446–622, *Hecuba* 1109–292, *Supplices* 399–580. The other eight scenes are in plays later than the first Attic speeches (i.e. after 421), except *Alcestis* 614–733 (*c*.438 BC), where rhetorical influence is not readily discernible.

[53] After mentioning a major κακόν to which Theseus had subjected Heracles, Alcmene says: ἀλλὰ δ᾽ οἳ᾽ ἐμηχανῶ κακὰ σιγῶ· μακρὸς γὰρ μῦθος ἂν γένοιτό μοι.

improbable in a rhetorical hypophora (1009–15). A hypothetical inversion (εἰ μὲν . . . ἂν . . . νῦν δέ) (1022–7) leads to an emotional plea (1028–31), conventional in an epilogue.[54]

Medea's speech contains a vestigial diegesis (narration) (475–87), but its structured progress breaks down in emotion. Her adversary coolly but self-consciously divides his defence under clear heads: he analyses her motives (526–33) and her gains (534–44) and balances these with his own motives in a passage which contains hypophora (567–8), hypostasis (569–70), and a generalized misogynistic statement (569–75).

In *Hecuba*, another early play (429–7 BC), Odysseus, speaking like a rhetorician (or sophist), as he often does in Attic tragedy, tries to explain to Hecuba the necessity of her daughter Polyxena's sacrifice at the tomb of Achilles. One of his arguments concludes with a pathetic paradox: οὔκουν τόδ' αἰσχρόν, εἰ βλέποντι μὲν φίλῳ χρώμεσθ', ἐπεὶ δ' ὄλωλε, μὴ χρώμεσθ' ἔτι; (311–12). A similar argument describes a paradoxical non-hypothetical situation in 592–8, introduced by οὔκουν δεινόν, the more common formula for pathetic paradox in the orators. Later in the play, a passage which Lloyd (97) rightly describes as 'one of Euripides' most sophisticated pieces of forensic rhetoric' (1187–237) begins with a short invective against clever speakers (1187–94), addressed to Agamemnon as a prooemium (1195: φροιμίοις). In it Hecuba attacks the immorality of Polymestor's behaviour from several angles, first suggesting possible motives through questions (1201–5) and supplying the discreditable answer—personal gain (1206–7)—then contrasting what he *should* have done with what he actually did (1217–32) and underlining the consequence of his wrong action with hypothetical inversion (εἰ . . . ἂν . . . νῦν, 1228–32). She concludes by turning back to Agamemnon, summarizing the overall consequence for his reputation (1232–7). Rhetorical division is apparent throughout her speech. The only other play by Euripides which probably preceded the earliest extant Attic speeches is *Supplices* (c.421). Although it is an intensely political play, the plot affords few opportunities for rhetorical invention. However, Theseus' generalizations about the bounties which man has devised for the development of civilized life (195–218) are also

---

[54] Here in the form of a wish, ὀλοίμην . . . , with asyndeton: ἄπολις, ἄοικος, φυγὰς ἀλητεύων χθόνα. Lloyd, *The Agon in Euripides*, 47, remarks: 'Hippolytus' defence evokes the lawcourts to a greater extent than any other speech in Euripides.'

the subject-matter of epideictic oratory, while observations about the importance of law (312–13), especially written law, for individual freedom (429–37) are equally commonplace in forensic and epideictic oratory. The formal and detached character of the *agon*-scene in this speech may be compared with that in *Heraclidae*, as Lloyd has suggested (79); and its central theme, democracy, establishes its generic affinity with deliberative oratory. Finally, it is impossible to read the character-sketches of the seven heroes (860–918) without recalling rhetorical techniques, but precise parallels are difficult to make, and the existence of a rhetorical model for these sketches must remain an open question.

Figures of language are the common property of poets and prose-writers, though different tendencies may be noted. Polyptoton, etymological figure, and epanadiplosis (*geminatio*) are notably commoner in Sophocles and Euripides than in prose, and anaphora is at least as common. Though not without interest, this tells little about influence or affinity. Figures of thought are more revealing. In addition to the instances already mentioned, paraleipsis occurs in Euripides *Heraclid*. 951, *Electra* 946, and *Orestes* 16, 27; aposiopesis in *Orestes* 1145, 1161, aparithmesis (*enumeratio*) in Soph. *Electra* 261 ff., Eur. *Troades* 919 ff., correction in Eur. *Iph. Aul.* 460, *Orestes* 18, Soph. *Electra* 273, οὐκ . . . ἀλλὰ antithesis (or pleonasm) in *Iph. Aul.* 1269–71, *Orestes* 576–8, *Helen* 957, Soph. *Ajax* 1250–2, *Ant.* 456–7, *O.T.* 810, 855, procatalepsis in Eur. *Orestes* 665.

As a trenchant lampoonist of sophists, rhetoricians and demagogues, **Aristophanes** might be expected to have frequent, if parodic, recourse to rhetorical artifice.[55] Two of his plays which are most concerned with oratory also happen to precede the earliest extant speeches for the courts. In *Acharnians* (425 BC), the speech of the protagonist Dikaiopolis to the Assembly (really addressing the audience (οἱ θεώμενοι)) begins with a variant of the conventional apology (496–8).[56] His speech consists mostly of dramatic narrative, anaphorically divided (ἐντεῦθεν . . . , 528, 530, 535, 539), with antistrophe (. . . οὐχὶ τὴν πόλιν λέγω, 515–16) and procatalepsis (ἐρεῖ τις, 540); and it concludes with a long sequence of asyndetic

---

[55] See C. T. Murphy, *HSCP* 49 (1938), 69–113; N. O'Sullivan, *Alcidamas, Aristophanes and the Beginnings of Greek Stylistic Theory* (Stuttgart, 1992), 106–50.

[56] The speech being deliberative rather than forensic, Dikaiopolis' apology, for addressing the sovereign People's Assembly though he is a mere beggar (πτωχός), may be a variant of the apology of a young speaker taking precedence over his elders (Dem. 4 *Phil. I* 1).

genitives (546–54).[57] These latter may well be a parody, taken to an extreme of bad taste, of early attempts, perhaps illustrated in the *technai*,[58] at periodic structure.[59] The poet's description of his long-term mission to arm his fellow-citizens against deceit by politicians includes reference to the clever fawning styles of visiting diplomats and their use of fair words (636–40). The performance of Gorgias on the Leontinian embassy (427 BC) would have been fresh in the minds of his audience, the younger members of which, in particular, would have been inspired to emulate it.[60]

The *dikasteria* are central to the plot of *Wasps* (422 BC), and a number of passages in it have a distinctly rhetorical flavour: 488 ff.; 548 ff. (which deploys devices of emotional appeal); 650 ff. (which contains a prayer in a prooemium, a subsequent rarity, see n. 42); 950 ff., where Bdelycleon begins his defence of the dog Labes thus:

χαλεπὸν μέν, ὦ 'νδρες, ἐστὶ διαβεβλημένου
ὑπεραποκρίνεσθαι κυνός, λέξω δ' ὅμως.

Gentlemen, it is difficult to speak in a slandered dog's defence, but I will try none the less.

In *Knights* (424 BC) there is a comic reference to the topos of audience-flattery in prooemia (1340–4, cf. 215–16). But for further examples of rhetorical material one must turn to the 'women's plays', all of which are too late to meet the present purpose.[61]

THE EARLY RHETORICAL TRADITION: SUMMARY

The results of the foregoing search for doctrine, topoi, types of argument, and rhetorical material in literature preceding the first Attic oratory must now be brought together. The product of this

---

[57] See also the asyndeton in the famous description of Pericles' oratory (530–1): Περικλέης οὐλύμπιος ἤστραπτ' ἐβρόντα ξυνεκύκα τὴν Ἑλλάδα.

[58] Ultimately: but an immediate source for a few lines and phrases in Dikaiopolis' speech has been found in Euripides *Telephus*. See D. M. MacDowell, *Aristophanes and Athens* (Oxford, 1995), 60–2.

[59] In *Ad. Herenn.* 4. 12. 18 the use of such long sequences is listed as one of the faults of composition to be avoided. This shows the influence of Aristotle (*Rhet.* 3. 9), who was reacting against the practice of Isocrates.

[60] See *Acharnians* 678 ff. for description of rhetoric as a young man's art.

[61] 'Speeches' making obvious use of rhetorical forms and commonplaces are *Lys.* 507–97, 1122–61 (411 BC); *Thesm.* 383–432, 466–519 (411 BC); *Eccl.* 151–88, 216–40, 587–94 (*c.*392 BC).

exercise is a kind of composite *techne*, the entire content of which one may assume to have been available to a speechwriter plying his trade from about 420 BC.

The only general doctrine that seems to have governed oratorical composition from its beginnings is that of *division*. The Sicilian pioneers taught that a speech should have a prooemium, a central section containing the case proper as argued by either side (the *agon*—'contest'); and an epilogue. Viewed from later practice, the absence of a clearly defined section for narrative is interesting, since this suggests a prime area for the development of individual talent. The *Tetralogies* observe a mainly tripartite division, with little narrative, and even those theorists who taught after narrative had been used to good effect by the first speechwriters seem to have devoted most of their attention to subdivisions of the proof.[62] But our composite *techne* must begin at the beginning. The topoi, types of argument, and rhetorical figures are in italics.

Prooemium

The conditions which a speaker needed to create at the beginning of his speech would have been universally understood. He had to win his audience's goodwill. The specific topoi designed to realize this aim are:

Flattering the jury by (1) *expressing confidence in their fair-mindedness* (*Tetr.* 1. 4. 1; Aristoph. *Knights* 1340–4).

(2) *sympathizing with them in their difficult task* (*Tetr.* 3. 3. 1).

In order to stress his own difficulties he may advert to:

His inexperience and/or ineptitude as a speaker[63] (Eur. *Hipp.* 986–7) (variant).

Disadvantage arising (1) *from his status, e.g. being a poor man* (Aristoph. *Acharnians* 496–8) *or a young man* (esp. in deliberative oratory).

---

[62] Plato, *Phaedrus* 266c–267a: Theodorus of Byzantium belonged to the generation after Thrasymachus and Gorgias (Cic. *Orator*. 39), and was thus a contemporary of Lysias. See Blass *AB* i. 259–62. Euenus of Paros was a sophist well known in Athens as a teacher of ἀνθρωπίνη and πολιτικὴ ἀρετή at the time of Socrates' trial in 399 BC (Plato, *Apol.* 20b; *Phaedo* 60d).

[63] It is logical to assume that this plea by an Athenian litigant in the classical period (420–322 BC) must refer to his delivery and his performance on the stand, since the text of the speech itself was the work of a skilled professional speechwriter. Yet this topos may have its origin in the pre-professional era of litigation, and may perhaps be regarded as a survival from that era.

(2) *from his character* (esp. *from his retiring, non-litigious disposition* (*apragmosyne*)). (*Tetr.* 2. 2. 1).[64]

Yet in a complex case, he may need to

Apologize for having to argue cleverly (*Tetr.* 2. 2. 2, 4. 2, Eur. *Med.* 522–5).

Adverting to advantages enjoyed by his opponent, he may refer to his:

Preparation[65] (*Tetr.* 1. 1. 1, 2. 3. 3).

Cleverness, esp. at ingratiation (Aristoph. *Acharnians* 636–40).

Lack of Danger (*Tetr.* 3. 2. 1).

The other topoi which the early tradition assigns to prooemia are:

Abundance (of evidence, arguments etc.) (*Tetr.* 2. 3. 1, cf. Soph. *Philoc.* 1047).

Ascription of Motive to the opponent (*Tetr.* 3. 2. 1; Eur. *Hec.* 1206–7 (enmity)).

Finally, the injection of *Emotional Appeal* into prooemia seems, on the evidence of the *Tetralogies* and Euripides (see *Med.* 465–74, *Heraclid.* 941, *Hipp.* 936–45), to have been a firmly recommended practice, to which some of the above topoi readily lent themselves. This usually included *self-pity*, through which a litigant might *deplore the danger he faces* (especially in capital cases) (*Tetr.* 1. 2. 1–2; 1. 4. 1); or he may simply bemoan his misfortune in general (*Tetr.* 1. 2. 1, 1. 3. 1, 1. 4. 1–2, 2. 2. 2).

In spite of its containing some of the topoi most commonly found in later prooemia, the early tradition clearly did not exhaust the possibilities, but left ample scope for the Attic orators to exercise their ingenuity in this part of the speech. Most noteworthy is the absence of a formal statement of the case to be proved or answered (*prothesis*).

Narrative

Scope for innovation was to be immeasurably greater in respect of narrative, for which our early models seem to have offered little exemplary guidance. Its development as a distinct part of a speech seems to have been due to the first Attic orators, especially Lysias and Andocides; but it is not wholly absent from the *Tetralogies*. In

---

[64] See n. 33.

[65] παρασκευή: this topos was to be associated not only with time but also dishonest intent.

3. 1. 6 we find what may be termed 'economical narrative', in which a bare minimum of facts are recounted, describing only the act of killing. Elsewhere the facts of the cases emerge through, or have to be inferred from, the arguments. Models for expanded or continuous narrative were, however, to be drawn from other genres. Historiography at this stage of its development proved less useful than drama. The tragedians had many opportunities to exercise their narrative skills, but the best example of a narrative in a quasi-forensic setting is Aristophanes *Acharnians* 515–39, a truly dramatic narrative with rhetorical features. Narrative was to come into its own in real lawsuits, in which litigants had real-life stories to tell.

Proof

The lack of a distinct role for narrative in early theory leaves only an undifferentiated central section, which contains the topoi, forms of argument and figures of thought that combine, without clearly-defined division,[66] to present the speaker's side of the contest (*agon*) and his rebuttal of his opponent's case.

Generically established in the early tradition, and often implied when not stated explicitly, was *Argument from Probability* (eikos)[67] (*Tetr.* 1. 1. 2–4, 2. 3, 5–8, 1. 4. 5, 9; Eur. *Hipp.* 1007–20), species of which include

    Biographical Proof (Pistis ek biou) (*Tetr.* 1. 2. 12); (rebuttal of: *Tetr.* 1. 3. 8).
    Character-Types (*Tetr.* 3. 3. 2, 4. 8. Cf. Aristot. *Rhet.* 2. 12. 14).
Topoi:
    Praise of the Law (*Tetr.* 2. 4. 8; Eur. *Suppl.* 312–13, 429–41).
    Intention (dianoia) (*Tetr.* 3. 4. 4–5).
    Reversal of Accusation (peritrope, translatio criminis) (*Tetr.* 2. 2. 6–8, 3. 9, 4. 6; 3. 2 *passim*, 4. 7–8).
    Universalizing (Particular to General) (*Tetr.* 1. 3. 7; 2. 4. 6).
    Status (stasis) (Aeschyl. *Eum.* 585 ff.; *Tetr.* 2. 2. 3; 3. 2. 3).
    The Evidence of Slaves (*Tetr.* 1. 2. 7–8, 3. 4).
Forms of argument, and argumentative formulae:
    Double-Catch (Dilemmaton): (Tisias v. Corax (see p. 3)).

---

[66] But the need for division and subdivision was felt by some theorists: Plato, *Phaedrus* 266c–267a mentions Theodorus of Byzantium and Euenus of Paros.

[67] See n. 6; also C. Kuebler, *The Argument from Probability in Early Attic Oratory* (Chicago, 1944).

Petitio Principii (Tetr. 1. 1. 1, 4. 5).

Pathetic Paradox[68] (οὔκουν δεινόν (αἰσχρόν, etc.) . . . ;) (Eur. *Hec.* 311–12, 592–8).

Reductio ad Absurdum (Eur. *Alc.* 699–702).

A Fortiori (Comparative) Argument (Eur. *Hipp.* 451–61; *Tetr.* 3. 2. 2).

Hypothetical Inversion (Eur. *Med.* 488–91, 585–7; *Hipp.* 1022–7; *Hec.* 1228–32. In *Tetr.* a fixed formula had not become established).

Interrogation (Aeschyl. *Eum.* 855 ff.).

Figures of thought:

Rhetorical Question (passim).

Question and Answer (Hypophora) (Eur. *Hipp.* 1009–15. Elsewhere in Euripides: Lloyd, *The Agon in Euripides*, 29–30).

Anticipation (Procatalepsis) (Tetr. 3. 2. 3; Eur. *Suppl.* 962 (Lloyd 73–4)).

Hypostasis ((εἰς) τοσοῦτο (τόλμης etc.) . . . ὥστε . . .) *(Tetr.* 2. 3. 4–5; 3. 3. 5).

Paraleipsis (Eur. *Heraclid.* 951–2).

Concession (Tetr. 1. 2. 10; 3. 4. 7).

Correction (Tetr. 1. 4. 2).

Finally, early uses of themes which later became standard in deliberative oratory—justice and expediency—have been noted in Eur. *Heraclid.* by Lloyd (73–4).

Epilogue

The two main components of the epilogue, summary and emotional appeal, are established in the early tradition. The latter would typically contain an earnest adjuration to convict or acquit, giving grounds which include, on the prosecution side, *The Interest of the Community* and *Example to Others (Tetr.* 1. 3. 11) as well as that of individual justice; and, on the defence side, especially appropriate in homicide cases, *The Plea for Time (Tetr.* 3. 4. 11):

Summary (Anacephalaiosis) (Tetr. 1. 1. 9; 2. 4. 9–10; 3. 3. 7).

[68] This type of argument, which usually contains a comparative element, was classified under the head of *argumenta ex contrario* by G. Gebauer, *De Hypotacticis et Paratacticis Argumenti ex Contrario Formis quae reperiuntur apud Oratores Atticos* (Zwickau, 1887). My name for it attempts to take account of the emotional content which it usually has. J. J. Bateman, *Phoenix* 16 (1962), 164 remarks that the function of this type of argument 'is emotional rather than logical'.

Emotional Appeal (Pathos): Couching the plea for acquittal or conviction in language which evokes anger or compassion (Eur. *Hipp.* 1028–31; *Tetr.* 1. 1. 10–11; 1. 2. 13; 1. 3. 10–11 (the irreversibility of a capital penalty); 2. 2. 11–12; 3. 2. 9; 3. 4. 10–11).

As is the case with prooemium and narrative, the range of topoi which the Attic orators include in their epilogues is wider and more varied than that found in the early tradition. In the *Tetralogies*, perhaps because of their brevity, this section is not thoroughly developed.

2

ANTIPHON

Antiphon is the earliest of the Attic orators by a generation (born c.480 BC). Dearth of biographical detail is unsurprising in his case, since he shunned public attention throughout a career which combined rhetorical writing with political conspiracy. Thucydides, his admirer, credited him with masterminding the oligarchic revolution of 411–410 after years of clandestine preparation (8. 68). Its failure led to his trial and death. His literary legacy, by contrast, was permanent. He comes down as the first man to publish speeches written for others.[1] Some of the surviving titles of lost or fragmentary speeches suggest a political programme or affinity,[2] and a less clearly definable political background may be discerned in the extant full speeches. All concern homicide. They contain few indications as to their date, though they are probably all products of his later years. There has been little scholarly opposition to the tentatively expressed opinion of Blass (AB i. 192–3) that the speech Against the Stepmother is the earliest, but there is less agreement over the dates of the other two speeches. Without a high degree of conviction, I accept the arguments which assign Death of a Chorus-Boy to 419/18 and Murder of Herodes to 417/16.[3]

---

[1] This statement is based on the simple fact that no forensic speeches earlier than Antiphon's were known to his biographers (Vit. X Or. 832d). For other sources and evidence, see Edwards GO i. 21–3.

[2] On the Tribute of Lindos and On the Tribute of Samothrace may have been written in support of subject-allies against an oppressive Athenian democracy, or perhaps more specifically in support of the oligarchic factions in those places. Cartledge, in Nomos (1990), 51–2 reasonably suggests that Antiphon hired out his expertise to oligarchs facing litigation in the years of preparation for the coup of 411.

[3] See B. D. Meritt, The Athenian Calendar in the Fifth Century (Harvard, 1928), 121–2; K. J. Dover, CQ 44 (1950), 44–60.

1 *Against the Stepmother*

This case of alleged poisoning, brought by the stepson of the
accused and defended by his half-brother (her son) posed serious
problems to the prosecutor. In the first place the poison was administered to the victim, the speaker's father, by a third person who
was executed soon after the alleged crime, stretching and hence
weakening the chain of guilt, and adding to the circumstantial
nature of the evidence. Secondly, that evidence was itself peculiarly
tenuous, there being no witnesses as to fact. Faced with these difficulties, Antiphon had to use literary and rhetorical means to create the required prejudice against the accused.[4]

The speech is highly charged with emotion from the beginning,
with the speaker pleading for punishment (τιμωρία) and expressing amazed outrage at his brother's behaviour. The **prooemium**
(1–4) begins with conventional references to the speaker's inexperience, due to youth. But it is joined by two other topoi not previously encountered—apology for the necessity of litigation and
deprecation of conflict between relatives.[5] A more subtle feature of
this prooemium is the pervasive petitio principii that a murder has
been committed and the guilty are known and must be pursued.[6]
The other point which needs to be stressed at an early stage is the
forethought and planning (ἐξ ἐπιβουλῆς καὶ προβουλῆς, 3;
προνοίας, 5) and persistence (μὴ ἅπαξ ἀλλὰ πολλάκις, 3) that
preceded the murder, because the defence have alleged that the
fatal poisoning was accidental.

The simplest way to account for lack of evidence is to blame
the other side for that lack, and this Antiphon proceeds to do
(5–12). In this procatasceue the argument is conducted, mostly in
general terms, and at somewhat disproportionate length, around
the refusal of the defence to allow slaves in their power to be tor-

---

[4] For full discussion of the problems and Antiphon's solutions, see S. Wijnberg, *Antiphons
Eerste Rede* (Amsterdam, 1938); A. Barrigazzi, *Antifonte: Prima orazione* (Florence, 1955); also
J. H. Thiel, 'Antiphontea', *Mnemosyne* 56 (1927), 81–92; U. Albini, *Maia* 10 (1958), 38–65,
132–45.

[5] Nevertheless the chances that both these topoi occurred in earlier *technai* are high: in
particular, if Sicilian rhetoric had its beginnings in litigation over disputed property (Cic.
Brut. 12. 46), family quarrels must have figured in some at least of these. Certainly the topos
became firmly established (Lys. 32 *Ag. Diog.* 1; Isaeus *passim*; Dion. Hal. *Lys.* 24).

[6] The early reference to 'murderers' (φονεῦσι (1) . . . φονῆς (4)) is joined by an indig-
nant paradox that they are being defended by one who should be avenging his father's killing
(4–5).

tured to obtain evidence. This behaviour is taken as a tekmerion (indication) of guilt (11), and the speaker adds that if he had behaved similarly, his opponent would have drawn the same inference.[7] But he protests too much about the importance of these slaves' evidence. From what he himself says, they were able only to confirm that the stepmother had been caught administering a potion to her husband on a previous occasion. They could only have given an opinion as to her purpose, and they would be unable to refute her allegation that the potion was intended as a love-philtre (9–10). Hence their evidence would have been both irrelevant and indecisive.

Lacking evidence, the speechwriter must try to persuade the jury through the way he relates the facts of the case. Thus the **narrative** becomes the most important section of the speech.[8] Events preceding the poisoning serve (prodiegesis, 14–18) to establish motive—the *pallake* ('concubine')[9] was about to be discarded by Philoneos, and the stepmother was 'being wronged' ($\dot{a}\delta\iota\kappa o\hat{\iota}\tau o$) (14–15)—and more importantly to show the degree of planning and premeditation that went into it (see 3, 5). While the women schemed and deceived (the *pallake* was duped by the stepmother into believing that she would be administering a love-philtre), the male victims are represented sympathetically: Philoneos is a 'gentleman' ($\kappa a\lambda\acute{o}\varsigma\ \tau\epsilon\ \kappa\dot{a}\gamma a\theta\acute{o}\varsigma$), who sees his good friend off on his journey with a party and a sacrifice, while the latter is simply an unsuspecting and undeserving victim. This impression is sharpened by pathos in the narrative of the fatal act itself (18–20). The *pallake* pours out the poisoned wine 'for them to make a libation—prayers never to be fulfilled, gentlemen of the jury' (19). There is also a short moment of drama as the two victims 'lay hold of their slayer as they drink their last draught' (20).[10] Immediate reference to the swift retribution that overtook the *pallake* makes effective way for

---

[7] Antiphon uses this standard argument in 5 *Her.* 38, and its counterpart, refusal to submit his slaves to torture, in 6 *Chor.* 27. B. Due, *Antiphon: A Study in Argumentation* (Copenhagen, 1980), 17 notes the implied attempt here to contrast the defendant's base motives with the upright motives of the speaker.

[8] Due, *Antiphon*, 20, describes it as 'the broadest and most vivid in the extant speeches of Antiphon'.

[9] Her servile status is argued by C. Carey, 'A Note on Torture in Athenian Homicide Cases', *Historia* 37 (1988), 241–2.

[10] G. Vollmer, *Studien zum Beweis antiphontischer Reden* (Hamburg, 1958), 50, and Due, *Antiphon*, 20, follow Gernet (Budé) in noting the quasi-tragic atmosphere created by the mention of Clytemnestra (17).

the vehement plea[11] that the real culprit should suffer a similar fate.

In 23 Antiphon carefully avoids saying what the defence's plea would be,[12] insisting on the contrary that murder had been the intention,[13] and that it was the victim of the violent crime who deserved pity, not the perpetrator. The passage (23–7) contains no new facts or proofs, but depends for its effect upon rhetorical questions and amplification. His final attempt to persuade by argument is one of probability ($\epsilon\grave{\iota}\kappa\acute{o}s$) (28–30): removal or avoidance of witnesses is the typical device of persons contemplating a crime.[14] The speech ends quietly and gravely with the image of the gods watching the outcome (prosopopoiia—the first oratorical appearance of this figure, which later finds regular use in epilogues).

All the rhetoric of the speech is directed towards establishing the stepmother's personal guilt, and all facts and arguments that tend to disprove this are marginalized or obscured. One might imagine, for example, that the *pallake*, intent on her private quarrel with Philoneus, made no mistake when she gave him a lethal dose, and that she gave same dose to the other man to eliminate him as a witness. She is the thorn in the prosecution's side, since her possible motive casts doubt on the intention they ascribe to the stepmother.[15]

6 Death of a Chorus-Boy[16]

In this as in the previous speech, inferences are strongly drawn from the behaviour of the opponents, but in all other respects it is different. It is a defence speech which depends centrally upon the unchallenged and unexamined statements of witnesses; and the speaker is not a young and inexperienced man, but one whose

---

[11] 21–2: Note esp. amplification: $\grave{\epsilon}\lambda\acute{\epsilon}ov$ $\kappa\alpha\grave{\iota}$ $\beta o\eta\theta\epsilon\acute{\iota}as$ $\kappa\alpha\grave{\iota}$ $\tau\iota\mu\omega\rho\acute{\iota}as$ . . . $\grave{\alpha}\theta\acute{\epsilon}\omega s$ $\kappa\alpha\grave{\iota}$ $\grave{\alpha}\kappa\lambda\epsilon\hat{\omega}s$ . . . $\grave{\alpha}\theta\acute{\epsilon}\mu\iota\tau\alpha$ $\kappa\alpha\grave{\iota}$ $\grave{\alpha}\nu\acute{o}\sigma\iota\alpha$ $\kappa\alpha\grave{\iota}$ $\grave{\alpha}\tau\acute{\epsilon}\lambda\epsilon\sigma\tau\alpha$ $\kappa\alpha\grave{\iota}$ $\grave{\alpha}\nu\acute{\eta}\kappa o\upsilon\sigma\tau\alpha$ $\kappa\alpha\grave{\iota}$ $\theta\epsilon o\hat{\iota}s$ $\kappa\alpha\grave{\iota}$ $\acute{\upsilon}\mu\hat{\iota}\nu$.

[12] He writes $\varDelta\epsilon\acute{\eta}\sigma\epsilon\tau\alpha\iota$ . . . at the point where procatalepsis might be expected: a formula such as ($\grave{\iota}\sigma\hat{\omega}s$) $\grave{\epsilon}\rho\epsilon\hat{\iota}$ . . . followed by a statement of the precise plea, viz. that the potion was intended as a love-philtre.

[13] 26: $\grave{\epsilon}\kappa o\upsilon\sigma\acute{\iota}\omega s$ $\kappa\alpha\grave{\iota}$ $\beta o\upsilon\lambda\epsilon\acute{\upsilon}\sigma\alpha\sigma\alpha$.

[14] Cf. 5 Her. 43. This could well be a standard topos, but here it is invested with a degree of pathos (29–30).

[15] On her part, see further E. W. Bushala, 'The Pallake of Philoneus', *AJP* 90 (1969), 65–71.

[16] See H. M. ten Berge, *Antiphons Zesde Rede* (Nijmegen, 1948); K. Freeman, 'The Mystery of the Choreutes', *Studies in Honour of Gilbert Norwood* (Toronto, 1952), 85.

wealth made him a suitable appointee as *choregos* ('chorus-master') as well as a natural client for Antiphon. It was through that appointment that he found himself facing trial after a boy in his chorus, named Diodotus, had been accidentally poisoned by a drink which had been given to improve his voice.

This seasoned public man's **prooemium** (1–10) is suitably full of lofty sentiments and gnomic generalizations,[17] of which some appear for the first time: 'having a clear conscience' (1); 'time and experience teach mankind' (2); 'most men's lives rest upon hopes' (5); beside these are more mundane topics which have already been encountered: faith in good laws (2) (*Tetr.* 2. 4. 2) and in the jury (10) (*Tetr.* 1. 4. 1); the dire finality of a capital verdict (3–4 hinted at in *Tetr.* 1. 4. 11; cf. 5 *Her.* 87–9, 95); and ascription of motive to the prosecutor (7) (*Tetr.* 3. 2. 1) (here, in a word, διαβολή[18]). This prooemium contains the first extant summary of the plan of the speech: 'reply, narrative, defence' (ἀποκρίνεσθαι . . . διηγήσασθαι . . . ἀπολογήσασθαι, 8).

Whereas in the last speech the prosecutor uses a scene-setting narrative of prior events (prodiegesis) to establish motive, the defendant in this speech uses one (11–13) to show how he performed his duties as chorus-master in a normal and conscientious way. This was necessary because the death took place in his absence—a fact which was at once the basis of his defence and a possible ground for criticism. He seeks to avert the latter by detailing the duties assigned to Phanostratus, his son-in-law, and to Ameinias (see below) and Philippus, 'to ensure that the boys should receive the best possible training and lack nothing because of my preoccupation' (13).

The subsequent division of the speech is complex, with narrative playing a subordinate but subtle part, interwoven with the argument which it serves—a technique which was to develop in the hands of later orators. The main statement on which the speaker rests his case, that he 'neither told the boy to drink the poison, nor forced him to do so, nor gave it to him to drink, nor was present when he drank it', is made twice (15, 17), encasing the

---

[17] Due, *Antiphon*, 72 takes this idea further, finding 'the constant use of general reflections to support a particular case' a distinctive characteristic of Antiphon's argument in general. For later critics, it was a characteristic of the Grand Style.

[18] On διαβολή as a theme in 5th-cent. literature, see E. A. Gondos, *Auf dem Weg zur rhetorischen Theorie: Rhetorische Reflexion im ausgehenden fünften Jahrhundert v Chr.*, Rhetorik-Forschungen 10 (Tübingen, 1996), 15–22; on this speech, 18.

confirmation of it by witnesses and giving a compact unity to this all-important section. Nevertheless, his position is difficult. It seems clear that a chorus-master could not delegate his responsibilities, at least not to the extent of blaming someone else when things went wrong, otherwise he would have done just that. One man in particular, Ameinias, might have been blamed, since he was experienced, having been previously chosen by the Erechtheid tribe 'to recruit and care for its choruses at various festivals' (13). That he chooses not to pursue this line of defence indicates its likely inefficacy. For the present he falls back on ascribing the boy's death to *tyche* ('chance', 15), the same agency that would be responsible for his own fate, if he were convicted (1). But he knows that will not be enough.

Much of the rest of the speech is concerned with exposing the prosecutor's base motives. Generalizations about the currency of truth and falsehood and a contrast between cases involving planning and secrecy and the present one, in which the prosecution are said to admit that the boy's death was not the result of premeditation or design (19), lead to the first **narrative**,[19] which describes the behaviour of the prosecutors on the day of the boy's funeral, at which time the defendant was prosecuting them before the Heliaea (20–4). He tells how he had repeatedly challenged them (προὐκαλούμην (23) . . . προκαλουμένου (24)), to question witnesses, and asks that their refusal to do this should be taken as an indication of the truth of his claim and the weakness of their case (30–1, on which see Due, *Antiphon*, 57–9). It suits the defendant's purpose to elevate the importance of witnesses as providing the clearest and most reliable proof (ἔλεγχοι . . . σαφέστατοι καὶ πιστότατοι, 25), and this theme is enlarged upon with hypothetical inversion (εἰ μὲν . . . ὅπου δὲ . . . ὅπου μὲν . . . ὅπου δὲ, 29–30).[20]

The commonplace statement[21] that the speaker could rest his case at this point (33) signals the broadening of the charge (dilata-

---

[19] The prosecution will have narrated the death of the boy with all the pathos that could be extracted from that harrowing event: it was the very last thing on which the defence would wish to dwell.

[20] Part of this, one of several elaborate periods in the speech, is worth quoting as a description of the ingredients of an ideal case: ὅπου μὲν γὰρ λόγῳ τις διδάσκοι περὶ τῶν πραχθέντων, μάρτυρας δὲ μὴ παρέχοιτο . . . τεκμήρια δὲ αὖ τοῖς μαρτυροῦσιν ὅμοια μὴ ἀποφαίνοι, ταὐτὰ ἄν τις ἔχοι εἰπεῖν, εἰ βούλοιτο. ἐγὼ τοίνυν τούς τε λόγους ὑμῖν εἰκότας ἀποφαίνω, καὶ τοῖς λόγοις τοὺς μάρτυρας ὁμολογοῦντας καὶ τοῖς μάρτυσι τὰ ἔργα, καὶ τεκμήρια ἐξ αὐτῶν τῶν ἔργων.

[21] Later a frequent transitional formula, it appears here for the first time.

tion) against the prosecutors. This necessitates recounting facts that have already been mentioned (20–1), but this time emphasis is laid on contrasting the prosecutor's behaviour towards the defendant on the day of the boy's death with their accusation of the defendant on the day of the funeral. This inconsistency enables him to make the crucial inference that in those three days they had been persuaded by his enemies (34). He then goes on to explain that he was about to prosecute these enemies before the council for embezzlement, and that a murder charge against him would have banned him from proceeding (35–6). He describes, in a long period,[22] how their attempt failed, and, graphically,[23] how his accusers were reconciled with him.

The prosecutors failed initially to register their murder charge against the defendant because the incumbent King-Archon was too near the end of his official year (41–3).[24] The rules were clear, yet they complained that this archon had acted in the defendant's interest. Then, after a new archon had assumed office, they failed to register their charge for fifty days. Their behaviour in both these matters provides a tekmerion (41, 44) of the lack of substance in their charge, and their own realization of it. As he went about his daily duties, religious and political, as a councillor, they could have debarred him from them but did not do so.[25]

With that inference clearly drawn from the prosecutor's earlier behaviour, it remains only to raise the emotional temperature, conventionally, in the concluding sections, by deploring their rashness in finally bringing the charge against him. The 'tumid rhetoric'[26] (47–51) is notable stylistically for its periodic structure and amplification. Of interest also is the fact that a clear epilogue is lacking, and this is perhaps to be linked to the subject-matter: there is a passing reference only to the reason for the initiation of the present trial—because the defendant was proposing to investigate the activities of the state's Financial Officers (the *Poristai*, *Poletai*, and

---

[22] 37–8. It falls into two antithetical halves: τότε μὲν . . . ἐπειδὴ δέ . . . with the main clauses beginning the first half and ending the second, giving a solid, unified effect.

[23] 40: 'standing with me on the platform, accosting me and conversing with me, and with each of us addressing the other by name.'

[24] See C. Carey, *Trials from Classical Athens* (London and New York, 1997), 73, who notes this difficulty as an aspect of the 'designedly cumbersome procedures for homicide'.

[25] The rhetorical effect of the period in 45–6 would be to portray the frustration of the prosecutors seeing their enemy operating freely on the political stage, and knowing that they had little chance of gaining revenge for his successful lawsuit against them.

[26] So Dover, *CQ* 44 (1950), 48.

Practores, 49). This passing reference suggests that the whole matter was to be raised and aired more thoroughly in the second speech for the defence, when also a full epilogue might be expected.

5 *The Murder of Herodes*

The most admired of Antiphon's speeches in antiquity,[27] this is also the longest and most accomplished of those that have survived, and the one with the strongest political associations. The defendant Euxitheus[28] is a young man from Mytilene, on the island of Lesbos. A subject-ally of Athens, the city had been ruled by oligarchs and had risen against Athenian rule in 428 and been crushed (Thuc. 3. 2–6, 8–19, 25, 27–50). Euxitheus stresses the reluctance with which his father had been involved in the revolt (76); but he was one of Mytilene's richer citizens, having served more than once as a *choregos*. As a citizen of a recently dissident subject-ally, whose family might be reasonably suspected of complicity, or at least sympathy, with the organizers of the revolt, Euxitheus, accused of murdering an Athenian citizen, must have faced the prospect of trial before an Athenian jury with some trepidation.[29] He was a natural client for Antiphon, the titles of whose lost speeches show that he espoused the causes of subject-allies who claimed exposure to abuses of power by the Athenian democracy.[30]

Three aspects of the case made it an attractive one to defend. There was no body, no direct evidence as to the manner of Herodes' death, and Euxitheus was not the only possible suspect.

[27] *Vit. X Or.* 833d. It has also received most attention in modern times. See F. Scheidweiler, *Rh. Mus.* 109 (1966), 319–38; H. Erbse, *Rh. Mus.* 120 (1977), 209–27; U. Schindel, *Nachr. der Akad. der Wiss. in Göttingen* 8 (1979), 1–41; Edwards *GO*; M. Gagarin (1989).

[28] The name does not appear in the speech, but is supplied by Sopatros (Walz iv. 316).

[29] This prospect arose from the prosecutors' actions in bringing him to trial, which he describes in 9–13. He has been indicted as a 'malefactor' (κακοῦργος). This seems to have been a device used to secure the persons of aliens (perhaps especially subject-allies, thus relating to Antiphon's own political interest in the case). κακοῦργοι were subject to summary arrest (ἀπαγωγή) and detention, but an Athenian charged with murder faced a more elaborate procedure which did not, however, involve immediate imprisonment. Antiphon makes the most of the rhetorical points which the prosecutors' actions afford, arguing that their procedural irregularity ('you have invented laws to suit yourself', 12; 'you have turned yourself into a lawmaker', 15) has led to more serious illegality, involving sacrilege, in the conduct of the murder trial (11–12). He also meets the disadvantage of a Heliastic trial (rather than one before the famously fair and objective Areopagus) with conciliation ('not that I wish to evade trial before you, the people', 8).

[30] See n. 2.

The two men were among several passengers on an open-decked ship which sailed from Mytilene, and was forced to seek shelter from a storm. They landed near Methymna, where they trans-shipped to a covered vessel in the harbour, and took to their cups. During their carousal Herodes left the ship and was never seen again. Euxitheus is able to furnish witnesses who confirm that he did not leave the boat that night. But it is over the reliability of witnesses that he is obliged to argue his case, because his prosecutors have extracted contradictory evidence from these same witnesses.

The **prooemium** combines convention with invention, initially contrasting in a hypothetical inversion (Ἐβουλόμην μὲν . . . νῦν δὲ) inexperience in speaking with experience of misfortune, then exploring the hazards facing the inexpert speaker through a sequence of carefully crafted antitheses.[31] Invention is also at work in 4, where the common topos of appeal for a fair hearing is amended to captatio benevolentiae, with paraleipsis: 'I shall not ask for a fair hearing, as an honest jury will automatically grant that.' Another common topos which receives more elaborate treatment than before is that of the special danger facing a defendant: here are added the ideas of chance, and of alarm inducing under-performance (6–7).

The following section (8–19) has the character of a separate plea, with its own introductory prothesis (πρῶτον μὲν . . . διδάξω, 8), and has little direct bearing on the question of the defendant's guilt or innocence. He claims that the wrong procedures have been used: charged with murder, he has been summarily arrested and imprisoned as a 'malefactor' (κακοῦργος); and he is being tried before the popular court (Heliaea), not the Areopagus.[32] Reforms in legal procedure made not long after this speech introduced 'counter-prosecutions' (paragraphai) at which alleged irregularities, if proved, could prevent an intended trial from taking place. These were effectively obstructive pleas, or demurrers.[33] No such procedure was yet available to Antiphon, so that he was forced to include

[31] 2: οὐ μὲν . . . οὐ δὲ . . . ἐν τούτῳ . . . 3: πολλοὶ μὲν . . . πολλοὶ δὲ . . . (anaphora). There is an apparent incongruity of style with the character of the speaker.

[32] See n. 29. On apagoge of kakourgoi see M. H. Hansen, *Apagoge, Endeixis and Ephegesis against Kakourgoi, Atimoi and Pheugontes* (Odense, 1976); Todd *SAL* 117–18, 330–1 (this speech).

[33] Isoc. 18 *Against Callimachus* is the earliest example of a paragraphe. See D. M. MacDowell, 'The Chronology of Athenian Speeches and Legal Innovations in 401–398', *RIDA* 18 (1971), 267–73.

this rhetorically unpromising section in his defendant's speech, able to extract from it only the general idea that the prosecution, by their allegedly illegal procedure, cannot be trusted to present a fair case.[34] Nevertheless he makes the best of this line of argument, censuring the prosecutors as strongly as he can by means of frequent apostrophe (12–13, 16—where he also uses dilemmaton effectively), and concludes the section with dignified pathos (18–19).[35]

The **narrative** is economical and fragmented: more than in the other speeches, Antiphon ensures that what he recounts leads to the inferences he requires, and these inferences are drawn piecemeal so that the jury registers them immediately and individually. 20–1 takes us only to the transshipment, 21 (καὶ πρῶτον μέν)–2 draws the inference, noting that the two men were fellow-passengers by chance, and that likewise the landing and the transshipment were unplanned. He then resumes his story (23–4). The two crucial facts are stated at the outset and underlined with succinct force: '*it is clear* that he [Herodes] left the boat and did not board it again, whereas I did not leave the boat *at all during the whole of that night.*'[36]

From the few other facts surrounding the alleged murder, which a jury might find of neutral significance, Antiphon turns to the much more fruitful examination of the behaviour of the prosecution. What follows affords excellent illustration of the scope of argument from probability.[37] Firstly, he considers their version of the facts, and seeks to undermine its credibility by exposing its incoherence and inconsistency. Why was a charge not made against Euxitheus immediately (25)? Because the prosecution needed time to fabricate their evidence.[38] Yet a jury might think that perhaps *one* of their stories could be true: those stories are admittedly

---

[34] There may be some significance in the defendant's allegation (9) that he is the first victim of this particular misuse of ἔνδειξις κακουργίας. As a Mytilenean a few years after the revolt, Euxitheus might easily have become the subject of a harsh precedent, especially one designed to prevent him from leaving the city. See n. 29.

[35] πρῶτον μὲν ἀπαρασκευότατον γενέσθαι με . . . ἔπειτα κακοπαθεῖν τῷ σώματι . . . ὄνειδός τε αὐτῷ τε ἐμοὶ περιέθεσαν . . . εἰς τὸν βίον ἅπαντα.

[36] 23: καὶ ὁ μέν ἐστι φανερὸς ἐκβὰς ἐκ τοῦ πλοίου καὶ οὐκ εἰσβὰς πάλιν· ἐγὼ δὲ τὸ παράπαν οὐκ ἐξέβην ἐκ τοῦ πλοίου τῆς νυκτὸς ἐκείνης. Both statements are emphatic, but the second, more contentious statement is given the greater emphasis.

[37] 25: σκοπεῖτε τὰ εἰκότα.

[38] He has already registered this conventional plea, though with unusual force, emphasizing his accusers' determination to ruin him, in 19: καίτοι χαλεπόν γε τὰ ἐκ πολλοῦ κατεψευσμένα καὶ ἐπιβεβουλευμένα, ταῦτα παραχρῆμα ἀπελέγχειν. (Edwards GO i. 85 notes this as the first instance of a recurrent theme of the speech.)

incomplete, but he can only counter them with his own version of what happened. Much more damaging for the prosecution are the probabilities to be drawn from their treatment of the two key witnesses. One, a slave, under torture gave a version incriminating Euxitheus, but retracted it when he knew he was to be killed.[39] Antiphon makes the prosecutors' behaviour seem bizarre in the extreme by means of the first extant para prosdokian (38): 'In other cases, it is the victim who quietly seizes an informer and then makes away with him: in this case, it is the very men who have arrested the slave in order to investigate the affair who have made away with the man who was informing against me.' The probability-arguments are drawn together for maximum effect (43–5): the slave's retraction, the general improbability that a murderer would recruit an accomplice, the likelihood that such a crime could not be committed without attracting attention, and the difficulty of removing evidence: 'how can these things be probable, gentlemen?' So great is the importance of the slave's evidence and the probabilities to be drawn from the prosecutor's handling of it, that these arguments are repeated in 46–52, with the added fact that the slave-witness was purchased by the prosecution (47) with a view to killing him (perhaps illegally[40]) after he had given them the answers they wanted. This section is at once earnest and modest in tone, beginning with a reminder of the danger facing the defendant, and ending with a minimalist plea that equal weight of evidence for and against him should produce an acquittal.

Having reinforced his best probability-arguments by repetition, Antiphon can now pass on to his most difficult obstacle, the alleged letter to Lycinus. His problem here is not so much the letter itself, the existence of which he is able to discredit (53–5), as the fact that a third party, clearly an acquaintance of the accused, who knew about his financial circumstances (58, 63), was an enemy of

---

[39] His fate is portrayed with some pathos (41): ἀπώμωξεν ἐμέ τε καὶ αὐτὸν ὡς ἀδίκως ἀπολλυμένους. This is preceded (37) by a deft application of the test of probability to the unfortunate slave's two actions: εἰ μὲν γὰρ ἐκ τοῦ εἰκότος ἐξετασθῆναι δεῖ τὸ πρᾶγμα, οἱ ὕστεροι λόγοι ἀληθέστεροι φαίνονται. ἐψεύδετο μὲν γὰρ ἐπ' ὠφελείᾳ τῇ ἑαυτοῦ, ἐπειδὴ δὲ τῷ ψεύδεσθαι ἀπώλλυτο, ἡγήσατο τἀληθῆ κατειπὼν διὰ τοῦτο σωθῆναι ἄν.

[40] See Edwards, ad loc. The positive evidence of 47–8 should figure largely in any discussion. The killing could be defended only on the ground that the slave's admission of complicity rendered him liable to judicial execution, of which the killers might claim to be the agents. But Antiphon naturally adopts the most obvious course and accuses the prosecution of murder.

Herodes (62). His solution is to go on to the attack, switching from refutative to confirmatory arguments, and concentrating on negative motivation rather than on trying to explain Lycinus' involvement. Whereas in *Death of a Chorus-Boy* the study of motivation is spread over much of the speech, here Antiphon deals with it summarily (57–9). Enmity? None existed between him and Herodes. Favour? Profit? Denied (explanation in 63). Fear? Denied.[41] He then tries to dissociate his motives from those of Lycinus, but does so in two stages, first arguing that Lycinus had no more reason than himself for murdering Herodes (60–1), then covering himself by saying, by means of concession (62), that even if Lycinus did desire Herodes' death, Euxitheus lacked motive (profit, favour) to act for him (63). By these arguments he deals as thoroughly as necessary with the embarrassing Lycinus, but without dwelling on him for too long.

The idea that an accused man should be expected to try to identify the guilty party seems to be early (*Tetr.* 1. 2. 2). Here (64–6) Antiphon exposes its weakness by arguing that the innocent man is the person least suited to engage in such speculation. This leads to the topos of the hazard of convicting on uncertain evidence in capital cases, and the argument is illustrated by the first of many historical examples (paradeigmata) used by Attic orators.[42] All three illustrate how wrongful conviction and the irrevocable penalty were avoided, but they differ from one another. With the murder of Ephialtes, the case is simply that no culprits had ever been discovered, and his companions were not required to conjecture who they were (unlike Euxitheus) (68). In the second case, the true culprit failed to make his escape, and his conviction saved his fellow-slaves in the household (69). The third case was one of false accusation and execution of nine out of ten Hellenotamiae for embezzlement (69–70). The survivor was rescued when his inno-

---

[41] He uses hypophora (ἀλλὰ δείσας . . . ; ἀλλ᾽ . . . ἀλλὰ χρήματα . . . ἀλλ᾽ οὐκ ἦν αὐτῷ) followed by a *translatio criminis* (arguing that Lycinus' financial difficulties made him more likely to commit crime for profit than the defendant).

[42] No doubt historical examples were particularly suited to deliberative oratory, as Aristotle says (*Rhet.* 1. 9. 40), but by making their first extant appearance in a forensic speech they illustrate the artificiality of his deliberative/forensic/epideictic trichotomy. *Rhet. ad Alex.* 8 does not make the distinction of genre, but regards the use of examples as supplementary to probability-argument. Here it supports a recommended course of action. In later deliberative and epideictic oratory it could have a protreptic purpose (example for imitation), on which see Dem. 18 *Cor.* 95, with my note (*GO* v. 202). Further on historical examples in oratory, see Ch. 3 n. 29.

cence was discovered. Thus the three examples are arranged in order of gravity, the last being the most compelling one to introduce the stern advice to deliberate without anger or prejudice, 'the worst possible counsellors'.[43]

The political dimension of the case comes most clearly to light in the following section (74–80), and here Antiphon may have found little to guide him in earlier theory. It is pleading rather than argument, and it became customary to deploy such rhetoric at this point in the speech. He confesses to his city's 'mistake', which they will always regret (79), but claims that slander against his father has been actuated by the usual motive of sycophantai—money. A wealthy citizen of a state which has recently revolted would have been an easy target for their callous attacks. But they should not be encouraged (80).[44]

Further recession from both evidential and argumentative proof is to be noted in 'signs furnished by the gods' (81–3).[45] They were coming to the end of their useful life as rhetorical material by this time,[46] finding a more natural environment in drama.

In the long **epilogue** (85–96 (end)) Antiphon abandons the conventional emotional appeal and summary of defence against the charge itself and concentrates on restating the paragraphic plea, reinforcing it with the topos of the irrevocability of capital verdicts (87, 91, 95).[47] Instead of demanding outright acquittal, the defendant is made to ask for a retrial, blaming his accusers for 'making

---

[43] ἀλλὰ πρότερόν γ' εὖ βουλεύσασθε, καὶ μὴ μετ' ὀργῆς καὶ διαβολῆς, ὡς τούτων οὐκ ἂν γένοιντο ἕτεροι πονηρότεροι σύμβουλοι.

[44] This is one of the first of very many attacks on sycophantai in the orators. In *Death of a Chorus-Boy* the prosecutors appear to have been hired by the defendant's enemies (35–6). This differentiates them slightly from the sycophantai in this speech, who stood to profit directly from success.

[45] 81: τὰ ἀπὸ τῶν θεῶν σημεῖα.

[46] Yet the popular outrage at the mutilation of Hermae at Athens (415 BC, around the time of this speech), strongly suggests that an Athenian jury at this time would have been impressed by religious arguments involving pollution, especially in a case involving homicide or impiety. Hence it is relatively unsurprising to find the last occurrence of this curious type of ἄτεχνος πίστις in Andocides 1 *Myst.* (137–9).

[47] In these arguments Antiphon adopts an earnest, philosophical tone, aimed at making the jury look to their own moral obligations rather than the question of the defendant's guilt: φόνου γὰρ δίκη καὶ μὴ ὀρθῶς γνωσθεῖσα ἰσχυρότερον τοῦ δικαίου καὶ τοῦ ἀληθοῦς ἐστιν· (87); ἐν μὲν γὰρ ἀκεστῷ πράγματι καὶ ὀργῇ χρησαμένους καὶ διαβολῇ πιθομένους ἔλαττόν ἐστιν ἐξαμαρτεῖν· μεταγνοὺς γάρ τις ἔτι ἂν ὀρθῶς βουλεύσαιτο· ἐν δὲ τοῖς ἀνηκέστοις πλέον βλάβος τὸ μετανοεῖν καὶ γνῶναι ἐξαμαρτηκότας (91). He even manages to insert the topos of voluntary and involuntary crime (92: cf. *Tetr.* 3. 1. 6; 1 *Ag. Stepmother* 27).

two trials out of one' (85).[48] The simple conclusion to draw from this is that the defendant's case is shaky, but this would ignore the particular circumstances of the trial. The new trial would be a δίκη φόνου, which unless special conditions obtained for aliens, would be held before the Areopagus, which consisted mostly of senior ex-officials who might be less susceptible to the popular prejudice that was rife in the Heliaea, and more likely to judge in strict accordance with the law. In particular, they might take an unfavourable view of the prosecution's killing one of their main witnesses, while the passage of time might weaken the impact of his evidence. In spite of these particular circumstances, however, the line taken in the epilogue does suggest that this was a difficult defence, and the publication of the speech displayed Antiphon's talents at their most acute.

ANTIPHON: SUMMARY

The three court speeches of Antiphon show clear advances on the *Tetralogies* in technique, style, and use of topoi. All three prooemia contain innovations. In 1, charged emotion centres around abhorrence at conflict between relations. In 1 and 5, the opponents' abuse of slaves' evidence is examined in two extended procatasceuai (1. 5–12, 5. 8–19). The prooemium of 6 contains the first summary of the plan of a speech. In that of 5 the standard topoi are invested with stylistic adornment, notably antithesis and parison; and the plea for a fair hearing is amended to a captatio benevolentiae.

Narrative, a relatively minor feature of the *Tetralogies*, comes into its own, especially in 1. It is used to supply not only facts but motives, and pathos is injected into it at climactic moments. In 5 the bare facts are told in separate narratives in order to draw the necessary arguments most effectively from each. Interweaving of narrative and argument is no less cleverly used in 6, where there is also a more direct attack on the opponent's character.

Antiphon's reputation as both pioneer and perfecter of argument from probability arises chiefly from its prominence in 5, a case

---

[48] To this variant of the topos of blaming the opponent for initiating litigation, one may add the ideas that the defendant faces greater danger than the prosecutor (89) and the speaker's confidence in the jury (93), all usually found in prooemia rather than epilogues.

ideally suited to its deployment, where it is applied both to actions immediately surrounding the alleged murder and to the prior and subsequent behaviour of other principals, notably the prosecutors. That speech also contains the first historical example, or rather a comparison of three, and the beginnings of a political atmosphere, which was to be replicated many times in later oratory.

All three epilogues contain emotional appeal, although 5 depends more on grave adjuration. But recapitulation has not yet become established as an essential part of this section.

Stylistically, Antiphon's distinct voice seems to have aimed to set oratory, or at any rate written oratory, apart from everyday speech, suspended between the poetic and the philosophical. In particular, taste for abstraction is to be found in the use of rare abstract nouns and neuter participles and adjectives, as is an archaic flavour in the language of tragedy and earlier prose.[49] These characteristics mark Antiphon as a pioneer in prose style no less than in oratory.

---

[49] See Blass *AB* i. 126–32; C. Cucuel, *Essai sur la langue et le style de l'orateur Antiphon* (Paris, 1886).

3

ANDOCIDES

Second in the canon of ten Attic orators, Andocides was probably the least esteemed.[1] He was not a professional writer of speeches for others: all of his surviving orations were spoken by him on his own behalf, and he does not seem to have been a regular public speaker. But a deliberative speech by him has survived, and it is the earliest surviving example of this genre of oratory.

Perhaps because of false pride,[2] the speech with which he tried to secure his return from exile[3] struck the wrong general tone with his popular (Assembly) audience and failed in its purpose. However, closer examination of it reveals a certain degree of purely technical competence.

---

[1] Herodes Atticus, the most famous orator of the Second Sophistic, on being complimented with the accolade that he was 'one of the Ten', is said to have replied: 'At least I am better than Andocides!' (Philostr. *Vit. Soph.* 2. 1. 565). Little critical opinion of him has survived. The *Life* (*Vit. X Or.* 834b–835b) confines judgement of his oratory to its concluding sentence: ἔστι δ' ἁπλοῦς καὶ ἀκατάσκευος ἐν τοῖς λόγοις, ἀφελής τε καὶ ἀσχημάτιστος. Hermogenes' longer critique, which is concerned purely with style (*Id.* B 11 (Sp. ii. 416–17)) emphasizes general lack of clarity and organization. For modern criticism, see S. S. Kingsbury, *A Rhetorical Study of Andocides* (Baltimore, 1899); G. A. Kennedy, *AJP* 79 (1958), 32–43; Commentaries: D. M. MacDowell, *Andocides: On the Mysteries* (Oxford, 1962); Edwards *GO* iv (1995).

[2] He was the scion of a distinguished and wealthy Athenian family, earlier generations having had connections with the Alcmaeonids. (See MacDowell, *Andocides*, 1–2.) It may not be too fanciful to suppose that connection claimed with an even more distinguished ancestor, the god Hermes (*Vit. X Or.* 834c (Hellanicus)), who was also the god of Rhetoric, could have persuaded Andocides that he had innate oratorical talents.

[3] The Decree of Isotimides, which excluded from public places any man who had admitted to implication in the Mutilation of the Hermae, may have been aimed personally at Andocides. It made life at Athens intolerable for him, so he retired from the city (415). Later he was formally exiled (411–410?), but returned briefly on persuading the Prytaneis to allow him to address his speech *On his Return* to the Assembly. The tone of the speech suggests that he was still feeling his grievances keenly, but there is no precise indication as to when he made it. The years 408 or 407 would suit the known facts, with a *terminus ante quem* of 405. Further on his political career, see A. Missiou, *The Subversive Oratory of Andocides* (Cambridge, 1992).

2 On his Return

The idea that an orthodox prooemium, with the standard pleas and summary statement of the case to be defended, may not be effective where there is strong prejudice, was recognized in the fourth century and stated much more fully later. The remedy was the ephodos, or 'oblique approach'.[4] Andocides' first speech is the earliest to display this sophisticated type of **prooemium**, and to a difficult case. Instead of his plea for his return, the subject on which he focuses is the benefits he can bestow on the city. He has found considerable help from the handbooks in the early part of his speech. He begins with a prescribed prooemium-construction, a hypothetical inversion (εἰ μὲν . . . οὐδὲν θαυμαστὸν ἐνόμιζον· ὅπου μέντοι δεῖ τὴν πόλιν ἐμέ τι ποιῆσαι ἀγαθὸν . . . δεινότατον ἁπάντων χρημάτων ἡγοῦμαι . . .), which is closely followed by a dilemmaton (εἰ μέν γε . . . εἰ δὲ μὴ ταὐτὰ ἡγοῦνται . . . συμφέρειν (2–3), used again in 7). In 25 he uses one of the standard gnomai about γνώμη,[5] and makes one attempt at captatio benevolentiae.[6] But for most of the speech he allows his own character to take over, to the exclusion of organized rhetorical argument—his pugnacity as he attacks his unnamed opponents, calling them 'either the most stupid of mankind or the worst enemies of the city' (2), and accusing them of cowardice (4); his arrogance as he dwells on the supposed 'relief from evil' which his disclosure of the identity of the mutilators of the Hermae brought to the people (8); and, throughout, his egotism. This is always close

---

[4] *Rhet. ad Alex.* 29 1436b–1437a proposes different approaches according to a speaker's reputation. Thus a man who has been the object of διαβολαί, and 'is under suspicion of some bad behaviour in the past' (ἐκ τοῦ παροιχομένου χρόνου ἐάν τις ὑποπτεύηται εἰς πονηρίαν τινα), should complain about past treatment in the courts and elsewhere and say that his misfortune on those occasions is sufficient punishment. This matches both Andocides' situation and his reaction to it: 'All men are born to meet with good fortune and with bad . . . suffer misfortune . . . deserve sympathy' (6–7). Cf. Aristot. *Rhet.* 3. 15. 3: 'error, misfortune, necessity'. The idea of the 'oblique approach' is elaborated in later prooemium-theory (Cic. *Inv.* 1. 17 (where the part relevant to Andocides is 'where the thing is substituted for the person, so that the hearer's attention is transferred from what he hates to what he favours' (*interponi oportet . . . pro homine rem, ut ab eo quod odit ad id quod diligit auditoris animus traducatur*, 24). Cf. *Ad Herenn.* 1. 6.

[5] εἰ γὰρ ὅσα οἱ ἄνθρωποι γνώμῃ ἁμαρτάνουσι, τὸ σῶμα αὐτῶν μὴ αἴτιόν ἐστιν, ἐμοῦ τὸ σῶμα τυγχάνει ταὐτὸν ἔτι ὄν, ὅπερ τῆς αἰτίας ἀπήλλακται, ἡ δὲ γνώμη ἀντὶ τῆς προτέρας ἑτέρα νυνὶ παρέστηκεν. Cf. Antiph. 5 *Her.* 5–6, 92.

[6] 10: εἰσῆλθέ μοι, ὥσπερ εἰκός, ἐπιθυμία τῆς τε μεθ' ὑμῶν πολιτείας ἐκείνης καὶ διαίτης.

to the surface, even when he is making fleeting admissions of his guilt in the affair of the Hermae (7, 10, 15). In the **narrative** (13–16) describing his reception on his return, he portrays himself as a tragic figure, beset by wholly unexpected hostility[7] and cruelly imprisoned, but steadfast in his desire to serve his city.[8] His skill in using a short narrative to portray character is to be used to even greater effect in his next speech, but it is already manifest in this one.

Yet in the end its aggressive egotism disqualifies the speech as an organ of persuasion. Enumeration of services was, of course, a standard topos, but Andocides tries to argue that his services were superior to others', and he disparages these (17). An eclectic (or desultory) recourse to rhetorical procedures, without clear division and definition of objectives, made this, both literally and theoretically, an unsuccessful speech, though it already shows a talent for vivid description and emotional appeal which becomes Andocides' *forte* when he makes his second defence.

1 On the Mysteries

Andocides returned to Athens, probably under the general amnesty of 403. Far from opting for a quiet life, he seems to have assumed immediate political ambitions. These ambitions explain his prosecution of Archippus, a mere ten days after his return:[9] a successful lawsuit would have been a useful beginning to his relaunched public career. Tenure of the offices of *gymnasiarch* and *architheoros* followed.[10] But high political profile led to the recrudescence of old enmities and rivalries with his peers, and the trial for which he composed his longest and best speech arose from his quarrel with the most powerful of these rivals, Callias, son of Hipponicus, who,

---

[7] Expecting the congratulations of the Athenians for supplying their fleet at Samos with timber for oars, he was charged by Peisander, the leader of the revolutionary oligarchs, with supplying 'the enemy' (i.e. the Athenian fleet, whose leaders and men had affirmed their adherence to democracy).

[8] 16 (last sentence): ἀλλ' ὅμως καὶ ἐκ τούτων τοιούτων ὄντων ἀπαλλαγεὶς οὐκ ἔστιν ὅ τι ἕτερον ἔργον περὶ πλείονος ἐποιούμην ἢ τὴν πόλιν ταύτην ἀγαθόν τι ἐργάσασθαι.

[9] [Lys.] 6 Ag. Andoc. 11. He accused Archippus of mutilating his family's Herm. (Andocides explains how this Herm escaped mutilation at the hands of the Hermocopids in Myst. 62.)

[10] These offices were leitourgiai, imposing expense upon their holder, so that the efforts of men like Callias and others to secure Andocides' appointment to them show not that he was popular but that he was wealthy.

in 400, prosecuted him for profanation of the Mysteries.[11] Understanding of the speech depends to a large extent on this fact—that the issue was not one of quest for justice, or even requital, but one of winning precedence over men who oppose one's political ambitions. Attacks upon these men occupy over one third of the speech.

For his **prooemium** (1–10) he plays safe this time, adhering to the conventional topoi, and reeling them off in rapid succession— his enemies' preparation (1, 6), his voluntary presence, trusting in a fair trial (2–3), his plea for goodwill (6) varied with a request for *more* than that accorded his opponents; his aporia (8), which he presents in a kind of thinking-aloud process; a second captatio benevolentiae (9) which touches on the limitations of his oratorical skills,[12] and the conventional summarized plan (prothesis, 10), covering his defence against the charge of profanation of the Mysteries (i.e. down to § 33).

After thus demonstrating quite thorough knowledge of the standard topoi of prooemia without adding significantly to them, Andocides then settles down to what he does best—telling a story. His narrative technique is quite different from Antiphon's in spite of sharing his choice of a style that is paratactic, simple, and clear. In general, he lets the story tell itself without the comments and asides which inform Antiphon's narratives. But he uses a number of devices designed to animate the action and win the sympathetic involvement of his audience. Live speech is the most obvious and effective of these.[13] Pythonicus' accusation of Alcibiades in the last-minute debate prior to the departure of the Sicilian expedition (11) is certainly dramatized by the report of his actual (?) words, and something of the atmosphere of the debate itself is recreated. Other features of the first **narrative** (11–18) are frequent asyndeton,[14] especially in the opening sentences of paragraphs, giving the

[11] Andocides attended these religious rites in 400 while still under accusation, or at least suspicion of committing impiety in 415.

[12] In asking the jury not to ῥήματα θηρεύειν ('chase after words'—i.e. solecisms), he affects a certain lingering diffidence in his oratorical ability.

[13] However, it seems to have found no place in early rhetorical theory. Aristotle and [Anaximenes] (*Rhet. ad Alex.*) say nothing about it. The earliest recognition of it is in *Ad Herenn.* (*sermocinatio*, 4. 52. 65). Quintilian (9. 2. 29–31) includes it under the general heading of προσωποποιίαι ('personifications') and notes that it 'lends wonderful variety and animation to a speech'. On its use by the orators, see J. Trevett, 'The Use of Direct Speech by the Attic Orators', *Lo Spettacolo delle Voci* 2 (1995), 123–45.

[14] On asyndeton in Andocides, see MacDowell, *Andocides*, Appendix P.

impression of a desire to move rapidly on to the next episode of a
story; and tense variation, with frequent historic present tenses
alternating with aorist.

In 19–24 Andocides subjects the prosecution's version of his and
his father's behaviour to the test of probability. Even in his use of
this standard procedure there is a degree of animation.[15] In 21–2
there is more live speech, but here 'direct speech' is a more accurate
description, since the words are put in the mouth of Speusippus by
Andocides.[16]

After ending his account of the informations (μηνύσεις) laid
concerning the profanation of the Mysteries (27–8), Andocides
summarizes the points proved, but his vehemence, both in attacking his opponents[17] and in defending himself, gives these sections
the strong flavour of peroration.[18]

As he turns to the second indictment, concerning the mutilation
of the Hermae, he faces even greater difficulties. Beside the abom-
ination in which this gross act of sacrilege was still held, there was
his undoubted implication. He was present at the drinking party
where the escapade was proposed (61) and, though he claims to
have opposed it, might have become directly involved but for a fall
from his horse, which left him bedridden with concussion and a
broken collar-bone. His only practical course was therefore to represent himself as the one man who saved others from death by his
information against the true miscreants, hoping to establish a kind
of moral superiority over those who made false accusations by
showing their venal motives. Of these accusers the most dangerous
was Diocleides, and Andocides deploys his narrative skill[19] to show

---

[15] λόγον οἶμαι πάντων δεινότατόν τε καὶ ἀνοσιώτατον λέγοντες. . . . καίτοι τί
ἐβουλόμην, εἰ ἐμήνυσα μὲν κατὰ τοῦ πατρός, ὡς οὗτοί φασιν, ἱκέτευον δὲ τὸν
πατέρα μείναντά τι παθεῖν ὑπ᾽ ἐμοῦ; Characterizing the effrontery of the prosecutors is
an essential aim.

[16] By giving the actual words which Speusippus *could* have used to meet the challenge of
his opponents, Andocides creates a hypothetical situation in order to show its impossibility.
See S. Wilcox, *The Destructive Hypothetical Syllogism in Greek Logic and Attic Oratory* (New
Haven, 1938), 36–7.

[17] Note the argument by reversal of accusation in 30: ἐγὼ γὰρ πολὺ μᾶλλον ἐκείνων
κατηγορῶ . . . ὅτι ἠσέβησαν.

[18] Reminding the jury of their solemn oath (31) and their obligation to acquit an innocent man and punish his accusers, he signals a pause when he asks them to show their
approval (δηλώσατέ μοι, 33) so far, before he restarts with renewed confidence. Andocides
may have got the idea of 'two speeches in one' from Lysias 12, where there is a clear break
at 39.

[19] The use of *oratio obliqua* is perhaps intended to hint at the story's falsehood.

how cleverly Diocleides convinced the authorities with his story of his moonlight sighting of the Hermocopids at work. Recital of the telling detail elaborates the premeditation of the malice, which is exposed when the whole story turns out to be a fabrication. Its effect at the time, however, was dramatic. Those identified by Diocleides were imprisoned, and the scene was set for Andocides' act of salvation. His description of it is calculated to abide in the jury's minds, recalling as it does the sights and sounds, lamentations and entreaties that attended those traumatic events (48–53). Direct speech, as before, plays an important part, as Andocides responds to the plea of his cousin Charmides to reveal the names of the guilty so that the innocent might go free (49–50). He also presents his own thoughts in the form of direct speech (51). Although he has the frankness to make it clear that his concern was mainly for members of his own family, he also mentions three hundred potential victims (51). It is vital for him to do this, because he has to counter the stigma attached to informers by showing that his action benefited the whole city. The reasoning that led him to his decision is very clearly given (57–9). His information sent four guilty men into exile, but saved him and his family from destruction and the city from fear.

As observed in the beginning, this trial centres around personal quarrels, and these arose directly out of Andocides' disclosures. It is his next task to show (63 ff.) how he incurred the hostility of Meletus and Euphiletus. To show their lawless character in the worst light, he gives their words in direct speech (63): 'Now if you see your way to keeping quiet and saying nothing, you will find us just as good friends as before. If you do not, our enmity will be stronger than any new friendships you make through your betrayal of us.' Then he shows how they misapplied the revised laws that had come into force after the restoration of democracy (71–91). The function of this detailed account is to provide a foil for the attack which he is about to launch on his enemies, one by one: 'And now, gentlemen, consider my accusers and their relation to the laws. They prosecute others, but what is their position?' (92). There follows a catalogue of illegalities committed by Cephisius, Meletus,[20] and Epichares ('the worst of rogues, and proud of it', 95; 'practised villain', 99); and Andocides ends the section with a chilling but brilliantly effective

[20] This is a different Meletus from the one mentioned above. On the name and its owners' identities, see MacDowell, *Andocides*, Appendix M 208–10.

para prosdokian, as he imagines transplanting the present trial to the time of the Thirty, with Charicles, one of its most feared members, as inquisitor (101):

> 'Tell me, Andocides', he would have asked, 'did you go to Decelea and fortify it against your country?' 'I did not.' 'Well, did you ravage the land, and plunder your fellow-citizens by land and sea?' 'Certainly not!' 'And I suppose you did not fight against the city at sea, or join in the demolition of her walls, or help put down the democracy, or secure your own return by force?' 'No, I have done none of these things.' 'Then do you expect to escape the death-penalty which so many others have suffered?'

Andocides had made many enemies, but the most powerful and dangerous, and the man ultimately responsible for his indictment,[21] was Callias. He prefaces his attack on him with a brief historical excursus on the themes of amnesty (μὴ μνησικακεῖν) and concord (ὁμόνοια) (106–9), both of which Callias' action contravenes.[22] Artistically, this provides variety, with an interval between two passages of invective, a comparatively new and unfamiliar form of oratory at this time. The origins of his quarrel with Callias are unclear, but it culminates in a contest over the hand of an heiress, one of the daughters of Andocides' uncle, Epilycus. As a cousin, he had a stronger claim than Callias, who tried to press his case by claiming her for his son.[23] Andocides threatened to test it in court, so Callias decided on pre-emptive litigation. The section in which Andocides explains these matters (117–19) has the clarity of a good inheritance-speech, but also the Andocidean trademark of live speech. Thereafter he launches into a scurrilous attack on Callias. The women in his life seem to have had a hard time, and we read of attempted suicide (125), pregnancy, denial of paternity, mother and daughter in the same marriage-bed—though not, apparently, at the same time (126–7). The lurid account ends with the question 'There are three women with whom his [the son's] father will have cohabited. What ought this son be called? Oedipus, Aegisthus, or what?' (129).

The style of the speaker has by now become more like that of a raconteur than a litigant—the form of address he might have used when exchanging gossip and other pleasantries with the fellow-

---

[21] He paid Cephisius 1,000 drachmae to bring the case.

[22] Historical example, here drawn from Athens in the early 5th cent., could be used, as it was by Lysias (12. 63) to illustrate by contrast as well as by analogy.

[23] See MacDowell, *Andocides*, 207; Edwards *GO* iv. 185.

members of his club (ἑταιρεία). But there is a return to textbook oratory in 136 with the standard reference to the behaviour expected of prosecutors (cf. Antiph. *Tetr.* 2. 4. 1, 5 *Her.* 94), and there is an interesting reminiscence of 5 *Her.* 81–3 in 137–9[24] (note the corresponding positions in the two speeches). Formality takes over to the end of the speech, and there is a political colouring as he once more urges concord (140), praises the leitourgiai of his ancestors (141–3), and represents himself as a tragic but reformed figure, with much to contribute (144–5).

The **epilogue** (146–50) is impassioned and well-stocked with rhetoric.[25] However, it lacks a summary.

3 *On the Peace with Sparta*

Following his successful defence, Andocides resumed his political rehabilitation, and after seven years, during which he must have become one of the regular speakers in the Assembly, he was one of four ambassadors chosen to go to Sparta (392 BC) to explore the possibilities of peace after the Corinthian War. He delivered this speech soon after his return. It is the first surviving text of a deliberative speech composed by an orator and addressed to a real historical situation. Fuller discussion of deliberative oratory will find its place when the works of Isocrates are examined, but some of its main characteristics are to be noticed in this early example of the genre.

Study of the deliberative speeches in Thucydides shows speakers developing their arguments around a few constant themes and creating tensions between them. Of these the two most important are justice (or honour) and expediency,[26] but the latter gains ground as

[24] The prosecution had apparently anticipated that Andocides would argue, as Antiphon has made Euxitheus do, that his safe return from several sea voyages is a sign of divine favour. If he is to be believed, their rather feeble explanation of his survival was that the gods had saved him so that he should be ruined by Cephisius, the present nominal prosecutor. For his part, he affirms the favour of the gods, adding that pirates and war at sea could have been their agents.

[25] Note esp. the chiastic καίτοι οὐκ ὄνειδος. . . . τότ᾽ ἦν ὄνειδος (146), the anaphora with antithesis πλείστας μέν . . . πλείστας δέ . . . (147), and the hypophora τίνα γὰρ καὶ ἀναβιβάσομαι δεησόμενον ὑπὲρ ἐμαυτοῦ; τὸν πατέρα; ἀλλὰ τέθνηκεν. ἀλλὰ τοὺς ἀδελφούς; ἀλλ᾽ οὐκ εἰσίν. ἀλλὰ τοὺς παῖδας; ἀλλ᾽ οὔπω γεγένηνται (148). There is also an a fortiori argument (149).

[26] See M. Heath, 'Justice in Thucydides' Athenian Speeches', *Historia* 39 (1990), 385–400. Later teaching is divided on the question of precedence: Aristot. *Rhet.* 1. 3. 5, 6 seems to give it to expediency: τέλος . . . τῷ μὲν συμβουλεύοντι τὸ συμφέρον . . . οἱ

the war progresses. These speeches provided Andocides with
recent texts on subjects germane to his own, and to these he could
add memory of oratory he had heard or which his older friends
could recall.[27] It has no formal prooemium:[28] he immediately tackles his first problem, which is his audience's belief, based on past
experience, that alliance with Sparta tends to promote oligarchy. In
the prescribed way, of which he later shows explicit approval (29,
32) he argues against this belief by means of historical precedents,[29]
all of which illustrate that, made at the right time, peace treaties had
proved expedient in the past. The theme of *expediency* (συμφέρον)
thus dominates this section (3–12). Apart from the extraordinary
confusion of facts which these contain,[30] the most interesting feature of this part of the speech is the goodwill expressed towards the
Spartans. That sentiment may lie behind the inconsistency between
the uses of the term *spondai* in 3 and in 11: in 11 *spondai* are defined
as 'the dictation of terms by the winners to the losers', whereas in
3 they herald a negotiated peace by which the Spartans allowed the
Athenians to prosper and rebuild their strength. This goodwill is an
essential ingredient of his central argument, and it leads ultimately
to a very striking generalization in 28: 'Now what causes me the
greatest dismay, Athenians, is our inveterate fault of invariably
abandoning our more powerful friends and choosing the weaker,

συμβουλεύοντες τὰ μὲν ἄλλα πολλάκις προίενται, ὡς δὲ ἀσύμφορα
συμβουλεύουσιν ἢ ἀπ' ὠφελίμων ἀποτρέπουσιν οὐκ ἂν ὁμολογήσαιεν· whereas in
Rhet. ad Alex. (11 1424b 29 ff.) the justice of a cause and the reliability of potential allies take
equal place with argument of opportunity (καιρός) in a speech *for* an alliance, and take second place after inopportuneness in a speech *against* an alliance (1425b: πρῶτον μὲν ὡς οὐκ
ἀνάγκη ποιεῖσθαι νῦν αὐτήν, εἶθ' ὡς οὐ δίκαιοι τυγχάνουσιν ὄντες).

[27] I accept in general the common view that demegoric speeches were not written down,
and therefore not published. But there may have been exceptions, as when major political
issues were central to the debate. See my article 'Xenophon, Critias and Theramenes', *JHS*
88 (1968), 128–35.

[28] Aristotle (*Rhet.* 3. 14. 12) notes that a prooemium is usually unnecessary in a deliberative speech.

[29] See Ch. 2 n. 42. Main studies: K. Jost, 'Das Beispiel und Vorbild der Vorfahren bei
den attischen Rednern bis Demosthenes', *Rhetorische Studien* 19 (Paderborn, 1936); K.
Schmitz-Kahlmann, 'Das Beispiel der Geschichte im politischen Denken des Isokrates',
Philol. Suppl. 31. 4; L. Pearson, 'Historical Allusions in the Attic Orators', *CPh* 36 (1941),
209–29; S. Perlman, 'The Historical Example, its Use and Importance as Political
Propaganda in the Attic Orators', *Scripta Hierosolymitana* 7 (1961), 150–66; M. Nouhaud,
L'Utilisation de l'histoire par les orateurs attiques (Paris, 1982).

[30] On the historical blunders of Andocides and others, see R. Thomas, *Oral Tradition and
Written Records in Classical Athens* (Cambridge, 1989), who shows how family traditions could
distort historical events (pp. 119–23, 201, 204). Omission is a no less useful device: Missiou,
The Subversive Oratory of Andocides, 63–5, notes how he passes over the tyranny of the Thirty.

and of going to war for the sake of others when, as far as we ourselves were concerned, we could remain at peace.' This is raw,
chauvinistic expediency in its extreme form. While epideictic oratory could still praise the unselfish idealism of past Athenian foreign
policy,[31] Andocides, the practical orator speaking within recent,
disillusioning memory of defeat and loss of empire, uses the type of
argument most calculated to persuade people who were looking for
the shortest route to a recovery of power and prosperity. And he
answers their possible objections directly (37 ff.): the building of
walls and ships, which would be allowed under the terms the
ambassadors had obtained from Sparta, might not lead to immediate recovery, but were an essential preliminary to it. The means of
achieving empire were varied, and compounded of persuasion,
bribery, stealth, and force (37–8). Thanks to the diplomacy of
Andocides and his fellow-ambassadors, the people now had a
choice (41): to resume either their pursuit of advancement with the
assurance of Sparta's acquiescence, or war against her aided by inferior allies (Argos and Corinth). The case could hardly have been
argued more convincingly. Its main thrust is certainly utilitarian
and amoral; yet it does contain a section (13–20), notably rich in
rhetorical devices,[32] in which Sparta is represented as acting with
justice in victory, on which he comments: 'Yet what terms of peace
would they have faced from us, if they had been beaten in only one
battle?' (19). The shift back to the theme of expediency is gradual,
and a degree of deception is involved: Sparta has shown forbearance, and advantage may be taken of that. This argument will have
been favourably received by many of his audience at a time when
revival of imperial ambitions was in the air. But Andocides sedu-
lously tries to lead his audience away from thoughts which glorify
military adventurism.[33] He also passes over the advantages which
Sparta expected from the terms of peace. Her diplomacy was aimed
not only at Athenian, but also at Persian compliance. By settling
her differences with Persia, she hoped to win freedom to assert her
hegemony in Greece. But the price demanded by Persia was control over the Greek cities of Asia Minor, with many of which the

[31] [Lys.] 2 *Epitaph.* 68 (contemporary with this speech); Isoc. 4 *Paneg.* 79, 80; Plato,
Menex. 239b, 240e.
[32] Questions, including hypophora (14); concession (16); para prosdokian (Sparta's surprising magnanimity) 17–19.
[33] So Missiou, *The Subversive Oratory of Andocides*, 47 n. 1.

Athenians had ancestral ties and recent alliances. Consideration of these factors, which no doubt opposing speakers raised and likewise expounded in terms of justice and expediency, prompted the Assembly to vote against the peace, and in 391 BC the ambassadors were exiled. It may be deduced that Andocides had underestimated the abiding hostility felt against Sparta. In view of consequent events—the King's Peace (386 BC), which gave Sparta a free hand in Greece with Persian support—Andocides' suggestion that objectors to the peace should make constructive counter-proposals, and his insistence on openness (33–4) and the people's responsibility (40–1), may be additions incorporated in the published speech by way of vindication. This might also explain his complaint (35) about the fickleness and contrariness of assemblies—hardly to be seen as conciliatory in a speech which was actually delivered. Indeed, the circumstances of the speech's publication invite speculation, since he is not known to have returned to Athens. Perhaps his friends published it in the hope of securing his recall, or as a political pamphlet to canvass the advantages of a *rapprochement* with Sparta.

ANDOCIDES: SUMMARY

The surviving speeches of Andocides belong to three phases of his public life—his exile (*On his Return*), his rehabilitation (*On the Mysteries*), and his subsequent career (*On the Peace with Sparta*). The mere fact that he passed through and survived these phases in a period of such political turbulence proves that he was a resilient and adaptable communicator, who learned from his mistakes. But he also retained and developed characteristics which gave his oratory individuality. The effectiveness of the rhetorical sophistication that he could show in *On his Return* was undermined by its overall egotistical, sometimes hectoring tone. In *On the Mysteries* he fell back on standard topoi in the conventional parts of the speech, but gave full licence to his natural talent for telling stories, conducting lively dialogues, and denigrating opponents. Indeed, the animation generated by live or direct speech, the informal, almost knockabout style of some of the narrative (and indeed the variety of circumstances in which narrative is used)—are traits of a natural orator; and this informal style may have been more influential than we can know, since the works of its exponents are less likely to have been published and preserved for posterity. At least one other orator, however, seems to have found it congenial—Aeschines, another speaker who relied on natural gifts.[34] Informality also seems to have been a characteristic of Hyperides, whom some critics regarded as the most roundly gifted of the orators. Assessment of Andocides' ability as a deliberative orator is again vitiated by failure, but *On the Peace with Sparta* shows gritty realism in its insistence on expediency, and well-deployed rhetorical features.[35]

[34] Points of resemblance between Andocides and Aeschines have been long recognized. Kingsbury, *A Rhetorical Study*, examines these, and the differences, in his ch. 5.

[35] See Edwards *GO* iv. 108–9. This volume also contains [Andocides] 4 *Against Alcibiades*. See pp. 131–6 for a full discussion of the question of authenticity. I concur with its negative conclusion.

4

LYSIAS

The most prolific and successful speechwriter before Demosthenes, Lysias maximized his opportunities to write with freshness and originality by free choice of clients.[1] The development of forensic oratory in his hands was further advanced by two external factors: the growing recognition, to which he responded, of the genre as literature, which could be read, appreciated, and criticized like the established genres;[2] and the speechwriter's need to attract more clients, which led him to publish those of his speeches which most effectively displayed his skills.[3] His productive life spanned a period exceeding twenty years, ample time in which to find and explore new means, adapted to the political climate and literary tastes of the age as well as to each client's needs, of convincing Athenian juries. Twenty-three complete and twelve incomplete speeches survive,

---

[1] These show no uniform political affinities: Lysias wrote both for ordinary citizens like Euphiletus (Speech 1) and for wealthy property-owners who may have felt no particular affection for the democracy which he himself, naturally, professed to espouse. The unidealistic words of the speaker in Speech 25. 8 (οὐδείς ἐστιν ἀνθρώπων φύσει οὔτε ὀλιγαρχικὸς οὔτε δημοκρατικός, ἀλλ᾽ ἥτις ἂν ἑκάστῳ πολιτεία συμφέρῃ, ταύτην προθυμεῖται καθεστάναι, 'No human being is naturally either an oligarch or a democrat: each man strives to establish whichever constitution works to his advantage') found application in Lysias' own practice. Ability to pay his fee was sufficient qualification for most of his clients. On the question of the political affinities of Lysias' clients, see Dover LCL 47–56.

[2] Plato Phaedrus furnishes the best evidence for Lysias' literary reputation (228a, 258d, 278c). There it is made clear that his writings were widely read and enjoyed, but this has to be squared with the fact that his surviving oeuvre consists almost entirely of speeches for the courts. Isocrates (Paneg. 11) deplores the literary status accorded forensic oratory; and the survival of so much of it long after it could have been useful for attracting clients or instructing litigants is hard to explain except in terms of a lively critical readership.

[3] This need might cause him to select successful cases, but more important was the necessity to demonstrate his ability to handle difficult cases. Dion. Hal. Lys. draws particular attention to his inventiveness in cases lacking direct evidence (15: δηλοῦσι δὲ μάλιστα τὴν δεινότητα τῆς εὑρέσεως αὐτοῦ οἵ τε ἀμάρτυροι τῶν λόγων καὶ οἱ περὶ τὰς παραδόξους συνταχθέντες ὑποθέσεις, ἐν οἷς πλεῖστα καὶ κάλλιστα ἐνθυμήματα λέγει καὶ τὰ πάνυ δοκοῦντα τοῖς ἄλλοις ἄπορα εἶναι καὶ ἀδύνατα εὔπορα καὶ δυνατὰ φαίνεσθαι ποιεῖ.)

together with over 100 fragments.[4] Length is not necessarily a guide to interest: some of the shorter speeches are the most innovative and entertaining. But the examination begins with the first speech in the Corpus. As elsewhere, examination of individual speeches follows their chronological order as far as this can be established. Some speeches, however, are undatable. The first speech is one of these.[5]

1 *The Killing of Eratosthenes*[6]

Euphiletus, a cuckolded husband who has caught his wife's adulterer *in flagrante delicto* and killed him on the spot before witnesses, is accused of intentional homicide by the dead man's kinsmen, who have also claimed entrapment. The difficulty of this case lies in a conflict between ancient law and contemporary custom. Euphiletus' prosecutors were able to represent him as a murderer because adulterers were rarely killed, so that a jury might be expected to feel prejudice against a man who forsook the usual remedies—monetary compensation and/or various forms of physical humiliation—and, more seriously, suspicion of his motives for observing the letter of the law.

[4] The Corpus contains several speeches which are probably not by Lysias. For an attempt to identify these using statistics, see S. Usher and D. Najock, *Comp. Hum.* 16 (1982), 85–105.

[5] But see n. 6. For the chronology of the surviving speeches, see Dover *LCL* 44–6. The latest, 26, is to be assigned to 382/1. Statistical evidence reinforces historical evidence for the spuriousness of 20, leaving 403/2 as the date of his earliest datable extant speech, 12 *Against Eratosthenes*. 445/4 is a better guess for his date of birth than the traditional year 459 (Dion. Hal. *Lys.* 1, 12; *Vit. X Or.* 835c), which is based on the unsure assumption that he went to Thurii, aged 15, at its foundation (443). See Blass *AB* i. 341–5; Dover *LCL* 42; Usher *GO* i. 125–6; C. Carey, *Lysias: Selected Speeches* (Cambridge, 1989), 1–2. For a modern defence of the earlier date, see U. Schindel, *Rh. Mus.* 110 (1967), 32–52. For further biographical details, see Speech 12 (below).

[6] If this Eratosthenes is correctly identified with the 'tyrant' prosecuted in Speech 12, we have a *terminus post quem* of 403 for this speech. The strongest reason for this identification remains that proposed by Kirschner, the rarity of the name. Against this, however, must be set Davies's *argumentum ex silentio* (*APF* 185): absence of reference to Eratosthenes' infamous political past is indeed extraordinary and probably decisive. It may even rule out Davies's suggestion that he may have been a younger relative, since litigants' vituperation routinely included members of their opponents' families. The opportunity to draw a parallel between political and personal *hybris* would have been too good to miss. For a revival of Kirschner's view, see H. Avery, 'Was Eratosthenes the Oligarch Eratosthenes the Adulterer', *Hermes* 119 (1991), 380–4. His argument (381) that Lysias the speechwriter would not have aired his personal prejudices in a speech written for a client might be valid if the person attacked had been merely a private enemy instead of a publicly reviled figure. But see K. Kapparis, 'Is Eratosthenes in Lys. 1 the Same Person as Eratosthenes in Lys. 12?', *Hermes* 121 (1993), 364–5 for a cogent restatement of the arguments against identifying the two Eratosthenes.

Since the narrative of the bare facts immediately surrounding the killing could not overcome this prejudice and suspicion, Lysias resorted to artifice dressed in simple clothing.[7] But even in the **prooemium** (1–5) forthrightness conceals originality. Absent are pleas which stress the speaker's disadvantages; and instead of flattering the jury, he asks that they put themselves in his position, seeing him as a victim instead of a perpetrator of a crime (so Carey, *Lysias*, 64)—a crime which is abhorred throughout the Greek world. In his summary of the case he has to answer, he fails to mention the charge of entrapment. In the **narrative** (6–28) he tells a straightforward story, starting with a prodiegesis (6–9) describing the early, serene years of his married life, and leading to the events immediately preceding the discovery of his wife's adultery.[8] Everything seems to happen naturally, but each action contributes to a portrait of Euphiletus' character which is intended to convince the jury that he would have lacked the ingenuity necessary to form any plan of entrapment or abduction, or indeed to interpret obvious signs and deduce their consequences. He appears naïve,[9] but Lysias recognizes the danger of overstressing this characteristic, so he also makes him trusting[10] and considerate.[11] But the portrait is still unsatisfactory, as some dicasts might yet identify him with the stock comic figure of the unknowing cuckolded husband.[12] In order to be congruent with his killing of Eratosthenes, his character needed to have masterful, even potentially violent elements. These are to be found in the narrative, though their presence is not acknowledged by some commentators.[13] He is master in his own

---

[7] This speech exemplifies *par excellence* the 'artlessness which is the product of art' praised by Dionysius (πεποίηται γὰρ αὐτῷ τοῦτο τὸ ἀποίητον (*Lys.* 8)).

[8] The contrast is sharply marked (7: ἐν μὲν οὖν τῷ πρώτῳ χρόνῳ . . . πασῶν ἦν βελτίστη . . . ἐπειδὴ δέ μοι ἡ μήτηρ ἐτελεύτησε, πάντων τῶν κακῶν ἀποθανοῦσα αἰτία μοι γεγένηται), the first of several bitter asides intended to gain sympathy.

[9] He is even made, in one aside, to deplore his own gullibility (10: οὕτως ἠλιθίως διεκείμην . . .), but still he conscientiously describes climactically all the signs of his wife's deceit: the baby's crying, artificially stimulated (11), his wife's locking the door (13), the banging of the street door during the night, her wearing cosmetics while still supposed to be mourning the death of a relative (14), the most suspicious sign.

[10] His trust is made to appear logical, the result of a good early relationship and the birth of their child (6).

[11] Again, the image of the kind husband who changes the domestic arrangements to make it easier for his wife to nurse their baby, will have elicited mainly sympathy from a jury.

[12] See Aristoph. *Thesm.* 478 ff. and Carey, *Lysias*, 61 for examples in later literature.

[13] Carey, *Lysias*, 62 says that Euphiletus' anger 'is not stressed', and suggests that 'irascibility would not be a good defence in a homicide case', no doubt relying on passages

house as he orders his wife to see to their baby's crying and becomes angry when she is slow to obey him (12). His reaction to the discovery of his wife's adultery is one of suddenly released emotion, mirrored in the style.[14] Lysias' use of live speech for Euphiletus' confrontation of the conspiring servant-girl, whom he threatens with violence (18), and again when he confronts the adulterer in the bedroom and assaults him before killing him (25), is surely intended to dramatize the character of a man whose natural impulsiveness readily expresses itself.

There is less scope for disagreement about the difficulties posed by Euphiletus' actions prior to the killing, because these actions cannot but make him appear capable of planning, which could, in a jury's mind, extend to the entrapment of which he is accused. But the plan, as described by Lysias, is a simple one, and its ultimate intention is deliberately obscured.[15] Moreover, he has already answered, indirectly through his narrative, another basic question which would have occurred to some jurors—that of why he did not confront his wife directly with his knowledge—by portraying her in detail (10–14) as a consummate liar and dissembler. She would have denied everything and ended the liaison, leaving him with no evidence on which to act within the law.

Simple narrative adds details which imply lack of planning—his entertainment of his friend Sostratus and the latter's departure (22), the absence of some of his neighbours (though he finds enough at home to witness the denouement)—and fulfilment of the requirement of the law—the discovery of the couple in bed, and the fact that Eratosthenes was not killed while seeking sanctuary at the hearth (25, 27).

expressing general sentiments about anger, such as Lys. 10. 30, 19. 2. This, however, discounts the concept of 'just anger': a man may surely give full rein to his anger, which will be the more violent if he is naturally quick-tempered, when he discovers that the integrity of his family has been violated. Even on a more disinterested level, juries are often urged to show 'just anger' towards miscreants (Lys. 12. 2, 20, 30, 80; 31. 11), so it is difficult to believe that they would have disapproved of violent anger in a personally affected individual.

[14] 17: note esp. tense variation and the repetition of the striking clause μεστὸς ἦν ὑποψίας ('I was full of suspicion') (see S. Usher, *Eranos* 63 (1965), 103, GO i. 225). The repetition draws no comment from Carey, who appears to find no tension in the passage, describing it on the contrary as 'The leisurely re-enactment of his reasoning'.

[15] 21: ἐπ' αὐτοφώρῳ . . . τὸ ἔργον φανερὸν γενέσθαι, εἴπερ οὕτως ἔχει: the servant-girl's task is no more than to alert Euphiletus when Eratosthenes has entered the house and enable him to ascertain the truth. 'In the act' confirms that the requirement of the law is met (30). Lysias has had to weigh the risk of pointing to conspiracy against the need to provide a detail that legalizes his action.

The items of direct evidence (atechnoi pisteis) are neatly summarized in 29: Eratosthenes admitted his guilt and sought to win
release by payment of a sum of money in compensation. Euphiletus
chose to invoke the letter of the law, which provides for summary
execution of an adulterer. After quoting the law and its ramifica-
tions, and explaining the reasoning behind it (30–6), he turns to
argumentative and rhetorical evidence (entechnoi pisteis), first
refuting his opponents' allegations with probability- (eikos-) argument, deducing these from the facts in the narrative (37–42), then
dismissing the standard motives of enmity, fear, and gain (43–6).
These sections are conventional. In the **epilogue** (47–50) he gives
the speech unity by insisting that he has upheld the law, which he
represents, as in the prooemium, as unambiguous and unequivocal.
Indeed, he has been its agent.[16] While the prooemium is not without its idiosyncrasies, the vividness and the main originality of the
speech lie in the portrayal of Euphiletus' character in the narrative,
which, while serving the needs of the defence, has also proved subtle enough to elicit differing interpretations from commentators.

12 *Against Eratosthenes*

The lives of Lysias himself and his family form the background to
this speech, the only one that he certainly delivered on his own
behalf. His father Cephalus came to Athens from Syracuse. The
family had been wealthy before his migration (Plato, *Rep.* 330b),
and remained so, owning a shield-factory which thrived during the
long years of war. They moved in the upper circles of Athenian
society while supporting the democracy, and seem to have escaped
the prejudice and suspicion suffered by some resident-aliens
(*metoikoi*, 'metics') in wartime, ironically to fall victim to it after
peace was made. The Thirty Tyrants, needing money to maintain
the Spartan garrison which propped up their regime, chose wealthy
metics as the readiest source, and arrested ten of them, including
Lysias and his brother Polemarchus. Lysias escaped from his captors,
but Polemarchus was killed. After the Thirty had been deposed and

---

[16] This may be the effect sought by the hieratic pronouncement of sentence which
Euphiletus is made to make before he kills Eratosthenes (27). (Notice, however, that the
words are introduced by ὅτι, leaving room for conjecture as to what was actually said, both
on the scene and at the trial; and the literary requirements of the published speech placed it
at a point of further removal from reality.)

the democracy restored (403 BC), Lysias brought one of their number, Eratosthenes, to court, accusing him of the murder of his
brother.[17]

Two major problems faced Lysias, one personal, the other political. As to the former, he could not fix individual responsibility on
Eratosthenes, who, though he arrested Polemarchus, did not kill
him. This fact forces Lysias to search for the opportunities
Eratosthenes may have had to let Polemarchus escape: but some of
the jury would have had first-hand experience of the ruthlessly
thorough methods of the Thirty. On the political side, he has to
contend with Eratosthenes' association with Theramenes, who,
though one of the Thirty, had died at the hands of the extremists
led by Critias, and enjoyed a degree of posthumous sympathy.[18]
Lysias' response to this dual challenge is, in effect, to write two successive speeches. The first is a clearly divided forensic oration
(1–40: **prooemium** 1–3; **narrative** 4–24; **proof** 25–36; **epilogue**
37–40). The second is a political invective, initially against
Eratosthenes (41–61), then against Theramenes (62–78).[19] In the
long concluding section (79–100) the theme is one not of individual but of collective guilt. Indeed, this is already adumbrated in the
prooemium, where reference is made to 'their crimes' (αὐτοῖς
. . . εἴργασται, 1) and 'the defendants' (τοὺς φεύγοντας . . . τῶν
φευγόντων, 2), and the conventional specification of the charge,
which would have to be against the named defendant, is omitted.

[17] Under the terms of the 'amnesty' (μὴ μνησικακήσειν, Xen. Hell. 2. 4. 43) sworn by
all parties after the restoration of the democracy (403 BC), those of the Thirty who had survived could retain full rights if they successfully submitted to investigation of their conduct
in office (euthyna). Eratosthenes may have done this, or have been about to do this, when
Lysias invoked another of the terms of the settlement, that the amnesty did not exonerate
those guilty of homicide (on which see Rhodes CAP 468–70; P. Cloché, La Restauration
démocratique (Paris, 1915), 259–62; R. J. Bonner and G. Smith, The Administration of Justice
from Homer to Aristotle, ii (Chicago, 1930), 195). Murder still carried a taint of pollution which
was too strong to be expunged by political legislation. For the sequence of events surrounding Lysias' prosecution of Eratosthenes see Usher GO i. 235–6; and for a thorough
examination of this episode of his career, when he briefly enjoyed full citizenship under a
decree of Thrasybulus, only to be deprived of it under a decree of Archinus, see T. C.
Loening, Hermes 109 (1981), 280–94.
[18] See B. Perrin, 'The Rehabilitation of Theramenes', AHR 9 (1903), 649–69; L. van der
Ploeg, Theramenes en zijn Tijd (Utrecht, 1948); M. C. R. Giammarco, 'Teramene di Stiria',
Parola del Passato 28 (1973), 419–25; P. Krentz, The Thirty at Athens (New York and London,
1982).
[19] Lysias may have had good career reasons for framing his prosecution in this way—to
display his versatility so as to attract not only litigating clients but also men hoping to make
their way in politics.

He even converts the private motive of ἔχθρα into a public one (πρὸς τὴν πόλιν, 2). The combination of *difficulty* with *abundance* (1 ἄπορον ... καὶ τοσαῦτα εἴργασται) is new.

The **narrative** is a model of factual clarity, yet it contains enough personal judgements and reflections[20] to arouse sympathy for the speaker and prejudice against his opponents. This combination of apparent simplicity and persuasive formation of opinion becomes a central characteristic of Lysianic narratives. The underlying purpose of this one soon becomes plain: it is to represent Eratosthenes and the rest of the Thirty as having been motivated by pure greed, unalloyed with political idealism or any patriotic intention. Lysias applies himself to this purpose almost at the outset, devoting only the first sentence (4) to prodiegesis, a brief reference to his family's thirty years' residence in Athens. Beginning with the Thirty's decision to arrest certain metics, and their reasons for doing so (5–7), the narrative concentrates first on the arrest of Lysias himself (8–16) by Peison and Theognis. This story has a minor climax as Peison sees the contents of Lysias' money-chest and removes it bodily after swearing to allow him to escape in return for one talent only (10–11); but the rhetorical highpoint comes in 18–19, after Polemarchus has been arrested and made to drink the hemlock:

And as he was being carried dead from the prison they did not allow a funeral to be conducted from any one of our three houses, but they laid him out in a small hut they had hired. We also had many cloaks, yet they refused their request for one for his burial; but one of our friends supplied a cloak, another a pillow, and others what they each happened to have, for the burial. They had seven hundred shields of ours, they had all that silver and gold, with bronze, jewellery, furniture and women's clothes, all in quantities exceeding their expectations, and a hundred and twenty slaves, the best of which they took for themselves and the rest they handed over to the public treasury. But the action which illustrates their character and the extremes of insatiable greed that they had reached was this: on first entering the house, Melobius tore from her ears the gold earrings which Polemarchus' wife happened to be wearing.[21] Thus we received no pity from them even regarding the smallest part of our property.

[20] e.g. 5: οἱ τριάκοντα πονηροὶ καὶ συκοφάνται ὄντες. 7: λαμβάνειν δὲ χρήματα περὶ πολλοῦ ἐποιοῦντο. 14: ἡγεῖτο γὰρ ἅπαν ποιήσειν αὐτόν, εἴ τις ἀργύριον διδοίη.
[21] Further on this climactic moment, see C. W. Wooten, 'The Earrings of Polemarchus' Wife', *CW* 82 (1988), 29–31; E. K. Borthwick, 'Two Emotional Climaxes in Lysias *Against Eratosthenes*', *CW* 84 (1990), 44–6; J. A. E. Bons, 'Lys. 12. 19: The Earrings Again', *Hermes* 121 (1993), 365–7.

With motivation thus melodramatically established, Lysias has yet to focus guilt upon the named defendant. Eratosthenes is mentioned for the first time in 16, but he is connected straightway to a vital piece of evidence: that he had arrested Polemarchus 'in the street'. Armed with this, Lysias is able to argue in the proof (26, 30) that Eratosthenes could have allowed Polemarchus to escape, whereas if Polemarchus had been caught in his own house arrest would have been unavoidable. This argument might have been decisive, but Eratosthenes has relied on a plea which the jury, with their knowledge of the extremism of the leaders of the Thirty,[22] might accept—that he was an unwilling agent of their cruelty. Lysias realized that this position must be attacked at the outset of the proof, and he chooses a novel method, apostrophizing the defendant with direct questions (erotesis).[23] As a quick and dramatic way of gaining an admission which leads to an absurdity, it undermines Eratosthenes' claim and exposes him to further attacks. To meet Eratosthenes' claim that he had actually spoken in opposition to the killings, Lysias deploys a sophistical eikos-argument,[24] and follows it with a classic example of reductio ad absurdum.[25] He then draws argument from the vital piece of evidence (16 above) before concluding that Eratosthenes 'felt not pain but pleasure at what was being done' (32).

The concluding sections of the purely forensic part of the speech (34–40) are very rich in rhetorical devices and topoi, as if Lysias was aiming to display his panoply of oratorical skills. Every sentence contains artifice.[26] Of especial interest is the reference to the 'standpoints' staseis, Lat. status, according to which later rhetoricians

---

[22] Lysias naturally does not draw much attention to these men—Critias, Charicles, and their hetaireia—because to do so would point up ideological differences within the Thirty and the relative moderation of Theramenes and his supporters, who included Eratosthenes.

[23] See Rhet. Graec. (Sp. i), 166–7; E. M. Carawan, 'Erotesis: Interrogation in the Courts', GRBS 24 (1983), 209–26.

[24] 27: οὐ δήπου γὰρ ἐν τοῖς μετοίκοις πίστιν παρ' αὐτοῦ ἐλάμβανον. In order to test his loyalty after his public dissent, the extremists would have sent him to kill a leading democrat rather than mere resident aliens. Hence he must have been a trusty adherent to their cause.

[25] 29: νῦν δὲ παρὰ τοῦ ποτε καὶ λήψεσθε δίκην, εἴπερ ἐξέσται τοῖς τριάκοντα λέγειν ὅτι τὰ ὑπὸ τῶν τριάκοντα προσταχθέντα ἐποίουν; see J. J. Bateman, Phoenix 16 (1962), 168.

[26] 34: concession and a fortiori (comparative) argument; 35: the topos of example and precedent (cf. Antiph. Tetr. 1. 3. 11); 36: historical pathetic paradox (οὐκ οὖν δεινὸν . . .); 37: concluding formula (ἠξίουν ἱκανὰ εἶναι τὰ κατηγορημένα), which is however followed by general political arguments, and turns out to be a bridge to the epideictic excursus on Eratosthenes' career.

defined lawsuits. Lysias says that Eratosthenes must show either that he did not arrest Polemarchus (question of fact, στάσις λογική, *status coniecturalis*), or that he did so justly (question of justice, στάσις νομική, *status iuridicialis*). The presence of *staseis* in Lysias (see also 13 *Ag. Agorat.* 49, 51, 84; 29 *Ag. Philocr.* 5) is one of many indications that later theory had its origins in the earliest practice. (See Ch. 1 n. 47.)

Section 41 opens with the formula Πολλάκις ἐθαύμασα ('I have often marvelled'),[27] and the style becomes more periodic and expansive. A new start has been made, and we are reading the earliest example of one of the two types of epideictic oratory, censure or denunciation (ψόγος, κακολογία, *vituperatio*).[28] The characteristics of this genre of oratory, later elaborated by Isocrates, are detailed and stylistically balanced comment on the facts,[29] opinion unrelated to them,[30] description of what ought to have been done,[31] and direct appeal to his audience to express their anger.[32]

The *kakologia* of Theramenes (62–78) calls for a different technique and different emphasis. It is appropriate that a figure now dead should be compared unfavourably with one belonging to remoter history,[33] but it was sure to be difficult to arouse a jury's posthumous resentment against a man who had excited such varying passions. Lysias must constantly be pointing to Theramenes' relationship with 'you, the people' (τὸ ὑμέτερον πλῆθος, 66, 67) and to his selfish and treacherous disregard for their best interests.

[27] The earliest instance of a formula which, with variants, was subsequently used in many discourses: it begins works as diverse as Isocrates *Panegyricus* and Xenophon *Memorabilia*.
[28] The other is, of course, praise or encomium (Gorgias, *Helen* 1). Theorists offer little discussion of the themes of censure: Aristotle (*Rhet.* 1. 9) merely lists those of praise and says that those of censure are their opposites; and they receive similar treatment in *Ad Herenn.* 3. 6. 10–16. Quintilian (3. 7. 19–21) lists some topics; *Rhet. ad Alex.* 35 1441b advises interestingly that censure should be based on facts (narrative). There is an extended exercise in Aphthonius *Progymn.* 9 (Sp. ii. 40–2) and a shorter entry in Aristides *Tech. Rhet.* (Sp. ii. 506). In the absence of much specific teaching, Lysias' early contribution to the genre is of particular importance.
[29] e.g. 44: οὕτως οὐχ . . . ἀλλὰ καί. . . .
[30] e.g. 51: ἀλλ' οὗτος τὴν μὲν πόλιν ἐχθρὰν ἐνόμιζεν εἶναι, τοὺς δ' ὑμετέρους ἐχθροὺς φίλους. The speaker's judgement is given more prominence than the narrative, but facts play an important part, as recommended by *Rhet. ad Alex.* 35 1441b.
[31] e.g. 47: καίτοι εἰ ἐσωφρόνουν . . . 48: εἴπερ ἦν ἀνὴρ ἀγαθός . . . 50: χρῆν δέ. See G. Gebauer, *De Hypotacticis et Paratacticis Argumenti ex Contrario Formis quae reperiuntur apud Oratores Atticos* (Zwickau, 1887), 209.
[32] § 58.
[33] 63: the antithesis with Themistocles, who built the walls against the Spartans' will, produces a telling *paradeigma*.

A narrative (72–6) recounts the crowning event, the Assembly at which Theramenes presented the terms of peace which he had negotiated with Lysander, and reminds the jury of how the Thirty Tyrants came to power. He has no need to distort the facts here,[34] so bitter is the recent memory of their rule. But he concludes the *kakologia* with a resounding rhetorical flourish (78: πάλαι καὶ νεωστὶ καὶ μικρῶν καὶ μεγάλων αἰτίου γεγενημένου . . . δικαίως μὲν . . . δικαίως δ' . . . τῶν μὲν παρόντων καταφρονῶν, τῶν δ' ἀπόντων ἐπιθυμῶν, καὶ τῷ καλλίστῳ ὀνόματι χρώμενος δεινοτάτων ἔργων διδάσκαλος καταστάς).

Eratosthenes is accused once more as an individual (81): otherwise he is linked with his fellow-tyrants (79, 81, 87); and as to Polemarchus, their victim, silence. Again, there is no conventional recapitulation of the events leading to his killing, since this would weaken the specific charge by reminding the jury that the crime cannot be pinned upon Eratosthenes alone. Lysias makes collective responsibility the abiding theme of these later chapters,[35] and the crimes of the one and the many tend to merge together, converting a lawsuit into a political statement. It cannot have helped him win the case, but it is really his only recourse against a man who was generally thought to have been the least culpable of the Thirty (89: καίτοι λέγουσιν ὡς Ἐρατοσθένει ἐλάχιστα τῶν τριάκοντα κακὰ εἴργασται). He disappears from the scene altogether in the concluding chapters (92–100), which attempt to unite the contending parties of the City (92–4) and the Piraeus (95–8) in condemnation of the Thirty.[36] The speech ends with a succession of topoi and figures.[37] The final sentence, asyndetic, and elliptical,

[34] The earlier part of the account is not, however, free of distortion, as when Lysias says that Theramenes was 'not forced by the Lacedaemonians' (70) to agree to the demolition of the walls.

[35] See esp. 84–5, where Eratosthenes' boldness is explained by the support he expects to receive from his companions, who hope his acquittal will benefit them.

[36] Lysias reserves the strongest rhetoric for the sufferings and struggles of the Piraeus party, his own side: 95–8 passim, esp. 97: ὅσοι δὲ τὸν θάνατον διέφυγον, πολλαχοῦ κινδυνεύσαντες καὶ εἰς πολλὰς πόλεις πλανηθέντες καὶ πανταχόθεν ἐκκηρυττόμενοι, ἐνδεεῖς ὄντες τῶν ἐπιτηδείων, οἱ μὲν ἐν πολεμίᾳ τῇ πατρίδι τοὺς παῖδας καταλιπόντες, οἱ δ' ἐν ξένῃ γῇ, πολλῶν ἐναντιουμένων ἤλθετε εἰς τὸν Πειραιᾶ. Period with antithesis, alliteration and oxymoron. The language resembles that of contemporary epitaphioi (97: ἄνδρες ἀγαθοὶ γενόμενοι... ἡμάρτετε. Cf. [Lys.] 2 Epitaph. 24–5).

[37] 99: topos of abundance (see Glossary under aporia): the 'too numerous to mention' topos, with which the speech began. 100: the second instance of prosopopoiia in oratory (see p. 30). Whether it was Lysias who established it as a figure especially suited to epilogues must be uncertain, but if he did, his example was followed by Isocrates (6 Archid. 110), and Lycurgus (Ag. Leocr. 150).

was doubtless imitated in many lost speeches. Aristotle paraphrases it closely in the final sentence of his *Rhetoric*.[38]

The above analysis suggests strongly that Lysias intended his first oration to establish him as the supreme all-rounder of his generation in the genre of oratory, an ambition which he may have realized.[39]

13 *Against Agoratus*

Lysias has given his unnamed client in this case the longest and most vehement speech in the corpus, apart from his own. Similarity of subject-matter partly explains this: the Thirty had induced Agoratus to lay information against certain men, chiefly democrats, who opposed the terms of peace with Sparta negotiated by Theramenes. One of these, Dionysodorus, was the speaker's cousin and brother-in-law (1). Agoratus was a man of little significance, a mere tool, yet he, not they (as in 12) is the main object of attack. Passage of time may partly explain this: the prosecution was brought a few years after their fall (83: Blass suggests '398 or later'), by which time popular hatred of the Thirty and fear of oligarchy had subsided somewhat, as the restoration of Andocides seems to indicate. But Lysias, his personal grievance against the Thirty still unredressed,[40] saw an attack on one of their minions as the only remaining way to pursue it. Further personal interest, and hence further explanation of the peculiar intensity of the speech, may perhaps be found in some form of family relationship, deducible from the victim's name.[41] However speculative such an idea may be,

---

[38] 100: Παύσομαι κατηγορῶν. ἀκηκόατε, ἑωράκατε, πεπόνθατε, ἔχετε· δικάζετε. (Aristot. *Rhet.* 3. 19. 6: εἴρηκα, ἀκηκόατε, ἔχετε, κρίνατε).

[39] Dion. Hal. *Lys.* 1. Although Socrates is made to disparage him in the *Phaedrus*, Plato's treatment of him as the model of popular oratory is an acknowledgement of his standing.

[40] The prosecution of Eratosthenes had probably failed. See Rauchenstein edn. (1899), 18–19.

[41] Two speculative linkages need to be made; but then there are two sets of nominal coincidence. Lysias and his brothers Polemarchus and Euthydemus lived in Thurii between c.430 and 412 (Dover *LCL* 42). A Dionysodorus and his brother Euthydemus were sophists who specialized in forensic speechwriting and teaching the art to others, and migrated from Chios to Thurii (Plato, *Euthyd.* 271b–272b, 283c, 288a–b). Now whereas the tradition that Lysias learned rhetoric at Thurii 'from Tisias and Nicias' (Dion. Hal. *Lys.* 1) is predictably vague, Plato's *mise en scène* of these two sophists in *Euthydemus* gives them contemporary substance. If it was they who taught Lysias, the possibility of a resulting friendship, or of something even closer, may be considered. Bearing in mind that they are old men, like Socrates, in the dialogue, one could assign to it a dramatic date some time after 412, when

Lysias certainly makes his client speak with force and confidence, making no pleas for allowance for his own shortcomings or disadvantages, but speaking straightway of the jury's sacred duty (Προσήκει, 1, 92, 96, 97; ὅσιον, 3, 4, 93) and of just revenge (τιμωρεῖν, τιμωρεῖσθαι, 1, 3, 40, 76, 92, 93, 94, 95, 97). Such an assured performer could well be a member of a family steeped in forensic and rhetorical skills.

The political aspect of the case is established at the outset and constantly kept in view: Dionysodorus and other victims are friends, and their persecutors enemies, of the democracy.[42] The first of the narratives, which dominate the speech, recounts events immediately following the destruction of the fleet at Aegospotami, in accordance with the division which Lysias has outlined at the end of the **prooemium**.[43] Initially, this **narrative** shows no advance in technique on those in Speech 12. There are just enough subjective observations to indicate the speaker's bias,[44] while the story is told clearly and dispassionately until it reaches the point where the terms of peace negotiated by Theramenes are revealed (14–15). At this point the style becomes antithetical and periodic (ἀντὶ μὲν τοῦ . . . ἀντὶ δὲ τοῦ . . . ὁρῶντες . . . 16 ποιήσασθαι), and Lysias strives successfully to create a conspiratorial atmosphere. The story of the recruitment of Agoratus into the oligarchs' plan and the subterfuge used to make him seem a reluctant informer is told in some detail, because it is essential that he should not be allowed to have appeared unwilling. This is a major difficulty for the prosecution, especially as they have had to concede, indeed

they, along with Lysias and his brothers, had left Thurii for Athens. The Dionysodorus of this speech was an Athenian citizen, since he was a taxiarch (13), but he could also be a relative of the sophist if one of their common ancestors migrated to Chios, an island on steadily friendly terms with Athens until the Ionian War. The other nominal coincidence may perhaps be explained by adoption: the son of the sophist Euthydemus may have been adopted into Lysias' family. (Incidentally, was this the Euthydemus who rejected the sexual advances of Critias (Xen. Mem. 1. 2. 29–31)? That would afford another explanation of the Thirty's hostility to Lysias' family, but one too indelicate to include in a published speech.)

[42] Note the recurring phrase τὸ πλῆθος τὸ ὑμέτερον (1, 2, 9, 10, 16, 17, 92; δῆμος, 20, 51).

[43] 4: πρῶτον μὲν ᾧ τρόπῳ ὑμῖν ἡ δημοκρατία κατελύθη καὶ ὑφ' ὅτου (5–17), ἔπειτα ᾧ τρόπῳ οἱ ἄνδρες ὑπ' Ἀγοράτου ἀπέθανον καὶ δὴ ὅ τι ἀποθνῄσκειν μέλλοντες ἐπέσκηψαν (18–42).

[44] 9: Θηραμένης, ἐπιβουλεύων τῷ πλήθει τῷ ὑμετέρῳ . . . 12: ἐπιβουλεύοντες καταλῦσαι τὸν δῆμον. Bias and distortion are explored at some length by A. Schweizer, Die 13 Rede des Lysias: Eine rhetorische Analyse (Basel, 1936), though his study is concerned primarily with division and correspondence with rhetorical theory.

assert (18), that Agoratus was no more than a pawn in the oligarchs'
game-plan. Their first step must be, at least, to establish that he was
a willing pawn. The point is hammered home in the narrative at
every opportunity (19: ὡς δὲ ἑκὼν ἐμήνυσε . . . 28: νῦν δὲ ἄκων
μὲν προσποιεῖ, ἑκὼν δὲ πολλοὺς καὶ ἀγαθοὺς Ἀθηναίων
ἀπέκτεινας. 29: ἑκὼν ἀνέστη Ἀγόρατος ἀπὸ τοῦ βωμοῦ) and
taken up again in the proof (52–3). But the difficulty remains, and
to overcome it Lysias seeks to stir emotions by recreating the most
poignant moment in the story (39–42):

Now when the death-sentence had been passed on them, gentlemen, and
they had to die, each man sent for his female next-of-kin—sister, mother
or wife—to visit them in the prison, so that they could embrace their
people in their final farewells before ending their lives. And Dionysodorus
sent for my sister, his wife, to come to the prison. On hearing his request,
she appeared, dressed in a black cloak, which was natural in view of her
husband's tragic fate. In the presence of my sister, after disposing of his
possessions as he thought fit, he named Agoratus as the man responsible
for his death, and laid upon me and Dionysius here, his brother, and all
his friends, the solemn duty of vengeance on his behalf against Agoratus.
And he charged his wife, believing her pregnant by him, that if she should
bear a son, she should tell the boy that Agoratus had killed his father, and
bid him exact revenge for his murder.

This description of a scene of pathos attains new levels of emotional
appeal in oratory,[45] but also has a practical purpose: to invest the
prosecution of Agoratus with a sense of religious duty. The adjura-
tions of dying men were potent weapons against the accused; and the
rhetoric which follows is hardly less powerful and concentrated.
Beginning with an expression of anguish[46] and the first oratorical
example of eironeia,[47] the account (44–8) of the Thirty's seizure of
government dwells upon its tragic consequences for his audience.
The contrast between this kind of narrative, in which expression of
subjective feeling takes precedence over the retailing of facts, and the
swift-moving action of narratives like 12. 8–20, illustrates the variety
of which Lysias is capable in narrative, a quality which marks him off
from all other orators except Demosthenes.

---

[45] The prison scene in Andoc. 1 *Myst.* 48–50 is superficially comparable, but lacks the
sad, portentous solemnity of the present passage. Carey has rightly pointed out that Lysias
achieves his emotional effect with few emotionally charged words, relying on the telling use
of external detail.

[46] 43: ἀνιῶμαι μέν.   [47] 44: ὡς σφόδρα ὑμῖν ἐλεεῖν προσήκει Ἀγόρατον.

Very little confirmatory argument is needed to prove the fact of Agoratus' information, and his willing agency (49–54), but he has tried to deflect blame by accusing others of menusis. Lysias counters this, and even exploits it, by showing how the actions of the two named informers proved them to be men of better character than Agoratus, yet they were condemned to death by the people.[48] This is the beginning of a graduated comparative argument, because Lysias now turns to the character of the men condemned to death[49] by Agoratus—distinguished generals and patriotic citizens (62–3). This is followed dramatically by a sudden descent (64): 'Such, you see, was the character of these men whom Agoratus either killed or sent into exile. And who was he?' Not only he, but his father and brothers, are subjected to scrutiny. This, the most conventional and least edifying part of the speech (64–85), contains one interesting item—reference to the event which won for Agoratus his citizenship.[50] Lysias neatly exploits the rhetorical opportunity afforded by this with a dilemmaton (75): If Agoratus has claimed falsely to have killed Phrynichus, he is culpable; if his claim is correct, he must have committed greater crimes under the Thirty to have redeemed himself in their eyes for the killing of a fellow-oligarch.

Before concluding, Lysias deals with two technicalities. The warrant for Agoratus' arrest contained the words 'caught in the act' (ἐπ' αὐτοφώρῳ), which at this time was the formula required in making an arrest (ἀπαγωγή) and need not literally describe its circumstances, as Agoratus tries to argue.[51] The second seems more difficult to counter. Agoratus has appealed to the amnesty, from which only 'the Thirty and the Ten and the Eleven and those who

---

[48] The less reputable of the two, Menestratus, is represented as having been forced by Agoratus' information to turn informer himself; while Aristophanes is portrayed as a man of principle, and, for maximum contrast, Lysias places his death immediately before his description of Agoratus' background and character (64–85).

[49] Lysias writes ἀπέκτεινεν, which listeners might construe as an aorist before the context established it as a conative imperfect: 'Agoratus killed the democratic heroes from Phyle!'

[50] 70–5. On the murder of Phrynichus, see Thuc. 8. 92. 2 and Dover ad loc. pp. 309–10. Agoratus is listed as a benefactor of the city on a stele honouring his killers (Meiggs and Lewis GHI 85, pp. 261–3). That stele does not seem to correspond with those quoted by Lysias, but there is agreement that many conspirators were involved and that controversy over their rewards was prolonged.

[51] See MacDowell AHL 130–40, esp. 133; others have argued for varying degrees of precision in the application of the term: M. H. Hansen, Apagoge (Odense, 1976), 48–53, cf. Todd SAL 80 ('caught in such a way that it is clear that he was the criminal').

ruled the Piraeus' were excluded ([Arist.] *Ath. Pol.* 39. 6). Lysias'
argument here (88–90) certainly runs against the spirit of the
amnesty, but prosecution for murder may have been excepted from
it.[52]

In the **epilogue** (91–7) he insists on the religious duty of the jury
to punish a murderer. This conventional adjuration acquires a
political side when he adds that acquittal would be tantamount to
affirming that the victims had been justly killed (94). Lysias is still
at war with the Thirty (96), and we leave the speech with the feeling that his vehemence may have been wasted in a cause that had
been weakened by the removal of the chief villains.

34 *On the Constitution*

Preserved by Dionysius as an example of Lysias' style in the deliberative genre, this fragment has an interest disproportionate to its
length. Firstly, its subject-matter seems to make it closely contemporary with Speech 12, and hence important in a study of development. Secondly, it contains political arguments which seem
independent of the requirements of winning a particular lawsuit.
Having suffered under the Thirty, Lysias used the speech as an
opportunity to present the political credentials which would enable
him to live and practise his trade in Athens without fear under the
restored democracy. In it the speaker[53] opposes a motion by
Phormisius to limit the franchise to landowning Athenians, which,
if approved, would limit the electorate to about five thousand. At
a time when democratic sentiment was at its strongest, notwithstanding the amnesty, Lysias' persuasive powers were not to be
taxed unduly. He is able simply to say that the oligarchs and crypto-
oligarchs are up to their old tricks again, exploiting the people's
short memories or masochistic tendencies.[54] To win maximum
support he must appeal not only to extreme democrats, of whose
vote he could be sure, but to those with moderate means. That is
why he feels it necessary to say (3) 'I would not be excluded
because of property or birth, but am in both respects superior to

---

[52] See n. 17.
[53] Dion. Hal. *Lys.* 32 describes him as 'one of the prominent politicians'. As a metic,
Lysias could not have delivered it himself.
[54] 1: ἐξαπατῆσαι ζητοῦσι τοῖς αὐτοῖς ψηφίσμασιν οἷσπερ καὶ πρότερον δὶς ἤδη
. . . ἐπιλησμονέστατοι ἢ πάσχειν ἑτοιμότατοι κακῶς . . .

my opponents.'[55] He is appealing to the moderately wealthy by
showing that he is one of them, and arguing that a broad franchise
is to their advantage because, on the basis of past experience, it is
more likely to bring political stability. On the other hand, that same
experience has shown that they have not prospered under oligarchic tyranny. It is all clear and logical, and coloured by his own
family's treatment at the hands of the Thirty.[56]

Now supporters of Phormisius could adduce an argument which
might play upon the fears of the people.[57] 'What if the Spartans
object?' (6) Lysias poses the question and answers it directly with
another question: 'What will our people gain by doing as they say?'
On the face of it, this is dangerous advice so soon after defeat, and
with a Spartan garrison still encamped on the Acropolis. But Lysias
had made his own assessment of the likelihood of Spartan intervention, based on their past record, which showed them incapable
of achieving lasting conquest, a failing which led them to be unam-
bitious and conservative. This was, of course, a popular Athenian
view of Spartan foreign policy, but it was also a remarkably clair-
voyant perception of the immediate situation, especially as the
speech was probably composed before the reincorporation of
Eleusis into the Athenian state, which seems to have elicited no
protest from the Spartans.[58] Lysias shows further understanding of
Peloponnesian inter-state politics by his reference to the Argives
and the Mantineans (7) as examples of states which have exposed
the limits of Spartan power.[59] The argument proceeds with
another example, but it is used in an original way, to point a contrast and advocate an opposite course (9):

We thought it a wise course to allow our land to be ravaged, as our
interest lay in neglecting a few things in order to conserve many advantages; but today [νῦν δέ, temporal, instead of the logical sense found in

[55] i.e. he has no personal reason for opposing an oligarchic franchise, since he would
qualify for it.

[56] 5: 'The oligarchs' propaganda (λόγῳ μὲν . . .) is directed against democracy, their
actions (ἔργῳ δὲ . . .) against your property.'

[57] Aristot. *Rhet.* 2. 5. 3 lists 'the enmity and anger of those able to injure us in some way'
as one of the sources of fear. The dispulsion of his audiences' fears was a standard task for a
deliberative orator. Among the many devices used, a speaker might counter fear by profess-
ing his own confidence (Thuc. 6. 33. 4) or turn it to advantage by saying that fear can lead
to urgent and constructive action (Thuc. 6. 33. 9).

[58] Xen. *Hell.* 2. 4. 43; [Aristot.] *Ath. Pol.* 40. 4 (401/0 BC).

[59] Lysias may have derived some of this understanding, and also up-to-date news, from
his guest-friend Thrasydaeus of Elis (*Vit. X Or.* 835f).

hypothetical inversion, 'as it is'], when the battle has deprived us of all
these, and our native land is all that is left to us, we know that only this
hazardous course (κίνδυνος) offers hopes of deliverance.

The pathetic paradoxes[60] which follow are more conventional, and
the speech breaks off in the middle of some 'fighting talk'. Indeed,
both the tone of the speech and its central message may have established it in the political literature of the time as the first reassertion
of Athenian sovereignty and independence after the Peloponnesian
War.

25 *Subversion of the Democracy: Defence Speech*

In spite of the title attached to his speech in the manuscripts, the
unnamed defendant[61] is not facing a graphe, but a dokimasia (see
10, 14). His is the earliest[62] of four such speeches in the corpus (the
others being *For Mantitheus, Against Euander, Against Philon*), and
the richest in political argument. Closeness in time to the tyranny
of the Thirty explains this feature, but also made this defendant's
task the most difficult. The attacks of sycophants, which he frequently deplores, are no doubt due to his wealth. They would have
adduced the fact that he still seems to be wealthy after living under
the tyrants as evidence that he had avoided their depredations by
contributing voluntarily to their treasury, and acting supportively
in other ways. But they appear not to have levelled specific charges
against him. The defendant's task is therefore, from the purely
technical viewpoint, not difficult. He calls no witnesses or other
direct evidence, but faces the more undefined challenge of dis-
pelling suspicion and prejudice. His method is to begin by foment-
ing these same feelings against his accusers.[63] By this time certain
standard arguments against sycophants were in use and appear

---

[60] 11: δεινὸν γὰρ ἂν εἴη ... οὐκ οὖν αἰσχρὸν ...; the first is quoted incompletely,
inaccurately, and without attribution by Aristotle, *Rhet.* 2. 23. 19. At least his reference to it
proves that the speech was still in general circulation some two generations after its composition.

[61] T. M. Murphy, 'Lysias 25 and the Intractable Democratic Abuses', *AJP* 113 (1992),
544–5, deduces that he is a 'disaffected aristocrat claiming intellectual ascendancy over the
democratic rank and file and moral ascendancy over current leaders of the restored democracy'.

[62] 400/399: see M. Weissenberger, *Die Dokimasiereden des Lysias* (Frankfurt, 1987), 86–7.

[63] For this technique in prooemia see Aristot. *Rhet.* 3. 14. 7 (ἐκ τοῦ ἐναντίου); *Rhet. ad
Alex.* 26 1142a (τὸν δ' ἐναντίον κακολογεῖν).

here,[64] but the suggestion that these are incompetent because they have failed to describe the extent of the Thirty's atrocities (2) may be an adaptation to a novel political situation. Of more interest than topical innovations, however, is the thematic unity which Lysias imposes on the speech by the statement which he makes at the beginning of the **proof** section (8):[65]

Now firstly it must be borne in mind that no human being is naturally either an oligarch or a democrat: each man strives to establish whichever constitution works to his advantage, so that it is largely up to you to see that as many men as possible desire the present constitution.

This statement of the all-importance of self-interest in deciding political allegiance accords with contemporary thinking,[66] but this is the first time we find it used in a forensic context. Lysias follows it with examples[67] of politicians who have changed from demagogues into oligarchs and back again between 411 and the present (9–11). He now applies this principle in a review of his own career, effecting a smooth transition to an essential part of a dokimasia-speech: he shows how all his leitourgiai were performed under the democracy, and he contributed more than was required (13).[68] This generosity disqualified him for honours under the oligarchy, and he subsequently did nothing that would ingratiate him to them (14–17). His difficulty seems to be that his claims are all negative—he had no hand in the establishment of the oligarchy, made no arrests, laid no charges and made no gains—yet his inaction under the Thirty might be interpreted as acquiescence. His best course is therefore to compare himself with the active miscreants rather than try to rival the active saviours of democracy (18).

---

[64] 3: the preferred victims of sycophants are 'men who have done no wrong' because they tend also to be *apragmones*, men who shun the limelight and will consequently part with their wealth rather than face public attention.

[65] There is no continuous narrative: argument closely follows individual statements of fact throughout the speech.

[66] For the idea that συμφέρον-argument was preferred to δίκαιον-argument in Thucydides' speeches, see M. Heath, 'Justice in Thucydides' Athenian Speeches', *Historia* 39 (1990), 385–400.

[67] Phrynichus and Peisander are named, but not Theramenes, the arch-turncoat, popularly nicknamed *Kothurnos* after the tragic boot which fits either foot (Xen. *Hell.* 2. 3. 31). Perhaps the speaker was one of his adherents, like Eratosthenes. Lysias had in common with his client an ability to adapt his politics to changing circumstances.

[68] The reason he gives for doing so (cf. 16 *For Mantitheus* 17) is 'that if I suffer a misfortune at any time I should be able to defend myself better'. That is to say, he could bring to future litigation a favourable character-reference which might save him.

The speaker leaves his own case at this point, and returns to general political argument, the underlying theme of which is *concord* (ὁμόνοια). After an introductory section (19–20), he shows how the fall of the Thirty began through internal discord due to their wickedness (πονηρία) which thus proved a more potent force than the military power of the returning democrats (22): a bold argument to a jury which probably included some of these men. Scarcely less bold is his censorious reference to the democrats who assumed control after the expulsion of the Four Hundred (25–6), but they have a necessary place in the argument because they represent the forces of discord as clearly as their political opponents. It is the persistent extremists on both sides, and sycophants, who most threaten concord (28–30). Now the extremists come from the ranks of the returned democrats (31–3).[69] The speech breaks off after urging the jury to abide by their agreements and oaths, i.e. the amnesty, which was invoked at this time more especially by men suspected of oligarchic sympathies. The missing text must have returned to positive pleas in support of the speaker's case. Commentators have rightly noted that the speech as a whole has the flavour of a political pamphlet.[70]

21 *Defence on a Charge of Receiving Bribes*

This fragment merits examination because it is the first extant detailed statement of a litigant's public services (leitourgiai). Blass (*AB* i. 497–8), followed by Jebb and Lamb, proposes 402 as the probable date: the defendant was 18 in 411/410 (1), and he describes leitourgiai he has performed down to 403 (4). It begins immediately after the main proof section, the conventional point at which to begin such statements. The speaker, who is undergoing audit (euthyna) for an unspecified office, is accused of malpractice, including the acceptance of bribes (21). More serious, however, than possible hostility arising from any specific offence during his recent office, may have been the popular resentment still felt against those who had survived the Battle of Aegospotami, of whom the defendant was one (9). He makes the best he can of this by describing how he saved not only his own ship but also that of a fellow-trierarch, Nausimachus of Phaleron; and he makes the fur-

---

[69] See n. 61.   [70] See Weissenberger, *Dokimasiereden*, 86–8.

ther point that no *strategos* was sailing with him (i.e. he did not rescue one of the men responsible for the disaster). Whereas the main facts and evidential arguments about his administration may have required only a routine treatment, critics found oratory worth preserving in the extended statement of a litigant's public services and consequent inferences as to his character ($\pi \iota \sigma \tau \iota s$ $\dot{\epsilon} \xi$ $\ddot{\eta} \theta o v s$ $\kappa a \iota$ $\beta \iota o v$), of which this is the first extant example.

In order to enable the jury to draw the desired inferences as to 'what sort of a man he is' ($\pi \epsilon \rho \iota$ $o \iota o v$ $\tau \iota v \delta s$ $\ddot{o} v \tau o s$, 1), the defendant not only gives precise details of expenditure but constantly refers to the victories that he won: with choruses (1, 4), and in games (3), including naval games (5). This could, of course, be the vaingloriousness of a young man, but, more tellingly, it serves the practical purpose of magnifying his expenditure: he won because he hired the best, and therefore the most expensive, performers. This leads smoothly to his trireme, equipped for the more serious business of war, and chosen for his flagship by Alcibiades (6–7), whom the jury would remember for his expensive tastes.[71] The rhetoric here is progressively logical (8): 'Well, how much money do you think I spent on such a ship? How much harm did it do the enemy and how much benefit to the city? The best proof is this . . .', and he tells how he rescued his own ship and that of Nausimachus at Aegospotami through having hired one Phantias, 'the best steersman in Greece'.

Willingness to spend his wealth for the good of the city, and actually having ample resources, are two qualities which a man facing a charge of accepting bribes would have found very useful to claim. We may perhaps assume that, in the lost narrative and proof, he will have argued that a man with his wealth would have had no need to succumb to bribery.[72] In the extant part the emphasis is upon his patriotism: the idea that truly distinguished public service required the expenditure of more than the amount demanded by the law appears for the first time in this speech, to be elaborated later in the speech *For Mantitheus*. For it he now asks for no reward,

---

[71] Thuc. 6. 15. 3. Like the speaker, Thucydides' Alcibiades was not afraid to speak of his victories (6. 16. 2–3). Tolerance of self-praise for victories and success was greater in ancient Athens than in modern Western society. See Dover *GPM* 233–4, who notes that '*philonikia* was treated as a virtue in the earlier part of the fourth century', being associated with *philotimia*, the worthy pursuit of honour.

[72] One of Pericles' strengths was his incorruptibility (Thuc. 2. 60. 5, 65. 8; Plut. *Per.* 15–16).

just permission to keep what is his (11). Loss of it, however, would be less painful than the dishonour incurred (12)—treatment which would, moreover, discourage others from following his patriotic example. The state's self-interest is thus placed ahead of his personal feelings: it needed willing and honest contributors, not men who would skimp and try to evade their responsibilities. Characterization of the speaker as a man confident in his case is strongly drawn as he pronounces himself 'a far better steward of my property than those who control for you the property of the state', and he follows this with an even bolder adaptation of the topic of reversal (16):[73] 'In my opinion, gentlemen—and let none of you be vexed by this—it would be much more just for you to be said by the Commissioners to be holding my property than for me to be prosecuted now for holding Treasury funds.' He then rounds off the section neatly with a collocation not found before, asking the jury to take cognizance not only of his public services, but also of his behaviour as a citizen, saying that the most difficult of public services is to be orderly and self-controlled in his private life. Added to the opening catalogue of his leitourgiai, this has a thematically unifying effect. The rest of the speech, which contains typical arguments against sycophants (20) and a final plea including a pathetic image of his destitute family 'wandering about in sore straits', contains conventional epilogue-material.

30 *Against Nicomachus*

The defendant in this case was an 'inscriber' or 'transcriber' of the laws (τῶν νόμων ἀναγραφεύς, 2) between 410 and 399 BC. That office must have been purely clerical or secretarial, at least nominally,[74] and herein lies a major difficulty for his prosecutors: they

---

[73] This was originally used against an opponent to argue that he, not the speaker, should be the one accused (Antiph. *Tetr.* 2. 2. 8–9).

[74] The precise status of *anagrapheis* is one of several problems concerning the legislative reforms of 410–401. See esp. A. R. W. Harrison, 'Law-Making at Athens at the End of the Fifth Century BC', *JHS* 75 (1955), 29–35; N. Robertson, 'The Laws of Athens, 410–499 BC: The Evidence for Review and Publication', *JHS* 110 (1990), 43–75; P. J. Rhodes, 'The Athenian Code of Laws, 410–399 BC', *JHS* 111 (1991), 87–100. The transitional character of Athenian legislative processes in these years seems to be recognized by the latter's statement (p. 91): 'I suspect that the *anagrapheis* were given a task whose nature was not at first fully thought out but was gradually clarified as questions came to be asked and answered.' See also S. Todd, 'Lysias Against Nicomachus: The Fate of the Expert in Athenian Law', in L. Foxall and A. D. E. Lewis (eds.), *Greek Law in its Political Setting* (Oxford, 1996), 101–31.

are attacking a mere functionary, whose long tenure of office could be due to satisfactory performance of the minor duties of inscribing, copying, and filing away laws, and producing them when required. The duration of his tenure may also have had a political dimension, which also forms the background to the trial: those maintaining him in office were influential democrats (he was in exile during the regime of the Thirty), and all he did was with their approval.

The prosecutor is a Councillor (23) and Nicomachus, who may have been a persuasive speaker (24), might counter-attack by repeating an earlier accusation of past oligarchic activities (7: ὡς ἐγὼ τῶν τετρακοσίων ἐγενόμην). In turn he casts doubts upon Nicomachus' democratic credentials by referring to his part in Cleophon's trial and condemnation (10–12), but this could be disputed, or undermined with a similar argument to that used by Agoratus and Eratosthenes, who pleaded that the Thirty compelled them on pain of death. He needs more brutally aggressive arguments, and impugning Nicomachus' ancestry (the 'δοῦλος ἐκ δούλων' gibe), as he has done with Agoratus, is one of the best he can find against another powerfully supported opponent. Other difficulties had to be met. Nicomachus' work had included additions to the sacrificial laws (17–20), and there was an obvious danger of being accused of sacrilege if these laws were questioned. But Lysias provides his client with two arguments to deal with this. The first is a form of the recurrent one accusing Nicomachus of promoting himself from mere transcriber to legislator, here by claiming precedence for his laws[75] over those inscribed on the tablets and pillars (17–19). His second argument is that Nicomachus' 'laws' had damaging financial consequences, diverting money from the established sacrifices, and inflating the overall cost of sacrifices at a time of financial difficulty (22), which he describes in graphic terms.[76] Here the argument subtly broadens with the sentiment that the worst counsellors are heard when the treasury is low,[77] and Nicomachus' profligacy becomes a potential encouragement for

---

[75] i.e. the laws in his copy, which omitted some and added others (19–20) to those on the tablets and pillars. The prosecutor is saying that Nicomachus perpetuated rather than removed inconsistencies between the publicly inscribed laws and his written records of them.

[76] 22: τοὺς δὲ νεωσοίκους καὶ τὰ τείχη περικαταρρέοντα.

[77] Cf. Aristoph. *Knights* 1356–61.

others.[78] On the contrary, he should be punished and thereby become an example to others (24).

The rhetoric in the following section (26–30) contains the usual summarizing of possible pleas by means of hypophora, conventionally placed,[79] but then the speaker is made to criticize the jury, contrasting them with their prudent ancestors and representing them as irrational (28). Forceful language is used[80] and he urges them to repent (30: ὑμῖν μεταμελησάτω τῶν πεπραγμένων). In a section normally reserved for attacks on the opponent's character, Lysias has, to an unprecedented and seemingly dangerous degree, charged the dicasts with serious faults and misjudgements.

The sinister presence of Nicomachus' sponsors is clear in the **epilogue** (31–5). Some 'politicians' will try to 'beg him off' (31: ἐξαιτησομένων . . . φίλων . . . τῶν τὰ τῆς πόλεως πραττόντων). Their influence is such that Lysias does not dare to attack them individually—they remain nameless, grey figures—and he feels safer concentrating on Nicomachus with the 'one against many' argument, here for the first time.[81] He does not, however, formally recapitulate the main charge against him on his own, but briefly, in the penultimate clause of the speech, urges punishment for 'those who nullify your legislation'.[82] But a clear case that Nicomachus had acted illegally has not been made. It is reasonable to suppose that this attack on the *anagrapheus* who has served longest in the interests of the democratic party was an expression of conservative discontent and a reaction against popular extravagance. If this supposition is correct, it was a bold speech to make at the time of the trial of Socrates.

---

[78] For this topos, see 1. 48, 12. 85 (πολλὴν ἄδειαν ποιήσετε). It is also used to end the speech (33–4).

[79] i.e. near the end of the proof and forming a bridge between it and the epilogue. Cf. 6. 46; 24. 24.

[80] 29: ὃ δὲ πάντων δεινότατον . . .

[81] 32: 'that he, a mere individual . . . should try to persuade you, who are so many . . .' Cf. 7. 33; 24. 13, 22; 31. 31.

[82] 35: ἡμεῖς . . . παρακαλοῦμεν . . . τοὺς τὴν ὑμετέραν νομοθεσίαν ἀφανίζοντας. The plural subject has suggested to some that the speech is a deuterologia. But in § 2 the speaker uses the paraleiptic formula πολὺ ἂν ἔργον εἴη λέγειν, suggesting that all the details of the case for the prosecution have yet to be revealed, and it is he who has to decide what to omit in the first instance. Second speakers usually refer to τὰ κατηγορημένα at an early stage (e.g. 28. 1).

31 *Against Philon*

Perhaps more remarkable than its content is the style of this speech, which is a curious mixture of fifth-century grandeur and a more contemporary balanced antithetical structure: while notably rich in gnomic expressions[83] and replete with hiatus, it also contains some elaborate periods and paronomasia.[84] Thus it both looks backward to Antiphon and forward to Isocrates.[85] The case was heard in the Council some time between 403 and about 398.[86] The speaker is a retiring Councillor opposing the entry of an incoming one in a dokimasia. Philon left the city, along with many other citizens, on the accession to power of the Thirty, and the only offence of which he can be accused is failure to return with the democrats at the earliest opportunity. Lysias' solution to the problem is to base his attack on a broad moral front,[87] and he begins in that mode with deinosis, noting Philon's audacity. He follows this with a novel combination of the *paraskeue*-topos and the topos of abundance:[88] 'so many are his crimes that my preparations to indict them have been difficult' (3). In the same way, he adapts the inexperience-topos to the defendant's crimes, and invites others who are 'more able (δυνατώτεροι) than me at speaking' to supplement his account.[89] The thrust of the broadly-based attack is adumbrated in the prothesis (5–7), where the requirements of patriotism are

---

[83] e.g. 6: πᾶσα γῆ πάτρις . . . 11: καθέστηκε δέ τι ἔθος . . .

[84] Periods: 1–2, 5–6, 8–9, 17–18, 32; paronomasia: 11: γνώμη . . . συγγνώμης, 17: δυστυχήματα εὐτυχήματα, 24: τιμωρηθήσεται . . . τιμήσεται, 26: οὐ περὶ τοῦ βουλεύειν ἀλλὰ περὶ τοῦ δουλεύειν.

[85] The close succession of conventional topoi in the prooemium is typically Antiphontean, while the high frequency of οὐκ . . . ἀλλὰ antithesis compared with μὲν . . . δὲ is similar to the proportion in Isocrates. (The latter's forensic speeches are contemporary.) Some artificial strain is even apparent, when balance is imposed on disparate topoi, as in 2: οὐ μέντοι γε ἰδίαν ἔχθραν οὐδεμίαν μεταπορευόμενος, οὐδὲ τῷ δύνασθαι καὶ εἰωθέναι λέγειν ἐν ὑμῖν ἐπαρθείς, ἀλλὰ τῷ πλήθει τῶν ἁμαρτημάτων αὐτοῦ πιστεύων, καὶ τοῖς ὅρκοις οἷς ὤμοσα ἐμμένειν ἀξιῶν.

[86] The later date is favoured by Blass (*AB* i. 481) and tentatively accepted by Carey, *Lysias*, 189.

[87] Thus he foreshadows the approach of Lycurgus in a similar case, *Against Leocrates*.

[88] Cf. 10. 1; 12. 1.

[89] The speaker may not here be depreciating his own oratorical ability, since he has earlier referred to his 'ability and practice at speaking' (τῷ δύνασθαι καὶ εἰωθέναι λέγειν ἐν ὑμῖν ἐπαρθείς, 2), but simply implying that others might be in a position to speak with greater authority about misdeeds of which he had no direct knowledge. (In spite of τῷ δύνασθαι above, one would expect δεινότεροι rather than δυνατώτεροι if the speaker were describing simply his oratorical ability.)

described in a periodic sentence (5–6: τούτοις . . . ἡγεῖσθαι), which he follows with the statement that he will show how Philon failed to meet them.

The style of the **narrative** is periodic and antithetical, contrasting Philon's actions with those of his fellow-citizens (τὰ ἐναντία ἅπασι τοῖς ἄλλοις πολίταις ἐποίησε) in the dominant main clause of the period (8–9): . . . Οὗτος γὰρ . . . ἐποίησε . . . πολίτης εἶναι. The effect is dignified but contrived, very different from the natural simplicity of the narratives of the two Eratosthenes-speeches. It soon turns to generalization (10–11)[90] and the moral tone is maintained (11) with the commonplace that the sins of the poor and the weak might be excused, but this is contrasted with the defendant's status—he was neither physically disabled nor penurious (12). Elaboration on the idea that he 'betrayed both sides' (13–14) adds to the imbalance between factual narrative and argument.[91] A possible explanation of the shortage of facts in the narrative, and the consequent need to bolster it with rhetoric, may be found in the unusual formula of the following procatalepsis (15),[92] which suggests, as Carey has said, that the accuser is not fully informed of Philon's line of defence. He is left with a paucity of facts on which to work. Once more an artificial antithesis is brought into play: Philon's anticipated plea, that he was incapacitated from aiding the democratic cause in person (15–16) is contrasted with his predations upon elderly citizens in outlying townships (17–18)—presumption contrasted with alleged fact, which gives the latter a certain authenticity, to which the accuser adds a minor item, Philon's mother's decision to leave her funeral arrangements in the hands of another, not her son (21–2), making the most he can of it with a comparative argument.

The concentration of rhetorical devices in 24–6[93] is not accidental. The accuser has to face Philon's strongest argument, that no law disqualified people who had chosen to live abroad from seek-

---

[90] The oxymoron ἑκούσιον δυστύχημα is derived from the sophistic ἑκούσιον ἁμάρτημα (Antiph. 5 Her. 92, Tetr. 3. 1. 6).

[91] §§ 8–23 have been regarded as 'narrative', but facts and actions are confined to 8–10, 16–18, 21–2, about half the section.

[92] Ὑπολείπεται τοίνυν αὐτῷ λέγειν . . . ('Now it remains for him to say . . .') instead of 'I hear he is going to say . . .' (cf. 27).

[93] Hypophora, pathetic paradox with paronomasia (δεινὸν γὰρ . . . τιμωρηθήσεται . . . τιμήσεται, 24); comparative argument with etymological figure (ζημίαις ἐζημιοῦτο) and parechesis (βουλεύειν . . . δουλεύειν), involving hyperbole.

ing office on their return (27).[94] Against this the rhetorical weapons
are hyperbole and comparison: there is no law because such a
heinous crime was inconceivable.[95] If desertion from one's battle-
post is a crime (see 14 *Against Alcibiades*), then deserting one's city
is a greater crime (28). What Lysias does not admit, of course, is that
it is also a less clearly definable crime, since a man might leave the
city without appearing personally responsible for endangering it;
and in the present case, the defendant had left along with many
other citizens in face of the tyranny of the Thirty. He uses two
rhetorical questions to press his argument (28, 29), and the comparison involving metics adds colour if not substance to it.

Two practical arguments complete the proof section, introduced
with formulaic ἐνθυμήθητε (31). Firstly, the jury are reminded that
they are assessing a potential Councillor, and this is done effectively
with questions: 'What sort of a Councillor do you think he will be,
who has, in various ways, been unpatriotic?' It is important, before
ending, to draw attention to the exacting criteria by which candidates should be audited. Secondly, the defendant's supporters are
attacked (32) and accused of condoning his treasonous conduct.[96]
The idea of self-condemnation by his own action (33) is peculiarly
suited to a dokimasia. In the brief **epilogue**, as at the start, he
claims an abundance of material, some of which he will omit, and
returns more directly to the question of audit-criteria (see 31
above). Here he says, 'To judge who are worthy to sit as
Councillors you need only to turn to yourselves, and the civic
qualities which won you your audit.' It is a timely reminder that
Philon was not being tried for a crime, but being assessed for his
character. This being so, the absence of the sort of descriptions of
minor misdeeds that feature in other speeches which actually

[94] [Aristot.] *Ath. Pol.* 8. 5 appears to cite such a law, but the agreement of prosecutor and
accused here must tell at least against its application at the time of this speech. For discussion
of the problem, see Carey, *Lysias*, 198–200, Rhodes *CAP* 157–8.

[95] Cf. Lys. 14 *Ag. Alc.* 4 (Carey, *Lysias*, 152); Lycurg. *Ag. Leocr.* 9 (A. Petrie, *Lycurgus:
The Speech against Leocrates* (Cambridge, 1922), 70). The orator asks the jury to become lawmakers in such cases. Neither Aristotle nor Anaximenes mentions this topos specifically in
their otherwise thorough discussions of approach to the direct evidence of the law (*Rhet.* 1.
1. 15; *Rhet. ad Alex.* 36 1443a, where it is assigned, as in the present speech, to procatalepsis
preceding recapitulation).

[96] The usual practice of elevating the style in the section immediately preceding a short
epilogue is adopted here. The period τότε δέ . . . κατεργασαμένων (32) contains repeated
τότε, the metaphor τὰ δὲ ἆθλα αὐτὴ ἡ πολιτεία ἔκειτο (cf. 1. 47), polysyndeton (καὶ . . .
καὶ . . . καὶ . . . μήτε . . . μήτε) and emotive sentiments (freedom, succour, and treason).

depend less on them than the present speech, suggests that its special stylistic effects are the speechwriter's way of making an impression on the Council which the evidence on its own would not achieve.

The stylistic features noted, and the contrived moral emphasis in a case where purely legal issues seem unsubstantial, suggest that the publication of this speech was intended to broaden its author's literary appeal. Through it, he might expect his readers to regard him as a master of the old and the new styles, and able to adapt the finer patriotic sentiments of an earlier age to his own and future generations.

32 *Against Diogeiton*

Dionysius of Halicarnassus preserves the introduction, the narrative, and most of the proof of this speech as an example of Lysias' style in forensic oratory. It is the last of his speeches that may be dated with reasonable certainty to the end of the fifth century.[97] Dionysius' reasons for choosing it are instructive. For him, the **prooemium** 'has all the virtues that a prooemium ought to have' (*Lys.* 24), by which he means that it follows the rules laid down in the handbooks (οἱ κανόνες οἱ τῶν τεχνῶν). This discourages expectations of originality, and indeed there is nothing novel to note: even the sentiment, frequently expressed in the inheritance speeches of Isaeus, that disputes between relatives are to be deplored, is expressed here not for the first time.[98] The first part of the **narrative** (4–8), in which the arrangements made for his estate by Diodotus, and events down to his death, are described, is factual and devoid of the comment that we have noticed in some of Lysias' other narratives. But a complete change arises when Diogeiton's wardship comes to an end. Here Lysias devises a dramatic scene, gives Diogeiton a live part, and describes the emotional reactions of the affected relatives as he informs them of his plans (9–10). The actual words of his gruff, arrogant dismissal of the boys[99] create a

---

[97] Diogeiton had been guardian of Diodotus' estate for seven or eight years (9: ὀγδόῳ ἔτει) since the latter's death in 409. If the elder son litigated immediately on reaching his majority, as seems likely, the case came to court in 401 or 400.

[98] See Antiph. 1 *Ag. Stepmother* 1.

[99] 9: 'Now I have spent a lot of my own money on your upbringing. So long as I had the means, I didn't mind, but now I myself am in difficulties. So, now that you have officially come of age, you must look to your own livelihood.'

greater degree of shock than would have been achieved by the mere report of them. It also creates a persona for him—selfish, callous, and hybristic—which the jury will retain in their minds as they hear of his subsequent actions. It is into this highly charged scene[100] that the most striking personality in the speech makes her entry. The boys' mother is also Diogeiton's own daughter. At a meeting of the family, reluctantly attended by Diogeiton, she recites an itemized account of his income and expenditure. Live speech is used at the beginning of this account (12–13) as the mother swears that it is true; and she speaks again to describe the situation which Diogeiton has just created. Her performance here attains even greater heights of emotion (15–16):

After that, with so much money in your possession, you had the audacity to say that these boys' father left them two thousand drachmae and thirty staters—just the amount that was left to me, which I gave you after his death. And you thought it right to cast these children of your own daughter out of their own house without shoes, without attendant, without bedding, without clothing, without the furniture which their father had left them, and without the money which he had deposited with you.

We are told that those present were deeply affected by her words, being reduced initially to inarticulacy, then to tears (18). Lysias clearly wants the jury to feel the same. The spectacle of a daughter confronting her father and convicting him of monstrous maltreatment of his grandchildren is powerful real-life drama, and live speech finds its most natural, and hence most effective setting when the conversation is between relatives or acquaintances. But we hear only one side of it in this dramatized form. The assault on Diogeiton is sustained in the **proof** (19 ff.), as details of the expenses he claimed to have incurred in the boys' upbringing and in his own leitourgiai are given, and the amounts challenged and refuted: the account is laced with the various formulae of deinosis (20: ὃς ἐτόλμησε . . . εἰς τοῦτο ἦλθεν ἀναισχυντίας . . . 21: ἐφ' ᾧ ἡμεῖς οὐχ ἥκιστα ὠργίσθημεν. 22: . . . πενεστάτους ἀντὶ πλουσίων ἀπέφηνε. 24: ὃ δὲ πάντων δεινότατον . . .). He has proved a worse enemy to them than any of the family's avowed foes (22).

[100] Lysias' description of the relatives' emotions (10–11) is one of his most forceful and pathetic passages: ἐκπεπληγμένοι καὶ δακρύοντες . . . οἰκτρῶς ὑπὸ τοῦ πάθους διακείμενοι καὶ ἀθλίως ἐκπεπτωκότες . . . ὅσον πένθος ἐν τῇ ἐμῇ οἰκίᾳ ἦν ἐν ἐκείνῳ τῷ χρόνῳ.

The novel device of making a woman (the mother of the plaintiff) a leading character with a speaking part serves to emphasize
the extremity of the grievance felt by the family at Diogeiton's
behaviour.[101] Live speech makes her a compelling figure in itself,
but it also enables her to express graphically her willingness to
swear on the lives of her children (13), and her reasonableness in
not criticizing Diogeiton for rearing his children in comfort (17).
The speech could easily have become a dry catalogue of income
and expenditure. Instead Lysias has made it into a story of family
tragedy and the pain of trust betrayed, with victims and a heroine,
and one clear villain.

17 *On the Estate of Eraton*

This speech can be dated to 397.[102] In spite of its extreme brevity,
it contains all the conventional parts, and is therefore certainly not
a fragment and probably not an epitome. Two talents borrowed by
Eraton from the speaker's grandfather had not been repaid on his
death, and his father obtained a verdict against Erasistratus, the only
son of Eraton still resident in Attica. Subsequently the state confiscated all Eraton's property. The present case is a dispute (*diadikasia*)
between the speaker's family and the state, the former seeking to
retain that part of Eraton's estate (i.e. that inherited by Erasistratus)
which they had won in court three years earlier.

The case affords little scope for rhetoric. Lysias has decided to
give his client a subdued persona as he seeks only partial restitution
of the estate.[103] But there is a certain ambivalence in his adaptation
of the topos of inexperience, as reference is made to the speaker's
desire to 'be someone of account'.[104] This must be a concession to

---

[101] 11: She is made to express her conventional reluctance to speak in the presence of
men, but says that her family's present misfortunes compel her to do so. Her appearance as
a speaking character also enables the speechwriter to sidestep the procedural bar on women
appearing as litigants (so Todd *SAL* 203). Further on her performance, see J. Trevett, 'The
Use of Direct Speech by the Attic Orators', *Lo Spettacolo delle Voci* 2 (1995), 139–40.

[102] See 3 (archonship of Xenainetus 401/400), 5 (the property at Sphettus let for three
years from that time).

[103] The residual estate of Eraton had been valued at over one talent (7), obviously less
than the two talents which the speaker's grandfather had lent to Eraton. Yet instead of claiming the whole of this, the speaker is prepared to concede two-thirds of it to the state (6),
leaving him with only 15 minae (7), one-eighth of the amount of the original loan.

[104] 1: βούλεσθαί με ἄξιον εἶναί τινος.

the speaker's known ambition for some public office[105]—perhaps he was about to undergo a dokimasia—but he has to weigh this against the difficulties inherent in engaging in a dispute with the state, whose representatives are the very dicasts before whom he is standing. His speech gives the facts simply and clearly in three short narratives (2–3, 5, 6–7) with witnesses' testimony. There are no rhetorical proofs and no emotional appeal. Indeed, absence of rhetorical resource extends to the style, which is unpolished— notably rich in hiatus and containing comparatively few figures of language or thought—in keeping with the small scale. Lysias has decided to play safe in his first surviving speech for a client against the state. Even though that client cannot be portrayed as the typical quiet citizen (*apragmon*), avoidance of slickness, flamboyance, and other manifestations of over-confidence or lack of humility must be his aim, and he achieves it neatly and effectively in this little speech.

18 *On the Confiscation of the Estate of Eucrates*

The first word indicates that this is a concluding fragment.[106] The fact that the opening sections contain a *laudatio* of a famous, if controversial Athenian, Nicias, son of Niceratus, and his family, readily accounts for its preservation. The style of this part is suitably epideictic, with long periods.[107] In the first period antithesis is used to contrast Nicias' willing promotion of the public good with his unwilling involvement in policies which led to the disaster of the Sicilian Expedition. This may well have become a standard defence of Nicias in the later rhetorical schools. The second period is a more complex structure,[108] and its subject is a defence of his brother Eucrates, more relevant to the present case. It is clear that Poliochus, against whose proposal the speech was made,[109] will impute oligarchic sympathies to Nicias' family, so it is vital that the

[105] Such an ambition would explain his reference to competence in speaking on matters which do not concern him personally (1).

[106] ἐνθυμήθητε: one of the words frequently used by Lysias to remind a jury of important arguments and facts, either in the epilogue itself (3. 46, 4. 18, 10. 31, 12. 94, 19. 63, 31. 31) or somewhat earlier, though in the latter part of a speech (21. 15, 22. 17, 30. 21). Jebb's (*AO* i. 230–1) dating of this speech to 396 or 395 is probable: it seems clear that Sparta and Athens were not at war: the Corinthian War of 394–387 had not yet begun.

[107] 2–3: ἐκεῖνος γὰρ ... λέγειν. 4–5: Εὐκράτης τοίνυν ... καταδεδουλωμένον.

[108] Note its elongation through clauses dependent on ἐξόν, a frequent Isocratean device.

[109] Galen, vol. 18. 2 p. 657 Kühn, calls the speech *Against Poliochus*.

speaker should refute this. The concluding clauses of the period (5: μᾶλλον εἵλετο. . . . ἀπολέσθαι . . . καταδεδουλωμένον) portray Eucrates almost as a martyr to the cause of democracy, while his nephew, Nicias' son Niceratus, also died at the hands of the Thirty because of his devotion to the democracy. A pathetic formula introducing a dilemmaton effectively seals this section.[110]

The account of the behaviour of Nicias' other brother, Diognetus, who also 'held no office under the oligarchy' (10), cleverly turns to good account a relationship which was potentially embarrassing but was also common knowledge—his family's long-standing friendship with one of the royal houses of Sparta. We are told that Pausanias was moved by his family's sufferings under the Thirty to turn against their tyranny.[111] The resulting situation is tailor-made for a pathetic paradox: 'Surely it will be shocking, gentlemen of the jury, after being pitied as children by an enemy who had come to aid the oligarchy, for us, who have proved our good character, to be stripped of our property by you, whose fathers gave their lives for democracy?'[112]

About halfway through the piece attention turns briefly to the defendant Poliochus (13). We should like to know more about him. He is portrayed not as a mere sycophant but as a man with political ambitions who sees victory in a suit against a powerful family as a means of promoting his career, especially if that victory meant overturning a previous verdict in their favour (14). The speaker then moves to a more generalized discussion of the ethics and practicalities of the confiscation of property, with conventional references to *homonoia* ('concord') and *stasis* ('faction') (17), punishment (18), and remembrance of past wrongs (19). An interesting hint of a more or less concerted attack on the property of wealthy families at this time may be found in 20 in the phrase τὰ ὑπὸ τούτων δημευόμενα ('the properties being confiscated by these men'). However this may be, the strongest possible argument

[110] 8: καίτοι τίνες ἂν ἡμῶν εἴησαν δυστυχέστεροι, εἰ ἐν μὲν τῇ ὀλιγαρχίᾳ ἀποθνήσκοιμεν εὖνοι ὄντες τῷ πλήθει, ἐν δὲ τῇ δημοκρατίᾳ ὡς κακόνοι ὄντες τῷ πλήθει ἀποστεροίμεθα τῶν ὄντων;

[111] According to Xenophon (*Hell.* 2. 4. 31), Pausanias was sympathetic towards the democrats from the beginning of his term of command, but P. Krentz (*The Thirty at Athens* (Ithaca and London, 1982), 100–1) seems to believe that it was Diognetus' appeal which finally decided Pausanias to begin negotiations with the democrats.

[112] Lysias uses a similar pathetic paradox in 15 (οὐκ οὖν αἰσχρόν . . .). Gebauer, *De Hypotacticis et Paratacticis*, 140–1 also notes the paronomasia κυρίους . . . ἀκύρους, and remarks that such word-play is a common feature of this type of argument.

against such confiscations is that willing donation by patriotic owners of wealth is a healthier and more reliable method of raising
money for the state. That argument appears here for the first time.

14 *Against Alcibiades, for Desertion*

Addressing a jury of soldiers, perhaps not long after the campaign of
395, the speaker in this deuterologia[113] introduces a spirit of cama-
raderie with an original formula: πειράσομαι ὑπὲρ πάντων τῶν
πεπραγμένων μεθ᾽ ὑμῶν αὐτὸν τιμωρήσασθαι. His purpose is
to complete the task of discrediting the famous Alcibiades' delin-
quent son. However, he faces two difficulties. The first is that the
younger Alcibiades has actually served, in the cavalry (8, 11); and
the fact that the jury are urged to become *lawmakers* (νομοθέται)
seems to indicate that existing law did not decisively condemn his
conduct.[114] The second problem appears to be Alcibiades' influential relatives and supporters. Lysias finds it necessary to argue at
length against listening to their pleas (16–23). For both these problems a bipartite solution suggests itself: exploitation of residual prejudice and resentment against the family, and attack on the character
of the defendant. The latter is not without subtlety. Lysias suggests
that the effrontery of Alcibiades in flouting the law and serving in
the cavalry without audit was prompted by his belief that he would
not have to face punishment because, unlike his patriotic and law-
abiding companions, he believed that, after the battle, 'the city
would not be able to exact punishment from the wrongdoers' (10).
This allegation was pregnant with treasonous implications. Here
was the son of the man who had gone over to the Spartan side at
the height of the Peloponnesian War and done the city incalculable
damage, looking to Spartan success and inviting the worst accusations of oligarchic sympathies. Much of the succeeding rhetoric is
more conventional, including the topos of *example to others* (cf. 12.
35), here reinforced by the idea of punishing 'the most conspicuous

[113] The first prosecutor, Archestratus, has quoted the relevant laws and examined the primary evidence (3).

[114] The prosecutor refers only briefly to the law requiring those wishing to serve in the
cavalry to submit to audit (8). Perhaps Archestratus has already dealt with this, but it seems
more likely that such a law would be applied irregularly in times of war. There also seems
to be room for doubt as to whether a man could be condemned for desertion when there
has been no battle (5). The attempt (6–7) to condemn Alcibiades for desertion because he
did not serve in the infantry is sophistical.

offenders' (τοὺς ἐπιφανεστάτους τῶν ἐξαμαρτανόντων, 12). He launches his main attack on the younger Alcibiades (24) with the claim that a jury should listen to accusers' accounts of defendants' misdeeds with the same attention as they give to defendants' own accounts of their merits and services. This is the first extant occurrence of an effective counter-argument to the plea for sympathy (συγγνώμη), with which diffident litigants try to persuade juries to acquit them. An account (25–31) of the defendant's alleged debaucheries begins with reference to his father as his model, and the paradoxical idea that he thought he could not achieve distinction in his later career unless he could show himself a complete scoundrel in his youth; and Alcibiades senior reappears at the end (31) in the pathetic paradox with which the section ends:

Yet he has been in the habit of insisting that it is unfair, when his father received gifts from the people on his return, that he should have to face slander because of his father's exile. But it seems to me that it would be shocking if, after depriving the father of those gifts, considering them to have been undeserved, you should acquit this man, though he has done wrong, on the ground of his father's good service to the city.

The rest of the speech is concerned with the career of Alcibiades senior, and here Lysias joins a debate which had begun in his lifetime. He has little difficulty in refuting the parallel which Alcibiades junior has drawn between his father's treason, and the democrats' withdrawal to Phyle and their subsequent war against the Thirty (32–3),[115] but it is interesting that he finds it necessary to misrepresent events in Alcibiades' subsequent career.[116] He is probably repeating the popular charges made against Alcibiades at

---

[115] The same shifty sophistry is apparent in his argument as in that attributed to his father by Thucydides (6. 92. 4: 'I am a patriot not in a state where I am wronged, but where I have lived in security: the country I am attacking does not seem to be mine any longer, but rather I am trying to recover what has ceased to be mine').

[116] His sketchy treatment of Alcibiades' career after his recall (36 ff.) is at least right on one point, that he did not have enough 'power' to fulfil the tasks assigned to him (37). Accusations of embezzlement of public money may have originated with his enemy Thrasybulus (Plut. *Alc.* 36), and his constant shortage of funds to pay his sailors obliged him to leave a subordinate, Antiochus, in command of the fleet. This officer ignored his express instruction not to engage Lysander, and lost the Battle of Notium (407/6 BC: see J. Hatzfeld, *Alcibiade* (Paris, 1951), 312 n. 1). Alcibiades was blamed, and went into exile for the last time. But he did not 'surrender the ships to Lysander with Adeimantus' (38) at Aegospotami: on the contrary, he rode from his castle in Thrace to warn the Athenian generals of the weakness of the position they had chosen for their encampment, and was rebuffed (Xen. *Hell.* 2. 1. 25–6; Plut. *Alc.* 36–7).

the time of his final exile. However much these were canvassed, it is clear that a contrary tradition survived him.[117] In particular, arguments that dilated upon Alcibiades' manifest enmity with the Thirty (Isoc. 17 *Team of Horses* 40 ff.), whom Lysias has to marginalize in the present speech (39 only), would have served to increase residual popular regard for him.[118] Such were the feelings, which were not without their elements of romance and nostalgia, that a litigant attacking the memory of a dead hero no less than the record of a living descendant, must oppose.

Thus Lysias had limited material with which to work, and had to resort to distortion in order to make the most of what he had. It is perhaps surprising that he does not make more of service in the cavalry as a relatively safe privilege of the wealthy, thereby feeding the jury's envy.[119] However, generalized criticism of 'men such as these' (41), 'these men' (46), finds its place towards the end of the speech (41 ff.),[120] underlining the political aspect of the case and raising once more the question of comparison with Isocrates' speech for the same client. The speech *On the Team of Horses*, a defence of the younger Alcibiades, was written perhaps a short time before the present speech (*c.*397 BC). Stylistic comparison of the two speeches seems to point to influence: the Lysianic speech, while containing slightly less $\mu\grave{\epsilon}\nu \ldots \delta\acute{\epsilon}$ antithesis and shorter sentences, has an almost identical incidence of $o\grave{\upsilon}\kappa \ (\mu\acute{\eta}) \ldots \grave{\alpha}\lambda\lambda\acute{\alpha}$ antithesis and comparable homoeoteleuton and parison,[121] all characteristically Isocratean features. It is difficult to avoid the inference of a reply in kind, in a literary and political rather than a purely forensic contest. It would be natural to find Lysias representing the democratic point of view, while Isocrates, at this time on the lookout for wealthy pupils for his school, supported a member of one of the most illustrious Athenian families.

[117] The most extended surviving expression of this tradition is the first part of the speech *On the Team of Horses* by Isocrates, in which the Younger Alcibiades defends the memory of his father, who is portrayed as a patriot and a friend of the people (25, 28, 36) who brought nothing but glory to his city (30, 32). That speech contains a comparison between Alcibiades' return and that of the democrats (12–15) similar to the one ascribed to Alcibiades junior in this speech (33).

[118] Plutarch *Alc.* 38 says that the people of Athens believed 'that he would not look on passively at the triumph of the Spartans or the outrages of the Thirty'.

[119] This topic may have been thoroughly explored by Archestratus: it is touched on obliquely in 9 ($\kappa\alpha\grave{\iota}\ \tauο\grave{\upsilon}\varsigma\ \piο\lambda\epsilon\mu\acute{\iota}ου\varsigma\ \check{\epsilon}\delta\epsilon\iota\sigma\epsilon$).

[120] Cf. 12. 81ff.

[121] Sentences 67: 88·5. $\mu\grave{\epsilon}\nu \ldots \delta\acute{\epsilon}$ 64: 52·5. $o\grave{\upsilon}\kappa\ (\mu\acute{\eta}) \ldots \grave{\alpha}\lambda\lambda\acute{\alpha}$ 24: 23·75. homoeoteleuton 30: 25. parison 2: 2·5. (Isoc. figures first, Lysias figures proportionally adjusted to length).

7 *On the Olive-Stump*

This case was heard before the Areopagus, probably a year or two
after the alleged offence, which may be assigned to 397 or 396.[122]
The defendant was accused of uprooting from his land the stump
of one of the olive trees which were thought to be scions of
Athena's olive tree on the Acropolis.[123] Hence he has an initial
problem: he can offer no material proof that he has not removed
an object which is patently absent. As in Antiphon's *Murder of
Herodes*, there is no *corpus delicti*, but in Athenian trials this did not
necessarily benefit the defendant, especially in cases involving possible religious sanction.[124] In the present trial, the defendant has to
explain the absence of the sacred stump from his land. He alleges
that the prosecution have changed their charge at the last moment
from that of the removal of a sacred tree to the removal of an
enclosed stump (σήκος).[125] This reference to the irregular behaviour of the prosecution is once more reminiscent of *Murder of
Herodes*, but the defendant's own account also raises questions.
After a short catalogue of previous owners (4), he says: 'So I consider my task to be to prove that, when I acquired the plot there
was neither an olive-tree nor a stump upon it.' Now this land had
suffered two possible sources of degradation: a period of three years
(7) during which it was untenanted after it had been confiscated
from Peisander, and the frequent incursions of Spartan armies into
Attica after their occupation of Decelea. The bleak picture which
he paints of these times on the land (5–8) may be an attempted
diversion from his central difficulty. *Trees* might be burnt or
chopped down by marauding Spartans, but it is hard to envisage

122 Blass dates the speech to '395 or later' (*AB* i. 591, 647). See also Carey, *Lysias*, 114.

123 This was the famous tree that was burnt to the ground during the Persian assault on
the Acropolis. Herodotus (8. 55) tells how it put up fresh shoots 'to the height of a cubit' on
the day following the fire. This revivability, of which this is an extreme example, in trees of
such great economic importance lies behind the law prohibiting their destruction, which
however could be applied in practice only to those trees which could be denominated 'state
property', and exempt from the landowner's axe and plough.

124 E. Heitsch, 'Recht und Taktik in der 7 Rede des Lysias', *Mus. Helv.* 17 (1961), 213–18,
dwells on the significance of the religious element, and puts it in its historical setting. It
accounts for the severity of the penalty: nominally death ([Aristot.] *Ath. Pol.* 60. 2), but by
this time exile and confiscation of property (see §§ 3, 32, 41).

125 2: the crops from fruit-bearing sacred olive trees (ἐλάαι μορίαι) were collected sep-
arately, a process which also required some form of registration. The defendant says that his
accusers' enquiries from the collectors (τοὺς ἐωνημένους—'those who had bought the
contract to collect') yielded nothing to incriminate him.

their raiding parties on their short visits *uprooting* olive-stumps.[126]
This work would be done mainly by farmers wishing to grow other
crops, and such men were absent from the land for three years
(410–408). Suspicion must inevitably fall on the active cultivators
of the land. He ends this section (8) with a neat comparative argument: 'And yet, if you release from blame those who have cultivated the land throughout this period, surely those who bought it
in peacetime should go unpunished by you.' But in the light of his
insistence on the absence of both sacred tree and sacred stump from
his land five days after he took over the plot, on the evidence of the
first tenant Callistratus (9), why does he find it necessary to refer to
the exoneration of men *who had uprooted trees*? The answer may, of
course, be double insurance, the procedure of a cautious, punctilious pleader (see below); but suspicions may linger.[127]

After the atechnoi pisteis, comprising the testimonies of his tenants Demetrius and Proteas, who presumably corroborated his
claim, he turns to refutation of motive, the only possible one being
that of gain (κέρδος), measured here against the probability of
detection. Added to this novel combination is a no less innovative
treatment of character—not allowing it to emerge through action,
as in *The Killing of Eratosthenes*, but explicitly describing the traits to
which the defendant wishes to lay claim (12):

Now formerly, councillors, whenever people alleged that I was a clever,
punctilious person, unlikely to do anything at random and without cal-
culation, I would resent it, regarding it as an exaggeration. But now I
should be glad if you all held this opinion of me: for then you would
expect me, if I were to engage in such an act, to weigh the gain I should
make from removing the stump against the loss from preserving it, and
what I should achieve if I escaped detection against what I should suffer
at your hands if I were caught.

[126] He seems to affirm that they did by saying (7): 'It is hardly surprising that (εἰ followed
by the imperfect indicative) they uprooted (ἐξέκοπτον) the sacred olives at a time when we
were unable to protect even our own personal property.' He hoped the jury would readily
and unthinkingly blame the Spartans.

[127] Carey (*Lysias*, 117) notes with suspicion the defendant's failure to call Apollodorus or
Anticles, owners of the land before him (4), as witnesses. But these were hazardous times:
either or both, or the latter's tenant, could have been victims of the Thirty, or of the returning democrats, or casualties in the Corinthian War. Yet some evidence from these missing
years might be expected, and Carey (117–18) is right to point to the five days in 403 during
which he had sole charge of the land before he let it out to a tenant.

After this he summarily dismisses poverty as a possible reason, and dilates upon the practical dangers of exposure.[128] But in the jury's mind now dwells the portrait of a cautious man who would never take such risks. The impact on them of the defendant's concentrated self-characterization would be immediate. Again, he has no actions to narrate, so that the medium of character-portrayal is not available to him. The explicit self-description marks a clear development in Lysias' technique, and its presence is felt throughout the otherwise routine probability-arguments in 16–19.

The apostrophe to his accuser Nicomachus (20) marks a change of direction. The defendant's complaint of delayed litigation is a standard device against an opponent whom he wishes to brand as a sycophantes.[129] The defendant is able to capitalize on his failure to produce witnesses (20–2), but carefully ensures that Nicomachus cannot exploit his own weakness—another example of double insurance.[130] This also takes the form of repeated statements.[131]

The defendant switches briefly to his own state services (30–3) before returning to criticism of Nicomachus' irregularities in a standard argument about the reliability of slaves' testimony (34–7). This discontinuity may be an implementation of his overall strategy to keep his own personality constantly in the jury's mind. We have learnt quite a lot about his circumstances as well as his character: he has owned several plots of land (24); he may have enjoyed some favour under the Thirty (27); he is wealthy enough to have performed expensive leitourgiai (31, 41); and he has enemies (18, 27, 39, 40). He completes the portrait with a brief moment of pathos (41):

I shall be the most hapless of men if I am unjustly driven into exile: I am childless and alone, my house would be abandoned, my mother would be in utter penury, and I should be deprived of a land I cherish, after serving her many times on land and sea, and being a law-abiding citizen under both democracy and oligarchy.

But this is the only display of emotion that the defendant allows himself. The **epilogue** (42–3) is a model of precise recapitulation, in keeping to the last with the persona he has fashioned for himself;

---

[128] Blackmail is added to other dangers as a witnessing slave would, through his knowledge, become his master.
[129] Nicomachus is so characterized in 38–9.   [130] 23: dilemmaton.
[131] In 25 and 29 he denies having been punished for encroachment, and he claims lack of profit for himself in 17 and 32.

and we are left with an impression of a defendant who has not only won all the arguments but whose instinct for self-preservation is too strong to allow him to have taken chances in the hope of small gain.

3 *Against Simon*

This defence in a case which may have been heard not long after the campaign of Coroneia (394),[132] concerns rivals in homosexual love, the object of their infatuation being a Plataean boy named Theodotus. As both sides dispute most of the facts and have witnesses to their version of them, the speechwriter turns once more to character-portrayal, this time comparative and antithetical, requiring a more rhetorical technique than that used for Euphiletus in Speech 1. But in the background lies a difficulty, which is his client's age: the embarrassment of the ageing lover could not be concealed.[133] His solution to this problem is to adapt the 'reluctant litigant' topos,[134] but he does so in an original way. He admits shame (3,9: $αἰσχυνόμενος$) and the fear of being ridiculed for his foolishness (9: $ἀνόητος$; see also n. 133), but asks for indulgence for his human follies (4). Lysias thus portrays another client as having venial character-flaws. This one is more timorous than Euphiletus, flattering the jury (2) and pretending to be baffled in the face of his opponent's effrontery (1, 10). Yet in the narrative he is constantly on the attack,[135] interpreting his own, and, much more, colouring his opponent's actions in terms of his character more forcefully than Euphiletus is made to do.[136] The contrast between the antagonists

[132] § 45: precisely how long after that campaign is a guess; Blass (*AB* i. 578) suggests 'around 392'.

[133] Homosexual affairs between adults and between young men and boys did not excite popular disapproval (Carey, *Lysias*, 93), but the adage 'There's no fool like an old fool' (cf. 3: $φαίνωμαι\ παρὰ\ τὴν\ ἡλικίαν\ τὴν\ ἐμαυτοῦ\ ἀνοητότερον\ διατεθείς$) was considered as true in matters of love in ancient Athens as it is universally today. The defendant's age is not mentioned, an omission which allows only one deduction—that he was a younger man than the prosecutor.

[134] For $ἀπραγμοσύνη$ as a civic virtue, see Aristoph. *Wasps* 1040; Dem. 18 *Cor.* 308; Carey, *Lysias*, 93; modern discussions: W. Nestle, '$Ἀπραγμοσύνη$ zu Thukydides II 63', *Philol.* 81 (1926), 129–40; V. Ehrenberg, 'Polypragmosyne: A Study in Greek Politics', *JHS* 67 (1947), 46–76; L. B. Carter, *The Quiet Athenian* (Oxford, 1986) (rev. D. Whitehead, *JHS* 108 (1988), 253).

[135] See O. Büchler, *Die Unterscheidung der redenden Personen bei Lysias* (Heidelberg, 1936), 67.

[136] Note esp. the frequency in the speech of hypostasis (correlatives of the type $εἰς$ $τοσοῦτο\ τόλμης\ (ἐλθεῖν)\ \dots\ ὥστε$): nineteen examples, the highest in the corpus.

is drawn in the first sentence of the **narrative** (5: ἐγὼ μὲν εὖ ποιῶν
. . . οὗτος δὲ ὑβρίζων). It is indeed a story of hybris, of reckless
and relentless violence by Simon and his friends, who break into
women's quarters (6), carry out assault (8), ambush (12), and kid-
nap (16), the latter despite the protests of onlookers, who later assist
the victims of the attacks (18)—a clever device, recording public
reaction which a jury might choose to replicate. Contrasted with
all this is the speaker's decision to leave town in order to avoid violence (13–14). He thus represents himself as the moderate man suffering at the hands of the hybristic man, whose actions and attitudes
are described in the strongest terms.[137]

He begins the **proof** (21–44) with Simon's least sustainable
claim, that he had formed an agreement with Theodotus in the
sum of 300 drachmae, and that the speaker had seduced the boy
(ἀπέστησα, 22), presumably by outbidding him. The nature of
such an agreement might make witnesses difficult to find or even
irrelevant, and airing it could expose the parties to ridicule.[138] The
other charges that Simon has made are rebutted by showing his
statements to have been incompatible with his actions. Rhetorical
questions are used to appeal to the jury's sense of probability (29,
32: τῷ γὰρ ἂν δόξειε πιστὸν . . . and 30, 33, 34). Of the charges,
those alleging assault (27–8) are of particular interest, since, if true,
they would explain the effort the defendant has made to represent
himself as the aggrieved party who has consistently backed away
from confrontation (32–6) and has used only the minimum force
when necessary (37). But the most ingenious argument is reserved
to prepare for his strongest point—that Simon has delayed his prosecution for four years. This argument (38–9) combines inverted
hypothesis with comparative (a fortiori) argument for the first time
in extant oratory: 'If I had been the attacker, I should have faced
the severest penalties, yet I am facing those penalties now when I
am the victim.'

Before concluding, Lysias deploys two moral arguments. The
first concerns the application of the law to his case. In order to
inflict the maximum damage on his opponent, a prosecutor alleged
'wounding with intent' (*trauma ek pronoias*), i.e. the intention of

---

137 e.g. 7: ἀτοπώτατον πρᾶγμα καὶ ἀπιστότατον ἐποίησεν, εἰ μή τις εἰδείη τὴν
τούτου μανίαν.
138 See Carey, *Lysias*, 103, who points out that either Theodotus' age or his servile status
would probably have disqualified him from making legally binding agreements.

committing murder. The defendant, in the standard way, here argues the purpose of the lawgiver, which may be assessed by the severity of the punishment of exile. The second is a brief attack on his opponent's character—shorter than usual, but in keeping with the retiring persona which he has created for himself.[139] The **epilogue** (46–8) contains the conventional summary (anacephalaiosis, 46).

16 *For Mantitheus*

Recently elected to the Council, but subsequently challenged at his dokimasia on the ground that his name appears on the register (*sanidion*, 6) of those who served in the cavalry under the Thirty, Mantitheus has to overcome both direct evidence and, more difficult and insidious, political prejudice and suspicion. He is able to rebut the former by showing that he was abroad until the final days of the regime of the Thirty, and by arguing the unreliability of that register (4–8). He might persuade a jury on those points, but it is clear that he has made some implacable enemies during his short career.[140] They will have portrayed him as an arrogant young man of oligarchic, perhaps pro-Spartan sympathies. His defence must call attention to those of his actions which refute such charges, and a narrative technique which swiftly draws inferences from actions is required. This technique is perfected in this speech. He ends a short account of his private life, which contains the usual assertions of generosity with slender means, with a general claim: 'never to this day has a single person ever had any grievance to lodge against me' (10). His description of his public behaviour is coloured at the outset as he calls it 'proof of my seemliness' ($\tau\epsilon\kappa\mu\acute{\eta}\rho\iota\upsilon\nu$ $\tau\hat{\eta}s$ $\dot{\epsilon}\mu\hat{\eta}s$ $\dot{\epsilon}\pi\iota\epsilon\iota\kappa\epsilon\acute{\iota}as$, 11). Again, his own interpretation of the situation and of the opinions of others comes to the fore as he describes his decision to serve as a hoplite rather than in the cavalry (13). In 14 we hear his views about his payment of campaigning expenses and his generosity, 'not because I was wealthy, but to set a good example to others'. Later he is advising his commander to dispatch his

[139] Note the paralcipsis ($\tau\grave{a}$ $\mu\grave{\epsilon}\nu$ $o\mathring{\upsilon}\nu$ $\mathring{a}\lambda\lambda a$ $\dot{\epsilon}\acute{a}\sigma\omega$): so also in 46. He wishes to end as soon as possible.
[140] It is unusual for a defendant to complain so early in a speech (here in the opening sentence) of the prosecutor's desire 'to do him down by every possible means'. Elsewhere these enemies appear only fleetingly (11, 18–19).

battalion without drawing lots (16). In sum, the self-portrait he
gives the jury is one of unvarying propriety and unstinting, almost
quixotic, patriotism. Indeed, it verges on improbability, and where
he dissociates himself from 'all the younger men, who choose to
spend their time in dicing and drinking and other such
debaucheries' (11), he is in danger of seeming priggish. Lysias must
have thought that the risk of exaggerating the conventional topics
was necessary and/or worthwhile in this case; necessary, possibly
because prejudice against this client was particularly strong.
Evidence for this may be found in 18, where he feels obliged to
mention his habit of wearing his hair long.[141] The argument that
mere appearance should not excite prejudice is not in itself convincing, since it could be argued that dress is used, especially by
younger people, to make a statement about their affiliations. Lysias
realizes this, and follows it with an argument which is more powerful because it has a sinister contemporary resonance: 'There are
many who engage little in debate and dress soberly, but have caused
great mischief, while others for whom such things have been a
matter of no concern have done you valuable service.' The jury
cannot have failed to think of the oligarchs who planned the revolution of 411, and especially Antiphon, who 'did not appear before
the people or willingly engage in any lawsuit' (Thuc. 8. 68. 1). By
contrast, the bold, forthright young man who defends his candida-
ture for the Council in this speech is not afraid to display his oratorical skills. Lysias has given him a highly polished oration, notable
for periodic sentences (*passim*, but especially 3, 10, 16, 20–1) and
for avoidance of hiatus. The latter feature is yet another example of
Lysias' versatility. It may also be pertinent to point out that this
speech is probably later than the first forensic speeches of Isocrates.

19 *On the Estate of Aristophanes*

Nicophemus, the father of Aristophanes, served with Conon in his
mainly successful naval campaigns of 398–397, but both father and
son were subsequently executed without trial. An expedition to

---

[141] Hamaker's emendation of MSS τολμᾷ to κομᾷ is perhaps the most brilliant in the
Corpus Lysiacum. The habit was adopted by some knights, but was also a Spartan custom
viewed with distaste at Athens, especially at this time. Mantitheus' need to emphasize his
choice of serving as a hoplite rather than in the cavalry, and to disclaim involvement in the
regime of the Thirty, is thus partly explained by the image he has projected of himself, and
which he must now counteract.

assist Euagoras against the Persians in Cyprus in 390 appears to have
been organized by them, and its failure may mark a low point in
Athenian fortunes, after earlier hopes of renewed imperial power
had not been realized.[142] This is therefore another case in which
the speaker must employ tact before a probably unsympathetic
jury, at a time when the Athenian treasury was under great strain,
and popular frustration was strong.

Lysias' client's sister is Aristophanes' widow. The client's father,
whose death may have been recent (62), betrothed her to
Aristophanes on Conon's suggestion (12), having himself become
a friend of Conon.[143] This friendship could prove embarrassing in
the present case, not because Conon was unpopular at Athens since
he was dead by now (4), but because his exploits must have brought
great wealth, some of which people would assume to have found
its way into the pockets of his friends. Hence, when the estate of
Aristophanes, and with it his public liabilities, became the responsibility of the speaker's father, the popular perception would be that
there was plenty of money to claim, justly or unjustly, for the public treasury. The speaker's task must therefore be to argue from all
possible angles the improbability of the existence of great wealth in
the hands of any of the principals in the case. But with tact, from
beginning to end.

While the **prooemium** (1–6) is packed with commonplace
topoi,[144] there is a certain amount of interlacing, which is distinctive. The topos of inexperience appears in different forms in 1 and
2, interlaced with that of the opponent's preparation (2 and 3). The
plea for a fair hearing is made straightforwardly first (2), then modified to ask that the defendant be heard with the greater sympathy
(3). The speaker is working with standard material when he
deplores the irrevocable harm done by false accusers (4–5), but here
again there is something distinctive: the speaker affects innocence

[142] The specific reason for their execution can only be conjectured. So too the place of
execution: C. J. Tuplin, 'Lysias XIX, the Cypriot War and Thrasyboulos', *Philol.* 127 (1983),
170–7, challenges the common view that they were brought to Athens, and tends to a date
for the speech closer to the war (i.e. 390/89). The only other information we have is that
Conon appointed Nicophemus harmost of Cythera (Xen. *Hell.* 4. 8. 8). Jebb's suggestion
(*AO* i. 236) that they were found guilty of 'treachery or embezzlement' would explain the
apparent relentlessness with which the state pursued their surviving relatives.

[143] Willingly forming ties, however indirect, with such an illustrious figure, as he himself frankly admits (13).

[144] To such an extent that some commentators have thought it a 'stock proem' (Carey,
Lysias, 9, who also suggests comparison with the prooemium of Andoc. 1 *Myst.*).

of such matters with the clause ὡς ἐγὼ ἀκούω ('or so I hear', 5), and even more strikingly, greater ignorance than his audience of the wicked ways of the world when he says 'for I hear, and I think most of you already know, that slander is the most pernicious thing of all' (5). The argument in 6 about the abatement of a jury's anger carries the standard topos, which related originally to capital cases (Antiph. 5 *Her.* 73, 86–8), to a new point. Lysias knows that his client has a hard task, needing the greatest tact, to win the jury over in this case.[145] Why this tact is necessary becomes immediately apparent.

Nicophemus and Aristophanes were put to death without trial (7). Their offence must have been thought extremely serious (see above). The speaker can therefore do little but pass over the affair as quickly as possible (paraleipsis: 'But I shall pass over these matters, for I could achieve nothing'), but no harm is likely to be done by deploring the misfortune of their surviving families (8–9). The immediate task, however, is to establish the credit of the speaker's own family, since they are now in charge of the estate and would be liable to any further confiscations that the court might decree. This task is not easy: indeed, the rhetorical problem is well summarized by the speaker (11): 'It is difficult to defend oneself against an impression (opinion—δόξαν) which some people have of the wealth of Nicophemus, and of the shortage of money in the city.' He has to contend both with a general human tendency, to assume that people who have enjoyed wealth in the past have retained it, and with the perhaps more dangerous popular mood at this particular time. Lysias is judicious to point out these difficulties before the main **narrative**, which begins at 12.

The two families require different treatment. The speaker's account of his own family emphasizes marriages made not for money but from moral approval.[146] His father refused to betroth his daughters to wealthy men who were prepared to take them without dowries because he judged them to be 'of bad family' (κάκιον γεγονέναι, 15). He now has to fit his brother-in-law Aristophanes into this scheme, and yet avoid connecting his own family too closely with a man who has been condemned to death.

---

[145] The unparalleled use of the word χαρίσασθαι (2) adds to the impression of a defendant ingratiating himself to the jury. The *ingénue* is not without his wiles.

[146] 14: his father married the daughter of Xenophon, son of Euripides, 'a man not only known to be a good citizen but also thought worthy by you to be a general, as I am told'.

This he does in a clever linking passage (18), before going on to describe the career of Aristophanes, who emerges as an archetypal patriotic man of action (19–23). Attention is drawn particularly to his lavish expenditure in the pursuit of glory, and considerable detail is provided (24–7) to prove that Aristophanes used up practically all his money and needed to borrow. By contrast, the period of his career after the Battle of Cnidus (394) receives less coverage. Yet it seems clear that his fortunes changed around this time.[147] Lysias, however, moves quickly on to highlight the upright behaviour of his client's family in the matter of the confiscation (31):

Again, consider this: in all other cases where you have confiscated the property, not only have you not had any furniture to sell (i.e. it was destroyed or looted), but even the doors were torn away from the apartments; we, on the other hand, as soon as the confiscation was announced and my sister (Aristophanes' widow) had left the place, posted a guard in the deserted house, in order that neither door-timber nor utensils nor anything else might be lost.

This remarkable description of an act of honesty and public spiritedness, supported by a pathetic appeal (33), diverts attention from what may have been the most profiteering period of Aristophanes' career.[148]

Further diversion from the dubious career of Aristophanes comes through two types of example. The first begins with a hypothesis (38), an innovation which serves the needs of the situation because it introduces an acceptable person, Timotheus, son of Conon, and gives a precise account of Conon's estate (39–41). This leads to comparative argument: the estate of Nicophemus and Aristophanes must have been a mere fraction of Conon's (42–4). This is followed by more straightforward examples of estates which have proved smaller than expected. People airily assume, in particular, that holders of state offices acquire great wealth (49). Another hypothesis based on an example, that of Diotimus, in recent memory (ἔναγχος, 50),[149] illustrates not only the folly, but also the danger of believing such assumptions. He was thought to have amassed

---

[147] In 29 we read of him performing two *choregiai* and one *trierarchia*. It must be assumed that he had suddenly acquired considerable wealth, perhaps from Conon's booty. This was the money for which the state was pursuing his heirs.

[148] In 36 he says it is *probable* that Conon shared only a small part of his prizes with others, but since these donations took place far from Athens, he could have no means of knowing.

[149] This gives an approximate date for the speech—soon after Diotimus' command (388/7).

a fortune of forty talents, but appeared in person to refute that claim: what if he had died abroad, and his relatives had been faced with it? Their hypothetical situation is similar to the actual one faced by the defendant. The last example, that of Alcibiades (52), is of some interest. Lysias would not have risked introducing him unless some degree of his former popularity had been restored by the time of the speech.[150]

In his otherwise conventional pistis ek biou (55–9) the speaker maintains his tactful persona, reasserting his retiring nature (apragmosyne) (55) and apologizing for having to detail his own and his father's services and expenses (56: συγγνώμην ἔχετε). The idea that true character cannot be concealed for long (60) may well be a commonplace, but this is its first appearance in Attic oratory. The speech has of necessity been longer than average, because the process of breaking down popular prejudices and misconceptions depends less on single items of evidence than on the cumulative weight of impressions.

27 Against Epicrates

This case was heard around the same time as the last,[151] and against a similar background of a weakened treasury and frustrated Athenian imperial ambitions. We have only the concluding part.[152] Falk should be followed in deleting καὶ τῶν συμπρεσβευτῶν (1), since this Epicrates is charged not with misconduct on an embassy but with embezzlement when serving as a treasurer (3). A well-tried topos of prosecution reappears here: the need for an example to be made of offenders in order to make others behave more responsibly (7).[153] But hostility to this type of offender is carried a stage further than before in 8, where it is suggested that such men might justly be condemned and punished without trial because

---

[150] It was presumably possible to excite resentment against him at the time of Lysias' speeches Against Alcibiades (the Younger) (395/4); but the frustration of Athenian ambitions, which form the background to this speech, would have led many to remember his exploits sympathetically, as Lysias invites them to do here.

[151] Or a short time earlier, perhaps 390/89.

[152] Rather than a deuterologia: the formula Κατηγόρηται . . . and the use of ἐνθυμεῖσθαι are most closely paralleled in the concluding sections of full-length speeches (e.g. 12 Ag. Eratos. 81, 94).

[153] Cf. 12. 35 (close verbal parallel: ἤκουσιν . . . εἰσόμενοι).

their acts were so notorious.[154] Also, fear is expressed that they may escape through their eloquence: the most effective example to others is that in which eloquent wrongdoers receive condign punishment (5). Portrayal of the wealthy but dishonest holders of public office attains a new level of harshness as reference to lei-tourgiai, conventionally laudatory, is here used critically: men who perform them and still remain rich (10–11).[155] An unusually strong note of indignation is sounded, though in the now familiar form of a paradox, in 12: 'Most extraordinary of all ($\pi\acute{a}\nu\tau\omega\nu$ $\acute{v}\pi\epsilon\rho\phi\upsilon\acute{\epsilon}\sigma\tau\alpha\tau\sigma\nu$[156]), whereas in private suits it is the victims who weep and arouse pity, in public suits it is the wrongdoers who attract sympathy, and you, the wronged, who pity them.' The theme of the rich and eloquent being able to flout the law thus re-emerges, and is present to the end.

28 *Against Ergocles*

While the previous speech is mainly argumentative and sophistical, this closely contemporary piece, another concluding fragment, or possibly a synegoria, is remarkable for its expansive, periodic style.[157] It reflects even more starkly the tensions of those times— the fleet is breaking up for lack of money, yet individual citizens are enriching themselves while serving in it (2). The hyperbolic topos of the guilty deserving many deaths, with which the piece begins, has been used before (12 *Ag. Eratos.* 37; 13 *Ag. Agorat.* 91). But the attack on the same group of wealthy wrongdoers is carried a stage further with accusations of oligarchic ambitions (7):

No sooner are they rich than they abominate you, and plan thenceforth not to be your subjects but your rulers, and, fearful of losing their booty, they are prepared to seize territory, establish an oligarchy, and do everything they can to expose you, day after day, to the most terrible dangers.[158]

[154] Distinction is drawn, in a Prodicean manner, between the literal sense of $\mathring{\alpha}\kappa\rho\iota\tau\sigma\varsigma$ (='without an actual trial') and its conceptual sense (='unjudged'). There is also a third sense, 'judged, but unfairly', on false testimony and through *sycophantia*.
[155] The argument here also contains an undercurrent of resentment against the *nouveaux riches* (9).
[156] The only occurrence of the word in the *Corpus Lysiacum*.
[157] Noticed by F. Berbig, *Über das genus dicendi tenue des Redners Lysias* (Küstrin, 1871), 10–11. Periods: 4–6, 12–13, 14.
[158] The link between corruption and a desire to establish oligarchy is made again in 11, but failure to press it strongly relegates it to the status of a standard charge against wealthy, or supposedly wealthy, officials.

Scarcely less forceful is the argument that the jury should clear themselves of any suspicion of collusion with this and other corrupt officials by condemning him today (9): it is not Ergocles alone, but the whole city that is on trial. This is a development of the 'example to others' argument, which is stated more explicitly a little later (11). Otherwise no new ground is covered in the rest of the speech, which contains the same charge of self-enrichment under democracy that was used in the previous speech.

29 *Against Philocrates*

This is, as it were, a postscript to the speech *Against Ergocles*. Philocrates was Ergocles' friend, who seems to have survived his condemnation and execution. Now he is accused of holding a residual sum of thirty talents from Ergocles' estate.

Even shorter than *Against Ergocles*, the speech is written in a similarly periodic style,[159] and contains an ingenious inversion of the prooemium-topos of *abundance* (10 *Ag. Theomn.* 1; 12 *Ag. Eratos.* 1). Here, instead of saying that he has many witnesses, he points to the dearth of them as probability-evidence[160] that Philocrates did indeed have the money, which he used to bribe witnesses not to testify. Again, Ergocles' money has not come to light: who is more likely to have it than his friend, whom he also appointed as his purser (χρημάτων ταμίαν, 3)? Another passage, while not breaking new ground, confirms previously noticed rhetorical division (5):

I think, gentlemen, that Philocrates can defend himself in two ways, and in two only: he must prove either that Ergocles' money is held by others, or that he was put to death unjustly, having embezzled none of your property, and having taken no bribes.

For the fourth time (see Ch. 1 n. 47) we have clear reference to στάσεις: the στάσις λογική (*status coniecturalis*) or question of fact (two questions of fact here); and the στάσις νομική (*status iuridicialis*), or question of justice or law.[161] Elsewhere the fragment

---

[159] Berbig, *Über das genus dicendi*, 11.

[160] Dover (*LCL* 57) notes that Lysias uses probability-argument in this speech without actually using the word εἰκός.

[161] This is one of a number of items of evidence to be found in the Attic orators, which refute the main thesis of T. Cole (*The Origins of Rhetoric in Ancient Greece*, Baltimore, 1991), that rhetorical theory was formed mainly in the 4th cent. and later.

breaks no new ground. The idea that crime against the state is more serious than similar crime against the individual is couched in pathetic paradox in 9 and 11, and is implicit in much of the other argument. But in such a short piece there is little scope for development. Indeed, its precise nature is difficult to determine. It is styled $E\Pi I\Lambda O\Gamma O\Sigma$ in the MSS: absence of factual statement confirmed by proof and testimony shows that it is unlikely to be a complete speech. Yet there is no reference to an earlier exposition of the case ($\kappa\alpha\tau\eta\gamma\acute{o}\rho\eta\tau\alpha\iota$ . . . $\tau\grave{\alpha}$ $\kappa\alpha\tau\eta\gamma\rho\rho\eta\mu\acute{e}\nu\alpha$); the reference to dearth of witnesses would be a topos more suited to a prooemium than an epilogue; the only parallel reference to $\sigma\tau\acute{\alpha}\sigma\epsilon\iota\varsigma$ occurs just over a third of the way through *Against Eratosthenes* (37); and the speech ends without the recapitulation or emotional appeal usual in epilogues. These features may point to an opening fragment of a speech, which owes its preservation to its association with the speech *Against Ergocles*.

22 *Against the Corndealers*

Though it is of great interest as an historical document,[162] rhetorical scope seems at first sight to be somewhat limited by the fact that one, at least, of the accused admits the main charge, that he has bought more than the legally allowed amount of corn (5), claiming only that he did so on the instructions of the corn-inspectors (here called $\mathring{\alpha}\rho\chi o\nu\tau\epsilon\varsigma$ rather than their technical title, $\sigma\iota\tau o\phi\acute{\nu}\lambda\alpha\kappa\epsilon\varsigma$).[163] Refutation of this claim would seem to require only denial on the part of the officers concerned, but we also read that popular indignation at profiteering in times of shortage had led to a demand for the summary execution of the profiteers (2), and that the speaker had opposed this and thereby incurred odium (3). He must therefore show himself to be a severe and uncompromising prosecutor. He does this nowhere more effectively than in the following passage (14):

[162] The evidence it contains concerning commerce, economics, and the politics of the corn trade, has attracted frequent attention. See P. H. Kohns, 'Die staatliche Lenkung des Getreidehandels in Athen', Festschrift Oertel, Bonn, 1964, 164–6; R. Seager, 'Lysias and the Corndealers', *Historia* 15 (1966), 172–84; G. R. Stanton, 'Retail Pricing of Grain in Athens', *Hermes* 113 (1985), 121–3; C. Tuplin, '$\Sigma\nu\mu\pi\rho\acute{\iota}\alpha\sigma\theta\alpha\iota$ in Lysias *Against the Corndealers*', *Hermes* 114 (1986), 495–8; T. Figueira, 'Sitopolai and Sitophulakes in Lysias' Against the Corndealers', *Phoenix* 40 (1986), 149–71.

[163] Lysias uses *erotesis*, as he has done with another defendant who admits the charge but disclaims responsibility (*Against Eratosthenes* 25). See Carawan, '*Erotesis*'.

Their [sc. the corndealers'] interests are the opposite of other men's: they profit most when, on the city's receiving bad news, they sell their corn at a high price. Such is their pleasure at your disasters that they find out about them before others, or make up their own rumours—that you have lost your ships on the Pontus route, or they have been captured by the Lacedaemonians on their outward voyage, or the trading ports are under blockade, or the truce is about to be broken. And they have carried their *enmity* to such a pitch that they choose the same crises as your foes to plot against you. For, just when you find yourselves worst off for corn, these men snap it up (ἀναρπάζουσι) and refuse to sell it, in order that we should not argue about the price, but be glad enough to come away with corn bought at any price, however high. Thus there are times when, although we are at peace, *we are besieged by them* (ὑπὸ τούτων πολιορκούμεθα).

This portrayal of 'the enemy within' (sharpened in the italicized words) is one of Lysias' most memorable creations.[164] He reinforces it with the idea that this class of traders has for a long time (πάλαι, 16) been acting against the public interest. The sequel is no less charged with powerful rhetoric: comparative argument (16); hypothetical inversion (17); pathetic paradox (18); the topos of example (19–21—one of the most elaborate instances). The jury could not, after this, suspect the speaker of selfish motives.[165] He has made the most of a forensically unpromising case.

10 *Against Theomnestus*

This case seems to have arisen out of a remark made in the stress of the moment by the defendant in another trial, which he won. Add to this the excellence of the speech which Lysias has written for this client in his only extant action for slander (δίκη κακηγορίας), and we face an intriguing set of questions. Was there something, apart from the payment he received, which attracted Lysias to this seemingly trivial yet difficult case? Why was his client sustaining a public attack on Theomnestus which had already failed once? Was there a political aspect?[166] Perhaps most interesting, was this a test-

---

[164] It also prefigures at least one later creation—Aeschines as portrayed by Demosthenes in the *De Corona* (280–1, 291–2, 308, 313, 323).

[165] The speaker's opponents may have argued that his advocation of the due process of law rather than summary punishment was prompted by a desire to be bought off by the corndealers.

[166] This may be suggested by the speaker's reference to his father's death under the Thirty (4), which he precedes with these words: 'I am thirty-two, and it is nineteen years since your return' (i.e. 403 BC). This dates the case to 384/3.

case in which literal interpretation of the law could be successfully challenged by invoking its spirit?

In the short **prooemium** (1–3) he seeks to avoid an accusation of litigiousness by recognizing the triviality of slander, considered generically, but he excepts the charge of patricide (3). The effectiveness of this, showing both unselfishness and family loyalty, will have been enhanced if his father had been prominent among the opponents of the Thirty.[167] He has made a confident start, managing a jibe at Theomnestus' father (2) after beginning with a claim to have many witnesses. In the short section dismissing the charge of patricide (4–5) the possible political aspect of the charge becomes clearer when he says: 'At that age [i.e. thirteen] I neither knew what an oligarchy was, nor would I have been able to rescue him from the wrong that he was suffering.' It seems that Theomnestus had implied that the speaker's inaction might have been due to sympathy with the regime of the Thirty. This was a desperate attempt to extricate himself, which the speaker is easily able to scotch. He also shows by probability-argument that he had greater reason for wanting his father alive than dead (5). This done, he can turn to the main argument to which Theomnestus has been forced to resort.[168]

Theomnestus' argument is simply that he has not used the actual words forbidden by the law (τὰ ἀπόρρητα) in his slander, and is therefore not subject to its penalties. Lysias' attack on this position is direct and immediate (7): ἐγὼ δὲ οἶμαι δεῖν ὑμᾶς οὐ περὶ τῶν ὀνομάτων διαφέρεσθαι ἀλλὰ τῆς τούτων διανοίας. By invoking the 'meaning' rather than the 'letter' of the law, he adverts the jury to the intention of the legislator and asks them to exercise their common sense of what is reasonable.[169] This is the first extant

[167] He describes his father as οὕτω πολλοῦ ἀξίου γεγενημένου καὶ ὑμῖν καὶ τῇ πόλει. For the possibility that he was Leon of Salamis (Xen. *Hell.* 2. 3. 39 gives him a similar reputation), see A. Andrewes and D. M. Lewis, 'Note on the Peace of Nicias', *JHS* 77 (1957), 179 n. 10.

[168] It may indeed be the only argument that Theomnestus offers, if he restricts himself to restating what he said at the preliminary hearing (*diaita*) (6).

[169] Aristotle, *Rhet.* 1. 13. 17, touches on this distinction in the context of the idea of 'equity' (τὸ ἐπιεικές), which is said to be achieved by looking μὴ πρὸς τὸν νόμον ἀλλὰ πρὸς τὸν νομοθέτην, καὶ μὴ πρὸς τὸν λόγον ἀλλὰ πρὸς τὴν διάνοιαν τοῦ νομοθέτου. In a wider discussion of the relationship between 'law' and 'equity' (*Eth. Nic.* 5. 10. 3–4, 1137ᵇ) he points out that, because law is a general statement, individual cases cannot be covered by it. In such cases application of the principle of equity can act as a corrective (ἐπανόρθωμα). On the whole question, see M. Hillgruber, *Die zehnte Rede des Lysias* (Berlin, 1988), Appendix.

example of this precise distinction.[170] The argument is devastatingly straightforward. Murderers are murderers whether you call them ἀνδροφόνοι (the forbidden word) or say ἀπεκτόνασί τινας: the lawgiver cannot include all the words for 'murder' in the text of the law, so a single word covers all synonyms (7). The defendant himself is apostrophized: would he decline to prosecute someone who accused him of beating his parents if he did not use the forbidden words πατραλοίας and μητραλοίας? Other examples follow, and this sequence of direct questioning personally discredits the defendant. One (9) is of interest for reasons other than the fact that it concerns the charge for which Theomnestus had himself been prosecuted.[171] The text of one of the laws concerning cowardice in battle contains the word ἀποβεβληκέναι (sc. τὴν ἀσπίδα). By this time ἀποβάλλειν was more commonly used in its other, weaker sense, 'to lose', and the current words for the offence were ῥίψασπις and ῥῖψαι τὴν ἀσπίδα.[172] In another example, the text of the law contains a word which had changed its meaning: Ἐπεγγυᾶν δ' ἐπιορκήσαντα τὸν Ἀπόλλω (17) referred to the swearing of an oath; but in Lysias' time ἐπιορκεῖν meant 'to forswear, break one's oath'. Texts of other laws contained words which were no longer in current use, and in each case he gives the current word. Thus the current word for δρασκάζειν is ἀποδιδράσκειν; for ἀπίλλειν, ἀποκλήειν: neither of the archaic words is found elsewhere. It is possible to imagine that some of the grandeur of the old text is lost in Lysias' modern substitutions; πεφασμένως πολοῦνται (19) sounds more impressive than his φανερῶς βαδίζειν, but perhaps Aeschylean grandeur is less appropriate for a description of prostitutes plying their trade than for some other activities. In any case, these examples serve to press home his argument admirably. No less revealingly, they reflect a specific interest with which he is associated by later critics: the

[170] Related distinctions regarding the law, such as those between intentional and unintentional homicide and questions of responsibility for death, do of course arise in earlier oratory (Antiphon, Second and Third Tetralogies). But the present case is concerned not with redefining the nature of the alleged offence but with showing that it falls within existing law, as it would be understood by fair-minded people.

[171] Lysias makes the most of his inconsistent behaviour with a pathetic paradox (13).

[172] Debate about this particular example would have been complicated by the difficulty in deciding such cases, e.g. whether a man had shown unpardonable cowardice in taking flight, or whether he lost his shield through incompetence during combat. Plato (Laws 944b) proposes to distinguish between a 'loser' and a 'thrower-away' of arms. Evidently the distinction was not made at the time of this speech.

standardization of written Attic prose.[173] He, more than any other orator, saw that the lawcourt was a place for clarity (or apparent clarity), where a jury of ordinary citizens, sometimes faced with difficult decisions, should at least have them explained in familiar terms.

When the needs for persuasion were more urgent, however, rhetorical artistry must be deployed. Although Theomnestus has had to resort to pedantry in the present weak case, he has been successful in two previous related cases, one as defendant and the other as prosecutor.[174] Lysias' method is a continuance of this agonistic, antithetical setting: straightforwardly, of himself, who did not throw away his shield in battle, with Theomnestus, who did (22); and emotionally, of the tragic *peripeteia* of his friend Dionysius (24–5):

Who would not pity Dionysius for the disaster which befell him, a man of proven valour in times of danger, who on leaving the court said that that was our most unfortunate campaign, in which many of us died, and those who kept their arms had been condemned for false witness on indictment by those who had thrown theirs away; and that it would have been better for him to have been killed on that day than face such a fate on his return.

Powerful as this passage is, it contains an element of caution; two allusions to Theomnestus' crime of throwing away his shield fall short of defining it explicitly, presumably because of his earlier acquittals. The speaker must content himself later (30) with a sarcastic reference to them: 'I have personally twice acted as witness in this man's case, for I was not yet aware that you punished the men who had seen the deed, but pardoned those who had thrown their shields away.' Style and rhetorical ornament combine

---

[173] Dionysius of Halicarnassus singles out Lysias (*Lys.* 2) as both pioneer and paragon: 'He is completely pure in his vocabulary (ἑρμηνείαν), and is the perfect model of the Attic dialect, not the archaic dialect used by Plato and Thucydides, but that which was in general currency in his day . . . none of his successors surpassed him.' Cf. Cicero, *Orator* 81 on the characteristics of the Plain Style: *Ille tenuis orator, modo sit elegans, nec in faciendis verbis erit audax et in transferendis verecundus et parcus in priscis in reliquisque ornamentis et verborum et sententiarum demissior.* Earlier (29), while arguing against a narrow definition of Atticism, he says that Lysias should be called 'Attic' not because he is *tenuis atque inornatus* (sc. though he is), but *quod nihil habeat insolens aut ineptum.* Both critics agree that an important component of the Plain Style, of which Lysias is the model, is avoidance of the strange and the inapposite, which undoubtedly includes vocabulary.

[174] An apparent reference later (29) to Theomnestus' tall stature and dashing appearance suggests that he was, on a purely physical level, a formidable opponent.

artistically in these closing sections. A perfectly constructed period
(22: ἐγὼ δὲ ἑωρακὼς ... λήψομαι) is followed by Lysias' most
forceful hypophora (23: τίνος ὄντος ἐμοὶ ἐγκλήματος; πότερον
ὅτι δικαίως ἀκήκοα; ἀλλ' οὐδ' ἂν αὐτοὶ φήσαιτε. ἀλλ' ὅτι βελτίων
καὶ ἐκ βελτιόνων ὁ φεύγων ἐμοῦ; ἀλλ' οὐδ' ἂν αὐτὸς ἀξιώσειεν.
ἀλλ' ὅτι ἀποβεβληκὼς τὰ ὅπλα δικάζομαι κακηγορίας τῷ
σώσαντι; ἀλλ' οὐχ οὗτος ὁ λόγος ἐν τῇ πόλει κατεσκέδασται).
His reference to his father's services (27) is cast in a rhetorical
mould rather than as a conventional recital: emphasis is laid on his
sharing in the common dangers (μεθ' ὑμῶν ἐκινδύνευσε); and his
death under the oligarchy δι' εὔνοιαν τοῦ ὑμετέρου πλήθους
identifies him decisively with the jury. It is his opponent and his
family who are the outsiders: the memorials of his father's valour are
hanging in the city's temples, whereas those of his opponent and his
father are hanging as trophies in the temples of her enemies (28).

The late and brief rebuttal of an excuse made by Theomnestus,
that he uttered the slander in anger (30), must indicate that the
prosecutor did not expect to make much of it, knowing that it
would not necessarily be accepted.[175] The end of the speech is conventional: by summarily making the point that acquittal of
Theomnestus would be tantamount to convicting him (the
speaker) of patricide, he focuses the jury's mind on the future consequences for him of their verdict.

24 *For the Invalid*

Lysias' literary reputation depended not only upon his forensic oratory, but also upon essays in the other genres.[176] It will be argued
here that the present speech belongs to a category which transcends
genre, to which Lysias contributed in common with other sophistic writers, the paignion ('play-piece', *'jeu d'esprit'*).[177]

[175] A jury would consider the circumstances in which Theomnestus' anger had arisen, and he would no doubt supply them with that information, suitably coloured.

[176] Dion. Hal. *Lys.* 1: he also quotes passages (27–33) illustrating Lysias' style in forensic, epideictic and deliberative oratory; *Vit. X Or.* 836b; Plato's description of him, put in the mouth of Phaedrus (228a), δεινότατος ὢν τῶν νῦν γράφειν, however it may be intended to serve his purpose of providing himself with a 'precise target at which to aim his criticism of the rhetorical culture of his own and the preceding age' (R. Hackforth, *Plato's Phaedrus* (Cambridge, 1952), 17), must substantially reflect Lysias' actual status. This status becomes clearer in 257c where we read of Lysias being disparaged as a logographos by an unnamed politician.

[177] Dion. Hal. *Lys.* 3: περὶ γὰρ δὴ τῶν ἐπιστολικῶν αὐτοῦ καὶ ἑταιρικῶν καὶ τῶν ἄλλων, οὓς μετὰ παιδιᾶς ἔγραψεν, οὐδὲν δέομαι λέγειν.

Suspicion should immediately be aroused by the trivial nature of the subject and the way the speaker refers to it (26):[178] 'I am neither giving an account of public money which I have handled, nor have I held any state office for which I am now undergoing an audit: my speech is about a mere obol.' To a reader familiar with the lighter works of contemporary sophists, this would have put the subject on a par with 'encomia of bumble bees and salt',[179] and there would be nothing more natural than for Lysias to choose the genre for which he was best known for an excursion into parody. The many incongruities of scale, emphasis, and structure, can be explained by this supposition.

Taking the last first, although the **prooemium** (1–3) and prothesis (4–5) seem normal enough, they are followed by a narrative which is wholly inadequate (5–6),[180] and leads to a passage of emotional appeal where a real speech would be expected to refer to witnesses and/or documentary evidence. And the passage itself (7–8) looks like a ready-made exercise[181] which does not quite fit into the context. Using comparative argument and pathetic paradox, it refers to his growing older and weaker, but earlier he has said (6) that he does not yet ($ο\mathring{v}πω$) have children. The plea is generalized by the use of the plural ($το\grave{v}s$ $ο\mathring{v}δ\grave{\epsilon}ν$ $\mathring{\epsilon}χοντας \ldots το\grave{v}s$ $κα\grave{i}$ $το\hat{\iota}s$ $\mathring{\epsilon}χθρο\hat{\iota}s$ $\mathring{\epsilon}λειvο\grave{v}s$ $\mathring{o}ντας$), as might be expected in a handbook written for an indeterminate clientele. Next, instead of dealing with the grounds for doubting his poverty in straight succession, he inserts between them a piece of inconsequential sophistry (11–13) portraying a topsy-turvy state of things[182] which could result from his losing the case: he could stand for the archonship (which was open only to able-bodied men), and his opponent

---

[178] Lysias, like Gorgias describing his *Helen* as a $πα\mathring{\iota}γνιον$ (12), leaves his reference to the character of his case until the end in order to achieve a maximum effect of para prosdokian.

[179] Isoc. 10 *Helen* 12.

[180] It is notably lacking in precise facts on the vital question of his income, and is self-contradictory: he says that his business is $βραχ\acute{\epsilon}α$ $δυναμ\acute{\epsilon}νην$ $\mathring{ω}φελε\hat{\iota}ν$, then that the dole is his sole source of income. (Typically of the whole speech, there is possible ambiguity in $πλ\grave{η}ν$ $τα\acute{v}της$.)

[181] It is a standard argument about poverty and old age, such as would be found in a handbook. (Aristot. *Rhet.* 2. 8. 9–10. Radermacher *AS* 71–2.)

[182] The description of a *mundus perversus*, as suggested by P. Harding (in I. Worthington (ed.), *Persuasion: Greek Rhetoric in Action* (London and New York, 1994), 203), is certainly a feature of the speech. For a worthy attempt to treat the speech as serious forensic oratory, see C. Carey, 'Structure and Strategy in Lysias 24', *G & R* 37 (1990), 44–51; also D. A. Russell's chapter 'Ethos in Oratory and Rhetoric', in C. Pelling (ed.), *Characterization and Individuality in Greek Literature* (Oxford, 1990), 365–442.

could apply for the dole. The next charges with which he deals are one of his general behaviour, that he is 'hybristic, violent, and utterly abandoned', and that his shop is a den of vice. Neither of these was likely to have been made in a real trial without the adduction of specific acts. His prosecutor is much more likely to have targeted the amount of trade which he carried on in his shop, which was near the agora, as evidence for his wealth. Next, to counter the charge against his character, he produces another set of commonplaces (15–17)[183] about the powerlessness of the poor when compared with the rich, even managing one on the young and the old (17), and against that of having disreputable customers he merely counters with a claim that they are a cross-section of the population of Athens. In a real case one would have expected him to name some well-known respectable customer(s), if he could. Hence there is an agreeable irony in his transition to emotional appeal, when he says (21) 'I have argued the principal points: why is it necessary to dwell seriously on trifles, as my opponent does?' The appeal to emotion, though conventionally placed, is out of all proportion to the length of the speech as a whole (22–5); and nowhere more than here does the grandeur of the rhetoric (rodomontade?) seem to point to parody.[184]

The question of scale has to some extent been covered in the above consideration of structure. Of a speech of average, or slightly less than average length, over half consists of oratory which provides no assistance to a jury's efforts to reach an objective and just verdict. What it does provide, however, is entertainment; which leads us to the remaining question, that of emphasis. The presence of humour alongside pathos in this speech has long been noticed.[185] Now Attic oratory, and especially early Attic oratory, is for the most part[186] an earnest and serious genre. Antiphon was proverbially grave and austere, and, outside this speech, Lysias provides very few instances of humour. Yet here we have a speech in which it is present, in the

---

183 Blass *AB* i. 638.

184 Ancient critics would identify the Grand Style in these sections, with their reference to the deity, fortune, and the city; antithesis and hypophora; long words but simple sentence-structure. See [Longinus] *Subl.* 9, 18; Dion. Hal. *CV* 22, *Dem.* 38.

185 Blass *AB* i. 637: ' . . . burlesque tone . . . The whole speech is like a parody on defence through pathos, and this form is constantly set in comic contrast with the triviality of the case in hand.' Thus he to some extent anticipates my position, but falls short of it. Harding's sensitive examination of the speech (see n. 182) is in a chapter entitled 'Comedy and Rhetoric', but he too eschews the logical extreme.

186 Andocides is the only exception, and he uses humour sparingly.

forms of both parody and straight jocosity, from the very beginning.
The topos of gratitude for the opportunity to give an account of his
public life (1), obviously intended for use by a man ambitious to
pursue a public career, like the young Mantitheus, is here given to
an older man whose life has been played out in the shadows. There
is a touch of farce, typical of parody, in the claim that he 'deserves
praise rather than envy' (cf. 'better citizen', 3). The aposiopesis 'If
it's my wealth he's after . . . ' (2) is obviously funny, but may also be
parodic in that aposiopesis was recommended by the handbooks for
prooemia, but as a restraint on ill-omened utterance.[187] Elsewhere
there are jokes designed to ridicule the idea that he is wealthy: the
hypothetical antidosis (9), the comparison of the dispute over his
wealth with that over a (wealthy) heiress (14); and simple burlesque
with the picture of the defendant using two sticks when other
invalids use one.[188] Perhaps most significant for my main thesis is
the suggestion (18) that the prosecutor is 'not serious but playful:
indeed, it is not his desire to persuade you that I am of that nature,
but to make me into a comic character, as a kind of artistic touch':
it is difficult to imagine such a suggestion being made in a real trial,
but it could easily have a literary purpose, as a kind of conceit alluding to the intended character of the whole piece, of which later
readers of it might not be aware.

Parody of the kind envisaged by Blass (AB i. 637) is a matter of
language and style. Apart from the set-piece passages (7–8, 15–18),
and the example of Grand Style already discussed (n. 184), there are:
καὶ γὰρ οἶμαι δεῖν, ὦ βουλή, τὰ τοῦ σώματος δυστυχήματα
τοῖς τῆς ψυχῆς ἐπιτηδεύμασιν ἰᾶσθαι (3); εἰ γὰρ ἐγὼ
καταϲταθεὶς χορηγὸς τραγῳδοῖς προκαλεσαίμην αὐτὸν εἰς
ἀντίδοσιν, δεκάκις ἂν ἕλοιτο χορηγῆσαι μᾶλλον ἢ ἀντιδοῦναι
ἅπαξ (9); ἐγὼ γάρ, ὦ βουλή, πάντας οἶμαι τοὺς ἔχοντάς τι
δυστύχημα τοῦτο ζητεῖν καὶ φιλοσοφεῖν, ὅπως ὡς
ἀλυπότατα μεταχειριοῦνται τὸ συμβεβηκὸς πάθος (10).
Elsewhere some unusual vocabulary is used: ἐλεημονέστατοι (7),
φιλαπεχθήμων (24). The speech also contains a high incidence of
hyperbaton and rhetorical question.[189] Finally, the effect on a jury

---

[187] See Usher GO v. 170.   [188] Making him an engagingly eccentric figure.
[189] i.e. compared with the Lysianic average. Of these hyperbaton is perhaps the more significant, as a feature of carefully crafted sentences and emphatic word-order, suited to a
composition intended for literary enjoyment rather than practical use. Examples: 3: τοιαύτῃ
κεχρημένος συμφορᾷ τούτου βελτίων εἰμὶ πολίτης. 6: πρόσοδος δέ μοι οὐκ ἔστιν
ἄλλη πλὴν ταύτης. 25: μεθ᾽ ὑμῶν εἱλόμην κινδυνεύειν ἁπάντων.

achieved by the juxtaposition of humour and pathos would have
found approval with a later orator/critic,[190] but Athenian juries of
the fifth and early fourth century were not, to judge from the
forensic speeches which have survived from that period, yet ready
for sudden changes of mood. But those who looked to the speech
for literary entertainment (as Plato's Phaedrus might have) would
enjoy its deft touches and its chameleon character. From our point
of view it is arguably the most original speech in the Corpus
Lysiacum, the first surviving parody in the genre of forensic
oratory.[191]

26 *Against Evander*

This concluding fragment of a prosecution speech in a dokimasia is
the latest datable speech in the Corpus Lysiacum (382 BC). The case
against Evander was lost, as his name appears among the archons of
the following year. But the speech shows Lysias at his most inventive in adapting existing topoi, and at his most adventurous in his
vocabulary. His chief rhetorical problem is that by this time some
of the old arguments about oligarchs seem tired and overworked,
while Evander's own part in the events of 404–403 is obscure, and
not clarified, at least in the surviving part of the speech. He also has
a political problem. Evander was sponsored by the influential
Thrasybulus of Collytus, who had secured the disqualification of
the speaker's friend Leodamas in order to promote him. Thus
expression of bitterness becomes a natural feature of the speech.[192]

The fragment comprises mainly a procatalepsis, anticipation of
the arguments and pleas expected from the defendant. The latter
will recite his father's leitourgiai: Lysias' novel answer to that is that
when money is thus used to gain influence with a view to over-
throwing the democracy, it deserves not praise but condemnation
(4). His answer to the 'quiet citizen' argument (5) is equally novel:
the claim becomes hollow when the claimant's powers to act

---

[190] Cicero, enumerating the qualities of the ideal orator (*Brutus* 322), mentions his ability to 'turn the jury briefly to mirth and laughter . . . to anger . . . to tears . . . and to what-
ever emotion the case demands'.

[191] The fact that the speech is not datable does not reduce the probability of this, provided that Lysias is its author.

[192] This appears early, as when (2) he accuses the Council of 'naïvety' ($\epsilon\dot{v}\dot{\eta}\theta\epsilon\iota\alpha$, cf. 5
$\epsilon\dot{v}\dot{\eta}\theta\epsilon\iota\varsigma$) for allowing oligarchs who served the Thirty subsequently to participate in democratic government (3).

otherwise are shown to have been curtailed. Less interesting rhetorically[193] is his reply to the urgent claim that failure to make an appointment would interfere with the sacrificial ceremonies. The speaker turns from particular to general by arguing that attention should be focused on Evander's likely behaviour, based on his past record, during the rest of his time in office. The argument in 9 is the now familiar pathetic paradox, though forcefully put.[194] The comparative argument in 10–11 may illustrate the difficulty arising from the passage of time. The speaker wishes to accuse Evander of serving in the cavalry and on the Council under the Thirty, but when he is made to say (10): νῦν δέ, ὅτε μὴ μόνον ἱππευκὼς μηδὲ βεβουλευκώς, ἀλλὰ καὶ εἰς τὸ πλῆθος ἐξημαρτηκὼς φαίνεται . . . there is an element of uncertainty in the statement.[195] In 11–12 the 'one and many' argument[196] is adapted, in order to show the special importance of the office of archon, by comparing it with that of a Councillor, who is only one of five hundred. Pointed reference to sensitive areas of the archon's administration then makes good rhetoric: what if the trial of murder cases should fall to a man who ought himself have been tried for murder; or control over heiresses and orphans be given to the man responsible for their state (12)? Routine dismissal of motive (here χάρις, 15) follows. More interesting is 16–17, which is an objection to the general character of the amnesty of 403.[197] Here Lysias argues that the view of the people is not so liberal, and that they recognize different degrees of patriotism and reward or condemn them accordingly. This was how the amnesty worked in practice: with a choice of candidates for office, people were free to

[193] But of interest to constitutional historians. See P. J. Rhodes, *The Athenian Boule* (Oxford, 1972), 177–8.

[194] Weissenberger, *Die Dokimasiereden des Lysias*, 225 notes the chiastic structure in δι' οὓς . . . οὗτοι . . . ἄρξουσι, καὶ κύριοι γενήσονται . . . ἦν . . . ἐλωβήσαντο. The articular infinitive ἐν τῷ ἕκαστον δικαίως ἄρχειν is also an unusual construction in Lysias.

[195] Participial clauses dependent on φαίνεσθαι are negated with οὐ(κ) when the required sense is 'clearly, manifestly to . . . '. The use of μή here must signify doubt or equivocation: 'it seems that he may . . . '. The difficulty of the passage was noted by P. Müller, *Das Lysias Rede gegen Evander* (Merseburg, 1873), 18, who proposed to amend the text. Weissenberger (*Die Dokimasiereden des Lysias*, 223) thinks emendation unnecessary, since the weight of the argument is upon εἰς τὸ πλῆθος ἐξημαρτηκὼς φαίνεται. But the element of doubt remains.

[196] See Lys 7. 33; 24. 13, 22; 30. 32.

[197] According to the agreement brokered by the Spartans (Xen. *Hell.* 2. 4. 38), the only men excepted from the amnesty were 'the Thirty, the Eleven, and the Ten who ruled in the Piraeus'.

prefer those with wholly clean records of conduct where these presented themselves. Thus is the 'argument of precedent' ('Your treatment of my case will affect all others') refuted. It also affords Lysias the opportunity to indulge in a little flattery of the jury by inferring their good sense with epicrisis (εἰκότως, 17).

A final piece of rhetorical invention is an adaptation of the conventional pistis ek biou in 21–2. Instead of reciting services directly, he makes his opponent Thrasybulus the subject and says 'He will not be able to say that I took part in the oligarchy . . . or that my father did . . . or that my ancestors . . . ' Then with these are contrasted immediately the heinous crimes of his opponent (23). Lysias also uses a number of words rare in Attic prose: ἐπισύροντα, διακλέπτοντα (metaph.) (3); ἡσυχιότητα, ἀσελγαίνειν (5); ἐλωβήσαντο (9); καθήκειν (12); προσενθυμηθῶσιν (13); μισοδημίαν (21). There is also evidence of an avoidance of hiatus.[198] It is intriguing to contemplate the direction which Lysias' oratory might have taken, both rhetorically and purely stylistically, if his creative lifespan had been longer. Perhaps it would have become more difficult for Dionysius of Halicarnassus to mark him down as 'the perfect model of the Attic dialect' (Lys. 2).

4 Malicious Wounding: A Defence

This is the most Lysianic of the remaining speeches, but like them it is undatable and lacks prooemium and narrative. The quarrel between the principals is over the ownership of a slave-girl. The defendant must persuade the jury that the quarrel had been trivial and was now resolved. Two interesting points arising from this speech are the idea, noted by Jebb (AO i. 280), that a challenge to antidosis could be presented as evidence of ill-will; and the handling of the charge of pronoia.[199] Forensic and rhetorical usage of that word had broadened its meaning to 'intention to kill', creating added danger, but also opportunity, for the defendant, who can argue in this speech that, if he had intended to kill the prosecutor, he would have armed himself with a knife, not merely struck him

---

[198] The examples of attachment of αὐτόν to a relative noted by Dover (LCL 139) may be so explained.

[199] In the MSS the speech is entitled Περὶ Τραύματος ἐκ Προνοίας. For pronoia as 'intent to kill', see Carey, Lysias, 109 (n. on 3. 41). The way the present speaker argues on the assumption that he is being accused of attempted murder provides the strongest ground for believing in this extended meaning of pronoia.

with his fist (6). The speech also has the stamp of Lysianic characterization, with contrast used for the first time: we have thumbnail
sketches of the paranoid, atrabilious prosecutor whose excesses
include making false claims, and the easy-going defendant (8–10),
who, like any normal man, accepts feminine fickleness, is prepared
for a reasonable settlement of differences, and speaks rather dismissively of the whole affair (17, 19). Of interest also is one of the
clearest distinctions between the meanings of 'semeion' and 'tekmerion' (12). Here semeion is applied, almost in passing, to the
opponent's 'proofs', while full weight is placed on the speaker's
tekmeria.[200]

5 For Callias

Sympathy with a respectable fellow-metic may have prompted
Lysias to write this short speech for one of his friends to deliver,
apparently at a time when a rash of *sycophantia* was breaking out in
the city (2). Callias' slaves, joining in the spirit of the time, had
denounced him for impiety in the hope of winning their freedom.
Lysias has crammed his client's speech with commonplaces—
successive hypothetical inversions (1–2), topoi of lesser danger (4),
common concern and example to others (5). An epilogue is lacking.

6 Against Andocides

All the remaining speeches in the Corpus are of more or less questionable authenticity, and will be treated summarily. The spuriousness of *Against Andocides* has been argued many times.[201] It could
be contemporary with Andocides *On the Mysteries* if it was actually
delivered at his trial (399), but it can, at best, only have been a
deuterology for the prosecution,[202] and its unrelieved religiosity

---

[200] In Aristot. *Rhet.* 1. 2. 16–18, a *semeion* is a sign from which general probabilities might
be deduced, which might be fallible, whereas *tekmerion* is a proof which can be reduced to
syllogistic argument, and is therefore logically irrefutable.

[201] L. Hölscher, *Quaestiones Lysiacae* (Erfurt, 1857); W. Weber, *De Lysiae quae fertur contra Andocidem oratione* (Leipzig, 1900); G. Begodt, *De Oratione κατ' Ἀνδοκίδου* (Münster,
1914), who attributes the speech to Meletus; Blass *AB* i. 562, 568; Jebb *AO* i. 281. Statistical
evidence (Usher and Najock, *Comp. Hum.* 16 (1982), 104, see also p. 100 on vocabulary
richness) places it third behind Speeches 8 and 9 in the scale of divergence from Lysianic
norms.

[202] In spite of the use of procatalepsis (13), the speech, at least in the form in which it survives, contains too little primary evidence to have been the first speech for the prosecution.

gives it an unreal and old-fashioned atmosphere, while its tone, as
Blass observed, is sycophantic (in the fourth-century sense of that
word). The first part is missing, and we join it as the speaker
describes, by way of example, the unhappy fate of a man who had
acted impiously. As MacDowell observes,[203] it contains no argued
proof of Andocides' guilt. But the speech is by no means without
vigour, protesting against the prospect of an acquitted defendant
standing for the archonship (4) in spite of his recent turbulent
career (6); appealing to unwritten laws (10), portraying Andocides
as suffering from god-sent madness (22–3), a soul-tortured fugitive
(28–9), yet impudent in his claims to have benefited the city (35–6).
Whoever wrote it may reasonably have thought that he did not
need the aid of another speechwriter.

9 *For the Soldier*

This little speech seems to be complete. The defendant's name is
Polyaenus (5), and he is threatened with confiscation of his property (*apographe*) for being rude about magistrates in public. But
there have been irregularities in his treatment by the authorities,
and he explains these, attributing personal enmity to the officials
concerned, who may not have been the magistrates (generals), but
mere secretaries (*grammateis*, *syngrammateis*). Having argued this
cogently, MacDowell[204] concludes that 'the text shows how it was
possible for secretaries to have considerable power over administrative and legal procedures', and that 'This speech is an attack on
the improper use of bureaucracy'. It is one of those speeches whose
historical interest exceeds its rhetorical interest.

8 *Accusation of Slander*

This piece seems even more remote from the lawcourts than
Speech 24 *For the Invalid*, at least in the sense that a forensic context is absent. In the first half of it, the speaker delivers a tirade
against fellow-members of some kind of association or club, but we
do not learn his actual grievance, that one of them has tricked him
over a loan he has made, until §§ 10–11. He ends by resigning from

203 D. M. MacDowell, *Andocides: On the Mysteries* (Oxford, 1962), 14.
204 'The Case of the Rude Soldier (Lysias 9)', *Symposium: Vorträge zur griechischen und hel-
lenistischen Rechtsgeschichte* (1993), 153–64.

the club with bitter recrimination, but not seeking redress at law. The presence of an unusually large amount of word-play, parison, antithesis, and an array of other rhetorical devices, may seem to suggest that this is another paignion, though it is much less likely to be by Lysias than Speech 24.[205]

20 *For Polystratus*

The preserved text appears to be a conflation of perhaps two speeches.[206] Add to this the fact that the two parts (1–10, 11–25) begin abruptly, and it becomes clear that normal critical methods cannot be applied to it. The context is political, and the time is not more than a few years after the Revolution of the Four Hundred (411–410). Polystratus has been accused of implication in the oligarchic coup, and his defenders have to contend against the fact that he held an official post under their regime (that of *katalogeus* ('registrar'), 13). The first speaker's piece reads like the concluding part of a proof, with general probability-argument and hypophora (3) used to discredit the idea of Polystratus as an oligarchic revolutionary. The second speaker expands this into a contention that Polystratus was a reluctant functionary whose sympathies were actually democratic. This speaker draws his speech to a proper conclusion, with the first extant inversion of the topos of parading one's family before the jury to elicit sympathy, here used with comparative argument (35, see also 16, 19). Although the style is at times tortured and the sentences unusually short and clipped, it seems clear that both speakers had access to technical expertise. Other rhetorical features and topoi include pathetic paradox (10), 'example to others' (31); and the end is a strong emotional appeal. If the conclusion is drawn from Plato *Phaedrus* that Lysias was a well-established writer several years before the death of Socrates

[205] The most thorough case for its spuriousness is made by P. A. Müller, *Oratio quae inter Lysiacas fertur octava* (Westphal, 1926), who assigns it to the 2nd or 1st cent. BC. The suggestion that it is a paignion may originate with T. Bergk, *Griechische Literaturgeschichte*, iv (Berlin, 1887), and is cited with approval by A. Darkow, *The Spurious Speeches in the Lysianic Corpus* (Bryn Mawr, 1917), 40, who accepts the speech as genuine.

[206] This hybrid feature is analysed by A. Andrewes and K. J. Dover in A. W. Gomme, *A Historical Commentary on Thucydides*, v (Oxford, 1981), 201: they note that the defendant is οὗτος until § 11, when he becomes ὁ πατήρ. Any possibility that the speaker throughout is a middle son of at least three sons (28–9) of Polystratus, is ruled out by the fact that they are all referred to in the third person in § 4.

(399 BC), he could well be the author of the two speeches from which this piece was made by an unknown compiler.

23 *Against Pancleon*

A cluster of non-Lysianic usages in this otherwise competent but unremarkable and undatable speech should arouse suspicions.[207] It is a reply to a special plea (paragraphe) by a man who claimed to be a Plataean, thereby enjoying Athenian citizen-rights. The speaker uses narrative to rebut this claim, describing his own enquiries among genuine Plataeans, who denied any acquaintance with him. He then tells how it transpired that he was not only not a Plataean, but not even a free man (12). His story speaks for itself, and requires no rhetorical artifice, though its periodic sentence-structure is noteworthy.[208]

LYSIAS: SUMMARY

Lysias made no radical changes to the overall structural framework which he inherited from Antiphon, but expansion of the non-argumentative parts of the speech, especially narrative, gave his oratory a more varied literary character while still fulfilling forensic requirements. Already in his prooemia he shows inventiveness in adapting or combining existing topoi, selecting those which accord with the impression he wishes to convey of his client, which may require making him seem bolder than convention recommended.[209] The richness of early materials for proof made innovation difficult for Lysias in that section, but he shows a constant awareness of the need for clarity of both argument and expression, and devises counter-arguments to conventional pleas.[210] Procatalepsis (anticipation)

---

[207] See S. Usher, 'The Speech against Pancleon', *CR* NS 16 (1966), 10–12. These usages include: formulaic instruction to stop the water-clock (4, 8, 11, 14, 15), the use of πρῶτον μὲν . . . ἔπειτα δὲ (4, 5–6) rather than the Lysianic (and usual Attic) πρῶτον μὲν . . . ἔπειτα, ἐκ + genitive with instrumental force (= 'by' with passive verb, an occasional Herodotean usage) (5); and some ἅπαξ εἰρημένα: a remarkable number of anomalies in so short a speech.

[208] See Büchler, *Die Unterscheidung*, 68.

[209] See esp. prooemia of Speeches 1, 16, 24. For combination of topoi, see Speech 31. On variety in Lysianic prooemia, see P. Grau, *Prooemiengestaltung bei Lysias* (Würzburg, 1971).

[210] See Speech 14; Speech 26 (adaptation of pistis ek biou for use against opponent). Further on Lysianic argumentation, see J. J. Bateman, *Phoenix* 16 (1962), 157–77.

comes into its own in Lysias, and probability-argument assumes a variety of guises, from the straightforward, as in Speech 19, to the psychological (arising out of character), as in Speeches 1, 3, and 7.

Lysias' best narratives are much more than simple recitals of the facts of the case. He uses them to give his client a certain persona. This may have been easier to do if the given persona coincided faithfully with the actual character, but a credible effect could be achieved by judicious underlining of existing traits. It should be assumed that all actions and statements in a Lysianic narrative are included with a purpose, most commonly that of illustrating a character whose probable behaviour on other occasions is thereby circumscribed. Thus the careful client in Speech 7 is unlikely to have destroyed the olive-stump, the timorous elderly prosecutor in Speech 3 is unlikely to have been the instigator of violence, and the simple rustic Euphiletus, as portrayed in Speech 1, is unlikely to have planned the entrapment of Eratosthenes, but might act forcefully when confronted with the actual adultery. Narrative is also the medium through which literary horizons are broadened. In addition to passages of drama or pathos, such as those found in 12. 8–20 and 13. 39–42, and lively scenes such as the family meeting in 32. 12–17, Lysias speaks at times like a politician, condemning the regime of the Thirty (12. 41–61) and the careers of Theramenes (12. 62–78) and Alcibiades (14. 30–40), and praising the patriotism of clients like Aristophanes (19. 18–23). Passages like these, and also the discussions found in speeches for clients accused of political crimes, like 25 and 34, foreshadow the deliberative oratory of later years—that of Aeschines, Lycurgus, and, pre-eminently, Demosthenes.

Less originality is to be found in Lysianic epilogues, although he seems to be the first to introduce dramatic prosopopoiia (12. 100). Speeches often seem to end rather abruptly, and any appeal to emotion tends to be brief. It is this tendency that led Dionysius to contrast him with more emotional writers (*Dem.* 2, 4, 13 esp.[211]). But a quiet ending seems to have been characteristic of most Greek oratory, with pathos for the most part to be found elsewhere; and Lysias continued this trend. His position is pivotal in the development of Attic oratory, though few others were able to match his variety of style, which included the ability to marshal massed forces

[211] ὅταν δ' εἰς τοὺς ἀποδεικτικοὺς ἔλθῃ λόγους, ἀμυδρά τις γίγνεται καὶ ἀσθενής, ἐν δὲ δὴ τοῖς παθητικοῖς εἰς τέλος ἀποσβέννυται.

of rhetoric when the underlying argument was weak (as in Speech 31). Dionysius was at least right in his general judgement (*Lys.* 1) that Lysias 'left few of his successors with the opportunity of improving on his performance' in the main oratorical media.

ISOCRATES LOGOGRAPHOS

In the course of his long life (436–338 BC) Isocrates had two distinct literary careers. Most of his published writing is the product of his school and its programme, and will be considered later. But he began by writing speeches for the lawcourts, a profession which he subsequently disowned and disparaged.[212] Six speeches from this early period survive, five of which are to be assigned to the years 403–393, the sixth, *Aegineticus*, to *c.*390. This corpusculum is thus contemporary with much of the Lysianic corpus, and must be examined in close proximity to it.

21 *Against Euthynus*

This and 18 *Against Callimachus* are the earliest datable Isocratean speeches (403/2), and the first of his six forensic orations. The question of authorship is raised by the frequency of hiatus, a clashing of final with initial vowels elsewhere scrupulously avoided by Isocrates, but it may be laid to rest by the presence in abundance of other stylistic features associated with him—homoeoteleuton and parison, in which it exceeds the average for the corpus by factors of $2\frac{1}{2}$ and 3 respectively.

The survival of the short piece (it is incomplete, lacking an epilogue) is readily explained: it is an exercise in standard probability-argument (*eikos, ek tekmerion,* 4), applied to the circumstances immediately following the fall of the Thirty Tyrants at Athens, in a case where no witnesses or documents provided direct evidence. The plaintiff Nicias left three talents with the defendant when he fled the tyranny, but received only two back from him on his

---

212 See Usher *GO* iii. 5, 151 (on *Paneg.* 11). Isocrates probably became a logographos from financial necessity, under circumstances similar to those faced by Lysias after the tyranny of the Thirty. He disowned the profession as part of his promotion of his paideia, and his pupils and friends backed him (Dion. Hal. *Isoc.* 18).

return. Probability is applied to Nicias' motivation in proceeding. Would he have done so vexatiously? No, because he was reasonably wealthy, a poor speaker (5), and short of supporters,[213] unlike Euthynus (13) and also related to him (8–9). To these are added probabilities of peculiar relevance to the period of the Tyranny: wealthy people like Nicias were wont to keep a low profile (11–15), shunning avoidable exposure to the money-hungry Thirty. Finally, the speech illustrates another standard technique, that of reversal (*peritrope*) (19: 'It is easy to use on Nicias' behalf arguments similar to those employed in Euthynus' defence . . . '). Interesting if read in isolation, the speech does not mark its author as an innovator.

18 *Against Callimachus*

More interesting, as the first surviving example of a *paragraphe* (counter-suit),[214] this speech concerns the violation of the Amnesty of 403 through litigation. The victim of such litigation would be the first speaker in the paragraphe, effectively becoming the prosecutor. Reflecting the new situation, the speaker here gives a preliminary narrative expounding the law of Archinus (2).[215] The **narrative** proper (5–11) tells quite simply how success in recovering rightly confiscated money had encouraged Callimachus to try his luck further in the courts; and he prepared his ground so well that the speaker's friends advised him to settle. This whetted Callimachus' appetite for more, but his greed now provides the speaker with some very telling arguments, which he deploys adroitly (12–18). Callimachus' attempt to deny that an arbitration had taken place, at which he had accepted an award of 200 drachmae, is met by specific *tekmeria*, based on *eikos* (sing.), and this is followed by a general probability argument (16: *ek ton eikoton*

---

[213] The speaker is not Nicias but someone speaking on his behalf because he has no ability as a speaker (ἀδύνατος εἰπεῖν) (1). This category of disability is not among those listed in *Rhet. ad Alex.* 36 1442b 13–17 among the reasons for *synegoria* (pace M. Lavency, *Aspects de la logographie judiciaire attique* (Louvain, 1964), 104), and it runs counter to the principle, often enunciated by scholars, that the Athenian courts required litigants to plead on their own behalf. However, one cannot be sure that Nicias did not appear briefly, before giving way to his more able advocate. Demosthenes 36 offers the closest parallel, where an advocate appears for Phormio, who is old, an ex-slave, and a foreigner.

[214] See MacDowell *LCA* 213–16, who assigns the speech to the year 400.

[215] On Archinus, see C. Hignett, *A History of the Athenian Constitution to the End of the Fifth Century BC* (Oxford, 1952), 295–7.

(plur.)) that the speaker's character, based on past behaviour, ruled him out as a likely vexatious litigant. This clears the way for the subject of the paragraphe (19). Here the rhetoric is more straightforward. Examples of stronger cases being dropped in deference to Archinus' Law (21–2) and others not being initiated (23) serve to show that the law is being observed, and they are followed by a broader plea for the observance of covenants (29–34), and a special plea not to heed Callimachus' complaints (35–41). Alternation between the personal and the general is established in the next section, the subject of which is the opinion which the outside world is likely to form as a result of this trial (42–4); and it is followed by another, more sustained attack on Callimachus (47–57) and a contrasting account of the speaker's record in the closing stages of the war. A narrative of his services (59–61) decisively casts the spotlight on the speaker, and it remains there in the concluding sections (66–8). This is a shrewd tactic in a paragraphe, in which the chief aim is to deflect litigation rather than obtain a conviction. Isocrates shows his acquaintance with the rhetorical devices in current use at the time,[216] but, notwithstanding the political background—the speaker and Callimachus having differing views, with Callimachus aligned with the democrats to the extent that he felt it unsafe to live on in Athens under the Thirty—he remains much more detached from the ideological conflict than Lysias.

16 On the Team of Horses

This is the closing section of a defence in an action for damage (*blabe*) which seems to have taken place a few years after the death of the famous Alcibiades (i.e. some time around 397 BC). His son and namesake has answered the main charge, that one of the four-horse chariot teams which his father had entered at Olympia (perhaps in 416) had belonged to the city of Argos, and he had misappropriated it.[217] But the surviving part of the speech is a defence by the son of his father's career and character. This is no doubt why it was published, to be appreciated by a small readership who retained an abiding admiration for the most mercurial and colourful personality of the previous generation.

---

[216] e.g. hypothetical inversion (1, 37, 51), paraleipsis (10), procatalepsis (13), pathetic paradox (15, 21, 24–6, 39).

[217] J. Hatzfeld, *Alcibiade* (Paris, 1951), 140 concludes that the charge was well-founded.

Although a defendant accepted the convention that he must defend his father's name as an extension of his own pistis ek biou (e.g. Antiph. 5 *Her.* 74–9), the time he could devote to it was obviously limited. The present piece is too long to have been accommodated in the speech delivered at the actual trial, and must have had an independent literary existence as an encomium. As such it is unique, and may express Isocrates' view at the time of its composition.[218] The parallel drawn between Alcibiades' effort to win back his country by going to Sparta (10–11), and the exiled democrats seeking the aid of any 'city, friend, or stranger' (13) to secure their return is novel, if strained. The following description of the perils facing Athens on his return is enough to show the full measure of his achievement (16–21), and this section may correspond with that in the original speech. But a fresh start is made at 25, with a more or less conventional epideictic genealogy. His Alcmaeonid lineage is used to establish him as a friend of democracy (28), and this sits comfortably alongside his worthy ambition (29) and distinguished service. Even his competition at Olympia is explained in patriotic terms;[219] and more is said of his democratic credentials (34–8) and of the way in which his personal fortunes have gone hand in hand with those of the city. The rhetoric here is inventive. The topos combining abundance with difficulty, used by Lysias,[220] is changed from a prosecution-topos into a topos of praise; and there may be an attempt to portray the eagerness of youth when the young Alcibiades says: 'for always what has not yet been said seems more important than the arguments that have already been presented to you' (39). He manages to combine the idea of his father's loyalty with that of his importance (40–1) by showing how the Spartans pursued him even after the defeat of Athens.[221] Contemporary colour is provided by the reference to Charicles,

---

[218] In *Busiris* 5–6, Isocrates describes Alcibiades as 'far superior to his contemporaries'. He offers a more balanced view of his exploits in *To Philip* 58–61, which is closer to the informed 4th-cent. view of Alcibiades—a mixture of admiration for his defiance of adversity and dismay at the damage he did to Athenian interests. Cf. Dem. 21 *Ag. Meidias* 143–6: here his career exemplifies the Athenian people's intolerance of *hybris* in their leaders, even those of the greatest ability like Alcibiades.

[219] The belief that success of individuals at the Games brought glory to their cities was universal (Pindar, *Ol.* 4. 10; Lys. 19 *Aristoph.* 63; and Alcibiades' own claim in Thuc. 6. 16. 2). But the idea is rejected by Isocrates himself in *Paneg.* 1.

[220] 10.1 and 12.1, on which see Usher *GO* i. 230, 237.

[221] 'in the belief that they could place no reliance upon the city's word if they merely demolished her walls, but failed to destroy the man who could rebuild them'.

one of the cruellest of the Thirty (42), and by the apostrophe to his
opponent Teisias (43). The final plea, in which he catalogues the
sufferings he has already experienced under the Thirty, is strong but
full of conventional arguments.

17 *Trapeziticus*[222]

This speech takes its name from the defendant, the banker Pasion,
whose business and family figure in several other Attic speeches
(Dem. 36, and all the speeches truly ascribed to his son
Apollodorus). It is the most accomplished of Isocrates' forensic
speeches, and one of his latest.[223] The subject itself would have
touched many citizens—the scope for fraud in banking, due to its
dependence on trust—and presented a rhetorical challenge because
of the absence of witnesses from banking transactions (2), and other
reasons arising from events. The unnamed prosecutor, son of
Sopaeus, a wealthy subject of King Satyrus of the Cimmerian
Bosporus, had deposited money with Pasion after he had set out on
a tour.[224] He soon received news that his father Sopaeus had been
arrested under suspicion of conspiracy, and Satyrus had ordered his
agents abroad to secure his money and the return of his son. The
latter was placed in an ambiguous relationship with Pasion. He had
to trust him with his money, but at the same time involve him in a
kind of fraud—that of concealing the amount of his deposit from
Satyrus' agents—which gave Pasion something akin to the power
of a blackmailer over him, and might be expected to reduce a jury's
sympathy with his plight. The speechwriter needed considerable
powers to counter this, and Isocrates, in one of the longest continuous **narratives** in early oratory (3–23), concentrates his fire on
the character of Pasion.[225] Starting by planning *with* him, he subsequently plotted *against* him.[226] His later actions confirm this, as

222 Lit. 'The Banker'.
223 393 BC. See § 36 (written after the destruction of the Spartan fleet at Cnidus, 394); and
§§ 3, 57 (King Satyrus still alive (died 393/2: Diod. Sic. 14. 93, 1)).
224 4: κατὰ θεωρίαν suggests a sightseeing trip (cf. 4 *Paneg.* 182), but this intention seems
to have been overtaken by the events described in 5 ff.
225 The case seems tailor-made for techniques pioneered by Lysias, which Isocrates may
have studied. Why did not the speaker, who was not indigent, enlist Lysias' services? Perhaps
because Lysias would have been reluctant to assist litigation against a fellow-metic who had
achieved a status in Athenian society similar to that of his own family.
226 7: βουλευομένοις ἡμῖν . . . 8 Πασίωνα συμβουλεύειν . . . ἔγνων αὐτὸν
ἐπιβουλεύοντα τοῖς ἐμοῖς.

he temporarily removes the slave Cittus, who was privy to their plans (11–12), and later is prepared to go to any lengths to avoid having his testimony examined under torture (16, 17, 53). But Pasion is also erratic and unpredictable, subject to sudden changes of mood, from tearful chagrin (12) to impudent audacity (14), then remorse (or discretion) (15), followed by humility (22); then audacity again (23). For his characterization of the defendant, Isocrates had the Lysianic model in 12 *Against Eratosthenes*, where the actions of the Tyrants are used to show their overriding greed. But Isocrates' task here requires greater tact and subtlety. Pasion was an associate of wealthy men, and consequently influential,[227] but he faced a changed situation when Satyrus exculpated Sopaeus (11–12), and the defendant had no further need of their secret agreement. Isocrates has to keep the jury's attention focused on Pasion's callous dishonesty and represent his adaptation to a new situation in terms of unreliable character. He must also use relentless logic to expose the inconsistency of his claims with his actions, and he does this most thoroughly in 25–44. This is followed by less rigorous probability-argument, with a return (53) to main proof and an informal ending, where the speaker alludes to his wealth and his alien status, and material evidence of his goodwill to the Athenian people.

19 *Aegineticus*

An early case of disputed inheritance,[228] this speech is also singular in that the hearing took place not in Athens but in Aegina. Thrasyllus, a travelling soothsayer, fathered two daughters by different women. The first became the speaker's opponent, the second his wife; but the estate in question is that of his son Thrasylochus. The speaker appears to be on very firm ground: Thrasylochus had adopted him and secured a blood-line for the next generation by giving him his sister in marriage; whereas his opponent was Thrasylochus' half-sister who, because of the adoption, had no legal claim on the estate, at least in Athenian law.[229]

[227] For his status, see Trevett *ASP* 156–65. Some of his actions described in this speech show that he had the assurance to pervert judicial procedures for tactical advantage (12–14, 49–50).

[228] If 394/3 is its date (so Jebb, Norlin), or even if Blass's dating (390) is preferred, it is earlier than Isaeus 5, the earliest of his datable speeches (389). Certainly Isocrates had no Isaean models to follow.

[229] A law of Solon established the principle that a man without legitimate issue had complete freedom to adopt an heir to his estate (Isae. 2 *Menecl.* 13). It may be assumed that a

The speaker assiduously records details of the relationships, social and emotional, between the different parties, using narrative extensively as in the previous speech. A description of family affinities, forged both collaterally and by descent, includes events leading naturally and inevitably to the speaker's adoption by Thrasylochus on his deathbed (12). This is contrasted with the opponent's behaviour (30–3). She never visited him during his long illness, and did not attend his funeral: now she wishes to 'make him her brother' (*adelphizein*, 30), 'as if she was related to his money, not to him'. But she does not contest the fact of the speaker's adoption by Thrasylochus, only its propriety.[230] Instead of furnishing probability-argument about the testator's intentions, the speaker has only to confirm his established position, so he provides further facts which widen the circle of the relatives who shared mutual affection, but exclude the opponent. A device speculating on the likely feelings of the now dead Thrasyllus on the whole matter (42–7) is similar to a prosopopoiia, but with even more dramatic immediacy than usual, as he is confidently added to the list of those who would approve of the speaker's adoption (47), a striking rhetorical coup.

Confidence, indeed, is the prevalent mood from the start,[231] and it appears well conceived, as the legality of his adoption cannot be disputed. So why does the speaker need more justification? The answer may be sought in an objection attributed to the opponents (36–7), that his own family background did not match that of Thrasylochus. It may be the case that, in these island communities, the personal opinions and prejudices of the people concerned could count for more than the letter of the law, and their approval must be sought, whether they were relatives, like the speaker's brother-in-law Sopolis (38–41), or members of a jury (Aeginetan in this case). His speech recognizes this special need, and the **narratives** (5–14, 18–29) which form the backbone of the speech tell how he earned his adoption by his devotion to Thrasylochus; and it concludes by reminding the jury of the wishes of the members of

---

similar law obtained on Aegina, Ceos, and Siphnos (12–15), but perhaps custom and precedent limited its application.

230 34: οὐ μέντοι καλῶς οὐδ' ὀρθῶς φασὶν αὐτὰς [τὰς διαθήκας] ἔχειν.

231 2: unlike most other litigants, but like Lysias' Mantitheus (16. 1) and his Invalid (24. 1), he is 'almost grateful' to his opponents, and expects to be deemed 'worthy of an even greater reward'. The opponents have not, apparently, disputed the validity of the adoption on the statutory grounds of the adopter's madness, senility, subjection to duress or the influence of a woman (on which see MacDowell *LCA* 101).

his family and their descendants (47–8), but at the same time reaffirming that the law is on his side and should be upheld (49–51). The high moral tone of the speech led Blass to describe it as *ein epideiktisches Kunstwerk*, and to deny it the character of a genuine court-speech. Yet he also notes that Isaeus adopted its technique of divided narrative. Thus it seems to foreshadow trends in both Isocrates' own development and in that of the genre of forensic oratory.

20 *Against Lochites*

From what may well have been a routine case of assault, this concluding fragment of the prosecution (introduction, narrative, and proof are all missing) amplifies and politicizes the crime. Lochites, a young aristocrat, had struck the prosecutor, who styles himself 'poor and a man of the people' (19). Contempt for the law, in its extreme form, could lead to oligarchic revolution (10), as it has done in recent Athenian history.[232] This is the strongest example of the rhetorical magnification that is applied to the subjects of the case. Among the others, the assault itself is an example of *hybris*, which is not like other offences but a *koinon pragma*, a matter of concern to the community as a whole, and uniquely abominated (2, 15). The injury suffered is not merely physical, but involves humiliation and dishonour (5). Thus far there is nothing very novel: but the hyperbole that follows certainly is (6). *Hybris* should excite the same indignation as theft or even sacrilege (*hierosylia*). The political overtones also serve to amplify the charge: in 12–13, the impression is created of revolutionary forces still at work; and they are present again in the concluding sections, where the jury is urged to resist the threat posed to their democratic rights by people who break the law.

On the evidence of these six speeches, Isocrates could have continued his logographic career with considerable success. He has shown himself to be an intelligent if not particularly inventive speechwriter, who knows how to use existing techniques and topoi

---

[232] Lochites was too young to have participated in the oligarchy of 404–403 (§ 11), but we are not told by how much. The reference to the destruction of the Long Walls in the same section could still have been made after their reconstruction in 393, so it does not provide a reliable *terminus ante quem*.

but does not add significantly to them. He can also write clear and effective narrative, but his attitude to it seems purely utilitarian and he does not give it a distinctive role. Individuality is to be noted in the introduction of epideictic features in Speech 16, while 19 ends with some colourful rhetoric. But the characteristic qualities of Isocratean art, which centre upon his prose style, come into their own in the longer discourses.

5

ISAEUS

Innovation in forensic oratory was difficult after Lysias. In adapting and standardizing the array of topics, formulae, and rhetorical devices which he inherited from Antiphon and the early tradition, he found effective and economical expression for them. After Lysias, the recurrence of so much material, together with a common dialect and, to a large extent, common vocabulary, tended to confer on much Attic Oratory a certain uniformity, some degree of which Isaeus could not avoid.[1] Again, the fact that his career seems to have begun as that of Lysias was nearing its end,[2] in the same city and among the same clientele, guaranteed Lysianic influence. Yet shrewd observers could discern that in Isaeus' hands the genre responded to changing times.[3] The precise forms which this response took will be the subject of this chapter; but the search for them must be preceded by some essential facts about the orator.

Very little of significance is known about him.[4] The dominant fact in the biographical tradition of Isaeus is his connection with Demosthenes, who engaged him as a full-time private tutor in preparation for his lawsuits against his fraudulent guardians. This tradition had several consequences, including perhaps the selection of his speeches made by the Hellenistic librarians. It is clear from fragments that Isaeus wrote speeches for a variety of types of

[1] Awareness of this tendency may lie behind the observation of Dionysius of Halicarnassus (*Isaeus* 2) that Isaeus 'modelled his style upon that of Lysias, and anyone who was unfamiliar with the two orators . . . would find many of their speeches difficult to assign to the right author'.

[2] Isaeus' earliest datable extant speech is 5 (390/89 BC); Lysias' latest is 26 (382 BC, see Dover *LCL* 44).

[3] See esp. Blass *AB* ii. 500, who sees 'the influences of a later period, in which the old simplicity had completely given way to modern artifice and cunning'.

[4] Jebb (*AO* ii. 262–9) makes the most of what firm information we have. For our purposes the fact that he was numbered among the first pupils of Isocrates (perhaps in 393–390) is of more interest than his disputed Chalcidian origin. Dion. Hal. *Isaeus* 1 and *Vit. X Or.* 839e–f have a common source.

lawsuit, but the eleven complete speeches which have come down
to us all concern inheritance.[5] The attitude of literary critics compounded this view of his limited function in the development of
the genre. They tended to seek, and hence to find, mainly characteristics which seemed to anticipate Demosthenic usage. On the
other hand, there is no attempt to minimize his debt to Lysias, so
these two influences compete in ancient criticism and complicate
the modern critic's task. His best course is to look to them for general guidance only, and to approach the speeches with an eye, and
an ear, for novelty in any form it may take.

An increasingly flexible attitude to the conventional division of
a speech, already to be seen occasionally in Lysias, is adopted by
Isaeus as a matter of course. Prooemia may contain some of the
conventional topoi, but speeches are sometimes launched *in medias
res* with some of the main statements of a case. Narratives have
become mostly brief and multiple, the purpose of each being not
so much to tell a story which creates an atmosphere and constructs
a picture of character, as to provide the essential material for proof,
which tends to follow piecemeal in a succinct and a forceful form
which has original features, as will be shown. Finally, one can usually be sure that there are good strategic or tactical reasons for the
chosen form of attack or defence: Isaeus' reputation for cleverness,
which could include dissimulation and misrepresentation, was
probably well deserved.[6] The first speech in the corpus combines
these with most of his other qualities to a remarkable degree.[7]

---

[5] The longest fragment, known as Speech 12, *For Euphiletus* and preserved by Dionysius,
concerns the rights of citizenship. Adoption is involved in all the other speeches except 8,
hence L. Rubinstein, *Adoption in IV Century Athens* (Copenhagen, 1993) becomes a major
source beside the earlier authorities.

[6] Dionysius' characterization (*Isaeus* 3–4) both dwells specifically on Isaeus' rhetorical
artifice (3: [σύνθεσις] περιεργοτέρα τις καὶ σχηματισμοῖς διειλημμένη ποικίλοις
. . . δεινότητι τῆς κατασκευῆς), mentioning in particular his skill in argumentation and
emotional appeal (3: μέχρι πολλοῦ προάγει τὰς τῶν ἐπιχειρημάτων ἐξεργασίας
σχημάτων τε μεταβολαῖς ἐναγωνίων καὶ παθητικῶν ποικίλλει τοὺς λόγους); and
underlines his willingness to use all means, fair or otherwise, to win—'blackening his opponent's character and out-generalling the jury' (πρὸς μὲν τὸν ἀντίδικον διαπονηρεύεται,
τοὺς δὲ δικαστὰς καταστρατηγεῖ). But some modern critics may have accepted the latter judgement too readily. Harrison (*LA* i. 122 n.) rightly disapproves of the scepticism frequently expressed by Wyse in his great edition regarding factual statements about the laws
in Isaeus. The orator was too careful to rely routinely on blatant falsehood. His 'reputation
for chicanery and deception among his contemporaries, and for being clever at devising
speeches for the worse cause' (Dion. Hal. loc. cit.) was earned purely by his technical skills.
Lysias, no less adept at deceit, escapes critical censure by parading his skills less overtly.

[7] Chronological order is followed, as far as this can be established, but the first and third

1 On the Estate of Cleonymus

This speech affords immediate illustration of Isaeus' methods. Having no issue, Cleonymus had left his estate to certain relatives. The will, though made some years earlier, was undoubtedly authentic. Yet the claimants, his nephews, have the boldness to state at the outset that Cleonymus bequeathed his property to them in his lifetime.[8] This head-on assault[9] characterizes the speakers as victims, suddenly deprived of their patrimony by shameless relatives and forced to come forward from a retiring life to contest their rights in court. Already the required ingredients are there: the statement that the speakers were brought up in Cleonymus' house, and forms of protestation,[10] whose presence in numbers is a feature of shaky cases. Having appeared in summary form in the opening sections (1–2), the initial falsehood is repeated (3), further unconfirmed claims are added, and the protestation amplified (5–8) with more elaborate references to the shamelessness of their opponents, with a new, altruistic twist to the old topos of the undesirability of litigation between kinsmen (6):

I regard it as the worst thing about my present troubles, not that I am being unjustly placed in danger, but that I am in dispute with kinsmen, against whom even to defend oneself is not good; for I should not regard it as a less unfortunate act to injure them, my relatives, in my own defence, than to have been the original victim of injury at their hands.

With this Isaeus immediately contrasts the attitude of the opponent—vengeful, shameless, and greedy. He has crammed a lot into

---

speeches provide no information whatsoever as to their dates. On the various methods that have been used to try to date the speeches, see R. F. Wevers, *Isaeus: Chronology, Prosopography and Social History* (The Hague, 1969), 9–33.

[8] ἐκεῖνος γὰρ ζῶν μὲν ἡμῖν κατέλιπε τὴν οὐσίαν. Some editors, finding such boldness incredible, have amended κατέλιπε to conative imperfect κατέλειπε ('tried to . . . wished to . . . '). But Isaeus is typically committing a petitio principii, presenting as a fact what he hopes to prove by subsequent argument.

[9] An alternative opening to the conventional, more leisurely prooemium (see Andoc. 2 *Ret.*). The word ἔφοδος was used, perhaps in the 4th cent., to describe it, and Isaeus was an exponent of it, according to Dionysius (*Isaeus* 3). In *Rhet. ad Herenn.* 1. 4. 6, 1. 6. 9 it is, I think misleadingly, identified with *insinuatio*, the 'subtle approach', which 'steals into the mind of the hearer by circuitous dissimulation' (Cic. *Inv.* 1. 20); though the purpose and the effect are likely to be the same.

[10] 2: 'Our opponents have become so shameless that they are seeking to deprive us even of our inheritance—not because they are ignorant of what is just, but because they are fully aware that we are helpless.'

this **prooemium** (1–8), stating and restating his main claim and characterizing his client and his opponents.

His next task is to explain how the 'wrong' will came into existence. Cleonymus made it because of enmity with the speakers' uncle, Deinias, and fearing that the latter would obtain control of his estate if he should die before they reached adulthood. They go to some lengths (11–12) to affirm that Cleonymus' hatred was against Deinias, not them. This is followed by positive evidence of Cleonymus' regard for them (12): 'He took us into his house and brought us up, and rescued our property when our creditors were scheming against it.' The narrative is suspended at this point, giving way to the main argument on which they base their claim (13): 'It is from these acts rather than from the will that his intention should be discerned.' Of this Wyse (197) rightly says: 'The reasoning is sophistical.' Cleonymus' kind treatment of them could equally be interpreted as compensation for not making them his heirs. However, Isaeus does not rely exclusively on it, but returns to more 'facts'. The narrative resumes (14) with Cleonymus' deathbed attempt to change his will. The incompleteness of the account is deliberately designed to reflect maximum discredit on Poseidippus, one of the present beneficiaries who is made both to disobey the dying man's order to fetch the official, and to send away an official who had come.

Having made the most of the circumstantial facts that he alleges, Isaeus summarizes his line of argument (17):

I think, gentlemen, that in any dispute about an inheritance, if the claimants can prove, as we can, that they are closer both in relationship and affection to the deceased, all other arguments are superfluous.

The idea that subjective argument has greater validity than objective fact is applied again and again in this speech. In the following section (18–21) the topic is probability (*eikos*), and it is instructive to see Isaeus' individual way of handling it. The opponents have claimed that Cleonymus sent for the magistrate in order to correct his will, while still confirming it in their favour. Isaeus contrasts the probabilities (18):

Now consider which is the more likely, that Cleonymus, having become friendly towards us, wished to cancel a will which he had made in anger, or that he was devising a more secure way of depriving us of his property?

Then he underlines the contrast by referring to the normal behaviour of men in such circumstances (19):

All other men repent of wrongs they have done to their relatives in moments of anger: Cleonymus is represented by my opponents as wanting, when he was on terms of the closest affection with us, still further to confirm the will which he made in anger.

He then goes on to say that such behaviour on Cleonymus' part would indicate that he was mad, adding that the death of Deinias, the object of his enmity, made it even more illogical.[11]

He now proceeds to draw probabilities from his opponents' behaviour (22–3). If, as they allege, Cleonymus summoned the official in order to confirm the will in their favour, why did they turn him away? Here Isaeus adds the idea of risking Cleonymus' anger, actually assuming the role which the opponents had made for themselves and following it through to its logically absurd conclusion—'they preferred to incur his enmity rather than secure this inheritance' (22). Turning from their behaviour to their version of Cleonymus' intention (to 'amend' (epanorthosai) the will), he points out that it was already complete.[12] 'Amendment' could only mean the alteration of a will with which he was dissatisfied (26).

At this stage the jury will have been impressed by Isaeus' relentless rational assault on the different angles of the case, but an injection of emotion is needed for the sake of emphasis or variety. This comes (26–9) in an attack on the sheer effrontery of the opponents.[13] This was no doubt effective on its own, but also makes them receptive to a possibly dubious allegation, that Cleonymus had recently quarrelled with the speakers' opponents (31–2). This seems a rather late point at which to introduce such an important piece of evidence. In Lysias one can be sure that it would have been a prominent item in the original narrative. For Isaeus it provides a

---

[11] These arguments illustrate Isaeus' multiple approach, an idiosyncratic technique which may lie behind the distinction drawn by Dionysius in *Isaeus* 16, when he says that Lysias uses the enthymeme, whereas Isaeus favours the epicheireme. In Dionysius the contrast is between 'thorough exposition instead of brevity, of detail rather than outline, of greater amplification and exaggeration of the facts'. In practical application, the first of the above probabilities would have sufficed in Lysias, but Isaeus follows it with a generalization and a reference to time, which enhances the improbability.

[12] 24: οὗτος ὅρος ἐστὶν τῶν δωρεῶν ('This meets every definition of a bequest'). The language of logic—the will is unambiguous, and fully realizes the intention of the testator.

[13] 26: καίτοι σκοπεῖτε ... τὴν ἀναισχυντίαν αὐτῶν ... 27 ἔτι τοίνυν τούτων ἁπάντων ἀναιδέστατος ... 28 πάντων δ' ἂν εἴη θαυμασιώτατον ... 29 ... ἀλλὰ ταῦτα μὲν, ὦ ἄνδρες, πολλὴν ἀπιστίαν ἔχει. 28 also contains a good comparative argument.

new impetus, and is assumed to be a fact in the rest of the speech,
along with the idea that Cleonymus 'rejected' (35: *apedokimasen*, a
word with a decisive legal connotation) his original will. The
speaker's assumption henceforth is that the validity of the will has
been totally undermined. The argument now proceeds as if the case
was one of intestacy. In such cases, the question of greater affinity is
paramount, and in the present one the speaker can argue both closer
kinship and closer ties of affection. Isaeus pointedly imagines the
opponents admitting this,[14] and in the pathetic paradox which follows[15] kinship and friendship are the only factors considered.

Another even more telling paradox rounds off the next argument, in which Isaeus seems not only to be attacking the laws of
testacy themselves, at least by implication, but also introducing the
concept of equity. Having drawn attention to the obligation which
next-of-kin have to care for old or indigent relatives,[16] he says (40):

> Your verdict will be neither just, nor in your own interest, nor in accor-
> dance with the laws, if you are going to force men's closest relatives to
> share in their misfortunes, but, when money has been left, to allow any-
> one rather than them the right to possess it.[17]

A subtle shift in approach to the jury is discernible in the sequel.
He appeals both to their power and their good sense: 'You should,
and indeed you do,[18] give your verdicts in favour of affinity . . .
you all know what family relationship is, and cannot be deceived
as to its nature . . . ' The section is rounded off (43) with the third
statement that Cleonymus cancelled his will, this time with an
antithesis in reverse chronological order: 'He revoked it when in
his right mind, but made it in anger.' This sets the stamp of finality
on the revocation.

In the short **epilogue** (48–51) there is no conventional summary. Instead Isaeus reintroduces the idea that the opponents'

---

[14] 37: ἀγχιστείαν . . . φιλίαν . . . ὥστ᾽ οὐ χρὴ παρ᾽ ἡμῶν, ἀλλὰ παρ᾽αὐτῶν τούτων
πυνθάνεσθαι τὸ δίκαιον.

[15] 38: πάντων δ᾽ εἴη δεινότατον, εἰ . . .

[16] 39: this was enshrined in Solonian law (Aristoph. *Birds* 1354; Dem. 24 *Ag. Timocr.* 103;
Lys. 13 *Ag. Agorat.* 91). See Rubinstein, *Adoption*, 64–8.

[17] The arguments in 44–7 explore further the question of equity, using hypothesis and
reversal: 'If Cleonymus had survived and the speakers died . . . If Pherenicus or one of his
brothers had died . . . '

[18] Aristophanes' comic portrayal of the power of juries in *Wasps* 546 should not be taken
at face value, but they could clearly override the authority of a will if they thought it was a
forgery or the product of any other irregularity. (Cf. Aristot. *Prob.* 29. 3 950^{b}6.)

claims would convict Cleonymus of insanity. This might be effective as a final plea to a jury who did not wish to damn the memory
of a dead man. But Isaeus also gives the game away at last when he
says that Cleonymus 'wished to revoke the will' (50). The speech
concludes with a dilemmaton (50) followed by a pathetic paradox
(51). It is perhaps Isaeus' most resourceful, not to say unscrupulous
speech, displaying most of his characteristics of insistent logic, with
arguments rammed home by frequent repetition, and inconvenient
facts marginalized or depreciated. Stylistically it lacks some of his
trademarks, but these will become apparent in other speeches.

5 *The Estate of Dicaeogenes*

The family at the centre of this case was wealthy and distinguished.
The first Dicaeogenes had been a general, the second a trierarch,
killed at Cnidus in 411 BC. It is with the character and behaviour of
the third Dicaeogenes that Isaeus is concerned in this, the earliest
datable speech in the Corpus (389 BC). Two related difficulties
faced his opponents, the claimants. The first, shared by other clients
of Isaeus in the extant speeches, was the existence of heiresses.
Dicaeogenes II had four married sisters, three with issue. Now he
had bequeathed two-thirds of the estate to them equally, and the
remaining third to a son of his aunt by a certain Proxenus of
Aphidna, who had held the office of Hellenotamias in 410/9. This
was Dicaeogenes III. The other difficulty was simply the passage of
time, which worked in favour of the plans of this latter crafty oper-
ator. The original settlement lasted for twelve years, but during that
time one of the heiresses died and two of the others were widowed.
Dicaeogenes III had bided his time to good effect: heiresses without husbands were vulnerable. He now produced a will which gave
him the whole estate, and fortune seemed to aid him further when
Polyaratus, husband of the eldest heiress, died before he could contest it. Time continued to favour him: another ten years passed
before a new generation of contestants could come of age. When
one of these, Menexenus II,[19] son of Cephisophon by the third
heiress, seemed likely to succeed, Dicaeogenes offered to settle
with him, but failed to carry out his agreement. This dereliction

[19] This is the Menexenus III of Wyse's account. His Menexenus II is a son of
Dicaeogenes III who plays no part in the case. Menexenus III, the speaker in my account,
is Menexenus IV in Wyse.

was a signal for full litigation against Dicaeogenes by the claimants: their spokesman was Menexenus III, his speechwriter Isaeus.

The speech begins with the briefest statement of the situation,[20] such as in most previous speeches would have come at the end of a conventional prooemium. But it does contain a hypothetical inversion,[21] one of the regular constructions in earlier (and later) prooemia. No less strikingly abrupt is the early introduction of *atechnoi pisteis*, here witnesses as to the fact of Dicaeogenes' agreement with his co-heirs. Here we learn that the action is technically against Leochares, Dicaeogenes' surety, and that he intends to treat the question of the inheritance 'from the beginning' (5). Whether or not this was Leochares' intention,[22] it gave Isaeus the opportunity he wanted to examine the activities of Dicaeogenes over a long period, and to build up the most damaging portrait of the man and his character. Why did Isaeus see this as his best line of attack? One might have thought that discrediting the second will, by which Dicaeogenes had claimed the whole estate, would have produced a decisive result. Indeed, we are told that the witnesses to it were convicted of perjury (15). Yet in the initial narrative no mention of it is made at the point where it should have been expected (7–8).[23] We are not being told everything we need to know about the second will or about some other means by which Dicaeogenes had been able to hang on to his initial gains. This ability is evidently strong enough to have persuaded Isaeus to utilize it by a process of perversion and degradation: to show that all his actions are those of a morally corrupt character. But initially he is seen as mad (8). Then his action in expelling his relatives from their property is described, together with its moral implications in order to underline his callousness (10):

He was at once these people's guardian, master, and legal opponent, and they met with not the slightest degree of pity from him through their rela-

---

[20] Blass (*AB* ii. 522 n. 3) calls it 'a kind of προκατασκευή'.

[21] Οἰόμεθα μέν ... ἐπειδὴ δέ ...

[22] The device of procatalepsis (anticipation). Material for this may have been presented at the preliminary hearing (anacrisis), at which litigants learned, in outline, the content of their opponents' case. (See Harrison *LA* ii. 94–105 for a full account of the evidence for anacrisis.) Its rhetorical possibilities included attributing to them weak material which could be triumphantly demolished; and, as here, one litigant's 'intention' could be used by his opponent to justify a scale of treatment which suits his purposes.

[23] Dicaeogenes is merely described as making a claim for the whole estate, *alleging* that he had been adopted as sole heir by the claimants' uncle (ἠμφισβήτει ἡμῖν ἅπαντος τοῦ κλήρου, φάσκων ἐφ' ὅλῃ ποιηθῆναι ὑπὸ τοῦ θείου τοῦ ἡμετέρου).

tionship, but were rendered orphans, bereft and penniless, and wanting even in life's daily necessities. This is how Dicaeogenes here, their nearest kinsman, discharged his duties as their guardian.[24]

This section, which Isaeus admits to be a digression (12), is rounded off with an extreme example of Dicaeogenes' *hybris* (11):

He added insult to injury by reproaching and criticizing him for wearing heavy shoes and a coarse cloak, as though it was Cephisodotus who was wronging him by wearing such shoes, and not he who was wronging Cephisodotus by having reduced him to poverty by robbing him of his property.

This incident adds a new and cruel twist to an old sentiment—that a fortunate man should never upbraid a fellow-human with his misfortune because fortune is fickle[25]—since here the upbraider has himself been responsible for the other's misfortune.

The broken narrative resumes (12). Menexenus II,[26] who had been pursuing his own claim independently, was finally outwitted by Dicaeogenes III, and now once more made common cause with his cousins, including the speaker. The account of how Dicaeogenes' witnesses to the second will were discredited, and how Leochares intervened on his behalf to block the adjudication of the estate to the claimants, is straightforward (12–18) and shortened with paraleipsis (17). Before proceeding with a more ample vituperation of Dicaeogenes, Isaeus prepares for maximum effect by a portrayal of the claimants as moderate men.[27] All Dicaeogenes' actions are interpreted, with the aid of *eikos*, as attempts to delay compliance with his agreements, and he is represented as lying and prevaricating at every turn. His success is explained by his very unscrupulousness.[28]

---

[24] Damaging comment continues in the sequel: καὶ ὃ πάντων δεινότατον . . . εἰς τοῦτο ὕβρεως καὶ μιαρίας ἀφίκετο.

[25] See Dover *GPM* 269.

[26] Isaeus sums up his actions unsympathetically with a neat chiasmus, 14: ἀφεὶς γὰρ τοὺς μάρτυρας καὶ ἡμᾶς προδοὺς ('he let off the accused witnesses and abandoned us' (i.e. he failed to pursue his suit against Dicaeogenes following the offer of an out-of-court settlement)).

[27] 19: 'Having been thus treated by Leochares, though it was within our power to have him deprived of civil rights, having obtained against him a conviction for perjury, we chose not to do so, but were satisfied to recover what was ours and be done with him. But having behaved thus towards Leochares and Dicaeogenes, we were tricked by them, gentlemen . . .'

[28] 23: οὐκ ἄν ποτε οἰόμενοι αὐτὸν ἐναντία οἷς ὡμολόγησε πρᾶξαι . . . 24: . . . ἀπῄειν ὑβρισμένος ὑπὸ τοῦ Δικαιογένους.

In the following sections Isaeus provides further instances of
Dicaeogenes' disregard for agreements, but his account contains
indications of a difficulty which his clients have created for themselves in their dealings with him. The rhetoric reflects their frustration (25):[29]

Our opponents endorse those parts of the agreement they made when
they are to their advantage, even if they are not in writing, but they deny
the validity of what is contrary to their interests unless it is in writing.

It is significant that agreement in writing is not mentioned in other
transactions in which Dicaeogenes or his associate Leochares (27)
defaulted. This makes the claimants seem trusting, but perhaps too
much so. They also excused Dicaeogenes payment of revenue due
to them from the property in consideration of liturgies which his
extra wealth obliged him to perform.[30] The contrast of character
that is being built up between the claimants and the defendant
reaches a climax in a general antithesis in 30,[31] followed by further
examples of their forbearance.

Isaeus sets about drawing the essential strands of his case together
in 34. As Leochares is technically the defendant, a final attack on
him is essential. The questions to the jury and the emotional plea
are conventional, but the bold use of the word *katepsephisato* ('condemned'), when the action was one of failing in support (i.e. condemning by silence) is characteristic of this orator. But the main
attack is on the character of Dicaeogenes (35–47), strategically
placed towards the end so that it will be freshest in the jury's memory. It is one of the longest, bitterest, and most comprehensive in
Attic oratory, as well as being one of the earliest: there is nothing
to compare with it in Lysias. It is divided into public and private
misdeeds. Isaeus tries to turn his portrayal of him as a reluctant and
half-hearted discharger of his civic duties,[32] characteristically
defaulting when he could (38), to serve his clients' case by means

---

[29] Symploke (ἃ μὲν . . . γέγραπται, ἃ δὲ . . . γέγραπται) followed by a fortiori argument (26).

[30] This accords with the character of *metrioi politai* which they have given themselves.

[31] 'When earlier we had the power to punish Dicaeogenes and deprive him of what he
had, we chose not to take anything belonging to him but were satisfied merely to recover
what was our own. He, on the other hand, when he had us in his power, stripped us of what
he could and tried to ruin us, as if we were his enemies and not his relatives.'

[32] From the fact that the choruses which he financed came fourth and last in their con-
tests (36), it is to be deduced that he paid the lowest prices for poor trainers, and/or engaged
them for the shortest time.

of a comparative argument (38): 'Indeed, gentlemen, how should there be any surprise that he tricked me, a single citizen, when he acted in this way towards all of you in the assembly?' This acts as a link between the two parts of the invective.[33] An account of Dicaeogenes' treatment of his relations and friends follows (39–40), then full force is given to the final assault, firstly by recounting the patriotic deeds of the forefathers whose property Dicaeogenes has despoiled,[34] then by turning on Dicaeogenes himself with a dramatic apostrophe (43):

It is the property of these men, Dicaeogenes, that you inherited and have wickedly squandered, and having cashed it you now plead poverty. On what did you spend it? For you have obviously not spent anything on the city or your friends.

The concluding sections are coloured with rich vocabulary[35] and sharp interrogation[36] with hypophora.[37] Most unusually, and here for the first time, the apostrophe is maintained to the very end, as the speaker denies Dicaeogenes any share in the glory he might claim from his ancestor Harmodius, which he has repudiated by joining the claimants' family in order to steal their money. Isaeus shrewdly realizes that a conventional epilogue would blunt the impact of this fierce attack, so he eschews it altogether.

As has been suggested earlier, there are enough clues in the speech to indicate that Dicaeogenes has somehow managed, in spite of morally reprehensible behaviour towards his relative, to avoid serious infringements of the law, and even at times to use it to his advantage. In those circumstances Isaeus' best recourse has been to excite the jury's personal prejudice against him so that they will take the most serious possible view of his misdemeanours.

---

[33] For this type of comparative argument (one against many), cf. Lys. 24 *Inv.* 22.

[34] The passage (41–3) has a certain old-fashioned dignity (e.g. the use of τοῦτο μὲν ... τοῦτο δέ, and chiasmus: πάσας μὲν χορηγίας ἐχορήγησαν, εἰσήνεγκαν δὲ εἰς τὸν πόλεμον χρήματα πολλὰ ὑμῖν, and the final assault).

[35] 43: καθιπποτρόφηκας ... κατεζευγοτρόφηκας ... 44: καλινδεῖται.

[36] 45: διὰ τί οὖν ἀξιώσεις σου τοὺς δικαστὰς ἀποψηφίσασθαι, ὦ Δικαιόγενες;

[37] A more complex variant of the conventional hypophora, beginning with an alternative question and ending in a sentence with a repeated key phrase, 45: πότερον ὅτι ... λελῃτούργηκας ... καὶ ... ἐποίησας; ἢ ὡς ... εἰργάσω, καὶ ... ὠφέληκας; ἀλλ' οὐδέν σοι τούτων πέπρακται. 46: ἀλλ' ὡς στρατιώτης ἀγαθός; ἀλλ' οὐκ ἐστράτευσαι ... πολίτης ὢν οὐδ' ἐστράτευσαι.

10 *On the Estate of Aristarchus*

After the vigorous rhetoric of the previous speech, the next, in
probable chronological order[38] breaks little or no new literary
ground. The **prooemium** is packed with commonplaces
('unequal terms', 'inexperience of the speaker', 'preparation and
cleverness of adversary', 'reluctant litigation'). There is also a hypothetical inversion[39] and a commonplace transitional phrase[40] leading to the **narrative** (4–6), in which the circumstances of the case
are explained quite straightforwardly.

At the centre of the case is an heiress, the mother of the speaker.
She had inherited the estate of her father Aristarchus after the
deaths of her brother Demochares and her sister (unnamed). She
also had a surviving brother, Cyronides, but he had been adopted
by his maternal grandfather, Xenainetus, and so passed out of the
immediate family of Aristarchus, and hence out of contention for
his estate. But certain key figures had their own designs. Of these
probably the most influential was Aristomenes, brother of
Aristarchus. He had assumed guardianship of the estate on his
brother's death. The fact that he did not claim the heiress in marriage, as he should have been expected to do according to normal
practice, suggests that machinations of some kind were afoot.[41]
Aristomenes did two things to weaken her claim to the estate: he
married her to a husband outside the family, and married his own
daughter to Cyronides, to whom he gave control of the estate. His
family's hold on it was maintained by the registration, after
Cyronides' death, of the latter's second son, Aristarchus II, as the
posthumously adopted son of Aristarchus. The speaker's difficulty
is compounded by three facts: that Cyronides had actually paid
some debts owed from the estate; that the posthumous adoption of
Aristarchus II had been officially confirmed by the relevant archon;
and that its effect was to nullify his standing as the grandson of
Aristarchus. His strongest line is to insist that Cyronides, by his
withdrawal from the family, had forfeited irrevocably his right to

---

[38] Speech 10 seems to have been delivered during the period 378–371 (so Wyse, Jebb,
Forster, and Wevers, relying on an apparent reference to the Theban War as in progress in
§ 22).

[39] 1: ἐβουλόμην . . . νῦν δέ: a very common *schema* in prooemia from earliest oratory.

[40] § 3: πειράσομαι διδάσκειν.

[41] Marriage would not realize his aim, since the estate would pass to her children; though
presumably he could ensure that she remained childless.

the estate. This he does, stating the legal position without embell-
ishment (8–10);[42] likewise with the adoption of Aristarchus II
(9–10). Emotion hardly breaks the surface of his flat statements as
its illegality is argued.[43] But the section ends vigorously enough as
the speaker confidently challenges his opponents to point to a law
which supports their claim.[44]

He then (15) notes that his opponents have resorted to argument
as well as the laws, and suggests that this indicates diffidence. This
is the first extant example of the use of entechnoi pisteis being
interpreted as a sign of weakness, though it is easy to imagine that
orators might have argued thus on more than one occasion. Here
the speaker counters his opponents' probabilities with an improbability—that they would have arranged an adoption into an insolvent family. But he has yet to deal with what may have been his
greatest difficulty—the lapse of time between the alleged usurpa-
tion of the estate and the present claim. The adoption of
Aristarchus II had been allowed to stand, and he had remained in
possession of the estate until his death some time during the
Theban War (378–1). The reason which the speaker gives for this
might be calculated to win a degree of sympathy from a jury: he
says that in order for his mother to lay claim to the estate she would
have to marry back into the family; that this would mean divorcing her husband (the speaker's father (unnamed)), a course of
action which was repugnant to him because of his love for her. Yet
while approving of such devotion, the jury might still be a little
cynical, and wonder whether it was the validity of Aristarchus II's
tenure that was the real deterrent to pursuit of this claim. As an
additional difficulty, we read that the claimant had 'unfortunate
difficulties with the public treasury' (20), i.e. he had become a state
debtor, which deprived him of citizen rights, including that of litigation. He can only fall back on a plea for justice (21–2). His final

---

[42] The passage contains two items of interest to legal historians: that adoption (here *eis-
agoge* ('introduction into the deme', see Rubinstein, *Adoption*, 38–45)) is always carried out
by a will (9); that disposal of property greater than a bushel of barley is not permitted to a
minor or a woman (10). Later (12) an important law, that the property inherited by a woman
must pass ultimately to her sons, is inserted parenthetically in a pathetic paradox (θαυμαστὸν
. . . εἰσποιῆσαι), a complex variant of an established type of argument.

[43] Neither Aristarchus I nor his son Demochares could have adopted Aristarchus II: the
former because he had a legitimate son, the latter because he was too young at the time
alleged.

[44] 14: ἐγὼ μέν, ὦ ἄνδρες, σαφῶς ἐπίσταμαι ὅτι οὔτε Ξεναίνετος οὔτε ἄλλος
οὐδεὶς τῶν ἀνθρώπων ἕξει ἀποδεῖξαι . . .

effort is a contrast between his own behaviour and that of
Xenainetus, his chief opponent (25):

But I suppose it is not enough for Xenainetus to have squandered the
estate of Aristomenes in his pursuit of boys,[45] but he also assumes that he
should dispose of this estate in the same way. I, on the other hand, gentlemen of the jury, though I am short of means, endowed my sisters in
marriage, giving what I could; and conducting myself as a responsible citizen, I perform the duties assigned to me, and serve in the army: so I
demand not to be deprived of my mother's estate.

Thumbnail character-contrasts of this kind are a distinguishing
Isaean feature. The speech ends quite neatly with a conventional
summary of what the speaker claims to have proved (26).

8 On the Estate of Ciron

For this difficult case, involving much wealth (2, 25), Isaeus has
written his best speech, or at least the one most generally admired
for its rhetorical resource.[46] Few cases could have called more
urgently for the speechwriter's ingenuity. In the absence of a will,
the death of Ciron brought forth two claimants to his estate. Isaeus
supports the claim of Ciron's grandson against that of his nephew.
In a straightforward case he should have been confident of success,
as descendants preceded collaterals. But his client is the son of
Ciron's daughter, and his opponents are claiming that she was ille-
gitimate.[47] As such a claim would be difficult to prove or disprove
by direct evidence, entechnoi pisteis come into their own. These
take the form of general probabilities deduced from the behaviour
of Ciron towards the client's mother, but this defensive material is
supplemented by attack, in particular on Diocles, the brother of
Ciron's second wife, the man behind the nominal opponent. As
there are no provably damaging facts for or against his client, Isaeus
approaches the case in a leisurely manner, intent on building a
gradual picture of the relationships and personalities. This leisurely
approach becomes apparent at the outset.

---

[45] καταπεπαιδεραστηκέναι.

[46] Blass (AB ii. 555) called it 'Ein Musterstück von Isaeus' Beredsamkeit', confirming this
later by reference (558) to its use by Demosthenes and Dinarchus.

[47] The fact that the opponents appear to have made comparatively less use of arguments
based on male precedence (cf. Dem. 43 Ag. Macart. 51, where the clause κρατεῖν δὲ τοὺς
ἄρρενας καὶ τοὺς ἐκ τῶν ἀρρένων should not be read out of context) seems to establish
their relative weakness.

The **prooemium** (1–5) is one of his longest. Although, like that of Speech 10, it contains conventional topoi, they are assembled towards the end.[48] Most of what is said is designed to adumbrate the main attack. First, his client indignantly denies the opponents' claim, as being insulting to him personally, that Ciron died without legitimate issue. Secondly, he focuses on the real villain of the piece, and arch-schemer, Diocles of Phyla, who is actually in the strong position of holding the property in question. With the prothesis following (6), in which he sets out the two points which he has to prove, that his mother was the legitimate daughter of Ciron, and that descendants have precedence over collaterals, Isaeus has in effect aired the main issues twice, and given his own version of vital facts, before the main part of the speech has begun.[49]

Things all look deceptively simple in the short **narrative** (7–8). The jury are told baldly that Ciron married the speaker's grandmother, that she bore him the speaker's mother, and died after four years of marriage.[50] His mother married twice. Her first husband Nausimenes died insolvent, so Ciron did not recover the dowry of 25 minae which he had settled on her. Consequently, her dowry when she married again, to the speaker's father, was only 10 minae.[51] But the fact that Ciron dowered her twice is offered as proof that he regarded her as his legitimate daughter. As there is little more that he can say by way of proof, he turns at this point to the main possible source of direct evidence in order to show how the opponents have denied access to it. The household slaves, over whom Diocles now has control, could have testified under torture to the other's marriage and the speaker's legitimacy; but Diocles has refused the challenge (the *proklesis es basanon*). The standard

---

[48] 4: request for a fair hearing; 5: the opponents' preparations (which include false witnesses); the speaker's inexperience; flattery of the jury's fairness.

[49] As in Speech 1, Isaeus uses the prooemium to state as fact what he has to prove (1: 'For, although our grandfather Ciron did not die childless but has left us behind him, the sons of his legitimate daughter . . . ').

[50] Curiosity might be stirred by the italicized words in 7 ἐκείνη μὲν οὖν συνοικήσασα οὐ πολὺν χρόνον, τεκοῦσα τὴν ἐμὴν μητέρα, μετὰ ἐνιαυτοὺς τέτταρας τὸν βίον ἐτελεύτησεν. The verb συνοικεῖν can occur in a tragic or sympathetic sense, meaning 'she was unable to share her life with him for long'; but Isaeus could be trying to conceal something behind this usage.

[51] He cleverly represents this as cause and effect, in the same sentence (8: τὴν προῖκα οὐκ ἀπολαβὼν ὅσην ἔδωκε . . . χιλίας δραχμὰς προῖκ' ἐπιδίδωσι). Blass (AB ii. 556), noting 'the negligible size of this dowry compared with the first', assumes that the opponents would have made much of this.

inference drawn from such a refusal (11) is followed by the commonplace on the value of this type of evidence—that slaves tend to
tell the truth under torture (12). The advantage of introducing this
otherwise rather tedious material arises from the fact that the opponents have employed free men, and Isaeus can now draw an effective contrast (13):

And will my opponent, the most shameless of men, expect you to believe
his fabricated stories and lying witnesses, while he thus declines such a sure
method of proof? Our behaviour has been quite different. Since it was we
who first demanded that torture be applied in respect of the evidence
which was about to be given, and he refuses this—in these circumstances
we shall consider that you ought to believe our witnesses.

This is a good example of what ancient critics had in mind when
they contrasted the enthymeme with the epicheireme. The simple
proposition (enthymeme) is given in the first sentence. The rest of
the statement elaborates upon it and makes the whole into an
epicheireme.[52]

A concise interrogative style[53] suits the application of *eikos*-
argument to the comparative credibility of witnesses (14). But it
also enables him not to test the probability too closely. The
emphatic form adopted conceals this weakness. A contrasting style
is used as the speaker elaborates on his grandfather's behaviour
towards his grandchildren (15–16). Ciron always had them by his
side when he was performing sacrifices and ceremonies and attending festivals. Isaeus seems here to be deliberately stirring the jury's
emotion (16):

And when he sacrificed to Zeus, Guardian of the House, a ceremony to
which he was especially devoted, to which he admitted neither slaves nor
free men outside his own family, and performed all the rites himself—we
took part in it and laid our hands with his upon the victims and placed our
offering side-by-side with his, and took part in all the other rites; and he
prayed for our health and wealth, as he naturally would, being our grandfather.

The criterion of acceptance, now firmly established as a substitute
for actual evidence of the speaker's mother's legitimacy, is applied

---

52 See n. 11. For the argument, cf. Dem. 30 *Ag. Onet.* I 37–8.
53 With anaphora: τίνας εἰκὸς ... μεμαρτυρήκασι τοίνυν ἀκοὴν οὗτοι ... τίνας
εἰδέναι ... ἀνάγκη. μεμαρτυρήκασι τοίνυν ...

to the next generation, which includes his father (18–19). The argument is conducted with Isaeus' now familiar thoroughness.[54]

The first extended encounter with the villainous Diocles follows (21–4). This is a **narrative**[55] which is long enough to give an idea of his character. It tells how he tried to have the best of both worlds by avoiding the expenses of Ciron's funeral and seizing his estate. Details of the interaction between the relatives differentiate this kind of narrative from the economical recital of facts in 6–8. It is the type of narrative in which Lysias excelled: Isaeus writes in a somewhat more complex style, but finishes with imaginary live speech (24), cf. the first quotation from Andocides (1 *Myst.* 101):

Yet had I not been Ciron's grandson, he [Diocles] would never have made these arrangements with me, but would rather have said: 'Who are you? What right have you to carry out the burial? I do not know you: you shall not set foot in the house!'

Thus even Diocles himself is forced to admit the closeness of the speaker's affinity with Ciron. The state of the argument is drawn together in a series of questions (28):[56]

What should make you believe what has been said? The witnesses' evidence, I think. And why believe that? Because of the torture—that seems reasonable. But why disbelieve my opponents' statements? Because they decline to face that test—that conclusion is unavoidable. How then could anyone prove that my mother is a legitimate daughter of Ciron by any method other than that which I am following?

With the question of his mother's legitimacy thus decided, he proceeds (30) to that of descendants versus collaterals (his opponent is Ciron's nephew). The clarity of this section has led commentators to accept its main contention, that the existence of female issue did not prevent the estate from passing to descendants. But the matter might have been put beyond doubt by the citing of a specific law.[57] The section concludes with two argumentative proofs

[54] He follows the statement that his father introduced his children as born of an Athenian mother duly married, and no fellow-wardsman (*phrater*) objected (19), with a longer statement, in periodic form (καίτοι ... γνησίαν Κίρωνος) of hypothetical probability. This is another type of epicheireme.

[55] It begins with the conventional γάρ (21: ἧκον γὰρ κομιούμενος ...).

[56] This is a new variant of hypophora, with question followed by suggestion, followed by subjective comment.

[57] Wyse (609) complains of this omission. Perhaps no single law could cover the possible permutations of contending relationships. Again, female descendants came within the laws governing heiresses, who were normally married to their nearest eligible male relative, who was likely to be a collateral.

of the precedence of descendants over collaterals. The first invokes
the law: it is descendants who shoulder obligations to fathers,
mothers, and grandparents: therefore, if they can be prosecuted for
neglecting them when they are indigent, how can it be right for
others to inherit when they leave a substantial estate (32)? Very
ingenious, but Isaeus is deliberately obscuring the primary purpose
of the law, which obliged children to tend their parents in their old
age (gerotrophein, see n. 16), a physical but not necessarily a financial
provision. The second is a summary comparison, by means of questions and answers (cf. 28 (above and n. 56)), of descent and collateral relationship.[58] This leads to an a fortiori conclusion, that if a
descendant precedes a brother, he must precede a nephew (the
opponent).

The rest of the speech, one quarter of its length, concentrates on
Diocles, his devious machinations and his character. He has somehow[59] acquired physical control over the estate, and thereby has
become, in practical terms, the speaker's main adversary. Diocles
had plotted for a long time, since the deaths of his sister's sons by
Ciron. The speaker makes much of his patient deviousness, as he
bides his time until Ciron's death. Then he acts quickly.[60] He
makes sure that his nephew (the opponent) pays the funeral
expenses, as a means of confirming his claim. Here as elsewhere
Diocles is represented as playing a double game, initially demanding money from the speaker, then claiming that his nephew had
paid and 'stealthily thrusting me aside'.[61] The speaker then tells the
jury how he frustrated Diocles' plan by making sure that he and not
his opponent defrayed the expense for the ninth-day offerings, 'in
order to eradicate their sacrilege'.[62] He even enlisted the counsel of
an expert in sacred law. But Diocles has won a partial victory, and
at this stage his misdeeds may not seem to have amounted to outright criminality. It is only through exposure of his other depredations that the portrait of a professional fraudster and profiteer
emerges. These involve physical violence, including murder
(41–2). The attack on Diocles gathers momentum, and the rhetoric

---

[58] Neatly encapsulated thus (33): ἡ μὲν γὰρ ἐξ ἐκείνου γέγονεν, ὁ δὲ μετ' ἐκείνου.
[59] 'He gradually persuaded Ciron to let him handle his financial affairs and manage his
real property, cajoling the old man by his attentions and flattery until he had the whole estate
in his grasp' (37).
[60] Ἐπειδὴ τάχιστα ἐτελεύτησεν . . . (38).   [61] ὑποπαρωθῶν (38).
[62] ἵνα αὐτῶν ἐκκόψαιμι ταύτην τὴν ἱεροσυλίαν (39).

keeps pace.[63] The urgency of the speaker's plea becomes clear as he tells of the damage which Diocles' success would inflict on him and his family (43–4). Summary is combined with emotional appeal (45). There is no formal epilogue, but another abrupt ending, this one extraordinary in that it consists of an unadorned statement that Diocles had been taken in adultery.[64]

4 On the Estate of Nicostratus

Dating of this speech depends on the acceptance of an emendation to the text.[65] Although it is a supplementary speech by a friend of the claimants, it is not without rhetorical interest. The problems of the case, both real and contrived, arise from Nicostratus' eleven-year sojourn and death abroad. His cousins, the brothers Hagnon and Hagnotheus, are contesting the genuineness of a will produced, with witnesses, by their eventual opponent[66] Chariades. After the shortest possible introduction (hardly a prooemium) (1), the speaker explains how Chariades has tried to rebut the brothers' claim of relationship by confusing Nicostratus' identity, 'inventing another father for the dead man' (6), hoping thereby to create a diversion from their easily achieved purpose of discrediting the will (5). Through this line of argument they insist on relationship as the only valid criterion of the right to inherit, but Isaeus also has a novel way of attacking the main obstacle to success—the will itself. He does this by proposing changes to the law. Whereas the commonplace topos has previously been praise of the laws (earliest

[63] Note esp. the novel elaborated form of hypostasis in 43: Οὕτω τοίνυν ἀσελγὴς ὢν καὶ βίαιος . . . οὐκ ἀγαπᾷ . . . ἀλλ' . . . ἥκει . . . ἀποστερήσων . . . εἰς κινδύνους καθίστησιν.

[64] A practical, though not a literary, explanation of this bald reference to Diocles' adultery may be the fact that a *graphe hybreos* against him was pending, his opponent's speechwriter being none other than Isaeus (Theon, *Progymn.* 1; Sp. iii. 63. 29).

[65] 7: ἐξ Ἀκῆς Valckenaer, Scheibe for ἑξάκις MSS; the reference could then be to the assembly of an army under the Persian satrap Pharnabazus for an expedition against Egypt in 374 BC (Ake = Acre, mod. Akko, on the northern coast of Israel). The emendation is accepted by Wyse (369). Blass (*AB* ii. 541) is more non-committal ('[V] perhaps correctly . . .'). Jebb (*AO* ii. 322) prefers to regard the date as 'uncertain'. C. Carey, *Trials from Classical Athens* (London and New York, 1997), 127 accepts 374 as the probable date.

[66] In 7 he describes in a series of rhetorical questions how, on hearing of Nicostratus' death abroad, many claimants appeared, with their hair cut and wearing black; how (10) these 'swooped (ᾄξαντες—a poetic word, used of the rapid descent of birds and ghosts) upon the estate of Nicostratus', some with preposterous claims (8), while Chariades bided his time. The problem of multiple claimants to estates of men who died abroad was frequent (21–2).

example: Antiphon, *Tetr*. 2. 4. 2), here he recommends alteration
of laws that have been abused (11), or rather the establishment of a
new law which gives greater precedence to proven relationships
over statements of witnesses. He justifies this proposal ingeniously
by arguing that witnesses to wills do not face the same risk of exposure, if false, as other witnesses, because their strongest potential
exposer is dead (12). Other reasons for mistrusting the use of such
witnesses are added (13–14).

There follows a discussion of the basic tenets of the law of inheritance, but it skirts around the central issue of the validity of the will
of Nicostratus until 18, when it is obliquely approached in an
examination of Chariades' behaviour towards Nicostratus during
his lifetime (distant connection), and especially after his death
(neglect of funeral rites) (18–20). The rest of the speech contains
mostly conventional material: topic of reversal (23), comparison of
character (27–9), and a concluding hypothetical inversion claiming
that his clients are not vexatious (*philopragmones*, 30). He has done
passably well with largely intractable material.

9 *On the Estate of Astyphilus*

This is another case of a contested will, inviting comparison with
Speech 1, though the claim of closer relationship advanced there
could not be used in this speech. The claimant is only a half-
brother of Astyphilus (both having as their mother the sister of
Hierocles), while the opponent, Cleon, is his cousin, and the
holder of the contested will, in which his son was adopted by
Astyphilus. The will was deposited with his uncle, Hierocles,
whom the speaker characterizes as Cleon's collaborator, though he
was not a beneficiary, nominally at any rate. The claimant's only
effective course is to prove that the will was a forgery.

The speech lacks a formal prooemium, or even an ephodos like
Speech 1. It begins with a carefully detailed **narrative**, the focus of
which is on the actions of Cleon around the time of Astyphilus'
death. The coolness of the account suggests that Isaeus may be
engaging in individual characterization of a sober, self-possessed
client, for whom also the conventional pleas associated with
prooemia would be inappropriate. The two essential points of these
opening sections (1–5) are the false concoction of the will, necessary to establish an otherwise impossible claim, and the fact that

Cleon did not conduct the funeral and other obsequies of Astyphilus.[67] But Hierocles is no less a key figure,[68] and Isaeus executes a double stroke when he says (5–6):

> On hearing this (i.e. about the will), I went to the house of Hierocles, being well aware that he was on very close terms with Cleon, though I never thought that he would dare to lie against the wishes of Astyphilus now that he was dead.

He thus both effectively dismisses the will as false, and blackens the character of Hierocles at an early stage.

Still, the claimant faces a major difficulty, which he acknowledges (7): he was abroad at vital times before and after the death of Astyphilus, and therefore has to rely on statements and behaviour of the various parties, including those hostile to his purpose. He can point to probabilities regarding Astyphilus' testatory intentions: in order to give his wishes maximum effect, he should have summoned as witnesses to his will his kinsmen, then his wardsmen, and demesmen. But the speaker is supposed to be proving that there was no will, and his statement[69] falls short of this. He does not strengthen his attack on this simple fact by saying that Astyphilus' *anangkaioi* ('close associates': Lat. *necessarii*) knew nothing about the will. Indeed, his choice of that word could suggest that some of his relatives did know about it. But this might go unnoticed in the face of this Isaean sophistry (10):

> But in my view, since the dispute is about a will and about the adoption by Astyphilus, more weight should be attached by you to the evidence of his close associates, when they state that they were not present on so important an occasion, than to those who had no connection with him testifying that they were present.

The inference is that Astyphilus is unlikely to have made a will witnessed by men outside his immediate family circle: it is a probability which a jury might consider, but, as Wyse observes,[70] he could have had good reasons for not involving them. In his usual thorough way, Isaeus adds supporting arguments: that Cleon himself

---

[67] For the conduct of a man's funeral as one of the recognized tokens of a claim to his estate, see the conduct of Diocles in Speech 8. 38–9.

[68] He is a sort of *éminence grise*, like Diocles.

[69] He can only say (9) that Astyphilus did not summon 'any of those persons' (i.e. those specified above).

[70] p. 631: 'he did not want angry scenes with jealous relatives.'

would have divulged the content of the will to secure his son's
inheritance, and that Astyphilus, if he had wanted it to remain
secret, would have used no witnesses at all; and he concludes this
section with a restatement (§ 13 = § 8).

The next attack on the will (14–15) depends on comparative
argument: why should Astyphilus make a will before departing on
a relatively less hazardous expedition, when he had not done so
before more hazardous ones? The weakness of this argument is
such that it has to be supported by a long questioning appeal for
disbelief.[71] But Isaeus returns to firmer ground with the sequel: this
may be the first example of what later rhetoricians called *Ordo
Homericus*, by which the weaker arguments were sandwiched
between stronger ones.[72] For Isaeus now turns to allege bitter
enmity (arising from a family quarrel about land, on which the
speaker does not venture to comment), between Cleon and
Astyphilus, which would establish a strong improbability that the
latter would adopt the former's son as his heir. This is the first of
two 'even greater proofs',[73] and it appears to be well-attested.
However, no attempt is made to blacken the character of Cleon. It
is against Hierocles that the fiercest fire is directed (22–5). His
forgery of the will is taken as a fact, from which imputations of
ingratitude to both Astyphilus and the speaker's father
Theophrastus, and of rapacity and conspiracy, are drawn.[74] He is
alleged (25) to have gone round offering to produce a will in favour
of anyone who was prepared to share its proceeds with him. The
need for this extreme allegation is the fact, which Isaeus cannot
deny, that Hierocles was not a beneficiary under the will in question. But even by reinforcing it with the charge of slandering the
dead (26), he cannot prove the spuriousness of the will, so he
explores another line, that of affinity. As we have seen in Speech 1,
that topic can yield some very promising rhetorical material. Here
we have the speaker's father Theophrastus cultivating Astyphilus'
estate for him (28), giving his sister in marriage (29), attending religious ceremonies with him (30), more than discharging the duties

---

[71] 15: τῷ οὖν ἂν ὑμῶν φανείη πιστὸν . . . (πῶς τοῦτον πιστὸν ἤδη;) . . .
ἐκπλεύσαντα τελευτῆσαι;

[72] The most famous example of this arrangement is Demosthenes *On the Crown*. See
Usher *GO* v. 17.

[73] 16: ἔτι μείζω τεκμήρια.

[74] Beginning with an apostrophe, 23: οὐδετέρῳ αὐτοῖν τὴν ἀξίαν χάριν ἀποδίδως·
ἐμὲ ἀποστερεῖς . . .

of a stepfather. It remains to draw a strong contrast between this relationship and that between Cleon and Astyphilus to complete the picture. This Isaeus does (31–3), summarizing and underlining earlier argument. Though typical of his method, his insistence here may be in response to a particular line taken by his opponents. Earlier (27) he has undertaken to show that, even if he had borne no relationship to Astyphilus, he has a better right to his property than his opponents. Though a recognized rhetorical figure (concession), it appears here to be offering an unnecessary hostage to fortune, unless it is designed to rebut an opponent's argument. Interest focuses on the speaker's father, Theophrastus. As Astyphilus' stepfather, he was strictly outside the immediate family, linked to it by marriage to the sister of Hierocles, widow of Euthycrates, the father of Astyphilus. In listing Theophrastus' good deeds (28–30) Isaeus has implicitly acknowledged his ambiguous status (otherwise they would be unremarkable duties). Perhaps the opposition have made even more of it, arguing to undermine the speaker's *anchisteia* ('relationship'). Hence the deployment of arguments which do not depend on it.

The **epilogue** (34–7) begins with a summary of the claims made by both sides, an unusual departure from convention. Unusual also is the appearance here rather than in the prooemium of the topos of the plea for protection against a clever speaker (35). The final emotional appeal (36–7) cleverly concentrates on sentiment rather than reason, in the form of the dishonour that would be done to the memory of Astyphilus if his wishes were flouted.[75]

6 *On the Estate of Philoctemon*

Euctemon of Cephisia was a man of great wealth who died at a great age (96) in 365/4 or 364/3. It is his estate that is the subject of this case. His three sons predeceased him, but the last to die was Philoctemon, probably around 376. Childless, like his brothers, he had adopted his sister's son Chaerestratus as heir to the estate which he assumed would be his on his father's death. The precariousness of such an arrangement is obvious in itself, but in this case it seems to have been compounded by the uncertain handling of the situation by Chaerestratus, who did not formally apply to have his

[75] For an examination of dating and prosopographical problems, see D. Welsh, 'Isaeus 9 and Astyphilus' Last Expedition', *GRBS* 32 (1991), 133–50.

inheritance confirmed.[76] It may have been his hesitation that encouraged other relatives to make their claim. These became his opponents in the present case. The names of two are given, Androcles and Antidorus (47), but their main claim is on behalf of two alleged sons of Euctemon by a second marriage. In the face of this challenge, Chaerestratus' task[77] seems clear enough: to prove the illegitimacy of these two sons. Most of his speech is directed to this end.

After a short **prooemium** (see n. 77), the **narrative** states the main facts briefly, but dwells at greater length on their interpretation and on cause and effect. Again, the simplicity[78] of the opening sentence conceals crucial questions: 'Philoctemon of Cephisia was a friend of Chaerestratus here, and died after bequeathing to him his property and adopting him as his son. Chaerestratus, in accordance with the law, claimed the estate.' We are not told at this stage that Chaerestratus' claim was made not on the death of Philoctemon, but on the death, some twenty years later, of Euctemon; and that 'the estate' in question is the whole estate of Euctemon. Yet it seems from the following narrative that the opponents are disputing the will and estate of Philoctemon, as it is of his life and arrangements for succession that we hear initially (to § 9). The central theme of this section is the spuriousness of the opponents' claim that Philoctemon did not make a legal will. But this is not the main issue of the trial, and could have served only to damage the credibility of Androcles and his friends in preparation for the real contest.

That contest begins with the introduction of the rival claimant (10), sponsored by the now discredited Androcles, whose title to the estate is challenged by the counter-claim that Euctemon was not known to have remarried and had children by that second marriage (11). This statement is intended to colour what follows, and it seems to gain authority when he describes how the claimants were unable initially to state who their mother was, and were only able to identify her as Callippe, daughter of Pistoxenus, after a

<hr/>

[76] The reason for his action, or inaction, is obscure.

[77] The present speech is actually delivered by a friend of Chaerestratus (1). The fact that this is almost the only point made in the prooemium (1–2) suggests that a previous speaker had delivered the main prooemium. For the unusual form of the pathetic paradox ἄτοπον ... γενήσεται, see Wyse. It seems slightly weak and truncated compared with most Lysianic examples.

[78] Blass (*AB* ii. 508) remarks that such a narrative style is even plainer than that of Lysias.

period of preparation.[79] But Isaeus examines her status and her age thoroughly enough for any reasonable judge to doubt whether she was ever married to Euctemon (14–16). When he turns to the latter, by seeming to look at events from the old man's point of view, he is able to impart an attractive tragic flavour to the story (18):

Euctemon lived for ninety-six years, and for most of that time was regarded as a fortunate man, since he had considerable property, and had children and a wife, and in all other respects enjoyed a reasonable degree of prosperity. In his old age, however, a serious misfortune befell him, injuring his whole house and causing him great financial loss, and setting him at variance with his nearest relatives.

Euctemon's misfortunes are recounted in a developing narrative (18–24). In his dotage, he becomes the easy dupe of one of his tenants, an ex-prostitute named Alce, who persuades him to introduce one of her sons by another man to his phratry. On being frustrated in this by his *phrateres* and by Philoctemon, he threatens to marry another woman and adopt her children. This persuades Philoctemon to acquiesce in his father's original plan regarding Alce's son, and to agree to his being settled on one of the farms in the estate.[80] The series of questions in apostrophe probe the logic of Euctemon's action from various angles, in Isaeus' characteristically thorough way (25–6).

The story is resumed after the death of Philoctemon. Euctemon makes a will confirming his agreement with Philoctemon limiting the inheritance of Alce's son, but then succumbs to a conspiracy between Alce and the speaker's opponents to carve up his own crumbling estate between them (29–30), and is persuaded to revoke the will.[81] Then, persuaded by them, he sells part of the estate to the value of three talents. Methodically and with utter callousness, they are dismantling it. As Euctemon approaches his final days, they plan their final outrage (35):

[79] This *paraskeue* enabled them to be ready with their story, 13: εὐθὺς ἔλεγον ὅτι Καλλίππη μήτηρ. But *paraskeue* is associated with falsehood (πρᾶγμα πλάττοντες ἀναιδείᾳ ὑπερβάλλον καὶ οὐδὲ γενόμενον).
[80] This was probably Philoctemon's best practical course to protect his own inheritance. He had much to lose by antagonizing his father. Euctemon appears to have controlled the whole estate, having given no part of it to Philoctemon (38), who could not legally prevent his father from making gifts to persons outside the family.
[81] Alce seems to have been the instigator: the speaker's opponents had 'fallen under her influence' (ὑποπεπτωκότες τῇ ἀνθρώπῳ).

They then immediately began plotting for the residual estate, and devised the most shocking plan of all,[82] which deserves your close attention. Seeing that Euctemon was completely worn out with age, and could not even get up from his bed, they began to look for ways of securing control of his property when he died. And what did they do? They registered these two boys (i.e. the sons of Alce) before the archon, as adopted children of the sons of Euctemon who had died,[83] naming themselves as guardians, and requesting the archon to grant a lease of the dwellings on the estate, as being the property of orphans.

This next stage in breaking up the estate and pocketing the proceeds was thwarted by some unnamed public-spirited citizens, but another opportunity, requiring quick action, came with the death of Euctemon. Isaeus makes the most of this stock situation with another of his descriptions of the behaviour of his opponents at this sensitive time (39):

> When Euctemon died, they had the audacity, even while he was lying dead in the house, to shut up the slaves, so that none of them might bring the news to his daughters or his wife or any of his relatives.

These relatives were unable to gain access to the house for two days, during which the opponents removed the furniture. The picture of the old man's house being ransacked while his body lay within it awaiting burial is one which will have stuck in the jury's mind. The narrative, by now Isaeus' longest (10–42, with short intervals), has served its purpose in characterizing the unscrupulous and unfeeling greed of his client's opponents. He now seeks further to discredit Androcles by exposing inconsistencies in his two claims. Having first attempted to register the sons of Alce as children of Philoctemon and Ergamenes (see § 35, quoted above), he now seeks to register them as sons of Euctemon. Isaeus is careful to examine and dismiss the conditions which might have made this re-adoption possible (44). Regarding the second claim, to the hand of Euctemon's daughter as an heiress to a fifth of his estate, he points out that Androcles has already testified that Euctemon has a legitimate son. The total impression is of an immoral but desperate

---

[82] πάντων δεινότατον πρᾶγμα κατεσκεύασαν.

[83] Philoctemon and Ergamenes. Although Euctemon had retained nominal control over the whole of his property, he must have made an agreement with his sons that a specified share of the estate was theirs. This seems the best way to make sense out of the reference in 38 to property owned by 'Euctemon with his son Philoctemon' (Εὐκτήμων μετὰ τοῦ υἱέος Φιλοκτήμονος).

adventurer, clutching at any means, legal or illegal, of securing a
lien on a very lucrative property. Particular point is given to it by
invoking the religious implications of a woman of Alce's reputation
entering temples and performing rites there and at the family tombs
(49–50).

The extended concluding argument (see next paragraph) begins
(51) with a weighted comparison of the merits of the two
claimants: the one a prostitute's son and the other the nephew and
legally adopted son of Philoctemon. Isaeus then shows how the
two possible arguments against Philoctemon's will—that it was illegal (52) and that it was never made (53–4)—can be rebutted. For
the latter proof he resorts to rhetoric,[84] sensing the weakness of the
argument.[85] There is some repetitive padding in these concluding
sections, most of it intended to augment the jury's indignation.
Rhetorical devices abound.[86] Not directly relevant, but performing
its usual function of persuading the jury to favour the speaker
uncritically, is the conventional recital of leitourgiai.

The **epilogue** proper begins at 62, although restatement and
summary of some of the argument in the preceding sections led
Blass (AB ii. 550) to place its beginning at 51. Now Isaeus focuses
the jury's attention[87] on the two essential questions: the opponents'
diamartyria ('protestation') against Philoctemon's will, and the legitimacy of the children whom they wish to make his heirs. That is
made to appear the logical order, since all attempts at legitimizing
and adopting new heirs fail through irrelevance if his will stands
and his chosen heir Chaerestratus is confirmed. But it does not take
account of the twenty years during which Euctemon, to greater or
lesser effect, possessed and controlled the estate after Philoctemon's
death. It is also interesting that Isaeus tries to insist on atechnoi
rather than entechnoi pisteis—the evidence of witnesses to the

---

[84] Note the live speech, and following symploke: 53 οἷς μὲν . . . μαρτυρεῖν . . . οἷς δὲ
. . . μαρτυρεῖν.

[85] While dwelling on the fact that Androcles himself was not present when Philoctemon
made his will, he ignores other possible means of his learning about it. For other criticisms
of this passage, see Wyse 538–41.

[86] Rhetorical questions (56–7); an especially effective pathetic paradox (58). Note also,
ironically, a reference to his opponents' attempts to win through by rhetoric (59), including
an occurrence, very rare in practical oratory, of a technical rhetorical term, παρεκβάσεις
('digressions').

[87] πρὸς ταύτην αὐτὸν κελεύετε τὴν ἀπολογίαν ποιεῖσθαι ('insist that he makes that
the subject of his defence'): a rare attempt by an orator to dictate his opponent's case. Cf.
Aeschin. 3 Ag. Ctes. 202, 205.

alleged marriage of Euctemon rather than rhetorical proofs, which would presumably dwell on details of his intimate relationship with Alce, and afford opportunity for emotional appeal. If he lost this case, it was not through neglecting the material available to his opponent.

11 *On the Estate of Hagnias*

Connection between this oration and Demosthenes 43 *Against Macartatus* enables the critic to see the other side of the case more clearly than usual.[88] The speaker and defendant is Theopompus, whose relatives are indirectly challenging his title to the estate by prosecuting him for the maltreatment of an orphan, the son of his brother Stratocles. Conflicting claims to the valuable estate of Hagnias (II) originated, of course, from his childlessness; thence from the heiress whom he adopted and who died. Although Hagnias had allowed for this contingency and appointed Glaucon, his uterine brother, as proximate heir, other relatives opened up the whole question of succession. The first challenge came from Hagnias' second cousin, Eubulides, and it was maintained after his death in the interest of his daughter Phylomache II by Sositheus, who claimed her hand as her closest male relative. But an array of second cousins (perhaps as many as five) lined up to contest Phylomache's title. The process by which one of these, Theopompus, emerged victorious, is obscure: the original claim of Glaucon and his immediate relatives looks stronger on paper, and Isaeus' decision to ignore that claim seems a bold and unscrupulous course. But the case, as presented, is full of unexplained difficulties. They are best confronted in an examination of the speech itself.

Instances of direct attack, dispensing with conventional preliminaries, have already been encountered in the speeches of Isaeus. The beginning of the present speech is unparalleled in Attic oratory in that it refers to and discusses laws—in this case those of succession. Having described them (1–3), the speaker applies them to the relationships in the case. His argument that the orphan son of Stratocles has no title to the inheritance under them concludes with an aggressive questioning of the opponent (5) and criticism of both

---

[88] That speech (§ 31) also provides an approximate date—361/60 or a little earlier. For a modern study, see W. E. Thompson, *De Hagniae Hereditate: An Athenian Inheritance Case* (Leiden, 1976).

his performance and his morality (6). The purpose of this unorthodox beginning is to impose upon the jury the idea that the speaker
has the law on his side before examining the details of his difficult
case. That these opening sections are technically introductory is
affirmed in 7, where the conventional topoi for ending a
prooemium appear.[89]

The impression of the speaker acting in accordance with the law
is extended into the narrative (8–10), in which Theopompus is
careful to say that he contested none of the provisions of Hagnias'
will,[90] in spite of being more closely related to him than the lega-
tee, his niece. But her death opened up the contest, which again
was taken up initially not by the speaker, but by Phylomache,
daughter of Eubulides, who had since died. Now Eubulides was
Hagnias' cousin, but through the female line (his mother was
Hagnias' aunt); whereas Theopompus was descended purely
through the male line, being the grandson of Stratius, who was the
brother of Hagnias' grandfather.[91] Once more a law is cited, this
time the one which gives precedence to male collaterals and their
male descendants, but only up to the first generation (11). He cleverly uses this stipulation to construct a comparative argument (12):

[The legislator] has placed our children outside the right of succession.
How, then, can those to whom, even if I were dead, the law does not
award the estate of Hagnias, suppose that, while I am still alive and have
a legal right to the property, they themselves have any title to it as next-
of-kin? Surely their claim is void.

The pathetic paradox which follows is unusually complex, being a
period[92] which includes an antithesis between the contending parties and comment on his opponents' conduct (13–14):

Is it not, therefore, shocking, that, whereas the laws have expressly given
me the right of inheritance but placed my opponents outside the requisite

[89] The presence of these topoi (summary of what is to be proved, and undertaking to state
the facts from the beginning) also removes any doubts about a possible missing opening.

[90] 9: ἡμεῖς δ' οὐ πώποτ' ἠξιώσαμεν ἀμφισβητῆσαι πρὸς τὰς ἐκείνου διαθήκας.

[91] However, he exaggerates his *angchisteia* by styling himself 'the son of a cousin': he is
the son of Charidemus, who is a cousin of the *father* of Hagnias, Polemon. But the word
ἀνεψιός is used of a variety of collateral relationships, so less should be made of this than is
made by Wyse (686–7).

[92] οὔκουν δεινὸν . . . governs main and subordinate clauses down to . . . 14 ἥκειν. A
further instance of Isaeus' way of complicating and augmenting standard rhetorical topoi
may be seen below (17), with hypostasis (εἰς τοσαύτας δ' ἀπορίας κατέστησαν . . . ὥστε
. . . ἐν δὲ ταῖς ἀγχιστείαις ὁμολογουμένως οὐκ ἔστιν, which contains extended
antithesis and explains precisely the difficulty of persuasion which faced his opponents.

degree of kinship, this man should dare to act the pettifogger and choose
the moment when I am laying claim to this estate, not to bring an action
against me for that, paying the required deposit, but to pursue a vexatious
suit in the name of this child and expose me to potentially great damages?

These two rhetorical arguments present Theopompus' case, thus
far, in a most persuasive form. He has followed the laws of succession to the letter, and can express justified indignation that his
opponents are not prepared to do the same. The status of the
orphaned son of Stratocles is the same as that of his own children,
for whom he will make no claim.

A **narrative** describing the actual process by which Theopompus
persuaded an earlier court of his superior claim (15–19) further
establishes the justice of that claim, and makes effective contrast
with the false allegations of collusion by his opponents, which he
refutes with a combination of counter-statement and probability-
argument (20–4).[93] This section of the speech is rounded off
(27–31) with an elaborated explanation of the opponents' failure to
litigate at an earlier time.[94] As is his way, Isaeus not merely gives
the simple reason—that they did not have a sustainable case—but
discusses in detail the priorities of the relationships. This is followed
by a summary of the position so far. It is made to seem very
straightforward: the alternatives open to the opponent are either to
claim the estate by right of kinship, or prove that the speaker agreed
to share it.

A short piece of invective (36) precedes a change of course into
mainly factual narrative which adds nothing to the legal argument
on which he has so far mainly relied. After claiming that the opponent in his speech has relied on emotional appeal, dwelling on the
orphan's poverty and Theopompus' avarice and meanness in his
dealings with the family of Stratocles, he attempts to rebut this by

[93] Note also 24 (dilemmaton followed by hypophora, a new combination): 'He declares
that I agreed, if I won my suit against the present possessors of the estate, to give the child a
half-share of the inheritance. Yet if the child had any right to a share by virtue of his relationship, as my opponent claims, what need was there for this agreement between me and
them? (25) If, on the other hand, they had no claim by right of kinship, why should I have
agreed to give them a share, when the laws have given me right of succession to the whole
estate? Was it then impossible for me to make my claim without their consent? But the law
gives free rein to anyone who wishes to make a claim, so that they could not possibly make
this allegation. Did they then have some evidence relevant to my case, without which I was
unlikely to win the adjudication of the estate? No, I was claiming by right of kinship, not
by a will, so that I had no need of witnesses.'
[94] For the raising of this question in oratory, see Usher *GO* v. 175.

giving details of their respective fortunes (40–50). From these it
emerges that Stratocles had acquired substantial additions to his patrimony from his relatives, so that its total value comfortably
exceeded that of the speaker's property, including the estate of
Hagnias, which is still subject to an adjudication. The extant text
of the speech ends with an offer to pool the estates of the speaker
and the orphaned son of Stratocles, and divide the aggregate
equally. The overall implicit argument, that a jury's decision should
be determined not only by the legalities but also by the relative fortunes of the litigants is common enough in Attic oratory, but rarely
argued in as much detail and with such vehemence as here.[95]

2 On the Estate of Menecles[96]

This and Speech 7 are among the latest surviving speeches of Isaeus,
belonging to the years 354–3. Childless by both his wives, Menecles
adopted the brother of his second wife. The adoption remained valid
until his death twenty-three years later, when it was challenged by
his own brother on the ground that the adoption had been made
'under the influence of a woman', one of three mental conditions
under which, according to Solonian law, a man's will could be challenged.[97] In his speech Isaeus includes the question of sanity which
would have been linked in the jury's mind with the main condition,
and the medium he chooses to convey the impression of a natural,
civilized, and legal course of events is narrative (3–12, 14–18), after
a short and very conventional **prooemium**.[98] The **narrative** is a bal-
ancing act of characterization and motivation. Menecles, on finding
himself childless by his second wife, decided, in his considerate way,
to arrange for her to marry Elius of Sphettus (8–9) so that she should
have the opportunity to bear children. He parts from her on friendly

[95] He alludes to his opponents' 'embezzlements' (τῶν παρακλεπτομένων, 44), to be
dealt with in a later part of the speech which has been lost, and refers to their 'slander'
(διαβολή, 47, 50) and lies (οὐκ ἄξιον τοῖς τούτου λόγοις πιστεύειν, 47).

[96] Rubinstein, *Adoption*, 33–4 begins her discussion of adoption *inter vivos* by referring to
12–14 of this speech.

[97] The other two were madness and senility according to [Aristot.] *Ath. Pol.* 35. 2, who
reports that the law was modified by the Thirty. It seems to have been restored after their
departure, with categories of disability added (Dem. 46 *Ag. Steph.* II 14, drugs, disease, and
constraint). But of these, 'influence of a woman' is surely the most interesting, modifying as
it must the conventional view of the subordinate position of women in Athenian society.

[98] The prooemium contains a hypothetical inversion Ἡγούμην μὲν ... ἐπειδὴ δέ, the
topos of reluctant prosecution, and plea for goodwill. Reference to the opponent's impiety,
which according to Wyse (236) 'strikes the keynote of the whole oration', is not distinctive.

terms. Now it is necessary to admit this in order to explain Menecles' decision to adopt her brother. But the speaker must not attribute too much mutual affection to the parting couple. The reason for his choice of her is made to appear purely logical (11):

He could find no nearer relative than us. He therefore approached us and said that he thought it right, since fate had decided that he should have no children by our sister, that he should adopt a son out of the family from which he would have wished to have a son of his own in the course of nature.

His reasoning is given extra force by live speech (12), but there is no mention of his ex-wife. Later, the whole situation is explained (19–20):

That Menecles was neither insane nor under the influence of a woman, but in his right mind when he adopted me, you can easily deduce from the following facts. In the first place, my sister, with whom my opponent's argument has been mostly concerned, and under whose influence he says Menecles adopted me, had remarried long before the adoption took place; so that, if it had been under her influence that he was adopting his son, he would have adopted one of her boys, for she has two. But gentlemen, it was not under her influence that he adopted me as his son: his chief motive was loneliness, and, secondly, the other causes I have mentioned, and the goodwill which existed between him and my father; and thirdly, because he had no other relative from whose family he might have adopted a son. These were the motives which at the time induced him to adopt me; so that it is quite clear that he was not insane or under the influence of a woman, unless my opponent wishes to describe his loneliness and childlessness in these terms.

It certainly adds conviction to the speaker's argument that he can point to more likely adoptees than himself, assuming his sister's influence over Menecles, and the introduction of her sons by Elius also marks the passage of time. Yet his failure to state precisely how long after he parted from her he adopted her brother is curious, unless he thought it immaterial, because he was quite prepared to concede that he remained on close terms with her and the rest of her family, as his adoption of her brother showed.

Turning to attack, he opens with an effective hypophora (21),[99]

---

[99] Although it is bipartite rather than tripartite, as it usually is in earlier oratory, the second part of the first pairing (the 'answer') is amplified (. . . ἄπαιδα αὐτόν καθιστάς· οὐχ οὕτως οὗτός ἐστι φιλοχρήματος). Note also the vehement challenge: δειξάτω γάρ οὗτος ὑμῖν. ἀλλ᾽ οὐκ ἄν ποτε δύναιτο.

summarily suggesting and dismissing alternative candidates for adoption by Menecles. The attack is intensified as the speaker accuses his opponent (his uncle by the adoption) of denying Menecles the right to adopt anyone through his opposition to the adoption of the only suitable heir. This portrayal of the spite[100] of his opponent is sustained, but adds nothing of substance until his motives are examined more closely (27). Here again envy (*phthonos*) is prominent, but to it is added greed, with a new account (28–34) of a quarrel between Menecles and his brother, who made a successful claim on his estate.[101] After thus reducing the speaker's inherited share to a fraction of its original size, he covets the rest. The rhetoric does not break new grounds, though the reversal of charge in § 40 (*peritrope*) is as good as may be found anywhere:

It is clear, I think, to you all that it is admitted by my opponents themselves that Menecles was not insane, but that it is much rather my opponent who is insane now when, after settling his quarrel with us and sworn oaths, he has again come forward in violation of what he has agreed and sworn, and demands that I should be deprived of these poor remnants of the estate.

This rounds off a second argument against Menecles' insanity, stronger than anything that has gone before because his opponents are his 'witnesses, not in word but in deed' (38). But the main argument here is against the unreasonable behaviour of the opponent, whose greed flouts the dying wishes of Menecles and the living obligation of the speaker. The pathetic paradox through which this is expressed is a good example of how Isaeus elaborated and refined existing rhetorical devices.[102]

Summary and entreaty make up the **epilogue** (44–7) in the usual way. His insistence of the religious duty to Menecles—not only his own but the jury's—is maintained to the end.

---

[100] 23: ἐπίφθονον πρᾶγμα καὶ οὐ δίκαιον ποιῶν.

[101] Wyse says little about the circumstances of this claim: they are best explained by E. S. Forster, *Isaeus* (Loeb; London, 1927), 38–9.

[102] 42–3: νυνὶ δὲ δεινὸν τὸ πρᾶγμα καὶ αἰσχρὸν εἶναι τῇδε νομίζω, εἰ ἡνίκα μὲν ὁ Μενεκλῆς εἶχέ τι, τότε μὲν ἔδωκα ἐμαυτὸν υἱὸν αὐτῷ ποιήσασθαι, καὶ ἀπὸ τῆς οὐσίας τῆς ἐκείνου, πρὶν πραθῆναι τὸ χωρίον, ἐγυμνασιάρχουν ἐν τῷ δήμῳ καὶ ἐφιλοτιμήθην ὡς υἱὸς ὢν ἐκείνου, καὶ τὰς στρατείας, ὅσαι ἐγένοντο ἐν τῷ χρόνῳ τούτῳ, ἐστράτευμαι ἐν τῇ φυλῇ τῇ ἐκείνου καὶ ἐν τῷ δήμῳ· ἐπειδὴ δὲ ἐκεῖνος ἐτελεύτησεν, εἰ προδώσω καὶ ἐξερημώσας αὐτοῦ τὸν οἶκον ἀπιὼν οἰχήσομαι, πῶς οὐκ ἂν δεινὸν τὸ πρᾶγμα εἶναι καὶ καταγέλαστον δοκοίη, καὶ τοῖς βουλομένοις περὶ ἐμοῦ βλασφημεῖν πολλὴν ἐξουσίαν παράσχοι;

7 *On the Estate of Apollodorus*

The speaker in this case, Thrasyllus, has a real problem. The formalities of his adoption into his deme by Apollodorus were not
completed before the latter's death, leaving his estate vulnerable to
counter-claims by relatives who were actually closer than
Thrasyllus. Isaeus tackles the problem at the outset, but in a more
oblique way than, for example, in Speech 1. As in that speech, the
usual prooemium-topics are dispensed with, but in this speech he
launches into an obfuscating comparison of two different procedures of adoption—the one in which all the formalities are
observed, and the other, when only a sealed will, made in haste, is
deposited in secret with a trusted private individual. Now he says
that it is natural for the latter procedure to attract counter-
claimants; but that his adoption had been made in the open.
However, the issue is not one of openness and secrecy, as will
emerge later, but of the completeness of the adoption procedures.
Yet the contrast will have made the jury more sympathetic to the
speaker's case when the steps toward his adoption are described in
detail (13–17). In order to explain the adoption of a comparatively
distant relative (Thrasyllus was Apollodorus' step-nephew), ties of
affection and/or debts of honour must be shown; and the medium
for this is narrative, which serves also to undermine the opponents'
claims by describing actions which illustrate the hostility that
existed between them and the testator. In this speech, the **narratives** are skilfully constructed to meet these particular requirements. They are separate, but certain figures play key parts in each.
In 5–10, the main purpose is to establish the bonds of friendship
between the testator and Archedamus, his step-uncle. But the discreditable part played at each stage by Eupolis, whose daughter was
the counter-claimant, is of no less importance, and his early actions
prepare us for the more direct portrayal of his hostile relations with
the family of Apollodorus in 11–13. Then the speaker returns to
the central question of his adoption, and this time the narrative is
unusually detailed, giving a step-by-step account of Apollodorus'
actions, beginning with the tragic frustration of his original hopes
(14):

Now Apollodorus had a son whom he brought up and cherished, as was
only natural. As long as this son lived, he hoped to make him heir to his
property. But when he fell ill and died in the month of November last

year, Apollodorus, while disheartened at his ill-fortune and repining his old age, did not forget those who had treated him kindly in earlier years. So he came to my mother, his own sister, for whom he had a greater regard than anyone else, and expressed a wish to adopt me, and asked her permission, which was granted.

We then hear how the speaker went to live with Apollodorus and managed all his affairs; how he was conducted to the family altars and to a meeting of his phratry. Isaeus gives details explaining the solemn importance of these introductions, as if to convince us that these were the only formalities that really mattered. Then, before narrating his registration with his deme (27–8, see below), Isaeus tries to weaken his opponents' position by rather complex legal arguments, whose relevance is not immediately obvious (18–26). In these sections he uses an extended comparative argument: Thrasybulus, a grandson of Eupolis, has not claimed the estate, though his title, through male precedence, is stronger than that of the claimant, the daughter of Eupolis; therefore the basis for the latter's claim must be insecure. A simple proposition (enthymeme) could be formulated thus: 'My adoption has been acknowledged by Thrasybulus, who might have a claim, but challenged by Eupolis' daughter, who has a weaker claim; therefore Eupolis' daughter should also acknowledge my adoption.' In Isaeus' hands this is amplified by citing a parallel case involving the estate of Eupolis' son (19–20), and a quotation of the law which states male precedence (20), making the whole passage into a prime example of an epicheireme. The probability that the whole proposition was legally flawed[103] may explain Isaeus' recourse to complication.

Having displayed his talent for complicated and perhaps misleading argument, Isaeus now shows how he can use narrative to the same effect (27–8). It is, as Wyse says (570), a stroke of daring to introduce members of his client's deme into his speech, as it seems clear[104] that Apollodorus had died before they could complete the formalities of adoption by admitting him into their number. Yet a listening jury might think that everything necessary had been transacted when they heard that Apollodorus 'informed his fellow demesmen that he had adopted me as his son . . . and he begged them . . . to enrol me in the public register as Thrasyllus the

---

[103] See Wyse 560–1, 565; Harrison *LA* i. 147–8. Isaeus himself provides a possible reason why Thrasybulus made no claim, even though he rejects it in a procatalepsis (23).

[104] Isaeus does not actually record the death of Apollodorus. See next note.

son of Apollodorus . . . the members . . . took the oath over the
victims and registered my name in accordance with Apollodorus'
behest'. The missing requirement was the presence of the adoptee:
he was attending the Pythian festival at Delphi, so that his deme-
registration must have been of a provisional nature, the procedure
for which is obscure. Again, the death of Apollodorus in his
absence is passed over,[105] even though it constituted the gravamen
of the whole case. This is Isaeus at his most devious.

With a neat transitional antithesis[106] he turns to argue more conventionally the improbability that Apollodorus would have left his
estate to these opponents. Generalization about the ideas that influence men as they contemplate mortality—the continuity of their
family and the conduct of their own funeral rites—is applied to the
specific behaviour of the daughters of Eupolis, one of whom is the
nominal opponent, towards their own brother (30–2).[107] He then
says more about his own proven character. Here, instead of the
usual mechanical recital of leitourgiai, he links it to that character
(34–5) and hence to the good sense of Apollodorus in choosing
him as his heir (36). There is a seamless logic to the argument, and
he reinforces it by reference to the state services of the father of
Apollodorus before concentrating, with renewed vigour, on those
of Apollodorus himself (40):

What public service did he fail to perform? To what war-tax was he not
the first to contribute? What duty has he shirked? When he organized the
boys' chorus, he was victorious, and the famous tripod still stands as a
memorial to his worthy ambition. And what is the duty of the law-abiding citizen? Was it not his duty, when others were trying to take by force
what did not belong to them, to do no such thing himself but only to try
to preserve what was his own? Is it not his duty, when the state needs
money, to be among the first to contribute and to conceal no part of his
fortune? Such a man was Apollodorus.

He then offers his own services for favourable comparison (41–2).

The **epilogue** is clearly marked (43–5), with summary of the
relationship on which the speaker bases his claim (43). Wyse (584)

---

[105] Thus 28 [Ἀπολλόδωρος] οὐκ ἐποιήσατό με ὑὸν is necessarily translated as pluper-
fect, because Apollodorus was now dead.

[106] 29: ἔχθρας μὲν παλαιᾶς αὐτῷ πρὸς τούτους οὔσης, φιλίας δὲ πρὸς ἡμᾶς καὶ
συγγενείας οὐ μικρᾶς ὑπαρχούσης: looking summarily both backward and forward. The
first example of its kind.

[107] Hence there is a comparative element in the argument: 'how much worse will their
posthumous treatment be of Apollodorus, a more distant relative'.

describes this as 'an effective piece of rhetoric',[108] and this effectiveness derives largely from the contrast between his claims and those of the opponents—not one usually made in epilogues. Wyse also pertinently notes that entry into the deme-roll is not mentioned. The speaker focuses tenaciously to the end (45) on relationship for his legal claim, and terms of intimacy for his moral claim.

3 On the Estate of Pyrrhus

According to the law, stated clearly in this speech (68), a man without sons but with daughters could leave his estate to the person of his choice only if the daughters were included.[109] Yet Pyrrhus, whose only child was a daughter, was able to leave his estate to Endius, his sister's son, whose succession was apparently not disputed and who enjoyed the estate for twenty years until his death. It is hardly surprising that the speaker, Endius' brother, makes the most of this in his concluding argument, but most of his speech is devoted to discrediting the claim of Phile, Pyrrhus' daughter, which is presented by her husband Xenocles. The validity of that claim depends on whether Pyrrhus had been legally married to her mother. It seems that the opponents had been unable to produce conclusive proof of the marriage, so the way is open for the speechwriter to dispute the question of fact with the rhetorician's standard argument, the test of probability: Was Phile's mother the sort of woman likely to have been chosen by Pyrrhus for his wife? Her brother Nicodemus is technically the defendant (4, 25), and he is facing a charge of bearing false witness (pseudomartyria), in that he testified falsely to his sister's marriage to Pyrrhus.

The opening is an example of ephodos, similar to that of Speech 1, and here as there the matter in contention is stated as fact: Pyrrhus was 'without legitimate children'.[110] There is no true prooemium: the speech moves straight into an account of the

---

[108] Blass (AB ii. 555) also notes the 'epideictic ornament', of which antithesis is a major component. § 44, a period with multiple οὐκ ... ἀλλά antithesis with parisosis, shows strong Isocratean affinities.

[109] σὺν ταύταις: cf. 42 οὔτε δοῦναι οὐδενὶ οὐδὲν ἔξεστιν τῶν ἑαυτοῦ ἄνευ τῶν θυγατέρων. This meant that the adoptee had to marry the daughter, or, if there were more than one, provide for them from the estate, including possibly a dowry for them when they married. See Rubinstein, Adoption, 92.

[110] 1: ἄπαις γνησίων παίδων.

claims lodged by the opponents after the death of Endius, which
led to successful charges of false witness against both claimants, of
whom Phile's husband Xenocles, who had attested her legitimacy,
was convicted of perjury (3), while Nicodemus, who attested his
sister's marriage to Pyrrhus, was discredited through the condemnation of one of his witnesses (4).[111] The series of questions which
follows (8–10) describes the normal steps taken by or for a recent
widow—recovery of her dowry, arrangements for her maintenance or for her remarriage—and asks why none of these was followed in his sister's case. Here he makes his first insinuation as to
her character: Why were there no suitors? (10):

Has anyone else taken this man's sister in legal marriage, either of those
who had dealings with her before our uncle [Pyrrhus] knew her, or of
those who associated with her during their marriage, or of those who did
so after his death? For it is clear that her brother has *made her available* on
the same terms to all those associating with her.

In one swift, deadly sentence Isaeus condemns Nicodemus as a
pimp and his sister as a prostitute.[112] Then he expands on this
theme by describing how she behaved like a *hetaira* even in her husband's house. Events there furnish persuasive probability-argument
(14): 'No one surely would dare to serenade a married woman, nor
do married women accompany their husbands to banquets or think
of dining in the company of strangers, especially casual ones'.

The next sections (17–27) illustrate Isaeus' method of turning
the contradictory evidence of witnesses to advantage. The argument is prefaced by an elaborated concession (*synchoresis*): instead of
saying simply: 'But suppose, for the sake of argument, that Pyrrhus
did marry Phile's mother', he says (16–17):

Let us consider the circumstances in which it might be imagined that a
marriage with such a woman in fact took place: for young men before this
time, after falling in love with such women, and finding themselves
unable to control their passion, have been induced by their madness to
ruin themselves in this way.

---

[111] The language used against Nicodemus is strong (4: ἀναισχυντότατον . . . ὅς γε
ἐτόλμησε): by decrying his part in the earlier litigation Isaeus is trying to anticipate his conviction in the present trial.

[112] Maximum effect depends on the acceptance of Reiske's emendation ἐκδέδωκεν for
MS ἐδεδώκει. ἐκδίδωμι carries the required ambiguity, either of giving in marriage or of
hiring out for mercenary purposes. The effect would be much less pointed with δίδωμι,
though possible.

But who are the witnesses to the union? Again we find not the simple question, but reference to the importance of the event (18), to which only one witness, Pyretides, was brought, and he has since retracted his deposition. This is accompanied by generalizations about the choice of witnesses—close associates used for deliberate acts, chance bystanders for unforeseen events (19); eye-witnesses for direct evidence, but acquaintances of repute for written depositions (20). Now Xenocles, we are told, observed these distinctions when he was laying claim to part of Pyrrhus' estate, yet failed to do so in the more important matter of Pyrrhus' marriage to Phile's mother, employing not so much unknown, as disreputable witnesses (22–3). The succession of these two instances of generalization followed by application produces a different type of epicheireme from those so far encountered. But what purpose is served by this elaboration? An awkward piece of evidence has to be negotiated: Pyrrhus' three uncles, Lysimenes, Chaeron, and Pylades, have borne witness to the marriage (26). The best he can do with this for the present is to say that the only witness claimed by Xenocles is Pyretides (see above), and that the principles of witness-choice which he has just established do not apply in the case of this marriage, as Pyrrhus would not wish his close relatives to know about it because it was discreditable to his family (27). He has cocooned the unsatisfactory evidence about witnesses (positive and negative) in rhetorical figuration and topoi, capping it with a petitio principii (27 above) and seeking to avoid bare exposure of its weakness.

He seems on firmer ground when he observes the absence of a dowry for the marriage (28–9), where probability-argument serves him well, as he is able to contend that both dowry and witnesses were the more necessary for a woman of this character. Suspicious too, is the confusion over the name of her daughter (Phile or Cleitarete?) Isaeus has a barrage of questions enquiring the purposes and implications of this, but leaves it inconclusively to return to the issue of the dowry (35–9). Here too probability is used in a tortuous argument. In order to explain their failure to secure the return of the dowry after Pyrrhus' death, the opponents said that it had been *atimeton*, i.e. it had not been subject to an official valuation, making it a private, informal arrangement which could not be upheld in law. The speaker, on the other hand, who thinks that no dowry was returned simply because there was no marriage, argues

that such a private arrangement would have been financially hazardous and therefore highly unlikely.

The legitimacy of Phile is the next matter for consideration. It is
examined methodically from the viewpoints of the principal characters. Initially, we return to the first point made in the speech: the
succession of Endius, and the failure of Nicodemus to contest it in
her favour (40–1). Next, when Phile was married to Xenocles, surely
Nicodemus would not have stood passively by without once again
raising the question of her status as the legitimate daughter of
Pyrrhus (45)? Isaeus does not merely note these failures, but
describes the official process by which a protest was filed, and adds
that this could have been done with impunity (47). Then there is
Endius' part. How could he have flouted or ignored Phile's claims,
or indeed been so improvident as to have not married her himself
and so secured the succession of his next generation, if she had truly
been the legitimate daughter of Pyrrhus? (This is a summary: Isaeus
puts these points as questions in different forms, 48–53.) Turning
from Nicodemus and Endius, he now examines the behaviour of
Phile's husband Xenocles. He had been married to her for eight
years (31), and therefore may not have been involved in the estate
when it was adjudicated to Endius. Isaeus tries to exploit the possible
chronological confusion in tracing his actions. He is said to have
denied the validity of the adjudication, but we are not told when this
denial was made, and are therefore not in the position to relate it to
his failure to claim the estate for his family after Phile had produced
children (56). The re-establishment of the family line through
descendants seems a strong motive, likely to be backed by law, but
Endius' family must have had claims too. Recognition of these,
rather than admission of his wife's illegitimacy, may have been the
reason for Xenocles' inaction in respect of the estate. Another line
of argument about his conduct is really a practical extension of the
last (59–61): if his wife's claim to the estate had been incontestable,
Xenocles would have taken possession of it without applying to the
archon. But we are not told about possible contestants who might
have made this physically impossible. Finally, why was not Phile
claimed by one of her uncles (63–5), since the law allowed this and
there was money as bait?[113] But here again both time and opposi-

---

[113] Not willingly forgone by anyone, as Isaeus drily observes (66): οὐδεὶς γὰρ
ἀνθρώπων μισεῖ τὸ λυσιτελοῦν, οὐδὲ περὶ πλείονος τοὺς ἀλλοτρίους ἑαυτοῦ
ποιεῖται.

tion may have been factors. In the absence of vital information, we can only note yet another example of Isaeus' thorough multi-faceted method, through which he explores all that should be expected of the parties (assuming that they acted in accordance with the law, 68), if the premiss of Phile's legitimacy were fulfilled.

The various steps of the argument are summarized with greater clarity in the concluding sections (72–80), but Isaeus' observance of this standard procedure in epilogues is a relative matter. The **epilogue** retains the scale and closely argumentative character of the main body of the longest speech in the corpus. The hypophora in 72–3 is typically placed, but is extended in form to a remarkable and novel degree:

From all this, gentlemen, and from what actually happened, it is easy to see how far these have exceeded other men in shamelessness. For why did our uncle, if he left a legitimate daughter, adopt and leave my brother as his son? Had he nearer relatives than us, whom he wished, by adopting my brother, to exclude from the right of claiming his daughter? In the absence of legitimate sons of his own, he neither has nor ever had a single relative nearer than us; for he had not brother or sons of a brother. But, it may be urged [the characteristic ἀλλά in hypophora], he might have adopted some other relative and given him the possession of his estate and his daughter. Yet what need had he openly to incur the enmity of any one of his relatives, when it was in his power, if he had really married the sister of Nicodemus, to introduce the child, who has been declared to be her offspring, to the members of his ward as his own legitimate child, and leave her sole heiress to all his estate, and direct that one of her sons should be introduced as his adopted son?

In the end, it is the conduct of Pyrrhus himself, largely negative though it is, that provides the most decisive proof, and this is summarily introduced in the central section of the epilogue (72–6). Then he turns to the jury with a sequence of questions, demanding that they put them to the opponents. This is an effective adaptation of a common device, while the use of questions in general has been one of the major features of a speech which has been relentlessly argumentative to the last.

12 For Euphiletus

The preservation of this substantial fragment by such a canonical arbiter of literary style and taste as Dionysius of Halicarnassus must prompt the reader to examine it closely for the peculiar qualities which he found in it, and perhaps for others besides. The case concerns not inheritance but the rights of citizenship,[114] and appears to have arisen from a recent census at Athens that had resulted in the exclusion of the defendant, whose elder half-brother here speaks on his behalf. We join the speech at or near the beginning of the **proof**, after the main facts, confirmed by witnesses, have been stated. Of these facts, the most important is that Euphiletus is the natural son of Hegesippus, not an adopted alien as alleged by his opponents.

The speaker moves first to consideration of motives for such an adoption, in order to dismiss them. Probability plays a part: how likely was his father to have adopted another son when he already had legitimate sons by his first marriage, and therefore no need of an heir and nothing to gain, but, in immediate financial terms, something to lose,[115] from the adoption (2–3)? How likely were relatives falsely to confirm Euphiletus' legitimacy, when it meant that each of them stood to receive a smaller share of the estate (4)? Thence he runs through a list of relatives—brothers-in-law, uncles, and other kinsmen—who had better motives for denying than for confirming his legitimacy: this is an aspect of the 'thoroughness and attention to detail'[116] which Dionysius praises in this speech, and is indeed characteristically Isaean, as has been found in his other speeches. While using the commonplace motive of gain, he looks at the slightly differing forms of it as it applied to the various persons he lists, even considering degrees of altruism (6). He also interlaces the unacceptable consequences of perjury (4, 6) to clinch its improbability.

The prominence given to oaths sworn by the principals (9–10) is, at first sight, puzzling. Wyse (720) rightly says that their value as atechnoi pisteis had become discredited by the time of the orators; and it is clear that standard arguments for and against them[117] had

[114] Hence it is compared by Blass (*AB* ii. 570–1) with Demosthenes 57 *Ag. Eubulides* (q.v.). Both speeches may have arisen from legislation in connection with the revision of the citizen-lists proposed by Demophilus in 346/5. If this is correctly taken as a guide to its date, Isaeus was an active speechwriter for at least 46 years.

[115] A nice twist is given to the *kerdos*-topos as the cost of Euphiletus' upbringing (3: οὐ μικρὰ δαπανήματά ἐστιν) is placed on the other side of the balance.

[116] *Isaeus* 16: πάντ' ἀκριβῶς ἐξειργασμένα.

[117] *Rhet. ad Alex.* 17; Aristot. *Rhet.* 1. 15. 28–9 (see E. M. Cope's *Introduction to Aristotle's Rhetoric* (London and Cambridge, 1867), 202–5).

been available for a long time. Moreover, other contemporary recorded instances of oath-taking for evidential purposes involve its alleged abuse.[118] But there may be reason to suppose that the oath first cited here, that of a mother confirming the paternity of her child, commanded exceptional respect.[119] In the present speech, Isaeus introduces less convincing oaths on the back of the respected mother's oath, typically amplifying his argument with more questionable material (another feature influencing Dionysius' choice of this fragment to illustrate his methods). In the two concluding sections (11, 12) contrasting types of argument involving the opponents are used: in 11 it is the honesty of the speaker's witnesses compared with the futile machinations of the opponents; and in 12 a hypothetical plea for parallel treatment, using correlative construction.[120] They illustrate the unflaggingly fertile inventiveness of Isaeus which Dionysius was trying to exemplify, in a speech which seems to have avoided the padding which afflicts some of his other extant oratory.

ISAEUS: SUMMARY

On comparing Isaeus with his predecessors, formal and technical development is to be found in three main areas: division, argument, and rhetoric. The detached, topos-rich prooemium of earlier oratory, while still identifiable in some speeches (8, 10), has given way to either the shortest of introductions (4) or, more characteristically, an abrupt and direct engagement with the main body of the case (as in 1, 3, 5, 11—the latter beginning with a discussion of the relevant law). Then Isaeus' attitude to narrative is different from that of Lysias: his use of it almost exclusively as a vehicle of factual presentation linked to argument leads him to break it up in a manner more reminiscent of Antiphon, and it is the pressing

[118] Dem. 39 *Ag. Boeot. I* 4, 25–6; 49 *Ag. Timoth.* 65–7; 54 *Ag. Conon* 26, 40.
[119] Aristotle (*Rhet.* 2. 23. 11) gives this oath as an example of rhetorical induction (ἐπαγωγή) (i.e. based on the probability that women always discern the truth 'about children'), and (importantly) cites examples from the courts in which this premiss has been upheld, including Dem. 39 (last note above), in which Plangon, mistress of Mantias, proclaimed the legitimacy of her sons by him after privately agreeing to refuse the oath, and her *volte face* destroyed his case, forcing him to acknowledge them and enroll them in his phratry.
[120] ὥσπερ οὗτοι ... ἂν ἔφησαν ... οὕτω τὸ νῦν ἡμῖν.

thoroughness of that argument that is Isaeus' most distinctive contribution to the genre.[121]

Amplification, repetition, and interrogation[122] give his argumentation a new intensity. It is also characteristic of him to introduce peripheral detail, and this includes at times material which makes him an important source for legal historians: indeed, his legal expertise even on occasion prompts him to criticize existing laws, at least by implication (1. 39–47, 4. 11–12). It is matched by the ingenuity and vehemence he brings to his attacks on chosen individuals, such as Dicaeogenes III in Speech 5 and Diocles in Speech 8: in this level of vituperation his nearest predecessor is neither Antiphon nor Lysias, but Andocides. In rhetorical usage he is not so much an innovator as an elaborator, under whose pen familiar devices are complicated (e.g. hypophora in 3. 72–3 and pathetic paradox in 11. 13–14), and combined (e.g. hypostasis with *ouk . . . alla* pleonasm, in 8. 43). Epilogues tend to be short, lacking anacephalaiosis and often emotional appeal, but sometimes containing unusual features: Speeches 5 and 7 end with protracted apostrophe addressed to the opponent. Finally, the speeches have been shown to contain many instances of Isaean dissimulation, petitio principii, over- and under-emphasis. Although Isaeus has been regarded as the closest forerunner of Demosthenes, he is a very individual orator whose sum total of characteristics is not replicated in any of his predecessors or successors.

---

[121] Conversely, his narratives could exceed those of Lysias in simplicity.

[122] Rhetorical question is an almost ubiquitous device. For this and other features, see W. W. Baden, *The Principal Figures of Language and Figures of Thought in Isaeus* (Baltimore, 1906); also C. A. Robertson, *Tropes and Figures in Isaeus* (Princeton, 1901); E. M. Linke, *De Elocutione Isaei* (Leipzig, 1884); and, in general, Léon Moy, *Étude sur les Plaidoyers d'Isée* (Paris, 1876) (admired by Blass *AB* ii. 498).

6

DEMOSTHENES
LOGOGRAPHOS
(Part I)

The biographers indicate an unbroken tradition of forensic speech-writing between Isaeus and his pupil Demosthenes. Indeed, the early start which his fraudulent guardians obliged him to make to his career in the courts caused doubt to be cast on the authenticity of his first speeches: some sources suspected their precocity, and concluded that Isaeus had written them.[1] In this chapter, however, while clear echoes of Isaeus will be noted as they are found, attention will be directed mainly towards any signs of a new and individual approach to the standard procedures. Style also assumes particular importance in an author who had observed the growing acceptance of oratory as a literary genre, and was able to draw on his own studies of the best prose writers of recent years in creating for himself an individual voice.[2]

Demosthenes was born perhaps five years after the first extant speech of Isaeus, in 384/3.[3] The family misfortunes which culminated in his early forensic debut began with the death of his father and namesake when he was 7 years old, leaving him a decade of minority (377/6–367/6). By the will of Demosthenes senior, of the deme of Paeania, his nephews Aphobus and Demophon were appointed trustees of his estate. Aphobus was to marry his widow Cleobule with a dowry of 80 minae and the family home, and

---

[1] *Vit. X Or.* 839f; Libanius *Vit. Dem.* p. 3 R; Zosimus *Vit. Dem.* p. 147 R. On the authenticity of 29 *Ag. Aphobus III*, see E. M. Burke, 'A Further Argument on the Authenticity of Demosthenes 29', *CJ* 70.2 (1974), 53–6.

[2] Thucydides and Isocrates were, in their very different ways, the strongest influences on his style. See Dion. Hal. *Dem.* 9–10; 16–22; *Thuc.* 52–5; and Usher GO v. 21–3.

[3] So Blass *AB* iii. 4–10; Sealey *DT* 247. MacDowell *DAM* 370–1 prefers 385/4. Inclusive or exclusive counting from fixed dates produces the difference.

Demophon was to marry his daughter with a dowry of two talents (120 minae).[4] A third trustee, Therippides of Paeania, an old friend, was also appointed, but seems to have played only a small part, for good or ill, in the story. The villain of the piece, in Demosthenes' account, was Aphobus. He received the dowry, but neither married Cleobule nor provided for her upkeep.[5] As to what happened in the following years, we are no doubt too dependent on the sole testimony of Demosthenes, but it seems clear that the initially prosperous business, which had been worth almost fourteen talents and employed over fifty slaves making swords and furniture,[6] went into decline. After an agreed contraction in size,[7] the assets of the estate seem to have been eroded by a mixture of mismanagement and deliberate effort to make a quick profit by realizing capital, which was subsequently frittered away. Yet the only certain effect of Aphobus' stewardship of the estate is Demosthenes' grievous disappointment at the smallness of its value (8). He did not enter adulthood in total poverty.[8] Opening proceedings against his guardians in 365/3, he was wealthy enough four years later to perform a trierarchy. In view of these facts, approach to the 'guardian-speeches' (27–31) may be made in a spirit of healthy scepticism, which should in turn heighten alertness to any new rhetorical skills which they display.

27 Against Aphobus I

The clearly defined **prooemium** (1–3) is conservative in its choice of topoi, though the technique of running them together shows a

---

[4] He arguably had the best deal, receiving the largest dowry immediately, with ten years to enjoy it before marrying Demosthenes' sister when she came of age (29 *Ag. Aphob. III* 43).

[5] Cleobule's brother-in-law Demochares remonstrated with him for this: he is an important witness, being a comparative outsider and having no material gain in prospect, but providing early evidence of Aphobus' maladministration.

[6] This made Demosthenes' father rich enough to serve as a trierarch (27 *Ag. Aphob. I* 64).

[7] 27 *Ag. Aphob. I* 18: 'My father left me an income of thirty minae from the factory; and after the sale by these men of half of the slaves, I *was to receive* the proportionate sum of fifteen minai (πεντεκαίδεκά μοι μνᾶς γίγνεσθαι κατὰ λόγον προσῆκεν)'. This strongly suggests that the disposal of these slaves was prescribed in the will.

[8] He received a normal education (18 *Cor.* 257; cf. 27 *Ag. Aphob. I* 46, his tutors cheated of their fees). The private tuition he received from Isaeus would not have been cheap, nor would an impecunious student have approached the famously expensive Isocrates, even to ask to purchase a part of his course (*Vit. X Or.* 837d–e).

new smoothness.[9] There is also a mixture of frankness and precision, later Demosthenic hallmarks, in the second limb of the otherwise conventional hypothetical inversion with which the speech begins:

But since he has avoided letting those who have clear knowledge of our affairs decide about them, and has come before you, who have no accurate knowledge of them, it must be in your court that I try to win my just claims.

This replaces the typical *plea* for justice and a more general reference to arbitrators. Individual stylistic touches are also present,[10] but for the most part the main stylistic influence is Isocratean.

A short **narrative** (4–5) concentrating on essential facts, without comment, follows the Isaean rather than the Lysianic model. Even when he is narrating the act of embezzlement, economy is observed (6). But this reserve is only temporary: condemnation of the act, when it comes, is fulsome (7),[11] and remains in the jury's minds as the necessary but potentially tedious itemization of the assets of the estate is given (9–11). But a general tone of clinical calmness returns: even as he narrates Aphobus' occupation of the family home after his father's death (13) his main concern is with material gains and disposals, and the reactions of others to these. He is gathering witnesses in preparation for the main proof.

In the **proof** (17–59) his task is to expose the fraud in its various aspects. He finds limited opportunity for rhetorical invention[12] as he sets about refuting the defendant's explanations of shortfalls in revenue, including one claim that the factory was idle for a time, though he was himself making ongoing purchases of raw materials (20), and another contradictory claim that a slave named Milyas had charge of everything (22). As this is a prosecuting speech, the jury would not know how Aphobus would avoid such inconsistencies

---

[9] 2: 'I know, men of the jury, that it is difficult, with my whole fortune at stake, to litigate against men who can speak and prepare their case well, when I am wholly without experience of affairs because of my youth.'

[10] 2: μέχρι γε τοῦ τὰ γεγενημένα διεξελθεῖν καὶ αὐτὸς ἀρκούντως ἐρεῖν.

[11] 7: 'When you have learnt the precise details of these matters, you will know that, of all those who have ever acted as trustees, none have more shamelessly or openly plundered (διηρπάκασιν) an estate than these men.'

[12] The pathetic paradox in 28, however, is well-balanced and effective (note use of articular infinitive τῷ . . . γεγονέναι); and rhetorical questions are used pointedly, e.g. in 29: 'Is it a small sum drawn from some obscure source, which might easily have been miscalculated, or have they not manifestly plundered a total of nearly three talents from me?' (cf. 33). A series of questions marks the end of this section (38).

in his own account, but the prosecutor has to anticipate all possible arguments; and later readers of the speech would admire his thoroughness. Preoccupation with covering all possible arguments tends to push the personality of Aphobus into the background: apart from occasional outbursts against his 'shamelessness' (24, 31, 38) and an unqualified reference to his general character (22), it is not subjected to a detailed examination, nor enlarged upon by drawing on his previous actions, as would have happened in a speech by Lysias or Isaeus.

Demosthenes might have made more of his opponents' failure to produce his father's will (43), but this becomes a major issue after Aphobus' speech.[13] He passes on to other evasive and concealing actions of Aphobus. These are his behaviour before the arbitrator (49–51),[14] and an allegedly improvised statement designed to distract him from the main charges (53–5). From the way Demosthenes handles it, that statement may have posed a serious difficulty to him. Aphobus has alleged that Demosthenes' father had buried four talents in the ground and 'put his mother in charge of them'. Demosthenes says that he is worried lest, if the jury believed this statement, they would think him rich and be less sympathetic (53). But his real worry may be that other more general considerations might make them doubt the degree of deprivation which he was claiming. His involvement of Aphobus in this produces effective rhetoric (dilemmaton, 54):

When one asks him upon what he has spent so much of my money, he says he has paid debts for me, and so represents me as poor; yet, when he so desires, he makes me rich, it seems, seeing that my father left so large a sum in the house.

And this short example is followed by a similar but more elaborate argument (55).[15] He is clearly very anxious to scotch this claim, because it would add to existing suspicions of his wealth. These sections contain the cleverest rhetoric in the speech: it is used to polarize the argument. The hiding of the four talents could have been a precautionary measure which met a kind of halfway con-

---

[13] It is possible that desire to avoid repetitiveness in the published speeches caused Demosthenes to excise some of the discussion of the will from the first speech.

[14] Cf. Lys. 10 *Ag. Theomn.* 6 (a brief reference); 54 *Ag. Conon* 26–7 (a whole section).

[15] Summarized thus: 'If my father had not trusted them, he would not have told them of the four talents; if he had trusted them he would not have set it aside from the bulk of the estate.' The intricacy of the argument is very reminiscent of Isaeus.

tingency that might arise neither from complete trust nor complete mistrust—a kind of insurance, albeit a substantial one, against a variety of ways in which things could go wrong. It is also interesting that Aphobus was unable to lay his hands on this money: Demosthenes uses this fact to deny its existence, but it may have been a well-kept secret. It is even possible that his mother's refusal to reveal it was in some way related to Aphobus' failure to marry her. At all events the possible existence of a sum of money which made Demosthenes wealthy would have undermined his case in the jury's eyes, and required the detailed attention it receives. The intensity with which this section closes confirms its importance (57).[16]

The emotional temperature of the speech reaches a climax in the long and elaborate **epilogue** (60–9),[17] though this section begins with a sinuous period containing typically Isocratean subordinations (60–1),[18] an unusual medium through which to summarize the main financial features of the case. After an apposite comparative argument (63) and a pathetic paradox (64), there is a new device to flatter the jury, comparing them with the defendants:

They have done away with the will . . . and greatly increased their capital. You, on your part, do not behave in this way towards those who wrong you: when you pass judgement against them, you do not take away all that they have, but in pity for their wives and children you leave something even to such men as these.

The concluding sections (66–9) are unusually full of emotional pleas, the outstanding one being a prosopopoiia:[19] 'Loudly would my father groan, I think, if he saw me, his son, at risk of being forced to pay a sixth of the dowries and legacies given by him to these men . . . '

Demosthenes already stamps his individual personality on the genre of forensic oratory in this early speech. After initial restraint in the interest of clear exposition, he gradually strengthens the

---

[16] Note the sequence of rhetorical questions, with epanadiplosis: οὐκ ἔστι ταῦτα, ὦ ἄνδρες δικασταί, οὐκ ἔστιν . . .

[17] So Blass (AB iii/1. 227–8: 'sehr ausgearbeitete').

[18] Note esp. the favourite Isocratean ἐξὸν following two genitive absolutes. Further on the style of Isocrates, see S. Usher, BICS 20 (1973), 39–67. The decision to place the main chapter on Isocrates after those on Demosthenes in this book is dictated by considerations of continuity and genre.

[19] Here, however, he follows earlier usage: see Lysias 12 Ag. Eratos. 100 (Usher GO i. 252); Isoc. 6 Archid. 110.

focus on Aphobus' role, though always keeping the financial details
in the foreground and not broadening his personal attack.
Arguments are mounted from varying angles in the Isaean manner,
but the emotional content of the concluding sections surpasses anything found in that orator.

28 *Against Aphobus II*

This speech is a reply to a specific charge made by Aphobus in his
defence, and therefore itself assumes the character of a defence-
speech. The charge could hardly have been more exasperating:
Aphobus sought to explain the absence of any record of the total
value of Demosthenes' father's estate by the claim that Gylon, his
maternal grandfather, was a state debtor, so that revelation of his
assets would have aroused the interest of treasury officials. With this
background, it is hardly surprising that this short speech should begin
with emotion, though here it is unusually intense.[20] In the rest of the
prooemium (1–2) Aphobus' claim is characterized as an unproven
allegation or pretence,[21] as shown by his underhand last-minute sub-
mission of it, by which he attempted to 'ambush'[22] his opponent.

A brief statement showing how his relatives have openly avowed
their wealth by performing public services (3–4) contains an element of probability, in that such openness would have been
unlikely if there had been anything to hide. But attention soon
reverts to Aphobus and his co-trustees. Here the underlying
assumption is that the relevant documents did exist (5: 'It was their
duty, as soon as my father died, to call in a number of witnesses and
to bid them seal the will'), but they had withheld them, expecting
their own word to be accepted (6).[23] Lively apostrophic questioning of the opponents (7–10) exposes the irrationality of their explanations and the irregularity of their behaviour. But Aphobus
himself is the chief enemy: ignoring defence against the charge he
had brought, Demosthenes seeks to generate resentment against
him by painting a narrative scene around his father's deathbed

---

20 Πολλὰ καὶ μεγάλ' ἐψευσμένου πρὸς ὑμᾶς Ἀφόβου πρῶτον, ἐφ' ᾧ μάλιστ'
ἠγανάκτησα τῶν ῥηθέντων.

21 1: πρόφασιν . . . οὐδεμίαν παρέσχετο μαρτυρίαν.

22 ἐνεδρεύειν (cf. Lys. 1 *Eratos.* 49) (in the epilogue—elsewhere such metaphors are rare
in prooemia).

23 Demosthenes adds a note of sarcasm: ἄξιόν γε πιστεύειν αὐτοῖς ὅ τι ἂν περὶ
τούτων λέγωσιν.

(14–16). Here style creates the desired effect. The dying man's instructions are given the maximum effect of meticulous care and elaboration of detail by incorporating them in a single long period, in which he also manages to include reference to symbolic religious acts, followed immediately by an outburst against Aphobus' impiety.[24] This is periodic writing which achieves both practical and dramatic effect. It also runs exactly counter to the Isocratean idea of a period embodying a single theme.[25]

Focus on Aphobus is nowhere better illustrated than in the merely passing reference made to Thrasylochus of Anagyrus (17). He tried to help Aphobus and his co-trustees to delay Demosthenes' suit by challenging him to an 'exchange'.[26] Now Thrasylochus was the brother of Meidias, who later emerged, in a celebrated lawsuit, as one of Demosthenes' bitterest enemies;[27] and that enmity originated, at least in part, from an incident arising from this exchange. Demosthenes accepted it, but tried to delay its implementation while he completed his case against his guardians. This brought Thrasylochus to his door, together with his brother.[28] In the later speech (78–9) their hybristic behaviour in breaking in and abusing his family is described graphically, but here Demosthenes is content to pass over the episode quite tamely. He is concerned exclusively with the prosecution in hand; and, of course there is the consideration that, at this stage of his career,[29] the danger of making too many influential enemies was to be avoided. He concentrates for the rest of the speech on his own plight, with some impassioned rhetoric sustained to unusual length.[30] But he ends on a practical and conventional note by

---

[24] 15: ὁ γὰρ πατήρ . . . 16: . . . ὧν οὗτος ὁ πάντων ἀνοσιώτατος . . . ἐπιβεβουλευκώς.

[25] e.g. philosophia in 4 Paneg. 47–9.

[26] Antidosis: a procedure devised to secure the fair allocation of state duties (leitourgiai). A man who thought that one of these duties had been unfairly imposed on him could claim that another man was wealthier, and offer to exchange property with him to confirm his confidence in his claim. See M. Christ, 'Liturgy Avoidance and Antidosis in Classical Athens', TAPA 120 (1990), 147–69.

[27] See Speech 21 Against Meidias.

[28] Agreement to antidosis gave either party the right to inspect the other's property.

[29] The assumption that Demosthenes conceived early ambitions to become a rhetor depends on the tradition that he heard, and was inspired by Callistratus while still a student (Plut. Dem. 5; Vit. X Or. 844b–c).

[30] 20 (epanadiplosis with asyndeton): βοηθήσατε . . . βοηθήσατε . . . σώσατε, ἐλεήσατε . . . ἱκετεύω, ἀντιβολῶ πρὸς παίδων, πρὸς γυναικῶν . . . οὕτως ὄναισθε τούτων (oath), μὴ περιίδητέ με . . . He also seeks sympathy for his mother.

reminding the jury that a verdict in his favour would make him a willing contributor to the public service (24).

29 Against Aphobus III (For Phanus)

In a desperate move to salvage his case, Aphobus demanded that Demosthenes surrender Milyas, the foreman of his sword-factory, for examination under torture, alleging that he had managed everything, including the financial side of the business (27 Ag. Aphob. I 19, 22). Demosthenes refused this demand on the ground that Milyas had been set free by his father on his deathbed, and further claimed that Aphobus had himself admitted this manumission at an official hearing witnessed by his own brother Aesius and two other men, Philip and Phanus. Aphobus knew that the only way to win was to accuse these men of giving false testimony; while fear of a reopening of the whole case in the event of their conviction prompted Demosthenes to defend them.[31]

In the opening part of the speech, however, he chose to concentrate on the character of Aphobus.[32] This was practical, since the argument turns mainly upon the reliability of witnesses; but it had an immediate and distorting effect on the form of the **prooemium** (1–5), which is over twice as long as that in the first speech, but the conventional topoi are packed into the first section; the rest is a protracted and verbose tirade against Aphobus. The style shows strong Isocratean influence,[33] and a certain youthful prolixity in the use of no fewer than three hypothetical inversions (1 (twice) and 2–3); and old ground is retrodden here as he describes Aphobus' depredations (3), and he returns to these more fully later. But the prothesis (5) is clear enough in spite of being unusually long-winded.

It is difficult to discern any subsequent division along conventional lines. What seems to start as **narrative** (e.g. 6–7) soon focuses on a particular question, initially Aphobus' decision to

---

[31] Thus he is technically a *synegoros* to Phanus. We do not know whether any action was taken against or for Philip.

[32] Initially, compared with himself: 1: πότερός ποθ' ἡμῶν ἐσθ' ὁ πονηρός. Later (4), 'greedy and vile', and (13) a *sophistes*.

[33] Note esp. frequent antithesis, including οὐκ . . . ἀλλά (2, 3, 5 (twice)), periods (esp. in 3, 5), amplification (1: μείζω καὶ δεινότερα, ἴσοι καὶ κοινοὶ, διδάξαι καὶ διηγήσασθαι, 2: ὠμῶς καὶ πικρῶς, 4: αἰσχροκερδείας . . . καὶ μιαρίας, 4: δικαιοτέραν καὶ εὐορκοτέραν, and almost total absence of hiatus (2 exx., end of § 3).

impugn one particular witness from the many who had testified in his trial (7–10), while refusing testimony under torture from a slave who was present and recorded his admission of Milyas' manumission (11–12). His attitude to slaves' evidence is shown to be inconsistent (14), and the decision of Aesius is easily explained by his inability to give evidence helpful to his brother (15–18), while Aphobus himself prevaricated (19–21).

At this point a distinction between two types of proof drawn by Demosthenes, but not by previous orators, should be examined. In 10 he says, of the evidence he will present in 11–22:

Now I will prove clearly to all of you that this testimony is true, not by means of probabilities or arguments devised to meet the present case, but with reasoning which will, as I believe, commend itself to all of you as just.

Now the proofs in 11–22 are the logical or reasonable conclusions drawn from particular actions: Aphobus refused the offer of the slave/scribe because his testimony would damage him; Aesius chose the option of not testifying because his testimony would damage Aphobus. Actions such as these, when subjected to reasoned interpretation, become 'sure signs' (*tekmeria*, 16),[34] which are the strongest *entechnoi pisteis*. After drawing the required conclusions from these primary sources of rhetorical proof, he says he will turn to 'probabilities' (*eikota*, 22). These turn out to be the standard motives in earlier oratory—friendship, enmity, gain (22–4),[35] which indeed are subsumed under the class of *eikota* in fourth-century and later theory.[36] Hence Demosthenes could here be either following a restriction placed on the scope of *eikota* by recent theory, or creating it himself. In earlier oratory, *eikota* included *tekmeria* drawn from a wide range of actions.

The rest of the speech is used as an opportunity to restate the main case, on which Aphobus has been convicted, and to show that the outcome has not been affected by Aphobus' inability to use the testimony of Milyas. It is given some dramatic moments, such as the actual wording of the indictment (31), and live speech (51). There are numerous rhetorical touches, though none not already

---

[34] Aristot. *Rhet.* 1. 2. 16–17.

[35] Cf. Antiph. 5 *Her.* 57–8; Lys. 1 *Eratos.* 43–4 (here also the fear of malicious prosecution (*sycophantia*): it is interesting to see Dem. here adding this charge against Aphobus (25); perhaps reference to a handbook suggested this to him).

[36] *Rhet. ad Alex.* 7. 1428a–b; *Ad Herenn.* 2. 2. 3.

observed. Alongside the prolixity noticed above, there are instances of the more characteristic Demosthenic concentration.[37] But the major curiosity of the speech is the fact that Phanus is not referred to as the defendant until almost the end (58). Again, although cases of false witness might reasonably refer at some length to the lawsuit that occasioned them (as happens, for example, in Demosthenes 45 *Ag. Stephanus I*), the amount of digressive material here seems excessive. Finally, the summary material distributed loosely throughout the long **epilogue** (50–60) concerns only in a general way the case in hand. There is some reason to doubt whether Aphobus had actually pressed his prosecution of Phanus, since he left the city to reside in Megara after the main trial (3). It may therefore be concluded that we have an embellished version of the speech prepared for the trial, published no doubt partly to establish a final record of the duplicity of Aphobus, but mainly to demonstrate to potential clients the variety of techniques he was able to deploy in difficult cases.[38]

30 *Against Onetor I*

After his success in court, Demosthenes still faced the task of collecting the damages awarded, amounting to ten talents. True to past form, Aphobus had disposed of his real estate before his departure for Megara, and the farm in question in the present case was valued at only a tenth of the total damages. But Demosthenes was forced to fight even for this, and the anger born of his frustration is clear throughout the speech. On trying to take possession of the farm, he had found Onetor living in it. The latter's sister had been married to Aphobus, who, on divorcing her, had mortgaged the farm to him as security pending the return of her dowry. The suit is one of ejectment (*dike exoules*). The rhetorical interest centres upon how Demosthenes deals with an opponent who is his enemy only by the accident of his relationship with Aphobus.

---

[37] e.g. locutions such as οὐκ ἠδικημένος συκοφαντεῖς (41), τὸ μισθοῦν τὸν οἶκον ἠφάνιζεν (43); and the rapid listing sequence τὰ μὲν ἀνηλωκέναι, τὰ δ' οὐ λαβεῖν ἔφη, τὰ δ' οὐκ εἰδέναι, τὰ δὲ τὸν δεῖν' ἔχειν, τὰ δ' ἔνδον εἶναι, τὰ δὲ πάντα μᾶλλον ἢ ὅπου παρέδωκεν εἶχε λέγειν.

[38] His next speeches follow closely in time, and at least some of the wealth which enabled him to undertake a trierarchy in 360/59 was probably derived from his earnings as a logographos. See on *Ag. Meidias* for a speech without a trial.

The course he adopts is to take an offensive line. Onetor, described as 'far more difficult to deal with than him [Aphobus], and more deserving of punishment' (1), drove him off the land 'in a most outrageous manner'.[39] Onetor continues to be coupled with Aphobus, being portrayed as a co-conspirator[40] using all the devices (*paraskeuai*, 3) of falsehood and misrepresentation, prepared to protect Aphobus and even stand trial (4–5) because his own financial interests are bound up in the outcome of his brother-in-law's suit against Demosthenes. In this speech the idea of *paraskeue* is extended beyond its previous conventional associations, connoting not merely the speechwriter's 'preparations and devices', but the long-term contrivance of the principals to ensure that a part of Aphobus' estate should not be adjudicable to Demosthenes in the expected event of his losing his case against him (10):

From the very first, then, it is admitted that the dowry [for Onetor's sister] was not paid to Aphobus, and that he did not acquire control of it. And it seems very likely that, for the reasons which I have just mentioned, they chose to continue their liability for the dowry rather than incorporate it into the estate of Aphobus, which was in such jeopardy.

Demosthenes then lists, in the thorough manner to which Isaeus' tutorship would have trained him, all the circumstances which might have excused failure to pay the dowry, and shows that they did not apply, leaving only mistrust of Aphobus' ability to repay it (10–13). Connection between the marriage and subsequent alleged divorce and Demosthenes' lawsuit is then confirmed (14–17), and the opponents' claim that the dowry had in fact been paid is refuted, using probability-argument (19–24).

Further confirmation of the bogus character of the whole arrangement is provided by Aphobus' continued cohabitation with Onetor's sister. Assuming that he did this for material rather than sentimental reasons, his behaviour would ensure that Onetor continued to live in the farm and thus deny it to Demosthenes.[41] To prove the simple fact of this cohabitation, the offer of a slave to

[39] 2: ὑβριστικῶς ὑπ' αὐτοῦ πάνυ ἐξεβλήθην.

[40] 3: συναποστερεῖ τέ με τῶν ὄντων τῷ ἑαυτοῦ κηδεστῇ.

[41] The method of divorce chosen—the wife leaving the husband (*apoleipsis*: ἀπολελοιπυῖαν, 25) rather than his dismissing her (*apopempsis*)—may have assisted their plan if the procedure for the return of a dowry (or, as in this case, the property hypothecated as security for it) was more complicated, and hence more protracted after *apoleipsis*. Such complication would arise not from the dowry-returning procedures but from those which the wife had to follow to legalize her divorce (written notice lodged in the archon's office).

provide direct evidence under torture is made and refused, and the usual conclusion drawn by Demosthenes. Fact and conclusion are juxtaposed (26):

When I saw, jurors, that after the woman's divorce had been registered with the archon, and the defendant had alleged that he had taken a mortgage on the farm as security for her dowry, Aphobus continued to hold and cultivate the land and live with his wife as before, I realized that all this was fiction and deceit to cover up the facts.

The inconsistencies and anomalies inherent in the actions of both Aphobus and Onetor are drawn together in a sequence of three pathetic paradoxes, surely unparalleled up to this time (29–30).[42] It is another example of Demosthenes' adroitness in adapting existing types of argument, and after it he returns to the theme of the wickedness of Onetor, complaining that he had never wronged him (31), yet had to witness his post-trial pleas on Aphobus' behalf (32). As he goes on to more evidence of Aphobus' cohabitation, it is difficult not to see in 29–32 an interruption, however rhetorically effective, to the main sequence of the argument, which itself at this stage becomes repetitive and derivative.[43] The speech ends without a clearly defined epilogue.

31 Against Onetor II

Demosthenes uses this second speech not to reply to Onetor's defence, but, avowedly at least (1), to mention a further inconsistency in this case—that he gave two different accounts of the value of the dowry he had paid to Aphobus. After making an initial valuation of 80 minae, he reduced this to one talent (60 minae), thereby reducing his claim on Aphobus' estate. According to Demosthenes, he did this through a mixture of conscience and perceived social pressure.[44] But he accords these scruples no indulgence, cheerfully

---

[42] 'And yet it is shocking (καίτοι δεινὸν . . .) that one of them should say that the land was mortgaged to him, when the mortgager is seen to be cultivating it; that he should claim that his sister has left her husband, when he is seen to have refused the test by torture on this very point; and that the one who is not living with his wife (as Onetor claims) should carry off all the produce and implements from the farm, while the man acting as guardian for the divorced woman, to secure whose dowry he claims to have taken a mortgage on the land, plainly shows no anger at any single one of these acts, but takes everything quietly. Is not the whole thing completely clear? Is it not an admitted plan to protect Aphobus?'

[43] There is close verbal correspondence between 37 and Isaeus 8 Cir. 12.

[44] 2: ' . . . he saw what your attitude was towards those who were too shameless in their wrongdoing, and came to his senses (ἔννους γίγνεται—note historic present).'

leading his probability-argument to the conclusion that Onetor is a liar (4), and pursuing him further with the charge of shameless behaviour (6), turning to apostrophize him. The latter figure is used here with a new argumentative intricacy (6–8):

With what end in view, Onetor, did you fix your mortgage-pillars on the house for the two thousand extra drachmae [20 minae], if the land was really worth more, instead of securing the two thousand drachmae also by mortgage of the land? Or, when it suits your plans to save all the property of Aphobus, is the land to be worth a talent only, and are you to hold the house on a mortgage of two thousand drachmae more; and with the dowry eighty minae, will you claim the right to hold both the land and the house? Or again, when this is not in your interest, is the assessment to be different, with the house worth a talent, because now it is I who am holding it, and what is left of the farm worth not less than two talents, in order that it may seem that I am wronging Aphobus, and not myself being robbed? Do you see that, while you masquerade as having paid the dowry, you are shown not to have paid it in any way whatsoever? For that would have been the honest and innocent way to behave [note typical Demosthenic abstraction and concentration: τὰ γὰρ ἀληθῆ καὶ μὴ κακουργημένα τῶν πραγμάτων ἁπλῶς], which is consistent from beginning to end, but you are proved to have done the opposite in my enemy's service.

Demosthenes is exploring different angles of attack on the character of Onetor, and with greater urgency than in the previous speech. Perhaps he does this because Onetor's defence has concentrated on dissociating him from Aphobus, or at least from Aphobus' misdeeds. However that may be, he uses hypothesis to add to his picture of Onetor's character as a fraudster and a trickster (9), just like Aphobus, then temporarily pretends concession[45] before returning to the attack, touching on other points of contention, using apostrophe again. The concluding sections maintain the intensity of this fiery little speech.[46]

---

[45] 10: 'But perhaps not all his acts have been of this kind, and he is not shown clearly to be a trickster from every viewpoint.'

[46] Esp. 14: 'We must look to the truth, not to arguments which this man has contrived . . . was it right for you to recover the whole amount, while I, an orphan who had been wronged and robbed . . . should be forced to suffer thus . . .'

41 *Against Spoudias*

The subject-matter of this speech rather than any internal chronological evidence points to an early date. It was natural for the
plaintiff (unnamed) in this dispute over a dowry to turn to a
speechwriter who had recently succeeded in a case involving one
(i.e. *Against Onetor*). He may thus have become Demosthenes' first
client.[47] He had married one of the two daughters of Polyeuctus,
who had promised him a dowry of 40 minae (4,000 drachmae), but
paid only 30, promising that his house would be assigned to him in
his will under an agreed valuation of 10 minae. In the meantime,
however, trouble arose on the other side of the family. The other
daughter of Polyeuctus had married Leocrates, but he divorced her
after a quarrel,[48] and Polyeuctus married her to Spoudias. On the
death of Polyeuctus, the agreement with the speaker that had been
ratified by Leocrates was disputed by Spoudias.

The scale of the speech is economical. Demosthenes' skill,
already noticed, in merging prooemium-topoi together, is seen
again in this **prooemium**.[49] The prothesis is likewise short and
neat (6). An early pointed contrast of character is remarkably fresh
and effective: 'The more gentle and civilized I have been in my
dealings with him, the more contempt he has shown me.' Spoudias
has been a frequent litigant (2, 24) and is clever (*deinos*, 12), so the
speaker is made to draw attention to positive qualities in himself
which will appeal more to the jury. The **narrative** (3–5) matches
the scale of speech, but ends dramatically with a typical question-
and-answer which summarizes the issue:

Now why have I told you this, men of the jury? Because I did not receive
the whole of my wife's dowry, but a thousand drachmae were left unpaid

[47] Blass (*AB* iii/1. 249–53) gives stylistic reasons as his main grounds for placing the
speech early. He notes avoidance of hiatus and Isocratean rhythms as symptoms of that orator's influence, while denying the speech any particular rhetorical power. See also R.
Ruehling. 'Der Junge Demosthenes als Verfasser der Rede gegen Spudias', *Hermes* 71 (1936),
441–51. The speech is of interest to legal historians as 'the sole literary instance adduced for
ἀποτίμημα as payment of dowry' (Harrison *LA* i. 298 n. 1).

[48] His quarrel was with Polyeuctus (4), his brother-in-law who had adopted him as his
son. On the basis of these affinities he had assumed family responsibilities—including that of
guarantor of the debt to the speaker. When he had cut his ties with the family, Spoudias,
having no such filial connections, felt no compunction about trying to grab as much of the
estate as he could.

[49] 2: danger/inequality/experience of opponent/inexperience of speaker/request for
attention—all in one sentence (καὶ νῦν κινδυνεύομεν . . . προσέχετε τὸν νοῦν).

with the understanding that I should receive them on the death of Polyeuctus; and so long as Leocrates was the heir of Polyeuctus, it was he who was responsible to me for the debt. But when Leocrates had *left the family*, and Polyeuctus was gravely ill, then I took a mortgage on the family house. Now Spoudias[50] is trying to prevent me from collecting the rent from it.

The italicized phrase must mean that Leocrates' adoption as Polyeuctus' heir was annulled. He thereby ceased to be a *cleronomos* (5), and Spoudias subsequently became one (7).[51] This leads to an important question: did Polyeuctus adopt Spoudias in place of Leocrates? It is difficult to avoid the conclusion that he did, and circumstances described in the speech suggest that Spoudias enjoyed a practical control over the disputed assets of the estate which the speaker could counteract only by recourse to forensic and persuasive skills. His opponent was the man in possession. He can only insist that, however strong his physical position, the law is above him, and the debts of the estate must be paid (7–11).

Spoudias, however, has not been passive, and his counter-claims are sufficiently serious to force the plaintiff to meet them at an earlier point than is normal in a prosecution. His clever opponent has apparently used a standard technique of reversal of accusation to go onto the attack[52] arguing that the 10 minae claimed by the speaker were pledged by Polyeuctus not in discharge of a debt but as a favour won by personal influence or pressure (12), and therefore had no legal sanction. Spoudias would have had to produce some clear and detailed evidence to support this claim, but Demosthenes restricts himself to probabilities, first concentrating on witnesses, whom he lists generically not specifically, but to good rhetorical effect, using asyndetic anaphora,[53] masking the narrowness of his attack. The idea that witnesses, by the simple fact of their presence, are unlikely to have given false testimony, must presumably have been used frequently enough, but it is expressed here with new clarity and vigour, matched by the swift turn from defendant to jury in the apostrophe that follows.[54] Then he applies probability

[50] Note the word-order: ἐξ ἧς διακωλύει με τὰς μισθώσεις κομίζεσθαι Σπουδίας.

[51] The speaker never describes himself as κληρονόμος, and the word is commonly translated as 'heir' (e.g. Harrison *LA* i. 124). The term κλῆρος was used of the estate as a whole.

[52] 13: μεταστρέψαντα τὰς αἰτίας ἐγκαλεῖν καὶ διαβάλλειν.

[53] τοὺς παραγενομένους . . . τοὺς εἰδότας . . . τοὺς ἀκούοντας . . . τοὺς τὸ τελευταῖον ταῖς διαθήκαις παραγενομένους.

[54] 17: ἀκριβῶς γὰρ ὅπως τουτουσὶ διδάξεις· εἰ δὲ μὴ πάντες ὑμεῖς ἀπαιτεῖτ' αὐτόν.

to the behaviour of Spoudias, who made no objection to Polyeuctus' will while he was still alive (17–18): indeed, it was sealed in his presence (20–4). This portrayal of Spoudias' disingenuousness is completed in the closing sections, as Demosthenes concludes that he has in fact already contrived to receive far more than his due share of the estate (28). There is no clearly marked **epilogue**. The speaker simply reaffirms the significance he wishes the jury to attach to Spoudias' unwillingness to submit the dispute to the arbitration of mutual friends (29–30 (14–15)). There is a nice touch at the end, where the jury are seemingly likened to those 'friends' when he says to them: 'You know how everything happened.' The last sentence may account for the brevity of the speech.[55]

55 *Against Callicles*

Complaints against vicious neighbours (1) are as ancient as literature itself,[56] but the motivation attributed to the defendant in this case marks its time and place. Callicles is characterized as a typical vexatious litigant (*sycophantes*,[57] a charge often made in fifth- and fourth-century oratory), but in this deservedly popular speech[58] the direct invective usually associated with that charge is largely avoided. Yet the speaker clearly has an uphill task in this action for damages.[59] He has been worsted in a series of previous suits, losing by two cases to one (2, 6–7). The dispute concerns the ribbon of land between the two properties which functioned as a natural watercourse during wet weather, and as a road at other times. Both parties had, at various times in the past, sought to protect their land from inundation, but the earlier litigation seems to have established that the walling done by the speaker's father Teisias had narrowed the road. He now seeks to have these earlier judgements reversed.

After the characterization of Callicles noted above, and a reference to the previous litigation, the **prooemium** contains another example of Demosthenes' economic technique of briefly combin-

---

[55] It also reasserts the plaintiff's amateurish persona: 'unless I have left something out through being forced to speak with little water left in the clock'.

[56] Hesiod, *Op.* 346.

[57] §§ 2, 6, 22, 26, 28, 33, 35.

[58] It was, for example, one of a very small number of private speeches included in the schedule of Demosthenes' oratory by London University when papers were set centrally at that institution.

[59] See H. J. Wolff, 'The dike blabes in Demosthenes, Or. LV', *AJP* 64 (1943), 316–24.

ing standard topoi.[60] Now a lengthy narrative would not have served his purpose, since it would have resurrected a number of points on which the earlier cases had been decided against him. He therefore concentrates on the single question[61] which offers scope for argument: whether the road was recognized by all parties as a watercourse, and hence whether there was a genuine issue, as distinct from a contrived grievance. The evidence he offers is the opponents' apparent indifference to his father's wall-building: if it had concerned them, they should have remonstrated with him at the time of its erection.[62] But they waited until Teisias was dead in order to take on his inexperienced son in the courts (7), with some initial success.

At this stage the speaker has established one point—the shameless greed of his opponent—and implanted doubts about another—the very existence of a recognized watercourse. By § 10 the disputed ground has become a 'road', down which water occasionally flows.[63] An owner of adjacent land thus has two reasons for building a wall—to demarcate it against trespass and encroachment, and to prevent inundation, both legitimate actions to protect private property. (The fact that Teisias' predecessor had been a 'townie' (astikos, 11) who neglected his country estate adds some credibility.) This completes a cumulative representation of legality, before the opponents' main charge is spelt out—that Teisias had 'walled off the watercourse'. In the next clause, however, the speaker is made to say: 'but I intend to show that this is private land and no watercourse'.

He thus discloses the true nature of the charge—encroachment—but deals with it swiftly through a kind of historical probability. The wall that is alleged to have narrowed and/or diverted the channel also enclosed cultivated trees and ancestral tombs (13–14), and these are unlikely to be found on a public right-of-

---

[60] 2 'I beg you all to listen to me and to give me your attention, not because I am going to show myself an able speaker, but in order that you may learn the facts themselves . . .'.

[61] Ἐν μὲν οὖν . . . παρέχομαι δίκαιον.

[62] 5. Note the use of live speech. The interpretation of an opponent's silence as passivity due to impotence appears here for the first time. It reappears in a political context in 18 *Cor.* 196–8 (assuming a more sinister form in 307–8).

[63] Had it been to his advantage, Demosthenes could here have resorted to the standard rhetorical technique of 'definition' (on which see Radermacher *AS* 69 for examples from Antiphon to Isocrates), in order to distinguish between a ὁδός and a χάραδρα. But it is in his interest that the distinction should remain blurred.

way.[64] This appears to have dealt effectively with the charge of
encroachment, leaving the way open for Demosthenes to explore
some of the logical absurdities that can be confected from the
opponents' position. What do they want his client to do? Let the
water flow through his land and then divert it back on to the road
and become the person directly responsible for any damage caused
by it to another neighbour's land (16–17), and incur a greater
penalty? The combination of comparative argument with a possibly humorous exasperation[65] is completely novel (18):

> But surely, if I am not going to divert the water into the road, I should be
> very rash to turn it on to my neighbour's land. For when the penalty for
> the inundation of the plaintiff's land from the road is fixed, what penalty
> am I to expect, by heaven, at the hands of those suffering damage from
> water overflowing directly from my land? But if, once I have got the
> water on my land, I am not going to be allowed to drain it off either on
> to the road or on to other land, what in god's name is there left for me to
> do, gentlemen of the jury? I presume Callicles will not compel me to
> drink it all up!

The mood of exasperation is maintained in the sequel, which brims
over with rhetorical devices—the pathetic paradox of Callicles
indicting the speaker for a deed (wall-building) which he himself
has done to protect his own property,[66] reductio ad absurdum by
universalizing,[67] and anticipation of a major point to be proved.[68]
Other landowners react (25) philosophically[69] in the face of such
natural disasters: his opponents go to court for damage which was
their own fault.

Now a change of approach comes in the form of a little **narrative** (23–4). He tells how his mother, on one of her customary visits to her neighbour after some rain, had seen the small extent of

---

[64] 13: 'Who would think of planting these in a watercourse? Nobody, surely! Again, who
would think of burying his own ancestors there?'

[65] Modern critics tend to see humour in it, but Aristides (*Tech. Rhet.* B δ (Sp. ii. 470))
uses the passage to illustrate βαρύτης 'indignation' (trans. Wooten on Hermogenes, *On
Types of Style* 2. 8), which he relates to absurdity (τὸ ἄτοπον) and sees as a strong reaction
to it.

[66] 20: ὃ καὶ πάντων ἐστὶ δεινότατον . . . Also 22: οὔκουν δεινόν.

[67] 20: 'And yet, if all those in this region who have been damaged through water flood-
ing their lands are to sue me, my whole fortune multiplied many times would not meet the
cost.' This purely factitious introduction of other (unlitigious) landowners is used to make a
contrast with his vexatious opponents in § 22.

[68] 21: πεπονθότες μὲν οὐδέν, ὡς αὐτίχ' ὑμῖν ἐγὼ σαφῶς ἐπιδείξω.

[69] 22: τούτους . . . τὴν τύχην στέργειν.

the damage done. In addition to achieving its main purpose of providing direct evidence,[70] this *narratiuncula* offers the jury an appealing picture of past neighbourly friendship, destroyed now by the litigious Callicles. But this is only an interlude. Argument returns with a reversal of blame, a familiar enough technique, but here pursued with great persistence (22, 27, 29). Himself responsible for the floodings, Callicles tries to blame his neighbour, whose forbearance[71] is contrasted with his outrageous pettifoggery (28). A sycophantes prepares his cases with care. Callicles has done this in a suit related to the present one: typically, he has devised a stratagem[72] involving the evidence of Callarus, a slave of the speaker, the effect of which should bring them gain from either outcome. This addition to the portrait of a sycophantes leads to a summary of that portrait in the **epilogue** (33), and a brief reminder to the jury that he tried to settle the dispute by arbitration. The speech ends abruptly.

51 *On the Trierarchic Crown*

The group of early speeches concludes with one which is not strictly forensic, since it is addressed to the Boule. The speaker, who is probably Demosthenes himself, argues his claim for the award of a trierarchic crown[73] against the claims of others. In form, the speech seems literary rather than practical: it reads like a political pamphlet against men who tried to evade their civic duties. But it is also cool and dispassionate as the writer approaches the subject from different angles and explores each thoroughly. In the

---

[70] As his mother would hardly seem an unbiased witness to the jury, he reinforces her testimony with an oath.

[71] 29: ἡσυχίαν ἔχω . . . 30: . . . στέργω τὴν τύχην. The speaker is so reasonable that he accepts that Callicles' measures to protect his land were sensible (30: τοῦτον φράττοντα μὲν τὰ ἑαυτοῦ σωφρονεῖν ἡγοῦμαι).

[72] 31: καὶ τοῦθ' ηὕρηνται σόφισμα.

[73] The swift manning and equipment of triremes could make the difference between winning or losing a campaign. However, citizens appointed to the leitourgia of trierarch did not necessarily assume their duty with alacrity, sometimes even paying others to perform it in their place (this speech, 16, 18 . . . μεμισθωκέναι τὴν τριηραρχίαν) if only because of the dangers it might involve. Yet the award of a crown to the first trierarch to present his ship in fighting trim was the meed of patriotism which only the worst sluggard would scorn. The expedition was bound for the Hellespont under the command of Cephisodotus in 359 BC. For the earlier trierarchy served (reluctantly) by Demosthenes (363?), see 28 *Ag. Aphob.* II 17, 20 *Ag. Meidias* 78: see MacDowell *DAM* 297-9 for the course of events which ended with Demosthenes' reluctant assumption of this first trierarchy.

prooemium (1–3) standard topoi are present, but in subdued yet artistic form: instead of general preparations and machinations, the opponents have 'neglected their ships, but taken care to make ready their orators'; and instead of a straight plea for goodwill, he claims that the Council should feel more of it for himself than for his opponents because he has shown clearer recognition of their expectations.

An epideictic style predominates in the rest of the speech, some of it based on antithesis between the speaker's and the opponents' actions and motives. 4–6 concerns the preparations of his ship, which have been superior to theirs in both quality and speed because he spent more money on hiring the best.[74] But arguments against the crowning of his rivals occupy a much larger proportion of the speech, and are more varied and resourceful.[75] His deployment of precedent (or example from the past) is conventional enough in itself, but he uses it as material for a paradox: in the past his rivals' behaviour would have incurred extreme penalties, but they demand reward rather than punishment! (8–10). Routine comparative argument follows (11–12), but when he begins to draw implications for the public good and the city's reputation from selfishly unpatriotic private actions, individuality emerges once more as the logical conclusion is reached (13–14):

and you alone of all people cannot travel anywhere without a herald's staff, because of these men's seizure of hostages and provocation of reprisals; so that, if one looks realistically at the matter, he will find that triremes like these have sailed forth not for your benefit, but for your disadvantage.

From his rivals themselves, he turns to attack their supporters (16–20). They too are interested only in personal gain (17), and are prepared to sacrifice both honesty and logic in their pursuit of it. The idea of faulty rhetoric as a sign of nefarious intent is certainly a moral advance on earlier perceptions of its flexible serviceability

---

[74] For a similar argument, see Lysias 21. 2–6.

[75] Any doubt about the authorship of this speech should be dispelled by a single sentence (10): οὐ γὰρ ἐπειδὰν ἐάσητέ τι τῶν ὑμετέρων ἀπολέσθαι, τότε χρὴ χαλεπαίνειν, ἀλλ' ἐν ᾧ τὰ μὲν ὑμέτερ' ἐστι σῶα, καθορᾶτε δὲ τοὺς ἐφεστηκότας δι' αἰσχροκέρδειαν οὐχὶ προσήκουσαν πρόνοιαν περὶ σωτηρίας αὐτῶν ποιουμένους. ('For the time to feel exasperation is not after you have allowed some of your possessions to be lost, but while they are still in your hands and you see those placed in charge of them failing through shameful avarice to make adequate provision for their preservation.') The prophylactic sentiment and the forceful style are unmistakably Demosthenic.

for both good and bad causes. Moral pressure, however dubiously applied in some of his cases, becomes one of Demosthenes' most potent weapons:

Then again, they show so little regard for a good reputation, and are so thoroughly convinced that everything else is of secondary importance to gain, that they not only have the audacity to contradict in their own public statements what they said before, but even now their statements are inconsistent.[76]

The more general dangers of bad rhetoric are then touched upon briefly (20). In a longer speech he might have developed this into a full dilatation, but, as Blass points out, the latter half of the oration is already a digression from the main theme. The stirring manner of the ending maintains its pervasive acerbity,[77] as the young (c.25 years old) orator blames his audience for ignoring speakers' mercenary motives and methods (cf. 15). If this was his debut before the Council, Demosthenes must have made a memorable impression.

DEMOSTHENES SYMBOULOS

The need imposed by my subject to follow chronological order is conveniently met in the case of Demosthenes by examining his private speeches in two sections separated by the speeches on public issues.[78] The earliest of the latter belong to the year 355.[79]

The virtual disintegration of the Second Athenian Confederacy in the Social War (357–355) left her politicians with limited options—a fact which may relate to a dearth of prominent names

---

[76] 17: the basic construction is familiar (hypostasis (οὕτως . . . ὥστε)), but has certain individual features, each of the two parts being biclausal, the first part having two articular infinitives (τοῦ δοκεῖν . . . πρὸς τὸ λαβεῖν). The sentence as a whole (to κελεύουσι) is periodic.

[77] 9: οὐχὶ φρίττουσιν ἐν ὑμῖν . . . 11: καὶ ποῦ τὸ πάντας ἔχειν ἴσον καὶ δημοκρατεῖσθαι φαίνεται . . . 15: . . . ὑμᾶς δ᾽, οἵτινες οὐδὲ πεπονθότες πολλάκις ἤδη φυλάττεσθε, τί τις καλέσειεν ἄν; 19: . . . ἀλλ᾽ ἱερωσύνην ἰδίαν αὐτοί τινα ταύτην ἔχοντες . . . 21: τοῦ τοίνυν τούτους ἀδίκους εἶναι καὶ θρασεῖς, οὐδένες ὑμῶν εἰσιν αἰτιώτεροι.

[78] Speeches concerning legislation, public behaviour and public finance meet the definition 'public' even though they are technically prosecutions of named individuals.

[79] For a summary of discussions on the dating of the early political speeches, see D. F. Jackson and G. O. Rowe, Lustrum 14 (1969), 54–5.

among them, in that it was not the time for grandiose schemes propelled by dominant personalities. Identification of the leading men and their policies is as difficult as the tasks that faced them, which were the recovery of the Athenian economy at home and of her influence abroad.[80] Entering politics in such uncertain times, Demosthenes needed to play himself in quietly; but he saw opportunities both for the city and for himself, and seized on both as they arose.

20 *Against Leptines*

The first characteristic to strike the reader on turning from the early forensic speeches to this speech is that of scale, and this demands explanation. It may be assumed that it and his other contemporary speeches[81] mark the beginning of Demosthenes' political career:[82] in which case the audience and readership that he wished to address had become wider, or at least had wider political and literary interests, than the limited numbers of potential clients for his forensic speeches. The emergence of this more sophisticated and less practically motivated readership in turn raises another question: whether literary form and philosophical content now became essential components of the published speech, even if this meant complete revision and expansion of the core material of the original oration. Certain features of the speech *Against Leptines* point to this probability. Although it was technically the second speech for the prosecution, it contains all the essential material, lacking only a full formal prooemium.[83] Again, the large part of the speech that purports to anticipate opposing arguments (procatalepsis, 105–33, see below) seems incongruous and improbable in a speech supposedly delivered after the first speech by the defendant.

[80] Two names figure in most discussions, those of Aristophon and Eubulus. G. L. Cawkwell, *JHS* 83 (1963) has argued (p. 48) that the latter 'may not have risen to great political importance until some time had elapsed after the Social War and until the credit he had gained in the interim as a financier was extended to his counsels on policy'. R. Sealey, *JHS* 75 (1955), 79–80 adds Androtion to the two above.

[81] Dion Hal. *Ep. ad Ammaeum* 1. 4 actually places 22 *Against Androtion* first, but assigns both speeches to the same year, 355/4. Here, in an attempt to account for the differences between two closely contemporary speeches with similar backgrounds (both are graphai paranomon), there is practical value in examining the more elaborate speech first.

[82] His ambition to become a politician is famously depicted by his biographers as fuelled by a quite extraordinary determination to overcome physical weaknesses by unremitting practice. (For details, see Usher *GO* v. 2–3.)

[83] So Schol. p. 445, 11 Dd. 1; Blass *AB* iii/1. 268.

In the later months of the Social War (357–355), with the city in severe financial straits, Leptines had tried to alleviate the burden on the treasury by reimposing leitourgiai upon those citizens who had been enjoying the exemption (ateleia) awarded for some past public service rendered by them or their ancestors. A delay of about a year before Leptines' proposal was attacked seems to have reduced, or even removed, his personal liability for it. The attraction of such a case to Demosthenes at the beginning of his political career was compelling: he could ingratiate himself with the influential class of wealthier citizens liable to perform state duties, while not having to alienate Leptines and his friends by attacking him personally.[84] The opening sentence sets the measured and conciliatory tone of the speech:

It is mainly because I think the state will benefit (sympherein) from the repeal of this law, gentlemen of the jury, and secondarily out of sympathy for the son of Chabrias, that I have agreed to support the prosecutors.

Public advantage is prior to personal attachment, as is reason to sentiment. Consideration of these polarities is a valid critical procedure in an examination of this and other Demosthenic speeches in public causes, because for these speeches he is drawing his models not from the forensic oratory of his tutor Isaeus, but from the speeches of Thucydides and, to a lesser extent, the political discourses of Isocrates. In the former, in particular, the topos of advantage or expediency (sympheron) competed or contrasted with that of justice (dikaion). The present speech offered Demosthenes the opportunity to explore these themes, and to expand their scope.

In an early paraleipsis[85] he temporarily shelves argument from justice, and the reasons given subsequently (3–10) for retaining the exemptions are practical and utilitarian,[86] supported by logic.[87] But a moral strand runs alongside, appearing first at 10 and broadening in 11–17, where he represents the withdrawal of exemptions as a breach of trust, which is contrary to the Athenian character; and

---

[84] Kid-glove treatment of the defendant is one of the features of the speech: 13–14 'he may be a good man, for all I know', 102, 137, 144 'not against him personally, but against his law'.

[85] 2: 'I shall leave unsaid the argument that it is not just to deprive all men of this privilege because you will find fault with some.'

[86] e.g. 5: πότερόν ποτε λυσιτελέστερον . . . (cf. 13).

[87] 2–3 is a reductio an absurdum, arguing that Leptines' bill would deprive citizens of their constitutional rights.

offers in support the first of several historical examples.[88] But practical advantage returns (18–23), and is the best line to meet one of the arguments used by Leptines, that too many public services fall upon the poor because of the exemptions. The reply to this (20–7) has both practical and moral elements: the revenue 'clawed back' by abolishing the exemptions would not compensate for the resentment and distrust which it would engender, whereas their retention would leave wealth available for the obligatory services.[89]

The only exceptions allowed by Leptines were the descendants of the tyrannicides Harmodius and Aristogeiton. This meant that distinguished foreigners who had been granted exemption for signal services would no longer receive it. Demosthenes chooses as his first example a man whose alienation would inflict the greatest harm upon Athenian interests. Leucon, who ruled over the Cimmerian Bosporus from 393 to 353, virtually controlled the supply of corn from Athens' chief foreign source, and was thus the prime example of the advantage of reciprocal exemptions from all restrictions that impeded the flow of trade.[90] The double damage Leptines' law would cause is described with rhetorical questions (34–5):

Do you not realize that this very law, if ratified, will withdraw the exemption, both from Leucon, and from those of you who import corn from his country? For surely no one imagines that he will tolerate the annulment of your grants to him and allow his own concession to you to continue? . . . In view of this, are you still considering whether you should remove this law from your statutes? Have you not made up your minds long ago?

After practical advantage, justice takes over, introduced by the emotional image of agreements carved in stone (36–7, reappearing in 64–6). Leucon himself is portrayed as a deeply wronged figure asking what he has done to deserve such punishment in return for his favour and trust towards Athens.

---

[88] These have made the speech a useful secondary historical source. The present one has a comparative (greater and lesser) element: in it the Athenians elect to repay a debt even to their recent enemies, the Lacedaemonians, after the fall of the Thirty Tyrants.

[89] There were no exemptions from war-tax (*eisphora*) or from trierarchies (26). Demosthenes underlines these exceptions with rhetorical effect (26–7: 'For money spent by the chorus-masters gratifies us theatre-goers for a fraction of a day, but money spent freely on equipment for war gives the city security for all time').

[90] Characteristically, Demosthenes has 'done his homework' on the figures, of which he gives details (31–2).

Remoter in time were the benefactions of Epicerdes of Cyrene. He opportunely saved from death a remnant of the Athenian expedition to Sicily (413 BC), so the exemptions he was granted were being enjoyed now by his descendants (47). Here the benefits to both parties are materially small, so more must be made of the moral factors—his sympathy and benefactions at the time of Athens' greatest disaster, for which he exacted no reward, thereby increasing the shame which should be felt at this treatment.[91]

A philosophical passage (49–50) recommending vigilance in maintaining good laws adds variety before the introduction of another example, the Corinthians who tried to shelter the defeated contingent of the Athenian army in their city after the Battle of Nemea (394),[92] a service which the Athenians were able to requite seven years later. How would Leptines' law strike a citizen of those times?[93] As this example, too, gives way to another philosophical passage (56–7), a new idea is introduced, which recurs frequently thereafter—that of envy: 'To give no reward in the first place is a matter of exercising human judgement; to take it away after giving it is the act of envy, and you must not seem to have felt that.'[94]

Shorter examples of rewarded benefactors follow (59–63), and then some hypothetical historical parallels are considered (61–3) before the section which serves as the centre of gravity of the whole speech, those of Athens' own citizens whose exploits have, in recent times, won them the coveted *ateleia* (67–86). The first of these, Conon, restored Athenian fortunes with Persian aid, and serves Demosthenes' plan well because he was lavishly honoured abroad (71), thus providing a link with the previous benefactors. This foreign recognition and his domestic fame outweighed the possible embarrassment arising from the fact that the living heir to his exemption was his son Timotheus, who had reached the summit of his career in 357, but was under indictment at the time of

[91] Note the powerful comparative argument here (47): 'If those who knew and experienced his generosity felt that it deserved this reward, while we, who have only heard the story told, shall revoke the gift as undeserved, how shall we not be guilty of exceptional wrongdoing (ὑπέρδεινον ποιήσομεν).'

[92] Xenophon, *Hell.* 4. 2. 23, mentions only the Corinthians who barred their gates to the Athenians.

[93] Prosopopoiia (55): 'If a man of those times . . . should hear this law which revokes the gifts which were then bestowed, how he would decry the wickedness of those who made the law . . . ' (cf. 87).

[94] The style is gnomic and old-fashioned: the sentence could have been written by a Thucydides or an Antiphon.

this speech after defeat in the Battle of Embata.[95] Now Conon afforded comparison with the great Themistocles, but this comparison had been made before, and to greater rhetorical effect because of an element of irony.[96] Of more immediate relevance was the career of Chabrias (see 1), and this receives laudatory treatment as it rounds off the central section (75–87). But the praise always contains a sharp edge of reproof for those who would undermine it by niggardly legislation (83):

And what shall we say, men of Athens, when the trophies he set up as general in your name stand plain for all men to see, but a part of the reward for those trophies is seen to have been snatched away?

In 88–104 Demosthenes outlines his own side's positive legislative proposals, which really amount to a restoration of the status quo, as he himself admits.[97] All he will do is to underline a provision of the old law that anyone could object to a proposed recipient, and his objection would stand if it were upheld in court. This draws him into a discussion of the safeguards laid down by Solon against hasty and contradictory legislation (90–4), concluding with the specific clauses of Leptines' law that contradict the existing law. Attention is focused increasingly on Leptines himself as he is challenged to make the correction himself, in the certain knowledge that his opponents would do so if he did not.[98] He politely accuses Leptines of ignorance of the relevant Solonian laws, and points a contrast with his own cleverness by a sophistical argument (102–3):

If Solon made a law that a man may, in default of legitimate children, give his property to anyone he pleased, not with the aim of depriving his next-of-kin of their rights, but in order, by making the prize open to all, to stimulate rivalry in mutual benefaction; and if you, by contrast, have proposed a law that the people should not be allowed to bestow on any man any part of what is theirs, how can you be said to have understood the laws of Solon?

Here the young Demosthenes, displaying his argumentative skills, has also exposed his inexperience. Not only is the parallel between

[95] Diod. Sic. 16. 21. 4. Timotheus' misfortune deprived Demosthenes of an otherwise ideal contemporary example. Iphicrates was also ruled out for similar reasons.
[96] By Lysias, 12 *Ag. Eratos.* 63.
[97] 89: 'And there is nothing novel in all this, nor any invention of ours.'
[98] 100: ἐγγυώμεθα, ὑπισχνούμεθα. Demosthenes also refers to that fearsome law, the bugbear of Athenian demagogues, which imposed the death penalty on those who broke their promises to the Assembly, the Council, or the Law Courts.

private and public munificence strained,[99] but also the idea of potential heirs responding to the prospect of a fat legacy by competing with their rivals in mutual benefaction is remote from reality, as a reading of a few pages of almost any speech of Isaeus would confirm.

His opponents have explored parallels of a more promising kind—the practice of other states (105–11) and that of Athens herself in former times (112–19); and they have insisted on the justice of such parallels. Demosthenes challenges this, saying that, while provocative, they are not just.[100] In oligarchic Sparta comparable privileges confer more power than in democratic Athens, where the people are supreme: in Thebes (darkly portrayed), their powerful men deserve no honour. In the prosperous Athens of old,[101] good men were rewarded with land and money, not immunity from tax (115).

To these two anticipated arguments, based mainly on justice, Demosthenes adds a further three: that the law proposed would still allow the state to make awards at its discretion (120–4); that the leitourgiai are religious duties, from which nobody should be exempted (125–30); that exemptions were open to abuse by bogus claimants (131–3). If an earlier observation on procatalepsis in a deuterology (n. 83) is recalled, it may be concluded that Demosthenes' replies to the arguments used in these five cases were programmatic rather than forensic—intended to air views which would cause his readers to credit him with a distinctive political personality. These were the importance of the bond of trust between the state and the individual (120–4, 131–4), and the sovereignty of the people (107), even over religious considerations (125–30). The train of thought is smoothly brought back to the idea of public reward as an incentive to public service, but reference to encomiastic oratory and prizes at games (141–2) is made without recourse to Isocratean artifice. The style seems deliberately clipped, with short sentences and avoidance of parallelism.

A review of persons who have defended Leptines' law (146–53) concludes the main body of this discursive oration. Such criticisms

---

[99] It reappears in a more suitable context in 136.

[100] 105: παροξυντικοί . . . πρὸς τὸ τὰς ἀτελείας ὑμᾶς πεῖσαι, οὐ μέντοι δίκαιοί γ' οὐδαμῇ.

[101] Now Athens can only *hope* for a prosperous future (115: νῦν δ' εὐπορήσει (euphemistic)).

as he makes of them are cool and measured, but even the octoge-
narian Aristophon does not escape criticism as his previous proposal
of a reward is compared with his present support for the opposite
policy (149). In tune with his attitude to other politicians in this
speech, Demosthenes' admonition of Cephisodotus (150) and
Deinias (151) is tempered with praise of their good qualities.

In a speech which has been concerned more with public policy
than with prosecution and legal technicality, the **epilogue**
(154–67), while performing its conventional function of drawing
together the main arguments in summary form, is allowed some
scope to expand on the practical aspects of the questions raised.
After showing the evil consequences of Leptines' law as drafted, he
graphically illustrates the necessity of precise definition by noting
the care with which Draco, a proverbially harsh legislator, distinguished between culpable and justified homicide (158).[102] He is
objecting to the wholesale abolition of exemption which Leptines
has proposed. What if heroes of the calibre of Harmodius and
Aristogeiton, the only exemptions allowed by Leptines, should
arise in the future (160)? Failure to reward men such as these will
cause the city to be regarded as untrustworthy, envious, and
mean.[103] The rational tone is maintained to the end as the speaker
urges the jury not to yield to the clamour, violence, and shamelessness of his opponents (166).

22 *Against Androtion*

The defendant in this case had a thirty-year political career behind
him and the seasoned skills which he had developed in the course
of it.[104] He was also currently unpopular with the wealthier class
because of his stewardship of the war-tax (*eisphora*), and had made
personal enemies besides. Two of these, Euctemon and Diodorus,
chose to attack him in the courts when he placed a proposal to

---

[102] 'Now Draco, in his laws on homicide, marked the terrible wickedness of killing
another man by banning the offender from the purifying water, the libations, the loving-
cup, the sacrifices, and the market-place. He listed everything likely to deter an offender.
Yet he never deprived a man of his right to justice, but defined the circumstances in which
homicide was justified, and exonerated the killer in those circumstances.'

[103] 164: ἡ δὲ πόλις . . . δόξει ἄπιστος, φθονερά, φαύλη παρὰ πᾶσιν εἶναι.

[104] 4: ἔστι . . . τεχνίτης τοῦ λέγειν καὶ πάντα τὸν βίον ἐσχόλακεν ἐνὶ τούτῳ.
Cf. 66: θρασὺς καὶ λέγειν δεινός. He had also been a pupil of Isocrates. See
P. Harding, 'Androtion's Political Career', *Historia* 25 (1976), 186–200.

grant a crown to the outgoing Council before the Assembly, without obtaining a preliminary decree by the incumbent Council. It is easy to see why Demosthenes should have welcomed the opportunity to write Diodorus' speech: it was another deuterology, giving scope for rhetorical display; the defendant was both skilful and unpopular—an ideal opponent for an orator trying to make his way in the wider political sphere; and he could exploit his role as speechwriter to make his client his mouthpiece, while hoping to enjoy a degree of immunity from direct reprisals in the event of defeat.

The mood of personal conflict is apparent from the start, but grows in intensity throughout. In beginning by briefly describing the false charges which Androtion had brought against Euctemon and himself, Diodorus assumes the jury's acceptance of revenge as a reasonable motive for his prosecution.[105] The **prooemium** (1–4) ends with the conventional plea for attention, but this is amplified with a warning against Androtion's rhetorical wiles. Justification for this warning is soon apparent, as Androtion is shown to have misquoted, by omission, the relevant law (5), and later to have taken the absence of a legal provision as permissive (8).[106] Demosthenes is able to describe the mood of protest within the Council when denial of the crown was broached (9–10), and goes on to explain why such importance was attached to the building of ships (12–16). Such historical passages, suffused with patriotism, become one of the special features of his deliberative oratory. The present passage also meets a need peculiar to the case. The importance of building triremes must be stressed, because Androtion has argued that the Council has in the past been awarded crowns without meeting that obligation (6–7). This dispensation is denied by the speaker (6), but it is probably the main weakness of his case, which he consequently has to pursue through personal attack. His choice of Androtion's hybris (1, 16, 54, 61) as his main vice fits his purpose well, as it is just such a man who will flout or deliberately misinterpret laws.

But Androtion remains a resourceful adversary, and Demosthenes has to devote about a third of his speech (17–46) to answering his clever arguments and the pleas of his friends. Demosthenes

---

[105] An assumption approved by contemporary ethics. See Dover *GPM* 182.
[106] 'The law, he says, forbids the Council to ask for a reward, if they have not built the ships: I agree. But, he says, it does not stop the Assembly from giving it.'

effectively deploys some conventional rhetoric in this section,[107] and delivers it in a lively style.[108] As to subject-matter, he is at pains to be seen observing correct procedure—witnesses and evidence— not relying on mere calumny (21–3) but upholding Solon's law, which barred immoral men like the defendant from addressing public audiences (31–2). The impatience of an ambitious young politician is to be seen when Demosthenes expresses the need to get rid of the corrupt clique of 'established speakers',[109] but the dif- ficulty posed by some of Androtion's arguments is obvious, espe- cially the mitigating one in which he has reminded the jury of his success in collecting war-tax (42). It must have been the potency of this and some of his other arguments which persuaded Demosthenes to turn to personal attack for the concluding part of his speech.

High-handed[110] treatment of his fellow-citizens made their lives worse than under the Thirty. The description evokes that evil time, and is also a comparison (52):

Now under the Thirty, we may hear, no man was left incapable of saving himself if he could hide in his house: what we denounce the Thirty for is that they arrested men illegally in the market-place. This man exceeded their brutality to such a degree that, though a politician in a democracy, he turned every man's private house into a gaol by leading the Eleven into your homes. What if a poor man, or a rich man who has spent a lot and is perhaps rather short of cash, should have to climb over the roof to a neighbour's house or creep under the bed to avoid being caught and dragged off to gaol, or should have to behave in some other unseemly way, suited to a slave rather than a free man, and be seen acting in this way by his wife, whom he married as a free citizen? And what if the cause of all this was Androtion . . . ?

---

[107] e.g. 22: definition; 23: reversal of charge; 41: dilemmaton. New formulae for pro- catalepsis: 35: . . . βέλτιον ὑμᾶς προακοῦσαι. 42: Οἶμαι τοίνυν αὐτὸν οὐδ' ἐκείνων ἀφέξεσθαι τῶν λόγων (litotes).

[108] The highpoint of a discussion on the modes of litigation open to different classes (which underlines the two-tier character of the Athenian court system) is an asyndetic ques- tion-and-answer passage (26), the first of its kind in oratory, but much imitated (see Denniston GPS 118–19): ἔρρωσαι καὶ σαυτῷ πιστεύεις· ἐν χιλίαις δὲ [δραχμαῖς] ὁ κίνδυνος. ἀσθενέστερος εἶ· τοῖς ἄρχουσιν ἐφηγοῦ· τοῦτο ποιήσουσιν ἐκεῖνοι. φοβεῖ καὶ τοῦτο· γράφου. καταμέμφει σεαυτὸν καὶ πένης ὢν οὐκ ἂν ἔχοις χιλίας ἐκτεῖσαι· δικάζου κλοπῆς πρὸς διαιτητὴν καὶ οὐ κινδυνεύσεις.

[109] 37: εἰ . . . τῶν ἠθάδων καὶ συνεστηκότων ῥητόρων ἀπαλλαγήσεσθε.

[110] 47: 'a shameless, reckless thief and a bully, fit for anything rather than public life in a democracy'.

This description compensates in vividness for a historical flaw in
the comparison. In Lysias' account, with which Demosthenes was
surely acquainted, the Thirty arrested him in his house (12. 8) and
his brother Polemarchus on the street (16, 26, 30). Lysias' escape
was more dignified than that of Androtion's imaginary victim, but
the only difference between his methods and those of the Thirty
seems to be that his were more efficient. Again, the young
Demosthenes has overplayed his hand, but his main purpose is kept
in sight—to portray Androtion as hybristic and disposed to treat
fellow-citizens like slaves (55, 68); and the taint of oligarchy lies
near the surface.[111] There is a new psychological insight as
Androtion's insensitivity is related to his vices (58), and the character Demosthenes has colourfully[112] created for him converts him
from a conscientious collector of war-tax into a tyrannical and universally abominated figure, with no mitigating virtue.[113] He makes
emotional capital out of Androtion's melting down of the golden
crowns, 'tokens of emulation and honourable ambition' (69–73),
quoting their inscriptions. He compares them with the great mon-
uments to Athenian patriotism, the Parthenon and the Propylaea,
and with the contrast which these provide, achieves a note of
bathos as he aims his last blow at his wretched opponent (78).[114]

24 Against Timocrates

Although this may be regarded as a companion-speech to the last—
it was written for the same client and contains several common
passages—its greater scale and complexity mark a significant stage
in Demosthenes' development. Here Diodorus is the first speaker
in another graphe paranomon. Timocrates had proposed the
offending law to protect his friends Androtion, Melanopus, and

[111] 57: 'The laws and the principles of the constitution do not uphold this [sc. the arbitrary seizure of private property], and you should guard these closely.' Oligarchs are the ultimate abusers of the property of others. See also 32.

[112] 59: . . . βδελυρίαν καὶ θεοισεχθρίαν . . . 63: . . . προπετείᾳ καὶ θρασύτητι . . .
64: . . . ἀναισθησίας καὶ πονηρίας.

[113] 69: 'Yes, he was indeed of this character in his public life, but he has managed some
things creditably. No, he has not, and the rest of his behaviour towards you has been even
more abominable . . . ' (A form of hypophora.)

[114] 76 . . . κτήματα ἀθάνατα . . . 77 . . . καὶ ἃ πᾶς τις ἂν εὖ φρονῶν εὔξαιτο . . .
78 . . . Ἀνδροτίων ὑμῖν πομπείων ἐπισκευαστής, Ἀνδροτίων, ὦ γῆ καὶ θεοί. καὶ
τοῦτ' ἀσέβημ' ἔλαττον τίνος ἡγεῖσθε (' . . . and the repairer of your processional plate
is Androtion! Androtion, by Heaven and Earth! What grosser impiety can you imagine than
that?').

Glaucetes, who had captured an enemy ship out of Naucratis while travelling on an embassy to King Mausolus of Caria, and retained the booty from it, though this was deemed to be the property of the state. The ambassadors had thus become state debtors; and Timocrates' law exempted these from imprisonment until the ninth prytany, if they gave sureties for their debt. Through their graphe paranomon Euctemon and Diodorus prevented the new law from operating, forcing Androtion and his colleagues to pay up, and pursued Timocrates with this further indictment.

Conventional division and topoi may be discerned in the opening sections. The **prooemium** (1–5) contains a pointed version of the attention-topos,[115] but its especial interest lies in its adumbration of the main themes of the speech, which are not primarily adversarial or forensic, but philosophical and political—the relationship between good laws, well administered, and the stability and prosperity of the state.[116] The personal note introduced in the **prodiegesis** (6–10), where the speaker's quarrel with Androtion is mentioned, promises a varied treatment later. The **narrative** of essential facts (11–14) is unique in its condensation and abruptness, using asyndeton to a greater degree than any previous narrative.[117] But one effect of this original treatment is to return the reader to central themes as quickly as possible.

Well-founded laws that have stood the test of time have been flouted by Timocrates (17–24), who has also ignored standard procedures in introducing his own (26–32). These two crimes combined stimulated Demosthenes' invention in this classic case of a graphe paranomon. The old topos of good laws is revitalized and enriched by contrast with bad legislators, but more important than this is the political dimension. The guardians of the laws are the people in their capacity as *dicastai* (36–7). The legal system was both the foundation of democracy and its protector. Hence suspicion of revolutionary, and especially oligarchic, intent must fall upon those who seek to undermine it. These are the main recurrent themes of the speech, which will have reassured his readers that his views

---

[115] 4: after admitting that it is a routine topos, he insists that it was never more appropriate than in the present case.

[116] 1: Timocrates' law is said to 'damage and impair the state' and (2) to rob the Courts of their powers.

[117] Ten successive sentences begin without connective particles. Note also the rapid succession of asyndetic verbs (13): ἐβόων, ἠγανάκτουν, ἐλοιδοροῦντο, ἀπέλυον τοὺς τριηράρχους.

were safely on the conservative side at a time of potential instability for the city.

But first he must expose the flaws in Timocrates' law and show how it conflicts with existing law. In the course of this exposure (43–89) corrections of drafting errors serve to advertise Demosthenes' own skills, the more so as he takes pains to represent Timocrates as both malign (48–9,[118] cf. 110) and later as clever, or at least experienced (100–1, 155–7). Then he displays his broader political vision as he shows (91–108) how the state depends on the prompt performance of leitourgiai. The passage is animated by typically sarcastic Demosthenic humour (93–4):

Now see how this fine fellow's law cripples and corrupts that process. His clause reads: 'if the penalty of imprisonment has been or shall hereafter be imposed on any debtor, he shall, on nominating a surety who undertakes to pay the money during the ninth prytany, be released from imprisonment.' Then where are our revenues? How shall any expedition be sent abroad? How shall we collect money, if every defaulter nominates sureties under this man's law instead of doing what he should? I suppose we shall say to the Greek world: 'Timocrates' law operates here, so please wait until the ninth prytany: we'll start the war after that.'

At this point the main charges against Timocrates have been established, and this stage is marked by a summary (108–9). This is the point on which the speech turns. In many earlier forensic speeches the latter half contains biographical material (pistis ek biou), but in this speech this is given a strong political colouring. After a lively introduction underlining the sinister motives and anti-popular sentiments of Timocrates and his friends,[119] they are subjected individually to attack, with hypophora; and other forms of question are used to add a degree of pungency (125 (esp.), 126–8). The jury is urged to make an example of these wrongdoers (131–8).

A logical sequence of thought now begins with the famous example of the Locrians and their stable laws (139–41), contrasted with constant innovation at Athens. Innovation equates with revolution in Athenian political vocabulary, and the chief motive of the innovators is the subversion of democracy (152): their method

---

[118] An elaborate hypothetical inversion in apostrophe: (48) καίτοι χρῆν σε, ὦ Τιμόκρατες ... (49) νῦν δὲ ...

[119] Note the extemporaneous formula μεταξὺ λέγων ... ἐνεθυμήθην (122). Also, § 122 is really an elaborate pathetic paradox, introduced dramatically (παράδοξόν τι, θαυμαστὸν ἡλίκον).

of achieving this being to secure special privileges for men of oligarchic bent like Androtion. The cabalistic machinations of contemporary politicians are described in terms which show the extent
to which they damaged the interests of the majority (157–9), and
this general description is followed by an individual illustration—
some highlights of Androtion's career (160–4) drawn from *Against
Androtion* (52–3). The common people, with whom Demosthenes
identifies himself,[120] are treated like slaves when he and his friends
exercise public office (166–9), while corrupt politicians of their
own ilk escape punishment. The picture of life under oligarchy is
complete. It remains to re-focus on the case against Timocrates.

    The complexity of Demosthenes' aims in this speech is reflected
in the variety of topics which occur in the long **epilogue**
(187–218). After reaffirming that Timocrates' law is 'undesirable,
illegal, and unjust',[121] he reviews its purpose,[122] and concludes that
its overall effect would be the Popular Court's loss of control over
penalties (190), and follows this with a philosophical passage distinguishing between laws governing public and private obligations
(192–3). But after this the focus is on the character and methods
(197–203), the motives (204–5) of Timocrates and his friends; and
the bad effects of his law are shown in order to press home his
guilt.[123] The argument is given emotional strength by introducing
Draco and Solon (211–13), and by reminding the jury of the
universal respect in which Athenian laws are held (210), and of
the military and naval power the city is able to wield because
of them.[124] Finally (217–18), the need to make an example of
Timocrates is stressed, and the speech ends.

23 *Against Aristocrates*

An opportunity to expatiate on foreign policy, and on other topics
through which he could show his grasp of the complexities of contemporary politics, was seized by Demosthenes when he wrote this
speech for a certain Euthycles. The case was heard a year later than
Against Timocrates, in 352/1, and was another graphe paranomon.

---

[120] 169: τῶν πολλῶν ἡμῶν.

[121] 187: ἀσύμφορος . . . παρὰ πάντας τοὺς νόμους . . . ἀδίκως ἔχων.

[122] 188–9 is a complex dilemmaton arguing that both claims of private and of public utility for the law fail.

[123] One effect is graphically likened to throwing open the prisons (208).

[124] He does not refer here to the law as an instrument of taxation.

The foreign lands in question were Thrace and the Hellespontine region, where Euthycles had served as a trierarch (5).[125] Here was the domain of the shifty king Cersobleptes, but the present trial was more directly concerned with Charidemus of Oreus, a mercenary commander in his pay who had earlier been granted Athenian citizenship for his part in negotiating the Peace of Chares (357). The defendant Aristocrates had proposed a further honour for Charidemus—that of inviolability, which not only made his assassin subject to summary arrest but also excluded any state which harboured him from all treaties with Athens. Behind these favours lay political expediency. Eubulus and his supporters sought through them to maintain friendly relations with Cersobleptes in order to minimize the commitment of Athenian forces to a region which was nevertheless vital to her trade links. Without, at this stage in his career, attacking Eubulus by name, Demosthenes sought to expose the hazards of such a policy by showing the character and motives of the mercenary and his paymaster.

The right tone of high-minded impersonality is set at the start. Demosthenes dissociates his client from the common herd of *rhetores* as he combines the topoi of the reluctant litigant and the inexperienced speaker (4–6). Thereafter, however, the divisions of the speech are, both logically and rhetorically, consummately skilful. A preliminary narrative (8–17) provides the essential historical background as it tells how Cersobleptes' Athenian backers cunningly and treacherously[126] exploited his enemies' goodwill towards the city to promote his ambitions, which conflicted with Athenian interests. Then in § 18, the subjects of each subsequent division are clearly stated:

That the decree is contrary to the laws (*para tous nomous*) (24–99).
That it is contrary to the state's interest (*asymphoron tei polei*) (100–22).
That Charidemus is unworthy to receive the privileges (*anaxios*) (123–95).

The didactic tone in which he demands piecemeal objectivity of his audience (20–1) has a new confidence, and he proceeds to show how the special law proposed for Charidemus conflicts with existing homicide law[127] and is itself ambiguous. Looking to his future

---

[125] His identity is preserved by Dion. Hal. *Ep. ad Amm.* 1. 4. Demosthenes could equally have been speaking for himself in § 5 when he refers to the trierarchy.

[126] 15: πῶς ἂν τεχνικώτερον ἢ κακουργότερον συμπαρεσκεύασαν ἄνθρωποι ...

[127] The speech is one of the main sources for Athenian homicide law. See MacDowell *AHL passim*, esp. 73–7. Sealey *DT* (1993) 131 finds Demosthenes' argument flawed, but does not examine the relevant passages (16, 27–9).

career, Demosthenes makes the most of the opportunity afforded
by this section to impress his audience with his own drafting skills,
as well as his profound respect for legal tradition. Aristocrates, by
contrast, has failed to define essential terms and deal with the particular circumstances, such as unintentional killing, which, under
existing law, would give rise to exceptions. Demosthenes constantly praises existing law for the very qualities which he finds
wanting in the legislation of his opponent, but otherwise mostly
eschews rhetoric[128] in a section concerned mainly with definition,
analysis, and legal history.

In the next section (100–22) the question of the state's interest,
frequently the dominant theme of deliberative oratory, produces
Demosthenes' first pronouncements on foreign policy. He shows
himself aware of the principle of counterbalancing power (102),[129]
as the internal quarrels of groups of states are the best guarantee of
security for their other neighbours. Then he applies it to Thrace:
favour shown to Cersobleptes through his general Charidemus
would alienate his enemies, who would not side with Athens when
he turned traitor on them (106). A combination of past interactions
and general patterns of human behaviour forms the basis of predic-
tion for Demosthenes: a formula which was to serve him well in
his later deliberative oratory is here deployed systematically for the
first time. Historical facts are closely bound up with argument, the
link between them being the psychology of the leading figures,
whose likely actions are deduced and thus form the basis of the policy which he advises. Immediacy and vigour are imparted to the
oratory, as elsewhere, by imaginary live speech (106) and questions
(106–7). Of interest, both to his audience and to modern readers,
are references to the early career of Philip II of Macedon (107–9,
111–13), but the psychology of princes with too much power is
drawn from the immediate context (114):

But why is there need to name Philip, or any one else? Cersobleptes' own
father, Cotys, whenever he was quarrelling with anyone, used to send his
ambassadors, and was ready to do anything, realizing that being at war
with Athens was an unprofitable exercise. But, as soon as he had all
Thrace in his power, he would seize cities, do mischief, go on a drunken
rampage, damaging first himself and then us in his desire to possess the

---

[128] Note, however, the pathetic paradox in 56 (οὐκοῦν δεινόν) which anticipates the latter attack on Charidemus.
[129] See Xen. *Hell.* 1. 5. 9; cf. Dem. 16 *Meg.* 4–5.

whole country—it was impossible to do business with him. For everyone
bent on wrongful gain tends to calculate, not the extreme difficulties he
may encounter, but the gains he will achieve if he is successful.

The psychological endnote becomes a Demosthenic trademark,
and Thucydidean influence is clear.[130] It serves to confirm a generalization, and in the other examples which follow the unreliability of these ambitious despots is illustrated, completing the
preparations for the case to be made against Charidemus personally.

This begins in 123. The paraleipsis in 125 is really only a delay of
the catalogue of Charidemus' offences against Athens, which
begins in 144. He is a mercenary commander, with no national loy-
alties and hence no moral restraints: to sponsor him would damage
the city's reputation (138–41), which had been upheld by inaction
in the case of another mercenary commander, Philiscus, killed by
Thersagoras and Execestus from Lampsacus. Demosthenes pursues
the parallel with Harmodius and Aristogeiton as far as he can. If the
decree of inviolability proposed for Charidemus had been applied
to Philiscus, a successful prosecution of the two Lampsacenes
would have ensued (143):

How then could you not have been guilty of a shameful and terrible deed
if, while erecting bronze statues of the men who performed a similar act
in your own city, and honouring them with lavish gifts, you had condemned to exile those who in some other country had shown the same
patriotic spirit?

A possible weakness of such rhetorical parallels as this (here reinforced by pathetic paradox) is that they are not true historical parallels. It is not known that Philiscus had, at any time in his career,
been disposed to serve Athenian interests. It was all the more necessary, therefore, when Demosthenes came to examine the career
of Charidemus, for particular emphasis to be laid upon his actual
hostility to Athens.

Demosthenes uses paraleipsis to establish the tone of a fair
critic,[131] contrasting himself with the 'mercenary speakers'[132] who

[130] Thuc. 1. 70 (portrayal of the Athenian character); 6. 24 (the mood of the Athenians
before the Sicilian Expedition). See also 1. 42. 4, 4. 62. 3–4 (the counter-argument).
Thucydidean sentiment is likewise to be noted in 134: 'and when a man is farther-sighted
than his friend, he should order things for the best, and not regard temporary gratification as
of more value than security for all time.'

[131] 148: . . . ἀλλ' ἐῶ ταῦτα . . . τὸν δικαίως ἐξετάζοντα. The catalogue of misdeeds
is to be long. By appearing judiciously selective (though actually mentioning Charidemus'
early misdeeds), the orator hopes to avoid the charge of mere invective.

[132] 146: τοὺς ἐπὶ μισθῷ λέγειν καὶ γράφειν εἰωθότας. See § 4.

deceive their gullible audience. Then his individual technique of
rhetorical narrative is deployed at length (149–59). According to
that technique, facts are not recited simply, but always interpreted
and related to an idea which the speaker wishes to impress on his
audience. In this case it is Charidemus' hostility to Athens.
Sometimes allusion to it is quite crudely overt,[133] but more often
his actions are closely related to their consequences, of which he is
shown to be fully aware. There are also oblique references to his
character, such as his ingratitude (151), and his malice is matched
only by his incompetence (155–6). Gradually a quasi-forensic case
is being made out against him, with documents adduced in proof
of his hostility; and the use of questions following those documents
(164) adds to the agonistic tone as it leads to further recital of
Charidemus' hostile actions (165–6) and other atrocities (169). By
his actions he has convicted himself of 'watching out for opportunities to harm our city', and they prove him to have been 'the city's
enemy'.[134] Demosthenes' ability to speak with first-hand knowledge about the politics of Thrace and its neighbours,[135] and even
to draw an analogy with the Greek mainland (182) gives authority
to his portrayal of Charidemus, and makes the conferment of honours upon such a man by Athens seem not only impolitic but
absurd (185):

All others who have received any favour from you have been honoured
for the benefits they have bestowed on you; Charidemus is unique in
receiving honours for the incompetence of his attempts to injure you.

In the closing chapters (196–220) examples from the past are
adduced as correctives to the excessive granting of rewards. Men
like Themistocles and Miltiades (196–7) were content with the
honour of having led and served, as their victories belonged to the
people who had fought. Today individual leaders wield too much
power and claim the credit and the material rewards that accompany it, reversing the old order, under which wealth was displayed
through public, not private buildings (207–8). 'The people were
then the masters, as they are now the servants, of the politicians'

---

[133] e.g. 150 'finding he could not do you any harm in that country . . . '

[134] 173: ἔργῳ ἑαυτὸν ἐξήλεγξεν ὅτι καιροφυλακεῖ τὴν πόλιν ἡμῶν . . . (cf. 183
. . . οὐδ' ἂν ὁντινοῦν καιρὸν παρείη); 175: Χαριδήμου δ' ἔργῳ φανεροῦ γεγενημένου
ὅτι τῆς πόλεως ἐχθρός ἐστιν.

[135] This authority was derived from his service as trierarch under Cephisodotus in the
region in 359.

(209). These and related topics are reused by both Demosthenes (in the *Third Olynthiac*) and Aeschines (in *Ag. Ctesiphon*). The speech concludes (215–20) with a summary of practical objections to the decree as drafted. These include its contradiction of existing law (recalling the main *paranomon* charge) and specifically the objection to summary action against Charidemus' killer.

14 *On the Symmories*[136]

While Demosthenes was honing his oratorical skills and publicizing his views on matters of public concern in the *graphai* against Androtion, Timocrates, and Aristocrates, the end of the Social War, which so weakened Athenian power, had brought with it alarms and emergencies which an aspiring politician could not afford to ignore. Of these, reports of renewed preparations by the Persian King to interfere in Greek affairs demanded reaction. The year was 354, and Demosthenes addressed the Assembly for the first time.

The **prooemium** (1–2) of this speech is best understood[137] as a personal statement of intent. In starting with a reference to a common epideictic topos, the praise of ancestors, and questioning its usefulness, he is alluding to the current practice of other speakers from the bema. The influence of Isocrates on some of these (Androtion was a pupil[138]) had deprived public oratory of the immediate practicality necessary for its effectiveness. This was a trend which Demosthenes proposed to reverse by his own example (2):

For my part, however, I shall simply try to tell you how best to make your preparations. This is how things stand. Even if all of us who are to address you should show ourselves clever speakers, you would surely be no

---

[136] Symmories were groups of wealthier Athenians so arranged in order to facilitate the collection of war-taxes (*eisphorai*), mainly for the equipment of ships. 'Tax-groups' or perhaps 'tax-syndicates' are possible translations of a word which describes a peculiarly Athenian institution. It had undergone changes since its introduction in 378/7, and at the time of this speech its 1200 members were arranged in twenty groups (§ 17). A number of the richest members of each group paid the tax promptly, and then recovered it, if they could, from their fellow-members. For a good succinct review of the evidence, and bibliography, see MacDowell *DAM* 368–73.

[137] It has puzzled some commentators, such as Pearson *AD* 24.

[138] See Blass *AB* ii. 19–20. Demosthenes seems to be repudiating Isocratean *macrologia* when he says that his speech would not be 'of futile length' (14).

better off.[139] But if one man, whoever he may be, could come forward and demonstrate convincingly the nature and size of the force that will meet the city's needs, and show how it will be provided, all our present fears will be dispelled. That is what I will try to do, if I am able, first giving you briefly my views about our relationship with the King.

The different aims of deliberative and epideictic (or display-) oratory are thus described by differences in both style and content. It would be difficult to overestimate the importance of Demosthenes' initiative for the future of the genre, which might otherwise have lapsed prematurely into an anodyne, deadening uniformity. True to his undertaking, after a shrewd review of the politics of Graeco-Persian relations (3–13) he devotes most of the rest of the speech to detailed practical proposals—the enlargement and redistribution of the tax-syndicates (16–17), reorganization of equipment for the navy (18–22), manning of ships (22–3), and financial provision (24–8), on which he interestingly advises delay until precise needs are known.[140] These preparations might make the King think again.

While showing awareness of the conventional topics of deliberative oratory—justice (or honour), expediency and possibility[141]—Demosthenes shows no inclination to treat each in a distinct part of his speech. This is a pointer to his future practice, which, as will be seen, favours flexibility. Now all that remains after the practical recommendations is to predict their probable effect, allaying fear that the King might raise a mercenary army which includes Greeks. Here the rhetoric seems hollow, even naïve, in the light of history.[142] Somewhat simplistic, too, is the argument about the Thebans (33–4). But there is also the right tone of idealistic patriotism, expressed hyperbolically, and firmly founded on the past (35–6):

[139] This is an apparent parody of the antithesis in the opening period of Isocrates' *Panegyricus* 2, where athletes are unfavourably compared with statesmen: 'for if all the athletes should double their physical strength, the rest of us would gain nothing thereby; but a single man could conceive a good idea, there would be benefit for all those who wish to share his intelligence.'

[140] At this early stage of his career, Demosthenes did not wish to antagonize the wealthier citizens by imposing burdensome taxes on them before the money was actually needed.

[141] 28: ταῦτα δὲ καὶ δυνατά ἐστιν . . . καὶ πράττειν καλὰ καὶ συμφέροντα.

[142] 32: 'Who is so benighted that he will sacrifice himself, his ancestors, his family tomb, and his native land, all for the sake of a small profit?' At that time, and even more in the time of Alexander, there were many such men.

Indeed, I cannot see that any of the other Greeks have reason to fear this war. For who of their number does not know that as long as they were united in their minds against the common foe, they enjoyed many advantages, but since they regarded him as a friend to help them in their mutual quarrels, they have suffered such evils as no one would have imagined for them even in a curse?

But the Greeks remain disunited, so caution is the final, as it has been the initial theme (3, 37–40). He advises that the recommended preparations be made quietly and unprovocatively. This advice blends well with the reassurance of the other main arguments. Elements of both justice and expediency are present in the summary with which the speech ends.[143] The economy of scale has excluded narratives and digressions. His proposals for reforming the trierarchy were not adopted, but the Athenians were only too ready to remain cautious in their dealings with the King. Thus the debut of Demosthenes before the Popular Assembly was more significant for the development of his own style of political oratory than for the course of his career as a statesman.

16 *For the Megalopolitans*

Hellenic inter-state politics, centred on the Peloponnese, form the subject of this second deliberative speech by Demosthenes. The Spartans sensed an opportunity to recover some of the power lost to the Thebans at Leuctra and Mantinea when, in 353 or 352, the latter were hard-pressed in their struggle with Onomarchus and the Phocians. Their pronouncements and preparations alarmed the Arcadians, whose league was centred on the newly-founded city of Megalopolis; while their immediate neighbours in Messenia had even more reason to fear that they would fall once more under Spartan rule. Both sent envoys to Athens pleading for help, and the present speech is probably to be assigned to the same year.

While maintaining his established role as an independent counsellor (1), Demosthenes defines it further here. Initial vagueness in referring to 'taking a general view' and 'advocating a middle course'[144] is soon replaced by a clear and hard-headed policy of

---

[143] 41: . . . ἄρχειν δὲ μηδενὸς μήτε λόγου μήτ' λόγου ἀδίκου . . . συμφέροντα πράξετε.

[144] 1: τὸ δὲ κοινῶς ὑπὲρ τῶν πραγμάτων λέγειν, 2: . . . ἂν τὰ μεταξύ τις ἐγχείρῃ λέγειν.

self-interest. It is in the Athenian interest that neither Thebes nor
Sparta should become too strong (4–5, cf. 23 *Ag. Aristoc.* 102).
Now the aggressor is Sparta: at what point should she be stopped?
Here the idea of degrees of justice is introduced to help resolve the
question (9): 'Now ask yourselves at which point your stand against
Lacedaemonian injustice would be fairer and more humane—with
the defence of Megalopolis or the defence of Messene?' But expediency must remain the final consideration (10): 'The proper policy is always to look to what is the just course of action, but at the
same time to take care that what we do is also going to be expedient.'

After this clear statement, argument for opposition to Spartan
expansionism relies to some extent on future probabilities: if we
oppose it, will they forget our past services to them and thwart our
attempt to recover Oropus? Will those same services count for
nothing when we side with the Arcadians? The idea that the
Spartans will show compunction in the face of Athenian moral
superiority[145] gives a new psychological twist to the topos of justice. But he seems to recognize its limitations as he returns first to
criticism of them (16), then to the more difficult question of
Theban involvement in the diplomatic calculations. Support for
Megalopolis could be interpreted as support for Thebes, her sponsor. With Thebes now set on the other side of the balance,
Demosthenes devises a general policy, in keeping with the 'general
view' and 'middle course' which he advocated at the outset,
whereby resistance to Spartan expansionism in the Peloponnese is
matched by support, however theoretical, for the independence of
Boeotian cities from Thebes (25–6). This even-handedness would
accord with the principle enunciated in 4–5, which remains the
basis of the argument in the closing sections of the speech, with
Athenian support for Megalopolis seen as an insurance against both
Spartan and Theban aggrandizement. Constant to the end also is
the primacy of expediency, which is the basis of friendship[146] and
hence of alliances. Compared with that of *On the Symmories*, the
mood of the speech is cerebral, calculating and unsentimental, even
when justice and fairness enter the argument: Demosthenes, still

---

[145] 14–15: the standard topos of the Athenian policy of aiding the oppressed may be an
attempt to repair the damaged psyche of his audience, for whom memories of lost maritime
empire and defeat in war were recent.

[146] 27: τὸ συμφέρον εἶναι τὸ ποιοῦν τὴν φιλίαν.

cautiously developing his ideas on foreign policy and uncertain of his audience's reception of them, sees it prudent to eschew rhetorical flourishes and concentrates on thematic unity.

15 *For the Liberation of the Rhodians*[147]

Secession from the Athenian League in 355 had been followed in Rhodes by the establishment of an oligarchy by Mausolus, satrap of Caria. Exiled democrats appealing to Athens could expect little popular sympathy, so that the orator espousing their cause faced a major test of his persuasive skills. Demosthenes chooses the boldest possible gambit: he pretends to assume that the required action is obvious to all (1), affording as it does the opportunity for Athens to win the goodwill of democrats everywhere (4). Rhetoric and self-assertion[148] are used to try to overcome popular prejudice, while self-interest again dictates the policy recommended. Recent precedent is invoked (his proposal to free the Rhodians is 'nothing novel' (9)), and the discussion turns almost imperceptibly to the prospects of success, based on the probability that the Rhodian oligarchs' sponsors[149] would not defend them. The idea that they would actually prefer that the Athenians rather than the King should assume control of the island, is arrived at by an intricate course of reasoning based on psychology which is typical of Demosthenes' oratory at this time (11–13).

But he is aware that reason alone could not reverse popular hatred of the dissident Rhodians, so he begins the second part of his speech by going along with his audience's prejudices. The Rhodians deserve the slavery that they have brought upon themselves (15–16). He makes his audience feel good by comparison with them in order to solicit its indulgence,[150] which will give them the chance to learn from their mistakes. But this is still not enough: what the Athenians must be made to feel is apprehension

[147] Edition: J. Radicke, *Die Rede des Demosthenes für die Freiheit der Rhodier (Or. 15)*, Beiträge zur Altertumskunde 65 (Stuttgart and Leipzig: Teubner, 1995).

[148] 4: θαυμάζω introducing a greater-and-lesser paradox, followed by reference to himself and his earlier speech *On the Symmories* and its effect ('I was the only speaker . . . Nor did I fail to convince you that I was right' (cf. 18 *Cor.* 179)). Note also the propagandistic use of 'liberation' to mean the restoration of democracy.

[149] Mausolus had died in 353. His wife Artemisia, who succeeded him, might be influenced by the King's fortunes in his attempt to reconquer Egypt (11–13).

[150] 15: βελτίοσιν αὐτῶν ὑμῖν . . . 16 μὴ μνησικακεῖν. The argument reappears in a slightly different form in 21.

for their own safety, and it is this realization that leads Demosthenes to launch upon a discussion of the dangers of oligarchy (17–20).[151] At one point his rhetoric becomes hyperbolic (19):

Seeing that Chios and Mytilene are under oligarchy, and that Rhodes and, I might almost say, all the human race is being seduced into this form of slavery, I am surprised that none of you thinks our constitution is also in peril, and fails to reason that, if all other states embrace oligarchy, it is inconceivable that they will allow your democracy to subsist.

Thus the restoration of the Rhodian democrats would reverse a disastrous trend. The following example of the Argives who sheltered Athenian democratic exiles during the tyranny of the Thirty is reinforced by a good pathetic paradox (23):

Then would it not be shameful, Athenians, if when the people of Argos were not cowed by the imperial might of the Lacedaemonians in those times, you, who are Athenians, should fear one who is a barbarian, and a woman at that? Indeed, the Argives could have complained that they had often been defeated by the Lacedaemonians, but you have conquered the King many times, and never once been beaten either by the King's slaves or their master.

The example is well chosen for its rich antithesis, but the dismissive attitude here struck to the power of the King contrasts markedly with the caution advocated in *On the Symmories*. His opponents' policy, by contrast, is characterized as inactivity justified by spurious morality ('pleading the rights of others' (25)). But, he argues, such considerations have never restrained those who have seen opportunities for aggrandizement (26–7): to be alone in making a moral stand is a sign not of justice, but of cowardice. The doctrine of an earlier age is still valid (28): 'I perceive that all men are accorded their rights in proportion to their power to assert them.' Obviously aware of previous debates, both those arriving at extreme conclusions like those led by Thrasymachus in Plato's *Republic* and Callicles in his *Gorgias*, and the more contentiously qualified identification of might with right in Thucydides, Demosthenes adds to them by distinguishing between inter-state politics, in which the extreme form still obtains, and internal administration, where private rights are upheld (29).

---

[151] The topicality of the subject is clear from 31, and from *Ag. Androtion* (q.v.). The *Areopagiticus* of Isocrates, published three or four years before the present speech, would have sharpened the controversy by seeming to dwell approvingly on the oligarchic elements of Athenian society.

The penultimate sections (30–3) contain a sinister variant of 'the enemy within' theme (cf. Lys. 22. 14–16). Hyperbole appears again: *all* other states have only external enemies to beat, but Athens also faces the more serious opposition of unpatriotic factions (31). A hypothetical inversion identifies them (32).[152] But the speech ends inconclusively. Instead of making practical recommendations, he refers, as he began, to a policy already agreed upon in principle[153] and makes a general call to action (35). The impression remains of a politician still feeling his way,[154] and seeking to gain the attention of thinking politicians by publishing his opinions on important matters.[155]

13 *On the Public Fund*

Little has been done to counter the view of nineteenth-century scholars that this speech is the work of an editor of Demosthenes' works, who may nevertheless have preserved his views, and also, to some extent, his expression of them.[156] The content appears to date it to 353/2,[157] and it shares common passages with the contemporary speech *Against Aristocrates*.[158] But words and phrases which reappear in the *Olynthiacs* and *On the Chersonese*, which are later, are more suggestive of a second hand, though it is possible that the present speech is the original source. Other features of the speech are equally open to differing, perhaps opposite explanations. It contains a disproportionately high number of words and expressions not found elsewhere in Demosthenes.[159] This is the strongest

---

[152] χρῆν τοίνυν . . . πολιτευομένους ὀλιγαρχικῶς . . . νῦν δὲ . . . τοὺς τῆς πόλεως ἐχθροὺς ἡρημένους, τούτους πιστοτάτους ἡγεῖσθε.

[153] 34: ἃ προῄρησθε.

[154] The tradition preserved by Dion. Hal. (*Ep. ad Amm.* I. 4) places the present speech after *Phil. I.* But the low-key reference to Philip in § 25, seemingly accepting that he is φαυλός ('insignificant'), if only for the sake of argument, makes that tradition difficult to accept.

[155] Criticism, like that in § 33, would be more acceptable to private readers of the speech than to the audience apparently addressed, since the former would automatically exempt themselves from it.

[156] So Blass *AB* iii/1. 401–3.

[157] See Cawkwell, *JHS* 83 (1963), 48, who follows Blass in assigning the speech to 353/2.

[158] 21: 196; 22: 198; 23: 199; 24: 200. In each case, slight differences point to condensation in Speech 13.

[159] 6: μίση (plur.), 8: ἐφορεύσουσαν, 12: ἐνέπλησε τὰ ὦτα, μετεωρίσας, 13: τὰ ὦτα ἰάσασθαι, 15: ἄοπλοι, ἀσύντακτοι, 16: παρερρυήκασι, 19: τελεσθῆναι στρατηγός, 24: οἰκοτρίβων οἰκότριβας, 30: κονιάματα.

evidence for non-Demosthenic authorship, but some of the suspect words may not be un-Demosthenic. The asyndetic privative adjectives in 15 (n. 159) resemble a similar collocation in 4 *Phil. I* 36.[160] The metaphorical expressions in 12, 13, and 19 add to a rich store of Demosthenic examples (see Ronnet, *Étude*, 149–76). These words and phrases are compatible with existing Demosthenic usage, lessening the probability of spuriousness. Then there is another feature which might be more difficult for another writer to counterfeit: the articular infinitive.[161] The speech contains a disproportionately high number of instances. A sceptic might note that fifteen of the seventeen occurrences are in the first half of the speech, and attribute this unevenness to a failure of stamina on the part of the imitator. But certain concentrated phrases have a distinctly Demosthenic flavour.[162] Certain passages in asyndeton, featuring infinitives in rapid succession (14, 32–3) likewise carry an authentic stamp which could have been difficult to replicate. Finally, the speech is replete with Demosthenic sentiments and policies, so that nothing in the subject-matter betrays another's hand.

If the speech is to be dated to 353/2, the passages, words, and phrases echoed in *Against Aristocrates*, *Olynthiac III*, and *Philippic I* are the originals, recycled in the later speeches. This gives it a kind of archetypal status in its author's mind, enhanced perhaps by the almost unparalleled reference to his own name in his political speeches (12–13):

It has been said before by some speaker, Athenians, not one of your number, but one of those likely to burst if these reforms are carried out, 'What good has ever come to us from the speeches of Demosthenes? He comes forth, whenever the whim takes him, and fills our ears with phrases, deplores our present state and praises our ancestors, raising our hopes and puffing us up before leaving the platform.' But if only I could persuade you to accept any of my proposals, I think I should bring about greater benefits to the state than many of you would think possible if I tried to describe them now.

This seems to suggest that the speaker, while not lacking self-confidence, felt he had arrived at a critical point in his political

---

[160] ἄτακτα, ἀδιόρθωτα, ἀόρισθ᾽ [ἅπαντα].

[161] For characteristically Demosthenic forms of the articular infinitive, see Usher *GO* v. 24.

[162] Esp. 7: ἄνευ τοῦ πρὸς τοὺς οἰκείους πολέμους οἰκείᾳ χρῆσθαι δυνάμει συμφέρειν.

career, where he at once sensed a decline in his influence and resolved to reassert it. The above claim is a general plea. The specific matter over which he chose to illustrate his abilities was, however, controversial. The Theoric Fund, which was a repository of surplus revenues distributed to the people in peacetime but used to finance military operations in wartime, raised moral questions which were large in relation to its actual size.[163] In this speech the principle that payment should not be gratuitous but related to services performed is argued without reference to any specific national emergency and without any clearly articulated proposals. This lack of a pressing programme enables him to rehearse, with considerable vigour at times, some of his favourite themes—a citizen- rather than mercenary army (4), patriotism against personal ambition (historical comparison: 18–21, 22–31), and hatred of oligarchy (8–9, 14). But the speech is best understood as a review of Demosthenes' position in Athenian politics and a restatement of opinions which had earned him a degree of respect in the past, and which he believed to be still valid and acceptable to most of his fellow-citizens.

4 Philippic I

Conflict between Philip II of Macedon and the Athenians had begun over Amphipolis in 357,[164] and they had been nominally at war since his capture of that city. Yet his actions were of only marginal interest to Demosthenes until 351, the probable date of the present speech.[165] Philip's anti-Athenian actions during those years included his capture of Potidaea (356), Pydna, Methone (354), and possibly Neapolis.[166] His subsequent involvement in the Sacred War threatened Athenian interests less directly than those earlier actions, but in 352 he chose to exploit dynastic instability in the Thracian Chersonese, and laid siege to Heraeum Teichos. The danger this posed to the Athenian corn-route provided

[163] 2: τἀργύριον μέν ἐστι τοῦθ', ὑπὲρ οὗ βουλεύεσθε, μικρόν, τὸ δ'ἔθος μέγα, ὃ γίγνεται μετὰ τούτου.
[164] Diod. Sic. 16. 8. 2; Cawkwell PM 36–7; Ellis PMI 63–4.
[165] So Blass AB iii/1. 300–1, followed by most scholars. In Against Aristocrates (352) Philip figures primarily as a paradeigma of an unreliable potentate (111–17), even though he is also described as 'our worst enemy' (121). The earliest reference to him in Demosthenes is Against Leptines 63.
[166] See Ellis PMI 72–3.

Demosthenes with a momentous theme, and hence an opportunity
to give renewed impetus and focus to a political career which had
seemingly stalled in the face of the rejection or disregard of his earlier proposals. The speech was to be a do-or-die effort.[167] This
surely called for innovation, but how much?

The **prooemium** (1) is brief and cautiously old-fashioned in
both form[168] and content.[169] But thereafter its author injects a new
urgency into the deliberative genre. This urgency is seen in the
direct appeal to his audience not to be downhearted (2), a rhetorical introduction of the theme of possibility (*dynaton*), which in previous deliberative oratory is preceded by arguments on expediency
and justice. Equally surprising is the quick switch to Philip, whose
assessment of the possibilities of the situation is based on an old
Thucydidean dictum.[170] He is further characterized through his
actions, indeed his hyperactivity, which acts as a magnet to
prospective allies (6). Demosthenes is exhorting his own people by
using the example of their enemy in a passage full of striking
phrases[171] designed to arouse them and prepare them for his specific proposals. The technique is to jump quickly from one point
to the next: Philip the insecure tyrant (8), his instability (9),
Athenian passivity, presented as a question (10).[172] Finally (10–12),
the argument used in 5 is expanded and animated with live speech:
passivity would create another Philip if rumours of his death
proved true, and Athenian power must be ready for deployment in
the region of conflict.

Practical recommendations (13–22), the rationale behind them
(23–7), and their cost (28–9) form the heart of the speech, but hor-

[167] So he implies in his concluding sentiments, when he says (51): 'I know it is to your
advantage to receive the best advice: I only wish I knew with equal certainty that the adviser
would benefit from giving it.'

[168] It is a conventional hypothetical inversion (εἰ μὲν ... νῦν δέ). Two of the 56
prooemia that have survived in the *Corpus Demosthenicum* (1 and 21—both containing hypothetical inversion) appear to have been drafted for this speech. On this practice and other
aspects of the composition of Demosthenic deliberative speeches, see F. Focke,
Demosthenesstudien (Stuttgart, 1929).

[169] Cf. Aristoph. *Eccl.* 151–5.

[170] 5: 'The property of those who are absent belongs naturally to those who are present,
and that of the negligent to those who are willing to exert themselves.' Cf. Thuc. 4. 61. 5
(esp.); also 1. 76. 2 and 5. 105. 2, which enunciate the 'law' that the strong rule over the weak.

[171] 8: ... τὰ παρόντα πεπηγέναι πράγματ' ἀθάνατα ... κατέπτηχε πάντα ... 9:
προσπεριβάλλεται ... περιστοιχίζεται (two hunting metaphors).

[172] πότ' οὖν, ὦ ἄνδρες Ἀθηναῖοι, πόθ' ἃ χρὴ πράξετε; ἐπειδὰν τί γένηται;
ἐπειδὰν νὴ Δί' ἀνάγκη τις ᾖ; cf. Thuc. 1. 71. 1, where the Spartans are characterized as
dilatory or passive.

tatory devices are never absent. First, the personal angle again (see n. 167): do not pass hasty judgement on my proposals, which are admittedly bold (14–15); put psychological pressure on Philip by your willingness to act (17–18), equipping a force which will wage constant war on him.[173] And the details are presented through questions and answers (20–2). Lively colour is given to the idea that command should be exercised by Athenian officers, who are at present employed on mainly ceremonial duties (26): 'You are like the makers of clay puppets—you choose your brigadiers and commanders for the market-place, not for the field of war.' Their presence would make the force a truly Athenian one.

The speech continues[174] in a more restrained mode, as he explains the advantages of a permanent force. Such a force would be first on the scene, enabling organized prevention, impossible in the past. This arrangement, like the force itself, should be permanent and statutory, like the festivals—a telling parallel made into a paradox, as organization of the city at peace is seen to be more timely[175] than in the dangerous circumstances of war. The section develops into a forceful criticism of past policy. At one point it borders on insult (40):

But you, Athenians, though you have the most powerful resources of all—warships, infantry, cavalry, revenues—have never to this day used any of them properly, but you always wage war against Philip in the same way as a barbarian boxes. For, when struck, the barbarian clutches the stricken spot, and if you hit him somewhere else, there go his hands. He neither knows how to defend himself nor how to look his enemy in the eye, nor does he wish to do either.

---

[173] 19: δύναμιν . . . ἢ συνεχῶς πολεμήσει καὶ κακῶς ἐκεῖνον ποιήσει. This 'harrying force' was to consist of 2,000 infantry and 200 cavalry (with transports), at least a quarter of its personnel being Athenian citizens, supported at sea by ten triremes. The larger force described in 16, consisting of fifty triremes manned entirely by Athenians, would be ready in an emergency to meet specific threats. For doubts, based mainly on cost, as to the feasibility of these proposals, see Cawkwell *PM* 81. Sealey *DT* 132–3 and Pearson *AD* 124–5 note the absence of the document detailing the sources of revenue. Demosthenes, like many other 4th-cent. politicians, had no military background.

[174] Dion. Hal. *Ep. ad Amm.* 1. 10 makes § 30 the start of a new speech, but most editors reject this. The main argument for continuity is the complete absence of introductory material, and an almost immediate allusion to the prospect of a vote. Most discussions of the speech assume its unity. For a review of these, see Jackson and Rowe, *Lustrum* 14 (1969), 59.

[175] Here the theme of *kairos* (36 . . . ὑστερίζειν τῶν καιρῶν . . . 37 . . . οἱ δὲ τῶν πραγμάτων οὐ μένουσι καιροὶ τὴν ἡμετέραν βραδύτητα καὶ εἰρωνείαν) is used to dwell on past tendencies. For its use as a rallying theme referring to the present, see *Olynth.* 1 2.

A further imputation of cowardice (42) is followed by urgent rhetorical questions (44):

Shall we not man the fleet ourselves? Shall we not march out with at least a proportion of our own citizens in the army, now if never before? Shall we not sail against his territory?

Demosthenes' ability to excite quickly changing emotions, so vividly described by Dionysius of Halicarnassus,[176] could scarcely find better illustration than in this passage.

There is no relaxation of criticism of the 'civilian mentality', or diminution of reforming zeal, in the closing chapters. The first readings of Philip's mind, later to be greatly amplified, appear here. He is 'drunk with the magnitude of his achievements and dreaming of further triumphs' as he finds none to oppose him (46). Demosthenes' advice has been uncompromising to the end, and the more admirable for his nervous realization that it could ruin him (51).

1 Olynthiac I

Populous and prosperous Olynthus was the leading city of Chalcidice, and a natural focus for Philip's expansionist ambitions. He had sought to realize these through diplomacy, and an alliance was made; but in 352 the Chalcidians became so alarmed at his power that they approached the Athenians for protection. Philip's reaction to this perceived breach of faith was delayed by his illness and military operations in the Chersonese in 351 and 350, but in mid-349, he began to attack the city. The Olynthians sent ambassadors to Athens to plead for help, and the Olynthiacs were Demosthenes' contribution to the debate.

Demosthenes is not the first speaker: the assembly already has before it logistical proposals, detailed and costed (20). This may explain the curious opening sentence: 'I imagine, Athenians, that you would give a great deal of money to have made clear to you the policy that was likely to benefit the city in the present circumstances.' He goes on to contrast the speaker who has a well-

---

176 *Dem.* 22: 'When I pick up one of Demosthenes' speeches, I am transported: I am led hither and thither, feeling one emotion after another—disbelief, anguish, terror, contempt, hatred, pity, goodwill, anger, envy—every emotion in turn that can sway the human mind.' The prosopopoiia in 42 (δοκεῖ δέ μοι θεῶν τις . . .) will have added to the effect.

considered plan with one speaking impromptu. Obviously he sees himself in the latter category, however disingenuously, and this frees him to concentrate on more abstract ideas. Listening to previous speakers, his audience had soberly to consider how much money they might have to spend: listening to him, they would be raised to a higher mental plane, while still deliberating to good purpose. The first idea, and the most compelling, is *Kairos* ('Opportunity'), personified and 'calling out almost with an audible voice'.[177] But the complex nature of the opportunity is analysed with cool acuity. Whereas Philip enjoys the advantages of autocracy in executing his military movements, he suffers its disadvantages in relation to the Olynthians, who have seen how he treated the Amphipolitans and the Pydneans and know that their very existence is threatened, as there is no appeal against the tyrant. So they will fight, if they know they can count on Athenian support. The speech continues in the same positive vein as *Philippic I* with a religiously coloured version of the argument used in that speech—that the gods had shown their favour by not punishing Athenian sloth (10–11), but to miss the present opportunity would be to show ingratitude to them. From this point he moves to the sure consequence of further Athenian passivity (15): 'By heaven, is anyone here so foolish as to fail to realize that the war will be transferred from there to here, if we are negligent?'

To the vivid description of Philip's hyperactivity (*philopragmosyne*) in *Philippic I* is now appended its logical conclusion: Philip laying siege to the Acropolis. How preposterous would this prospect have seemed in 349? Real enough, in the orator's estimation, to allude to it at greater length later (25–7).

He offers his recommendations in a summary form, without details—two separate expeditionary forces to be sent simultaneously, one to save the Chalcidic cities, and the other to ravage Philip's territory (17–18). The more contentious question of money is accompanied by sharper rhetoric—a correction[178] and a

---

[177] Cf. 18 *Cor.* 172, and Denniston *GPS* 32 for other exx. The idea was imbued with life in the 4th-cent. mind, as is attested by Lysippus' statue of 'him' at Olympia. 'Kairos stood on tiptoe in winged sandals, he had a razor in his right hand to recall the well-known Greek metaphor (*e.g.* Hdt. 6. *11*), he had a forelock to be grasped when he approached but was bald behind because once he is past no one can catch him' (T. B. L. Webster, *Art and Literature in Fourth-Century Athens* (London, 1954), 103 (my italics)). This theme links *Olynthiac I* to *Philippic I*, adding a further reason to those summarized by Vince (Loeb i. 203) for believing the traditional order of the *Olynthiacs* to be correct.

[178] 19: . . . προσδεῖ, μᾶλλον δ' ἅπαντος ἐνδεῖ τοῦ πόρου.

'reverse apostrophe', whereby the speaker himself is apostrophized.[179] By following an aggressive tone with swift disavowal (19): 'No! I am not proposing that [sc. that the money for the army should be raised from the Theoric Fund]', he manages to press the point while ensuring self-preservation, in full awareness that previous proposals to raise money by drawing on public funds such as the Theoric Fund had led to the indictment of the proposer. He then returns to safer ground with the *dynaton*-topos touched upon in *Philippic I* (8), here developed at greater leisure: Philip's problems after his initial successes, especially with his treacherous or recalcitrant allies. What is inopportune for him is opportune for Athens.[180]

But urgency must be stressed to the end. The forensic convention of using hypophora to round off the proof summarily is here adapted as a hortatory tool, with an imaginary question (25–6):

If Philip takes Olynthus, who is to prevent his marching hither? The Thebans? It may be rather harsh to say it, but they will readily join the invasion. The Phocians, then? They cannot even protect their own country without our help. Any others? 'But, my good fellow,' (someone may say), 'he will not wish to attack us.'

On the contrary, he argues, knowing the vulnerability of Athens by land, Philip would be mad *not* to attack, and loss of their own land would be more expensive than the cost of a war fought on someone else's. The **epilogue** (28) summarizes his recommendations in the usual way, while maintaining a hortatory tone and ending, like *Philippic I*, with a pure optative verb.

2 Olynthiac II

Whereas *Olynthiac I*, like *Philippic I* and sharing its main ideas, is a clarion call to action, *Olynthiac II*, like *Philippic II*, is more analytical and philosophical. In an unchanged situation, he must find new arguments, but there is also scope for elaboration of some already used. The interaction between these two groups of material is the main interest of this speech and the next.

---

[179] 19: ἄν τις εἴποι, 'σὺ γράφεις ταῦτ' εἶναι στρατιωτικά'; μὰ Δί' οὐκ ἔγωγε.
[180] 24: δεῖ τοίνυν . . . τὴν ἀκαιρίαν τὴν ἐκείνου καιρὸν ὑμέτερον νομίσαντας ἑτοίμως συνάρασθαι τὰ πράγματα. Note the preceding aphoristic statement (τὸ γὰρ εὖ πράττειν . . . χαλεπώτερον εἶναι), contrasting with the following paratactic (καί) clause describing swiftly moving and cumulative actions.

Athenian good fortune (favour of the gods), and hence her chances of success, have received a great boost in the form of Philip's enemies, now their potential allies (1–2). There is a brief, dark allusion to Athenian partisans of Philip,[181] but the king himself is to be the leading topic. Carefully avoiding the charge of mere abuse (5), in tune with the contemplative mood of the speech, Demosthenes argues that Philip's career, built on deceit and injustice, is doomed to failure, because he adds to his enemies with each act of treachery (8):

Now just as he gained power by these means, when each of his victims thought he was going to benefit them, so through these same deceits he is bound to be destroyed as his total selfishness is exposed.

Thus he adapts the old deliberative theme of justice (*dikaion*), using its obverse. Linked to it through the idea of goodwill (*eunoia*) is the companion theme of interest (*sympheron*) (9):

When an alliance is held together by goodwill, when all the allied states have the same interests, then the individual members are willing to remain steadfast, sharing the toil and bearing the hardships; but when a man has gained power by rapacity and crime, as Philip has done, then the first excuse, any minor slip-up, throws[182] and ruins him.

After briefly urging diplomatic activity backed by mobilization, he returns to broaden the moral argument, the first side of which is a much more detailed portrait of Philip and the nature of his power (14–21). While it draws on the well-established conception of the tyrant, as an isolated figure whose people do not share his aspirations and whose immediate companions are yes-men because he suppresses men of talent through jealousy and fear,[183] it contains some picaresque details (18–19):

Any moderately decent or honest man, who cannot put up with the daily drunken disorder and the lewd dancing, is pushed aside and disregarded. All the others in his court are robbers and flatterers, men given in their cups to the sort of dancing that I should hesitate to describe here . . . men

[181] *Philippic I* 18 is the only previous reference to them.
[182] πταῖσμα . . . ἀνεχαίτισε: the metaphor of the tripping horseman forms a chiastic core, as 'excuse' (πρόφασις) is the subject only of 'ruins' (διέλυσεν). See G. Ronnet, *Étude sur le style de Démosthène dans les discours politiques* (Paris, 1951), 171.
[183] The negative aspects of the tyrant's lot are very well described by Xenophon in his most accomplished dialogue, the *Hiero*: the tyrant's friendless isolation: §§ 3, 6; his need to suppress the best men: § 5.

who were expelled from Athens . . . low comedians who compose dirty ditties to raise a laugh against their fellow-boozers.

Such a society is organically[184] unstable, but positive action is still needed to overthrow it. In the concluding passages of the speech (22–31), morality is the binding theme, and the Athenians are to be its agents. They must set an example by their own activity, as Philip has done to his side, and they have themselves in the past (22–4), though not in recent times (25–8). Morality includes a sense of duty and the willingness to punish default, and the resolution to put the good of the state ahead of personal gain and partisanship (27–30).[185] It is clear that Demosthenes is still operating as an independent spokesman, as he ends with the plea that his audience should adopt the best advice offered (31).[186]

3 *Olynthiac III*

While the danger from Philip is still the subject under debate, the underlying theme of this speech is domestic politics, and specifically the impediments to effective action which the patriotic statesman has to overcome (12–13). It seems clear that, without new money, the costs of the action which Demosthenes has proposed could not be met. In *Olynth. I* 19–20, he had merely deplored the popular view that surplus money should be used 'for the festivals'. Now he actually names the Theoric Fund (10–11). But this highly contentious proposal[187] had to be hedged round with an array of hortatory themes, beginning with a studied version of the *kairos*-theme ('it requires thought and planning', 3), which begins with a reminder of Philip's first acts of aggression and Athenian reaction, or lack of it, to them (4–5), and ends with a contrastingly rapid[188]

---

[184] The simile of the body and its ailments compared with the state (21) is not one of Demosthenes' happiest as here used: it is reworked to greater effect in 18 *Cor.* 198.

[185] In § 30 he seems to be expressly attacking the class divisions in the city, with especial criticism of the poorer class, which 'has no other public duty than to condemn them [sc. the tax-paying classes]'.

[186] This apparent platitude acquires a special meaning in the political context. Supporters of leading men could expect a hearing out of all measure to the value of what they had to say. Demosthenes, still the outsider, needed to make the strongest case in order to compete with them.

[187] He uses a form of *aporia* to express his own anxiety (3): 'I am at a loss to know how I shall put them (sc. my proposals) before you.'

[188] 7: note the asyndeton: ὑπῆρχον Ὀλύνθιοι . . . ἐπράξαμεν ἡμεῖς . . . ἦν τοῦθ ὥσπερ ἐμπόδισμά τι . . . ἐκπολεμῶσαι δεῖν.

statement of the present position regarding Olynthus. The specific
reference to the Theoric Fund is sandwiched between this and
another, more straightforwardly hortatory passage, containing
some rhetorical flourishes[189] (14–20). Thus the impact of the core
proposal (11–14) is mitigated while its content is justified. He provides himself with further protection by a mixture of frankness and
dissimulation, introducing his proposal as a 'paradox', but avoiding
personal responsibility by suggesting the appointment of a board of
legislators (10).

With its main proposal made, the rest of the speech (21–36) is
long enough to suggest that it is intended as complementary to all
three *Olynthiacs*, and both its style and its subject-matter confirm
this. It is about the nature of Athenian statesmanship, and how this
has been determined by the degree of patriotic concern shown by
the citizens who elect them. Statesmen of the past placed the city's
interests ahead of their own popularity and aggrandizement, and it
prospered: those of today adopt the opposite priority, and it lan-
guishes. How was this change allowed to come about? (30–1):

Because then the people themselves, having the courage to engage in politics and serve in the army, controlled the politicians and were themselves
the dispensers of all benefits, while the rest were content to receive what-
ever portion of honour, authority, and favour they chose to bestow.
Now, on the contrary, the politicians command the favours and manage
everything, while you, the people, robbed of nerve and sinew,[190] stripped
of wealth and of allies, have become mere lackeys and hangers-on, content if these men dole out the Theoric Fund to you or let you hold the
Boedromia procession; and —bravest of all!—you thank them for granting what is your own.

Association of the impotence of the *demos* in a nominal democracy
with the Theoric Fund, supposedly a democratic institution, may
have seemed outrageous to some, but it matches the roughshod

---

[189] 18: καὶ νῦν, οὐ λέγει τις τὰ βέλτιστα· ἀναστὰς ἄλλος εἰπάτω, μὴ τοῦτον
αἰτιάσθω. ἕτερος λέγει τις βελτίω· ταῦτα ποιεῖτ' ἀγαθῇ τύχῃ (successive hypotheses in asyndeton). Hermogenes detected a tone of 'asperity' (τραχύτης) in 20: 'Surely it is
not in the character of sensible and worthy men to shirk your military duty because there is
no money, regarding such behaviour lightly; or to seize their arms to march against the
Corinthians or Megarians, but to let Philip enslave Greek cities because you are short of
campaign-rations.'

[190] 31: ἐκνενευρισμένοι καὶ περιῃρημένοι ... καθείρξαντες ὑμᾶς ... τιθασεύουσι
χειροήθεις αὐτοῖς ποιοῦντες: physical/medical and hunting, two of Demosthenes'
favourite metaphorical media. See Ronnet, *Étude*, 163–6, 170–1. Carey notes a similar complaint by Bdelycleon in Aristoph. *Wasps* 682–5.

mood of the first part of this concluding section. More metapho
follows. His audience are 'pent up in the city and enticed with
baits', like captive animals (31), (see n. 190, on p. 225), and he himself fears that he may seem too outspoken (33). This mood gives way
in the second part (33–6) to a cooler and clearer explanation of hi
moral and practical ideas regarding the dole: it should always meet
need rather than be given as a gratuity, which merely breeds apa-
thy;[191] and it should be a reward for necessary services, not an excuse
for idleness (34–5). Thus the proposed change to the status of the
Theoric Fund dovetails neatly into the rest of his political programme, which posits a restoration to full strength of the citizen army
and a commitment to the active defence of Athenian interests abroad

21 *Against Meidias*

Enmity between Meidias and Demosthenes dated from the latter'
early adulthood,[192] but it culminated spectacularly at the Festival o
the Dionysia in spring 348, at which Demosthenes, in full regalia a
choregos (chorus-master), was publicly punched in the face b
Meidias. At first Demosthenes contented himself with the publi
condemnation of Meidias in the Assembly, but after further provocation initiated[193] a formal prosecution in 347/6. As a forensi
speech composed by the litigant, it belongs with the guardian
speeches and the great orations against Aeschines. But it comes at
turning-point both in his political career and in his literary development, and should therefore be considered in its historical position.

Whereas in the *Olynthiacs* he is only too ready to scold and
berate his audience, the *leitmotif* of the first part of this speech
(1–35)[194] is Demosthenes' self-identification as one of them. The
share his experiences of Meidias' arrogance (cf. Lys. 10. 1), so hi
action is the same as theirs would be (1) (cf. Lys. 1. 1), and he ha

---

[191] This is portrayed through one of his earliest similes (33), that of the ineffectual diet.

[192] In 364/3, in a continuation of the dispute over Demosthenes' patrimony, Meidia
abetted his brother Thrasylochus. The two broke into his house in pursuit of a challenge t
exchange property (*antidosis*). For details, see MacDowell *DAM* 1–4.

[193] The contentious questions of whether the trial took place and whether the speech wa
delivered are discussed thoroughly but inconclusively by MacDowell *DAM* 23–8. In m
view, the public nature of Meidias' offence would have left him with a very shaky case. A
out-of-court settlement along the lines described by Aeschines (3 *Ag. Ctes.* 51–3) therefor
seems probable. See also n. 207.

[194] The **prooemium** (1–8) contains a succession of commonplace topics.

indeed pursued it, as it were, by popular demand (2–3). He is one of them (also 112: 'the rich . . . the rest of us'), and undertakes to concentrate on those of Meidias' offences that will excite universal indignation (15): his fellow-tribesmen have been insulted along with himself (19, also 126); and finally, as the logical highpoint, Meidias' insult has been against the office of *choregos*, not the individual holding it (31, 34). In the following disquisition on the laws (41–50), the central point is that an act of violence is, *per se*, an act against the whole state (45). Meidias is shown to have been exceptionally and gratuitously violent by comparison with others (62–76).

   An earlier forensic speech might have drawn to a conclusion at this point. However, examples are not lacking of prosecutions in which a chance is taken to blacken further the portrait of the defendant.[195] What is remarkable and unprecedented in the present speech is the scale of the digression, which comprises two-thirds of the speech. Another thematic thread runs throughout what is essentially a chronological catalogue of Meidias' misdeeds. It is his contempt for law, religion, and the rights of his fellow-citizens. The jury is told of his violent behaviour during his brother's *antidosis*-challenge (77–82), then of his attempts to corrupt, and then successfully to prosecute the arbitrator Strato. The latter is the subject of a passage of remarkable pathos (95–6):

This man, Athenians, is poor perhaps, but certainly not wicked. He is a citizen, who has served on all the campaigns while he was of military age, and has done no terrible wrong. Yet now he stands silent, deprived not only of the benefits common to all, but even of the right to speak and complain. All this he has suffered at the hands of Meidias, and from the wealth and arrogance of Meidias, because he was poor and friendless and merely one of the common people.

This is an epiphany of tragic import. Because he has been silenced by Meidias' wickedness, his mute presence[196] is at once noble and reproachful.[197] He has defied Meidias in the cause of justice, and

---

[195] Lysias *Against Eratosthenes* is an early example, where the character and actions of Theramenes are the subjects of a long digression. Isaeus regularly dilates upon the sins of his clients' opponents after dealing with the main issues.

[196] Meidias had secured his disfranchisement, which disqualified him from testifying in the lawcourts.

[197] Comparison may be made with the silence of Ajax when he encounters his enemy Odysseus in the Underworld in Homer, *Od*. 11. 563, which Longinus uses to illustrate that sublimity could be achieved without words (*Subl*. 9. 2).

forfeited his rights. The conventional device to elicit pity which
Meidias will use—parading his family, in rags, before the jury
(99)—will seem weak and contrived after Strato's silent performance, and the rhetorical questions and hypophora in 97–8 superfluous.

The catalogue continues, and along with it the characterization
of Meidias. Firstly, groundless charges of desertion and homicide
against Demosthenes (102–22), which he pursued 'letting neither
religion nor piety nor any other compunction stand in the way of
his accusation, and stopping at nothing (104) . . . these acts make
him my murderer (106)'. His ruthlessness makes him comparable
to a barbarian tyrant (106). He is relentless (109) and treacherous
(116–17).[198] Failure to prosecute him would have been tantamount
to dereliction of duty.[199] The section is concluded with a restatement of the theme of universal concern (123–7).

A hypothetical inversion ('Now if . . . but, as it is') marks the
beginning of a new section (128–42), an edited account of Meidias'
other misdeeds. The paraleipsis is unusually elaborate (129–30),
ingeniously excusing omission (129)[200] and pretending to offer a
random selection (130). Comparative argument (132), apostrophe
(133–5), and dilemmaton (134) give this section a formal rhetorical
flavour. The proximity of handbook rhetoric is also seen in 136,
where a summary of typical character-probability argument is
given: 'Does any of you know me capable of this? . . . Who among
you has ever seen me commit these offences? . . . These men are
lying against me out of spite.' But Meidias' character meets the
opposite probability, as many know from cruel experience, and it
has deterred his victims from prosecuting him. Further standard
topics occur towards the end of the section (141–2).[201]

---

[198] Meidias is given live speech to demand from the Council the arrest of Aristarchus,
then we are told how, on the previous day, he had visited him on friendly terms (117–18).
The word ὁμωρόφιος is used twice (118, 120): its association with homicide law colours
the whole passage and unifies the argument: if Meidias thought Aristarchus was a murderer,
he should not have come under the same roof as him, for fear of pollution. The argument
is tailor-made for pathetic paradox (120: καίτοι πῶς οὐ δεινὸν . . .).

[199] 120: εἰ τοῦτον ἀφῆκα, λελοιπέναι μέν, ὦ ἄνδρες Ἀθηναῖοι, τὴν τοῦ δικαίου
τάξιν, φόνου δ' ἂν εἰκότως ἐμαυτῷ λαχεῖν· οὐ γὰρ ἦν μοι δήπου βιωτὸν τοῦτο
ποιήσαντι.

[200] Demosthenes pretends to fear lest his own grievances might lose some impact if he
gives a full account of Meidias' other crimes.

[201] 141: prooemium-topoi: want of leisure, distaste for affairs, being a poor speaker, aporia: here used as excuses for avoiding litigation, but in practice more often used to elicit sympathy for a litigant who felt obliged to litigate. 142: the status coniecturalis: Meidias must prove

Comparison of Meidias with Alcibiades (143–50) has the two
men's hybris as a common factor, but it is really an extended a fortiori argument. Against Alcibiades' generalship, Olympic successes,
and patriotism Meidias can set nothing, but can match his predecessor's crimes, and even exceed them. To argue this requires editorial skill. We read of some of Alcibiades' transgressions, but the
full measure of the damage he did to the Athenian cause by going
over to the Spartan side is not recorded.[202] As to Meidias, any
claims he may have made to generalship or oratorical skill are dismissed (148, hypophora).

But Meidias' services to the state have been considerable.
Demosthenes' answer to this (151–74) is to compare them with his
own, showing in every instance how Meidias was a grudging contributor who devised ingenious methods of avoiding serving in
person,[203] and abused those offices to which he was appointed.

It remains to reaffirm the grounds for severe punishment of
Meidias, and this is done once again by comparison with previous
offenders (175–83). After that the attack intensifies. Meidias does
not deserve the even-handed treatment that a moderate man might
expect,[204] so conventional pleas for pity, including the appearance
of the family in court, should be ignored. (Here Demosthenes
obliquely solicits sympathy for himself as he mentions his childlessness (187).) He then anticipates Meidias' complaint that he is a
rhetor (189–92), but uses the word in its sense of 'political orator'
(and thereby gains some personal credit), whereas Meidias' concern
was with his forensic and litigational skills. He leaves his audience
with late disturbing thoughts as he first apostrophizes Meidias on
various manifestations of his anti-democratic attitude (193–204),
then refers to Meidias' supporters in a passage of especial interest

that he did not do what he is accused of. Demosthenes is trying to rule out other issues—
such as those of definition and justification (see M. Heath, *Hermogenes On Issues* (Oxford,
1995), 32–4). To consider these would have left Meidias with too much defensive material.

[202] The Spartans' fortification of Decelea is mentioned (146), but not the fact that it was
carried out on Alcibiades' advice; nor is mention made of his advice to send a Spartan general to command operations in Sicily.

[203] 166: 'What is the most suitable name for a trierarchy such as his? Shall we call it tax-
purchase, two-percent exemption, desertion, malingering and every name of that sort; or
"patriotism"?' (Cf. Andoc. 1 *Myst.* 133 for a similar if more humorous antonomasia.) It is an
effective way of depreciating an undeniable record of service.

[204] For the combination of internal anaphora (τούτῳ . . . τούτῳ) with asyndeton cf. 18
De Cor. 198, 274.

(205–18).[205] That interest is aroused by the appearance of Eubulus as the most influential of these and Demosthenes' enemy (205–7).[206] Eubulus is urged not to associate himself with Meidias' hybris (207): 'In a democracy there must never be a citizen so powerful that his advocacy can make one side submit to outrages and the other escape justice.' Other powerful friends of Meidias are mentioned, and they become the characters in an oligarchic scenario (209), enriched by live speech and irony: if such men came to power, no doubt they would treat anyone who crossed them with kind indulgence! This leads to a powerful plea urging support for his reliance on the law and refusal to be bought off.[207] He pleads for his personal security (221–2). The commonplace request 'come to my aid by upholding the laws' has never been as rhetorically[208] expounded as in these concluding sections. The final reference to the impiety of Meidias' act reintroduces one of the strongest of the speech's recurrent themes (35, 55, 104, 114, 120, 130, 199). With that as a cohering and unifying factor, the many digressive and amplifying components of the speech can be accommodated; and these elements combined mark the greatest forward stride in Demosthenes' development towards the great orations *On the Embassy* and *On the Crown*.

5 *On the Peace*

The fall of Olynthus in 348 spelt danger for the rest of Greece and marked a crisis in Demosthenes' career. Although he could still argue that his policy of stopping Philip early had not been tested, the practical situation now required cautious diplomacy, including negotiation with the enemy. The Peace of Philocrates (346) was

---

[205] MacDowell (*DAM* 11–12, 409) judiciously assesses the evidence which the passage provides for attributing political motives for the prosecution, and concludes that it falls short of proving that the dispute between the two men was political as well as personal.

[206] Demosthenes is at pains to disclaim responsibility for the enmity (205), and urges Eubulus not to make it a reason for supporting Meidias (206).

[207] Another scenario, with Demosthenes being publicly approached by the rich banker Blepaeus (215–16) amid popular uproar, was no doubt a graphic attempt to affirm to later readers that the trial did in fact take place. Perhaps perversely, one may therefore regard it as evidence that it did not.

[208] Note esp. 224: 'What is the strength of the laws? If one of you is wronged and cries aloud, will they run up and be at his side to assist him? No; they are only written texts and could not do this. Wherein lies their power, then? In yourselves . . . the laws are strong through you and you through the laws.'

the product of these negotiations, and it brought Philip to the heart
of Greece as president of the Pythian Festival (22). Demosthenes
had quietly switched his support to those advocating peace, but his
audience's memory of *Philippic I* and the *Olynthiacs* would still be
fresh, so that his credibility as a *symboulos* was about to be severely
tested.

Small scale and a relatively modest and subdued tone were
appropriate, as was absence of focused criticism. Within these limitations, however, there was scope for invention. In the
prooemium, beside the old theme of Athenian tardiness (2) and
the topos of the aporia of the present situation (1), the conventional
plea for a hearing is delivered with a new confidence,[209] carefully
balanced by feigned reluctance to talk about himself (4). He gives
three examples of advice which had been justified by events, in
which he shows some restraint in criticizing his opponents,[210]
while affirming his own courage in opposing bad but popular policies (7, 10). His claim to be heard is thus summarized (12):

In public matters, my judgements and calculations are disinterested
(*proika*), and no one can show that my policy or my speeches have been
influenced by private gain.

He delivers his actual proposals with cool clarity: do nothing to dis-
rupt the present peace, or offer enemies an excuse for war (13–14).
It is a holding, wait-and-see policy, in which alliances are seen as
unreliable for the present because no common cause is perceived
and existing enmities between the cities remain strong. There is a
certain resigned realism about all this, and he says little now about
Philip's ambitions beyond brief reference to his short-term aims.
Yet the speech is not wholly without rhetorical interest. Apart from
the striking metaphor *diaspan* ('torn apart' (5): see above), the analogy of money weighing down on the balance (*trytane*) with
bribery appears for the first time, to be used to great effect later (18
Cor. 298). He has modestly preferred to lay claim to luck and incorruptibility rather than 'cleverness' (*deinotes*, 11–12), but the speech
belies this disavowal. The paradox with which it ends is masterly
(25):

[209] 3: οἴομαι καὶ πεπεικὼς ἐμαυτὸν ἀνέστηκα . . . ἕξειν καὶ λέγειν καὶ
συμβουλεύειν . . .

[210] While saying that he was 'almost torn apart' by the advocates of aid to Plutarchus,
tyrant of Eretria, he does not name his recent adversary Meidias (see MacDowell *DAM* 5,
335, 407).

It is sheer folly and quite disgraceful, after negotiating with each of our neighbours individually in matters of vital importance to ourselves, to wage war against them now over this shadow at Delphi.[211]

6 *Philippic II*

Under the terms of the Peace of Philocrates, Philip had insisted not merely on peace but on alliance with Athens. To possible military reasons for this (which could have included a role for the Athenian navy in his future plans[212]), may be added a diplomatic one—that such an alliance would impede the plans of those at Athens who wished to renew hostilities. He followed this with conciliatory gestures towards Athens;[213] and even two years later, Philip had still not threatened Athenian interests directly, during which time Demosthenes and his friends seem to have lost popular support.[214] Philip was no doubt aware of this when he initiated the present debate by complaining of unwarranted Athenian hostility.[215]

Understandably in these circumstances, Demosthenes has to begin with commonplaces about the need for action rather than speeches, but he also attempts to create an impression of widespread resentment against Philip, and to generate even more, by referring at the outset to present discussions of his intrigues and violations of the peace, whose occurrence is stated as fact. In the absence of palpable dangers, he must resort, for the first time, to the moral imperatives which inform so much of his subsequent deliberative oratory. Moral attitudes must change, and all who speak and listen must choose the best and safest policy, rather than the easiest and most agreeable (5). But first he must convince his audience that Philip poses a real threat. Both these themes call for psychological

---

211 περὶ τῆς ἐν Δελφοῖς σκιᾶς: like the phrase ὄνου σκιά ('a donkey's shadow'), meaning something illusory or of no importance, the reference is to Philip's newly-won influence in the Delphic Amphictyony.

212 So Cawkwell *PM* 111. Sealey *DT* 161–2 doubts whether Philip could have been considering an invasion of Asia at this stage.

213 See Ellis *PMI* 130–1.

214 Evidence for this is to be seen in the condemnation of Demosthenes' ally Timarchus (345) in a political trial. Aeschines' speech is examined below (pp. 280–4).

215 According to the *Hypothesis* to this speech, Philip sent an embassy on which all his allies were represented, including the Argives and Messenians, whom he had promised to protect against the Spartans. Demosthenes had to speak not only against one of the ablest orators of the age, Python of Byzantium, but against an alliance of Greek states cleverly bound to Philip by perceived self-interest. See Cawkwell *PM* 123–5; G. Calhoun, *TAPA* 64 (1933), 1–17.

insight rather than straightforward argument, and no speech illustrates his command of this more tellingly than the *Second Philippic*. He begins by reasserting that Philip is indeed the enemy of Athens (6) and his use of the word *echthros* rather than *polemios* implies that the conduct of outright war was not necessary for enmity to be affirmed. Previously portrayed as merely an opportunist, now Philip is seen to be aiming at universal domination.[216] His path towards that goal is traced by imagining his thoughts (see esp. 17–19): friendship with Thebes rather than Athens would enable him to attain it, because the Thebans, like most other Greek states, looked to their own short-term interests,[217] whereas the Athenians had a long record, well known to Philip, of espousing only just causes (10–11). He might win over the Thebans by disabling the Phocians, and the Argives and the Messenians by curbing the Spartans, but the Athenians would stand firm, alone if necessary,[218] leaving no choice other than conflict.

This deliberately idealized view of Athenian patriotism makes political reality, when it is introduced, all the more stark and shocking. Demosthenes ends by putting the spotlight on his opponents (29–36), demanding that they be called to account for deliberately misrepresenting Philip's intentions. It is they who are responsible for the present situation (35):

While the danger is still in the future and events are coming to a head, while we can still listen to one another, I want to remind each of you who it was that persuaded you to abandon the Phocians and Thermopylae, which gave Philip control of the road to Attica and the Peloponnese, and who it is that has forced you to deliberate, not for your rights and interests abroad, but for your possessions here at home.

Thus the speech is directed at two enemies, not one. It is important to understand its dual character: it is not only a contribution, nor the only contribution[219] to the debate on Philip's complaint, but a foretaste of Demosthenes' personal crusade against 'philippizers'. In addition to being a persuasive formulation of foreign

---

[216] 7: τὸ πάνθ᾽ ὑφ᾽ αὑτῷ ποιήσασθαι.

[217] He describes the consequences of shortsightedness (20–5) by reworking a speech which he delivered to the Messenians, in which he warned them by example against trusting Philip's promises. It ends memorably: 'Every king, every despot, is the enemy of freedom and law: beware lest, in seeking to be rid of war, you find only a master.'

[218] 17: 'He seeks dominion, and has realized that you alone stand in his way.'

[219] He left the proposal of a reply to Philip to another speaker, probably Hegesippus.

policy, the *Second Philippic* is to be seen as the prelude to his contest with his most eloquent opponent, Aeschines.[220]

19 On the Embassy[221]

That contest with Aeschines came within a year, in the summer of
343. Both men had served on the embassies that had been sent to
negotiate and ratify the Peace of 346, in which Philip, from a position of superior military strength, won all his immediate objectives.
Demosthenes felt that, in order to save his own political career, he
had to dissociate himself from his fellow-ambassadors, and perhaps
from some of his own miscalculations.[222] His enmity towards
Aeschines, though intensely personal, was apparently recent in origin. Not a professional *rhetor* or a political heavyweight, and with
Philocrates already condemned, Aeschines seemed to offer him a
lifeline back to centre-stage in Athenian counsels. But the task of
proving substantive charges against him was fraught with difficulties.

The **prooemium** (1–8), includes (4) a conventional summary of
the charges: false reporting, false advice, failure to follow instructions, delay and lost opportunities, and the suggested reason for
these—corruption. Of these the last receives the most thorough
attention, and is made into the explanation of the other failings. Of
these the first involves inconsistency: Aeschines made contradictory speeches, for and against the original peace terms. Here
Demosthenes increases the force of the charge by allowing that
Aeschines was the first to see Philip's designs on Greece (10–12,
302–4), and won his place on the embassies on the strength of this.
The account of his performances in the Assembly after the return
of the second embassy stresses his great confidence in his diplomatic
achievements, but does so only in order to cast its sinister cause in
sharper light (27–8):

I want you to recall that policy of precaution and distrust of Philip which
this man chose when he was still unbribed, and compare it with the trust
and friendship that afterwards sprang up so suddenly.

---

[220] The debate took place less than a year before the trial of Aeschines. See P. Treves, 'La
politica di Demostene e la seconda orazione philippica', *Civiltà Moderna* (1935), 497–520 for
the close connection between the two events.

[221] The popular title 'False Embassy' (i.e. corrupt conduct by an ambassador) is a transla-
tion of παραπρεσβεία, a subjective word with little lexical and probably no legal authority
(see MacDowell *DAM* 224 on § 5).

[222] See Cawkwell *PM* 105 n. 27.

In the complicated sequence of events, Aeschines is established as Philip's agent, delivering his propaganda (37–8, 48–9), leading opinion and suppressing opposition in Athens, and causing the destruction of Phocis through deception. Demosthenes brings a new depth of pathos to his description of the desolation of that state (65–6):

Not long ago, when we were travelling to Delphi, we were forced to look upon that scene—houses razed to the ground, city-walls destroyed, the land bereft of its young men; only women, a few children and the old men stricken with misery. No one could find words to match the woes that afflict that country today . . . Who is the author of these wrongs? Who is the deviser of this deception? Is it not Aeschines?[223]

By contrast, Philip enjoys the good fortune of finding worse scoundrels than his purposes required (68). The picture of corruption is being amplified by purely rhetorical means, without the adduction of new evidence, while Aeschines' confident claims (72–9) are set against the grim reality of the political situation which he has created (83–90).

Up to this point the case against Aeschines has been based on general arguments. The defensive arguments assigned to him by procatalepsis are even vaguer—his complaint that he is being blamed for the war and the necessity to make peace (92–3)—and can be brusquely dismissed as irrelevant and replaced by serious arguments, once more marking the maximum contrast. Why, if he was really outmanoeuvred by Philip, did he not denounce him (106–7)? 'Because he was not cajoled and hoodwinked: he had sold himself and pocketed the money before he made his speech and betrayed us to Philip' (110). A more specific incriminating action follows. Aeschines, prior to the third embassy, stayed behind in Athens to counteract Demosthenes, but only until the ruin of Phocis was complete, whereupon he went off to Pella to join Philip in his celebrations (126–8), toasting his success in what amounted to a curse on his own fatherland.[224] This is one of the highpoints of the speech, at which the introduction of further direct evidence might have been expected in order to press home any advantage. But Demosthenes is working on a very broad canvas, and he digresses

---

[223] Reinforcing his moving description with prosopopoiia and pathetic paradox (66: . . . τοὺς προγόνους ὑμῶν, εἰ λάβοιεν αἴσθησιν, ψῆφον ἢ γνώμην θέσθαι . . . πῶς γὰρ οὐκ αἰσχρόν . . . ;), he places the blame squarely and solely on Aeschines.

[224] 130: κατηρᾶτο τῇ πατρίδι, ἃ νῦν εἰς κεφαλὴν ὑμᾶς αὐτῷ δεῖ τρέψαι.

on the subject of ambassadorial responsibility, illustrating how its effective discharge can enhance the respect in which states are held and the ambitions of potentates can be curbed (134–49), before returning to another incriminating action—the delay to the ratification of the oaths. This curious section (150–77) lacks focus or coherence, spending time on the irrelevant matter of Demosthenes' ransoming of prisoners and the trouble he had with his fellow-ambassadors. But its conclusion marks a clear point of division, as he summarily claims to have proved the main charges (177–8), and demands the punishment prescribed by the law.

The delivered speech may have ended at this point: the rest of it embellishes what has already been said, with an emphasis on attacking Aeschines' character (192–201, 241–55,[225] 285–7), and justifying his own actions (188–91, 234–6). The purpose was to complete the eclipse of Aeschines' political career. That it failed to do so cannot have been due to lack of rhetorical resource, as this latter half contains some of Demosthenes' best oratory: on the duties of ambassadors (183–4); Xenophron's banquet and the treatment of the woman from Olynthus (196–8); the novel hypothetical narrative ('Think of the story that will be told, if you acquit him . . . ', 229–31); the deploration of the 'disease that is sweeping through Greece' (viz. corruption of politicians, 259–62); examples of the treatment of men who had done positive good, but had offended, in former times, used for comparative argument (271–7); and the call for popular vigilance against power-seeking individuals, with its invocation of the divine (296–9). He is also able to give new life to a hackneyed epideictic theme by using dialogue (312):

What Greek or barbarian is there who is so gauche or ignorant or hostile to our country that, if someone were to say, 'Tell me, in all the country that is called Greece and lived in today, is there any part that would retain that name or be inhabited by the Greeks who now hold it, if the heroes of Marathon and Salamis, our forefathers, had not performed those glorious deeds in their defence?', there is not one man who would not affirm that all this land would have become the spoil of the barbarian.

The concluding sections of the speech are the most original from a structural standpoint. Instead of a conventional summary of charges

---

[225] Reference to the trial of Timarchus, who was convicted, was not likely to have been made in the delivered speech; and the literary colouring given to this section by the extensive quotation of poetry is likewise more suited to a published speech designed to be read privately than to the one delivered at the trial.

and proofs (anacephalaiosis), Demosthenes gives a narrative in which he reconstructs Philip's thoughts and actions in order to show that the treachery of Aeschines and his colleagues was an integral and necessary part of them (315–24). He finds space too for some more sarcastic references to Aeschines' thespian pretensions, warning against succumbing to them (337–9). A final detail signals a development in the oratorical genre: technically forensic, the speech has been concerned as much with political and deliberative matters as with those of law and personal guilt. It is therefore interesting to hear Demosthenes saying that it is 'expedient' (*sympherei*) that Aeschines be convicted, not merely 'just'; and earlier (203) he has distinguished as the two main issues (*staseis*) 'whether the deed was done, and whether it was advantageous to the state'.[226] In forensic oratory, the second of these issues was justice rather than advantage (Lys. 12. 34). It was highly desirable for Demosthenes, in a lawsuit where hard evidence was in short supply, to elevate it into a contest of statesmanship; and it is this that led him to give the standard deliberative topoi a part in his speech. But the deployment of these has had a broadening effect on the speech. In particular, the narrative of matters extraneous to the case reaches new lengths, and is perhaps its most original feature.

8 On the Chersonese

This speech was followed within a few months by the *Third Philippic* in 341 BC. Both speeches were followed by the action which Demosthenes recommended in them. As this fact sets them apart from most of the deliberative oratory that he had hitherto addressed to the Athenians, it is worth considering whether part, at least, of this difference could be attributed to the persuasiveness of the oratory itself.

On first inspection, many of the arguments in *On the Chersonese* are familiar. What we find, however, is a new force and directness. The issue of peace or war with Philip is no longer a matter of choice, but a just and necessary task.[227] Justice imposes itself on the debate, because Diopeithes, the general conducting Athenian

---

[226] ἢ ὡς πέπρακται τὰ κατηγορημένα δεῖξαι, ἢ ὡς πεπραγμένα συμφέρει τῇ πόλει.

[227] 7: οὐ γὰρ αἵρεσίς ἐστιν ἡμῖν τοῦ πράγματος, ἀλλ' ὑπολείπεται τὸ δικαιότατον καὶ ἀναγκαιότατον τῶν ἔργων.

operations in the Chersonese, was using coercive means of raising money to pay his troops,[228] conduct which could only strengthen Philip's influence in the area. He already besets the country with a large force, and is awaiting his opportunity (13–14). The removal of Diopeithes and the disbandment of his army would be exactly what Philip wanted (20); and yet his necessary action in keeping his force supplied was justified both by his need and by precedent.[229] In 31–2, after blaming Philip's belligerence for all the trouble, Demosthenes finds a new line in the complaint that his audience are readier to chastise their domestic politicians if they give unpalatable advice, than to face the more difficult task of punishing an external enemy. Live speech and dialogue occupy a greater part of this than of previous deliberative speeches, most effectively when it is put in the mouths of other Greeks—potential allies who upbraid Athens for her inactivity (35–7). Used in this way, live speech serves to represent a broad body of opinion—indeed, that of all Greece!—rather than the views of the speaker alone, which the listener has heard with tiresome frequency.

At the central point of the speech Demosthenes delivers the most forceful statement yet of Philip's attitude (39–40):

Firstly, Athenians, you must fix this firmly in your minds, that Philip is waging war with the city and has broken the peace: you must stop wrangling with one another about that. He is ill-disposed and hostile to the whole city and to its very foundations—and, I will add, to every man in it, even to those who think they enjoy his greatest favour . . . he is set on the destruction of our free constitution.

Philip is 'the inveterate enemy of constitutional government' (43), but with one target in his sights.[230] The full implication of his success is stressed in a recurrent word designed to achieve maximum shock: slavery, nothing less, would be the outcome for any other state, but for Athenians, who would not submit to that, total annihilation (49, 51, 59–60).

---

[228] See Cawkwell *PM* 131–2; Sealey *DT* 180–1.

[229] 26: 'Where do you think he looks for the maintenance of his troops if he gets nothing from you and has no private source from which to furnish their pay? To the heavens?' For the normal practice of raising money from theatres of war, see 25–6. He could have added the example of Alcibiades (Diod. Sic. 13. 69. 5).

[230] Note how assonance and repetition are used to reinforce this single-mindedness: πάνθ' ὅσα πραγματεύεται καὶ κατασκευάζεται νῦν, ἐπὶ τὴν ἡμετέραν πόλιν παρασκευάζεται, καὶ ὅπου τις ἐκεῖνον ἀμύνεται, ἐνταῦθ' ὑπὲρ ἡμῶν ἀμύνεται.

This dire prospect enables him to bring greater intensity to his attack on Philip's supporters. They should be 'abominated and crucified' (61),[231] for they are exploiting the uniquely democratic freedom which Athens affords and which includes the freedom to speak on behalf of her enemies. This hyperbole is supported by effective anaphora and antithesis (65–6): 'It would not have been safe to speak thus freely in Olynthus . . . it would not have been safe . . . in Thessaly . . . in Thebes . . . But in Athens . . . it is safe to speak on Philip's behalf.' Athens has material wealth but moral poverty: true riches consist of allies, credit, and goodwill (66).

In a speech dominated by argument, the question of recalling Diopeithes has become subordinate to defining and dramatizing Philip's designs and undermining, even terrorizing, his alleged Athenian supporters, the 'philippizers'. He still finds it necessary to attack them in the *Third Philippic*, but in that speech they are no longer the main target, so a degree of success may be assumed for the rhetoric of *On the Chersonese*.

9 *Philippic III*

For someone seeking novelty of thought, this speech begins disappointingly, even reverting to sentiments expressed in the *First Philippic* (9. 5 = 4. 2). The craftsmanship of the opening two periods may be admired, but such artistry is to be found elsewhere. More notable is the succession of examples of Philip's sudden and unheralded treachery leading to the question: if he behaves thus towards people to whom he has pledged friendship, is he likely to give warning of hostilities to you, his avowed enemies (10–14)?[232] Study of the discrepancy between stated and real intention, diplomacy and action then turns to Thrace, the Hellespontine region, Euboea and Megara (15–18), places of vital strategic and economic importance to Athens. Demosthenes brings the most urgent rhetoric to bear on these incursions, real or threatened (17):

I say that, when he interferes in Megara, sets up tyrannies in Euboea, marches into Thrace as he is now doing, intrigues in the Peloponnese, and

---

[231] μισεῖν καὶ ἀποτυμπανίσαι: the latter was the punishment for convicted homicides (Lys. 13 *Ag. Agorat.* 56); see MacDowell *AHL* 111–12.

[232] This adaptation of the *eikos*-argument of the lawcourts to politics corresponds with the Aristotelian distinction between the two genres—that deliberative oratory concerns the future, whereas forensic oratory concerns the past (*Rhet.* 1. 3. 4). The argument also contains a comparative (a fortiori) element.

engages in all his present military operations, he is breaking the peace and
waging war against *you*—unless, of course, you are prepared to say that
men who are bringing up siege-engines are observing the peace until they
actually train them on your walls!

With the immediate danger vividly described, he is able to examine the whole problem in greater depth. In 21–9 he offers an explanation of Philip's success which also points to the means of arresting
it. It begins (22) with an extension of the Thucydidean idea that
empires are the result of natural human opportunism in the face of
passivity (1. 76. 2, 4. 61. 5, 5. 105. 2) into the cause of all Greek
wars. But history shows how limits were set on imperial ambitions
by rival states, an impediment which Philip had not so far encountered. Now a careful scrutiny of the following argument reveals a
continuous thread. First, when Greek states opposed imperialism
they did so by alliance ('going to war in aid of the wronged party'
(24)), whereas Philip had been able to 'plunder and strip the Greeks
one by one' (22). The Greeks need to combine and make common
cause, but cannot because they are each entrenched (28), eyeing
one another with mistrust (35). The final call proclaims the remedy: after making our own preparations, we must call upon other
Greeks (71), summon, collect, instruct, and exhort them (73).[233]
For the first time, but by indirect implication, Demosthenes has
suggested why Philip is too strong for a single Greek state to overthrow him. In 47 he alludes darkly to present conditions being very
different from those of former times, as great advances have been
made in the arts of war. Later he refers to two of these—the
Macedonian phalanx (49) and siege techniques using *mechanemata*
('engines') (50). But he is in a rhetorical dilemma: if he amplifies
the effect of these technical advances, he will make resistance seem
impossible; yet he must keep focused on the reality of the danger.
So he deliberately discounts the first (49), and suggests that keeping
Philip as far away as possible will avoid the second (51), while
pitched battles should be avoided because 'he is better trained for it
than we are' (52). In the meantime, the most telling rhetoric dwells
on the psychological and moral aspects of the danger: the failure of
Greek patriotism (the onset of 'the Greek disease' again, 36–9) and
the licence allowed to traitors (see esp. 54–5).

---

[233] συγκαλεῖν, συνάγειν, διδάσκειν, νουθετεῖν.

Concern with revolutionary changes in Euboea (57–68) is greater than in any of his other speeches. That fact alone could account for its success, since the cities of Euboea were among Athens' closest neighbours, and the establishment there of regimes friendly to Philip should have been a stronger spur to action than almost any other danger. But there is more. Following a narrative of the fortunes of Euphraeus of Oreus, whose resistance to the 'philippizing' oligarchs was not backed by the *demos*, Demosthenes draws a chilling parallel with the situation at Athens (63), where the same advantages were enjoyed by pacifists and appeasers. The clear though unstated implication is that the fate of the people of Eretria and Oreus[234] awaits those who reject the stern demands of the patriotic statesman. But at Athens there is still time. After listening to his graphic portrayal of the sufferings of the Euboeans, his audience will have been more receptive than ever before to his proposals, introduced by a parable of the storm-tossed ship.[235] They are preparations for a defensive war, with even the possibility of delay entering the calculations.[236] Against an adversary whose ambitions and intrigues are widely pursued (27–8), as many allies as possible should be mustered, but their leader has to justify her position by making the largest contribution.

Athenian control over Oreus and Eretria was restored by expeditions commanded by Ctesiphon and Phocion, recommended by Demosthenes (Plut. *Dem.* 17. 1). This may have been his main achievement in the *Third Philippic*. But there can be little doubt that it also put many Athenians in the mood for the greater commitments that were to come.

Philippic IV

The surviving text of this speech could not have had a separate existence from its immediate predecessors. Sections 11–27 and

---

[234] 66: 'They are slaves, subject to the lash and sword.'

[235] 69: 'While the ship is safe, whether it be a large or a small one, then is the time for sailor, the steersman, and everyone else at his post to be on the alert, and to see that it is not founder through anyone's deliberate or involuntary action; but when the sea has gulfed it, zeal is futile.' A parable is a simile converted into a story. This one may be the [first] in Greek oratory. Others in 18 *Cor.* 194 (also nautical), 243.

[236] 72: he says that delay could be advantageous because 'the war is against an individual not the might of an organized state'. The instability of Philip's personal position (*Olynth.* 4–21) was increased by his active participation in his campaigns (18 *Cor.* 67), and his ill-[ness] around the time of this speech.

62–70 are drawn almost verbatim and entirely[237] from 8. 39–51 and
67. This wholesale transference of material[238] must have served the
needs of a literary composition rather than a speech to be delivered
in a live debate. Blass rightly noted an absence of a definite occasion or purpose[239] for it. But it does contain two recommendations, the nature of which may explain the form in which the
speech has survived. They occur in the central section (31–45),
flanked by the transferred passages. The first (31–4) is a reasoned
argument for applying to the Persian King for aid. This idea had
been touched upon briefly in *Philippic III* (71). The second (35–45)
centres upon the Theoric Fund, and is a plea for the abatement of
class antagonism. Now in their respective spheres of foreign
and domestic policy both topics were extremely contentious.
Rapprochement with the King was obviously anathema to those who
favoured it with Philip, while among their opponents awareness of
the King's overall policy of keeping the Greeks weak was as alive
as ever. Hence there may have been something approaching consensus on the subject among Athenians before Demosthenes proposed a change of policy towards him.[240] As to the other
contentious topic, the Theoric Fund, he tries to reconcile the attitudes of both rich and poor to it. The poor have benefited from
increased revenues in recent years, but the rich should not express
disgruntlement at this by refusing to maintain their contributions
(37–42). Equally, the rich have a real grievance when they see demagogues controlling the destination of these public moneys and
thereby acquiring undue influence (43–5). Previously (1. 19–20, 3.
11) he has seen the Theoric Fund primarily as a source of extra
money for the war; now, at a scarcely less critical time, its fair distribution is regarded as an agent of harmony between the classes, as
each has its rights.[241]

237 From other speeches: § 12 = 6. 17–18; also, § 30 οἱ μὲν γὰρ ἄλλοι . . . τὰ
πράγματα = 5.2.
238 The scale is proportionally greater than that found in earlier instances in *Against
Androtion* and *Against Timocrates*. Further on the relationship between *On the Chersonese* and
Philippic IV, see C. Adams, 'Speeches viii and x of the Demosthenic Corpus', *CP* 33 (1938),
129–44; S. Daitz, 'The Relationship of the De Chersoneso and the Philippica Quarta of
Demosthenes', *CP* 52 (1957), 145–62.
239 *AB* iii/1. 388.
240 The full effect of Demosthenes' oratory on the course of Athenian policy at this critical time is examined by H. Montgomery, *The Way to Chaeronea* (Bergen, 1983).
241 43: 'Athenians, we must share the citizenship justly among ourselves, the wealthy feeling safe to lead their own lives without fear, but prepared in emergencies to make over their

Thus the two newly argued topics are in their different ways surprising and contradictory of previously propounded views: surely
indigestible fare for a single speech to a live audience, as may be
guessed from the 'extreme fear' he expresses in introducing the second (35–6). Their juxtaposition at the centre of a discourse whose
other topics are either second-hand or unrelated to them has a
practical explanation: they were raised in two separate debates. The
first proposal (which was not necessarily prior in time) led, in 340,
to the dispatch of an Athenian embassy to the King's court, much
to Philip's chagrin (12. 6–7). The circumstances which prompted
the second, which contains no concrete proposals, must remain
obscure.

Notwithstanding its patchwork composition, and a generally
subdued, almost academic tone outside the transferred passages, the
speech is very Demosthenic in style. Passages which exhibit this
most conspicuously are 4–6 (nominal clauses), 39–42 (imagery),
46–50 (nominal clauses in patriotic/philosophical argument, comparison (*agora/polis*)). On the other hand, there is no final drawing
together of themes, summary of proposals or rallying call. Instead
there is a personalized attack[242] on hyperactive politicians who
advocate passive policies (72), and the now familiar complaint, in
condensed form, that their audiences too readily give ear to them.

---

property to the state for its defence; while the rest may regard state property as common
property and receive their due share of it, but must recognize that private wealth belongs to
the possessor.'

[242] He apostrophizes 'Aristomedes': perhaps 'Aristodemus' should be read, in which case
we know that Demosthenes proposed a crown for him for his service on the first embassy
to Macedon (Aeschin. 2 *Leg.* 17). Disillusioned friends become the bitterest enemies: here
one becomes the prime example of a mischievous politician.

7

DEMOSTHENES
LOGOGRAPHOS
(Part II)

Discussion now turns to the remaining speeches. These are all concerned with private lawsuits, except the *De Corona*, his masterpiece, which will be treated last. Some sixty speeches and other works are preserved under Demosthenes' name, but critical examination of them over many years, using various means,[1] has reduced the number of those accepted as authentic. Dionysius of Halicarnassus (*Dem.* 13) considered that there were 'not many more than twenty' private speeches in addition to the six he had mentioned. This provides a rough guide to the number of private Demosthenic speeches known and recognized in the Augustan period; and there is the further fact that he accepts as genuine two speeches (43 *Ag. Macartatus* and 48 *Ag. Olympiodorus*) which modern critics have tended to reject. When these two facts are applied to the modern list of 'authentic' speeches, which is substantially that of Blass, the fourteen titles which it contains must seem conservative, and consequently the seventeen speeches rejected as spurious may seem excessive. In the present early stage of Demosthenic authenticity-studies, my own observations lead me to include in the twenty speeches examined below some which others have rejected.[2]

---

[1] These include inferences drawn from chronology (the best criterion, where available), the incidence of hiatus (G. E. Benseler, *De Hiatu in Oratoribus Atticis et Historicis Graecis* (Freiburg, 1841)), and assessments of literary worth and technical competence which are, despite their subjectivity, not without value, and should be accepted until scientific examination of objective criteria can be conducted on the whole Corpus (see Ch. 4 n. 4).

[2] There remain eight non-Demosthenic speeches, not discussed in this chapter: 46 *Ag. Stephanus II*, 49 *Ag. Timotheus*, 50 *Ag. Polycles*, 52 *Ag. Callippus*, 53 *Ag. Nicostratus*, 59 *Ag. Neaira*, all of which may have been written for his own lawsuits by Apollodorus, son of Pasion (on their authenticity, see Trevett *ASP* 50–76); and 25, 26 *Ag. Aristogeiton I, II*.

The first group of seven private speeches—the five Guardian-speeches and the other two from the first period to 355 BC (55 *Ag. Callicles* and 41 *Ag. Spoudias*)—have already been discussed. The eight private speeches of the second period span about ten years (355–345),[3] and thus plot the orator's development in due sequence. Five (36 *For Phormio*, 37 *Ag. Pantaenetus*, 38 *Ag. Nausimachus*, 32 *Ag. Zenothemis*, 33 *Ag. Apaturius*) afford an opportunity to observe development in a single type of case, the paragraphe (demurrer or obstructive plea) and two are replies 'pros paragraphen' (37 *Ag. Lacritus* and 34 *Ag. Phormio*). The order of the subsequent twelve speeches is chronological as far as knowledge allows. But I begin with one of his most highly regarded private speeches.

54 *Against Conon*

This is a prosecution for serious assault, or battery (*aikia*). The plaintiff, Ariston, claims that he narrowly escaped with his life from a fracas in which Conon was the leader of a drunken gang. Conon has produced witnesses as to fact (31), and a secondary line of defence drawing on common human experience (13–14).[4] Models available to Demosthenes would include Lysias 3 *Against Simon* and the speech *Against Tisis*, which Dionysius of Halicarnassus compares with the present speech (*Dem.* 11–12), concluding thus (13): 'If we did not know from their titles who their authors were, I doubt whether many of us could easily decide which of the two was by Demosthenes and which by Lysias.' Although *Against Conon* is deservedly admired,[5] the task of finding new and distinctive features may prove hard. Stylistically, the individual Demosthenic stamp is lacking, which may argue for the earlier date suggested by commentators,[6] and the division is conventional.

---

[3] Or five years (350–345) if the later date for 54 *Ag. Conon* is preferred. But see below (n. 6).

[4] In this case, behaviour normal in young men ('boys will be boys'). For the theory, see Aristot. *Rhet.* 2. 12. 3.

[5] The publication of three English editions attests this: Sandys (1875), Doherty (1927), and C. Carey and R. A. Reid, *Demosthenes: Selected Private Speeches* (Cambridge, 1985).

[6] *c.*355 rather than 341. For discussion of the evidence, see Carey and Reid, *Selected Private Speeches*, 69. Both they and Blass (*AB* iii/1. 457) find it inconclusive. Bearing in mind his political preoccupations in 341, one could only express admiration for his protean ability to switch oratorical genres if that later date is correct.

From the very first word, however, Demosthenes takes hold of
his main line and never releases it:[7] 'Outrage, gentlemen of the
jury, was what I suffered at the hands of Conon the defendant
. . .' Not only the assault itself (though it is essential to establish its
extreme viciousness), but the conduct of the defendant and his
friends at every stage, must be shown to have been outrageous and
antisocial. Slanted narrative is the obvious medium through which
to convey this, and Demosthenes shows mastery of this, from his
initial description of the brutal drunken antics of Ctesias, Conon's
son, in camp at Panactum (3–6), to the much more detailed
account of the main fight and the near-fatal injuries which Ariston
sustained (7–12). Now the counter-argument that the matter was a
normal dispute between groups of young men (14) may have
acquired added strength from the nature of the groups in this case,
if they were in fact political clubs or *hetaireiai*.[8] In that case the jury
would regard injuries inflicted by rival members on one another
with little sense of outrage, and might even take an adverse view of
complaints by a loser in one of their routine battles. Ariston's narrative must contain nullifying detail. The early **narrative** (3) dates
the quarrel from the initial encounter, and tells clearly how Ctesias
and Conon's other sons started it and were blamed for it by the
general, who thus becomes an authoritative witness (4–5). The
main narrative brings the whole of Conon's drunken party to the
scene near the agora, where Ariston is accompanied only by
Phanostratus.[9] Unconscionable from the outset, Conon's behaviour shows excess in every particular: the violence of the assault,
the extent of the wounds inflicted, and his exultance in them
(8–9);[10] then, after graphic detail of Ariston's wounds and his
friends' reaction to them, a sequence of arguments (15–25) is
designed to deepen the jury's prejudice against Conon beyond the
mere rebuttal of his disclaimers. There is some discussion of a scale

---

7 Ὑβρισθείς: thereafter the verb occurs twelve times, ὕβρις nine times.

8 See M. P. O. Morford, 'Ethopoiia and Character-Assassination in the *Conon* of
Demosthenes', *Mnemosyne* 19 (1966), 241–8. References to names which they assumed
(*autolekythoi*, *ithyphalloi*, on which see Carey and Reid, *Selected Private Speeches*, 86–7), may
suggest such associations.

9 The use of the military metaphor ἀνεμείχθημεν ('we joined battle') (8) is revealing:
Ariston wishes to avoid appearing weak or pusillanimous; but the verb tends to be used of
several combatants on each side, and not an uneven contest.

10 'He began to crow, mimicking game-cocks that have won a fight, and his friends got
him to flap his elbows against his sides like wings.' This detail exposes Conon not only as a
participant but as the leader.

of legal remedies, curiously irrelevant to a case of almost sponta-
neous mayhem (18–23), but it ends in an effective comparative (a
fortiori) argument.

The various antics and ploys used by the defendants at the arbitration are described in a narrative even fuller of subjective comment
than the earlier account (26–9). This extended treatment of *extra
causam* behaviour serves the purpose of portraying Conon as hybristic towards the city's legal institutions no less than her citizens. This
is unusual, as are the deployment of live speech to discredit the character of witnesses (35–6), the use of procatalepsis to describe intended
actions rather than intended evidence (38), and the luridness of detail
in an attack on Conon's impiety.[11] This produces an antithesis which
leads to the most original rhetoric in the speech. Instead of swearing
an oath as an item of *atechnos pistis*, Ariston is made to do two things
with it: to use it to summarize the main charge, and to insist on the
oath itself as evidence of his truthfulness (41–2):

I swear by all the gods and goddesses that I have in very truth suffered at
the hands of Conon this wrong for which I am suing him; and that I was
beaten by him, and that my lip was cut so that it had to be sewn up, and
that it is because of this gross maltreatment that I am prosecuting him. If
I swear truly, may many blessings be mine, and may I never again suffer
such an outrage. But if I have sworn falsely, may I perish utterly. But my
oath has not been false, even though Conon should say so till he bursts.

Conventional warnings against pleas for pity and bad precedent
(43), and a brief reference to state services (44) bring the speech to
a close, but it has had its moments of pure inventiveness.

36 *For Phormio*

From the beginning of the fourth century, a citizen being prosecuted could initiate a paragraphe (counter-prosecution),[12] on the
ground that the suit was inadmissible for technical reasons, such as
the fact that he had already been released or discharged from the
impending claim, or that the claim was being made too late.[13] The

---

[11] 39: Conon and his friends devouring the sacrificial food set out for Hecate.
[12] See H. J. Wolff, *Die attische Paragraphe* (Weimar, 1966); Harrison, *LA* ii. 106–24;
MacDowell *LCA* 214–17, 219. On this speech, see H.-V. Beyer, *Über den Sachverhalt der
demosthenischen Rede für Phormion* (Berlin, 1968).
[13] 'Prescription', or 'statute of limitations' imposed time limits (five years for most cases
in the Athenian courts). Other grounds on which a paragraphe might be brought were: (1)

paragraphe afforded the litigant a singular advantage, turning him from defendant into prosecutor and giving him first hearing and the chance to make the first impression on the jury. Whether Demosthenes exploits this advantage with new techniques or by adaptation of old ones is the main question to be considered.

Phormio faced prosecution by Apollodorus, son of Pasion. The latter, in his old age, had made Phormio manager of his bank and shield-factory. In his will he confirmed Phormio's tenancy pending the majority of his younger son Pasicles, and provided that he should marry his widow Archippe. Apollodorus' resentment of the conferment of power over the family fortune upon an outsider (Phormio was an alien, though he was granted citizenship) might draw sympathy from the property-owners among a jury. So that sympathy must be reduced. But there is greater urgency for attack on the main charge, which is that of misappropriation. Instead of the summary of points to be proved, the **prooemium** (1–3) contains a summary statement of the obligations which Phormio has discharged (3).[14] Proofs of each lease follow (4–10), then probability-argument. Conventional narrative is dispensed with in the interest of sustaining the impetus of the attack on Apollodorus, whose rapacious and profligate character[15] has been the cause of the dispositions. Again, procatalepsis, which usually occurs later, here makes its first appearance early (18 (again, 33, 36)). The main arguments about the release and discharge have been made and summarized by 23–4, and the matter of the prescription (*prothesmia*) is dealt with in 26–7. The paragraphe proper is complete at this point, but the speaker intends to use his initiative to dispose of the matter for good, and this intention[16] accounts for the extension of the speech to the length reached in a full trial. Aware of possible sympathy for Apollodorus (see above), the speaker[17] shows how his resentment against Phormio is not justified, by giving examples of other enfranchised ex-slaves marrying their ex-masters' female

that the plaintiff had chosen the wrong legal process; (2) no category of *dike* covered the charge.

14 'Phormio has done many kindnesses to this man Apollodorus: he has duly paid and delivered up to the plaintiff everything of his which he had been left to control, and has been discharged of all further claims.'

15 8: ἁρπάζοντος δὲ τούτου καὶ πόλλ' ἀπὸ κοινῶν τῶν χρημάτων ἀναλίσκειν οἰομένου δεῖν.

16 2: ἀπαλλαγή τις αὐτῷ γένηται παρ' ὑμῖν κυρία.

17 Phormio's case is pleaded by unnamed friends (1).

relatives; and with the same purpose, he seeks to disparage (probably unjustly) Apollodorus' performance of leitourgiai, notably the trierarchy (41–2). The rhetoric intensifies with a long apostrophe (43–8), in which the speaker compares Apollodorus unfavourably with his father, whose career has resembled that of Phormio. Thus the usually pejorative 'rags-to-riches' topos is given a new, laudatory lease of life. The speech draws to a close in a flurry of oaths (51, 53, 61), a hypophora touching on the question of prescription (53) with an argument paradoxically using Apollodorus' litigiousness to explain his delay in pursuing his claims against Phormio (54–5);[18] and a final full-scale plea on Phormio's behalf, superimposing the idea of pity for his plight on any residual sympathy the jury might feel for Apollodorus. Demosthenes has used the advantage of the first strike not merely by turning defence into attack, but by pressing that attack home on a personal level with great intensity, though without employing any new techniques.

37 *Against Pantaenetus*

This paragraphe is one of the few literary sources on administrational aspects of mining in Attica, and the case also concerns the ownership and lease of land and property.[19] It does not, however, show a significant advance in rhetorical technique on the last speech, which may be five years earlier (350/49). The division is more conventional, with clearly marked **prooemium** (1–3) and **narrative** (4–17). A major difficulty faced by the speaker Nicobulus is that his business-partner Euergus has been defeated by Pantaenetus in a previous suit on the same charges (23). He begins his evidence and arguments by challenging and disproving all Pantaenetus' accusations against himself (18–44), but, since he has to guard against suffering the same outcome as Euergus, he also has to show that that outcome was unjust. He does this initially by exposing irregularities in the process against Euergus, which arose when Pantaenetus entered directly into litigation without prior examination by the archon (45–6). This gave him an advantage similar to that sought by Nicobulus from the present paragraphe—

---

[18] His clever argument is that Apollodorus delayed because he knew his case was weak, but his litigiousness got the better of him in the end.

[19] Hence detailed discussions of it by M. I. Finley, *Studies in Land and Credit in Ancient Athens, 500–200 BC* (New Brunswick, 1951, repr. 1973), 32 ff., Harrison *LA* i. 274–9. It is also one of the *Selected Private Speeches* edited by Carey and Reid (Cambridge, 1985), q.v.

that of striking the first blow without revealing the charges, and playing on the emotions of a jury which had not been provided with all the facts (47–8). In his reply the speaker resorts in turn to emotional appeal, maligning Pantaenetus himself directly (apostrophe) and his witnesses (48–9), and ridiculing his claims. The best rhetoric is to be found in the closing pages, where Nicobulus tries to counter the age-old popular prejudice against money-lenders, which Pantaenetus may have used in his suit against Euergus. He makes Pantaenetus say (52): ' "The Athenians hate money-lenders. Nicobulus is a nasty fellow: he walks fast, talks loud, and carries a cane; and all these things count in my favour." ' But the speaker goes on to argue that he has not engaged professionally in usury and never defrauded anyone, unlike his adversary. 'Such a man am I, Pantaenetus, who walk fast; and such are you, who walk slowly' (55).[20]

The concluding passage (58–60) recurs in the next speech, where it will be examined.

38 *Against Nausimachus*

Similar in form to *For Phormio* (direct examination of proofs without narrative), and sharing common passages with *Against Pantaenetus* (opening and conclusion), this speech is less distinctive than either, though the issue (claim for damages following abuse of guardianship) is different from both. As in those cases, time has elapsed (twenty-two years) since the alleged offence, and the speaker is able to invoke the law of prescription as well as that of release and discharge.

The speaker's father, Aristaechmus, had been guardian to Nausimachus, who was resurrecting his claim, now against the guardian's sons, that they had received money due to him and not handed it over. The speaker says that this claim had already been settled in a lawsuit (8, restated in rhetorical form (pathetic paradox) in 18), and argues, from the absence of subsequent claims (11), against the probability that any further monies were due. The arguments which he attributes in advance to his opponents (procatalepsis, 19–20) are designedly general, emotional and subjective. The passage common to this and the previous speech (21–2 = 37.

---

[20] Cf. Dem. 45 *Ag. Steph.* I 77 and Trevett *ASP* 170–1.

8–60) looks suspiciously like a commonplace used in dubious
ses, since it argues a fortiori that, since in the past plaintiffs have
leased defendants in serious cases (homicide, sacrilege), release
anted in less serious cases, such as the present one, should have
ual validity. No more convincing is the second anticipation
5–7), in which the opponents' parading of their trierarchies is
logically set against their profligacy, which is further underlined
7). It is a speech in which too much may have been concealed to
ake accurate assessment of its quality possible. The speaker's
bjective seems to have been more modest than that of Phormio's
lvocate.[21]

2 Against Zenothemis

his paragraphic speech, like the next, concerns a mercantile loan.
uch transactions were the essential motor of Aegean trade. In this
ase the lender was Demo, a relative of Demosthenes, and the
ader a certain Protus, who was to bring a cargo of grain from
yracuse. Now a condition of these 'bottomry' loans was that they
ere not repayable if the cargo was lost at sea, and this could be
xploited by men like Zenothemis and Hegestratus, who accom-
anied Protus, borrowed further money after the cargo had been
aded on the ship at Syracuse, set sail on it bound for their native
Iassilia, then plotted to sink it.[22] Demosthenes enjoys telling the
ory of how their plan misfired, but there are too many unan-
verable questions in the case, including the crucial one of the
wnership of the cargo, which Zenothemis had claimed and Demo
ontested.

The **narrative** of the attempted sinking and subsequent return
–14) is simple but vivid, and contains an ethical element at the
oint of the criminal act (5–7):

hen they were two or three days into the voyage, Hegestratus went
own by night into the hold of the ship and began to cut a hole in its bot-
m, while Zenothemis, pretending to know nothing about it, remained
n deck with the rest of the passengers. But the noise below attracted their
tention and, realizing that something wrong was going on in the hold,

---

[21] He could not have hoped that such a short speech could stop all further litigation, as
ormio's advocate intended in his case (cf. n. 16). See further, Harrison *LA* ii. 118; Blass
B iii/1. 482–5.
[22] Thereby 'bottomry' was degraded into 'barratry'.

they went below to assist. Hegestratus, caught in the act, was pursued from the scene and leapt into the sea, where he was drowned on missing the ship's boat in the darkness. Thus, an evil man met the evil fate he deserved, suffering what he intended others to suffer; while this man, his associate and accomplice, had been present at the crime and pretended to be astounded by it, yet still tried to persuade the captain and the passengers to abandon ship.

This portrayal of the determined roguery of Zenothemis will have been useful to Demo at this stage, but his title to the cargo is still a matter of dispute. This dispute is waged through live speech, in a new and more complicated form than before, with several persons participating (15–16). But Zenothemis is represented as adopting stonewall tactics, and since, as Blass noted,[23] the text of Protus' agreement with Demo is absent, we cannot assess the validity of his claim. And it turns out that he is not the only rogue. Protus, in order to salvage something from the whole sorry affair, seems to have conspired with Zenothemis (30) by letting his suit win against him by default (25–6), thereby incurring Demo's charge that he 'won for him a pettifogging scoundrel instead of the return of his loan'.[24] Finally, the text breaks off in mid-sentence, apparently some way from the end of the speech.[25] But Demosthenes has displayed some relish in attacking 'a gang of scoundrels in the Piraeus',[26] and at least ensures that his kinsman Demo emerges with more credit than any of the other principals.

33 Against Apaturius

This speech is less conventional than the last, in that it begins, at some length, with an explanation of the legal procedure governing mercantile actions, and the justification of a paragraphe when no contract has been made (1–2). The speaker's adduction of legal facts is consonant with his categorical denial that any contract was currently in force between himself and Apaturius (35): he claims that

---

[23] AB iii/1. 495.

[24] 26: συκοφάντην ἀντὶ χρημάτων αἰτιώμενοι τοῦτον ἡμῖν κεκομικέναι.

[25] At 31 he anticipates Zenothemis' argument that he had tried to enlist Demosthenes' services as synegoros, hoping to profit from his reputation. Without denying that he had approached him, Demo says that his relative had declined to act in that capacity, but the speech bears most of the traits of Demosthenic style.

[26] 10: ἐργαστήριον μοχθηρῶν ἀνθρώπων ἐν τῷ Πειραιεῖ. Blass (AB iii/1. 497) notes the lively 'charm' (Reize) of the style, and does not substantiate his doubts about Demosthenic authorship.

a certain Archippus (15, 22), not he, had lately[27] agreed to act as surety. But he was still involved (14–15, 21), and when the documents of settlement between Apaturius and Parmeno were lost (16–18), he became dangerously exposed to litigation,[28] and a paragraphe offered his best chance of salvation. In these circumstances, the case called less for any rhetorical novelty than for resort to well-tried devices: the topos of delay as evidence of a groundless charge (22), and probability deduced from behaviour (in this case, his own, 28–9). But this is another perplexing case which is obfuscated by the economical deployment of the relevant facts.

35 *Against Lacritus*

A plaintiff facing a paragraphe had to reply to his opponent's objections. Two such 'pros paragraphen' speeches survive among those ascribed to Demosthenes, both concerning mercantile loans.[29] Interest in comparing them is enhanced by the time which separates them.[30] Lacritus had objected to being prosecuted for a debt incurred by his dead brother Artemo on the ground that he personally had made no contract with the lenders, Androcles and Nausicrates. To the strength of his case he was able to add a certain personal prestige—he was a pupil of Isocrates who had also served as a legislator (*nomothetes*, *Vit. X Or.* 837d)—so that the challenge to the speechwriter was to counter these disadvantages.

His initial assault (*ephodos*) is extraordinary and novel. It is a powerful invective against a particular race of men—the Phaselites—characterizing them as inveterate financial fraudsters, who 'think the repayment of debts is like losing their own private property' (2), and are responsible for more lawsuits than any other race. For earlier models of such ethnic or local characterization one may look to Herodotus, the descriptions of physical qualities of peoples living in different climates and terrains found in the Hippocratic *Airs*,

[27] In 4–12 he describes earlier dealings he had had with Apaturius and Parmeno, but concludes (13): 'Since then I have had no transaction [or 'contract' (συμβόλαιον)], great or small, with the fellow.'

[28] See Harrison *LA* ii. 112–13.

[29] The other is 34 *Ag. Phormio* (see next note). The earliest speech *pros paragraphen* is [Lysias] 23 *Ag. Pancleon*.

[30] Perhaps over sixteen years. 351 is reasonably suggested for *Ag. Lacritus* by Blass (*AB* iii/1. 564); his date for 34 *Ag. Phormio*—327/6 (578)—may be too late, the only certain *terminus post quem* being 335 (§ 38).

Waters, and Places, or, less pertinently, the comparison of Athenian with Spartan character in Thuc. 1. 70,[31] and the general atmosphere of resentment against the corndealers as a class portrayed in Lysias 22; but as the beginning of a forensic speech it has no antecedent.

The long **narrative** (6–27) keeps the rascality of the opponents in continuous view with some remarkable language.[32] The style is notable for pleonastic antithesis, perhaps in an attempt to outdo Isocrates' pupil in his master's style.[33]

The personal attack on Lacritus is sustained throughout, returning latterly (40–1) to his education as a 'sophist' under Isocrates,[34] and using the rhetorical technique of reversal (*peritrope*) as the argument is turned to consider what Lacritus would have done in the role of prosecutor (44–5).[35] Thus Demosthenes tries to match the opponents' accomplishment, but his chief problem remains. In the long documents describing the agreement between the lenders and the borrowers, the name of Lacritus does not appear, either as guarantor of repayment or in any other capacity. Verbal undertakings from him seem to be all the speaker can invoke (15), while he makes as much as he can of his involvement (16: 'It was he who was organizing the whole matter'). He lumps together the perpetrators of the offending actions: 'they' and 'you' (plur.)[36] are constantly assumed to include Lacritus, who acts as spokesman (30–1), the sophist who could turn the worse into the better cause (41), and is also familiar with the workings of the law (48–9).[37] Once again,

---

[31] Carey persuasively suggests Eur. *Andromache* 445–63 as a better model of characterizing invective.

[32] 7 . . . πονηρίαν . . . 8 θηρίοις . . . 9 ἐτοιχωρύχθησαν . . . 24 πανουργίαι . . . 25 ὕβριν καὶ ἀναίδειαν . . . ὕθλον καὶ φλυαρίαν . . . 26 σεσυλήμεθα.

[33] e.g. 19: 'Instead of three thousand jars, these men did not put even five hundred on board the boat; and instead of having bought the quantity of wine they should have, they used the money however they pleased.' (Isocratean οὐκ . . . ἀλλὰ antithesis partly replaced by Demosthenic articular infinitive construction producing a similar antithetical construction (ἀντὶ τοῦ ἠγοράσθαι . . .).)

[34] If the speech is correctly dated to 351, the subject of the unpopularity of Isocrates' school had had recent currency: his apologia, the *Antidosis*, was published a little earlier.

[35] This provides a promising line of argument, as Lacritus is said to have pursued his dead brother's debtors. Proof of this would have established his liability in the present case, and it is surprising, or suspicious, that this is not given.

[36] Note esp. 46 ὑμῖν, which makes Lacritus himself a borrower.

[37] Pathetic paradox (47) and hypophora (47–8) strengthen the attack on the legal expert: (49) 'Instruct us (δίδαξον), Lacritus'; but he should only say 'what is just and according to the law'. The precise status of 'Lacritus the Phaselite' (15), who was said also to have been a legislator in Athens (see above), is not established.

we are unable to assess the extent to which Lacritus in his para-graphe had needed to dissimulate and pervert: we can only see how much rhetorical ingenuity Demosthenes needed to employ in order to offer his client some chance of success.

34 *Against Phormio*

In spite of its late date (see n. 30) the second speech pros paragraphen reads like an old-fashioned defence speech, with hackneyed topoi of inexperience and *apragmosyne* in the **prooemium** (1–2). The case requires less rhetorical treatment because, unlike in the previous two, there is no dispute as to the original existence of a contract. Chrysippus had lent 2,000 drachmae on bottomry to Phormio, but the loss of the ship on the return journey from the Crimea released Phormio from the contract; or so he claimed initially, and this was the ground of his paragraphe. But at the arbitration held before this came to court Lampis, the ship's captain, came forward with a story that Phormio had repaid the whole sum to him, and that it had been lost with the ship. It is easy enough for the speechwriter to point up the inconsistency of the two stories, and dialogue helps him to enliven his narrative (14–15). A new speaker, presumably a business partner of Chrysippus, takes over the attack.[38] He combines the fact that Phormio had been unable to dispose of his wares (dismissively called 'trash' (*rhopos*) by Chrysippus (9)), with his over-borrowing at Athens to produce an elaborate probability-argument rebutting Phormio's claim that he had repaid the loan to Lampis (21–8). Realizing, however, that positive proof of the existence of a sum of money was impossible, he turns (33) to the prior conditions of the original contract, and argues that Phormio has violated these by not placing on board goods to the value of the sums loaned. From this a picture of conspiracy emerges (34–5), followed by the most concentrated rhetoric in the speech,[39] which, however, breaks no new ground. Lampis is effectively represented as no less discreditable than Phormio.

[38] However, see J. Lofberg, 'The Speakers in the Case of Chrysippus v. Phormio', *CP* 27 (1932), 329–35, who argues that only Chrysippus speaks.
[39] 40–8: improbabilities of logically contradictory actions and statements; 43: pathetic paradox; 46: credibility of witnesses; 48–9: continuing sequence of *argumentum ex contrario*; paradeigma of an unnamed fraudster; 51: universalizing argument (public injury—lenders in general must be protected).

56 *Against Dionysodorus*

Closest in time to the previous speech[40] and also concerned with a maritime loan, this case involves not loss of cargo but sale for greater profit. The plaintiff refers to the violation of a specific law (10) which bound traders to sail to their agreed destinations. Invocation of this seemingly minor law rather than the major laws which forbade persons resident at Athens, both moneylenders (35 *Ag. Lacrit.* 51) and traders (34 *Ag. Phormio* 37), to traffic between other ports, must mean that these laws did not apply to the defendant Dionysodorus and his partner Parmeniscus because they were not Athenians, or even metics. This status complicated the rhetorical task of the speaker, who is named as Darius in the *Hypothesis*.

Hence we find him resorting to high moral tone in the **prooemium**. Darius and his partner made their loan in good faith, accepting the risks but expecting protection under the law (1–2). A précis of the whole case is presented (3–4) in a periodic style, an unusual mixture of rhetorical techniques. The author shows further taste for periodic writing in the long **narrative** (5–18), but it is occasionally careless and old-fashioned, as in § 10, where the singular subject of the main clause has two anaphoric participial clauses in the plural dependent upon it.[41] But he also uses dialogue to good effect (12, 15); the language is not without colour,[42] and his summary of Dionysodorus' actions in 19–20 in terms of protestation shows notable inventiveness. The **proof** has clearly defined sections. The **refutation** (21–36) contains some rather laboured argument (esp. 24–5) and standard topics and devices.[43] In the

---

[40] In 7 reference is made to Cleomenes' command in Egypt (ἄρξαντος ('who had become ruler')). If this assumption of command was recent, the *terminus post quem* for the speech is 332/1. The ingressive force of the aorist is used frequently in verbs denoting state (cf. βασιλεύω, πλουτῶ). (See Goodwin *MT* 55; Humbert, *Syntaxe Grecque* § 242 (p. 143), who quotes Thuc. 6. 55. 1: . . . πρεσβύτατος ὢν ῾Ιππίας ἦρξεν ('came to power').) The terminative force of ἄρξαντος adopted by the Loeb translator and by Carey and Reid (pp. 201–4), following Schäfer ('having ended his rule'), would place the speech after the death of Cleomenes in 323, and possibly after that of Demosthenes in 322. But the natural flow of the narrative is against that interpretation: 'Cleomenes came to power, and from that time did your city no small harm . . .' Hence the passage cannot be used to disprove Demosthenic authorship, and the earlier date is probably to be preferred.

[41] ὁ Παρμενίσκος . . . ἐξαιρεῖται τὸν σῖτον . . . καταφρονήσαντες μὲν . . . καταφρονήσαντες δὲ . . .

[42] 11: τούτῳ τῷ ἀρχιτέκτονι τῆς ὅλης ἐπιβουλῆς, 12: αὐτὸς ἑαυτῷ νομοθετῶν.

[43] Pathetic paradox (23, also 44); dilemmaton, framed interrogatively (32); reductio ad absurdum (35) (cf. Lys. 24. 13; 30. 32).

confirmation (37–47) apostrophe is used to go over the main points (39); rhetorical questions abound, and there is a singularly apt metaphor (44): 'You must not, Athenians, allow men of this character to have their own way, nor let them ride upon two anchors, expecting, if they win, to have what belongs to others, and if they fail to trick you, to pay merely the amount which they owe.' One may discern Demosthenic characteristics here, but some important ones are missing,[44] and the speechwriter also shows Isocratean influence in his use of long sentences and amplification. It is tempting to follow Carey and Reid in doubting Demosthenic authorship, but the speaker's concluding call to him by name to come forth in his support (50) would, as they say (*Selected Private Speeches*, 232), make his participation in the case, in some capacity, highly likely.

45 *Against Stephanus I*

A witness in Phormio's successful paragraphe (Speech 36), Stephanus was subsequently prosecuted by Apollodorus for bearing false witness (*pseudomartyria*). Demosthenic authorship of this speech would mean that he acted for both sides at different stages of the dispute, and considerations of style and technique point strongly to that probability.[45] The scale of the speech is explained by its inclusive purpose: not only the credibility of Stephanus, but the character of Phormio is to come under attack, because the ultimate purpose is to reopen the case against him.

The facts in question could be dealt with briefly. The short **narrative** (3–7) describes only the background, and leads straight into the application of clever probability-argument[46] to alleged procedural irregularities in Stephanus' deposition concerning the will of Pasion. Next, interpretation of the opponents' actions (15–26) their motives of greed and advantage (27–33, resumed later in 62). There is also some standard use of anticipation (43–7). But

---

[44] e.g. relative paucity of abstract expression, as in the use of articular infinitive constructions.

[45] There is also ancient testimony. In Plutarch (*Dem.* 15 and *Comp. Cic. & Dem.* 3) this double advocacy is an item in the tradition of Demosthenes' venality. Aeschines refers twice to his disclosure of his client's speech to his opponent (2 *Leg.* 165, 3 *Ag. Ctes.* 173), but does not mention the present speech, probably because writing speeches for opposing clients at different times was commonly viewed as unexceptionable. See Trevett *ASP* 53–61.

[46] Note esp. the dilemmaton in 13.

the speech really comes to life rhetorically at § 53, where the old
topos of the evil of conflict with one's kin assumes a new form:

It is a terrible thing to bear false witness against anyone, but it is much
more terrible and abominable to do so against one's kinsmen; for such a
man not only violates the written laws, but also the ties of natural affinity.

This is followed by the alleged theft of a legal document by
Stephanus; but the most inventive sections are the biographical
proof (pistis ek biou) against Stephanus (63–70) and the attack on
Phormio (71–6). In the former, Stephanus is described as a fair-
weather friend of prosperous men.[47] A period ending in a hyperbole (65)[48] leads to a succession of topics (66–7): whereas it is
reasonable to feel indulgence towards people who behave badly
because of poverty,[49] such behaviour in prosperous people is intolerable; obsessive greed (aischrokerdeia) as a failing in men already
prosperous;[50] and the external face or character which such men
present to society.[51] No such rhetorical guile is needed in the sav-
age but conventional exposure of the evils of the moneylender's
trade with which the assault on Stephanus' character ends. In 71–6
the attack is turned with equal venom on Phormio, 'the real opponent' (so Sandys, ii, p. xxxiv), of whose servile origins we are
reminded (71–2). Here the jury's worst instincts are invoked—
envy and hatred of a humble man who has made good, with class
prejudice added for good measure.[52] Phormio is still the target as
Apollodorus contrasts him with himself (77–84) in an inflated passage of irrelevant reminiscence; and the jury is left once more with
the image of the overweening ex-slave (86), but sight is not lost of
the original charge of false witness (87–8). This speech may be the
second extant Demosthenic oration of the 350s, preceded by 36 For

---

[47] 63: 'As long as Aristolochus the banker was doing well, this fellow followed him, keeping in step with him . . . But when he fell on hard times . . . Stephanus never stood by his
son . . .'

[48] εἶθ' ὃς εὐτυχούντων ἐστι κόλαξ . . . προδότης (summarizing previous section) . . .
τοῦτον οὐ μισεῖν ὡς κοινὸν ἐχθρὸν τῆς φύσεως ὅλης τῆς ἀνθρωπίνης προσήκει;

[49] Cf. Lys. 7 Sac. Ol. 13; Dem. 24 Ag. Tim. 123; 29 Ag. Aph. 22.

[50] Cf. Xen. Symp. 4, 35.

[51] Their mien belies their good fortune: they should appear cheerful, but are unsociable
and stand-offish. Cf. Theophrastus Char. 24. 8: the Haughty Man, who stoops down as he
ignores people, and straightens up again after he has passed them. Demosthenes seems to
have been the first orator to exploit popular prejudice against certain types of demeanour (cf.
37 Ag. Pantaen. 52, 54 Ag. Con. 34, 28 De Cor. 323), as distinct from dress (as in Lys. 16. For
Mantith. 18–19).

[52] 74–5: the ultimate insult of marrying into his ex-master's family.

Phormio, perhaps by a politically significant period, which could nevertheless have been quite short.[53] The next speech may have followed after a short interval.

39 *Against Boeotus I*

The defendant had laid claim to the name of Mantitheus, the prosecutor, through adoption: an unusual case (1), but one with serious implications for both men. It was normal for the eldest son to be named after his grandfather, and while Mantitheus could engage in quite effective, even entertaining rhetoric in pointing to the official confusions and anomalies which would arise from his having to share that name with another (7–12), the objection which he felt most strongly was to sharing the estate (6, 20). He could not give this the prominence he would have liked, because it would be a consequence of defeat rather than an argument supporting his case.[54] He tries forcefully[55] to show how his father Mantias' adoption of Boeotus was done under unfair pressure (2–5: **narrative** loosely appended to **prooemium**), and this tone of muted invective returns (13–18) with putative debts, tax-evasion, avoidance of military service, desertion—all ascribed to Boeotus in anticipation, on the basis of unspecified charges he is said to have faced (19).

Probability-argument to reinforce his denial of Boeotus' main claims (22–9) and the somewhat laboured use of dialogue to drive home the point of Boeotus' identity (30) leads to some more effective rhetoric.[56] But an even more notable section follows (34–7):[57] in a long apostrophe, Mantitheus urges a change of heart upon his opponent, even claiming altruistic motives (34–6):

---

[53] Cf. Harold Wilson's dictum 'A week is a long time in politics': perhaps too short for Demosthenes and Apollodorus to reach the *rapprochement* which might be needed. Its source, as suggested by Trevett *ASP* 145–7, may lie in contemporary politics. It is known that, in spring 348, Apollodorus proposed the allocation of Theoric funds to military expenditure rather than their distribution among the populace, and that Demosthenes was identified with this policy. The process by which they became political associates is less important than the fact of that association.

[54] However, by mentioning the objection twice, at the same points as two references to the testimonies to his enrolment, he gives coherence to this opening section of the speech (1–20).

[55] A 'gang of blackmailers' (ἐργαστήριον συκοφαντῶν) frightened and deceived his father.

[56] Prosopopoiia (or eidolopoiia) in 31; pathetic paradox in 33.

[57] Carey and Reid, *Selected Speeches*, 189 note a change of tone.

No one is trying to deprive you of these [sc. your rights]; certainly not I
. . . I too regard you as a kinsman . . . Why, then are you so contentious?
Stop, I beg you. Do not be so ready to be my enemy. I do not so regard
you—for even now, lest the fact escape your notice, I am speaking in your
interest rather than in my own in insisting that we should not have the
same name.

There are few other passages in the Attic orators in which a prosecutor calls upon his opponent to mend his ways, and therein lies
the unusual character of this speech.

40 *Against Boeotus II*

The same disputants meet again in this lawsuit, and we get a rare
record of the result of the last one. Victorious, the erstwhile
Boeotus is now Mantitheus (II) (18), and the estate has been
divided equally between the original Mantitheus (Mantitheus I)
and his two half-brothers. Still aggrieved, Mantitheus I is now
claiming exclusive right to his own mother's dowry, or a sum of
one talent representing it, and Mantitheus II is counter-claiming
the same sum for the dowry of his mother Plangon.

The style of the second speech is more expansive and periodic,
and the division more conventional, than that of the first. An
atmosphere of mixed pathos and hostility is established in the
prooemium,[58] and this is maintained in the full-scale **narrative**
(6–18), which contains some detail that might have been used to
advantage in the first trial, such as his early life as undisputed heir
(8–9). There is also some telling characterization, as the scheming
and duplicitous Plangon (10–11) is contrasted with the speaker, the
dutiful and law-abiding son (12–15); and the opponents' prevarication during the arbitration before the previous trial is mentioned in
order to discredit their success (16–18).

Turning to the counter-claim, he relies on general probability-
argument to the effect that Plangon's father, as a state-debtor, could
not have provided her with a dowry (20–3), whereas his own
mother, daughter of the wealthy Polyaratus and previously married

[58] 1: 'The most painful of all experiences, men of the jury, is to be addressed as "brother"
of persons whom one actually regards as enemies, and to be forced, as I am now, to come
to court because of the many cruelties I have suffered at their hands.' The topos of the
painfulness of litigation between relations has thus been transformed by an injection of hostility. Note also a call to the jury to show anger (5), usually a late plea.

ıto the family of Cleon, was so provided. The logic with which
e reinforces this argument is tortuous but based on legality.[59]
   The most remarkable of the previously undisclosed details is that
f the blows exchanged by the two men and Boeotus' attempt to
ıagnify his injuries (32). Now the latter has become a wicked con-
ɔirator,[60] who virtually forced the prosecutor into litigation, and
 even preparing to broaden the attack into a posthumous one on
ıeir father (45). Rhetoric contrasting the behaviour of true with
dopted sons towards their fathers (46–7) gives way to less relevant
rgument, with standard topics like that of unequal danger (55–6).
ʌ further generalized attack on the opponents' lifestyles (57) and
ıeir recourse to false evidence (58) leads to a neat summary of his
wn proof (60), and the speech ends. Did Mantitheus employ a
ew speechwriter for his second prosecution of his stepbrother?
'he difference in style between the two speeches is not great
ıough to suggest different authorship, and neither contains usage
ıat can be firmly pronounced non-Demosthenic.

7 *Against Eubulides*[61]

'his is an appeal (*ephesis*) to the Heliaea by a certain Euxitheus
gainst a decision by his deme to rescind his citizenship and reduce
im to the status of metic—a very serious matter for him, since loss
f his appeal could mean enslavement. Eubulides was apparently
ıe officiating demarch, though he is not so named in the speech.
ʌs Euxitheus' task is to vindicate his claim to citizenship, his speech
 in practice one of defence,[62] and some of the topoi he uses accord
rith that category. Of interest is the variant of the 'unequal dan-
er' topos, in which he asks for *greater* goodwill than that granted
is opponent (cf. Andoc. 1 *Myst.* 6; Lys. 19 *Aristoph.* 3), later justi-
ʃing his request by reminding the jury of his opponent's legal
nowledge (5). He has a tough task, a fact reflected in the elaborate
ıtroduction he makes to it. Apart from conventional material, he

---

[59] 26–7: that Mantias had recognized Mantitheus I's mother's status as his lawfully dow-
·d wife is proved by the fact that he acknowledged him ahead of Boeotus (as he then was)
ıd his brother Pamphilus, in spite of his affection for their mother Plangon.

[60] 34: ἐπίβουλος (also 43, cf. ἐνεδρεύων 45) καὶ κακοῦργος (also used as a legal term
ıalefactor')).

[61] Isaeus 12 *For Euphiletus* is concerned with the same type of case, and is probably to be
·ted around the same time, i.e. 345. See Ch. 5 n. 114.

[62] Note that the preposition in its title is *Pros*, not *Kata*, indicating opposition or reply to
·cusation rather than prosecution.

makes a strong plea against the admission of hearsay evidence, especially in the prevailing atmosphere.[63]

The sole purpose of the **narrative** (9–13) is to show that his case has not been properly heard. It is short but effective. Eubulides so organized the hearing that the vote on Euxitheus' case took place in the gathering darkness (9).[64] The latter is able to argue conclusively that this ruse had been devised specifically against him (15–16); and he has already given a reason why Eubulides had singled him out (8), so Euxitheus' account at this early stage is coherent, though two significant facts—his orphanhood and his demarchy (see below)—are postponed. Documented **proofs** of his father's (18–29) and mother's (30–45) citizenship follow, and complete the evidence. The latter section contains the theme of poverty, a state which might be expected to attract sympathy, but with Greek audiences this was by no means guaranteed.[65] The jury is led to suppose that the speaker's poverty has inflated the confidence of the powerful Eubulides, and that this is unfair. 'Do not dishonour the poor, for their poverty is a sufficient evil; and scorn still less those who choose to earn an honest living by toil' (36; cf. 45). A 'poor but honest' portrayal should effectively counter his slanders. At one point Euxitheus identifies his mother's career as a nurse (a lowly occupation) as the original source of those slanders (42), and later sharpens the focus by remarking: 'The present trial is concerned not with our fortune or our money, but with our descent' (45).

Questions of time and timing are now raised in order to discredit Eubulides. Having perforce accepted Euxitheus as a member of his deme for so many years, he chose a time of contention over the citizenship (see n. 63) to make his move against him: 'The earlier time would have suited one who was conscious of the truth of his charges, but the present time is opportune for a man motivated by enmity and malice' (49). Now we learn for the first time that Euxitheus was left an orphan (52), a potentially vulnerable state which Eubulides could exploit; but he turns even this to advantage

---

[63] A thorough revision of the citizen-list was under way at the time of the speech, offering open season to sycophantai and others with influence and enemies to injure.

[64] Perhaps a frequent device: for a famous antecedent, see Xen. *Hell.* 1. 7. 7 (the Trial of the Ten Generals).

[65] There was a tendency to link poverty causatively with crime, and an uncharitable assumption that, as a sign of divine disfavour, it was somehow deserved. See Dover *GPM* 109–10, 239.

by arguing that, as a mere child, he was unlikely to have bribed any relative to testify to his citizenship (54).

The next theme of the speech is Eubulides and his abuse of his office within the deme of Halimus (58–60), prefaced by a timely expression of confidence in the benevolent superior power of the Heliaea (56–7). But the invective, such as it is, is not sustained, and we return shortly to the question of Euxitheus' citizenship (61–2), and to another, wholly new fact—that he had himself held the office of demarch (63). The late appearance of this fact is perhaps not surprising, since it transforms Euxitheus from a poor victim to a political rival who had exercised power and thereby made enemies (63), and whose opponents (who are now a group, not an individual (64)), might go to extreme lengths to unseat him (64–5). Finally, he uses dramatic dialogue to summarize his main claim to citizenship (66–8), and the speech ends with a powerfully pathetic plea (70) which matches the gravity of the danger he faces. Demosthenes has kept the main evidence for Euxitheus' citizenship in constant view, and made as little as he can of awkward but unavoidable facts.

47 *Against Euergus and Mnesibulus*

Probably the earliest[66] of six speeches which owe their place at the end of this examination to their relative lack of merit,[67] this is, like 45 *Against Stephanus*, a prosecution for false witness. The two defendants have thwarted the unnamed speaker's attempt to prosecute a certain Theophemus, who had served as a trierarch, but failed to return the ship's tackle to the public store on quitting his appointment. Having said that he intends to rely less on direct evidence than on character-evidence (4), he gives a confused account (6–16) of the defendant's withholding of a key witness, which delays his explanation of the case itself (18 ff.). After establishing his own credentials by denying private enmity and showing that he acted in obedience to the laws, he gives an account of Theophemus' prevarications and deceptions which matches them in its tortuousness. The supposed main question, that of false

---

[66] Reference to the Law of Periander (358/7) in § 21 gives a *terminus post quem*. Blass (*AB* 1. 545) suggests 353/2 as the latest date for the present trial.

[67] The use of that criterion to decide the question of authorship is hazardous, but all six are stronger candidates for athetization than their predecessors.

witness, does not resurface until 47, after which the account of Theophemus' high-handed actions continues. In a speech dominated by narrative, there is not much use of the emergent facts to furnish logical argument. The best rhetoric is to be found in the later sections, which contain a pathetic **narrative** (52–61) modelled on that of Lysias 12. 8–20, a good dilemmaton argument (78) and final plea (79–81). But as a whole the speech is of interest for the legal procedures surrounding it rather than for the case itself.[68]

58 *Against Theocrines*

This is a public lawsuit (*graphe*) in pursuance of a formal accusation (*endeixis*).[69] The division normally adopted in private lawsuits, with narrative immediately following prooemium, gives way to the early introduction of the main direct evidence after an opening in an expansive, periodic style. This *endeixis* is in fact a counter-accusation. Epichares, the speaker, is seeking by that procedure to gain revenge for a verdict which Theocrines had obtained against his father.[70] He aims to disqualify Theocrines as a prosecutor by proving that he is a state debtor, and cites two actions (5–18, 19–21) through which he had incurred fines that were to date unpaid. His method is straightforward: while citing the laws, he represents Theocrines as a man who despises them,[71] making baseless charges (10) and tampering with witnesses (7); and subsequently conducts a more systematic demolition of his character. He is the arch-sycophant,[72] whose taint of evil ruined his own brother's political career. He is hypocritical and above all venal (29). Some of the facts of the present case emerge here, but are encased in an overall invective (30–2). He has threatened sundry people with vexatious action, but could invariably be bought off, while causing damage

---

[68] See Harrison *LA* ii. 131–2, who discusses it under procedure for counter-claims (*antigraphai*), in which the litigants had been involved at a prior stage. He also pronounces the speech as 'certainly not by Demosthenes'.

[69] There are only two other such cases in the Demosthenic Corpus, 25, 26 *Against Aristogeiton I, II*, and three elsewhere, Antiphon 5 *Murder of Herodes*, Lysias 6 *Against Andocides* and Andocides 1 *On the Mysteries*.

[70] The circumstances of the earlier *endeixis* are not wholly clear. The available information is presented by A. T. Murray in Loeb edn., vi. 312. Blass *AB* iii. 499 dates the speech to 344/3.

[71] 15: κρείττω τῶν νόμων, 29: παρὰ τοὺς νόμους ἦρχεν οὗτος.

[72] His name was used as a metonymy for 'sycophant' in 18 *Cor.* 313.

to the interests of both individuals and the state (33–9). His actions
are merged with those of sycophants as a class (40), who combine,
with self-righteous protestations, to act against law-abiding citizens
(41–5). It is one of the most analytical portrayals of the sycophant
that we have, and continues into the final section after the main
argument has concluded at § 56. The final part of the speech
(57–70) is divided into a plea for justice for his father and himself
(57–61, 68–70)—the former unable to plead for himself (60) and
the latter youthful and inexperienced (58, 60; cf. 1, 41)—and a
further attack on sycophants and their trade (62–5).[73] While
Demosthenic authorship is probably to be ruled out, the speechwriter is a polished and forceful artist.

48 *Against Olympiodorus*

The prosecutor Callistratus and the defendant are brothers-in-law.
They are seemingly both shady characters who have arranged a
carve-up of the estate of a certain Comon, in unequal competition
with others who may have had equal claims upon it, and subsequently fallen out through mutual deceit. The story told (the **narrative** predominates: 5–32) by the speaker naturally does not reveal
this. On the positive side, his self-characterization is consistently
bland, even beatific: he is mindful of his duty and family ties, even
under provocation (6), always law-abiding (27, 31, 41–2), and
altruistic (54–5). Absent from his account, however, is any clear
explanation of his prior claim. He styles himself simply *oikeios* (5),
and his narrative merely describes the tactics which the two of
them used to see off the other claimants, who at one stage managed
to win the whole estate from them (26–7).[74] Only one of these is
named (his brother Callippus at 10 and 22). The story is all about
the co-operation between the two principals and how it led to
treachery on the part of Olympiodorus because of the speaker's

[73] This last attack interestingly contains some of the arguments used to justify the activities of sycophants. Others, though not these, are discussed by Robin Osborne in his debate
with David Harvey in P. Cartledge *et al.* (eds.), *Nomos: Essays in Athenian Law, Politics and
Society* (Cambridge, 1990), 83–122). The present passage (63–4) provides evidence of their
perceived ambiguous role in society in the 4th cent.
[74] This happened, we are told, when Olympiodorus was called away on military service.
In order to restore the estate to both of them, he had to have the case (diadikasia) reopened
in his own name only, and hence, on winning (by dubious means, 31), he could renege on
his agreement with Callistratus.

loyalty to their agreement.[75] The **proof** (36–51) aims chiefly to expose inconsistencies in the defendant's behaviour, and contains one novel argument (46): 'If there were any truth in what he says, he should have stated it and proved it before the trial took place and before testing it with a jury's decision'. He is speaking in general terms, and saying that Olympiodorus should have exposed all his case to scrutiny at the anacrisis. Now the procedure at the preliminary hearing consisted mainly of questions,[76] which litigants might conceivably answer without revealing all the rhetorical ploys which they intended to use at the trial. So his claim is unrealistic, yet adds to the picture of Olympiodorus' dishonesty.

A final point of interest is the explanation offered for Olympiodorus' unreasonable behaviour: he is deranged, and acting under a woman's influence (53–4, 56). Such a person was disqualified from legally binding decisions by a law of Solon,[77] and invocation of that law at this late stage is a final desperate attempt to win a case in which the jury cannot have sympathized strongly with either side.

43 *Against Macartatus*

This is almost a retrial of Isaeus 11 *On the Estate of Hagnias*, and supplies names to the complicated stemma which are not found in that speech. Sositheus, the speaker, claims the estate for his young son following the death of the previous successful claimant Theopompus, father of the defendant. Generally thought not to be by Demosthenes, the speech contains enough of his characteristics to be genuine.[78]

Sositheus has to show that the adoption of Theopompus had been wrong, and to do this he must prove that his own branch of the family is the more closely related to Hagnias. The heart of the speech is a necessarily dry catalogue of names (19–30). The key

---

[75] While the case is technically one of damages (βλάβη), it also concerns inheritance, and a more precise account of relationships, and hence of rival claims, would have added clarity. But clarity is not what the speaker wanted.

[76] See Harrison *LA* ii. 94–105.

[77] For the full text of the law, see Dem. 46 *Ag. Steph. II* 14.

[78] While doubters may point to frequent hiatus, this is an unreliable criterion of Demosthenic authorship, and passages like the opening sentence, 9–10, 17, 38–41, bear the clear stamp of his style, while throughout the combination of periodic structure with forceful expression and didactic tone is characteristic.

figure in this is his own son, Eubulides III, whose adoption by his
grandfather Eubulides II, Hagnias' first cousin, brings him closer to
the *de cuius* than any of Theopompus' relatives could ever reach.
He refers to the original hearing as an exercise in deception (38–9);
and there is much repetitive recital of relationships. But the speech
also contains some useful information about the use of water-clocks
(8–9), and, most importantly, a major document on the laws of
inheritance (51). The speechwriter makes some effort at unfavourable characterization of the opponent in the early sections,
and manages to generate a fair amount of emotion in the concluding paragraphs as he talks about the rites due to the dead (63–7), the
threatened extinction of the house of Hagnias (73–7), and the
young Eubulides as the hope for its future (83–4).[79]

42 *Against Phaenippus*

Responsibility for public service was institutionalized at Athens in
several ways, but by none more contrarily than the *antidosis*
('exchange'). A citizen chosen to perform and fund public services
could nominate another to do them instead or exchange his property with him. The present speech is the main literary source for
the operation, or partial operation, of this procedure.[80]

The anonymous plaintiff had challenged Phaenippus to an antidosis, which he had accepted. The speech is concerned mainly
with the defendant's alleged attempts to impede its implementation
by falsifying and concealing the value of his estate. These are
described in a short **narrative** (5–9), which ends in a very
Demosthenic sequence (8–9).[81] The rhetoric is thus directed
towards exposing different facets of Phaenippus' unscrupulous and
illicit behaviour, and it gains effect from contrast with the honesty
and moderation of the plaintiff. The latter has suffered losses
through ill-luck (3), yet tried to meet his opponent's insolent

[79] On the estate and the two trials, see W. E. Thompson, *De Hagniae Hereditate: An
Athenian Inheritance Case* (Leiden, 1976). He dates the present speech to *c*.345 (p. 63). See also
.. Rubinstein, *Adoption in IV Century Athens* (Copenhagen, 1993), 41–2.

[80] It is not certain that the transaction was completed in the present case.

[81] 8: 'I sealed the buildings, as the law permitted me; he opened them. And he acknowledges that he removed the seal, but does not acknowledge that he opened the door, as if
men removed the seals for any other purpose than to open the doors. Then, I had forbid-
en that wood should be carried off; he carried it off every day except that on which I had
ssued the order' (asyndetic antithesis without μὲν . . . δέ, also articular infinitives). Cf. 18
or. 265.

prevarication as a reasonable citizen might.[82] The studious contrast
in their behaviour continues (14–15) before giving way to a summary of the challenge and a direct address to Phaenippus (apostrophe, 20–4), and it is curiously in that form that he describes the
deterioration of his own circumstances (21–2). Phaenippus, on the
other hand, is young, ambitious, and a breeder of horses (24)—and
therefore a possible object of the jury's envy, which the speaker
stimulates with a little sarcasm (25). The concluding appeal is
unusually pathetic;[83] the speech is studded with oaths and excla-
mations (6, 7, 17, 20), yet also has a rather informal atmosphere,
perhaps attributable to its late date.[84]

44 *Against Leochares*

This inheritance speech is of interest in the study of the laws of
adoption, though it raises as many questions as it answers. The
estate of the *de cuius*, the unmarried Archiades, had devolved on his
sister Archidice's line after he had adopted her grandson Leocrates
(I), an arrangement which other collaterals and their descendants
could not contest. But when Leocrates I returned to his old
Eleusinian tribe, and even more when his son Leostratus followed
him, and tried to have his second son Leochares adopted after the
death of his first son Leocrates II, the descendants of Archiades'
brother Meidylides, Aristodemus and his son (who is the speaker),
who had been unhappy with the adoption of Leocrates, decided on
litigation, basing their case primarily on closer kinship with
Archiades, and challenging the validity of vicarious adoption by a
person who is himself adopted.[85]

The length of the **prooemium** (1–8) may be attributable to real
disadvantages under which the plaintiffs labour—relative poverty
due partly to their earlier forbearance over Archiades' estate, and
unscrupulous and well-prepared opponents. It ends with a neat
summary of the central issue: whether descent or adoption was to

---

[82] 12: ἡγησάμενος δ' ἐγὼ καὶ μετρίου καὶ ἀπράγμονος εἶναι πολίτου . . .
[83] 31: 'Whither shall one turn if one fails to obtain your verdict . . . ?'
[84] The speech is usually assigned to the 320s: so MacDowell *LCA* 163. Blass *AB* iii/1. 506 suggests 330/29 as a *terminus post quem*. He likens it stylistically to the oratory of Hyperides (ibid. 509).
[85] 63: 'It is surely not just that an adopted son should bring other sons into the family by adoption: he may leave in it children born to him, but in default of these he must restore the inheritance to those related by blood.'

take precedence.[86] This is followed by a **narrative** (9–16) in which the plaintiffs' closer kinship through the male line is established,[87] and the jury are invited to compare their pedigree with that of Leocrates I, Leostratus, and Leochares (17–23), whose descent was through Archidice, sister of Archiades, and through adoption. So far so good; but they have a problem. If their claim had been strong, why had they acquiesced? They merely state that they did, without reasoned explanation: in 19 we are told that Meidylides was 'persuaded by the pleas of his relatives' to let Leocrates I remain in the family as the adopted son of Archiades; but they had no legal grounds for contesting Leocrates' inheritance. It was still legal for Leocrates I to leave his son Leostratus in possession of Archiades' estate when he returned to his old tribe, but subsequent events raise three questions—one for the contestants, another for legal historians, and a third for students of Greek Oratory. The three may be combined when considering the following passage (22–3), and many others like it:

Well, this same Leostratus, although he was an adopted son and had been left in the family of Archiades, himself returned, as his father had done to the Eleusinians, leaving in his place a lawfully born son and, *in defiance of the laws*, perpetuating the original adoption through the lives of three persons. For *how could it be other than contrary to the law*, when one, being himself an adopted son, returned to his tribe leaving adopted sons in his place?

Of the two phrases in italics, the first appears to state a definite law, but the second asks the jury to agree that it is being violated in the present case, or perhaps that it should be extended to apply to it.[88] This is the goal of rhetoric in this speech: to persuade the jury that the plaintiffs' interpretation, perhaps extrapolation, of existing law, is reasonable and equitable. They dwell on two points: the fact that Leostratus, like his father Leocrates I, had returned to his old tribe (26, 28, 35, 39, 47, 48); and the death of Leocrates II without issue (24, 44, 47–8, 63–4, 68). The latter point was of particular

---

[86] 7: ἀμφισβητεῖται δὲ παρὰ μὲν ἡμῶν κατὰ γένος ἡ ἀγχιστεία, παρὰ δὲ τούτων κατὰ ποίησιν.

[87] They also claim closer affinity through the female line (13), but that affinity arises only through the male line (Cleitomache, the speaker's grandmother, was the daughter of Meidylides, brother of Archiades).

[88] Perhaps in cases like this we are witnessing law in the making. On this passage, Rubinstein, *Adoption*, 59 writes: 'there is little reason to doubt that, technically, his opponents had acted in accordance with the law.' She also points out that the speaker appears to contradict himself in 63 and 68.

significance, because it meant that the final adoption, that of the
defendant Leochares, had had to be arranged not by the last
adoptee, who was dead, but by his father, who had already made
one adoption. It is understandable that other claimants to the estate
might intervene at this point. Their appeals to the jury in this
speech centre on the actions of Leostratus since his entry to the
estate (32–45). This is a different sort of narrative, soon turning to
argument and unfavourable interpretation. Surely, with the death
of Leocrates II, that branch of the family is extinct.[89] And if a family is extinct, there cannot be legitimate sons still alive: logic, albeit
sophistical, applied to existing law. Late reference to what purports
to be the relevant law of Solon, but without clear demarcation of
the actual text (64, and esp. 68), adds to uncertainty in what has
been a perplexing though intriguing case. Nothing helps us to date
it, and its style, though effective, has little individuality that would
help to identify its author.

18 De Corona[90]

Though it is neither the last nor the longest of his orations, this is
the only possible work with which to end an examination of
Demosthenes' oratory, since it encompasses the whole of his art,
transcending genre[91] and defining his position in both literature
and history. The case required him to compose an *apologia pro vita
sua*, because his political ally Ctesiphon had proposed, less than two
years after the Battle of Chaeronea,[92] that he be honoured with a
crown, for, among other services, 'having spoken and acted to the
best possible effect and been patriotic at all times' (57). Aeschines'
inevitable challenge took the form of a graphe paranomon against
Ctesiphon, which he finally brought to court in 330.[93] Here atten-

[89] 48: οὐκοῦν ἀνάγκη τὸν οἶκον ἐρημωθῆναι (note aorist infinitive: the matter is over
and done with, and no longer a possible matter of dispute).
[90] 'On the Crown': here given the Latin title by which it is best known, and which distinguishes it from Speech 51 *On the Trierarchic Crown*.
[91] It was technically a forensic defence speech, with Demosthenes appearing as synegoros
to Ctesiphon, whose speech was short and prefatory. But with policy and statesmanship as
its central themes, it had characteristics of a deliberative speech, except that it concerned the
past and not the future.
[92] i.e. early in 336.
[93] Possible reasons for the delay are discussed by G. L. Cawkwell *CQ* 2nd ser. 19 (1969),
166–73; H. Wankel, *Rede für Ktesiphon über den Kranz* (Heidelberg, 1976), 19–25 (summarized in Usher *GO* v. 13–14); and E. M. Harris, *Aeschines and Athenian Politics* (Oxford,

tion is concentrated on that part of the indictment by which both
orators laid the greatest store, which is Aeschines' charge that
Ctesiphon's citation (above) was false and therefore illegal:[94] the
two minor counts are dealt with in the discussion of Aeschines'
speech.

Demosthenes' immense task was to justify policies which had
ended in disaster and vindicate a personal career which had ended
in failure. To do this he had to reimplant in his audiences the spirit
which had set the ideals of freedom and patriotism above the aim
of mere survival. Invocation of 'all the gods and all the goddesses'
at the opening and the ending of the **prooemium** (1, 8) simulates
the opening ceremony of the popular Assembly, but also aims to
create a mood of quasi-religious solemnity; and even as conventional topics are used, each has a special feature appropriate to a
special defendant. Goodwill is reciprocal,[95] and the disadvantages
suffered by defendants are compounded in his case.[96] Cyclic thematic structure gives the prooemium unity and compactness (a
(§ 1) b (§ 1) c (§§ 1–2) d (§ 3) e (§ 4) d (§ 5) c (§§ 6–7) b (§ 8) a
(§ 8)), and prepares the jury mentally for his individual line of
approach. In the **prothesis** (9–16) the usual flat statement is
replaced by one blaming Aeschines for widening the contest. This
sets the tone of personal conflict, which never relents. Thereafter
the division of the speech is governed by three principles. The first,
called *Ordo Homericus* by the rhetoricians, required that, like the
weaker troops in the wise Nestor's contingent at Troy, the weakest part of the case should be shielded at front and rear by the
stronger elements.[97] The second, related principle was that
chronological treatment was best, because the last impression left

1995), 140–2. Alexander's conquest of Darius III and the failure of the revolt of the Spartan
King Agis against Macedonian rule would have left his enemies in Athens and elsewhere
fearful and demoralized. But Demosthenes and his friends were active, if intermittently, in
these years. See A. W. Pickard-Cambridge, *Demosthenes and the Last Days of Greek Freedom*
(London, 1914), 420 ff.; Cawkwell, *CQ* 2nd ser. 19 (1969), 170.

[94] The existence of a specific law forbidding false statements, especially such subjective
ones as Ctesiphon's, must be doubted, and Aeschines quotes no such law, merely referring
vaguely to 'all the laws' (*Ag. Ctes.* 50). See Usher *GO* v. 15.

[95] 1: 'I pray that I be granted the same goodwill by you as I have always held for the city
and for all of you.'

[96] 3: the inequality of the stakes for prosecutor and defendant is individually applied to
his case: (i) because he has his whole reputation to lose, and (ii) because in order to win he
must resort to self-praise in large measure, whereas people are happier listening to abuse and
accusation. In the event, Demosthenes makes sure that he satisfies their appetite for these.

[97] Homer, *Iliad* 4. 297–9; Quint. 5. 12. 14; Liban. *Hyp.* 9.

on the jury's minds was the strongest, and their memory of more recent events, carefully primed and channelled, could become his surest ally. The third principle was that of variety, especially in such a long speech. The resultant division, while it revolves around narrative, admits episodes which explore the entire gamut of human thought and emotions and include history, biography, and political philosophy. But all these are deployed in the service of their author and his case.

This is nowhere truer than in the **narrative** of events to 346 BC (17–52) and 346 to 340 (53–109). In the earlier account, their significance is weighed at every turn, with particular emphasis on the opportunities a divided and debilitated Greece offered Philip, who 'grew at everyone's expense' (19), corrupting the leading men of Greece, which at this stage excluded Demosthenes.[98] He joins the story after the Peace of Philocrates, and subjective language, judgement, and opinion crowd in even more strongly thereafter upon the facts (25 ff.), which become subordinate (43):

When you had been deceived by these men hiring out their services to him and reporting false news to you, and the wretched Phocians had been deceived and their cities destroyed, what happened? The detested Thessalians and the stupid Thebans regarded Philip as their friend, benefactor, and saviour. He was everything to them: they would not listen to any voice that spoke against him. But you viewed what he had done with suspicion and resentment, yet maintained the peace even so; for there was nothing you could do.

But alongside Philip's growing power, the jury is made to observe the Cassandra-like role of Demosthenes, who was 'constantly predicting it and protesting about it . . . but the states were diseased' (45): his vision and patriotism are contrasted with the 'inopportune negligence'[99] of the people and the misguided corruption of their leaders; and Aeschines is blamed, then apostrophized (51–2) for making the contrast necessary by 'bespattering [me] with the dregs of his own wickedness' (50).

More fundamental issues of statesmanship and patriotism assume prominence as Demosthenes comes to deal with the period of his own growing influence on events. Now narrative plays less part, and argument about policy takes over. In 66 he asks:

[98] He applies deliberately vague chronology to this general claim, and dissociates himself (dishonestly) from the prime movers of Athenian policy in these years.

[99] 46: ἀκαίρου ῥᾳθυμίας.

What was the proper course of action for the city when she saw Philip preparing to make himself master and tyrant over Greece? Or (and this is what matters most) what should I, a statesman at Athens, have said or proposed when I knew that, throughout history until I first mounted the rostrum, my fatherland had always competed for the first prize of glory and renown, and had expended more money for the sake of honour and the interests of Greece at large than the other states collectively have spent on their own behalf?

Hence his policy of opposing Philip at every danger-point, and the Athenians' support for that policy. At the same time, it was a proactive policy, whose proponent always risked the charge of warmongering. Demosthenes heads this off (68–86) by arguing that in every case Philip was the aggressor, and indeed some of the measures taken against him were proposed by other Athenian politicians, while Demosthenes earned a crown for his measures to prevent Philip from gaining a foothold in Euboea, and further credit for frustrating his designs on the Hellespontine grain-lifeline. Demosthenes manages to make even this example of self-interested intervention seem like one of high-minded altruism (94), and expands this argument as he draws this section to a close with an account of Athenian magnanimity towards her old enemy Sparta (96–8), and domestic measures to strengthen the fleet (102–9).

Thus Demosthenes has established his credit as a responsible and patriotic statesman before he comes (110–21) to the laws which Aeschines has accused Ctesiphon of breaking—proposing a crown for a magistrate while he is still in office and 'accountable' (i.e. yet to undergo audit); and proposing that the crowning ceremony should take place in the Theatre instead of the Council or the Assembly as the law prescribed. Insofar as those laws certainly existed, his case was weak. Of the two charges, the first was probably the more dangerous, and he meets it with sophistry, agreeing that he is 'accountable' for this whole public career (111) but creating a diversion by introducing his own private contributions in order to say that he is not required to give an account of them (112). Thus he sidesteps the main point, which is one of time. While doubts are possible about the application of both laws, especially the second,[100] Demosthenes is glad enough to divert

---

[100] This point is pursued further in the discussion of Aeschines' speech.

attention to Aeschines with his most vehement personal attack so far.[101]

The attack broadens and waxes in viciousness (129–59).[102] Aeschines, born in poverty and squalor, was destined for a career tainted by venality. No previous oratorical model prepares us for the scandalous detail here presented: Aeschines' father as 'a slave who wore thick fetters and a wooden collar' and his mother who performed 'daytime marriages', i.e. presided over obscene rituals (129). Later he will return to this biographical material with even greater energy (257–65). For the rest of the present section he concentrates on Aeschines' political career as a 'hireling politician' (131–59), interpreting all his actions according to that premiss. The smooth antithetical transition to the policies with which he opposed him (160) is deceptive, as this is a major turning-point. Events leading to the alliance with Thebes are described in a different kind of narrative to that encountered so far, full of action and scene-painting details designed to revive his audience's memories, as the burgeoning crisis is resolved by the timely courage of the protagonist (169–70):

It was evening. Someone brought a message to the presidents that Elateia had been taken. They were in the middle of their evening meal, but rose from it immediately at the news. Some of them drove the stallholders from their booths and set fire to the wicker-frames, while others sent for the generals and summoned the trumpeter. At dawn on the next day, the presidents called the Council to their chamber, and you made your way to the Assembly, and before the Council had deliberated and formulated its proposal, all the people were in their seats on the hill. After this, when the Councillors had entered and the presidents had announced the news that had been brought to them and introduced the messenger, and he had spoken himself, the herald asked 'Who wishes to speak?' And no one came forward. The herald asked the question many times, but still not a man got up, though all the generals and all the regular speakers were present, and their country was crying out in her collective voice for a man who would speak to save her . . . (173). Well, I was the man who came forth on that day and addressed you . . . I, alone of all the speakers and statesmen, did not desert my patriot's post in the hour of peril, but I was to be found there advocating and proposing the measures that your predicament required.

---

[101] 121: 'Why do you peddle slander, you wretch? Why do you fabricate arguments? Why do you not take a dose of hellebore [a reputed cure for madness] for your illness?'

[102] Aeschines had attacked Demosthenes' parentage (171–2), perhaps unprepared for the scale and venom of Demosthenes' reply.

That day was the high-point of Demosthenes' career, and the speech which he made then and followed up with diplomacy,[103] was a model of realistic appraisal balanced with optimism; and it halted Philip's advance.[104] But the alliance with Thebes also made the final disastrous battle certain. Demosthenes turns briefly but memorably[105] again on Aeschines before justifying his policy, which he does by appealing to history and the higher aspirations of the Athenian people. He challenges his audience to consider whether their ideals were inferior to those of their ancestors who fought at Marathon and Salamis, and this seasoned epideictic theme is given a new solemnity by being cast in the form of an oath (208):

But you cannot, you cannot have been wrong, men of Athens, when you took upon yourselves the peril of war for the freedom and salvation of all. I swear it by those of your ancestors who faced the dangers at Marathon, and those who stood in the battle-line at Plataea, by those who fought in the sea-battles at Salamis and Artemisium, and by those many others who lie in the public tombs, brave men, all of whom the city buried, deeming them all equally worthy of honour, not only the successful or victorious.

The sudden switch to abuse that follows this noble passage should not shock readers of Demosthenes' earlier oratory.[106] Thereafter **narrative** takes over again as the Theban alliance is consolidated by minor military successes, and other alliances secured (211–39).

Most of the rest of the speech explores different aspects of the contest between the two antagonists. Aeschines is the 'counterfeit orator' who misuses his dubious theatrical skills.[107] He is repeatedly accused of carping at the policies adopted while failing to offer alternatives and even appearing to rejoice at the city's defeat. Demosthenes, on the other hand, has performed the primary duty of a statesman, 'to see things at their beginnings, to anticipate them and to foretell them to others' (246), and his performance has earned the gratitude of his people, even after defeat (248–51).

---

[103] 179: 'I did not speak without proposing the motion, nor propose the motion without serving as ambassador, nor serve as ambassador without persuading the Thebans.' (*Climax*: see Usher *GO* v. 234.)

[104] Elateia, in Phocis, was a strategically important town on the route from Central Greece to Boeotia and hence to Attica. See Cawkwell *PM* 141–2.

[105] In 198 Aeschines' baleful appearances on the rostrum are likened to 'fractures and sprains which are stirred to life when some malady afflicts the body'.

[106] See Ch. 6 n. 176.

[107] 242: αὐτοτραγικὸς πίθηκος ('born tragic ape') . . . παράσημος ῥήτωρ.

Aeschines' invocation of Paideia in his penultimate sentence (260) stung Demosthenes into his first attack on Aeschines' parentage (127). Now he launches a full-scale *kakologia* of Aeschines' upbringing, the Aristophanic qualities of which will have amused his audience. The young Aeschines performing menial duties in his father's school, then later helping his mother with her initiation rites, and leading the noisy procession, is a figure of ridicule (258–62), but his later career has more sinister features. The unsuccessful stage actor becomes at home on the political stage, but only as the herald of adversity (263–4) and the spokesman of the city's enemies.[108] Demosthenes, by contrast, has used his oratorical skills on his country's behalf (277), not in pursuit of private ends—and this includes his litigation against Aeschines, whom he represents as a public enemy (278–84), who rejoiced in the city's disasters (291–2). It was Demosthenes' policy of forging alliances that gave Greece her best chance of freedom,[109] but on the battlefield the outcome was in the hands of fortune and the army's commanders (301–5). The focus returns to Aeschines (306–13), characterized as before but with added colour: the politician whose quietness spells malice, and who suddenly emerges from retirement, 'like the wind', when events have taken a bad turn (308), whereupon he may be heard in full voice, scarcely taking a breath, but saying nothing of substance. Demosthenes' final claim is on his own behalf, affirming his inflexible patriotism (320–3), and he ends with a strange prayer for the reform of his enemies and deliverance from impending fears (324).

The rhetorical richness of the *De Corona* consists more in devices of style than in argumentative ingenuity. It is a veritable thesaurus of imagery—simile[110] more notably than metaphor[111]—containing many figures of speech and language;[112] and its constant recasting of themes and literary forms display Demosthenes' protean talents in their ultimate form.

---

[108] 265: 'You have always served our enemies' interests in politics: I those of our country.'

[109] Rather than physical defences alone: 299 'My defence of the city was not with stone or bricks, but with arms, cities, countries, ships, horses and those prepared to defend all these.'

[110] §§ 153, 188, 198, 214, 308; and extended similes or parables: 122, 194, 243.

[111] §§ 11, 45, 61, 138, 168, 194, 227, 286, 296; $\tau\acute{\alpha}\xi\iota\varsigma$ (dead metaphor?): 173, 192, 304.

[112] §§ 3, 9, 11, 20, 69, 88, 100, 179, 208, 229, 242, 265, 268, 271, 297, 303, 313, 322, 324.

DEMOSTHENES: SUMMARY

While all Demosthenes' virtuosity is on display in the *De Corona*, it remains to identify his distinctive contribution to Greek oratory. Certainly his style has features which, by their frequent and well-judged deployment mark a definite stage of development. In particular may be noted the peculiar concentration obtained through the use of abstract noun phrases, especially the articular infinitive, which he uses more frequently than any other classical author.[113] To this may be added attention to emphatic word-order, as exemplified in the use of hyperbaton,[114] and his effective use of asyndeton.[115] These are all existing features which Demosthenes uses more often and to greater purpose than his predecessors. In the matter of vocabulary, however, he enters new territory, using with far greater freedom than his predecessors both imagery and neologism. On the level of purely rhetorical technique, on the other hand, the foregoing examination of most of his forensic oratory shows him using existing resources with a comparatively small number of innovations. Standard topoi may be run together in prooemia, where also may be found unorthodox openings like the furious outburst in *Against Aphobus II*, the racial invective beginning *Against Lacritus*, stark initial focusing of the issue, as in *Against Conon*. Elsewhere his clients are furnished with all the rhetorical aids, and a range of emotional expression, from violent attacks upon his opponent, as in *Against Stephanus I* and *Against Pantaenetus*, to the calm remonstration in *Against Boeotus I*. Expatiation after the conventional divisions have been observed, pioneered by Lysias in *Against Eratosthenes* and adopted routinely by Isaeus, is also a feature of many of Demosthenes' forensic speeches.

It is in his longer speeches and his deliberative oratory that we must look for the most novelty, and that novelty is a matter of literary intention realized through form and scale rather than identifiable technical or rhetorical innovation. The *De Corona* contains a few passages which reveal that intention:

---

[113] For some statistics, see Usher *GO* v. 24. Their use is related to the whole question of abstract expression, on which see Denniston *GPS* 28–9) (with statistics drawn from R. S. Radford, Diss. Baltimore, 1896) showing Demosthenic usage close to Thucydidean.

[114] See e.g. 18 *Cor.* 18, 262.

[115] See 18 *Cor.* 43, 117, 198, 215, 265; 24 *Ag. Timocr.* 11–13.

Just consider—for though the time for action has passed, the time for understanding such things is always present for men of sense (48).

Hear now the nature of those transactions . . . you will be greatly helped in your quest for knowledge of public affairs (144).

I ask you to listen attentively . . . so that, by spending a little time you will gain much experience for the future conduct of all affairs of state (173).

It seems clear from these sentiments that oratory, for Demosthenes, had become a medium of political education, and this accounts for the scale of the longer speeches, which is attained by disquisition on broader subjects of historical or political interest, such as legislative processes (in *Against Lept.* and *Against Timocr.*), and principles of foreign policy (in *Against Aristoc.*). This didacticism is more than a mere idiosyncrasy. Demosthenes no doubt published many of his private speeches for the same reasons as other forensic speechwriters; and the final form in which he published his graphai paranomon and his deliberative speeches was dictated to some degree by a politician's immediate need for self-promotion. But the scope and cerebral character of these speeches point to a desire to reach an enlightened and timeless readership which would derive greater benefit from them than from the academic exercises of Isocrates. Such readers would enjoy works which would give them the feel of the age in which vital decisions had to be made, serving as commentaries on the events and policies of the time; but they would also draw general instruction from them. Like Thucydides, he intended that his work should find a permanent place in literature and thought, and he ensured this by always pointing to the lessons to be drawn from events, and by characterizing them with the greatest clarity and force.

8

AESCHINES

The most celebrated, and possibly the most eloquent political opponent, forensic adversary, and personal enemy of Demosthenes, Aeschines also maintained a rival, or at least an alternative tradition in Greek oratory. He never wrote speeches for others to deliver and probably did not receive any form of systematic training, and his career became that of the non-professional (but not amateur) orator, whose speeches were concerned with his own affairs or his public career. Comparison with Andocides has often been made, and with reason,[1] but Aeschines had a technical advantage over his predecessor: he was one of a number of actors who turned from the stage to the rostrum, bringing with them their natural gifts of stage presence, strong, clear voice, and good delivery.[2] He could also draw on his experience in another job: he served for a short time as a junior secretary (*hypogrammateus*) to the Assembly. From the second of these early careers he acquired useful knowledge of laws and decrees,[3] and how to present them in legal arguments—an ability which he needed in all three of the lawsuits for which he composed his surviving speeches.

Those three orations are probably all that he published, and it can scarcely be doubted that his rivalry with Demosthenes, with which they are all primarily concerned, influenced the form in which they appeared to posterity. After his defeat over the Crown (see below), and retirement to Rhodes, Aeschines had only his literary reputation and his standing among his pupils to consider, if indeed he set up a school of rhetoric on the island, as tradition reports. His aim had to be the perpetuation of the contest with his

---

[1] e.g. by Jebb *AO* ii. 393. On a practical level, Aeschines incorporated Andocides' account of the Pentecontaetia (*On Peace with Sparta* 3 ff.), errors and all, in 2 *Leg.* 172–6.

[2] Demosthenes names two in the *De Corona*, Aristodemus (21) and Neoptolemus (116). Their services were valued especially on embassies.

[3] See E. M. Harris, *Aeschines and Athenian Politics* (Oxford, 1995), 30.

old rival, and this could only be done with the most polished oratory.[4]

1 *Against Timarchus*

Aeschines brought this *graphe* as a pre-emptive strike against his arch-enemy. Timarchus, a supporter of Demosthenes and an active politician in his own right, was intending to join him in his prosecution of Aeschines after the return of the second embassy to the court of Philip II of Macedon. The purpose of his indictment of Timarchus was to eliminate one of his prosecutors and discredit the other by association. He was wholly successful in the first, and temporarily successful in the second of those aims. The trial took place in the winter of 346/5.[5] He attacked Timarchus under the law which banned certain categories of citizen from speaking in the assembly, in this case those who had prostituted themselves and those who had wasted their patrimony. The incidence of prostitution as a main charge in an Attic speech is rare,[6] so Aeschines' handling of it is of critical interest.

It serves his purpose to rely on some of the conventional topoi in the **prooemium**. Of these the one given the most stress is that of himself as the 'moderate citizen' (1, 3, cf. 39), which serves to contrast him most effectively with the licentious defendant. But the opening section is otherwise ill-defined: no clear line marks its conclusion until § 39. Didactic and loftily patriotic (4–6), he will not lower himself to describe Timarchus' lewd acts (38, 52, 70, 71) except in the vaguest terms. He is also a champion of the laws (2)— effective again as he is proposing to rely on them. They feature

---

[4] This point is well made by Philostratus, *Lives of the Sophists*, Pref. (483): 'I think he [Aeschines] left behind him only orations that had been carefully composed (συγγεγραμμένους), in order not to fall far short of the premeditated creations (φροντισμάτων) of Demosthenes.' He contrasts this with the tradition that Aeschines was the supreme master of improvisation (18, 509).

[5] See H. Wankel, 'Die Datierung des Processes gegen Timarchos 346/345', *Hermes* 116 (1988), 383–6. E. M. Harris, 'The Date of the Trial of Timarchus', *Hermes* 113 (1985), 376–80, emphasizing the speed necessary, prefers 346.

[6] So Blass *AB* iii/2. 192; Todd *SAL* 107 ('no known cases'); K. J. Dover, *Greek Homosexuality* (Cambridge, Mass., 1978), 29–30; also the general discussion in D. Cohen, *Law, Sexuality and Society: The Enforcement of Morals in Classical Athens* (Cambridge, 1991), 176 ff., esp. 176–80. There was a practical distinction between privately conducted male prostitution, which would not have incurred severe automatic penalties, and the public appearance and behaviour of individuals known to have engaged in it, which was subject to the losses of rights (*atimiai*) outlined above.

very prominently here, not only receiving frequent praise (14, 17, 20, 24, cf. 177–8), but occupying the position normally held by the narrative,[7] and subjected to line-by-line analysis of purpose and effect. The dignity which they confer is enhanced by the introduction of august figures from the past—Themistocles and Aristides (25) and, above all Solon, the creator of those good laws. Here is a moment for complete contrast (25–6): the great lawgiver, as portrayed in his statue at Salamis, was an imposing restrained figure, setting the standard of decorum for his successors, 'who were too modest to speak with the arm outside the cloak'; but Timarchus 'threw off his cloak and leapt about like a gymnast (*epekratiazen*), his body in such a poor and wretched state through drunkenness and debauchery that right-thinking men covered their eyes in shame for the city, that we should allow such men to be our counsellors'.

The **narrative** follows the Rake's Progress of Timarchus' early adult life (40–70). In addition to the fact of his prostitution, it is necessary to emphasize that he enjoyed it, in order to counter a possible excuse of poverty (41–2). Section 44 contains a novel topos: this prosecution is easy, because the facts on which the charge is based are known to everyone. This has a preparatory function, as will shortly become apparent. Firstly, however, there are a few points to note about Aeschines' narrative style. He uses both short pieces, in order to make a particular point (43, 53), and longer 'stories' (53–65) containing contrasting passages of action. A passage describing extreme violence (58–9)[8] is narrated in the imperfect tense, while the following attempts at reconciliation and the defendant's ultimate treachery (60–1) are recounted using the historic present.[9] Both tense usages have their purposes: the imperfect to underline the *en train* of the action, the historic present to reflect the subjective concerns of the two miscreants, especially

---

[7] Noticed by Anon. Seguer. (Sp. i. 442). Hermogenes, *Inv.* 3. 2. discusses the consequences of this order.

[8] 'When he [Pittalacus, the second of Timarchus' associates] was becoming tiresome, behold, a mighty stroke on the part of Hegesandrus and Timarchus! One night when they were drunk, they with certain others, whose names I do not care to mention, burst into the house where Pittalacus was living. First they smashed the implements of his trade, and threw them into the street—various dice and dice-boxes—and other gaming tools—and killed the gaming-cocks and the quails which were the wretched man's pride and joy, and finally they tied Pittalacus himself to the pillar and gave him an inhuman whipping, so prolonged that even the neighbours heard the uproar.'

[9] ἔρχεται ... θέουσι ... πείθουσι ... λαγχάνει.

their desire to avoid the consequences of their earlier actions. He
continues to use the historic present in this way. As to proving
Timarchus' debauchery, these varied items of narrative are circumstantial, but their effect is cumulative.

Evidence and testimony might be reasonably expected at this
point. What Aeschines offers is extraordinary. In 71–93 he develops a new argument. He says, in effect, that witnesses to such acts
as the defendant's should not be expected to come forward because
they would fear to incriminate themselves. But another form of
testimony, ready and reliable, was to hand: that of deduction from
day-to-day experience and observation. If you see a man entering
a brothel, you know what he is intending to do (74–5).[10] Aeschines
reminds the jury that beliefs and prejudices based on just such
observation decide the outcomes of audits. A bad man's reputation
imprints itself on people's minds: that is why, when a man like
Timarchus uses words which can have a secondary, obscene meaning, an audience laughs at him (80), just as when the unworldliness
of a pious man like Autolycus causes laughter when double-
meanings of words arise in his dealings with Timarchus (81–4).
This all serves to make the jury receptive to Aeschines' assertion of
the value of general popular reputation as evidence. The rhetorical
conclusion of this is clear (85): the people's opinion *is* a *martyria*,
and further evidence, however formally presented, is superfluous.
The comparison of a *graphe* with an audit is, of course, flawed, since
the two were conducted under different rules, and its use by
Aeschines has naturally raised doubts as to the soundness of his case
(so Blass *AB* iii/2. 198–200). But this is of less concern here than
the argumentative position he has assumed, and which he amplifies
later. It makes him into a rebel against conventional forensic oratory, which relies for proof initially on direct evidence and argues
from it. He advocates reliance on the popular conception of a
defendant's character (90–1), which can bring about acquittal or
condemnation regardless of the eloquence of the man under trial
(92). Thus the skilled speechwriter has a severely limited role in
Aeschines' scheme of things: his advice is to 'rely on your knowledge and conviction, drawn from the past, not what is said today
about Timarchus' (93).

---

[10] This may be regarded as a form of *eikos*-argument, but the idea of human experience
plays a greater part in it than is usual in other oratory, where the argument is more readily
conformable to a syllogistic pattern.

More details of the profligacy and public abuses of Timarchus and his friend Hegesandrus are given, no doubt to the entertainment of the jury (95–115). At 116 a summary and a short internal **prooemium** mark a new departure (cf. Lys. 12. 41), but the underlying argument remains the same. Demosthenes, the clever rhetorician,[11] will demand documentary evidence (the tax levied on prostitutes) of Timarchus' activities. Aeschines puts in Timarchus' mouth the plea he thinks he should make (122), that he be judged on a general estimate of his worth based on his past life. Demosthenes has said that there is nothing more unjust than popular report (125): under the pen of Aeschines it achieves an apotheosis (128)[12] with poetic support (129).

The discussion now turns to homosexual friendships. Once more his opponents have well-tried arguments and literary and historical precedents (Achilles and Patroclus, Harmodius and Aristogeiton), and this time he goes along with them at first (132–52). Aeschines is the first extant orator to quote extended passages from the poets, a practice suited to his theatrical training and natural gifts; and for some of his audience, the words of dead poets carried more weight than those of living litigants. Modern examples of chaste love follow (155–7), but Timarchus and his associates belong to a different class (158–9), and the fact that the law condemns their activities means that contracts involving them cannot be valid (160–5).

Aeschines' dignified tone throughout most of the speech has concealed a certain discomfort he feels in discussing homosexuality, as he has had to confess his own *paidika* (136). Now, as he anticipates some of Demosthenes' arguments, the name of Alexander the Great appears for the first time in Greek literature. The passage (166–9) is cryptic, referring to the young prince performing at a banquet, presumably during one of the visits of the Athenian negotiators to Pella, and Aeschines objecting to remarks made about him by Demosthenes which he thought would be discreditable to the city. As this episode gives way to one about the sons of wealthy Athenians courted by Demosthenes, the main thrust of the argument seems to be that the latter's homosexuality was the worse

---

[11] Here also a teacher of rhetoric (117, 171, 175).

[12] As a divine agency spreading good news, Φήμη had an altar built to it in Athens after the Battle of Eurymedon (Pausanias 1. 17. 1). For a good discussion of the cult, see R. Parker, *Athenian Religion: A History* (Oxford, 1996), 155–6; and esp. 233–7.

because the more mercenary. But we are receding from the main issue, and the structure of the speech becomes more and more ragged as it approaches its conclusion. Miscellaneous arguments are strung together—the laws must not be allowed to be perverted by sophists (177–9), praise of the power of the Gerousia at Sparta to override the ill-directed rhetoric of demagogues, followed by early Athenian parallels (180–1, 182–4); and a succinct description of the defendant as 'a man masculine in body, committing the offences of a woman'. But he does not end before striking a memorably poetical yet rational note (190–1): do not blame the Furies of old tragedy for driving men to evil, for the wickedness that drives men to become pirates, brigands, and revolutionaries comes from within them. His own lusts are the Furies that torment such a man. The speech ends more quietly with an 'example to others' topos (192) and a call for civic solidarity. Aeschines must have owed his victory in large measure to his performance.

2 *On the Embassy*

The contest between Aeschines and Demosthenes took place some two years later, in 343. Comparison of the two published speeches is inevitable, but points of contact are difficult to find. Aeschines' plan is the simpler: he aims to discredit Demosthenes in every way—as a politician and as a person—exposing him as inconsistent, devious, treacherous, unpatriotic, and pusillanimous. Whereas Demosthenes' purpose of showing that Aeschines had been in Philip's pay required fairly elaborate deployment of probability-argument, Aeschines could rely on his favourite medium, narrative (with no little scope for entertainment), for the exposure of his enemy's sundry vices and misdeeds.

In the **prooemium** (1–11) the references to his own conflicting emotions (4), the cleverness (rather than preparation) of his opponent (1, 4) are fresh variants of existing topoi. But the whole central section of the speech is taken up with **narratives**, those of the First Embassy (11–56) and the Second Embassy (97–118) being separated by a review of the years from the fall of Amphipolis (357 BC). The purpose of this interruption of the chronological order may be sought in the main themes of these three narratives. Aeschines' account of the First Embassy has two aims: to show that the Peace of Philocrates, which gave Philip all he wanted, was advocated

mainly by Demosthenes and Philocrates working together (18, 20,
56), a fact which should remove any suspicion that he himself was
in Philip's pay; and to expose Demosthenes' faults through telling
details of his behaviour during the ambassadorial journeys and at
the hearing at Philip's court. In the narrative of the Second
Embassy, while the attack on Demosthenes is launched with
greater and more personal intensity (99), there is also more discussion of the inter-state political issues, in the course of which he tries
to make himself appear more statesmanlike than his rival. Now for
this to have full effect, some historical background was needed, and
this is why an account of the earlier years had to precede it.

The deflation of the braggart is the stuff of pure comedy, and in
the first narrative Aeschines makes the most of what must have
been the true story of Demosthenes' bout of stage-fright when he
stood for the first time before Philip, after boasting that he was
going to pour out 'fountains of eloquence' (21). Aeschines precedes
his narrative of that embarrassing scene (34–5) with a brief,
favourable glimpse of his own statesmanship as he gives a synopsis
of his speech to Philip (25–33), in which the tone and content are
far from ingratiating. The juxtaposition of the two performances
discredits Demosthenes' bribery charge and his diplomatic reputation with two swift strokes. Personal details describing Demosthenes' disagreeable manner (36), his use of peculiar words (21, 40),
and his superior posturing (49: 'rubbing his forehead in that portentous manner of his'), add substance to the characterization of his
enemy, and no doubt pleased those who found his foibles irritat-
ing. Less amusing but more relevant are actions which show
treachery towards his fellow-ambassadors—getting them to agree
with him that Philip, among other accomplishments, was a good
negotiator (41–2), and then contradicting them before the
Assembly when they so describe him (49–54). Charges made by an
ambitious politician who is also vain, inconsistent, and unscrupulous must be treated with deep suspicion: that is Aeschines' main
message in this section.

The narrative describing the decline of Athenian influence in the
north and Philip's advance (70–80) is sketchy in the extreme.
Serving Aeschines' immediate purpose rather than that of historical completeness, it aims to show that his patriotism, like his
Athenian pedigree (78), is of long standing. Though cautious
and conscious of the city's past mistakes (76–7), his policies were

honourable and sound, compared to those of Demosthenes
(79–86). The account of the second embassy is now delivered
against a clearer, or at least more detailed, background of politics
and diplomacy, and Aeschines represents himself as a wise counsellor (103–5, 113–16), opposed by Demosthenes who fawned upon
Philip shamelessly (109–12). However, in facing the fact of both
diplomatic and military defeat, he has to resort to a claim which has
a familiar ring to it (118, cf. 131):

> Fortune and Philip were masters of events, but I, of loyalty to you and the
> words spoken. My words were words of justice, and spoken in your inter-
> est; the outcome was not as we prayed it would be, but as Philip made it.
> So who is it that deserves your praise—the man who showed no desire to
> do anything whatever, or he who did all that he could?

Aeschines' sentiments are close to those expressed by Demosthenes
(18 *Cor.* 194, 303), but of course they pre-date them. Certainly they
provide a fitting introduction to a section in which he tries to show
how Demosthenes has misrepresented his words and actions, and
misread the whole political situation before the ruin of Phocis
(119–30), the causes of which he explains rather well (131–45). The
whole speech hinges upon this and the following sections, on
which he wants the jury ultimately to decide his fate. Proof from
past life (pistis ek biou) is, of course, a conventional part of a
defence speech: how does Aeschines handle it? Not content with a
laudatory account of his parents' lives (his aged father Atrometus is
present), he introduces contrasting items from that of his opponent
(148, 149). He is able to project feelings of proud loyalty for his
brothers Philochares and Aphobetus, who, like members of his
wife's family, have served the city with distinction. Dobson rightly
sees a new kind of pathos here (152),[13] and its impact adds force to
the probability-argument which follows it: 'with such affection for
my family, do you think I would have held the friendship of Philip
more precious than their safety?'

  With the jury's emotions thus primed, he turns on his opponent
with renewed savagery (153). Demosthenes has used his 'wicked
arts of rhetoric' to lie and cheat, but has gone too far and has not
been believed: he should not be believed now. But the main charge
against Aeschines, that of acting as Philip's agent for pay, now takes

---

[13] *GO* 178–9: 'aiming directly at the feelings of individual hearers for their own families,
rather than asking the assembly collectively to pity the victims of misfortune'.

second place to supposed complaints against his political conduct (160–3). Charges of inconsistency are met with counter-charges, though interestingly those made against Demosthenes concern his private dealings, not his public policies. These required a more subtle and general approach. The notorious inaccuracies of Aeschines' survey of fifth- and fourth-century history (172–8), taken over uncritically from Andocides, may distract us from the fact that it has a central theme—the war-mongering tendencies of generations of Athenian politicians.[14] The last reference to these leaves little doubt as to the individual the speaker has in mind (177):

But now men who had been illegally registered as citizens, ever latching on to the sick elements in our society, and following a policy of war after war, in peacetime prophesying danger, inflaming ambitious and susceptible minds, but in wartime never touching arms themselves, but becoming auditors and naval commissioners—men whose mistresses are the mothers of their offspring, peddlers of slander who deserve disfranchisement—these men are exposing the state to extreme danger by immorally flattering the people, trying to put an end to the peace that is the salvation of democracy, and in every way stirring up war, the destroyer of popular government.

And sight is not lost of the abominated enemy in the brief but impassioned **epilogue** (180–4). 'Save me from the Scythian rhetorician' (180); 'Fortune cast my lot with a slanderer, a barbarian, who cared not for sacrifices nor libations nor the shared table, but sought to intimidate all possible future opponents, and has come here with a trumped-up charge against us' (183). There is undoubtedly something uplifting and compelling about sincere hatred forcefully expressed: so Aeschines must have thought; and the result of this trial proved him right. Demosthenes' influence was not restored until events had decisively vindicated his predictions.

3 Against Ctesiphon

The final contest took place thirteen years later, in 330, six years after Ctesiphon proposed the crown for Demosthenes.[15] At 60

---

[14] 172: 'When certain men had stirred up trouble and finally brought us to war against the Lacedaemonians . . . '; 173: 'After men who were neither free by birth nor of moderate character had insinuated themselves into our body politic, we were finally involved in war again with the Lacedaemonians . . . '; 176: 'and at last, because of the pugnacity (ἀψιμαχίας) of our politicians, we sank so low as to see a Spartan garrison in our city'.

[15] For possible reasons for the delay, see Ch. 7 n. 93.

years of age, Aeschines saw it as his last chance to destroy his old
enemy. The grumblings of an old man are present (2–3: note the
convicium saeculi) in the **prooemium** (1–8), while to the tragic tone
noted by Blass[16] (following the scholia), may be added hypothetical inversion consisting of two complete and elaborate periods
(2–4), the second being particularly long,[17] giving an overall effect
of weight and dignity. This is an atmosphere which he wishes to
maintain as he moves straight on to the laws on which he bases his
graphe paranomon. They are the objective basis of his case.

The two sides are agreed as to the substance of Ctesiphon's
decree, though Aeschines does not quote it in full.[18] According to
him it violates two laws. The first unconditionally forbids the
crowning of magistrates while they are subject to audit (i.e. still
holding their office).[19] He shows how in the past some crownings
had been proposed for serving officials, but with a clause stipulat-
ing the completion of their audit before its award (11). Ctesiphon,
however, had 'overleapt this law' by expressly proposing the
proclamation of the crown 'before Demosthenes had given
account and faced audit, while he was still holding office' (12). This
seems clear, but his reference to 'men who try to crown those still
in office' (11) reduces that clarity and points to precedents.
Ctesiphon's leap now seems less bold—rather the final, logical step
in an evolving process. A similar difference between law and practice may have arisen in regard to the other illegality which
Aeschines claims. The law, according to him (32), required that the
crowning proclamation should take place where it had been
awarded, i.e. either in the Council or in the Assembly, 'and
nowhere else'. Yet Demosthenes can say that he, and countless
others, have been crowned in the Theatre on many occasions and
that the law had been amended, with good reason,[20] to allow this
(18 *Cor.* 120–1). Aeschines' protest that this would mean that contradictory laws stood side by side (37–40) seems suspiciously long-
winded, especially when followed by a lengthy, though interesting

---

[16] *AB* iii/2. 208.   [17] 3: ἐπειδὴ . . . 4 σεσίγηται . . . Ἀθηναίων.
[18] For the text see 18 *Cor.* 118.
[19] 11: [νόμον] διαρρήδην ἀπαγορεύοντα τοὺς ὑπευθύνους μὴ στεφανοῦν.
[20] The reason which Demosthenes gives—that such proclamations would encourage
patriotism among the largest possible numbers of citizens—suggests that the new provision
had official backing.

explanation of the origin of the law (41–4).[21] He cannot expressly
deny the existence of the amendment, but instead offers a logical
explanation of it which will restrict its application to foreign
crowns (45). It is almost as if he is legislating on his feet.

These uncertainties, as well as his own personal animosity, left
him little choice but to devote most of his energy and rhetorical
ingenuity to rebutting the short tribute in the proclamation, which
acknowledges Demosthenes' 'courage and bravery', in that 'he
never ceases to speak and do what is best for the people'. Aeschines
devotes four-fifths of his speech to this, regarding it as the most
important part of his prosecution.[22] But he has to be selective, and
a paraleipsis serves him well (51–2) by enabling him to allege a few
private breaches of faith by his enemy before saying that he is going
to concentrate on his public crimes (54). But he realizes that his
audience must be prepared more thoroughly than this to receive
the shocking accusations he is about to make, and he himself must
appear fair; so he resorts to a simile.[23] This careful preparation is an
involuntary testimony to Demosthenes' popular credentials as an
opponent of Philip.

Demosthenes was a prime mover of the Peace of 346, equally
with Philocrates. They promoted it with maximum zeal and
urgency, and were responsible for its unfavourable terms and disastrous outcome. This is what Aeschines seeks to prove, and he
describes, in a **narrative** accelerated by asyndeton (62–3), how they
co-operated in dictating the first decisions about the embassy. His
description of the actual negotiations and their reception at Athens
is in a more leisurely style (64–70) until the dramatic moment when
Demosthenes, determined that the terms of peace should include
an alliance, prompted one of Philip's ambassadors, Antipater, to
affirm that he would not agree to peace without one (71–2) and
won the vote. Without examining further the diplomatic options
open to Athens at this time of weakness, Aeschines concentrates on

---

[21] Interminable proclamations of crowns, other honours, and even manumissions of
household slaves, unauthorized and uncontrolled, had become the bane of the dramatic festival of Dionysus, delaying and interrupting performances. Further on this section, see
Harris, *Aeschines and Athenian Politics*, 144–5, 209.

[22] 49: ἐφ' ᾧ μάλιστα σπουδάζω.

[23] 59–60: the simile is prescriptive rather than merely descriptive: when prior expectations are proved wrong after accounts have been rendered, men accept the figures; so they
should do when Demosthenes' crimes have been proved. The analogy between objective or
arithmetical proof and proof which must depend on interpretation of reported fact is logically false but rhetorically plausible.

morality—Demosthenes' treachery to existing allies like
Cersobleptes, his duplicity (a Philip-hater who flattered the king
(73, 76), then rejoiced indecently[24] at his supposed death (77))—
but the application of morality to later events plays him false. When
Demosthenes saw the results of the peace he had propounded, he
changed his policy. To Aeschines this becomes a personal matter:
Demosthenes turning on his erstwhile friends—another act of
treachery—and opening up for himself a solitary path (80–1).[25]

Comparable failure to try to rationalize Demosthenes' policies in
other than personal terms is to be seen in Aeschines' account of
events in various quarters. In Euboea, when Demosthenes persisted
in advocating support for the Chalcidians after their treachery, it
was because they bribed him (85, 86), not because he saw advantages for Athens in such support. We read of the lengths to which
he was prepared to go in order to retain the alliance with Callias,
tyrant of Chalcis (94–102), but of no attempt to explain or even to
dispute the strategy behind this policy, only a list of the payments
Demosthenes was alleged to have received from the Euboean leaders (103). Philip and his ambitions, real or imaginary, have figured
remarkably little in Aeschines' version of Greek history up to this
point. And as the scene changes to Delphi and its environs in the
year 340 (106), Aeschines himself, by mischance,[26] takes centre
stage resurrecting an ancient curse against the Amphissian Locrians
for cultivating sacred land. His account of the exchanges that took
place in the Amphictyonic Council are quite full and dramatic. He
frankly admits that he was provoked by an interrupting Locrian
delegate into making an impromptu speech about the sacred
curse.[27] There is much to admire oratorically about the version of
that speech that he gives (119–20): it is as if he is inviting the jury
to marvel at his extempore virtuosity; and he enjoys telling how he

[24] Demosthenes' public display took place only seven days after the death of his own
daughter. Aeschines exploits this by saying that a man who showed such disregard for his
dearest kin could never be a good leader of the people.

[25] Here Aeschines' strong language of condemnation (referring to Demosthenes' 'innate
corruption, cowardice, and jealousy of Philocrates' bribes' and to his being 'an accuser of his
colleagues on the embassy', thereby seeking to gain favour with the people by his scandalous
treachery to his friends) suggests a certain frustration at his enemy's success in gaining a following, albeit from 'the enemies of public tranquillity' (82).

[26] He was serving as the junior Athenian representative (*pylagoras*) at Delphi after both his
senior colleagues, Meidias and Diognetus, had fallen ill.

[27] 118: 'As I listened, I was exasperated as never before in my life . . . well, *it occurred to
me* to call attention to the impiety of the Amphissians . . .'

carried the day, and the Delphic Amphictyony declared war on the Locrians (124). Looking back on subsequent events, and on how Philip was brought into central Greece as leader of the Fourth Sacred War, Aeschines says that Philip was in Scythia at the time (128), implying that his intervention could not have been foreseen.[28] Events proved him shortsighted, and his own version of them shows him still preoccupied with squabbles between the different states, with the leading figures acting in their own private interests (especially Demosthenes taking bribes: 114, 129, cf. 149). He failed to realize the extent of Philip's influence, even in his absence, through agents and friends, especially in Thessaly, and refused to recognize any disinterested motives in his enemy.[29] Yet his presentation of these parochial views is replete with lofty sentiments.[30]

The core of his indictment, and the part on which he might expect most support from the jury, is contained in 137–58. Here he identifies Demosthenes' three main mistakes or crimes, in rising order of gravity: failure either to realize or to communicate the fact that Philip was the enemy of Thebes more than the enemy of Athens (141–4); the negotiation of an alliance with Thebes on terms so unfavourable that vital powers were ceded, 'stealing the senate house and the democracy and carrying them off to the Cadmeia' (145–7); and insistence on prosecuting the war when both allies and enemy were ready to make peace. The tragic element in the last of these mistakes evokes a fine mixture of eulogy and invective from Aeschines (152–7). The interplay between the one form of epideictic oratory and its counterpart in the same piece

---

[28] Sealey (*DT* 192–3) appears to agree, noting that Philip had been fighting in distant lands since 342, so that the disputants at Delphi probably did not include him in their calculations. This makes Demosthenes' clairvoyance seem the more remarkable. Cawkwell (*PM* 141) grants substance to his view (18 *Cor.* 143) that Aeschines, by his rashness, was at least in part responsible for Philip's seizure of the leadership.

[29] e.g. in 125, Demosthenes opposed war against the Amphissians 'to earn his retaining-fee', not in furtherance of an alliance with their Theban friends. For a more favourable view of Aeschines' statesmanship and influence at this time, see Harris, *Aeschines and Athenian Politics*, 122–3. On Demosthenes' determination to prevent *détente* with Philip, see Ellis *PMI* 188–9.

[30] 130: 'But did not the gods forewarn us by words and signs, all but speaking with a human voice, to be vigilant? I have never seen any city given more constant protection by the gods, but more completely ruined by its politicians . . .' 132: 'Thus every possible event, whether hoped for or unexpected, has surely happened in our time! For the life we have lived is not that of normal human beings, but of characters in a tale of wonder . . .'

is both skilful and unusual until this time.[31] The men who died receive their due praise; but the man who sent them to their deaths deserves not crowning but condemnation. Was that crowning to be proclaimed in the same Theatre where the state-nurtured orphan sons of citizens who had died in battle were sent forth in ceremonial armour? Such an act would be obscenity bordering on madness (156).[32]

Now attention is focused on Demosthenes and his actions after the Battle of Chaeronea,[33] and the account becomes one of misjudgements and missed opportunities against a background of a character that contained a combination dangerous to the state—eloquence, venality, and cowardice (166–7):[34]

When he came forward and said, 'Certain men are pruning the city, certain men have trimmed off the shoots of the people, the sinews of the state have been cut, we are being matted and sewn up, certain men are drawing us like needles into narrow places.' What are these things, you sly fox, words or monstrosities? And again, when you whirled around in a circle on the platform and said, pretending that you were working against Alexander, 'I admit that I organized the Laconian uprising, I admit I am bringing about the revolt of the Thessalians.' You cause a revolt of the Thessalians? What? Could you cause the revolt of a village? Would you actually approach a house, let alone a city, where there was any danger? But if money is being paid out anywhere, you will lay siege to the place, though you will never act as a man should. If any stroke of luck should come of its own accord, you will lay claim to it, and attach your name to it; but if any danger should appear, you will take yourself off; and then if we recover our resolve, you will call for rewards and crowns of gold.

Up till now, Aeschines has argued economically and effectively in pursuit of his main objective—to discredit Demosthenes as a politician. In most of the rest of the speech (168–259) he is scurrilous and self-indulgent, disparaging his enemy's parentage (171–3), his relationship with Ctesiphon (213–14) and his character (215–19), and enlarging on one of his favourite themes—the superiority of the

---

[31] It is more subtle than the simple juxtaposition of eulogy and invective, such as may be noted in *De Cor.* 208–9, where the famous Marathon Oath is followed immediately by a violent attack on Aeschines.

[32] Rhetorically, this is an emotionally charged pathetic paradox.

[33] Neither orator, wisely, dwells on the battle itself; though Aeschines makes much of Demosthenes' alleged desertion (3 *Ag. Ctes.* 148, 175, 244, 253).

[34] Cf. 152: ὦ πρὸς μὲν τὰ σπουδαῖα τῶν ἔργων τῶν ἀνθρώπων ἁπάντων ἀχρηστότατε, πρὸς δὲ τὴν ἐν τοῖς λόγοις τόλμαν θαυμασιώτατε, and 174: δεινὸς λέγειν, κακὸς βιῶναι.

men and the democracy of bygone years (178–88, cf. 2), and also
of its legal procedures (193–6). This develops into complaints about
the conduct of the present trial and how they can be remedied
(197–212). The topics that arise thereafter are a mixture of antici-
pations[35] and uncoordinated criticisms of individual policies.
Continuing looseness of the sequence of thought is to be seen in
230–5. This section begins with a hypophora, with which he
appears to be bringing together the charges in summary form. But
he then allows himself two rhetorical flourishes (albeit effective
ones)—a comparison between the crowns awarded the state in the
past and the personal crown claimed by individuals, and a more
colourful literary simile—that crowning Demosthenes would be
like the Greeks in Homer crowning the wretched Thersites (231).
This is followed by a broadened discussion of the effect of what
would be an abrogation of their democratic responsibilities by the
jury, then a return to recent history (236–41). There seems to be a
new departure at 242, when Aeschines urges Ctesiphon to conduct
the main defence himself. We are expecting arguments against
allowing Demosthenes to take centre stage (that subject has already
been broached (200–1)), but instead we hear generalized moral
arguments against his crowning, then a roll-call of the great and
good, with standard eidolopoiia[36] which seems hollow when compared with what Demosthenes did with the same material.

Aeschines' defeat in this trial must be attributed to his failure to
tackle Demosthenes' main argument, which was for the maintenance and assertion of Athenian primacy. Avoidance of this, while
frequently referring to Athenian achievements in the past, prevented Aeschines from taking his arguments to their logical conclusions or indeed from sustaining them for any length of time.
And he cannot say, to the Athenians in their mood of factitious
euphoria in 330, that their city was now a second-class power.
Hence, for all its moments of brilliance, inchoateness and disorder
are recurrent faults of his speech.

---

[35] Or replies, in his published speech, to points made in the *De Corona*; 225–6 (of the
tardy physician) replying to *De Cor.* 243. Some of these points are absent from the
Demosthenic text (e.g. 228—Aeschines like a Siren).

[36] 259: 'Do you not think that Themistocles and those who died at Marathon and Plataea,
and the very tombs of your ancestors, will groan aloud, if the man who admits he negotiated with the barbarians against the Greeks shall be crowned?'

AESCHINES: SUMMARY

Among the recurrent words and phrases used by ancient critics to describe the oratory of Aeschines, the most individually descriptive emphasize its elevation and grandiloquence.[37] Qualities of voice and delivery appear to take precedence over the purely rhetorical and literary aspects of his oratory in much of this criticism,[38] but in that of Philostratus (*Lives of the Sophists* 18. 509), reference to his 'divinely-inspired manner in oratory',[39] however derivative it may be,[40] is peculiarly applicable to Aeschines' speeches. This manner is seen in his efforts, notably in *Against Timarchus*, to create a general atmosphere of dignity and decorum by dwelling on august individuals and institutions, praising the laws and expressing lofty sentiments. He reminds the jury of the divinity of *Pheme* (Report, Popular Opinion), the agency he wants them to accept instead of rigorously examined evidence (128), and calls to his aid the poets of epic and tragedy along with appeals to higher feelings.[41]

His contribution to the narrative tradition of Greek oratory may arise from the circumstances in which he found himself. Always dealing with personal enemies, when he comes to describe their actions there is an extra element of acerbity, present in both the shorter narratives,[42] and sustained in some longer accounts,[43] in

---

[37] Demosthenes himself begins this tradition (19 *Leg.* 255; 18 *Cor.* 133), though his use of the words σεμνολογεῖν, σεμνολόγος was ironic or critical.

[38] This is seen, for example, in Cicero's choice (*De Or.* 3. 28) of *sonitum* ('sonority') as Aeschines' peculiar attribute. Again, Dion. Hal. highlights his natural gifts (*Dem.* 35: ἀνὴρ λαμπροτάτῃ φύσει περὶ λόγους χρησάμενος).

[39] θείως διατιθέμενος . . . θείως λέγειν . . . ἀπ' Αἰσχίνου δ' ἤρξατο θεοφορήτῳ ὁρμῇ αὐτοσχεδιάζοντος. Cf. Quint. 12. 10. 23: *latior et audentior et excelsior*.

[40] See [Longinus] *Subl.* 13. 2, and D. A. Russell, *Longinus* On the Sublime (Oxford, 1964), 114–15.

[41] There is no good reason to believe Aeschines' procatalepsis in § 133, where he says he expects Timarchus to quote from Homer: that would have been quixotic against an opponent with Aeschines' theatrical background.

[42] In *Leg.* 34, Aeschines describes how, as his ambassadorial colleagues awaited Demosthenes' promised *tour de force*, 'this abject creature (τὸ θηρίον τοῦτο) uttered a ghost of a prooemium, mortified with fright', and after a short while dried up and stood in helpless silence. Elsewhere, he likes to draw attention to his enemy's mannerisms (36, 49) and to quote his words in order to expose his malice and inconsistency (54: . . . τὴν ἀνωμαλίαν αὐτοῦ καὶ τὸν φθόνον).

[43] e.g. *Ag. Ctes.* 71–105: Demosthenes 'seizes the platform' (71), 'forces the decision' (72); then there is his 'fawning' (κολακεία . . . 77 κόλαξ) on Philip's envoys (76); he is 'the accursed fellow who stands forth as accuser of the rest' (79), and in the ensuing confusion, he 'followed his own inborn corruption, along with his cowardice and jealousy of Philocrates' bribes' (81).

which almost every occurrence of Demosthenes' name is accompanied by a pejorative epithet or a condemnatory judgement of his action. This constant personalizing certainly makes for a colourful, if biased story. It is also instrumental in constructing a complex and destructive portrayal of his enemy's character. But his narratives have other artistic qualities too. By judicious selection, expansion, and juxtaposition, and a general impression of lucidity (he is a relatively 'easy' author), he conceals astute manipulation of his material.

Aeschines is capable of matching Demosthenes in tragic power, as when he laments the destruction of Thebes (3 *Ag. Ctes.* 133–6); capable also of carrying his audience's imagination along as he reminds them of the past (ibid. 186–7). Through these qualities and the others described, he may be judged to have made the most of his considerable talents: that these seem not to have included the use of many of the standard probative arguments, or the ability to read political situations other than in terms of domestic and personal rivalry, simply place him on a par with most politicians of his and other periods of Greek history, and representative of his time.[44]

---

[44] For the personal element, in its various manifestations, as an increasingly important feature of literature from the middle of the 4th cent., see the discussion in T. B. L. Webster, *Art and Literature in Fourth-Century Athens* (London, 1954), 98–100.

9

ISOCRATES SOPHISTES

The first pupils at Isocrates' Athenian school[1] probably began their four-year courses in 388 or a little later. In his tract *Against the Sophists*, he inveighs against his pedagogical rivals, criticizing the narrowness and impracticality of their teaching, with its concentration on dialectic ('eristic'),[2] and the excessive claims they made for it. It is a bid for pupils in a small market; but the text breaks off abruptly before revealing his own educational programme. We find elsewhere[3] that it is directed towards contemporary political studies, including issues of domestic, inter-state, and international importance. His stance gives rise to a number of contradictions: here is a man who sold practical knowledge, thereby meeting the definition of 'sophist', but who railed against that class; who wrote disparagingly about forensic oratory after himself earning his living, however briefly, by writing it; and whose chosen medium was, in its popular and published form, one of mass communication, yet he himself was forced, because of vocal weakness and a nervous temperament, to ply his trade behind the closed doors of his exclusive school.[4]

Most of his extant work stems from that school, and therefore reflects its teaching methods and the subject-matter taught. Again,

[1] *Vit. X Or.* 837b preserves a tradition that his first school was in Chios, where he had nine pupils. If this sojourn was for a few years after his latest forensic speeches (it could not have been before the first of them if he was in Athens at the time of the death of Theramenes: *Vit. X Or.* 837a), his Athenian school could not have opened earlier than *c.*388. His Chian sojourn is discounted by the many scholars who propose 393 or 392 for the beginning of his Athenian school.

[2] Isocrates' opponents are usually identified as the sophists Polycrates, Antisthenes, and Eucleides. But if the traditional date for the opening of Plato's Academy (387) is correct, it is at least possible that Isocrates is attacking his aims and methods.

[3] 15 *Antid.* 46–50, 270–7; 12 *Panath.* 2, 136.

[4] Cicero (*De Or.* 2. 22. 94) likened it to the Trojan Horse, because only leaders (*meri principes*) came out of it. They had paid fees to match their status. On Isocrates' vocal weakness, see 12 *Panath.* 9–11; 5 *Phil.* 81; and on its social and political implications, see Yun Lee Too, *The Rhetoric of Identity in Isocrates* (Cambridge, 1995), 74–112.

the uniqueness of Isocrates is to be stressed. The published discourses[5] are derived not from live cases in the courts or from actual political debates in the Assembly or the Council, but from the lucubrations of a small academic circle dominated by a single mind. This was persuasion of a peculiar kind. There was no clearly defined or urgent occasion for each discourse (e.g. an immediate decision to be made on peace or war): rather they are addressed to a general situation, or even to a general proposition. And this new, academic context is matched by a new medium: the style of the discourses is more elaborate and carefully wrought than that of previous oratory, giving some credence to his claim that their composition was 'beyond the powers of ordinary men' (4 Paneg. 11). A later critic noted this peculiarity, and pronounced them 'more suitable for reading than for practical use', except perhaps on ceremonial occasions.[6] Dionysius' criticism had a practical history: Isocrates' discourses were probably read at leisure, well away from the tumult of the popular assemblies and the lawcourts, by pupils, ex-pupils, potential pupils, and others with an interest in political debate. The mode of persuasion adopted for this more tranquil, philosophical[7] setting was unlike any previously devised. Isocrates has no clearly identifiable predecessors among extant orators, though both ancient and modern commentators have traced his literary lineage variously through the sophists Protagoras, Prodicus, Thrasymachus, and especially Gorgias. The deliberative speeches in Thucydides' *History* provide more substantial models than any of those shadowy figures, as will become clear when the examination has begun.

The political discourses (*politikoi logoi*) which form by far the largest part of his published work, are concerned with the persuasive presentation of ideas which will both equip his readers with knowledge or science (*episteme*) of matters political, and give a moral dimension to their thinking. The former faculty will enable

---

[5] As distinct from the 'speeches' delivered in the lawcourts. The discourses belong exclusively to the second part of his career, yet span some 42 years. I place them after Demosthenes and Aeschines for generic as well as chronological reasons.

[6] Dion. Hal. *Isoc.* 3: ἀναγνώσεώς τε μᾶλλον οἰκειότερός ἐστιν ἢ χρήσεως ... *Dem.* 4 *fin.*: πανηγυρικὴν μᾶλλον ἢ ἐναγώνιον.

[7] *Philosophia* has a specialized meaning in Isocrates, who used the word to describe his educational system, or *paideia*. It connotes the interactive study of practical (including international) politics, ethics, and rhetoric. See Usher GO iii. 7–9 and refs. in that section.

them to benefit their state by counsel and action,[8] while the latter
will fulfil an educative purpose, because the contemplation of
noble themes will instil sound character, which will transmit moral
conviction to the student's discourse,[9] and through it to his audience. The presence of this moral element is apparent to the critic
Dionysius, whose comments dwell constantly upon the moral
uplift conveyed by the different discourses: 'Who could fail to
become a patriotic supporter of democracy and a student of civic
virtue after reading his *Panegyricus*?' (*Isoc.* 5). 'What greater exhortation to justice and piety could there be, for individuals singly and
collectively for whole communities, than the discourse *On the
Peace*?' (*Isoc.* 7). 'Who would not become a more responsible citizen after reading the *Areopagiticus*?' (*Isoc.* 8).

The Isocratean *politikos logos* is thus an ambitious hybrid genre,
being neither practically deliberative nor ceremonial and epideictic, but designed to be cerebrally and morally stimulating through
the style with which themes are elaborated. Those themes replace
the *partitio oratoria* of forensic oratory, and the broad division which
they dictate demands a more general treatment. Hence, in spite of
the length of many of them, the structure and essential rhetoric of
the discourses can be described quite economically.

4 *Panegyricus*[10]

This is the discourse with which Isocrates announced his talents to
the literary and political establishments, and challenged their
authority, respectively as arbiters of style and as counsellors. It was
a long time in the making (ten to fifteen years[11]), during which
changing historical circumstances complicated the rhetorical task
which he set himself. This was to propound the idea of a
Panhellenic expedition against Persia under the joint leadership of

---

[8] Dion. Hal. *Isoc.* 1 (summarizing several Isocratean passages): τὴν ἐπιστήμην . . . ἐξ
ἧς τὸ βουλεύεσθαι καὶ λέγειν καὶ πράττειν τὰ συμφέροντα παραγίγνεται τοῖς
μαθοῦσιν.

[9] See 15 *Antid.* 276–7.

[10] Commentaries: Sandys (London, 1868, repr. 1902); Rauchenstein (Berlin, 1908);
Buchner (Wiesbaden, 1958); Usher (Warminster, 1990) (*GO* iii).

[11] Dion. Hal. *CV* 25 (p. 225 Loeb) ('ten years, according to the lowest estimate of the
time'), echoed almost verbatim by Quintilian 10. 4. 4; cf. [Plut.] *Vit. X Or.* 837f (ten or fifteen years); [Longinus] *Subl.* 4. 1–2 quotes a more colourful approximation from the historian Timaeus of Tauromenium: that it took Isocrates longer to write the *Panegyricus* than it
took Alexander to conquer Asia.

Athens and Sparta. Now by the time the *Panegyricus* was published (380 BC[12]), Sparta had exploited the terms of the King's Peace (386) to become dominant in Greece, and was in no mood to accept parity with any other Greek state. Since her physical supremacy could not be contested, other grounds for a partnership must be sought, but the balance could be achieved only by stating the Athenian case hyperbolically; and the main theme to be explored and elaborated is *justice (dikaion)*.[13]

Justice (i.e. the Athenian right to the leadership) is the issue in the main body of the discourse (21–132). Mythological and historical events all point to Athenian precedence (22–50)—the tradition that they were the original inhabitants of Attica (*autochthones*) (23–5), the ancient Attic cult of Demeter and Persephone (28–32) marking the very beginnings of civilization; early leadership in the making of laws and the establishment of friendly relations with other cities, including her festivals (33–45). All this, however, has been the material of epideictic oratory already, notably in Thucydides' Funeral Oration of Pericles (2. 35–46). Isocrates' original contribution begins when he turns to *philosophia* (47), introduced with a period which admirably illustrates his style at its most complex and inventive.[14] Style and thought go hand in hand: Athens was the natural medium for the symbiosis of literature and philosophy.

But primacy in the arts of civilization is not enough: the project is a war. Careful selection and interpretation of events is needed. Athens is portrayed as the defender of Greek freedom and the protector of weaker states (53). Mythology and early history serve him well once more, even enabling him to mention Athenian benefactions to Sparta (61–3). But most relevant is her role of Greek champion against the barbarians (66–98). Isocrates' treatment of the subject is idiosyncratic, dwelling as it does on abstract ideas in an epideictic style,[15] with emphasis on the education which made the

---

[12] In 126 the Spartan sieges of Olynthus and Phlius are described as being in progress.

[13] This is one of the themes regularly found in the deliberative speeches in Thucydides.

[14] For an analysis see S. Usher, *BICS* 20 (1973), 42–3. The initial accusative Φιλοσοφίαν creates suspense, which is resolved only on the arrival of the main verbs κατέδειξε and ἐτίμησεν, but a succession of participial clauses leads to further subordination, with ὁρῶσα governing nine further participial clauses.

[15] Note esp. 75–6, a passage in epideictic (Gorgianic) style (76: οὐ γὰρ ὠλιγώρουν τῶν κοινῶν, οὐδ' ἀπέλαυον μὲν ὡς ἰδίων, ἠμέλουν δ' ὡς ἀλλοτρίων, ἀλλ' ἐκήδοντο μὲν ὡς οἰκείων, ἀπείχοντο δ' ὥσπερ χρὴ τῶν μηδὲν προσηκόντων).

victors patriotic; and before turning to their actual achievements, he makes a rhetorical comparison with past victories (82–5). The Persian Wars are made into a contest of valour between Athens and Sparta,[16] an equal contest until the Battle of Salamis. The Athenian contribution to that decisive victory is the highpoint of the whole discourse (93–6),[17] and as elsewhere the physical prowess shown in actual combat is subordinate to the moral strength which caused them to fight against the odds.[18] This distinction affects the choice of subject-matter, as Isocrates himself admits (97–8):

As to the noises that accompany such actions, and the shouts and cries of exhortation which are features common to all sea battles, I do not propose to spend time describing these. (98) My task is to speak of the particular aspects of the story which justify our leadership and corroborate my earlier arguments.

Isocrates thus affirms that detailed narrative is alien to his type of discourse. The argument and the conviction that stem from interpretation of the facts are what matter. The Athenians have earned the hegemony, at least on their record down to 480, which he summarizes using questions, a technique used in forensic oratory (99). Events after that[19] tax their apologist's ingenuity more severely. During their period of empire (478–404) the Athenians had committed a number of widely condemned atrocities against their dissident allies. Isocrates faces this by going on to the attack, using the language of imperialism—'some of those [allies] who made war on us were harshly disciplined' (101), and 'it is impossible to control so many states without punishing those who offend' (102)—so that it is easy to forget that the Athenian empire started as a league of volunteer states. He further argues that the Athenians established their moral right to rule by their moderate use of their power (103–9).[20]

---

[16] So C. Eucken, *Isokrates: seine Positionen in der Auseinandersetzung mit den zeitgenössischen Philosophen* (Berlin, 1983), 156.

[17] The Athenians' 'finest hour' is appropriately described in one of Isocrates' best periods, in which the circumstances are outlined in preparatory genitive absolute and other participial clauses, leading to late arrival of the main clauses (οὐχ ὑπέμειναν . . . ἀλλ' αὐτοὶ μὲν . . . παρεσκευάζοντο . . . εἶχον), giving maximum suspense.

[18] See the opening period of the prooemium for the superiority of mental over physical prowess.

[19] The campaign of 479 BC, which ended in the Battle of Plataea, a victory won mainly by Peloponnesian infantry, is passed over.

[20] Note esp. the content and structure of the period σημεῖον δὲ τούτων . . . αἰτίαν ἐχόντων (177–9); the opening participial clauses describing the population and military strength of Athens and the strategic importance of Euboea are subordinated to the main idea

By contrast, Greek history since the fall of their empire has been characterized by confusion and oligarchic tyranny. In this vehement tirade (110–21) Isocrates is careful not to blame the Spartans directly, but it proves to be transitional. In 122 the argument takes a decisive turn. Justice is still the theme, as he reasons that leadership is deserved only by those who treat others justly, as the Spartans have manifestly not done. The conciliatory tone of 129–32 marks it as a concluding section.

In the deliberative part of the speech (133–56) the themes are expediency (*sympheron*, 133–7) and possibility (*dynaton*, 138–56). Concern with practical matters and the actual situation is reflected in a change of style, illustrating Isocrates' versatility.[21] Greek disunity has given the King a free hand, and yet his victims would be willing allies for the Greek cause. Isocrates tries two methods of approach here. First, a comparative argument: if the King is strong now, delay in attacking him might find him even stronger (138). Second, is he really as strong as he seems? Examples illustrating his ineffectuality (140–3) furnish the core of the *dynaton* argument, which then broadens into a discussion of barbarian degeneracy and its causes (150–6), a thoroughly explored topic to which he can add little.

The theme of justice returns briefly (157–9), but this time the subject is Persia as an enemy, not Athens as a leader. This is succeeded by the rallying section (160–9), and the theme is *opportunity* (*kairos*), a pervasive topic in Isocrates,[22] and one which Demosthenes later deploys to great effect, especially in the *Olynthiacs*.

The **epilogue** (170–89) revives some of the topics of the prooemium in a slightly different form: a scathing criticism of contemporary statesmanship adds to his earlier criticism of the sophists. As counterparts to the summary of evidence and arguments given at this point in forensic oratory, the themes of expediency (173–4), justice (175–84), and possibility (185–6) reappear briefly before an emotional epideictic finish that includes a simulated extempore note of modesty (187) in which the speaker apologizes for not doing justice to his theme.

---

expressed in the two clauses 'none of these considerations tempted us . . . but we allowed ourselves to live in poorer conditions than those who were classed as our slaves'.

[21] Note the relatively short, paratactic sentences in 136–7.

[22] See H. Wersdörfer, *Die ΦΙΛΟΣΟΦΙΑ des Isokrates im Spiegel ihrer Terminologie* (Leipzig, 1940), 55–72.

8 *On the Peace*

Whereas the *Panegyricus* of 380 celebrates an Athenian 'cultural empire' in an expansionist Panhellenic context, the political situation in 355, after Thebes had become the strongest of the Greek states, and Athens had been forced to accept the secession of her strongest allies, Rhodes, Chios, Byzantium, and Cos, from her Second Delian League, demanded a complete reassessment of what was possible and desirable. Isocrates was now over eighty years old and comfortably placed through the success of his school, and this added subjective to objective reasons for advocating a conservative policy. In fact he goes as far as possible by recommending that Athens abandon entirely her ambitions to rule others.[23]

Awareness of dangerous and bitter opposition from demagogues is present throughout the discourse (3, 5, 9–10, 14, 36, 39, 52, 121, 124–32). They have the attractive and popular arguments: the countervailing rhetoric must be of a peculiarly forceful kind. After formulating his main proposal to accept the secession (16), he explains the advantages of the resultant peace and adds moral arguments which reinforce them, the main one being that justice makes for willing subject-allies.[24] The mood changes at § 41, as a sequence of paradoxes exposes the weakness of popular thinking. 'We praise the exploits of our ancestors, yet employ mercenary troops to fight our own wars' (41–2, 44, cf. 47–8);[25] 'They liberated the Greek cities, but we seek to enslave them' (42); 'We glory in our citizenship yet admit outsiders into it'; 'We make many laws, yet ignore them' (50). More complex paradoxes follow (51–3). The style of this type of writing is basically antithetical, but it is also amplificatory, the first limb (the ideal) being introduced in order to emphasize the absurdity of the second, which represents the real situation. A simple stylistic form of this is οὐ (μὴ) . . . ἀλλά, an Isocratean speciality.[26] The contentious tone produced by these paradoxes may contain sarcasm,[27] and this tone is also maintained

[23] See R. A. Moysey, 'Isocrates *On the Peace*: Rhetorical Exercise or Political Advice', *AJAH* 7 (1982), 118–27.

[24] 30: ἐκ δὲ τοῦ δικαίαν τὴν πόλιν παρέχειν καὶ βοηθεῖν τοῖς ἀδικουμένοις . . . παρ' ἑκόντων τῶν Ἑλλήνων τὴν ἡγεμονίαν ἐλάβομεν.

[25] Isocrates thus anticipates one of Demosthenes' most frequent complaints.

[26] οὐ (μὴ) . . . ἀλλά occurs 61.2 times per 25 Teubner pages in Isocrates, only 42 in Lysias.

[27] e.g. 59: 'If we were prudent we should supply each other with money for our general assemblies; for the oftener we meet to deliberate, the more we promote the success of our rivals.'

by straight contrast between past (good) and present (bad), which may be made with other devices beside οὐκ . . . ἀλλά.[28]

The main arguments for the abandonment of imperial ambitions are moral and historical (63–94). Instead of the glories of the Athenian empire bruited in the *Panegyricus*, empire here is the fruit of reckless acquisitiveness, and Isocrates selects the worst disasters—the failed Egyptian Expedition of 460/59 (86) and the Sicilian Expedition (84)—in order to press his argument home. The didactic tone of 91, in which he shows the difference between 'tyranny' and 'rule', is a reminder of his status as an educator, and discussions in his seminars about the corrupting effect of power would surely have provided the background to much of the rest of this discourse. The example of Sparta[29] contrasts their earlier self-discipline with their behaviour after the King's Peace, and this overlaps with some traditional arguments about the evils of tyranny to both holder and subject (95–119), while the positive moral example of the Megarians (117–18), perhaps surprisingly,[30] reinforces the main argument. The discourse concludes with a catalogue of recommendations—to listen to good advisers, not demagogues (133), to treat allies as such, not as subjects (134), guard the city's good name and become a kind of policeman of the Greek peace (135–7), thus combining justice with advantage. After an even briefer summary (142), he ends on an academic note (145), urging his juniors (pupils?) to enlarge on his message.[31]

7 *Areopagiticus*

After his advice to abandon imperialism in *On the Peace*, this discourse marks a further stage in a policy of retrenchment.[32]

---

[28] e.g. (77–8, 92) ἀντί with verbal participle or articular infinitive.

[29] Note also 114, where he seems to be underlining the value of examples as he chides his audience for not appreciating it: ἃ γὰρ ἐπὶ τῶν ἄλλων ὁρᾶτε, ταῦτ' ἐφ' ὑμῶν αὐτῶν ἀγνοεῖτε.

[30] The history of Megara since the colonizing age had been mostly one of decline. Here Isocrates refers to their poor indigenous resources ('having to farm rocks'). Some of her colonies, such as Byzantium, had outstripped her in prosperity while maintaining connections with the mother-city.

[31] Further on this discourse, see J. Davidson, 'Isocrates Against Imperialism: An Analysis of *De Pace*', *Historia* 39 (1990), 20–36.

[32] W. Jaeger's attempt to place *Areopagiticus* immediately before the Social War (i.e. in 357) (*Paideia*, iii, trans. Highet (Oxford, 1945), 109–10, condensed from his article in *HSCP* 1941)) does not consider all the internal evidence, and is unconvincing. 355 (Jebb) or late 355/early 354 (Blass) remain the most probable dates.

Expansionism was associated with demagogy, cautious fore
policy with government by the experienced and the responsi
Isocrates here proposes the restoration of powers to the most ex
rienced and august body in the Athenian state, the Council of
Areopagus.

The discourse begins with a swift portrayal of over-confide
leading to disaster, a traditional tragic theme presented in an o
fashioned style.[33] Recent Athenian history conforms with this
tern: power and success have been 'dissipated'.[34] The problem
explained with succinctness, memorable imagery and gnomic fo
(13–14):

We neither have nor do we honestly try to create a constitution wh
can manage our affairs. And yet we all know that success does not co
to nor stay with those who have built the finest and strongest walls aro
themselves, nor with those who have brought together the greatest p
ulation, but rather to those who govern their state in the best and m
responsible way. For the soul of the state is nothing else than its const
tion, having as much power over it as the mind over the body.

Here Isocrates amends the old idea of men, not strong walls be
the bulwark of the city:[35] its constitution is what shapes its desti
The constitution that best served Athens in the past incorpora
democracy in the election of officials, but limited the pool fr
which they were drawn to 'the best and the ablest for each fu
tion' (22). This fell short of extreme democracy, but, he argues,
more democratic than election by lot, the method which s
ceeded it, which left the choice of government to chance (23).
people elected and called the officials to account: the officials, w
time and means, could devote themselves to the common ser
(27–8). The picture of everyone knowing his proper place
observing the proprieties, religious and secular, is further ideali
in the central section of the discourse (37–55), where an import
Isocratean element enters. The old Council of the Areopagus
not only a political institution, but also a guardian of the preva
ethos of good order (*eukosmia*, 37; *eutaxia*, 39). This responsibi

---

[33] Esp. in 4–5, where abstract nouns (πλούτοις, δυναστείαις, ἄνοια, ἀκολα
ἐνδείαις, ταπεινότησι, σωφροσύνη, μετριότης) are packed together, and 'freq
changes of fortune' are described in consecutive clauses.

[34] 12: διεσκαριφησάμεθα καὶ διελύσαμεν.

[35] Alcaeus Fr. 28; Soph. *O.T.* 56–7; Thuc. 7. 77. 7. Demosthenes 18 *Cor.* 299 buil
Isocrates' idea.

necessarily involved education of the young.[36] The Areopagus did for all what Isocrates' school did for an opulent few, and he is anxious that he should not be thought to be recommending an oligarchy (57–9, 70). Indeed, he seems to be more concerned with rebutting the charge of being anti-democratic than with formulating firm recommendations, and it is that anxiety that causes him to dwell instead on the historical past—the Thirty as the worst type of oligarchy (64–9) compared with the best type of democracy—that which showed its finest qualities under the amnesty of 403. And this gives way to a general eulogy of Athens (74–5) followed by a summary of the main arguments. Return to the 'constitution of our forefathers', the guarantor of prosperity at home and a good name abroad, has been and remains the constant theme (16, 76–8).

5 *To Philip*

The nominal addressee of this discourse is Philip II of Macedon,[37] but it was circulated among his associates, and delivered in some form to an audience.[38] Its theme, Philip's leadership of a Panhellenic expedition against Persia (16), thus becomes one of inter-state propaganda as well as personal exhortation.[39] Philip himself remains firmly centre-stage throughout, and the most distinctive characteristics of the discourse stem from this fact. But his descent from Heracles (105–27), who laboured for the good of mankind, serves to argue his Greekness (a very contentious matter), his unifying power, and his benignity, qualities which should commend him to Isocrates' wider audience.

The Peace of Philocrates (346)[40] meets with his approval, but he argues that it must be consolidated, because past experience shows that the Greeks will return to internecine conflict. That experience had provided the main theme of the *Panegyricus*, addressed to the Greek world at large, but persuasion of an individual is most

---

[36] See Too, *Rhetoric of Identity in Isocrates*, 212–13.

[37] He is addressed throughout in the second person singular.

[38] In 17 he says that 'some of his associates (τινες τῶν πλησιασάντων)' disapproved of it; and he ends the address by submitting it to the judgement of 'you my hearers' (155). On the other hand, in an interesting passage on the difference between spoken and privately read discourses (24–7), he places the present one in the latter category.

[39] Further on this, see M. M. Markle, 'Support of Athenian Intellectuals for Philip: A Study of Isocrates' *Philippus* and Speusippus' *Letter to Philip*', *JHS* 96 (1976), 80–99, esp. 81–92.

[40] *To Philip* was probably published in the same year. See G. Mathieu, *Les Idées politiques d'Isocrate* (Paris, 1925), 155–6.

effective when it dwells upon his own peculiar power to do what is required of him, more than upon justification of his command. Even the latter theme is coloured by duty.[41] The all-embracing theme is possibility (*dynaton*): of the reconciliation of the Greek cities (39–56, general conditions favourable); of Philip's using his special powers to promote it (57–67); and of success in the invasion itself (89–104). It is treated with more originality here than the subordinate theme of expediency (68–80, 90–127), in which there is much material in common with *Panegyricus*, though the example of the March of the Ten Thousand is sharpened here by direct comparisons between leaders—Cyrus (and Clearchus) and Philip. Isocrates' decision to end by insisting that Philip should behave as a benefactor is shrewd, in that it is calculated to reassure his wider audience as much as to exhort the king.[42]

6 *Archidamus*

From discourses in which Isocrates is the First Person, we turn to the longest in which the speaker is another character. Later critics recognized this authorial transference as a rhetorical exercise or *progymnasma*,[43] and it would have been viewed similarly by Isocrates' pupils and other readers.[44] Archidamus III, king of a Sparta recently beaten by Thebes at the Battle of Leuctra (371), urges his people to stand fast in the face of the defection of her Peloponnesian allies, and the Theban demand that Sparta recognize the independence of Messenia.

The first task is to establish the character or persona of the speaker: the other more or less conventional items which the **prooemium** (1–16) contains[45] are subordinate to this. Archidamus is willing to

---

[41] *dikaion*-theme, 30–8: 'Now I say that you ought . . . ' 32: 'it is not proper for you to ignore . . . '

[42] For further discussion, see S. Perlman, 'Isocrates' *Philippus*: A Reinterpretation', *Historia* 6 (1957), 306–17; and 'Isocrates' *Philippus* and Panhellenism', *Historia* 18 (1969), 370–4.

[43] Such exercises were called *ethopoiiai* or *prosopopoiiai*. See Nic. Soph. *Progymn.* 11 (Sp. iii. 489–90), who distinguishes these by the degree of fictionality: in ethopoiia the person is defined (i.e. he or she is a known historical figure); while in prosopopoiia the writer invents both person and character. *Archidamus* is thus an ethopoiia rather than a prosopopoiia.

[44] Thus to describe it purely as 'deliberative', as do Blass and Jebb, seems imprecise. The piece's academic character also renders hazardous any attempt to date it close to the events with which it is concerned.

[45] Including 'reluctance to come forward' (2) (Archidamus is new to the rostrum, like Demosthenes in *Phil. I* 1); and there is a purely Isocratean touch when natural endowments and training are commended above mere seniority (4).

die rather than accede to Theban demands. And he will do this because his cause is a just one, requiring a man like himself who values action above mere words (15). The basis of justice is past history: as in the *Panegyricus*, claims go back to mythological times, when the sons of Heracles had held both Messenia and Lacedaemon (17–23), a union sanctioned in recent times by the Delphic Oracle (31). But the fact of recent defeat makes the justice-argument difficult to sustain, and tests the rhetorician's ingenuity. Taking his stand firmly on justice,[46] he plays on the word itself, making it the common factor in four statements, one false in practice, surrounded by three which may be true in conception (35–6):

Men of character and reputation pride themselves on practising it [justice], and the best-governed states make it their prime concern; and further, I observe that past wars have all been decided not by superior forces but in accordance with justice; and that, in general human life is destroyed by vice and preserved by virtue.

The just course is also subject to fewer uncertainties than that which looks pessimistically at expediency. Here there is a clever blending of morality and pragmatism typical of Isocratean thought: withdrawal from Messene would be a self-inflicted injustice, and it would lead to more demands (39). More straightforward are the examples that follow of states which have successfully fought for righteous causes against the odds (41–6). But some sophistical rhetoric follows. In 49–51 is described the paradox of present policy: whereas it is normal for states enjoying prosperity to be conservative, while those faring ill work for change, the Spartans are at present passive in misfortune, even though they have no real choice but to risk battle. Isocrates raises the temperature here: the peace terms are 'not far removed from slavery'; they should not be 'rashly and shamefully' accepted. In 54–6 there is a succession of four pathetic paradoxes contrasting other times and other cities with Sparta today.

Armed with the favour of the gods and their own patriotic spirit, the Spartans might hope for success (59–61), but not alone. In the real world, however, allies would be hard to find, so the rhetoric in Isocrates' exploration of *possibility* (62–9) focuses on the plight in which Sparta's neighbours find themselves (65–6),[47] which should

---

[46] 35: 'No man could persuade me that anything is more important than justice'.

[47] 'They have been so devastated [lit. 'levelled with the ground'] by their misfortunes (ὡμαλισμένοι ταῖς συμφοραῖς) that no man can decide which of them are the most

cause them to desire her protection. But even without them, he is
resolved to fight, and here (70–80) he sets forth his plan. It is dras-
tic: to evacuate their city, as the Athenians had done before Salamis,
and fight a guerrilla war against the Thebans. A grim programme,
but the rewards for its success would be great. The last quarter of
the speech is positive and hortatory in tone, as befits a king:[48] past
glories (99–100) should inspire hope (103–4), but may not be emulated without a struggle (104–5). The **epilogue** (107–11) contains
epideictic language as it reasserts the theme of justice, and a
prosopopoiia (110).[49] Stylistically, Isocrates has aimed to give
Archidamus a lively persona, which is reflected in the highest frequency of hyperbaton in the corpus, and above average frequency
of rhetorical question.

14 *Plataicus*

This discourse may be best read as Isocrates' reply to the doctrine,
much debated in and before his time, that 'might is right'.[50] The
Thebans compelled the Plataeans to join their Boeotian League
(377/6), but the Plataeans, in hatred and fear, justified by events
(the destruction of their city in 373), made overtures to the
Athenians. The speaker is an anonymous Plataean, so his persona is
unimportant. The speech lacks distinctive stylistic traits, and its
main interest lies in its arguments.[51]

  The Athenians are posited as opponents of the 'might is right'
argument, and as champions, on the basis of their past record, of
ethical justice (1, 17, 39). The Thebans have done indescribable
wrong (4), and cannot represent their actions in terms other than

---

wretched; for not one of their states is unscathed, none whose neighbours are not ready to
do them mischief. Consequently their fields have been laid waste, their cities sacked, their
people driven from their homes . . . '

[48] But Isocrates has scrupulously observed the king's position. Spartan kings reigned
within a technically democratic but practically oligarchic constitution. Archidamus could
use the prestige of his office to promote his ideas, but his audience, whether it was the
Gerousia or the Ecclesia, must 'take counsel' (χρὴ βουλεύεσθαι, 97) and decide.

[49] Using that term in its commoner sense of the introduction of significant persons to create particular emotional effects (Lat. *conformatio*, *Rhet. ad Herenn.* 4. 53. 66).

[50] The Melian Dialogue in Thuc. 5. 86–113 ('the strong rule, the weak obey'); the opinion attributed by Plato (*Rep.* 336b–342e) to the sophist Thrasymachus ('Justice is the interest of the Stronger [i.e. the holder of power]').

[51] 7: 'It is the arguments with which they will hope to deceive you that we shall try to
expose.' The facts of Theban depredation of Plataea are not in dispute.

hose of exploiting naked power.[52] They have espoused morality
ıntil they thought they had superior strength (24), whereupon they
leploy specious and inconsistent arguments (24–5, 30–1). The
ırguments which attack their essential immoral position are moral
ınd historical: baseness and treachery are punished by the gods, as
he Thebans themselves have found (28); Theban power is a threat
o the equilibrium of the whole region (33–4), and will be self-
lestructive because it is exercised without justice, as the fate of
ıther unjust empires has shown (39–41).

As in *Archidamus* (62 ff.), and at a corresponding point in the
peech (42), the support which the proposed action is likely to
ıttract is mentioned. This is really another argument against assum-
ıng tyrannical power: many allies will join the ranks of their
ıpposers. It gives way to emotional justice-arguments,[53] conven-
ionally appearing as the speech draws to its close—kinship (51),
ıast services (57), and respect for ancient memories and places
58–9). Those of Isocrates' pupils who read and remembered this
liscourse would be well-equipped to speak persuasively at many
imes of crisis in their cities during this turbulent period of Greek
ıistory.

? *To Nicocles*

Ine of the most illustrious and appreciative[54] of Isocrates' pupils
vas Nicocles, son of Euagoras, Prince of Cyprus. Before the prince
ınstructs his people in *Nicocles*, his teacher instructs him on 'how a
ıuler should reign'.[55] This resolves itself into establishing and main-
aining his authority, and making his reign acceptable to his subjects
ınd tolerable to himself. The claim (8) that no previous author has
ıxamined the question, and that this is the first extant protreptic to
;ood monarchical government, may be true in strict generic terms,
ıut the instruction (42–3) to seek guidance from early didactic
ıoets reminds us of the present work's long literary ancestry.

---

[52] 10: πῶς ποτε τὸ δίκαιον κρίνοντες ταῦτα φήσουσιν προστάττειν ἡμῖν;

[53] §§ 45, 49, 53: pathetic paradox with a strong comparative component.

[54] See 15 *Antid.* 40. Nicocles was said to have paid Isocrates twenty talents for the pre-
ent piece or its companion *Nicocles* ([Plut.] *Vit. X Or.* 838a; Philod. 2 p. 178 Sudh.).

[55] 3 *Nic.* 11: ὡς χρὴ τυραννεῖν. Note how the juxtaposition of the last two words illus-
rates the neutrality of tyranny: there were good and bad tyrants. The main task of the dis-
ourse is to encourage Nicocles to be one of the former.

However that may be, the prince is encouraged to model his city
on contemporary Athenian ideals.[56]

The literary form of the new genre is drawn selectively but
inventively from those already in use. Thus the contrast between
material and moral gifts (1–2) is reminiscent of the opening of
Panegyricus,[57] but the special needs of kings are constantly kept in
mind throughout the **prooemium** (1–8), even where it is adapting topics from other genres. Thus the difficulty of the subject,
which is both a forensic and an epideictic topic, becomes the difficulties facing the king (4), arising from his isolated position; and the
topic of its importance (mainly epideictic), becomes its especial
importance in the present case, because a well-advised ruler can
benefit far more people than a well-advised private citizen (8).

Topics are introduced under separate heads (*kephalaia*) in the
central section of the discourse (9–39). The king should be superior to his subjects in wisdom and virtue,[58] qualities acquired by
moral education. This will train him to exercise 'philanthropia', an
outward (and material) show of concern for the well-being of his
subjects (15–16).[59] Advice is given on religion (20), friendship (21),
attitude to foreigners (the Athenian model again) (22), to the exercise of his authority (24), and to war (24–5). At this point almost
every successive imperative carries advice on quite distinct topics,
and summary becomes impossible. But there are unifying sub-
themes: self-control, *arete*, *paideia*. 40–53 enlarges upon an aspect of
the latter, as the value of certain serious literature as a source of
advice to rulers is affirmed. Here again the king must not be like
ordinary men, for whom entertainment rather than edification
decides their choice, but he must study what is likely to be useful
(50). Thus the discourse ends, as it has begun, on the themes of
study and advice, teacher and pupil.

3 Nicocles

The present discourse is an *ethopoiia*, but portrayal of the speaker's
character is a means to an end, which is the subject's acceptance of
the rule of a man who is imbued with the qualities of his teacher's

---

[56] e.g. the state is presumed to be administered by laws (17), even though the tyrant could
change them.
[57] So Eucken, *Isokrates*, 216.
[58] 10: φρονιμώτερον τῶν ἄλλων . . . 12: ταῖς ἀρεταῖς αὐτῶν διοίσεις.
[59] For a foreshadowing of Hellenistic monarchy in 15, 18–19, see Usher GO iii. 207–8.

deal ruler, which include above all the wisdom and eloquence to exercise his power beneficently and with popular assent.

The discourse falls clearly into three parts. The **prooemium** (1–13) is more or less detached from the rest, containing as it does restatement of a few generalizations about the proper use of speech and its educational value—ideas which he would have assimilated in Isocrates' seminars. 14–47 is a justification of monarchy, as the ultimate realization of the principle that the best should rule, since such government ensures justice and continuity (17–21), and also decisiveness (22–4).[60] As to personal justification, Nicocles cites his lineage (27–8, 42) and his administrative record, relating this to his virtues—justice (31–5), moderation (36–41). It is difficult to match the degree of self-praise in this section with anything written in prose up to this time.[61]

As Nicocles turns to the duties of his subjects, the change of style is more interesting than the subject-matter. The treatment under heads noted in *To Nicocles* has changed into an almost lapidary prescriptive manner, whereby orders are given, and reasons for them briefly appended. This style will be found in its extreme form in *To Demonicus*, where it will be discussed more fully. Among other more predictable recommendations, citizens are urged to be open in their dealings in a passage which suggests a monarch suspicious of dissident forces at work (53–4). Otherwise the advice is bland and unexceptional.

To Demonicus

The salient features of this discourse are extreme applications of the technique found in *To Nicocles* and *Nicocles*. They are prescription (in the imperative) followed by explanation (usually a clause headed by *gar*). It is a development of an ancient style, found widely in early moral writing and the gnomic poets, to whom Isocrates implicitly recognizes a debt (*To Nic.* 43). But features otherwise recognized as Isocratean appear alongside these (13): 'First of all, how respect for the gods, not only by sacrificing, but by honouring your oaths; for the former is merely evidence of your wealth,

[60] For the advantages of a unified command, esp. in times of crisis (e.g. war), see Dem. 1 *Olynth. I* 4; 8 *Chers.* 11; 18 *Cor.* 235. Isocrates himself addresses the same point later to the subject of these observations by Demosthenes, Philip II, in 5 *Phil.* 14–15.

[61] The date of the discourse is impossible to fix with precision: the period 372–65, assumed by most commentators, is the best guess.

but the latter betokens a noble character.' *To Demonicus* is close to the Isocratean average for *ouk . . . alla*, and close to *Panegyricus* for *men . . . de* antithesis. The conscious and systematic adoption of a gnomic style accounts for the very high incidence of internal *gar* (nearly four times the average for the corpus).[62] Certainly if *To Nicocles* could not be safely regarded as his work, the authenticity of *To Demonicus* would be in serious doubt. It is best seen as another example of his stylistic versatility.[63] As to its content, although it is to be assumed that Demonicus is a personage of some importance, he is not a king.[64] This makes the more notable the number of echoes in it of *To Nicocles* and *Nicocles*. Beside these, however, is to be found prosaic advice such as could be given to any ordinary person, such as training in self-control (21) and trustworthiness (22–3), and the avoidance of intoxication (32). Thus the discourse lacks the clear focus of the two pieces for Nicocles. It is more derivative in content, and the originality of the style lies in its prose form.

9 *Euagoras*

Isocrates' serious purpose and the programme of his school were the twin factors that converted the sophistic encomium into a new literary form. His claim to have broken new ground in the *Euagoras* (8), which has been accepted by most commentators, rests upon his choice of subject—a famous man recently dead (374 BC), not a figure from the mythological past or a group of heroic mortals, like the fallen celebrated in *epitaphioi*. This choice gave the work an educative value: his readers (not only the dedicatee, Nicocles son of Euagoras), could realistically emulate his achievements (5, 77 80), encouraged by the fact that he started from unpromising beginnings (66–8).[65] Conventional elements survive, such as reference to his divine and heroic lineage (12–18) and physical prowess (22–3), but the main thread that runs through the discourse is the subject's own *arete* (33, 65, 70). It guides all his actions, and care is taken to portray Euagoras (however implausibly) as always acting

---

[62] For the absolute and relative figures, see Usher, *BICS* 20 (1973), 46–7.

[63] The best defence of Isocratean authorship is still that of Sandys (1902), pp. xxxi–xl.

[64] He is urged to model his behaviour on royalty (36) rather than to act as to the manner born. But he is also expecting to rule in some capacity (37).

[65] Note how Isocrates creates a positive version of the old negative forensic 'rags to riches' formula: 'he turned the citizens from barbarians to Greeks, from cowards into warriors, from obscure individuals into men of note.'

'well' (*kalōs*), i.e. with moral rectitude.[66] Certain actions illustrate this general idea, while others show subsidiary qualities, such as steadfastness in adversity (27–9) and decisiveness (30), but they are narrated only to the degree of detail necessary for the illustration of those virtues. Here as elsewhere[67] Isocrates repudiates the historian's task, as a distraction from his own. But brief reference to other events and their agents does serve his purpose. Comparison is instructive, since it serves to measure achievement. Objectively, Euagoras' return is more glorious than the conquest by Cyrus the Great of his effete Median neighbours (35–9), and his campaigns in Asia are greater in extent than those of Greeks against Trojans (65–6); and subjectively, King Artaxerxes II regarded his war against Euagoras in Cyprus as more dangerous than the incursion into his own kingdom of his brother Cyrus with the Ten Thousand (57–60). Comparison is a distinguishing technique of the new encomium: in later Greek biography, especially Plutarch, it becomes a central feature. The germ of later biographical writing is also present in the broadly chronological treatment of Euagoras' career: his birth and childhood (21–2), exile and return (27–32), accession to power (35–9), performance as king (40–6) and specific actions (47–50)—a kind of proof of his good character (51) which attracted allies (52–7). Tactfully, Isocrates leaves the end of his subject's life in eulogistic obscurity (73).[68]

In both style and content, *Euagoras* retains and even builds upon the rhetorical techniques of his earlier writing.[69] Attention is constantly being drawn to the subject's good character and the greatness of his achievement. This epideictic treatment of biography keeps it distinct for the time being from historiography, but the two genres draw closer together a few years later under the pen of Xenophon in his *Agesilaus* (358), which contains a number of passages from his *Hellenica*. But the rhetorical elements introduced by Isocrates survived in various degrees of attenuation, and the view that biography begins with the *Euagoras* remains substantially correct.[70]

---

[66] Even as he seized power, the necessary acts of violence and impiety were done by someone else (25–6).   [67] 31: 4 *Paneg.* 97.

[68] It seems to have ended violently, so Isocrates celebrates his avoidance of the infirmities of extreme old age (71).

[69] It is especially rich in hypostasis (correlative constructions) and amplification.

[70] The *Euagoras* heads most historical surveys of ancient biography, starting with that of I. Bruns, *Das literarische Porträt der Griechen im fünften und vierten Jahrhundert* (Berlin, 1896). For a short but thorough review of influences in prose and poetry on *Euagoras*, see L. Pernot, *La Rhétorique de l'éloge dans le monde gréco-romain* (Paris, 1993), 20–2.

10 *Helen*

Isocrates wrote three pieces early in his career as a teacher, each in
a different way attacking his rivals. *Against the Sophists* is incomplete
and not oratory in any recognizable sense, and its main substance
reappears in a more elaborate form in the *Antidosis*. The *Helen*, on
the other hand, is a practical demonstration of his talent and
method, affording direct comparison with other sophists because
the topic was popular in their schools.[71] The paradox of a beauti-
ful heroine who brought evil follows the tradition of choosing a
controversial subject for a rhetorical exercise (cf. Gorgias *Palamedes*,
q.v. (Appendix B)). But Isocrates wants to introduce material of
practical educative value, and begins by criticizing his rivals for failing to do so.[72] He also makes a literary criticism of an unnamed
writer, who, while claiming to have written an encomium, has
actually written an apology (14).

True to his criticism, Isocrates keeps praise firmly in view
throughout, but the object of that praise for one third of the discourse is Theseus, not Helen (18–37). He is a better character to
fulfil the serious educative purpose that Isocrates has set himself. He
has the cardinal political virtues: ambition (23), the desire to benefit Greece, or at least his native city of Athens (25); knowledge of
war, piety (31), and the instincts of a popular monarch (34–7).
Helen makes her first appearance half way through (38), riding in,
so to speak, on Theseus' shoulders: that such a man should have
admired her is a proof of her merits, corroborated by 'all the kings
and rulers of that time' (39) who became her suitors. Praise remains
dominant: even Paris ('Alexander') is credited with reason (42–3,
45) rather than mere infatuation, and after his critics have been
silenced Isocrates is free to indulge in more extravagant praise of
Helen, and of beauty as the greatest inspirer of other virtues (55–9)
and a source of power to the holder (61–6). But there is a political
consequence of Helen's beauty which sets the work in the mainstream of Isocrates' programme: it unified the Greek world, and
ensured that it did not fall under the barbarian yoke (67).

[71] The *Helen* of Gorgias has survived, but Isocrates' *Helen* is probably not an attempt to
outdo Gorgias, whose piece is, by his own description (21), a παίγνιον (play-piece or *jeu
d'esprit*).

[72] 4–5: 'They should abandon this quackery (sc. eristic disputation) and pursue the truth,
to instruct their pupils in practical political matters, realizing that reasoned conjecture about
such useful things is far better than exact knowledge about useless things.'

11 *Busiris*

A more purely academic exercise on a remoter but more contentious subject, competing with the work of a named sophist,
Polycrates, the third of the early pieces contains a higher proportion of criticism than the Helen. Isocrates' own defence of the le-
gendary king of Egypt, who was variously accused of human
sacrifice and cannibalism, occupies only two-fifths of the discourse
(10–29). It is preceded by criticism of wrong emphasis (5) and
factual errors (8), and followed by a broader attack on Polycrates'
attitude to evidence (31–2) and disregard for the truth (36–8); and
this ends only after Isocrates has shown that Polycrates' 'defence' of
Busiris is not a defence at all, and that discourses such as his tended
to give 'philosophy' a bad name (49–50). In Isocrates' own defence
of Busiris, the king is indistinguishable from other conventional
hero-kings, except perhaps in the scale of his achievement: for he
is credited with conferring on the Egyptians almost all the civiliz-
ing institutions that excited the admiration of the Greeks in classical times, but especially those concerning religion. This is Isocrates'
counterblast to the king's detractors, of whose inhuman sins, real or
alleged, nothing more is said.

15 *Antidosis*

Isocrates' longest discourse defies conventional classification. It is
neither epideictic nor deliberative (1, 12 'a mixed discourse'). For
literary reasons, while admitting his pretence[73] he gives it some of
the trappings of a defence in a real trial.[74] It is a defence, but one
of his whole life, not on a single charge.[75] In fact the trial that took
place seems to have been an adjudication (*diadikasia*), at which
there was no prosecutor or defendant as such.[76] On being
challenged to an exchange of property (*antidosis*) over a trierarchy,

[73] 13: τὴν ἀπολογίαν τὴν προσποιουμένην μὲν περὶ κρίσεως γεγράφθαι,
βουλομένην δὲ περὶ ἐμοῦ δηλῶσαι τὴν ἀλήθειαν.

[74] 17–18: plea for a fair hearing and references to the 'jury', the 'prosecutor' and the conditions of a live trial (20–3); his opponent's confidence in victory (26), the 'penalty' which
he faces (28), 'the present trial' (167); and, the most outrageous touch of illusion, the introduction of the water-clock (320) at the end of a speech which is far longer than would have
been allowed in a real trial.

[75] See H. von Arnim, *Das Testament des Isokrates*, in Wege der Forschung 351, ed. Seck
(1976).

[76] See MacDowell *LCA* 145–6.

Isocrates had initially declined the leitourgia, but the court imposed
it on him (4–5). Presumably the exchange would have taken place
if he had still refused the trierarchy, but matters did not proceed
that far. He performed it (5), but exposure to public scrutiny had
uncovered widespread and intense prejudice against him personally, his school, and his opinions. He could reasonably put much of
this down to envy (8, 142), but to dwell on that would test even an
Athenian readership's tolerance of self-praise. His apologia required
a full and reasoned explanation of his *paideia*, with stress upon the
positive good it had done to its pupils and to Athens as a whole.

His approach to the subject is wide-ranging but not systematic
(140). A **prooemium** (1–29) may be discerned, leading to a statement of the charge 'that he corrupted young men by teaching them
to speak and win in the lawcourts contrary to justice'. This gives
him the opportunity to restate his oft-repeated denial of his past
métier of logographos, though not before he has shown his knowledge of forensic argument in a dilemmaton reminiscent of the
semi-legendary Corax v. Tisias lawsuit.[77] But sophistic cleverness is
not to be his ally. With its similar charge, Plato's *Apology of Socrates*
is to be a constant point of reference. This relationship is confirmed
not only by verbal parallels and common sentiments,[78] but the type
of argument used in *Antidosis* accords closely with Isocratean thinking, with its emphasis on the importance of 'opinion' (*doxa*) as the
instrument of deductive reasoning,[79] rather than with the Platonic
quest for absolute knowledge. The rhetoric that arises from this is
illustrated in 224–42. There critics of his teaching are asked why
men come to his school from all parts of the world and pay to be
his pupils. The answer is, that they think they will be improved by
the experience, as it costs no effort or expense to become wicked
(225). In the meantime, his enemies are 'irrational' (227) in their
prejudices.[80] Eloquence taught as it is in his school (i.e. directed
towards constructive political thinking), has been a characteristic of
all the best Athenian statesmen of the past (232–6). Conversely,
opinion concerning those who have misused the power of words
has been expressed most forcefully in public pronouncements

[77] 16: 'If I speak well, I may show that I am liable to the charges which he [sc. the pro-
secutor] has made about my cleverness; while if I happen to argue less ably than he has led
you to expect, you may take a poor view of my affairs.'
[78] The *Antidosis* passages are listed by G. Norlin, *Isocrates*, i (Loeb; London, 1928), p. xvii,
and the *Apology* passages are noted under the text in vol. ii.
[79] See Usher GO iii. 9.   [80] ἀγνωμόνως ἔχουσιν.

(237–8). To conclude his rather loose sequence of thought, Isocrates returns to the charge of corrupting the youth, refuting it with the earlier argument, that he has received gratitude, not abuse and litigation, from his pupils. Their opinion of his teaching is all that matters, and its effectiveness is corroborated by his enemies' desire to get rid of it (240–2).

Before this the discourse deals with the different components of his *paideia*, beginning with its literary form (44–50), illustrated with passages which treat the main subjects of his teaching and lead naturally to the establishment of a vital connection (86):

When anyone devotes his life to encouraging all his fellow-countrymen to be more noble and just leaders of the Greeks, how is it conceivable that such a man will corrupt his followers? What man with the ability to compose such discourses would look for bad speeches on bad subjects?

The very existence of a causal link between eloquence and morality was, of course, a matter of fierce contention; yet it is central to Isocratean dogma, and he argues for it at greater length later, in the most important passage in the discourse, 270–80. The defining argument is in 276–7:

Firstly, anyone choosing to speak or write discourses which are worthy of praise or honour, could not conceivably adopt subjects that are unjust or petty, or concerned with private disputes, but rather those which are great and honourable, of general human concern and for our common good. Secondly, he will select from all the actions of men which bear upon his subject those examples which are most seemly and beneficial; and, familiarizing himself with them through thought and evaluation, he will feel their influence not only in the preparation of the discourse in hand, but also in all the actions of his life. It follows, then, that the power to speak well and think right will go hand in hand with a man who approaches eloquence in a spirit of wisdom and honour.

This is probably the best that can be made of a difficult thesis. The contemplation of lofty ideas can shape character. But he has already had to admit that a really depraved nature cannot be so altered (274); and such characters occupy a good deal of space in the *Antidosis*, both his accuser 'Lysimachus' (his actual challenger's name was Megacleides), and the class of sycophantai to which he frequently refers.[81] But with the main focus on himself and the

---

[81] See esp. 21–4, 129–31, 142, 159–77 (an attack on them full of pathos and personal feeling), 309–19 (where the worst ills afflicting the state are blamed on them). For conflicting

achievement of his school, the well-tried device of example is his most effective weapon. Here, as often, Isocrates' originality is not so much that of conception as of development. The career of his most famous pupil, Timotheus son of Conon, is examined at far greater length (101–39) than previous paradeigmata, and Isocrates imposes a particular interpretation upon his account. Faced with the difficult fact that Timotheus had recently been tried and condemned (356 BC), he has to explain this by the human weakness, arising from envy, which makes men willing to believe slander against successful people, especially those who, like Timotheus, have not gone out of their way to make themselves popular, as a leader should do (129–34, cf. To Nic. 15–16). But his main purpose is to portray Timotheus as the ideal product of his paideia,[82] excelling in reasoning powers—which enabled him to make the most advantageous practical decisions (107–20, esp. 117–20)—but also in moral strength, which cemented friendships, promoted trust, and enhanced the city's reputation (121–8). The section ends with a selection of the advice which Isocrates had given Timotheus, and a tribute (138–9).

Thus Isocrates, the quiet, retiring citizen (144–5) whose influence has nevertheless been great and wholly beneficial, makes his defence through a multifarious medium (10). The reader needs patience and an appetite for listening to self-praise. Yet Antidosis is the most important work for the understanding of Isocrates' educational aims.

12 Panathenaicus[83]

His last discourse, completed shortly before his death in 338 at the age of 98, the Panathenaicus is avowedly about 'the achievements of Athens and the arete of our ancestors' (5), but is of interest mainly for the autobiographical material it contains, especially in his longest **prooemium** (1–40), and the insight it offers into his school and his teaching methods. But one early statement invites imme-

views on the nature and function of sycophantia, see the essays of R. Osborne and F. D. Harvey in P. Cartledge et al. (eds.), Nomos: Essays in Athenian Law, Politics and Society (Cambridge, 1990), 83–122.

[82] Further on the Timotheus-excursus, see E. Alexiou, Ruhm und Ehre: Studien zu Begriffen, Werten und Motivierung bei Isokrates (Heidelberg, 1995), 68–87.

[83] For an appreciation of this discourse, see A. Masaracchia, Isocrate: Retorica e Politica (Rome, 1995), 81–149.

diate investigation: in § 2 he writes of 'a style loaded with many rhetorical arguments, not a few antitheses and parallel clauses, and other figures which give brilliance to oratory and evoke noisy applause from an audience', then he claims to have abandoned it (3) as unsuited to his advancing years. Comparative figures for the relevant features of style give a mixed result.[84] Certainly, the figures for parison and homoeoteleuton are below the average for the corpus, and very much lower than those for the *Panegyricus*; though the two discourses are close in their figures for antithesis and correspondence. But curiosity is raised by the figures for sentence-length: sentences in the *Panathenaicus* are 50 per cent longer than the average, and are the longest in the corpus. Examination of other figures partially explains how this comes about: the figure for amplification far exceeds that of any of the other longer works; but this simple form of verbosity accounts only partly for the very long sentences. When these are examined individually, their structure is found to be flabby and laboured, unlike the best periods noticed in the *Panegyricus*.

In a review of his long life (5–21) he brings together previously mentioned topics—his weak physique excluding him from a public career (9), the international renown which his teaching has brought him (8), adding to these the benefit of good health (7)—and sets these against the relentless hostility of sophists and sycophants, adding politicians to these and painting them in more unfavourable colours than before (11–13). In his old age, Isocrates feels that envy and misrepresentation have denied him the reputation he deserves (15–18, 20–1), and he expresses that feeling antithetically. Now his task is summarily to correct that misrepresentation by listing the categories of people whom he regards as 'educated' (30–2),[85] before proceeding to his subject. This time (i.e. compared with the *Panegyricus*), he uses contrast with Sparta more thoroughly, now that tact is unnecessary. Sparta's successes served selfish ends, those of Athens all Greece (42–8). The Athenian empire was 'milder' than the Spartan, and consequently lasted longer (56); and degrees of severity are compared (62–73). So far there is coherence; but thenceforth it is sacrificed in order to

---

[84] See Usher, *BICS* 20 (1973), 46–7, 58–9.

[85] These are people who conform to his *paideia*—those able to exercise *doxa* in accordance with *kairoi* (the two central Isocratean concepts) (31), and behave as moderate, tolerant citizens. He demonstrates his own tolerance by restating approval of geometry, astrology, and 'eristics' for junior pupils (26–7).

allow him to parade his virtuosity, as he draws freely upon established forms and techniques. The digressive encomium of Agamemnon (74–87) is the first of these showpieces. As the archetypal Hellenic unifier, the Homeric king of Mycenae was an obvious subject for Isocrates' epideixis, personalized and idealized.[86] It has been variously interpreted, the polarities being a protreptic paradeigma for Philip, and Isocrates himself as a kind of literary leader of Greeks against barbarians.[87] After it comparison between Athens and Sparta gives way to unbalanced criticism of Sparta alone for a time (88–118), designed to give maximum force to the pure encomium of Athens which follows.[88] This draws upon earlier and diverse works—*Helen, Areopagiticus, On the Peace*—and these sources give it a hybrid, unfocused character, but with a strong political flavour (123–52). The comparison with Sparta now returns as he shows the consequences of her selfish foreign policy (153–72), before retracing his steps to her prehistory (176), and the establishment of her unique society—useful source-material for historians, but requiring cautious treatment (177–81). It is an important part of the picture of Spartan immorality and oppressiveness (see esp. 185–6), which he contrasts with Athenian justice and Panhellenic ideals (188). Now the account of early Athenian history in which the city emerged triumphant from wars against invaders (193–5), which in the *Panegyricus* (68–72) was simply part of a longer narrative, is here furnished with a moralistic coda (196): in spite of their success, the Athenians retained their true character.[89]

At this point, where political morality has become the main issue, Isocrates takes us briefly but interestingly behind the doors of his school.[90] 'Three or four' of his pupils join him in a 'revision' of the discourse, and he decides to call in a former pupil who had lived under an oligarchy and written approvingly of the Spartans. He answers Isocrates' strictures on them in short measure, but the

---

[86] Isocrates makes Agamemnon the sole persuader of the expedition, ignoring the oath sworn by all the princes on Helen's betrothal to Menelaus, and making it a national war between Greeks and barbarians (79–80).

[87] See Too, *Identity in Isocrates*, 132–40, who reviews opinion since that of Schäfer, advocate of the former view, and herself argues persuasively for the latter view. See also W. Race, '*Panathenaicus* 74–90: The Rhetoric of Isocrates' Digression on Agamemnon', *TAPA* 108 (1978), 175–85.

[88] He admits this in 123.   [89] See Alexiou, *Ruhm und Ehre*, 95–6.

[90] See R. Johnson, *AJP* 80 (1959), 25–36.

master replies to his 'bad arguments' reprovingly and at length. Two characteristics of his teaching are thereby illustrated: his authoritarianism, and his preference for *macrologia* over dialogue as the medium of instruction.[91] The two go together, and the resultant literary legacy is the Isocratean period. In the present discourse, the 'lecture within a lecture' (204–13) provides variety of a kind, and the errant ex-pupil is suitably chastened, but his subdued reply sets the master off on another disquisition (219–28). This is followed by some soul-searching, clearly intended to leave the reader with an impression of a self-critical teacher and author with pupils who had adopted his high literary standards, as the ex-pupil now demonstrates in an even longer speech (235–63). After that the *Panathenaicus* ends quite abruptly after a reference to the illness that had prevented its earlier completion (267–8). Isocrates has intimated his personal aims, hopes, and fears[92] as he takes his leave, with the magisterial advice to his readers to heed the words of those with experience and understanding.

ISOCRATES: SUMMARY

In his career as a teacher or sophist, Isocrates contributed to the development of rhetoric rather than oratory, and in certain limited though lasting ways. In the mainstream of his writings, existing literary genres were transformed. The traditional Funeral Oration, with its rigidly standardized topoi, and its immediate audience of bereaved and fearful citizens whose morale had to be maintained, perhaps for a continued conflict,[93] was the inspiration for *Panegyricus*, *On the Peace*, and *Areopagiticus*. But with a wider audience, an educational and political programme, and, most of all, a special style of writing in mind, Isocrates redefined epideictic literature, broadening its subject-matter and treating it on an unprecedented scale. Thus when earlier models are found—the fifth-century *Athenaion Politeia* for *Areopagiticus*, and the hortatory speeches of Thucydides for *Archidamus*—the Isocratean discourse is seen to range far more

---

[91] This seems to align him broadly with the sophistic tradition, at least as represented by Protagoras in Plato's dialogue, in which the sophist begins with a long speech (320c–328d) and later objects to participating in a question-and-answer sequence (334c–335d; cf. *Gorgias* 449b–c). Isocrates shares the sophistic love of display and monopolizing the stage.

[92] 271: δηλῶσαι βουλόμενος τὰ περὶ ἐμὲ γεγενημένα. . .

[93] Thuc. 2. 44. 3, 45. 1.

widely, embracing moral and philosophical ideas within a more complex structure. This transformation is seen too in *Plataicus*, where a historical background is provided for discussion of an ever-topical moral question, that of 'might is right'. There is also a range of creativity: *Euagoras*, with its emphasis on the *arete* of its subject, sets the pattern for future biography, whereas *To Philip*, in spite of its length, contains much material recycled from *Panegyricus* and presents it in a loosely argued form.

The protreptic discourses *To Nicocles* and *Nicocles* show Isocrates' versatility. The treatment under short 'heads' and their relatively simple style reflect their practical purpose; but the writing is still polished, and there is nothing contemporary to compare with them. But if they serve to prove Isocrates a master of two extreme forms of style, it is in the more complex form—the periodic—that his originality and influence are to be seen at their strongest.

In the best Isocratean periods organic topical unity is achieved within a structure containing many phrases or clauses, which may be balanced precisely as to their length, in pairs or more complex combinations, with the completion of the sense at or near the end. Additional features are the avoidance of hiatus (the clashing of final and initial vowels) and the use of rhythms.[94] No two Isocratean periods are alike, but the opening period of the *Panegyricus* contains most of the ingredients described above. Here the topic is the superiority of mental to physical endeavour in promoting the common good. The contrast is drawn so that the final argument and the final word ('intelligence' *dianoias*) goes to the preferred object:

I have often found it amazing that those who organized the first national festivals and established the athletic games should have thought physical success worthy of such great rewards, whereas to those who have laboured in private for the public good, and have trained their own minds so as to be able to help others besides themselves, they accord no mark of distinction, when it was to these men that they ought reasonably to have paid

---

[94] The subject of Prose Rhythm has always been, and still is, very controversial. Dionysius of Halicarnassus and other critics take its use for granted, but the extent of that use, the metrical rules governing it, and especially the question of whether or not it is confined to concluding words (forming *clausulae*) are matters of opinion. My own view is that prose rhythm was an instrument of balance, which explains Dionysius' comparison of its use with that of poetry (*Isoc.* 2): on this view it would serve to reinforce *parison* (clauses of equal length with words in corresponding positions) and *paromoion* (assonance or rhyme between clauses). Hence prose rhythm can occur wherever the writing is aiming at clausal balance. For an example of prose rhythm in operation, see Usher *GO* v. 26–8.

greater regard: for if all athletes should double their physical strength, the rest of us would gain nothing thereby; but if a single man should conceive a good idea, there would be benefit for all who wished to share his intelligence.

Study of the Greek text is, of course, necessary for a full understanding of the niceties of the style, but the balance and the thematic unity of the period are clear. The influence of this style was great. Among later Greek prose writers must be numbered Polybius and Dionysius himself, in his *Antiquitates Romanae*. But most conspicuous among his debtors was Cicero, who not only followed Isocrates in complexity but added to his practice in the matter of amplification, as seen in the following period (*Pro Archia Poeta* 3):

It may be a matter for surprise in some quarters that in an enquiry dealing with statute law, in a public trial held before a specially selected praetor of the Roman people, and a jury of high dignity, in the presence of a crowded audience of citizens, my speech should be made in a style out of keeping not merely with the conventions of the bar, but also with forensic language; but I beg for your indulgence, an indulgence which will, I trust, cause you no inconvenience, and which is so peculiarly applicable to the nature of my client's case; and I would ask you to allow me, speaking as I am on behalf of a distinguished poet and consummate scholar, before a cultivated audience, and the praetor whom we see occupying the tribunal, to enlarge somewhat upon enlightened and cultivated pursuits, and, in keeping with the character of one whose studious seclusion has made him a stranger to the anxious perils of the courts, to employ what is perhaps a novel and unconventional line of defence.

Cicero has taken to Isocratean *macrologia* wholeheartedly here and elsewhere. The historical progress of the period as a feature of prose is beyond my scope, but the characteristics of 'writing at length' which Isocrates established constitute his most lasting legacy.[95]

[95] On Isocrates and Cicero, see E. Laughton, 'Cicero and the Greek Orators', *AJP* 82 (1961), 27–52 (indicating the differences between the two); also, in general, H. Hubbell, *The Influence of Isocrates on Cicero, Dionysius and Aristides* (New Haven, 1913); S. E. Smethurst, 'Cicero and Isocrates', *TAPA* 84 (1953), 262–320. Further, on the historical style of Dionysius and its Isocratean connections see C. Maetzke, *De Dion. Hal. Isocratis Imitatore* (Breslau, 1906); S. Usher, 'The Style of Dionysius of Halicarnassus in the *Antiquitates Romanae*', *ANRW* ii. 30. 1 (1982), 817–38, esp. 822, 828–32.

10

LYCURGUS

The most august of the Attic orators, scion of a priestly family which claimed descent from Erechtheus, Lycurgus was Demosthenes' senior by a few years, and shared his hostility to the ambitions of Philip II. He came into individual prominence after the defeat at Chaeronea, as he assumed charge of Athenian finances for the exceptional period of twelve years (338–326); and the unusually full account of his work in the pseudo-Plutarchian *Life* shows how charge of the treasury, earned through his reputation for probity, gave him wide powers to legislate. It is perhaps to this reputation that he owed his administrative success. Aided by continuity, he was able, among other measures, to provide 400 triremes for the fleet and carry out extensive building projects in the city. Money for this seems to have come, in part, from private subscription: a source on which the state had always drawn, but never to greater effect than under the administration of Lycurgus,[1] surely because wealthy citizens believed that he would put it to good use. Another source of revenue, though probably not the greatest,[2] was successful prosecution leading to confiscations, and this introduces the side of Lycurgus' career that concerns the present discussion. He equipped himself as an orator by attending the school of Isocrates, and his training will have enabled him to present his policies persuasively to the Assembly. But all his extant oratory is forensic and most of the speeches are prosecutions which, if successful, would have led to confiscation of property. This would have happened in the case of the general Lysicles, prosecuted after Chaeronea (Fr. 10),

---

[1] His biographer mentions (*Vit. X Or.* 841d) one instance of 250 talents 'entrusted to him' on deposit by private citizens', which would have helped him to double the annual revenue from 600 to 1,200 talents (842f). The phrase τῶν χρημάτων εὗρε πόρους (Hyperid. Fr. 23) adds the idea of his ability to find unusual sources of revenue.

[2] See C. Mossé (trans. J. Stewart), *Athens in Decline 404–86 BC* (London, 1973), 82: 'But it was above all the activity of the port which must have provided Athens with its greatest resources.'

and no doubt in others where the circumstances are less clear. In the only speech of Lycurgus which survives complete, *Against Leocrates*, the prosecutor is able to exploit his prestige as he magnifies the injustice of the defendant's action, arguing that the case affects 'the integrity of our fatherland' (7).[3] Leocrates' crime had been to remove his entire household from Athens to Rhodes immediately after the news of defeat at Chaeronea. The rhetorical problem facing Lycurgus appears to be the non-existence at the time of his flight of any law forbidding it.[4] To this is added lapse of time. Leocrates' sojourn abroad had lasted almost eight years, and his trial took place a few months before that of Ctesiphon, in 330.[5] Then the general question may be asked: what public service was done through the pursuit of such a defendant, whose offence had done no palpable harm to the city? The answer is to be found in the persona of the orator and the whole tone of his speech.

The commonplace of the public-spirited prosecutor appears in its fuller form,[6] as it is an essential part of the speaker's self-characterization. The keynote of the **prooemium** (1–15) is the pursuit of strict justice, but establishment of a legal basis for the charge is replaced by hyperbole: the crime is so terrible that no adequate indictment or punishment can be devised (8), yet some must be found so that future generations may be deterred from repeating it (10). But so far the impression is one of a respected politician relying on his *auctoritas* to give a new lease of life to hackneyed topoi, perhaps too audaciously in the case of one topos—the repudiation of digression (11–12)—in view of much of the content of the speech.

The initial account of the essential facts is, however, economical enough (16–27), and shows how Leocrates not only went to Rhodes but gave false news of the plight of his city (18). Taking up residence in Megara, he next compounded his treason by flouting

---

[3] ὑπὲρ ὅλης τῆς πατρίδος. See also 14, 18–19. A. Petrie's edition (*Lycurgus: The Speech Against Leocrates* (Cambridge, 1922)) is still valuable.

[4] This may be deduced from the fact that Lycurgus does not cite any relevant law (the decree at § 37 appears to concern the mobilization of personnel for the city's defence); and it may be inferred from his plea to the jury to be 'not merely jurors, but lawmakers' (9).

[5] Aeschin. 3 *Ag. Ctes.* 252.

[6] 5–6: 'I began these proceedings not out of private enmity or litigiousness, but because I thought it shameful to allow this man to barge into the market-place and join the public sacrifices, when he had brought such disgrace on our country and upon you all.' Cf. Lys. 31 *Ag. Philon* 2 for the short form of the topos.

Athenian laws on the export of corn (26–7); but the orator at the same time draws attention to religious transgressions—the removal of the sacred family images and the quitting of Athena's city (26). The usual inference is drawn, though rather verbosely, from Leocrates' refusal to hand over his slaves for torture (28–35), and his departure is replayed with enhanced rhetorical ornament in a **narrative** charged with emotion.[7] This quality is scarcely matched by other Attic orators, but is even heightened in the following narrative (39–41):

When tidings of the defeat and the resulting slaughter had reached the people, and the city was in a state of anxious excitement at what had happened, hopes of survival rested upon the men who were fifty years of age or over. Free women could be seen crouching terrified in doorways, asking of passers-by whether their husbands, fathers, or brothers were alive—a spectacle unworthy of the city and themselves. The men, their strength gone in their advancing years, excused by law from taking the field, could then be seen throughout the city, destitute upon the road that leads from old age to death, with their cloaks girded up double around them. Many terrible things were happening to the city, and every citizen had suffered the extremes of misfortune; but the sight which would most surely have affected the onlooker and moved him to tears over the sorrows of Athens was to see the people vote that slaves should be freed, that aliens should become Athenians, and that the disfranchised should regain their rights—and all that in a nation which had formerly boasted that it was indigenous and free.

Here was a recurrent scene which later historians found occasion to describe,[8] and Lycurgus provides the best surviving model, owing little to previous narratives in its combination of stressed action, dealing with the plight of the weak and helpless, and judgement of its implications (here political).

---

[7] 38: 'To such a point did he carry his treason, that, so far as his decision went, the temples were abandoned, the posts on the walls were unmanned, and the town and city were abandoned. And yet in those days, who would not have pitied the city, even though he were not a citizen . . . Surely there was no one who hated the people of Athens so much that he could endure to see himself unenrolled in the army?'

[8] A close parallel is to be found in Livy 22. 7. 7 (after the Battle of Lake Trasimene): *Romae ad primum nuntium cladis eius cum ingenti terrore ac tumultu concursus in forum populi est factus. Matronae vagae per vias, quae repens clades allata quaeve fortuna exercitus esset, obvios percontantur . . . Postero ac deinceps aliquot dies ad portas maior prope mulierum quam virorum multitudo stetit, aut suorum aliquem aut nuntios de iis opperiens; circumfundebantur obviis sciscitantes neque avelli, utique ab notis, priusquam ordine omnia inquisissent, poterant.* See also Sallust, *Cat.* 31.

After a brief excursion into epideictic topoi as he praises the fallen at Chaeronea,[9] he returns to the attack, replacing narrative with argument based mainly on examples and precedents, and relying on the veneration which the jury would feel for his subjects—the Areopagus and the first Athenian legislators. But the example of the condemnation of Autolycus (see also Fr. 9) may not be directly comparable with the case of Leocrates, since Autolycus was an Areopagite who left Athens with his family at the time of the Battle of Chaeronea. Again, the severe principle attributed to Dracon, that the death penalty should be exacted without distinction between greater and lesser offences (65), is used by Lycurgus to support the argument that Leocrates deserved punishment even if no law was in place when he committed his offence. The ancient authorities somehow connoted a timeless sanction, confirmed by the prestige of the speaker himself, who is ruthless in his exploitation of it, anticipating an argument which Leocrates' supporters are unlikely to have used,[10] and committing a number of historical errors in his account,[11] even basing an otherwise effective a fortiori argument on one (71).[12]

Grand old patriotic themes and ancient oaths, delivered in a dignified style, continue to serve in place of argument based on evidence. A series of stories, all with a religious element and illustrating justice (the fate of Callistratus, 93) and self-sacrifice (95–100) provide the material for another, comprehensive a fortiori argument. But the use of myth in argument has hitherto been characteristic of epideictic rather than forensic oratory; and Lycurgus now introduces a feature that adds literary variety, which no doubt also had an impact in actual performance: the extensive quotation of poetry. The poet is his ultimate authority, the recognized teacher and moral guide for thinking men,[13] but also a potent co-

[9] 46–51. Dobson (GO 276, 279) correctly notes the influence of Isocrates, and might have referred specifically to 4 Paneg. 75–7 and 92, which Lycurgus may have had in mind when he wrote 49 νικῶντες ἀπέθανον.

[10] 68–74: comparison of Leocrates' withdrawal with the mass evacuation of the Athenians to Salamis before the battle in 480.

[11] See C. Hignett, Xerxes' Invasion of Greece (Oxford, 1963), 413–14: 'the tainted evidence of the orator Lycourgos'—namely the imputation that the Aeginetans intended to desert, and the 'howler' of substituting the name of Eteonicus for that of Eurybiades.

[12] Another case of false identity: the mediator Alexander of Macedon takes the place of Lycidas (or Cyrsilus) as the man who was stoned to death merely for proposing that Persian peace-terms be heard.

[13] For the traditional view of the poet as teacher, see Aristoph. Frogs 1009–10, 1054–6, quoted by R. M. Harriott, Poetry and Criticism before Plato (London, 1969), 105, at the beginning of a valuable chapter entitled 'The Poet and his Audience'.

persuader. Euripides (55 lines from his *Erechtheus*) is invoked to
dilate upon the glory of the sacrifice of a princess for her country;
Homer, more briefly, affirms that to die in battle for one's country
is no disgrace (*Il.* 15. 494–9); and Tyrtaeus expounds similar sentiments in 32 lines, followed by two famous inscriptions by
Simonides. A practice begun by Aeschines to display his histrionic
skills has become in Lycurgus a source of rhetorical material, protreptic and emotional rather than strictly argumentative.

Exemplary instances of punishment of traitors (110–23) and aspi-
rants to tyranny (124–7) maintain the diversion from Leocrates' special circumstances, but Lycurgus will still argue vehemently that he
deserves death more than they (131–4). He piles on the rhetorical
devices towards the end, including an original twist (141) when he
says that the jury should be accompanied by their wives and children
in cases of treason (instead of the defendant's traditional family
parade). He makes the most of the outrage of Leocrates the runaway
returning to share in the social and religious life of the city he has
betrayed (141–3), and ends with the usual warning that acquittal
would be tantamount to condonation, but not before a hypophora
(144) in the usual place (cf. Andoc. 1 *Myst.* 148) and a prosopopoiia
closely modelled on Lysias 12 *Ag. Eratos.* 99. Read in isolation, the
speech seems to be a rich and triumphant marriage of epideictic and
forensic rhetoric, combining pathos and vividness in its narratives;
but its debt to earlier oratory in both genres is always apparent, and
it falls short of the best of those models in structural compactness.

HYPERIDES

The ancient critics compare Hyperides with the best models of oratorical style, Lysias and Demosthenes. In the evolutionary process
conceived by Dionysius of Halicarnassus, Hyperides is one of the
'perfecters' (*teleiotai*),[14] a status which imposes limits on originality;
but to the author of *On Sublimity*, whose critique of Hyperides
is the best we have, he 'speaks with more voices'[15] than
Demosthenes, replicating all that master's good qualities except his
word-arrangement. While he comes second in every accomplishment, like a pentathlete, his versatility enables him to span the

---

[14] *Isaeus* 20; *Din.* 1.   [15] 34. 1: πολυφωνότερος.

whole emotional scale—to be sharply witty—both urbane and sarcastic[16]—and equally able to excite pity and narrate mythological
subjects. This description seems to identify him as perhaps the most
literary of the Attic orators, a quality which would account for the
assumption of later critics that his speeches were more widely read
and enjoyed than those of, say, Antiphon and Andocides, or even
Isaeus, the mentor of Demosthenes. The more unfortunate, therefore, and also the more surprising, is the exiguousness of the surviving corpus. None of the extant six speeches has come down to
us complete or unmutilated, and even necessary extensive restoration has left them in a tattered and fragmentary state.

Hyperides was about six years older than Demosthenes, and died
at the hands of Antipater's executioners within a few months of
him in 322. Early evidence of political ambition is to be found in
his prosecution of the prominent politician Aristophon in 362 (4
Eux. 28); and other prosecutions followed.[17] The probability that
none of these early prosecutions was successful may partly explain
his slow progress in politics. However that may be, in 343 he
arraigned Philocrates, who was condemned to death and withdrew
into exile (Dem. 19 Leg. 116; Aeschin. 2 Leg. 6; Hyperid. 4 Eux.
29–30). This not only announced the arrival of Hyperides as an
effective politician, but also aligned him with Demosthenes,
Lycurgus, and others who advocated active opposition to
Macedonian expansion. He was especially active in the aftermath
of the Battle of Chaeronea, proposing emergency measures for the
defence of the city (Vit. X Or. 849a), but only reappears in a purely
political role some thirteen years later as prosecutor of his former
ally Demosthenes in the scandal of the Harpalus affair (q.v. under
Dinarchus, below). The fragmentary surviving court speeches all
belong to this period (338–24).

1 For Lycophron

After five fragments containing conventional pleas and objections,
Hyperides mounts a bold attack on the prosecutor Ariston (2),

[16] id. 34. 2. Cicero (De Or. 33. 7. 28, Orator 31. 110), followed by Quintilian (10. 1. 77),
attributes acumen to Hyperides.

[17] (1) That of Autocles, who had been placed in command of an aborted expedition to
support a revolt against the Thracian king Cotys (362/1). See Dem. 23. Ag. Aristoc. 104. (2)
That of Diopeithes, who was a trierarch in 349/8, and was active in the Chersonese, leading a party of cleruchs, in 343/2.

characterizing him as a corrupt litigant (though not calling him a sycophantes), detailing his methods of extortion by using many verbs in the historic present tense with asyndeton. If the fragment is correctly placed here (by Blass), this is a remarkable pre-emptive assault. No less effective in arguing the absurdity of the charge of adultery against his client is his method of presenting it. His opponent, who was the orator Lycurgus, has alleged that Lycophron had actually approached his lover during her marriage ceremony, trying to persuade her to refuse her husband and 'keep herself' for him (3).[18] Now this woman was a sister of two famous wrestlers, Dioxippus and Euphraeus, both of whom attended the ceremony. Scarcely could Hyperides have had such a compelling probability-argument, and he makes the most of it (6).[19] But this is followed by a succession of commonplaces about the advantages enjoyed by prosecutors, leading to specific complaints about the methods and procedure of the prosecutor. For his defence he relies on straightforward pistis ek biou, listing his service as a knight and proclaiming his *apragmosyne* in other respects. Thus there is little else that is distinctive in the speech. The same judgement applies to the surviving fragment of a second speech for Lycophron.

2 *Against Philippides*

The extant concluding section of this graphe paranomon has a more political flavour, and an approximate date around the time of the death of Philip of Macedon (336). Philippides had proposed crowning the presiding officers (*proedroi*) for enabling the granting of honours to certain leading Macedonians for unspecified services to the Athenian people. By opposing this in court Hyperides showed that a defiant mood still resided in the minds of some, and his appearance as prosecutor in this case may have led some later sources, rightly or wrongly, to include his name among those whose surrender Alexander demanded a short time later (in 335).[20]

[18] διαφυλάξει αὐτήν.

[19] 'Was I so utterly insane that with so many people in attendance at the procession, including Dioxippus and his fellow-wrestler Euphraeus, both acknowledged to be the strongest men in Greece, I would not have shrunk from saying such things about a free woman in the hearing of everyone and not be afraid of being strangled on the spot?'

[20] Plutarch's list of only eight names (*Dem.* 23. 4) does not include Hyperides, who is however, named by Arrian (*Anab.* 1. 10. 4). For discussion of the list, see Sealey *DT* 203–4 L. Braccesi, 'A proposito d' una notizia su Iperide', *Riv. Fil.* 95 (1967), 157–62 (arguing for Hyperides' exclusion).

The attack on Philippides contains invective which is familiar from readings of other oratory directed against perceived pro-Macedonian politicians, though here the approach is more allusive, with a cryptic mention of 'one person who will be immortal' (Philip?), and only a passing reference to the Thirty (8). In a more lively vein, Philippides' riotous character is portrayed with the colourful word *kordakizon* ('dancing the *kordax*'), recalling the revelries (*kordakismous*) which, according to Demosthenes (2 *Olynth. II* 18), enervated the Macedonian court. Elsewhere, too, some of the rhetoric is animated: the hypophora in 10 leads nicely to some forceful argument dismissing a plea by the defendant's supporters and urging the opposite course.[21] The abrupt end of the speech, said to be due to a shortage of time (13), contains a conventional signing-off formula.

3 *Against Athenogenes*

A more substantial fragment, enough has been preserved of this speech to raise hopes that it will reveal some of Hyperides' individual qualities, especially his narrative technique. In fact, we join the speech in the middle of a narrative. The story is one of infatuation, gullibility, and consequent deceit. The accuser Epicrates, in order to possess one of the two sons of Midas, a slave who ran one of the perfumery businesses owned by Athenogenes, was persuaded to buy all three. But he found that he had also purchased their debts, and Athenogenes tricked him further into accepting the business itself, which was subsequently found to be in debt by five talents. Epicrates has behaved foolishly, and Hyperides must salvage some sympathy for him. A key figure to highlight in this is Antigone, the *hetaira* whose persuasive services Athenogenes has

---

[21] 11: 'And if anyone comes forward with the plea that he has twice been convicted for illegal proposals and that therefore you should acquit him, do the very opposite, for two reasons: firstly, because it is merely a piece of good luck, when a man is known to have proposed illegal measures, that you should catch him coming up for trial on the third occasion; and you should not spare him as if he were a good man, but get rid of him as soon as possible, since he has twice given proof of his character. Secondly, compare the case of false witness. You have excused people who have been twice convicted of this from giving evidence a third time, even of events at which they have been present.' The law offers some protection to men with previous convictions by not obliging them to testify in cases in which they are not the principals; but Philippides has chosen to risk the severe penalty for a three-time offender by initiating the present illegal proposal.

enlisted. She has acted out her role to perfection,[22] so his entrapment should not cause surprise.[23] Athenogenes, too, is a professional in the arts of deceit, 'a speechwriter, a trafficker, and most
significantly, an Egyptian' (3).[24] His plausibility is reinforced by live
speech (5), as he stresses the advantages of the arrangement he proposes, and lies blatantly about the debts.[25] At this point the speaker
pauses to explain Athenogenes' plan (7), and then vivid detail of the
completion of the transaction serves to complete the portrayal of
the arch-deceiver and his victim (8):

When I accepted his proposals he immediately took a document from his
lap and began reading the contents, which were the text of an agreement
with me. I listened to it being read, but my attention was concentrated on
completing the business I had come for. He sealed the agreement straight
away in the same house, so that no one with my interest in mind should
hear the contents.

The subsequent scene where Eucrates confronts Athenogenes also
has vivid elements, as a crowd gathers and joins in the obloquy, giving the Egyptian a 'shredding' (katatemnonton—a rare, probably
colloquial use of the word), thereby adding their testimony rather
as bystanders have done in Lysias 3 *Ag. Sim.* 16, and, less directly,
in Demosthenes 54 *Ag. Conon* 9. The attack on Athenogenes and
his deceptions is then maintained through apostrophe (13 ff.).
Comparative argument figures largely in this (15–16), but when he
comes to deal with the text of laws the reasoning becomes somewhat obscure and he returns shortly to direct recrimination
through apostrophic questions (18–19), and thence to more narrative describing further deception by Athenogenes, though with no
chronological reference-point (23–4). In Hyperides' hands the classical division of speeches seems finally to have been abandoned, as
he switches from narrative to proof and back again. But the final
attack on Athenogenes for his 'desertion of Athens' after
Chaeronea (29–35) is a conventional negative pistis ek biou.

---

[22] 2: 'Her manner when she said this could not have been more sincere . . . That is how
love, it seems, changes a man's nature, when it takes a woman as its helpmate.'

[23] 3: 'Perhaps there is nothing surprising, gentlemen of the jury, that I should have been
taken in like this by Antigone, a woman who was, I am told, the most talented prostitute of
her time, who has continued in her trade of procuress . . . '

[24] Cf. Dem. 35 *Ag. Lacr.* 1–3 (denigration of Phaselites).

[25] 6: ' "It is a tiny amount, and greatly exceeded by the stocks in the shop—sweet oil,
scent-boxes and myrrh"; and he mentioned other things.'

4 *For Euxenippus*

This short but complete speech is a synegoria, a fact which has mixed consequences. It gives little further illustration of Hyperides' narrative ability, since the first speaker (the defendant) has related most of the facts. On the other hand, it allows him to expatiate on certain legal and political subjects, and it is hard to avoid the idea that he used this licence freely in this speech with a view to publication and the promotion of his career.

The circumstances from which the prosecution arose are given only sketchily in the speech (14–17).[26] The first and main subject on which Hyperides focuses is legal procedure. Euxenippus had been prosecuted through an impeachment (*eisangelia*), a procedure intended for the serious public crimes which he lists (1), making the speech an important source, though one requiring careful assessment.[27] Hyperides has to argue that Euxenippus is being prosecuted because of his alleged Macedonian sympathies, and that the charge of bribery has been concocted as part of a co-ordinated political attack on him. His task is probably complicated by the fact that the increasing use, or abuse, of eisangelia was a reaction to the popular perception that corruption among politicians was becoming commoner at this time.

Hence his insistence on preserving existing practice (4–6), in a passage which contains a forceful asyndetic 'situation-result' sequence (6):

Someone commits a religious offence: there are public prosecutions before the King-Archon. Someone maltreats his parents: the Archon presides over his case. Someone proposes illegal measures in the city: there is the Board of the Thesmothetai. He does something requiring summary arrest: you have the authority of the Eleven.

---

[26] It arose from the restoration of Oropus and its surrounding land to the Athenians by Philip II in 338. After the division of that land into five portions, each allocated to two of the ten Athenian tribes, the claim was made that one portion was sacred to the god Amphiaraus. In order to settle the matter, it was decided that Euxenippus and two other citizens should sleep in the god's temple at Oropus. His communion with the god through a dream produced a ruling which allowed the two tribes to occupy the land. But this was disputed by a certain Polyeuctus, who became Euxenippus' prosecutor when he accused him of being bribed to report his dream.

[27] See M. H. Hansen, *Eisangelia* (Odense, 1975); P. J. Rhodes, 'Ἐισαγγελία in Athens', *JHS* 89 (1979), 103–14'; reply by Hansen: *JHS* 90 (1980), 89–95 (91–2 on the present speech).

Not an original device,[28] but it is effectively used here. He goes on to argue that eisangelia was intended for use against men who wielded real power to injure the state, and these included any politician (*rhetor*, 8): but Euxenippus is a private citizen (*idiotes*), and one advanced in years (13), and the prosecutor Polyeuctus has sought further advantage by trying to deny him the right to have a synegoros,[29] while calling for them in his own cases (11–13). Hyperides favours dilemmaton in his analysis of the main events (15, 17), breaking up the **narrative**. Polyeuctus' concern with revenge and his subjective indifference to factual truth is well summarized in a stark apostrophe (18): 'So if you had been acquitted at your trial, Euxenippus would not have lied about the god: because you happen to be convicted, must he be ruined?'

Switching abruptly to a more direct consideration of the pro-Macedonian charge, he deals with what may be assumed to be a piece of *eikos*-argument used by the opposition, the dedication of a cup to the statue of the goddess Hygieia by Olympias, the mother of Alexander, which Euxenippus was alleged to have allowed in some official capacity (19). Here Hyperides uses two very different arguments. Firstly, he criticizes Polyeuctus for choosing a minor example, instead of some action that was really harmful to Athens (20–1). He argues that it is the real quislings who are responsible for these actions, and their names are known to every schoolboy (22).[30] The second argument (23–6) is more subtle and concerned with diplomacy: Olympias' dedication at Athens should not be deplored but used to counter her complaint of an Athenian dedication at the shrine of Zeus at Dodona, in Molossian land under her rule.

The theme of Polyeuctus' misdirected prosecuting zeal is resumed (27 cf. 1–4), and contrasted by an autobiographical section, in which Hyperides maps his own career in the courts. The passage (28–30) certainly reads like a personal statement made for purposes unconnected with the trial, but designed to publicize a favourable image of himself as a fair litigant,[31] just as the argument

[28] The three examples in Dem. 18 *Cor.* (117, 198, 274) may, of course, be later than the present one, but Denniston (*GPS* 118–19) lists other examples, though most of these are not exact parallels.

[29] It must be assumed that this denial was in some way related to eisangelia, i.e. that precedent existed for this denial under that procedure.

[30] ἴσασι καὶ τὰ παιδία τὰ ἐκ τῶν διδασκαλείων.

[31] He claims that, unlike Polyeuctus, he has never prosecuted a private citizen, only public figures like Aristophon, Diopeithes, and Philocrates. These were, he would have said, proper *eisangeliai*.

in 23–6 represents him as a shrewd politician. This image is maintained as he approvingly cites examples of trials in which the juries
have upheld the rights of individuals even when the state stood to
gain financially by their conviction (33–5). Such fairness is actually
profitable to the city in the longer term, and the 'good citizen' who
realized this thinks like a statesman (37),[32] and his identity is easy to
guess. The **epilogue**, the only clearly defined section (38–41), is a
textbook assembly of conventional topics, summarizing and finally
dismissing the prosecutor's main arguments. It ends, however, with
an unusual apostrophe to the defendant.

6 *Funeral Speech*

The pervading impersonality, conformity to a fixed set of topics,
and epideictic style which characterized earlier epitaphioi will be
noted and examined in the next chapter. Hyperides' oration
deserves separate treatment because it is starkly different from
them. Here those who died in the early encounters of the Lamian
War, the final stand for Greek freedom against the successors of
Alexander (322 BC), are commemorated. The circumstances of the
war, in particular those of recruitment and leadership, were such as
to have a potential influence on the form of that commemoration,
and are to be weighed against the orator's own creative inclinations
and possible literary influences on him.

    The leader of the Greek army was Leosthenes. He was an
Athenian who had seen service before his election as strategos for
324/3 and 323/2. But the army which he led consisted largely of
mercenaries and included some who had served in Asia under
Alexander. He emerges as a larger-than-life figure, partly of his
own and partly of a bygone age, an erstwhile *condottière* acting on
his own initiative in a patriotic cause, assembling a force in the
Peloponnese and then travelling to Central Greece to recruit more
men before confronting Antipater and besieging him at Lamia
(323–2). Thus most of the early Greek successes in this ultimately
doomed campaign were due to the energy, leadership, and military

---

[32] 37: 'The good citizen is not the man to make some small additions to the public funds
in ways which cause an ultimate loss, not one who, by dishonestly producing an instant
profit, cuts off the city's lawful source of revenue. On the contrary, he is the man who is
concerned with keeping what will be profitable to the city in the future, to preserve harmony among the citizens, and safeguard your reputation.'

arete of Leosthenes. All this would have been difficult for Hyperides to suppress, and it must qualify any judgement made of the part accorded him in the speech; yet Hyperides could have conformed with past models, but chose to write a new kind of Funeral Speech. It is constructed around its hero.[33] He is first mentioned in the second line, and in the passage (4–8) that makes way for a detailed description on his career, a poetic simile of the City and the Sun (5) appears to be leading to generalized topics, but Hyperides repudiates these, combining hypophora with aporia in an unusual way (6–8).[34] They must give precedence to the general, 'for that is only fair' (9). Leosthenes is credited with a Panhellenic vision,[35] and the only **narrative** in the speech is devoted to his measures and campaigns (11–13). Later (35), the image of Leosthenes being greeted in the underworld by heroes of the mythical and historical past, who could not match his exploits (36–9), is an inventive combination of prosopopoiia and comparative argument. But invention extends beyond the personality of Leosthenes. Victories are won through the courage of the men in the ranks of battle (15), and Hyperides invests the two major encounters with Panhellenic symbolism, though with some loss of historicity.[36] He also specifies the causes for which they fought: freedom against tyranny, the rule of law against the arbitrary whim of the despot (20, 24), and the restoration of old religious practices in place of the worship of individuals—a curious choice in a speech with a central hero, but one giving the opportunity for effective rhetoric (21): 'Where reverence for the gods has been destroyed by Macedonian insolence, what fate must we expect for the rules governing conduct towards

---

[33] N. Loraux, *The Invention of Athens: The Funeral Oration in the Classical City*, trans. A. Sheridan (Harvard and London, 1986), 111–12: 'The figure of Leosthenes dominates the very structure of the epitaphios; each new passage begins with the great man's name.'

[34] 'At what point, then, shall I begin my story? What shall I mention first? Shall I trace the ancestry of each? To do so would, I think, be foolish . . . Am I then to touch on their education, and, as other speakers often do, remind you how as children they were reared and trained in strict discipline . . .'

[35] 10: 'He saw the whole of Greece demoralized . . . he realized that our city stood in need of a commander, and Greece herself of a city able to assume the leadership, and he gave himself to his country and the city to the Greeks, to achieve freedom.'

[36] The first battle was in Boeotian territory against Boeotians, not Antipater, whereas Hyperides represents it as revenge for the destruction of Thebes, the prime example of Macedonian tyranny; but that city was some way from the site of the battle, which took place near Plataea (Diod. Sic. 18. 9. 5; 11. 3–5). The second battle led only to the siege of Lamia, some way from the meeting-place of the Amphictyonic Council, and hence weakening the Panhellenic symbolism.

men?' Several other passages mark this as an epitaphios of rare inspiration. The fallen have not 'died' (27): 'it is not right (*themiton*) to say of men who have left this life in a noble cause, that they have died—they will join the ranks of the immortals . . . (28) Should we not say that they have been born anew, a nobler birth than the first?' They will always be remembered with gratitude by all future ages, whether in pure pleasure at their achievement or for the practical good they have done (34). The most remarkable epitaphios in Greek literature maintains its invention to the end with a balance between the individual nature of grief and collective patriotic sentiment (41), and another allusion to the defence of Greek religion by the fallen (43).

5 *Against Demosthenes*

Hyperides turned against his old ally over the Harpalus affair (see Dinarchus, below), but both men faced exile and death within eighteen months.[37] The speech is fragmentary, but it contains a forthright acerbity lacking in the other speeches. Apostrophe is used almost throughout; there is sarcasm (12) and some lively word-order, especially near the beginning. But otherwise there is nothing very striking about the language, and little light cast upon the details of the case. As in the other fragments, it seems that no clear division of the speech can be discerned, and virtual abandonment of conventional division now appears to have taken place irreversibly.

Conventionality seems to be even more remote from what became Hyperides' most celebrated case, his defence of the prostitute Phryne. That no text of his speech survives is hardly surprising, since the highpoint of the trial was visual, not oral.[38] Hyperides exposed his client's nakedness to the jury, and her salient features convinced them of her innocence of the charge of impiety. Setting aside the questionable logic of Hyperides' 'proof' and the jury's reported verdict, it is worthwhile to try to define the nature of such evidence. It is certainly direct rather than rhetorical and hence

---

[37] The trials took place in March 323 at the earliest (so E. Badian, 'Harpalus', *JHS* 81 (1961), 43). Plutarch *Dem.* 28.1 places Demosthenes' death in Pyanepsion (Oct./Nov.) 322; *Vit. X Or.* 849b gives the ninth day of the same month for Hyperides' death in one of his versions.

[38] *aspectus sine voce* (Quint. 2. 15. 9).

qualifies as atechnos not entechnos pistis. But it also involves emotional appeal rather than verbal testimony, and thence arises the flaw of ambiguous probability: different emotions are aroused in the spectators. At all events, no parallel Greek example of visual persuasion is recorded.[39]

Although brilliant efforts have been made to produce continuous texts of Hyperides' surviving oratory from disappointing fragments,[40] the means of assessing the validity of ancient criticism of it remain elusive; and the fact that one of the greatest of the critics compares him, in some respects favourably, with Demosthenes ([Longinus] *Subl.* 34. 1–3), adds both to our frustration and to our sense of loss.

APOLLODORUS

In seven speeches preserved in the Demosthenic Corpus the speaker is Apollodorus, son of Pasion the banker. He is the prosecutor in 45, 46 *Against Stephanus I, II*, 49 *Against Timotheus*, 50 *Against Polycles*, 53 *Against Nicostratus*, and 59 *Against Neaira*, and appears as defendant in the earliest speech, 52 *Against Callippus*. Following ancient testimony, I take Speech 45 to be the work of Demosthenes. Apollodorus' authorship of the remaining six speeches seems probable on the best evidence available,[41] and is accepted for present purposes. Since these include assessment of originality, it is particularly important to note that five of the six Apollodoran speeches (the exception being 59 *Against Neaira*) are to be dated to the years 369–359. Demosthenes' logographic career began towards the end of this decade. If he wrote Speech 45 and Apollodorus wrote Speech 46, some form of co-operation must be assumed, which could include compositional guidance; but

---

[39] The idea that 'the inspiration of the incident may have been the tradition that Menelaus spared Helen's life at the end of the Trojan War when he glimpsed her bosom' (Kennedy *APG* 250, quoting Eur. *And.* 628 and Aristoph. *Lys.* 155) unrealistically rationalizes the effect of Hyperides' *coup de théâtre*. Further on the case, see C. Cooper, 'Hyperides and Phryne', *Phoenix* 49 (1995), 303–15.

[40] The best of these is probably that of G. Colin (Budé; Paris, 1946). See Also G. Bartolini, *Iperide* (Padua, 1977).

[41] J. Trevett *ASP* summarizes earlier work and offers new statistical evidence in his chapter '*Authorship*' (50–76).

Apollodorus was some ten years the senior, so that the relationship is unlikely to have been simply one of master/pupil. Further examination of the six speeches will tend to confirm the older man's independence. More specifically, it will be argued that Apollodorus represents the continuance of the tradition of 'natural' oratory represented first by Andocides and later maintained by Aeschines.[42]

If the accepted date of *Against Callippus* (369/8 BC, Blass *AB* iii/1. 515) is correct, Apollodorus began writing speeches before Demosthenes. The speech shows that he knew about division, but it is the early statement of intention to concentrate on his opponent's character, to the subordination of the legal issue,[43] that establishes his individual method. In the present speech the unfolding of Callippus' character is a gradual process. As *proxenos* ('consular agent') of the Heracleots, he could claim an interest in the money deposited in Pasion's bank by the Heracleot merchant Lycon (5), but the way Apollodorus tells the story suggests that Callippus relied on his status as *proxenos* (10) rather than any true claim, and used it to try to intimidate Pasion. Apollodorus tells the story graphically, using live conversation, Callippus played a waiting game, encouraged to do so by Pasion's failing health (13–14), but Apollodorus can use this to his advantage (17–18): and to the picture of a calculating, unscrupulous opponent he adds details which refute Callippus' claim to have had connections with Lycon, and probability-argument interpreting his father's actions (25–7).[44] This **proof** section is short, and the speech ends without a summary. Apollodorus has drawn rather sparingly on the rhetorical sources available to him. A similar pattern of usage is to be observed in much of his later oratory.

Next in chronological order, *Against Nicostratus* (366/5, Blass *AB* iii/1. 519) is against an ex-friend and neighbour. The speech has what amounts to a lengthy **prodiegesis** in which Apollodorus recounts their former friendship and the benefits and trust he had bestowed on Nicostratus before showing the bearing of all this on the case; and Nicostratus' metamorphosis from grateful friend to

---

[42] For this relationship, see Trevett *ASP* 116–18.

[43] 1: μηκέτι περὶ τοῦ πράγματος μόνον λέγειν, ἀλλὰ καὶ περὶ αὐτοῦ τοῦ λέγοντος.

[44] This argument depends on assumptions about the power and influence of the *proxenos* Callippus on the one hand and the vulnerability of metics like Pasion on the other. A kind of inferiority-feeling is often just below the surface in many situations and arguments in the speeches of Apollodorus.

defrauding enemy slowly emerges (14–18). Details of the actual
charge are given piecemeal (2, 14, 19): it seems to have arisen from
a simple desire for revenge on Apollodorus' part against Nicostratus
and his brother Arethusius. The evidence against them is given
briefly (19–21), and Apollodorus turns once more to attack their
character (26–7) before ending.

The defendant in *Against Timotheus* is the famous son of a famous
father (Conon). He had borrowed from Pasion to pay his fleet. For
a foreign banker, the arraignment of a popular general before a
patriotic jury was a daunting prospect, and the reader feels this from
the beginning.[45] Apollodorus gives an unnecessarily detailed **narrative** of the loan (6–8), and the sequel is an even more rambling
story, which includes one of the longest sentences in Greek literature (9–13),[46] as it describes further misfortunes of Timotheus,
which evoked Pasion's sympathetic subvention (18). At the same
time he is careful to give precise details of times and transactions,
and makes a point of mentioning that Pasion believed in
Timotheus' intention to repay his debts (24), which accumulated
further through his agents after his departure on campaign, while
Pasion continued to rely on his reputation (35). Apollodorus
devises a probability-argument around that reputation (36–42); but
narrative resumes thereafter, and proofs are not marshalled
together. His technique has not developed at this stage.

Like the last speech, *Against Polycles* (359 BC (?)) is informative
on the subject of naval administration and logistics, but this time
Apollodorus is directly involved, and other implications of wealth
combined with alien status come under review. He had recently
served as trierarch beyond his legal term, and is able to contrast this
patriotic action with the tardiness of his opponent, who was
appointed to take over from him. **Narrative** predominates once
more[47] and it serves as the medium for more than usually sensitive
characterization. We learn from it that Apollodorus had been zeal-
ous in not one but two respects—serving over his time and paying
his crew lavishly. Now this could have attracted resentment along

---

[45] 1: 'None of you should find it incredible that Timotheus should have owed money to
my father.'

[46] Notwithstanding its length, the sentence is not a true period, but an unhappy example of *lexis eiromene*, in which clauses are strung together paratactically, without an organic
centre or a rounded conclusion which completes the sense.

[47] So Trevett *ASP* 84, who adds 'to the greatest extent' (i.e. in the Apollodoran
speeches). For the possible political background of the speech, see ibid. 130–1.

the lines of 'these rich metics can afford to show patriotism in the pursuit of their ambitions'.[48] So he devotes much of the narrative to careful details of incidents which illustrate his restraint and his opponent's arrogant behaviour. There is little indication that Polycles can or would contradict his account, and hence no assemblage of proof-material. He is content to tell the facts that show all his own actions to have been legal and patriotic, and also that it was not over-zealousness on his part that was the reason for Polycles' failure to take over the trierarchy on time. In fact, he seeks sympathy at a psychological moment (60–3) when he says that the prolongation of his command was painful because of family troubles. In spite of the usual lack of division, it is a subtle and effective speech.

Assuming closeness in time between the two speeches against Stephanus, the second (Apollodoran) speech would be the last of the early group of five (c.350). It is also the only deuterology in that group, and is concerned mainly with Stephanus' alleged procedural and testamentary irregularities (4–25). The discussion of the latter make it an important source for inheritance law. The speech may owe its preservation to this rather than to any literary or rhetorical merit.

Reward for his public services came to Apollodorus in appointment to the Council (349/8), but one of his subsequent proposals for financial reform[49] was opposed vehemently by a certain Stephanus,[50] who seems to have been motivated by pure envy. He secured his conviction in a graphe paranomon and followed this up with a trumped-up charge of murder, which failed, but convinced Apollodorus and his friends that attack on such an implacable enemy offered his only hope of survival. That meant prosecution in the lawcourts: hence the speech *Against Neaira*, the wife of Stephanus. Part of the scholarly attention this speech has received is due, no doubt, to the light it casts on Athenian citizenship-law;

---

[48] Note esp. the conversation he records (26) between Polycles and the pentecontarch Euctemon, who says that Apollodorus had incurred debts during his command, at which Polycles scoffs: 'Ah, the mouse has just tasted pitch—he wanted to be an Athenian.' The proverb (see e.g. Theocritus 14. 51) describes a cheeky character getting into trouble, and suits Polycles' attitude to an ambitious upstart. See also 34.

[49] See Trevett *ASP* 15–16: he proposed the allocation of surplus treasury-monies to military funds rather than to Theoric distributions.

[50] This was Stephanus of Eroiadai; the opponent in Speeches 45 and 46 was Stephanus of Acharnai.

but the fact that the title-role is played by the most-travelled and
perhaps most-feted courtesan in antiquity must account in large
part for its popularity. However, present interest is focused on
Apollodorus' performance. What has he learnt about speechwriting in the ten years or so since his last extant speech (this one may
be as late as 340)? He has developed the confidence to take full
advantage of the extra time-allocation in a graphe, so that this
speech is twice as long as the longest of its predecessors. There are
two speakers: Apollodorus takes over at § 16 from his supporter
Theomnestus, who has furnished the political background summarized above, and thereafter the division is clearer and more pur-
poseful than in previous speeches: 18–48: The Career of Neaira
(**Narrative**); 49: Summary; 50–84: The Career of Neaira's
Daughter Phano (mostly Narrative, but with Summary at 62–3 and
Digression on precedents for Athenian citizenship (74–8)). The
elaborateness of the rhetoric in the following section deserves
examination. The subject is enfranchisement, and the principle is
laid down that citizenship should be granted only to those who
have earned it by some distinguishing act or service to the people.[51]
To rhetoricize this Apollodorus constructs a complex comparative
(a fortiori) argument which begins with a long historical example—the *andragathia* of the Plataeans illustrated through their many
acts of friendship and devotion to the Athenians, which earned
them Athenian citizenship (94–104). Yet even these exemplary
Plataeans had qualifications imposed upon their enfranchisement
(105–6). Would it not be shameful to let stand the citizenship of the
world's most-travelled harlot after restrictions had been placed on
that of Athens' most-honoured allies? Apollodorus has certainly
learnt a great deal.[52] The speech still displays many of his old weaknesses—especially a tendency to let his sentences run to excessive
length through incoherent clausal structure. It is tempting to look
for literary influences, and an unsuccessful attempt to imitate the
smooth,[53] ordered *macrologia* of Isocrates may be detected. Pupils at

---

[51] 89: δι' ἀνδραγαθίαν εἰς τὸν δῆμον τὸν Ἀθηναίων ἄξιον ᾖ.

[52] The direct derivation of his Plataean narrative from Thucydides (2. 2–5, 71–8; 3. 20–4.
52–68), from whose account Apollodorus has withdrawn items discreditable to the
Plataeans, provides evidence that his learning was broader than the mere technical requirements of his lawsuits demanded. On the digression, see J. Trevett, 'History in [Demosthenes
59', *CQ* 2nd ser. 40 (1990), 407–20.

[53] Smoothness was achieved by Isocrates through avoidance of hiatus, but Apollodorus
seems to make little or no attempt to avoid it.

Isocrates' school were instructed to read and draw upon literature (see *To Nicocles* 40–53): was Apollodorus one of them at some time? However that may be, it was probably his relationship with Demosthenes that influenced his development more. While in general he comes nowhere near Demosthenes in the clarity and force of his writing, he deploys some of his individual characteristics, notably abstract expression (including the use of the articular infinitive), the occasional vivid turn of phrase;[54] and, perhaps from noting the success of a new generation of longer speeches like Demosthenes 20, 21, 22, 23, and 24, he was encouraged to spread his own oratorical wings in his prosecution of Neaira. Throughout his oratory, however, narrative is the dominant medium, giving way only on brief occasions to rhetorical artifice, formal proofs, and disciplined argument. Like Andocides, and to a lesser extent Aeschines, he was happiest when regaling his audiences with stories which embarrassed his opponents and showed his own actions in the most favourable light.[55]

DINARCHUS

Firmly in the next generation after the previous orators, Dinarchus lived into the third century BC. A Corinthian by birth (Dion. Hal. *Din.* 2), he came to Athens while still young, when Alexander was invading Asia, and became a pupil of Theophrastus, who was head of the Lyceum, having succeeded Aristotle.[56] His mature oratory

---

[54] See *Ag. Neaira* 55, 67 (noted by Trevett *ASP* 108); and n. 8 (above).

[55] On Andocides, Aeschines, and Apollodorus, see esp. Trevett *ASP* 116–19. Further on Apollodorus, see F. Lortzing, *De Orationibus quas Demosthenes pro Apollodoro scripsisse fertur* (Berlin, 1863); J. Sigg, 'Der Verfasser neun angeblich von Demosthenes für Apollodor geschriebener Reden', *JCP* Suppl. (1873), 395–434; L. Pearson, 'Apollodorus, the Eleventh Attic Orator', in L. Wallach (ed.), *The Classical Tradition* (Ithaca, NY, 1966), 347–59; Carey *GO* vi; M. Delaunois, 'Le Plan rhétorique dans les discours dits apocryphes de Démosthène', *AC* 31 (1962), 35–81.

[56] 323/2: if Dinarchus was 'still young' (ἔτι νέος (*Vit. X Or.* 850c), when he began his education, which seems likely, the date usually given for his birth, 361/60 (Blass *AB* iii/2. 292, Dobson *GO* 302, Burtt *MAO* ii. 161, M. Nouhaud and L. Dors-Méary, *Dinarque: discours* (Budé; Paris, 1990), p. vii, I. Worthington, *A Historical Commentary on Dinarchus* (Ann Arbor, 1992), 5), seems too early. On the other hand, his three surviving speeches were all written for the trials arising from the Harpalus affair in 323, by which time he must have acquired a reputation as a speechwriter. From this emerges the idea of a precocious talent being exercised in the lawcourts while its possessor was still completing his education.

belongs to the period of the oligarchy at Athens after the death of Alexander,[57] but none of this survives; and after being forced into exile, he spent fifteen of his later years hoping for recall to Athens, which he won in 292, only to become involved in a lawsuit for the recovery of money which he accused his friend Proxenus of losing or misappropriating (Dion. Hal. *Din.* 3). Fragments of the speech survive: it was the only one that he made in his own person, and we do not know whether he won the case. There is no reason to reject the general assumption that he did not survive for long after it.

These biographical data show Dinarchus at a disadvantage in any assessment of his originality, or even of his talent considered in isolation. The law of diminishing returns applies to him, at the end of the series, most of all the orators; and we almost certainly do not possess his best work. His surviving speeches must be approached with these reservations.

1 *Against Demosthenes*

Harpalus, a Macedonian grandee appointed treasurer at Babylon by Alexander before he marched eastward, had Athenian connections (including citizenship earned through supplying grain in time of shortage), and ambitions of his own.[58] As those ambitions had been based on the assumption that Alexander would not return from India, flight was Harpalus' only course when the king confounded his expectations. By the time Alexander arrived back at Susa early in 324, Harpalus had gone, taking as much of the treasure as he could carry. Driven to pursue his grand plan earlier than he had perhaps intended, he appeared off Cape Sunion with ships, men, and money, but the Athenians refused to let him land. The precise course of the intrigues that followed is very uncertain, but it is at least clear that leading Athenian politicians were involved in them. They led finally to Harpalus' admission to the city, where he was detained, while his treasure was stored in the Acropolis. It was his escape soon afterwards, together with the discovery that the money he left amounted only to half the sum he claimed to have brought,

---

[57] Dion. Hal. *Din.* 2: μάλιστα δὲ ἤκμασε μετὰ τὴν Ἀλεξάνδρου τελευτήν.

[58] See Badian, *JHS* 81 (1961), 22–3, who describes him as 'the man who intended to hold Athens against the King himself, and who has rightly been called a precursor of the Successors'.

that led people to suspect that he had bribed their leaders to let him
go. Demosthenes chose to grasp the nettle, and proposed an
enquiry. After six months[59] the Areopagus published a list of recip-
ients, appending the amount of the bribe paid to each. This was a
signal for prosecutions to begin. Dinarchus wrote the speeches
delivered against five of those named—Demosthenes, Aristogeiton,
Philocles, Hagnonides, and Aristonicus.[60] His speeches against the
first three form the basis of his extant oratory.

The speech *Against Demosthenes* is a deuterologia, a fact which
adds to the already difficult task of assessing Dinarchus' ability. The
first speaker, Stratocles, has presented most of the charges and said
much besides.[61] Dinarchus is thus left with little to do beyond
exhortation and re-emphasis in order to arouse emotion.[62] Perhaps
the most notable feature of the speech is the sustained energy of its
invective. Although there are vestiges of a conventional division,
with a narrative beginning after a general denunciation of corrupt
men (3), these soon disappear. The tone is set by an unprecedented
resort to apostrophe of the defendant immediately after this narrative has begun (4), and is maintained with further apostrophes, a
constant switching from jury to defendant, and the use of emphatic
figures of language.[63] The attack on Demosthenes is mounted on a
broad front, with criticisms of his past policies amplified by means
of many parallels drawn from other historical times and personages,
always to Demosthenes' disadvantage. A more extended historical
excursus towards the end (72 ff.) propounds and illustrates the thesis that the fortunes of states wax and wane in accordance with the
character and performance of their leaders.[64] Dinarchus brings a

---

[59] Din. 1 *Ag. Dem.* 45. Badian (*JHS* 81 (1961), 33–5) explains the delay by referring to
Demosthenes' influence both in Athens and with Alexander, both of which waned early in
323. See also Sealey *DT*, Appendix 8.

[60] Dion. Hal. *Din.* 10.

[61] 1: τῶν πλείστων προκατειλημμένων κατηγορημάτων may have a semi-techni-
cal meaning: 'most of the defendant's arguments have been anticipated [and refuted].' This
would mean that Stratocles' speech had contained a complete proof—πίστις (*confirmatio*)
and λύσις (*refutatio*).

[62] 2: ὑπόλοιπον ἡμῖν . . . παρακελεύεσθαι . . . ἵν' ὀργίζεσθαι μᾶλλον
παροξύνωμεν, δὶς περὶ τῶν αὐτῶν ἐροῦμεν.

[63] Anaphora (3, 28, 33), epanadiplosis (10, 27, 28, 29, 40, 46, 72).

[64] In his otherwise admirable *Historical Commentary on Dinarchus*, 29, Worthington,
analysing this speech according to his theory of ring-composition, finds correspondence
between this passage and 29–47. But the emphasis is different in the two passages. The earlier is concerned primarily with describing Demosthenes' misdeeds (29–36, 41–7); the later
passage begins with an unparalleled list of examples of good and bad fortunes experienced

new vigour to the long-established device of the historical paradeigma, frequently addressing his audience in the second person, and never losing sight of his target, whose destruction he demands as the single prerequisite for the city's salvation.[65] This is strong rhetoric; but even at this late stage of the speech we are still waiting for the evidence for Demosthenes' receipt of money from Harpalus. In this speech Dinarchus is content merely to cite the finding of the enquiry set up by the Areopagus, whose integrity he defends, and to urge action upon it (1, 47, 53). For the rest, he relies on loose probability-argument based on an interpretation of Demosthenes' past record. As the writer of the deuterologia (for an unknown speaker), Dinarchus may have been under instructions as to the line he should take, and his client chose him for the special qualities of trenchancy and vehemence which his speech displays. The style has other qualities which imitate and exaggerate the main features of earlier styles. He seeks to match Isocratean periodicity with some ponderous sentences, including a huge one (18–21) which loses its train of thought in a cascade of genitive absolutes and defies rational punctuation.[66] Asyndeton is widely used, most effectively in the short narrative passages (e.g. 32–3) and apostrophe (e.g. 83), where it becomes a means of variation. Hostility occasionally takes the form of sarcasm (e.g. 79, 81) or an adaptation of one of Demosthenes' favourite figures (e.g. in 82 he imitates the famous climax in 18 *Cor.* 179). Combinations of different influences make Dinarchus' style a heady cocktail, not without individual colour, but also marking his position at the end of a long tradition.

by states through their statesmen's actions, and proceeds to a *different* set of Demosthenes' misdeeds. The recurrence of themes is more simply explained by the recapitulatory function of epilogues. More subtle attempts to establish internal correspondence are ingenious rather than convincing.

[65] 77: 'Put to death this robber caught red-handed, this traitor who could not keep his hands off the gold brought to Athens, who has cast her into the most terrible misfortunes, this bane of Greece. Cast his body beyond the city's boundaries, and thereby give her fortunes the chance to mend and then, with this done, expect a happier fate.'

[66] The main verb οὐκ ἀποκτενεῖτε occurs at the beginning, removing all possibility of suspense. Thereafter the sentence is constructed (?) around two relative clauses, 18 ὅς . . . περιεῖδεν . . . 20–1 ὅς . . . οὐκ ἐτόλμησεν . . . , but these are detached from one another, giving rise to anacolouthon.

2 *Against Aristogeiton*

Another alleged recipient of gold from Harpalus, Aristogeiton had a certain notoriety,[67] so that Dinarchus' audience may not have regarded 'the worst character in the city, or rather in the whole world' as a hyperbolic description of him (1). That character is tailor-made for Dinarchus' invective style of oratory. The message is simple enough: punish the miscreant. 'Do not neglect your duty, or give up punishing criminals, but purge the city of corruption as completely as you can' (5). As in the previous speech, the findings of the Areopagus are taken to require no further corroboration or presentation of evidence, but this speech seems to be the first for the prosecution. It breaks off abruptly, but our text may also begin some way into the speech, since the opening sections contain no recognizable prooemium-features, but launch *in medias res*. Indeed, generalizations about the social consequences of failure to punish delinquency (3–4) belong conventionally to the later stages, as do detailed examination of character and life (18–19). The attack on Aristogeiton has all Dinarchus' usual pungency and rhetorical skill,[68] but the incompleteness of the speech confirms the shortage of evidence for a critical assessment of Dinarchus.

3 *Against Philocles*

The third alleged bribe-taker (*dorodokos*) may have been archon in 322/1,[69] and the name is linked to other offices (*strategos* (325/4) and *kosmetes* (324/3)). Even allowing for possible confusion of identity, he was surely a more substantial political figure than Aristogeiton. But once again we are dealing with a fragment, beginning without introduction and not naming the accused until § 5. Dinarchus is able to capitalize on Philocles' influence and make him appear as a dangerous subverter of the state (4–5, 8–10) who has abused high office (12–13). Where Aristogeiton is attacked mainly for his private life, the attack on Philocles is more like that on Demosthenes, on a smaller scale but using the same devices of indignation—calling directly on the jury to condemn him and

---

[67] Speeches 25 and 26 in the Demosthenic corpus are *Against Aristogeiton*. 25. 51–62 contains a lurid catalogue of his misdeeds, but he also emerges as a popular orator and politician 25. 64, 90; 26. 16).

[68] Note esp. the effective a fortiori argument in 15.   [69] Dion. Hal. *Din.* 9.

showing impatience at their reluctance (17). Historical comparative argument, as often used before in similar exhortation, serves him well ('You showed no indulgence to far better men in the past . . . why should you show any to this abominable man?'). Dinarchus shows some of Demosthenes' capacity for keeping up the pressure on his victims: a more representative selection of his *oeuvre* might have raised our estimate of his abilities.

II

CEREMONIAL ORATORY

Any search for innovation in this genre is immediately discouraged by the opening sentences of the earliest extant example of it, the Funeral Speech of Pericles. Thucydides makes him say (2. 35. 1, 3):

Most of those who have spoken in the past (ἤδη) have praised the man who added this oration to our funeral rites . . . and since our forefathers gave this custom their approval, I too must follow it and fulfil the wishes and expectations of each of you, as far as possible.

Whether or not a precise date for the earliest epitaphios can be established,[1] it is clear that this main sub-genre of ceremonial or epideictic oratory was already formalized and its contents were determined[2] even before the beginnings of Sicilian rhetoric.[3] Unlike the topics of forensic rhetoric, which were subject to the

---

[1] The attribution to Solon (Anaximenes Fr. 44) may be dismissed. Somewhat vaguer, yet less easy to discount, is the statement in Dion. Hal. *Ant. Rom.* 5. 17. 2–4, that the Athenians instituted the Funeral Oration 'in honour of those who fought at Artemisium, Salamis, and Plataea, and died for their country, *or to the glory of their exploits at Marathon*'. It has been correctly observed (by N. Loraux, *The Invention of Athens*, trans. A. Sheridan (Harvard and London, 1986), 57) that Dion. Hal. is using this information to prove the priority of the genre at Rome; but a later date for the first Athenian epitaphios would have suited his argument even better, while no greater occasion for its inauguration could have been conceived than the victories over the barbarians which formed the most constant topics of the later speeches.

[2] Although Thucydides' language in the above passage is imprecise, Pericles' undertaking to follow a custom (ἑπόμενον τῷ νόμῳ) and fulfil his audience's wishes and expectations (πειρᾶσθαι ὑμῶν τῆς ἑκάστου βουλήσεώς τε καὶ δόξης τυχεῖν) at least implies his realization that they would be expecting something they would recognize from past examples. And his first topic, praise of ancestors (36. 1), is the commonest in all epitaphioi. Later (44. 1) he identifies an established topic—commiseration with the bereaved—by repudiating it.

[3] Loraux (*The Invention of Athens*, 57–60) argues for the 460s as the time of the earliest public epitaphioi, mainly because praise of democratic institutions fits this period better than an earlier one. But there is little evidence that Athens' young democracy was in any way suppressed before that time. It is, however, interesting that Loraux's argument depends on the assumption that the topoi found in later epitaphioi were the same as those used in the earliest epitaphioi.

expansion and variation necessitated by different cases and evolving litigational procedures, those of funeral rhetoric were deployed in relatively unchanging circumstances: young men had died, their kinsfolk had to be consoled and convinced that their sacrifice, and future sacrifices, were worthwhile and in the best traditions of the city. Standardization of topoi was made the more inevitable by the general practice of saying little about the actual campaigns fought by the fallen. Those topoi are mostly fixed and historical, as is seen from the following list of those which occur in at least two of the extant epitaphioi:

Difficulty or Impossibility of Adequate Praise for the Fallen[4]
Praise of Ancestors' Exploits, in Mythical Wars against Amazons, Eumolpus, Eurystheus, Thebes under Creon, Trojan War
Persian Wars: Marathon, Artemisium, Salamis, Plataea
Athenian Identity and Achievements: Autochthonia, Dispensation of Divine Gifts
Leadership and Championship of Greek Freedom
Athenian Paideia, the source of their Arete and Justice
Consolation and Exhortation.

This wealth of topics left limited scope for novelty in a speech of finite length. The Lysianic Epitaphios[5] is the longest, because it is amplified through narrative. It also establishes a distinctive style for the genre—one of periods with balanced clauses, which is not particularly Lysianic but accords with the Middle Style which Isocrates adopted for most of his discourses. The marriage of complex sentence-structure with narrative, if not original, is carried to new lengths in the speech. Two features of this kind of narrative are characterization (e.g. of the Amazons in 4–5) and its frequent reference to its subjects' feelings and motivation (e.g. in 13–14, 24–5, 37–8). The primary persuasive motif is that the fallen are to be envied and emulated (ζηλωτοί, 69): if the bereaved and their sympathetic fellow-citizens depart with these thoughts uppermost in their minds, the speaker will have performed his task satisfactorily.

---

[4] Not in Plato Menexenus, but for its unique character, see below.

[5] The authenticity of Lysias 2 has long been disputed, and the statistical data it yields place it in, at best, a marginal position. But the more relevant question is that of the extent to which the author of the speech could have been influenced by what he perceived to be the requirements of the established genre. Many have noted parallels between this Epitaphios, Isocrates Panegyricus, and Plato Menexenus (see Loraux, The Invention of Athens, 345 n. 56). Such similarities seem to confirm the dominance of genre over individuality.

Demosthenes 60 contains a number of features which link it closely to the event it purports to commemorate, the Battle of Chaeronea, and to the known historical fact that Demosthenes was appointed to deliver an epitaphios for the fallen in that battle (18 *Cor.* 285–7). The speaker begins on a personal note by mentioning his appointment. After the conventional topics have been treated (4–17), he turns to the special circumstances of the battle, arguing that the outcome of such encounters is decided by the gods (21, 23, cf. 18 *Cor.* 192, 208) and the vagaries of generalship (21, 22, cf. 18 *Cor.* 145, 146, 195, 245, 303); and there is a quasi-forensic touch as he suggests the restrained behaviour of Philip after his victory is proof of the valour of the vanquished. But most interesting is the catalogue of the ten Athenian tribes (27–31), and the attachment of the usual mythical material to them severally. This would fit a military context, as the Athenian army in the field was arrayed by tribes, and this focused the competition for honour. The speech lacks many of Demosthenes' characteristic traits. He may have felt imprisoned by the genre, not to mention inhibited by the occasion; yet he has managed to introduce some fresh ideas.

Hyperides *Epitaphios* is remarkable enough to deserve separate examination (pp. 335–7). As for the epitaphios offered by Plato as a model in the *Menexenus*, where it is ascribed by Socrates to Aspasia, Pericles' mistress, it is, as one might expect, imbued with Platonic ideas, the main one being the necessity of approaching politics through philosophy.[6] In fact, the underlying purpose seems to be to demonstrate the proper use of funeral oratory as an organ of political education. This purpose explains the detailed discussion of historical events, such as the preliminaries as well as the campaign that ended at Marathon (240a–d), where the *arete* of the Athenians taught the rest of the Greeks how to resist the barbarians.[7] Lessons were to be learned too from later events, as the speaker closely follows Thucydides' diagnosis of the main cause of Athenian defeat in the Peloponnesian War,[8] when she says (243d):

[6] So L. J. Coventry, 'Philosophy and Rhetoric in the *Menexenus*', *JHS* 99 (1989), who points out (3–4) that the choice of Aspasia indicates a relationship with Thucydides' Funeral Speech of Pericles. She also rightly alludes to its parodic character, the main symptom of which is replication, and to some extent exaggeration, of stylistic features of the epideictic genre.

[7] 240c: ἐτόλμησαν διακινδυνεύειν οἱ Ἕλληνες ὑπὲρ τῆς σωτηρίας, μαθηταὶ τῶν Μαραθῶνι γενόμενοι . . . 241 c . . . παιδευθῆναι τοὺς ἄλλους Ἕλληνας.

[8] 2. 65. 11–12: 'Because they [Athenian politicians] were busy with their own intrigues for leadership of the people they embroiled state policy . . . but final surrender came only after their internal strife had caused their downfall.'

'we were defeated by our own dissension, not by others: even to
this day we are unconquered by those enemies, but we were our
own conquerors and brought about our own defeat.' The element
of praise survives in her interpretation of political events after the
end of the war: the Athenian people resolved their internal differences because their *syngeneia* made them *metrioi* (244); but criticism,
however mild, returns as she suggests that her countrymen have, if
anything, been too sympathetic towards others.[9] Thus after defining clearly the traditional purpose of the old epitaphios—to adorn
the fine deeds of the fallen with fine words, and thereby praise
them; to exhort the living; and to console the parents (236e)—
Plato sets out to show how the speech can have an educative function by commenting on past policies, not merely narrating events.

---

[9] 244c: λίαν φιλοικτίρμων ἐστι[ν ἡ πόλις] καὶ τοῦ ἥττονος θεραπίς.

12

CONCLUSION

The foundations of a flexible and sophisticated rhetorical system, embracing argument, interpretation of the law, and emotional appeal, were laid before the first extant practical oratory appeared shortly before 420 BC. Antiphon developed certain lasting techniques, notably the application of probability-argument to behaviour, the use of historical examples, and addressing the jury in terms of earnest adjuration. Andocides, an enigmatic figure, opted initially to ignore some of the basic rules. Later he acknowledged their efficacy, but also gave rein to his natural talent as a raconteur, at some sacrifice of structural discipline. The establishment of narrative as a distinct and occasionally dominant part of the speech is seen for the first time in the oratory of Lysias, where it serves purposes other than the mere presentation of factual evidence. These include characterization, the creation of an atmosphere favourable to his client or unfavourable to his opponent, and stimulation of the jury's sense of history and civic solidarity. While the literary form of oratory was thus shaped by Lysias, Isaeus is not only a major source for historians of inheritance law, but also introduces a new level of persistence and logical thoroughness into argumentation, and launches character-assaults with unprecedented vehemence.

   In the forensic speeches he wrote for a wide variety of clients, Demosthenes made use of all the available techniques without making substantial innovations. But for cases which brought him on to the political stage and gave him the opportunity to show his mettle as a statesman, he created a form of oratory and a style which brought the genre into competition with historiography and moralistic writing, and also with the contemporary political discourses of Isocrates. Hence perhaps the scale of the speeches *Against Leptines*, *Against Timocrates*, and *Against Aristocrates*. As his political career burgeoned, his hortatory and deliberative techniques developed around the themes of opportunity (*kairos*) and necessity rather than the traditional themes of justice and expediency. His rival Aeschines could match him in emotional appeal, and shared Andocides' narrative ability, but his ex-actor's easy command of the purely physical side of his art could not conceal his superficiality.

The remaining orators suffer the double misfortune of meagre representation and the law of diminishing returns. The fashion for quoting from the tragic poets, followed by Aeschines and Lycurgus, may be viewed as a symptom of decline, but Hyperides is fully able to generate tragic power without it in his Funeral Oration. Dinarchus' oratory shows technical competence, but his efforts to outdo his predecessors in stylistic complexity sometimes backfire. Apollodorus is guaranteed a future readership for his speech *Against Neaira*, but Isocrates, who developed a uniquely complex yet organized style which found many imitators in his own (Lycurgus) and later (Cicero) generations, is likely to remain an outsider to many scholars and students, who find his perceived élitism, manifested in his interest in oligarchy and monarchy, distasteful. The more balanced assessments of recent monographs are welcome.

Provided from the start with many of the essential materials, the orators found enough scope for innovation to make their individual contributions to the genre. The pioneer Antiphon, Lysias who established the ideal division and literary status of forensic oratory, and Demosthenes, who found a style which made oratory into a potent medium of political thought and persuasion: these are the outstanding contributors; but each of the remaining eight orators found his own personal way of adapting the traditional material to his purposes.

APPENDIX A

THE *TETRALOGIES*: DATE AND AUTHORSHIP

The second of these subjects is of less concern than the first for present purposes. My inclination is to accept Antiphontean authorship, for which I shall argue briefly after dealing with the main question. The three *Tetralogies* contain a single[1] possible reference to their time of composition. That reference is in *Tetr.* 1. 2. 12, where the defendant represents himself as πολλὰς καὶ μεγάλας εἰσφορὰς εἰσφέροντα. Now Thucydides (3. 19. 1) appears to assign the first *eisphora* ('war-tax') to the year 428 BC. The text reads: καὶ αὐτοὶ ἐσενεγκόντες τότε πρῶτον ἐσφορὰν διακόσια τάλαντα. Gomme, ad loc. (*HCT* ii. 278–9), while noting the natural sense of these words, suggests that the more difficult sense of 'for the first time in this war' accords better with the epigraphical evidence. This is presented and discussed by Meiggs and Lewis *GHI* 156–8, 161. The inscription describes financial decrees moved by Callias, dated, 'by common consensus' (*GHI* 156) to 434/3, and specifies a requirement of a special sanction by the Assembly for drawing money above the sum of 10,000 drachmae from Athena's treasury. It goes on (156 ll. 15–17) to forbid the use of this money . . . ἐὰν μὴ τὴν ἄδειαν ψηφίσηται ὁ δῆμος καθάπερ ἐὰν ψηφίσηται περὶ ἐσφορᾶς. The people are to have a power to authorize and control expenditure analogous to their power to raise taxes, and this analogy is pursued further in the next few lines. But its illustrative effectiveness depends on a general understanding of an established tax.[2] Returning to Antiphon's imaginary defendant, and to his claim (above) to be a payer of 'many great *eisphorai*', his multiple claim must be seen as adding a rhetorical flourish to a touch of realism rather than indicating a later date for the speech. Indeed, it could even be argued that its effect would have been the more vividly hyperbolic soon after the first imposition of the tax. Hence the earliest *terminus post quem* of 434/3 (earlier if the tentative suggestion of Meiggs and

---

[1] The resemblance of *Tetr.* 2 to a case discussed by Pericles and Protagoras (Plut. *Per.* 36. 3) has been used to argue for a date in the late 440s or early 430s (e.g. by G. Kennedy, *The Art of Persuasion in Greece* (Princeton and London, 1963), 130–1). But the perennial interest of the question for the application of the laws of homicide could cause it to be raised at any time.

[2] Meiggs and Lewis *GHI* 161: 'There may be a reference to εἰσφορά in a decree concerning Hestiaea, c.445–435 (*IG* i².42. 22 f.)'.

Lewis (n. 2 above) is accepted) may not be far from the actual date of the
Tetralogies. Now reliance on the easier interpretation of Thuc. 3. 19.
would yield a date soon after 428. But the epigraphical evidence seem
decisive, so that the only possible reference to time of composition in the
Tetralogies indicates an earlier date.[3]

As we turn to literary evidence, the presence of many Ionicisms in the
Tetralogies has implications for both date and authorship.[4] It would be natural to assume that they are a function of an earlier date, since the pre-
Attic prose that we have is predominantly Ionic, and we look to author
like Herodotus, Democritus, and the *Corpus Hippocraticum* for models o
it, and for parallel usages when measuring its extent in another author. Bu
in order to base a *terminus ante quem* upon this evidence, one must try tc
reduce the long list of Ionicisms[5] to those words, meanings of words, anc
constructions which occur only in the earlier period, and subsequently fal
out of use; and also (a more difficult and subjective task) to try and identify words which seem to be used naturally by the author, rather than ii
a self-consciously old-fashioned way in a desire to give a patina of age, anc
hence authority, to his writing. It is with these restrictions in mind that
note the following usages, found in the *Tetralogies* but not elsewhere ii
Antiphon (numbered-only refs. e.g. 1. 2. 7 = *Tetr.* 1. 2. 7):

ἀναγιγνώσκειν (= Attic ἀναπείθειν) 1. 2. 7: cf. Hdt. 8. 57, 100.
ἀθέμιστα (= Attic ἄνομα) 3. 3. 6: cf. Hdt. 7. 33, otherwise not in Attic
   prose exc. Xen. *Mem.* 1. 1. 9.
ἀνακλαίειν 1. 4. 1: cf. Hdt. 3. 14. 66.

[3] R. Sealey, 'The *Tetralogies* Ascribed to Antiphon', *TAPA* 113 (1984), 71–85, after not
ing the conflicting interpretations of this evidence (p. 78 n. 13), concentrates on the text o
Thucydides, and concludes by preferring the straightforward interpretation, namely that th
Athenians levied an *eisphora* for the first time in 428/7. But his discussion is inconclusive, an
in the course of it he has to consider the possible meaning of the key clause 'then was th
first time that they raised an *eisphora* as high as two hundred talents', which would fatall
undermine the evidential value of the passage, since on that entirely possible (even likely
interpretation, precedent was created by the amount of the levy, not its novelty.
[4] Dover (*LCL* 189–90), after drawing no firm conclusion from the historical evidence
writes: 'I attach much more importance to the fact that the language of the *Tetralogies* is i
part Ionic.' He has rightly regarded assumptions that they are written with a purely Athenia
audience and readership contemplating Athenian history and society, as unwarranted. Thu
both the *eisphorai* and the laws and institutions which figure in the *Tetralogies* might apply t
or be understood by Greeks living on either side of the Aegean; and the firmest evidence fo
dating the *Tetralogies* is to be found in their language.
[5] Since this feature was noticed by Van Herwerden, 'Antiphontea', *Mnemosyne* 9 (1881)
203, and W. Dittenberger, *Hermes* 16 (1871), 321, the catalogue of instances has grown
Scholars who have used them to support arguments for an early dating are H. Richards, C
20 (1906), 148–53; G. Zuntz, 'Earliest Attic Prose Style', *Class. & Med.* (1939), 121–44, an
'Once Again the Antiphontean Tetralogies', *Mus. Helv.* 6 (1949), 100–3, replying to P. vo
der Mühl, 'Zur Unechtheit der Antiphontischen Tetralogien', *Mus. Helv.* 5 (1948), 1–5.

Appendix A

Appendix A

ἀπειρημένον (in sense of 'forbidden'): common in Hdt., but in Attic 'renounced, tired, given up'.

ἀτρεμίζειν (= ἡσυχάζειν) 1. 4. 9 (psychological sense), 2. 4. 5 (physical sense): Hdt. also uses the verb in both senses: physical (9. 74); psychological (1. 185, 190; 7. 18; 8. 68).

βέλος (in metaphorical or generalized ('missile') sense) 2. 3. 6: poetic, pre-Euripidean.

ἐκ (= ὑπό of agent, with passive verb) 1. 4. 1: common in Hdt. (e.g. 3. 62, 6. 13, 7. 175, 8. 114, 9. 16). Marchant (edn. of Thuc. iii (1909), 183) notes five occurrences in Thuc., but says: 'The use is Ionic: not found in ordinary Attic prose.'

ἐλαφρός (in mental sense) 2. 3. 12: Pind. Nem. 7. 113; [Aesch.] PV 263; Hdt. 3. 154.

ἐπί + dat. (of purpose) 1. 2. 5: with nouns in this sense, in Hdt. (1. 68, 3. 119, 5. 6, 9. 37); Homer and drama; in Thuc. only with articular inf., forming a purpose-clause (1. 34, 38, 70, 71), evidently an idiosyncratic development of the older usage.

θερμός (1. 4. 5), θερμότερον (1. 1. 7), in metaphorical sense ('hot-headed'): in fifth-century drama but not prose, or in later prose.

καταδοκεῖν (Att. ὑποπτεύειν) 1. 2. 2, 3. 7: cf. Hdt. 3. 27, 6. 16, 8. 69, 9. 57.

καταλαμβάνειν (= καταγιγνώσκειν) 1. 2. 9, 1. 4. 11, 3. 4. 9.

λεπτός (in mental sense) 2. 4. 2[6]: Hippoc. 295. 25.

παραφρονεῖν (= μαίνεσθαι) 1. 2. 9: Hippoc. Progn. 39.

πένθος (Att. λύπη, or λυπηρόν) 3. 4. 1: Homer (many exx.); Hdt. 2. 1; 6. 21.

ποινή (Att. δίκη) 1. 1. 3, 4. 11: cf. Homer (many exx.); Hdt. 2. 134, 7. 134.

πρός + genitive (in the sense 'in (my) favour') 1. 4. 10, 2. 2. 2: rare outside Hdt. (1. 75, 124).

Three other usages seem to point in the same early direction. The last is of especial interest:

πειρᾶσθαι + participle, 1. 3. 1 (remarkably in a transitional formula, πειρασόμεθα ἐλέγχοντες, which is standardized in the infinitive in all subsequent occurrences).

πρότερον ἤ + subjunct. (normal Attic πρίν) 1. 1. 2: mainly Herodotean (5 exx., 1 only in Thuc. (7. 63)) (Goodwin MT § 653).

Optative in apodosis of an unfulfilled condition (3. 4. 4):[7] apparently a

---

[6] Here the combination λεπτὰ καὶ ἀκριβῆ may find an echo in Eur. Med. 529–32, usu-ally dated to 430 BC: σοὶ δ' ἔστι μὲν νοῦς λεπτός, ἀλλ' ἐπίφθονος | λόγος διελθεῖν | ὡς Ἔρως σ' ἠνάγκασε | τόξοις ἀφύκτοις τοὐμὸν ἐκσῶσαι δέμας. | ἀλλ' οὐκ ἀκριβῶς αὐτὸ θήσομαι λίαν.

[7] εἰ γὰρ μὲν ἄρξας τῆς πληγῆς τύπτειν καὶ μὴ ἀποκτείνειν διενοήθη, ὁ δὲ ἀμυνόμενος ἀποκτεῖναι, οὗτος ἂν ὁ ἐπιβουλεύσας εἴη. νῦν δέ . . .

survival from early (esp. Homeric) usage before distinction between potential and unreal conditions had become established.

Early (i.e. pre-430 BC) authorship may be concluded from the absence of these usages from prose certainly written after that date.[8] But to deduce from this that Antiphon was not the author of the *Tetralogies* would be illogical, and rash for reasons which may be summarized thus:

1. Simple statistical tests, such as counts of sentence-length and antithesis, do not show significant differences. In particular, the *Tetralogies* and *Murder of Herodes* are very close in both. (However, *Tetr.* are particularly rich in τε . . . τε correspondence.)

2. Antiphon 1, 5, 6 share with *Tetr.* a taste for coining, or using agent-nouns.[9]

3. A related common feature is a taste for a style loaded with nominal forms, associated by later critics with the Grand Style. Such a style may have a gnomic flavour. Good examples in 5. 73, 91, 6. 6 are paralleled in *Tetr.* 1. 4. 9, 2. 2. 2.

4. The emphatic combination of pronoun and demonstrative, αὐτὸς οὗτος: 1. 1, 6, 10; 5. 32, 38; 6. 37, 41, 46, 48: *Tetr.* 1. 1. 11, 2. 13. (However, the emphasis of an antithesis with τοῦτο μὲν . . . τοῦτο δέ (also common in Herodotus) is seen in 1. 1, 11; 5. 5, 11, 26, 31, but not in the *Tetralogies*).

Other similarities of tone and style may, of course, be due to the fact that all the speeches concern homicide. But the differences noted by previous critics[10] could be explained by the circumstances in which the two sets of speeches were written. In Speeches 1, 5, and 6 Antiphon is a practical speechwriter, in the *Tetralogies* a sophist and a theoretician. A variety of differences could arise from this; and they might be augmented by passage of time from the earlier theoretical to the later practical oratory. Therefore I conclude that there is no compelling reason to reject the tradition of Antiphontean authorship of the *Tetralogies*. Writing them before other Athenian authors had established a distinct dialect for Attic prose, he would also see positive advantages in using, or at least drawing upon, the prevalent Ionic dialect, since some of his clients were from the eastern seaboard of the Aegean, where Ionic was the literary *lingua franca*.[11]

---

[8] This includes the three surviving full speeches of Antiphon. For the best dating of these, see K. J. Dover, *CQ* 44 (1950), 44–60. See also Edwards *GO* i. 24.

[9] e.g. ἀνατροπεύς (*Tetr.* 1. 2. 1), διαγνώμονες (2. 3. 3), ἐλεγκτήρ (1. 4. 3), πράκτορες (2. 2. 6). Cf. αἰτίασις (6.6), γνωρισταί, δοξασταί (5. 94), ἐπιτιμηταί (5. 32), ὀπτήρ (5. 27). For a full list, see C. Cucuel, *Essai sur la langue et le style de l'orateur Antiphon* (Paris, 1886).

[10] See esp. Blass *AB* i. 152, who notes the 'regularity' and 'rounding' of the sentence-structure of the *Tetralogies*, which indicate to him that they may have been pieces for public declamation (ἐπίδειξεις) rather than for use by pupils.

[11] Titles of fragments include *On the Tribute of Lindos, On the Tribute of Samothrace*.

Dover's suggestion that the *Tetralogies* were designed for a Greek, rather than purely Athenian readership, now seems very attractive.[12] The language in which the author of the *Tetralogies* wrote is his own native Attic with an Ionic flavour, before Attic had become divested of Ionic influences. Parts of Herodotus' history were almost certainly in circulation in the 430s, whereas the dialect of the Pseudo-Xenophontine *Athenian Constitution* (*c*.425) is undiluted Attic, as is that of Antiphon's speeches. While a precise date cannot be given for the *Tetralogies*, both literary and historical evidence indicate the years immediately preceding the outbreak of the Peloponnesian War.[13]

---

[12] Acceptance of it would, of course, render irrelevant one of the main theses on which both early date and Antiphontean authorship have been challenged—that the laws on homicide cited and posited in the *Tetralogies* are not Athenian laws. The argument begins with the important articles of W. Dittenberger: 'Antiphons' Tetralogien und das Criminalrecht I', *Hermes* 31 (1896), 271–7; 'II', *Hermes* 32 (1897), 1–21; 'III', ibid., 21–41; 'Zu Antiphons Tetralogien', *Hermes* 40 (1905), 450–70. The continuing debate has tended to concentrate on this legal discrepancy, through discussion of the laws of justified and accidental homicide. Two recent articles attempt to reinstate Dittenberger's thesis. Sealey, *TAPA* 114 (1984), 71–85, argues for a date after the end of the Peloponnesian War, but on insufficient evidence; and he dismisses the Ionicisms as 'archaising' rather than 'archaic' (85), without suggesting a reason backed by contemporary literary parallels. C. Eucken concentrates on the narrower question in his 'Das Tötungsgesetz des Antiphon und der Sinn seiner Tetralogien', *Mus. Helv.* 53 (1996), 73–82, and emphasizes the irresolubility of the conflict with religion and natural law that any form of killing creates. M. Gagarin, 'The Prohibition of Just and Unjust Homicide in Antiphon's Tetralogies', *GRBS* 19 (1978), 291–306, notes (294) that it is only the defendants who introduce the blanket prohibition of all killing; and argues (304) that the law, which they invoke for their own rhetorical purposes, is not a piece of statutory legislation but a statement of a general moral position which is, however, quite consonant with Athenian law. For one of the most thorough presentations of the case for an early date and Antiphontean authorship of the *Tetralogies*, see F. D. Caizzi, *Antiphontis Tetralogiae* (Milan, 1969).

[13] Cf. D. A. Russell, *An Anthology of Greek Prose* (Oxford, 1991), p. xv: 'By about 430, Athenian domination had established Attic not only as the main vehicle of administration and litigation through the Delian League and as the main language of drama, but also as the medium of most prose literature.'

APPENDIX B

GORGIAS *PALAMEDES*

While strictly outside the scope of the main discussion because it is
model defence of a mythical hero, this piece deserves brief examination i
only for the fame of its supposed author.[1] It may be assumed that th
choice of defendant was designed to give Gorgias a testing case in whicl
to display his powers. Palamedes was accused of betraying the Greek cam
before Troy to King Priam for gold. Though in most versions of the myt
it is admitted that the main evidence (a letter 'planted' under his bed) wa
manufactured by his enemy Odysseus, his proverbial cleverness made hin
a formidable defendant. Gorgias therefore begins with simple tragic an
Homeric themes: the idea that dishonour is more to be feared than deat
(1), and the contrast between force and justice (2) (cf. [Aesch.] *PV*). Thu
he skilfully creates the august if unreal atmosphere of a Homeric cour
But his model speech must also be of practical use to its audience. Th
subject he has chosen restricts its scope. There is none for the exercise c
narrative skill, since Palamedes' case is based on the premiss that he ha
done nothing (5, 23). The **prooemium** (1–5) therefore has to prepare th
ground directly for the proof. He has to predispose the jury to believe hin
rather than his opponent. He does this by asking why Odysseus ha
accused him. The suggested reasons—his φθόνος, κακοτεχνία, o
πανουργία (3)—lead to an aporia: how can an innocent man defend him
self against an unscrupulous one? (4) With two swift strokes he has black
ened the accuser's character and gained the jury's sympathy. They wi
now agree with him that amorality is a more potent weapon for someon
bent on crime than cleverness. Finally (5), he states the heads under whic
he proposes to argue his defence—lack of opportunity, lack of motiva
tion. The prooemium thus contains the following topics which orator
used and rhetoricians prescribed: statement of the issue, opponent's moti
vation, complaint of the speaker's disadvantage, summary of propose
division.

Lack of Opportunity (6–12) is introduced with characteristicall
Gorgianic reference to λόγος (cf. *Helen* 8), though here it is a medium c

---

[1] Its published form in the Attic dialect raises the same authorial or editorial problems
the same author's *Helen*.

communication rather than persuasion. The effectiveness of the argument in this section is greatly enhanced by the vehemence with which it is put—with hypophora (7, 10, 12) and procatalepsis (9). The weakest arguments come first. The jury is asked initially (6) to accept that no meeting between Palamedes and the Trojans took place, and is then offered two unconvincing arguments (as distinct from evidence) for believing this. The first is a supposed language problem between Greeks and Trojans. Listeners who had read Homer's many accounts of meetings between the two sides would be unimpressed by this. Hence the concession ἀλλὰ δὴ καὶ τοῦτο γενέσθω (8). The second is a topos which could be serviceable in the right context, in support of material evidence—that traitors are trusted by neither side (cf. Dem. 18 Cor. 47, 295)—but acceptance of it on its own would lead to the conclusion that treason could never take place. These arguments are followed by two which explore practicality and probability: (i) how the meeting between himself and the Trojans could have taken place (9–11); (ii) how, assuming it did, the agreed plan (to destroy the Greek army in its encampment) could have been executed (12). Since he denies all the probabilities, the use of rhetorical question inviting a negative answer is effective here because it enables him to avoid detailed examination of the points raised.

Lack of Will (13–21) concerns ethical probability, centring on character. Firstly, in general, no man gratuitously courts ill-repute for ill-defined or unattainable objectives (13); then, in his own case, the motives of power (14), gain—where the shift to his own individual character is even more pronounced (15), and honour—shown to be an unlikely aim for a man of sense (16) are considered and found unrealizable. The logic of this sequence appears to be broken by the reference to the danger (οὐκ ἀσφαλές . . .) faced by a traitor (17), but it is necessary because the insecurity of the traitor's position affects his ability to realize another possible aim: to help his friends and harm his enemies (18).[2] It also marks a switch from positive to negative aims: to avoid some danger or punishment (19). The section ends (20–1) with an emotionally charged[3] picture of the traitor in exile living an unbearable life (πῶς ἂν οὐκ ἀβίωτος ἦν ὁ βίος . . .), parted from his dear ones and dwelling among barbarians who would trust him no more than his betrayed countrymen.

The Evidence (22–32): the speaker addresses his accuser (apostrophe), and asks for material evidence—time, place and means—of the alleged betrayal. The section contains a succession of the standard rhetorical arguments that could be applied to direct evidence: if you were present, how were you not implicated (22)? How can I provide witnesses to an action

---

[2] On this as a theme of popular morality, see Dover GPM 180 ff.
[3] The hypophora (with asyndeton and chiasmus) in these sections gives them an almost poetic flavour.

which did not take place (23)? Since you only have supposition (δόξα) and not knowledge on which to rely, you should not be believed (24). Next he refutes the damaging charge of cleverness (δεινότης)[4] by pointing out that the action of which he is accused is that of a madman, and one cannot be clever and mad at the same time.[5] 27 is a transitional paraleipsis, leading to a pistis ek biou (28–32), prefaced by the topos of the envy incurred by self-praise as a danger to defendants (cf. Dem. 18 *Cor.* 3). In 29 he makes the general claim that his life has been blameless. This negative claim logically precedes the positive claim that he has been an active benefactor of the Greeks and of the human race. Gorgias lists these, drawing on the mythological tradition concerning Palamedes, that he invented τάξεις πολεμικούς (30: later sources specified the posting of sentries[6]), written laws, the alphabet, weights and measures, accountancy, fire beacons, and the board game, draughts. In 31 Palamedes is made to argue that a man's concern with such benefactions is a sign (σημεῖον) of his good character. 32 mentions the different categories of people—young, old, rich, and poor—who receive attention in later rhetorical treatises,[7] and the exigencies of the present καιρός.[8]

For the **epilogue** (33–7), Gorgias makes two interesting adaptations which allow for the special nature of his mythical jury, Palamedes' fellow-chieftains: he repudiates a plea for pity, saying that justice and not emotion were likely to influence such men (33); and he says that a summary (anacephalaiosis) is unnecessary (37). This illustrates how, at this early stage, the prescribed rules could be waived in particular cases. The epilogue also contains the topos of irremediability of a wrongly executed capital sentence (34), found in homicide trials.[9] It warns the jury of the danger of ill fame (δόξα αἰσχρά) if they condemn him falsely.[10]

The *Palamedes* is not a model forensic speech, but an exercise in the deployment of certain topics and arguments in proofs. It observes division within the **proof** section, with the defendant considering first his own position and dividing it into opportunity (6–12) and will or motivation (13–21); secondly the evidence, addressing his accuser directly. Then come his claims of good character and benefits, the counterpart of the Athenian litigant's recital of his liturgies (28–33). For the epilogue, he

---

[4] Cf. Antiph. *Tetr.* 1. 2. 3; Lys. 7 *Sac. Ol.* 12.

[5] This is expressed through a dilemmaton (cf. p. 4).

[6] Pausanias 10. 31. 1; 2. 20. 3; Philostr. *Heroica* 10; Schol. Eur. *Orest.* 432; Servius on Virg. *Aen.* 2. 81; Tzetzes *On Lycophron* 384.

[7] Aristot. *Rhet.* 2. 12–17.   [8] Ibid. 1. 7. 32, 9. 38.

[9] Antiph. 5 *Her.* 91 (also in the epilogue).

[10] Gorgias may here be thinking particularly of the popular reputation of Odysseus with theatre audiences and readers of myths, for some of whom he was the arch-schemer devoid of scruples, as in, for example Sophocles' *Philoctetes*. Both Sophocles and Euripides wrote plays about Palamedes' trial.

makes a plea to reason rather than emotion, in keeping with the character that has been assigned to him by tradition.

The piece contains Gorgias' stylistic trademarks, though not in the degree of prolixity found in the *Helen*. The appearance of forensic topics and techniques in mainstream sophistic writing, perhaps in the early years of the fourth century, gives the piece a certain interest, since it reinforces other arguments for the literary status of forensic oratory at this time.

GLOSSARY

This list contains the technical terms used in the text, and some besides. Most come from ancient and modern rhetorical theory and literary criticism, where they serve to identify figures of language and thought, and rhetorical or schematized forms of expression and argument. There are also some legal and political terms. As listing under classified heads would defeat the aim of quick reference, comprehensive alphabetical order is used. Words listed in this Glossary are generally not italicized in the text.

a fortiori   See **comparative argument**.

agon   Contest, trial.

alliteration   Frequent occurrence of the same consonant in a passage.

amplification   Collocation of two or more synonyms or near-synonyms.

anacephalaiosis   Summary of heads or points proved, recapitulation: an essential part of the epilogue.

anacolouthon   The breakdown of grammatical sequence.

anacrisis   See **procatalepsis**.

anaphora   Repetition of the first word or word-group in parallel clauses or phrases.

antidosis   Exchange, or challenge for exchange, of property.

antistrophe (and **epiphora**)   Repetition of the final word or word-group in parallel clauses or phrases.

antithesis   Paired clauses or phrases containing contrasting thought (μὲν ... δέ, οὐκ ... ἀλλά).

antonomasia   Renaming, using a colourful, usually pejorative alternative.

aparithmesis   Enumeration of items for emphasis or clarity.

aporia   Difficulty or impossibility deplored, either negatively, as when a speaker faces influential, clever, or well-prepared opponents; or positively, when he claims that he has abundance of material or many different ways of approaching his case.

aposiopesis   Abrupt silence in mid-sentence, to signal speaker's reluctance to talk about an inauspicious, unpleasant, or absurd subject.

apostrophe   Turning aside to address someone or something other than the audience—usually one's opponent in a hostile way.

asyndeton   Absence of connectives between clauses—a deliberate device in Greek, in which connectives were the norm.

captatio benevolentiae   Topos (q.v.) of ingratiation (mostly in prooemium).

hiasmus   Parallel clauses with corresponding parts, in which the order of the second clause is reversed (AB>BA).

limax   Form of multiple chiasmus with sequence of ideas containing rising force. (See Dem. 18 *Cor.* 179.)

omparative argument   Reasoning from the greater to the lesser case (*a fortiori*), or the lesser to the greater.

oncession   Allowing one point in order to strengthen another: 'Even supposing what you say is true, I am still in the right . . . '

orrection   Replacement of a word by a stronger word: 'I should be obliged, nay compelled . . . '

orrespondence   'Both . . . and' parallelism (καὶ . . . καί, τε . . . καί, τε . . . τε).

efinition   Reinforcement of an argument by defining its terms.

einosis   Highly-charged rhetoric, esp. expressing alarm or outrage.

euterologia   Second speech for defence or prosecution. See also **synegoria**.

ialogismos   'Thinking aloud', when a character describes his own thought-processes in a narrative (e.g. Andoc. 1 *Myst.* 51; Lys. 12, *Ag. Eratos.* 15).

iatyposis   A generic word for graphic or vivid description, in a narrative which represents the action as unfolding before the very eyes of the audience.

iegesis   Narrative.

igression   A loosely relevant, semi-detached episode, such as an illustrative story or description.

ilatation   Broadening of a theme to include universal or general ideas.

ilemmaton   ('double-catch') argument presenting two conditions, one of which must be fulfilled, though the fulfilment of either is bad for the speaker or his opponent.

ivision   Demarcation of the standard parts of a speech—prooemium, narrative, proof (subdivided into confirmation and refutation), and epilogue (with final peroration).

okimasia   Examination of a candidate's credentials for office.

idolopoiia   Term used for the form of **prosopopoiia** in which dead persons, not merely absent persons are represented.

ikos   See **probability**.

ironeia   Sarcastic pretence or suggestion of the opposite of what is intended.

isangelia   Impeachment or arraignment.

nthymeme   Rhetorical syllogism, more loosely constructed than the logical syllogism and using **probability**.

panadiplosis   Repetition of a single word.

phodos   Indirect or oblique approach or assault on opponent, in prooemia.

epicheireme   More elaborate form of **enthymeme**, proving or def
ing component parts.

epicrisis   Brief judgement of an action, expressed as a postscript.

epitaphios   Funeral oration.

etymological figure   The collocation of words derived from the sa
root, as in, for example, cognate accusative.

euthyna   Audit of an outgoing official.

gnome   An aphoristic or epigrammatic statement.

graphe paranomon   Indictment for proposing an illegal measure.

hiatus   The clashing of final with initial vowels.

homoeoteleuton   Rhyming ends of clauses.

hyperbaton   Separation of grammatically cohering words (e.g. adj
tives from nouns which they qualify, articles from nouns).

hyperbole   Exaggeration.

hypophora   Sequence of short anticipatory (see **procatalepsis**) qu
tions with short answers by the same speaker.

hypostasis   Correlative constructions of the type 'He was so arrogan
to . . . ': a device of **deinosis**.

hypotaxis   Construction using both main and subordinate clauses, p
ducing organic and periodic sentences.

hypothetical inversion   Unfulfilled condition contrasted with real
'If X had been the case, we could have done Y; but as it is . . . ',
'since Z is the case . . . '.

interrogation (erotesis)   Questions answered in his own person by
opponent, who usually condemns himself out of his own mouth.

leitourgiai   Public services performed by wealthy Athenian citizens.

litotes   Feigned avoidance of exaggeration by negation of opposite: '
small matter'.

logographos   Writer of speeches for litigants to deliver in court.

menusis   Denunciation, laying of information against someone.

metaphor   Transference of a word from one field of activity to anot
to supply extra animation or colour to an expression: 'The state
sick' (medical metaphor) or ' . . . foundering' (nautical metaph
Novelty could be lost with time, and the old metaphor became int
changeable with the literal word. When we say, 'I've been hunt
everywhere for that screw-driver', no one pictures us handing the s
rup-cup back to the butler and riding off into the autumn mists in p
suit of our quarry. 'Hunting' has become a 'dead' metaphor.

neologism   The coining of new words.

orthoepeia   Correct spelling and usage of words.

paignion   Skit, play-piece, *jeu d'esprit*.

parable   Simile (q.v.), through detailed example. ('Just as when a . .

paradeigma   Example or precedent, usually historical, to illustrate
justify an argument.

paragraphe Lit. 'counter-prosecution': but actually a pre-emptive suit to prevent an impending prosecution. It could itself be answered in a speech **pros paragraphen**.

paraleipsis Transitional formula, 'passing over'. In true rhetorical paraleipsis, the subject is not passed over: 'I shall not discuss the fact that . . . ' (details follow). By this device dubious facts or arguments may be presented to a not-too-critical audience.

para prosdokian Any unexpected turn or conclusion to an argument.

parataxis Sentence construction using parallel main clauses rather than subordination as in **hypotaxis**.

parechesis Occurrence of same-sounding syllables in neighbouring words.

parekbasis Digression (q.v.).

parison Sentences constructed from clauses of equal length and with corresponding parts. Also called **isocolon**.

paronomasia Punning assonance.

partitio oratoria See **division**.

pathetic paradox The term used, in this book for the first time, to describe a form of argument which combines emotion with logic. The emotion comes in the opening formula: 'Is it not (would it not be) shocking (shameful, terrible, absurd) if, when X, which is undesirable, is not allowed to happen, Y, which is far more undesirable, is allowed to happen?'. The comparative element provides the logical backbone to an argument which can have many variants.

peritrope See **reversal of accusation**.

petitio principii 'Begging the question', representing as agreed fact that which has to be proved.

pistis Proof which may be purely evidential (**atechnos**) or argumentative and rhetorical (**entechnos**).

pistis ek biou See under **probability**.

polyptoton The use in close sequence of different cases of the same word. Related to **etymological figure** (q.v.).

probability (eikos) The criterion of most non-evidential argument: likelihood, decided by belief based on common sense and human experience. Both single actions and behaviour over a period create an impression of an individual's character, and hence a 'biographical proof' (**pistis ek biou**) of his guilt or innocence. Is someone who has behaved in such a way throughout his life likely to have behaved in the (contrary) way described on this occasion? Probability also included such concepts as chance and physical laws, and is often implied where not stated in an argument.

procatalepsis Anticipation of the opponent's statements, pleas, or arguments. A regular subdivision of the proof, which may include genuine material gathered from a preliminary hearing (**diaita** or **anacri-**

sis); but also material which the speaker can easily refute as spurious or irrelevant.

procatasceue More elaborate form of **prothesis**, with persuasive elements.

prodiegesis Preliminary or background narrative; account of prior events.

prosopopoiia Representation of absent or dead person(s) as interested observers of the present scene, or imagination of future scenes.

prothesis Summary of the elements of the case to be proved or disproved.

reductio ad absurdum Logical deduction which leads to a conclusion that is either impossible or ridiculous.

reversal of accusation (peritrope) A defendant arguing that his opponent is the party guilty of the crime in question, or of a greater crime.

rhetorical question Question asked for effect rather than in expectation of a reply.

semeion Sign or indication which falls short of certain proof. Cf. **tekmerion**.

simile Explicit comparison, using the words 'like' or 'as'. See also **parable**.

status (stasis) The issue, raised by questions as to fact (Was the act committed?), the nature of the alleged act (Was it murder or manslaughter?), and its legality.

sycophant(es) False accuser or vexatious litigant. Not used in modern English sense of 'toady', 'flatterer'.

symboulos Statesman, political counsellor.

symploke **Anaphora** (q.v.) and **antistrophe** (q.v.) combined.

synegoria, synegoros Supporting speech, speaker. See also **deuterologia**.

tekmerion Sure sign or indication (proof). Cf. **semeion**. See Ch. 4 n. 200.

topos (pl. topoi) Standard theme, as when a speaker praises the laws or says that a verdict will serve as an example to others, or pleads for time in a capital charge. In epideictic oratory, a topos could be a broad theme, the three main themes being *expediency*, *justice* (or *honour*), and *possibility*.

SELECT BIBLIOGRAPHY

Abbreviations used in references to frequently cited works are listed on pp. x–xi. More specialized books and articles appear in the notes.

GENERAL

BENSELER, G. E., *De Hiatu in Oratoribus Atticis et Historicis Graecis* (Freiburg, 1841).

BLASS, F., *Die attische Beredsamkeit*, i–iii. 2 (Leipzig, 1887–98, repr. 1962).

BONNER, R. J., *Lawyers and Litigants in Ancient Athens* (Chicago, 1927).

BONNER, R. J., and SMITH, G., *The Administration of Justice from Homer to Aristotle*, i–ii (Chicago, 1930–8).

BRUNS, I., *Das literarische Porträt der Griechen im fünften und vierten Jahrhundert* (Berlin, 1896).

BUCHHEIT, V., *Untersuchungen zur Theorie des Genos Epideiktikon von Gorgias bis Aristoteles* (Munich, 1960).

CAREY, C., *Trials from Classical Athens* (London and New York, 1997).

CARTLEDGE, P., MILLETT, P., and TODD, S., *Nomos: Essays in Athenian Law, Politics and Society* (Cambridge, 1990).

CHANTRAINE, P., *La Stylistique grecque* (Paris, 1951).

COLE, T., *The Origins of Rhetoric in Ancient Greece* (Baltimore, 1991).

DAVIES, J. K., *Athenian Propertied Families* (Oxford, 1971).

DENNISTON, J. D., *Greek Prose Style* (Oxford, 1952).

DOBSON, J. F., *The Greek Orators* (London, 1919).

DORJAHN, A. P., 'Anticipation of Arguments in Athenian Courts', *TAPA* 66 (1935), 274–95.

DOVER, K. J., *Greek Popular Morality* (Oxford, 1974).

EDWARDS, M. J., *The Attic Orators* (Bristol, 1994).

GOMPERZ, H., *Sophistik und Rhetorik* (Leipzig and Berlin, 1912).

GOODWIN, W. W., *Syntax of the Moods and Tenses of the Greek Verb* (New York, 1875, repr. 1965).

GUTHRIE, W. K. C., *The Sophists* (Cambridge, 1971).

HARRISON, A. R. W., *The Law of Athens*, i–ii (Oxford, 1968–71).

JEBB, R. C., *The Attic Orators from Antiphon to Isaeus*, i–ii (London, 1893, repr. 1962).

KENNEDY, G., *The Art of Persuasion in Greece* (Princeton and London, 1963).

KERFERD, G. B., *The Sophistic Movement* (Cambridge, 1981).

LÄMMLI, F., *Das Attische Prozessverfahren in seiner Wirkung auf die Gerichtsrede* (Paderborn, 1938).

LAVENCY, M., *Aspects de la logographie judiciaire attique* (Louvain, 1964).

LORAUX, N., *The Invention of Athens: The Funeral Oration in the Classical City*, trans. A. Sheridan (Harvard and London, 1986).

MACDOWELL, D. M., *Athenian Homicide Law* (Manchester, 1963).

—— *The Law in Classical Athens* (London, 1978).

MARTIN, J., *Antike Rhetorik: Technik und Methode* (in *Handbuch der Altertumswissenschaft* 2.3) (Munich, 1974).

MEIGGS, R., and LEWIS, D. M., *A Selection of Greek Historical Inscriptions* (Oxford, 1969).

NAVARRE, O., *Essai sur la rhétorique grecque avant Aristote* (Paris, 1900).

NOUHAUD, M., *L'Utilisation de l'histoire par les orateurs attiques* (Paris, 1982).

PELLING, C. (ed.), *Characterization and Individuality in Greek Literature* (Oxford, 1990).

PILZ, W., *Der Rhetor im attischen Staat* (Basel, 1924).

RADERMACHER, L., *Artium Scriptores* (Vienna, 1951).

RHODES, P. J., *A Commentary on the Aristotelian Athenaion Politeia* (Oxford, 1981).

ROMILLY, J. DE, *Les Grands Sophistes dans l'Athènes de Périclès* (Paris, 1988).

SÜSS, W., *Ethos: Studien für ältere griechische Rhetorik* (Leipzig, 1910).

TODD, S. C., *The Shape of Athenian Law* (Oxford, 1993).

UNTERSTEINER, M., *The Sophists*, trans. K. Freeman (Oxford, 1954).

VOLKMANN, R., *Die Rhetorik der Griechen und Römer* (Leipzig, 1885).

WARDY, R., *The Birth of Rhetoric* (London and New York, 1996).

WOLFF, H.-J., 'The Origin of Judicial Litigation among the Greeks' *Traditio* 4 (1946), 31–87.

WORTHINGTON, I. (ed.), *Persuasion: Greek Rhetoric in Action* (London and New York, 1994).

EARLY RHETORIC

ALY, W., *Formprobleme der frühen griechischen Prosa* (Philol. Suppl. 21.2, 1929).

BUXTON, R. G. A., *Persuasion in Greek Tragedy: A Study of Peitho* (Cambridge, 1982).

CORTÉS GABAUDAN, F., *Fórmulas retóricas de la oratoria judicial ática* (Salamanca, 1986).

ENOS, R. L., *Greek Rhetoric Before Aristotle* (Prospect Heights, Ill., 1993).

GERKE, A., 'Die alte τέχνη ῥητορική und ihre Gegner', *Hermes* 32 (1897), 341–81.

GOEBEL, G. H., 'Probability in the Earliest Rhetorical Theory' *Mnemosyne* 42 (1989), 41–53.

GONDOS, E. A., *Auf dem Weg zur rhetorischen Theorie: Rhetorische Reflexion im ausgehenden fünften Jahrhundert v. Chr.*, Rhetorik-Forschungen 10 (Tübingen, 1996).

HAMBERGER, P., *Die rednerische Disposition in der alten TEXNH PHTOPIKH* (Paderborn, 1914).

HINKS, D. A. G., 'Tisias, Corax, and the Invention of Rhetoric', *CQ* 34 (1940), 61–9.

KARP, A. J., 'Homeric Origins of Ancient Rhetoric', *Arethusa* 10 (1997), 237-58.

KENNEDY, G. A., 'The Ancient Dispute over Rhetoric in Homer', *AJP* 78 (1957), 23–35.

—— 'The Earliest Rhetorical Handbooks', *AJP* 80 (1959), 169–78.

LEES, J. T., *Δικανικὸς λόγος in Euripides* (Lincoln, Neb., 1891).

LLOYD, M., *The Agon in Euripides* (Oxford, 1992).

LOPEZ EIRE, A., *Los orígines de la oratoria en la Grecia clásica* (Zaragoza, 1994).

MURPHY, C. T., 'Aristophanes and the Art of Rhetoric', *HSCP* 49 (1938), 69–113.

SEGAL, C., 'Gorgias and the Psychology of the Logos', *HSCP* 66 (1962), 99–155.

SOLMSEN, F., 'The Gift of Speech in Homer and Hesiod', *TAPA* 85 (1954), 1–15.

WILCOX, S., 'The Scope of Early Rhetorical Instruction', *HSCP* 53 (1942), 121–55.

—— 'Corax and the Prolegomena', *AJP* 64 (1943), 1–23.

ANTIPHON

For Antiphontean *Tetralogies*, see Appendix A.)

ALBINI, U., 'Antifonte logografo', *Maia* 10 (1958), 36–65, 132–45.

BARIGAZZI, A., *Antifonte: Prima orazione* (Florence, 1955).

BERGE, H. M. TEN, *Antiphons Zesde Rede* (Nijmegen, 1948).

CUCUEL, C., *Essai sur la langue et le style de l'orateur Antiphon* (Paris, 1886).

DOVER, K. J., 'The Chronology of Antiphon's Speeches', *CQ* 44 (1950), 44-60.

DUE, B., *Antiphon: A Study in Argumentation* (Copenhagen, 1980).

EDWARDS, M. J., *Greek Orators*, i: *Antiphon* (Warminster, 1985).

ERBSE, H., 'Antiphons Rede über die Ermordung des Herodes', *Rh. Mus.* 120 (1977), 209–27.

GAGARIN, M., *The Murder of Herodes: A Study of Antiphon 5* (Frankfurt, 1989).

—— 'The Nature of Proofs in Antiphon', *CP* 85 (1990), 22-32.

—— *Antiphon: The Speeches* (Cambridge, 1997).

GERNET, L., *Antiphon: discours* (Budé: Paris, 1923).

FREEMAN, K., *The Murder of Herodes* (London, 1946).

HEITSCH, E., *Antiphon aus Rhamnous* (Wiesbaden, 1984).

MAIDMENT, K. J., *Minor Attic Orators*, i (Loeb; London, 1941).

SOLMSEN, F., *Antiphonstudien* (Berlin, 1931).

SCHEIDWEILER, F., 'Antiphons Rede über den Mord an Herodes', *F Mus.* 109 (1966), 319–38.
SCHINDEL, U., 'Der Mordfall Herodes', *Nachr. der Akad. der Wiss. Göttingen* 8 (1979), 1–41.
WIJNBERG, S., *Antiphons Eerste Rede* (Amsterdam, 1938).

ANDOCIDES

ALBINI, U., 'Per un profilo di Andocide', *Maia* 8 (1956), 163–80.
—— 'Rassegna di studi andocidei', *Atene e Roma* 3 (1958), 129-48.
DALMEYDA, G., *Andocide: discours* (Budé; Paris, 1930).
EDWARDS, M. J., *Greek Orators, iv: Andocides* (Warminster, 1995).
FURLEY, W. D., *Andocides and the Herms* (BICS Suppl. 65, 1996).
KENNEDY, G. A., 'The Oratory of Andocides', *AJP* 79 (1958), 32–43.
KINGSBURY, S. S., *A Rhetorical Study of the Style of Andocides* (Baltimo 1899).
MACDOWELL, D. M., *Andocides: On the Mysteries* (Oxford, 1962).
MAIDMENT, K. J., *Minor Attic Orators*, i (Loeb; London, 1941).
MAKKINK, A. D. J., *Andokides' Eerste Rede* (Amsterdam, 1932).
MARR, J. L., 'Andocides' Part in the Mysteries and Hermae Affair 415 B CQ 2nd ser. 21 (1971), 326–38.
MISSIOU, A., *The Subversive Oratory of Andokides* (Cambridge, 1992).
MORGAN, M. H., 'Some Constructions in Andocides', *HSCP* 2 (198 57–69.

LYSIAS

ALBINI, U., 'Rassegna di Studi lisiani (1901–1954)', *Atene e Roma* 14– (1954), 56–67.
—— *Lisia: i discorsi* (Rome, 1955).
BATEMAN, J. J., 'Lysias and the Law', *TAPA* 89 (1958), 276–85.
—— 'Some Aspects of Lysias' Argumentation', *Phoenix* 16 (196 157–77.
BERBIG, F., *Über das genus dicendi tenue des Redners Lysias* (Küstrin, 1871
BÜCHLER, O., *Die Unterscheidung der redenden Personen bei Lys* (Heidelberg, 1936).
CAREY, C., *Lysias: Selected Speeches (1, 3, 7, 14, 31, 32)* (Cambridge, 198
DEVRIES, W., *Ethopoiia: A Study of the Types of Character in the Oration Lysias* (Baltimore, 1892).
DOVER, K. J., *Lysias and the Corpus Lysiacum* (Los Angeles, 1968).
FERABOLI, S., *Lisia avvocato* (Padua, 1980).
FRANCKEN, C. W., *Commentationes Lysiacae* (Utrecht, 1875).

FROHBERGER, H., *Ausgewählte Reden des Lysias*, i–iii (Leipzig, 1866–71).
GERNET, L., and BIZOS, M., *Lysias: discours* (Budé; Paris, 1924, 1926).
GRAU, P., *Prooemiengestaltung bei Lysias* (Würzburg, 1971).
HILLGRUBER, M., *Die zehnte Rede des Lysias* (Berlin, 1988).
LAMB, W. R. M., *Lysias* (Loeb; London, 1930).
LATEINER, D., 'An Analysis of Lysias' Defence Speeches', *RSA* 11 (1981), 147–60.
LOENING, T. C., 'The Autobiographical Speeches of Lysias and the Biographical Tradition', *Hermes* 109 (1981), 280–94.
MEDDA, E., *Lisia: Orazioni*, i, ii (Milan, 1991, 1995).
MOTSCHMANN, W., *Die Charaktere bei Lysias* (Munich, 1905).
MÜLLER, F. A., *De Elocutione Lysiae* (Halle, 1887).
SCHINDEL, U., 'Untersuchungen zur Biographie des Redners Lysias', *Rh. Mus.* 110 (1967), 32–52.
SCHÖN, K., *Die Scheinargumente bei Lysias* (Paderborn, 1918).
USHER, S., 'Individual Characterization in Lysias', *Eranos* 63 (1965), 99–119.
—— 'Lysias and his Clients', *GRBS* 17 (1976), 31–40.
—— *Greek Orators*, i: *Lysias* (Warminster, 1985).
USHER, S., and NAJOCK, D., 'A Statistical Study of Authorship in the Corpus Lysiacum', *Comp. Hum.* 16 (1982), 85–105.
VOEGELIN, W., *Die Diabole bei Lysias* (Basel, 1943).
WEISSENBERGER, M., *Die Dokimasiereden des Lysias* (Frankfurt, 1987).
WALTZ, J., *Der lysianische Epitaphios* (Philol. Suppl. 29.4, 1936).
WINTER, T. N., 'On the Corpus of Lysias', *CJ* 69 (1973), 34–40.

ISOCRATES

ALEXIOU, E., *Ruhm und Ehre: Studien zu Begriffen, Werten und Motivierungen bei Isokrates* (Heidelberg, 1995).
BARWICK, K., 'Das Problem der isokrateischen Techne', *Philol.* 107 (1963), 42–60.
BRINGMANN, K., *Studien zu den politischen Ideen des Isokrates* (Göttingen, 1965).
BUCHNER, E., *Der Panegyrikos des Isokrates* (Weisbaden, 1958).
BURK, A., *Die Pädagogik des Isokrates* (Würzburg, 1923).
CLOCHÉ, P., *Isocrate et son temps* (Paris, 1963).
EUCKEN, C., *Isokrates: seine Positionen in der Auseinandersetzung mit den zeitgenössischen Philosophen* (Berlin, 1983).
HEILBRUNN, G., 'Isocrates on Rhetoric and Power', *Hermes* 103 (1975), 154–78.
JUDSON-WILLIAMS, H. LL., 'Isocrates and Recitations', *CQ* 43 (1949), 64–9.

JAEGER, W., *Paideia*, iii, trans. G. Highet (Oxford, 1945).

JOHNSON, R., 'Isocrates' Methods of Teaching', *AJP* 80 (1959), 25–36.

KESSLER, J., *Isokrates und die panhellenische Idee* (Paderborn, 1911).

MASARACCHIA, A., *Isocrate: Retorica e Politica* (Rome, 1995).

MATHIEU, G., *Les idées politiques d'Isocrate* (Paris, 1925).

MATHIEU, G., and BREMOND, E., *Isocrate: discours*, i–iv (Budé; Paris, 1928–62).

MIKKOLA, E., *Isokrates: seine Anschauungen im Lichte seiner Schriften* (Helsinki, 1954).

NORLIN, G., and HOOK, L. VAN, *Isocrates*, i–iii (Loeb; London, 1928, 1929, 1945).

SANDYS, J. E., *Isocrates: Ad Demonicum et Panegyricus* (London, 1902).

SECK, F., *Isokrates* (Wege der Forschung 351; Darmstadt, 1976).

STEIDLE, 'Redekunst und Bildung bei Isokrates', *Hermes* 80 (1952), 257–96.

TOO, Y. L., *The Rhetoric of Identity in Isocrates* (Cambridge, 1995).

USHER, S., 'The Style of Isocrates', *BICS* 20 (1973), 39–67.

—— *Greek Orators*, iii: *Isocrates* (Warminster, 1990).

WERSDÖRFER, H., *Die ΦΙΛΟΣΟΦΙΑ des Isokrates im Spiegel ihrer Terminologie* (Leipzig, 1940).

WILCOX, S., 'Criticisms of Isocrates and his φιλοσοφία', *TAPA* 74 (1943), 113–33.

DEMOSTHENES

ADAMS, C., *Demosthenes and his Influence* (London, 1927).

CALHOUN, G., 'Demosthenes' Second Philippic', *TAPA* 64 (1933), 1–17.

CAREY, C., and REID, R. A., *Demosthenes: Selected Private Speeches* (Cambridge, 1985).

CAWKWELL, G. L., 'Eubulus', *JHS* 83 (1963), 47–67.

—— 'Demosthenes' Policy after the Peace of Philocrates', *CQ* 2nd ser. 13 (1963), 120–38, 200–13.

—— 'The Crowning of Demosthenes', *CQ* 2nd ser. 19 (1969), 163–80.

—— *Philip of Macedon* (London, 1978).

CLOCHÉ, P., *Démosthène et la fin de la démocratie athénienne* (Paris, 1937).

CROISET, M., NAVARRE, O., ORSINI, P., HUMBERT, J., GERNET, L., and MATHIEU, G., *Démosthène: harangues, plaidoyers politiques et civils*, i–x (Budé; Paris, 1924–60).

DAITZ, S., 'The Relationship of the De Chersoneso and the Philippica Quarta of Demosthenes', *CP* 52 (1957), 145–62.

DRERUP, E., *Aus einer alten Advokatenrepublik: Demosthenes und seine Zeit* (Paderborn, 1916).

ELLIS, J. R., *Philip II and Macedonian Imperialism* (London, 1976).

ELLIS, J. R., and MILNS, R. D., *The Spectre of Philip. Demosthenes' First Philippic, Olynthiacs and Speech On the Peace: A Study of Historical Evidence* (Sydney, 1970).

FOCKE, F., *Demosthenesstudien* (Stuttgart, 1929).

FOX, W., *Die Kranzrede des Demosthenes* (Leipzig, 1880).

GOODWIN, W. W., *Demosthenes: On the Crown* (Cambridge, 1901).

JACKSON, D. F., and ROWE, G. O., 'Demosthenes 1915–1965', *Lustrum* 14 (1969).

JAEGER, W., *Demosthenes: The Origin and Growth of his Policy* (Los Angeles, 1938).

KIRK, W. H., *Demosthenic Style in the Private Orations* (Baltimore, 1895).

MACDOWELL, D. M., *Demosthenes: Against Meidias* (Oxford, 1990).

MATHIEU, G., *Démosthène, l'homme et l'oeuvre* (Paris, 1948).

MCQUEEN, E. I., *Demosthenes: Olynthiacs* (Bristol, 1986).

MONTGOMERY, H., *The Way to Chaeronea: Foreign Policy, Decision-Making and Political Influence in Demosthenes' Speeches* (Bergen, 1983).

NAVARRE, O., 'Le style oratoire de Démosthène dans les trois plus anciens plaidoyers politiques', *AC* 8 (1939), 5–13.

PALEY, F. A., and SANDYS, J. E., *Select Private Orations of Demosthenes*, i–ii (Cambridge, 1875).

PEARSON, L., *The Art of Demosthenes* (Meisenheim, 1976).

PICKARD-CAMBRIDGE, A. W., *Demosthenes and the Last Days of Greek Freedom* (London, 1914).

RONNET, G., *Étude sur le style de Démosthène dans les discours politiques* (Paris, 1951).

SCHÄFER, A., *Demosthenes und seine Zeit*, i–iii (Leipzig, 1885).

SEALEY, R., 'Athens after the Social War', *JHS* 75 (1955), 74–81.

——*Demosthenes & His Time* (Oxford, 1993).

SPENGEL, L., *Demosthenes Verteidigung des Ktesiphon: Ein Beitrag zum Verständnis des Redners* (Munich, 1864).

TREVES, P., *Demostene e la libertà greca* (Bari, 1933).

——'La Composition de la Troisième Philippique', *REA* 42 (1940), 354–64.

USHER, S., *Greek Orators*, v: *Demosthenes De Corona* (Warminster, 1993).

VINCE, J. H., VINCE, C. V., MURRAY, A. T., DE WITT, N. W., DE WITT, N. J., *Demosthenes*, i–vii (Loeb; London, 1930–1949).

VORNDRAN, L., *Die Aristokratea des Demosthenes als Advokatensrede unde ihre politische Tendenz* (Paderborn, 1922).

WANKEL, H., *Rede für Ktesiphon über den Kranz* (Heidelberg, 1976).

ISAEUS TO DINARCHUS

ADAMS, C. D., *The Speeches of Aeschines* (Loeb; London, 1919).

BADEN, W. W., *The Principal Figures of Language and Figures of Thought in Isaeus* (Baltimore, 1906).

BARTOLINI, G., *Iperide* (Padua, 1977).

BURKE, E. M., 'Contra Leocratem and De Corona: Political Collaboration?', *Phoenix* 31 (1977), 330–40.

BURTT, J. O., *Minor Attic Orators*, ii: *Lycurgus, Dinarchus, Demades, Hyperides* (Loeb; London, 1954).

CAREY, C., *Greek Orators*, vi: *Apollodoros* (Warminster, 1992).

CAWKWELL, G., 'Aeschines and the Ruin of Phocis', *REG* 75 (1962), 453–9.

COLIN, G., 'L'Oraison funèbre d'Hyperide', *REG* (1938), 209–66, 305–94.

——*Hyperide: discours* (Budé: Paris, 1946).

CURTIS, T. B., *The Judicial Oratory of Hyperides* (Chapel Hill, 1970).

FORSTER, E. S., *Isaeus* (Loeb; London, 1927).

GWATKIN, W., 'The Legal Arguments in Aeschines Against Ctesiphon and Demosthenes On the Crown', *Hesperia* 26 (1957), 129–41.

HARRIS, E. M., *Aeschines and Athenian Politics* (Oxford, 1995).

KINDSTRAND, J. F., *The Stylistic Evaluation of Aeschines in Antiquity* (Uppsala, 1982).

LENTZSCH, R., *Studien zu Isaeos* (Leipzig, 1932).

NOUHAUD, M., and DORS-MÉARY, L., *Dinarque: discours* (Budé; Paris, 1990).

PETRIE, A., *Lycurgus: The Speech Against Leocrates* (Cambridge, 1922).

RAMMING, G., *Die politische Ziele und Weg des Aischines* (Erlangen, 1965).

RUBINSTEIN, L., *Adoption in IV Century Athens* (Copenhagen, 1993).

THOMPSON, W. E., De Hagniae Hereditate: *An Athenian Inheritance Case* (Leiden, 1976).

TREVETT, J., *Apollodoros the Son of Pasion* (Oxford, 1992).

WEVERS, R. F., *Isaeus: Chronology, Prosopography and Social History* (The Hague, 1969).

WORTHINGTON, I., *A Historical Commentary on Dinarchus* (Ann Arbor, 1992).

WYSE, W., *The Speeches of Isaeus* (Cambridge, 1904).

INDEX OF SPEECHES

GENERAL INDEX

Helen 62 n. 28, 107 n. 178, 360
'rand Style 108, 358
'aphe paranomon 201–2
'eed 59–61, 156, 168 n. 115, 187, 190,
    257–8
.uardianship 171–80

lagnias 154–7, 266–7
lagnon 145
lagnotheus 145
larmodius 137, 198, 207
larpalus 329, 337–8, 344–6
.eads (topics) (*kephalaia*) 310, 322
.egesandrus 281–3
.egesippus 168, 233 n. 219
.egestratus 251–2
.eiress(es) 109, 111, 138, 143 n. 57
.elen 314, 363
.eliaea 32, 35, 40, 261, 263
.ellenotamiae 38
.ellespont 205, 239, 273
.eracles, Heraclidae 305, 307
.eraeum Teichos 217
.ermae, Hermocopids 39 n. 46, 42–9
.ermagoras 16 n. 47
.ermogenes 42 n. 1, 225
.erodes 34–8
.erodes Atticus 42 n. 1
.erodotus 88, 253, 356–8
.esiod 186 n. 56
.atus 83, 94, 112, 118, 183 n. 47, 244,
    266, 342
.ierocles 146–9
.ippias 5–6
.ippocratic Corpus 253–4, 356–7
.storical example (*paradeigma*) 1 n. 1, 38,
    41, 50, 62, 97, 120, 190, 255, 283,
    303, 318, 334, 345–6, 348
.storical passages 199, 217
.omer 1 n., 293, 361
.omicide, laws of 6–8, 10, 14–16, 198,
    206, 359
.moeoteleuton 118, 319
.monoia, *see* concord
.mosexuality 91, 280–4
.amour 108–10, 188, 203
.bris 92, 125, 135, 199, 201, 229, 246–7
.ygieia 334
.perbaton 109, 277, 308
.perbole 79, 99, 215, 239, 258, 325
.yperides 53, 268 n. 84, 328–38, 354
.pophora 17, 25
.Aeschines 293

Andocides 49, 51 n. 32
Antiphon 38 n. 41
Demosthenes 201 n. 113, 203, 222, 228,
    249, 254 n. 37
Gorgias 361
Hyperides 328, 331, 336
Isaeus 137, 143 n. 56, 156 n. 93, 158,
    167, 170
Lysias 76, 78 n. 93, 106, 115
hypostasis 15, 25, 91 n. 136, 135, 155 n. 92,
    169, 313
hypotaxis 6
hypothesis 97
hypothetical inversion 17, 19, 25, 43, 102,
    120 n. 126, 134, 138, 157 n. 98, 178,
    203 n. 118, 214, 218 n. 168, 228, 288

impeachment (*eisangelia*) 333–4
impiety 230
individualism 295 n.
inexperience, topos 18, 22, 77, 95, 138,
    205, 255
informality 268
inheritance, laws of 146, 267, 353
intention (*pronoia*) 15, 16, 24, 28, 30, 92–3,
    112
interrogation (*erotesis*) 25, 61, 101 n. 163,
    137, 167, 170
invective 62, 137, 156, 227–9, 236, 258–9,
    274, 276, 285, 331, 347
Ionic dialect 356–9
Isaeus 127–72, 261, 277, 353
    life 127
Isocrates 35, 62, 77, 87, 94, 118–26, 173,
    209, 254, 257, 278, 296–323, 342–3,
    346, 354
    life 118, 296, 319–21
    school 296, 309, 312, 314–16, 318–21,
    324, 343
    style 311, 322–3
Isotimides, decree of 42

Johannes Doxopater 2 n. 4
justice, topos 7, 25, 49–50, 193–4, 210–11,
    223, 237, 299, 301, 309, 354

kairos 50 n. 26, 219 n. 175, 221 n. 177,
    224, 301, 353
kakologia, see invective
kephalaia, see heads, topics
King's Peace (386 BC) 299

Lacritus 253–4

Philoctemon 149–54
Philomache 154–7
Philon 77–80
philosophia 297 n. 7, 299
philosophical tone 195
Philostratus 286, 294
Phocion 241
Phocis, Phocians 211, 235, 272
Phormio 247–9, 255, 258
Phormisius 68–9
Phryne 337–8
Phrynichus 67, 71
Piraeus 68, 252, 325 n. 2
    Long Walls 125
    party of 63
pistis, see proof
Plangon 260
Plataea, Plataeans 116, 308–9, 342
Plataea, Battle of 300 n. 19
Plato 110, 115, 214, 316, 351–2
    Apology 316
    Phaedrus 2 n. 4, 3 n. 6, 54 n. 2, 64 n. 39,
        106 n. 176, 115
Plutarch 257 n. 45, 330 n. 20
Plutarchus, tyrant of Eretria 231 n. 210
poets as teachers 309, 327–8, 354
Polemarchus 58–63, 201
Poliochus 83–4
pollution (*miasma*) 11
Polyaenus 114
Polybius 323
Polycles 341–2
Polycrates 296 n. 2, 315
Polyeuctus 184–6
    (Hyperid. 4) 334
polypragmosyne (philopragmosyne, philoneikia)
        221, 325
polyptoton 20
Polystratus 115–16
Poseidippus 130
possibility, topos 210, 218–19, 222, 301,
        306, 307
Potidaea 217
praise of the law, topos 13, 24, 145–6, 202,
        206, 280–1
precedent, topos 50, 76, 112, 247
    see also historical example
preparation (preparedness), topos 23, 45,
        77, 138, 151, 181, 268
prescription (*prothesmia*) 247–8 n. 13
Priam 360
probability (*eikos*) argument 3, 7, 10, 15,
        24, 353

Aeschines 282 n.
Antiphon 30, 36–7, 40
Apollodorus 340
Demosthenes 179, 181, 185, 228, 239
        232, 253, 257, 259, 260
Hyperides 334
Isaeus 130, 139, 142, 147, 163, 165, 1◄
Isocrates 118–19, 123
Lysias 61, 103, 115
procatalepsis (anticipation of arguments) 1◄
        20, 25, 78, 110, 113 n. 202, 116–17◄
        120 n. 216, 134 n. 22, 192, 197, 20◄
        n. 107, 235, 247, 257, 294 n. 41, 36◄
procatasceue 28
proclesis (challenge) 32, 141
Prodicus 4, 5, 99 n. 154, 297
prodiegesis 29, 31, 56, 60, 202
pronoia, see intention
prooemium 7–15, 19, 22–3
    Aeschines 280–1, 284, 288
    Andocides 43, 45
    Antiphon 28, 31
    Demosthenes 172–3, 176, 184, 186–7◄
        190, 199, 202, 209–10, 218, 231, 23◄
        248–9, 255–6, 260, 268, 271
    Gorgias 361
    Isaeus 128–30, 138, 141
    Isocrates 306–7, 310–11, 316, 318–19
    Lycurgus 325
    Lysias 56, 59, 65, 95, 103, 107
proof (*pistis*):
    biographical (*pistis ek biou*) 24, 73, 112◄
        121, 203, 286, 330, 332, 362
    evidential (*atechnos*) 58, 89, 134, 168,
        247, 338
    rhetorical or argumentative (*entechnos*)
        24–5, 81, 92, 139–40, 173, 179, 256◄
        266
prose rhythm 6 n. 17, 322 n.
prose style 41, 105, 197, 216–17, 243,
        311–12, 319, 346, 356–9
prosopopoiia 30, 63, 117, 124, 175, 195 n.
        235 n. 223, 259 n. 56, 308, 328, 336
pros paragraphen 116, 253–5
prostitution, prostitutes 104, 164, 331–2◄
        341–3
Protagoras 4, 5, 297, 355
prothesis 35, 45, 77, 107, 178, 271
Protus 251–2
proxenos (consular agent) 339
Proxenus:
    (Din.) 344
    (Is. 5) 133

Short Loan Collection

WITHDRAWN

UNIVERSITY
OF
GLASGOW
LIBRARY

Lightning Source UK Ltd.
Milton Keynes UK
UKOW052138270312

189703UK00001B/2/A